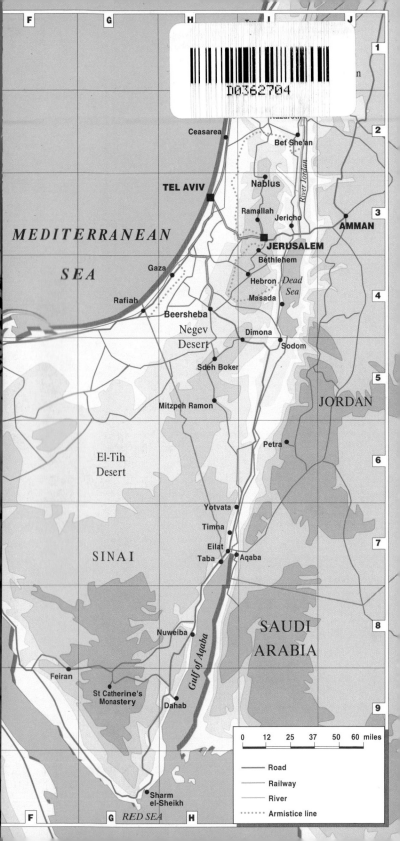

F G H I J

1

2

Ceasarea
Nazareth
Bet She'an

River Jordan

TEL AVIV
Nablus

Ramallah
Jericho
AMMAN

JERUSALEM
Bethlehem

MEDITERRANEAN

Gaza
Hebron
Dead
Sea
Masada

SEA

Rafiah
Beersheba

Negev
Desert
Dimona

Sodom

Sdeh Boker

JORDAN

Mitzpeh Ramon

Petra

El-Tih
Desert

Yotvata

Timna

Eilat
Aqaba
Taba

SINAI

SAUDI

Nuweiba

Gulf of Aqaba

ARABIA

Feiran

St Catherine's
Monastery
Dahab

Sharm
el-Sheikh

RED SEA

D0362704

| 0 | 12 | 25 | 37 | 50 | 60 miles |

Road
Railway
River
Armistice line

The region offers a unique opportunity to see, touch and briefly inhabit the scene of so many of the episodes recounted in the Bible; to reflect upon its heroes and heroines and imagine them in the setting in which they actually lived; to walk in their footsteps, contemplate the same landscapes, experience – as they did – the heat of the day and cool of the night, breathe the same scents and come as close as is humanly possible to the places and objects that were theirs in the hope of acquiring, like an echo from the past, some tiny part of the "holiness" of this Holy Land.

Photograph: The ramparts of Jerusalem, early 1900's

The overwhelming desire to capture something of this "holiness" has led believers, in the name of a piety only loosely connected to the beauty and reverence of the sites, to build a host of chapels, churches, basilicas, synagogues and mosques without being able to determine the exact events they are intended to glorify. But this does not mean they are merely pious inventions. Far from it. It simply means that the authenticity of a holy place has less to do with its archeology than the fact that tradition has chosen to honor a particular event in a particular place. It is the event rather than the place that is worthy of veneration.

Photograph: Village of Askar, east of Nablus, early 1900's

Essentially what this amounts to is an encounter between a God in search of humanity and pilgrims in search of God. The Holy Land remains a unique environment for this experience. Perhaps this is because the landscapes, the light, the scents and the silence have changed so little; or because similar dramas are still being enacted; or because the richness and variety of the encounters experienced there bear the mark of a presence which alone gives meaning to this country which is seemingly so small from without and yet so vast from within.

Photograph: Jaffa, the inner harbor, early 1900's.

THE HOLY LAND IS INHABITED BY PALESTINIANS, ISRAELIS, AND
CHRISTIANS OF ALL DENOMINATIONS.
IN ORDER TO REPRESENT THEM AS FAITHFULLY AS POSSIBLE, THIS BOOK
TELLS THE DIFFICULT STORY OF THE HOLY LAND IN THEIR WORDS.

THIS IS A BORZOI BOOK
PUBLISHED BY ALFRED A. KNOPF, INC.

NUMEROUS SPECIALISTS AND ACADEMICS HAVE
CONTRIBUTED TO THIS GUIDE: SPECIAL THANKS TO:
CLAUDE SITBON AND SLIMANE ZÉGHIDOUR.

EDITOR: Catherine Fouré
Assisted by : Florence Lagrange
and Grégory Leroy, Christine Papon
(travel information)
LAYOUT: Riccardo Tremori, Olivier Brunot,
Philippe Marchand, François Chentrier
GRAPHICS: Élisabeth Cohat *with* Brigitte Célérier,
assisted by: Valérie Gornot, Frédéric Danhez
TRANSLATION: Nathalie Le Jean,
Pascale Serck-Kérourérdan

ADVISOR: Jean-Olivier Héron.

NATURE: Philippe J. Dubois, Fréréric Bony *with*
Amir Ben David, Alexi Fossi and Sophie Nick,
Arié Issard, Philippe J. Dubois
HISTORY: Mireille Hadas-Lebel, Vincent Cauche,
Alain Dieckhoff, André Lemaire, Piere de
Miroschedji, George Tate
LANGUAGE: Ane-Marie Delcambre,
Mireille Hadas-Lebel, Eldad Beck
ART & TRADITIONS: Nadine Shankar,
Ammon Shiloah
RELIGION: Anne-Marie Delcambre, Michèle
Jarton, Rabbin Daniel Gottlieb, Azedine
Beschaouch
ARCHITECTURE: Suad Amiry, Carine Cohn,
Frère Louis-Marie, Pierre de Miroschedji
THE HOLY LAND AS SEEN BY PAINTERS:
Maurice Arama

BIBLICAL ITINERARIES:
Sister Cristilla Taudière
ITINERARIES IN THE HOLY LAND:
Séverine Mathorel *with* Michael Ben-
Joseph, Yves Boiret, Gérald Finkielsztejn,

Frère Louis-Marie, Cléry Guélaud, Mireille
Hadas-Lebel, Hamdan Taha, George Hintlian,
Michèle Jarton, Kathy Jones, André Lemaire,
Menahem Marcus, Roni Mishal, Pierre de
Miroschedji, M. and Mme. Hamzeh Natsche,
Sophie Nick, Émile Puech, Marie-Jeanne Roche,
Raphaël Rosner, Olivier Sanmartin, Anne Saurat,
Nadine Shenkar, Ayala and Claude Sitbon,
Abraham Avi Schwarz, Henri de Villefranche,
Catherine Weill-Rochant, Slimane Zéghidour

PRACTICAL INFORMATION:
Jean-Pierre Girard *with* Florence Lagrange,
Grégory Leroy, Christine Papon

ILLUSTRATIONS:
NATURE: Frédéric Bony, Anne Bodin,
Jean Chevalier, Gismonde Curiace, François
Desbordes, Claire Felloni, François Place,
Franck Stephan, Pascal Robin, John Wilkinson
ARCHITECTURE: Bruno Lenormand *with* Domitille
Héron, Jean-Benoît Héron, Jean-Olivier Héron
LITERATURE: Jean-Olivier Héron
ITINERARIES: Jean-Olivier Héron,
Domitille Héron, Jean-Benoît Héron
PRACTICAL INFORMATION: Jean-Olivier Héron,
Maurice Pommier
MAPS: Vincent Bruno *with* Stéphane Girel,
Isabelle-Anne Chatellard (colour), Dominique
Duplantier, Laure Massin, Patrick Mérienne
COMPUTER GRAPHICS: Paul Coulbois,
Emmanuel Calamy, Catherine Frouin-Marmouget
and Catherine Zacharopoulou (AFDEC)
PHOTOGRAPHY: Éric Guillemot, Patrick Léger
WE WOULD LIKE TO THANK:
Philippe Béguerie, Odette Kurz, Marie-Paule
Garçault, Yitzchak Gutterman, Philippe Henault,
Jean-Baptiste Humbert, Gilles Martin, Galit
Netzet, Jean-Cristophe Peaucel, Avner Rahan,
Elias Sanbar, Hilan Sibony, Faouzi Zayadine

TRANSLATED BY WENDY ALLATSON AND HELEN GRUBIN.
EDITED AND TYPESET BY BOOK CREATION SERVICES, LONDON.
PRINTED IN ITALY BY EDITORIALE LIBRARIA.

THE
HOLY LAND

KNOPF GUIDES

CONTENTS

NATURE, *15*

Geography and geology, *16*
Arava Valley, *18*
Negev Steppe, *20*
Wadis, *22*
Migrations, *24*
Coral reef, *26*
Fish and fishing, *28*
Mediterranean belt, *30*
Irrigation, *32*
Fruits and vegetables, *34*

HISTORY, *35*

Chronology, *36*
The Land of Canaan, *44*
The Kingdom of David and Solomon, *46*
The Hasmonean dynasty, *48*
Roman rule, *50*
Muslim Palestine, *52*
The Kingdom of Jerusalem, *54*
1948, *56*
Languages, *58*

ARTS AND TRADITION, *61*

Pottery, *62*
Oil lamps, *64*
Palestinian embroidery, *66*
Jewelry, *68*
Arab and Jewish music, *70*
Arab and Jewish dances, *72*
Food: bread, *74*
Olives, *76*

RELIGIONS, *77*

Origins and history of Judaism, *78*
Jewish festivals, *80*
Judaism in the Holy Land, *82*
Origins and history of Christianity, *84*
Christian festivals, *86*
Christianity in the Holy Land, *88*
Origins and history of Islam, *90*
Muslim festivals, *92*
Islam in the Holy Land, *94*
Calendar, *96*
Glossary, *98*

ARCHITECTURE, *105*

Synagogues, *106*
Churches, *110*
Mosques, *114*
Early architecture, *118*
Herodian architecture, *120*
Roman architecture, *122*
Byzantine architecture, *124*
Islamic architecture, *126*
Crusader architecture, *128*
Traditional Palestinian villages, *130*
Kibbutzim and moshavim, *132*
Nomads' tents, *134*

THE HOLY LAND AS SEEN BY ARTISTS, *135*

THE HOLY LAND AS SEEN BY WRITERS, *145*

SINAI, *167*

The Holy Scriptures, *168*
Saint Catherine's Monastery, *174*

SINAI

EILAT, *181*

Eilat, *182*
Eilat to Beersheba, *184*
The Nabateans, *188*

EILAT TO BEERSHEBA

BEERSHEBA, *193*

The Holy Scriptures, *194*
Beersheba to the Dead Sea, *198*
Masada, *202*
Qumran, a Sectarian "monastery", *212*
The Holy Scriptures, *216*
Beersheba to Jerusalem via Hebron, *220*
Architecture and water, *224*

BEERSHEBA
TO JERUSALEM

JERUSALEM, *231*

The Holy Scriptures, *234*
Walls and gates, *244*
The Citadel Museum, *252*
The Jewish quarter, *254*
Temple Mount, *260*
The Christian quarter, *266*
The Via Dolorosa, *268*
The Holy Sepulcher, *272*
The Muslim quarter, *280*
The Dome of the Rock, *284*

Al-Aqsa Mosque, *286*
Modern Jerusalem, *290*
The Israel Museum, *298*
Hadassah Synagogue, *304*
Jerusalem to Jericho, *310*
The tell of Jericho, *316*
Qasr Hisham, *318*
The Holy Scriptures, *324*
Jerusalem to Gaza, *326*
The monastery of Abu Ghosh, *328*

JERUSALEM

TEL AVIV, *337*

Jaffa, *338*
Tel Aviv, *342*
Ha'aretz Museum, *348*
Museum of the Diaspora, *350*
South of Tel Aviv, *352*
Wine, *354*
Tel Aviv to Rosh Hanikra, *356*
Underwater excavations at Caesarea, *360*
The Holy Scriptures, *362*
Hammam El-Pasha, *370*

TEL AVIV TO
ROSH HANIKRA

TIBERIAS, *375*

The Holy Scriptures, *376*
Tiberias, *378*
Lower Galilee, *384*
The Holy Scriptures, *386*
Tells, *394*
Upper Galilee and Golan, *398*
The Jordan, *406*

LOWER GALILEE

UPPER GALILEE

PRACTICAL INFORMATION, *409*

Useful addresses, *441*

APPENDICES, *461*

Bibliography, *462*
List of illustrations, *466*
Index, *473*

THE HOLY LAND

1. EILAT 2. AQABA 3. TIMNA 4. MITZPEH RAMON 5. BEERSHEBA 6. ARAD 7. GAZA 8. ASHDOD 9. HEBRON 10. JERUSALEM 11. JERICHO 12. TEL AVIV 13. NABLUS (SHECHEM) 14. HAIFA 15. SAFED (ZEFAT) 16. AKKO

1. RAS MUHAMMED 2. SHARM AL-SHEIKH 3. DAHAB 4. MOUNT CATHERINE 5. WADI FEIRAN 6. ST CATHERINE'S MONASTERY 7. MOUNT SINAI 8. NUWEIBA 9. TABA 10. EILAT 11. AQABA

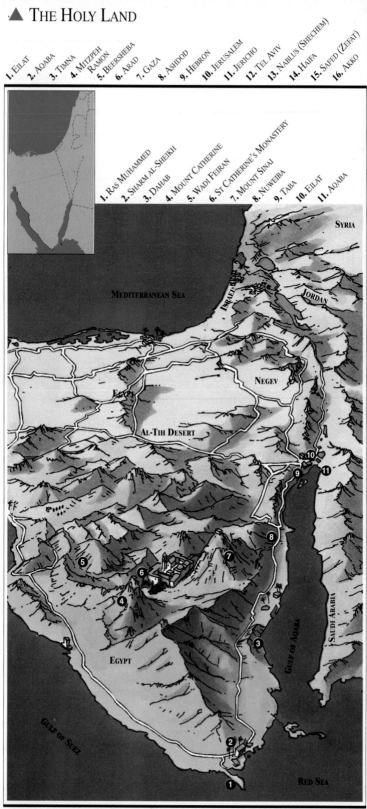

MEDITERRANEAN SEA

SYRIA

JORDAN

ISRAEL

NEGEV

EGYPT

AL-TIH DESERT

EGYPT

GULF OF SUEZ

GULF OF AQABA

SAUDI ARABIA

RED SEA

HOW TO USE THIS GUIDE

(Sample page shown from the guide to Venice)

The symbols at the top of
each page refer to
the different parts
of the guide.

■ NATURAL ENVIRONMENT

● UNDERSTANDING VENICE

▲ ITINERARIES

◆ PRACTICAL INFORMATION

The itinerary map
shows the main points
of interest along the
way and is intended
to help you find
your bearings.

The mini-map
locates the partic
itinerary within
the wider area
covered by
the guide.

●▲■◆
The symbols alongside a
title or within the text
itself provide cross-
references to a theme
or place dealt with
elsewhere in the guide.

★ The star symbol
signifies that a particular
site has been singled out
by the publishers for its
special beauty,
atmosphere or cultural
interest.

At the beginning of eac
itinerary, the suggested
means of transport to b
used and the time it will
take to cover the area a
indicated:

🚤 By boat
🚶 On foot
🚲 By bicycle
🕐 Duration

THE GATEWAY TO VENICE ★

PONTE DELLA LIBERTA. Built by the Austrians 50 years after
the Treaty of Campo Formio in 1797 ● *34,* to link Venice with
Milan. The bridge ended the thousand-year separation from
the mainland and shook the city's economy to its roots as
Venice, already in the throes of the industrial revolution, saw

🚶 Half a day

BRIDGES TO VENICE

NATURE

GEOGRAPHY AND GEOLOGY, *16*
ARAVA VALLEY, *18*
NEGEV STEPPE, *20*
WADIS, *22*
MIGRATIONS, *24*
CORAL REEF, *26*
FISH AND FISHING, *28*
MEDITERRANEAN BELT, *30*
IRRIGATION, *32*
FRUIT AND VEGETABLES, *34*

GEOGRAPHY AND GEOLOGY

The Dead Sea has record levels of salinity and – at 1,286 feet below sea level – is the lowest point in the world.

The Holy Land is a land of contrasts. It has some of the most diversified natural environments in the Middle East. This diversity can be explained by the undulating nature of the terrain, with its many folds and faults, and the combined effect of desert, tropical and predominantly Mediterranean climatic influences. The desert influence, due to the presence of the Saharan Belt, makes the summers extremely hot, while the low-pressure systems formed over the Mediterranean and southern Europe mean that winters are mild and wet. Subsoil and climate are two important factors in understanding the country's hydrology.

MEDITERRANEAN SEA

Tel Aviv ●

Fruit is grown in the sandy, fertile soil of the coastal plain, bounded to the north by Mount Carmel.

In Judea the transition between the desert and Mediterranean influences is at its most dramatic. The forests which covered the region over 1,500 years ago have almost completely disappeared as a result of human intervention.

Sea level (0 feet)

Level of the Dead Sea (1,286 feet below sea level)

Basalt

Marl and gypsum (Pleistocene)

Sand and sandstone (Pleistocene-Pliocene)

Chalk, marl and limestone (Eocene-Paleocene)

Limestone – dolomite - chalk (Upper and Middle Cretaceous)

Sandstone (Lower Cretaceous to Paleozoi

Magmatic rock (Pre-Cambrian)

/ Main faults

The Nahal Zin is a seasonal river that winds through the very heart of the Negev ■ 20.

GEOLOGY

The carbonated rock of the Cretaceous (limestone, dolomite, chalk) constitutes an important geological feature since its folding has formed the country's mountainous "backbone". The coastal plain consists of Quaternary sandstone, while part of Galilee is covered with basalt.

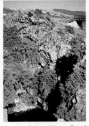

The foothills of Mount Hermon have a characteristically Mediterranean vegetation, which becomes increasingly alpine toward the summit. Snow is common until April.

Sudanese zone (subtropical savannah)
Mediterranean zone
Irano-Turanian zone (steppe)
Arabian-Sahara zone (desert)

BIOGEOGRAPHY

Israel lies at the intersection of four main biogeographical systems. Within a distance of less than 20 miles, between Jerusalem and the Dead Sea, the Mediterranean zone (2,625 feet) gives way to the eastern influence of the Irano-Turanian zone and the desertic influence of the Arabian-Sahara zone (656 feet), and then the oases of the tropical Sudanese zone of the River Jordan and the Dead Sea.

Source of the River Jordan

LAKE TIBERIAS (SEA OF GALILEE)
The hills around the lake are covered with black basalt rocks.

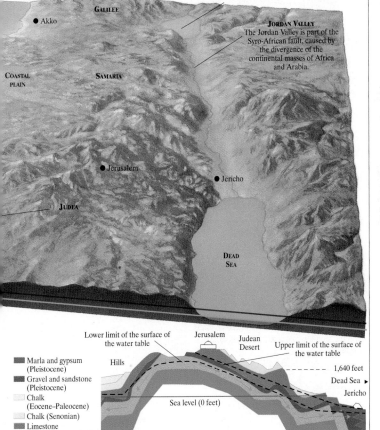

GALILEE

● Akko

JORDAN VALLEY
The Jordan Valley is part of the Syro-African fault, caused by the divergence of the continental masses of Africa and Arabia.

COASTAL PLAIN

SAMARIA

● Jerusalem

● Jericho

JUDEA

DEAD SEA

Lower limit of the surface of the water table
Jerusalem
Judean Desert
Upper limit of the surface of the water table

Marla and gypsum (Pleistocene)
Gravel and sandstone (Pleistocene)
Chalk (Eocene–Paleocene)
Chalk (Senonian)
Limestone (Upper Cenomanian)
Marl and chalk (Middle Cenomanian)
Dolomite and limestone (Lower Cenomanian)
Clay and marl (Lower Cretaceous)
→ Direction of flow of water table

Hills
1,640 feet
Dead Sea ►
Jericho
Sea level (0 feet)

HYDRO-GEOLOGICAL CROSS SECTION: JERUSALEM TO JERICHO. The high permeability of limestone, dolomite and sandstone allows around 30 percent of the rainfall to replenish the water tables – the country's main water reserves. Each year water flows into Lake Tiberias (Sea of Galilee) from Mount Hermon, the Anti-Lebanon mountains and the Jordan floods, generating 650 million cubic yards of water. The water tables of the limestone regions provide 520 million cubic yards, while the same quantity is pumped from the water tables of the coastal plain.

17

ARAVA VALLEY

Israel's Arava Valley is part of the great Syro-African
fault, which runs from East Africa to southern Turkey.
The region is in fact an extension of the Sudanese zone,
where summer temperatures can reach 118°F. Heavy soil
and wind erosion have formed its characteristic gravel
plains, sand dunes, alluvial fans and, in the lowest parts of
the valley, salt flats. The subtropical climate is further
evident in the presence of acacias, and some African
flora and fauna are at home here too.

Even the smallest wadis ■ 22 are colonized
by acacias.

ARABIAN GAZELLE
The Hai Bar Nature Reserve south of Yotvata
▲ 186, was created to protect rare species
such as the Arabian gazelle which is
disappearing from the Arabian peninsula.

STRIPED HYENA
This nocturnal animal can sometimes
be seen in broad daylight in the more
remote parts of the valley.

AFRICAN WILD CAT
The desert wild cat is leaner and has paler fur
than its European counterpart.

LITTLE GREEN BEE-EATER
These birds feed on ants, bees and other flying insects.

"ACACIA RADDIANA"
These tough trees give the valley its savannah-like appearance. They grow in the wadis where they provide food and shelter for a number of desert species.

"LORANTHUS ACACIAE"
This semi-parasitic plant lives on acacias. Its nectar is an important source of food for certain birds (including the sunbird).

DESERT LARK
This sturdy lark is a common sight on the gravel plains of the valley.

TRUMPETER FINCH
The trumpeter finch can be seen at dawn and dusk, when it comes to drink from the pools of the kibbutzim.

PALESTINE SUNBIRD
This beautiful little tropical bird feeds on insects and nectar.

HOOPOE LARK
Appears very different in flight, revealing a striking black-and-white wing pattern.

FAT SAND RAT
The fat sand rat feeds on plants that grow on the grassy plains of the valley.

LESSER EGYPTIAN JERBOA
Its specially adapted tail and hind legs enable it to make impressive leaps.

GERBIL
This nocturnal creature is found in the rocky areas of the valley.

ICE PLANT
Translucent projections on this plant's leaves absorb water and enable it to survive in this arid environment.

19

NEGEV STEPPE

In the northwest of the Negev, the desert gives way to arid steppe, a continuation of the Steppe Belt of the high plateau of central Asia which extends into Israel. The sandy terrain around Ze'elim is replaced by rocky steppe as the altitude increases, reaching heights of over 3,300 feet in places: Har Ramon, for example, overlooks a vast crater created by the erosion of the ridges of the Negev at their most fragile point. Part of the steppe's remarkable flora belongs to the Irano-Turanian botanical zone to the east, while its fauna includes animals, such as the wolf, not commonly found in the Holy Land.

The annual plants populating the sandy steppe between Beersheba ▲ *196* and Sdeh Boker ▲ *192* are dominated by grasses such as feather-grass, *Stipa capensis*.

HOODED CROW
Hooded crows are a common sight on the sandy steppe and cereal-producing plains around Urim and Ofaqim. They are never far from the kibbutzim where they find a plentiful supply of food.

This pale form of the red fox is well adapted to the arid conditions of the steppe.

DORCAS GAZELLE
This beautiful gazelle is a protected species throughout Israel. The careful observer will find it relatively easy to spot as it makes its way across the Negev.

BROWN HARE
With its pale fur and large ears (providing optimum ventilation), the brown hare is well adapted to the arid steppe environment.

Flowering clumps of "king's-rod", or branching asphodel, dominate the landscape in spring.

STONE CURLEW
The melancholy wailing cry, similar to the curlew's, of this nocturnal bird is heard from dusk onwards.

Female

Male

BLACK-BELLIED SANDGROUSE
These birds inhabit arid, rocky areas. They can be seen in the morning and evening when they gather noisily near water.

HOUBARA BUSTARD
The houbara bustard, hunted mercilessly from Pakistan to Morocco, has found a refuge in the Negev.

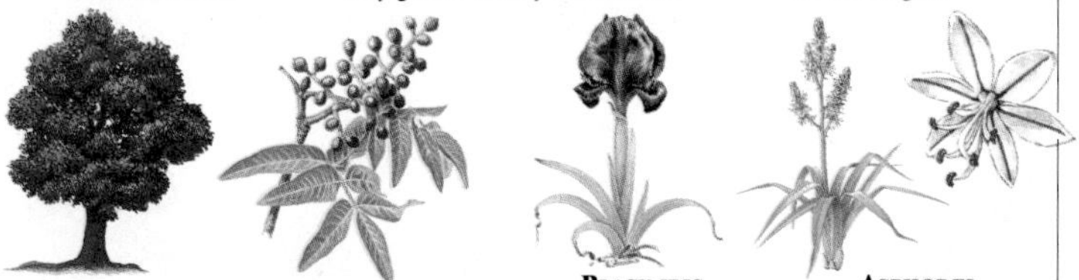

TEREBINTH
This tree dominates the Negev landscape. It is one of the oldest trees in the Holy Land and is closely associated with the Bible.

BLACK IRIS
This plant thrives in the chalky soil of the Negev and Judean deserts. It produces its striking, near-black flowers from March to May.

ASPHODEL
Great, flowering clumps of asphodel – ignored by grazing animals – dominate the landscape from January to April.

Dorcas gazelles move about in the early morning and late evening, remaining in the shade during the hottest part of the day.

CRESTED LARK
This bird is a common sight in rocky parts of the steppe.

Clumps of monospermic sagebrush

Houbara bustard

GRAY WOLF Wolves are still found in Israel, from the Judean Desert ▲ 330 to the Negev ▲ 187 and the Arava Valley ■ 18, ▲ 186. These naturally timid animals can sometimes be seen in open countryside, in broad daylight. In the mountains of the Negev they tend to be seen in winter, after snowfalls.

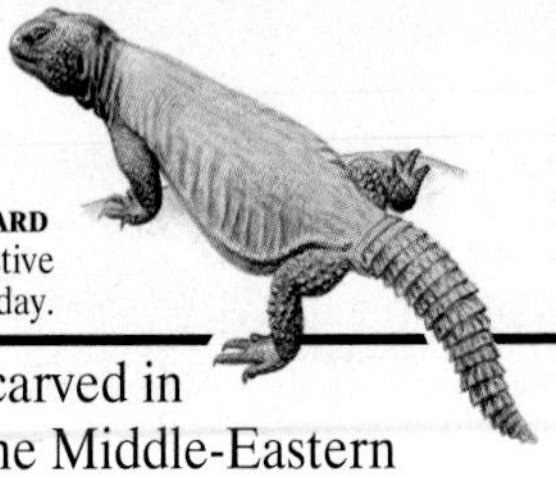

EGYPTIAN SPINY-TAILED LIZARD
This large lizard is particularly active
during the hottest part of the day.

The deep, steep-sided gorges, or wadis, carved in
the rock by ancient water currents, are the Middle-Eastern
equivalent of the North African wadis. They are a typical
feature of arid, desert landscapes and act as a kind of oasis
for wildlife. After torrential rains they are transformed, for
several hours and sometimes several days, into fast-flowing
rivers due to the low permeability of the soil. Shallow,
water-filled basins and permanent pools ensure the survival
of plants, animals and sometimes people. Some of the larger
wadis have been transformed into palm groves and sustain
a natural subtropical vegetation.

DESERT CISTANCHE
This parasitic plant
flowers in late winter
when the wadis are
relatively cool.

**CROWN OF THORNS
(CHRIST'S THORN)**
The spiny branches of
this tree are said to
have been used to
make the crown of
thorns worn by Christ
on the cross. Hence
its botanical name:
Ziziphus spina-christi.

After the early spring rains, flowers and grasses bloom briefly on the banks of the wadis.

Its toes are arranged like an elephant's.

ROCK HYRAX
The rock hyrax is about the size of a rabbit. It lives in colonies and feeds, mainly at night, on acacias. It can also be seen basking in the sun during the day.

NUBIAN IBEX
This large wild goat lives on the steep, rocky slopes of high cliffs. Ibex are a common sight in the Ein Gedi Nature Reserve ▲ *210*.

BLACKSTART
This slim gray bird haunts rocky wadis but also likes to perch in bushes and acacias.

FAN-TAILED RAVEN
The bird's short tail gives it a strange appearance when in flight.

SINAI ROSEFINCH
This timid little finch is only found in the Holy Land.

TRISTRAM'S GACKLE
Its loud whistling calls betray its whereabouts.

■ MIGRATIONS

STEPPE EAGLE. The steppe eagle, which nests in central Asia, migrates in February–March and again in late October–early November. In spring up to 75,000 individuals fly over Eilat ▲ *182*.

The position of the Holy Land – at the geographical intersection of Europe, Asia and Africa – makes it the biannual venue for a spectacular migration of birds. Rather than migrating across the sea, some of the larger, high-flying birds (birds of prey, storks and pelicans) prefer to fly overland between their winter quarters in east Africa and their nesting sites which stretch from eastern Europe to central Asia. In spring they fly up the Jordan Valley, via Eilat, while in autumn tens of thousands of birds migrate over central Israel and the Negev.

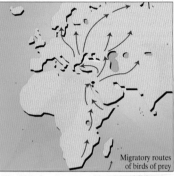

Migratory routes of birds of prey

The Holy Land acts as a "bottleneck" for the large, long-flight birds moving between their winter quarters and nesting sites. These birds cover thousand of miles using warm air currents to gain height.

LESSER SPOTTED EAGLE
Up to 142,000 of these birds have been recorded crossing central Israel in autumn *en route* to east Africa.

BLACK KITE

The black kite migrates in spring and is found in the Holy Land in March–April. Between 24,000 and 31,000 birds fly over Eilat on their way to eastern Europe and western Asia.

LEVANT SPARROWHAWK

Almost 50,000 individuals fill the sky above Eilat between mid-April and early May before flying on to central Asia.

STEPPE BUZZARD

The steppe buzzard nests in central Asia, migrating to Eilat in March–April and toward Jerusalem in September–November. Up to 460,000 individuals can be seen in spring.

HONEY BUZZARD

Up to 850,000 of these birds migrate, arriving in the Holy Land mainly in spring (early May) as they return from equatorial Africa.

BLACK STORK

Twice a year thousands of these rare storks fly over the Holy Land as they migrate from eastern Europe and Russia. As many as 3,500 birds were counted in a single day in March.

WHITE STORK

White storks fly over the Holy Land from February to April and August to September, mainly via the Jordan Valley ▲ 414. As many as 310,000 birds may migrate in a year.

Black stork

White stork

Steppe eagle

Lesser spotted eagle

Black kite

Honey buzzard

Steppe buzzard

Levant sparrowhawk

CORAL REEF

This colony of *Acropora* or Stagshorn coral has formed a clump which looks like a sunshade.

The Red Sea is part of the Syro-African fault and is famous for the wide variety and color of its fish, corals and other invertebrates of Indo-Pacific origin. In the Gulf of Aqaba alone there are around 120 species of soft coral. Coral reefs develop in warm, clear waters with a high salt content, little sediment and relatively little wave movement. Eilat is an ideal place from which to explore the underwater world of the coral reef.

The scales of the imperial angelfish go through several stages before reaching the full beauty of adulthood.

Blue-speckled parrot fish

The masked puffer fish is a member of the puffer family, and can inflate itself at the slightest hint of danger.

Soft coral *Dendronephtia*

Organ-pipe sponge

Red sponge

Sea slug *Chromodoris*

Sea urchin

Slingjaw wrasse

Giant clam

Fan worm *Sabella*

"Fire" coral

During the day the gray moray stays hidden in a crevice in the reef.

Sea anemone *Gyrostoma*

Banded *Amphiprion* or anemone fish

Banded coral shrimp

The biological diversity of coral reefs is truly remarkable. Corals, sponges, sea anemones, sea urchins, molluscs and prawns live together in harmony or even – as in the case of sea anemones with the anemone fish or *Amphiprion* – in symbiosis. Other species such as sponges act as filters.

The flying scorpion fish swims slowly through the semi-darkness of the reef in search of its prey (crabs and fish).

The greatest variety of fish is found near the reef, which provides both food and shelter.

The three types of reef – terrace, fringing reef and bottom rock – are defined in terms of depth. The intermediate reef has the widest variety of fauna.

Breaker
Barrier reef
Sea level
Coastal rocks
Lagoon
Rim
Reef wall
Fringing reef
Sandy slope

CORAL POLYPS
Polyps live in huge communities, growing on the calcareous skeletons of their predecessors. Over time, they form the coral reef.

The surgeon-fish, indigenous to the Red Sea, has a sharp spike at the end of its tail.

Butterfly fish – also known as "tobies" – live in shoals.

Blue tang, an endemic species, belongs to the "surgeon" family.

Anthias teaniatus

The red or tropical grouper rarely grows to more than 30 inches long. It lives in the cracks and crevices of the reef.

Anthias squamipinnis

FISH AND FISHING

Akko ▲ *376*, founded by the
Phoenicians, is one of the oldest
Mediterranean ports.

Fishing is an age-old tradition
which has been carried on in
the Holy Land since Biblical times. Although it is now a
secondary activity, large numbers of *lanchas* (motorized
dinghies), trawlers and *chincholas*, the local name for seiners,
can still be seen in the old ports of Akko and Jaffa and the
large modern ports of Kishon (Haifa) and Ashdod.
The 20,000–30,000 tons of fish caught in the Holy Land every
year consist mainly of sardines, red (or striped) mullet and
prawns. The variety of species caught has almost doubled
since the opening of the Suez Canal, which allows fish to
migrate from the Red Sea to the Mediterranean.

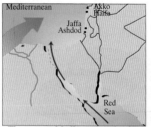

Migration of
Indo-Pacific species
Mineral salts from
the Nile

The eastern Mediterranean has been
colonized, via the Suez Canal, by Red
Sea species. These "Lessepsian"
species were named after the canal's
engineer, Ferdinand de Lesseps.

"LANCHAS"
Lanchas – motorized fishing dinghies between
23 and 33 feet long – are used for day or night
fishing, depending on the techniques used.

TRAMMELS
Trammels consist of three vertical series of
nets, placed close together near the rocks
and resting on the bottom.

TRAWLS
Grouper trawls or charaks are used at
night and located by means of buoys fitted
with storm lanterns. The most widely used
bait is horse mackerel (**1**) and live
cuttlefish (**2**) which attracts amberjack.

AMBERJACK
Amberjacks often
congregate around
metal wrecks.

CUTTLEFISH
This is not a fish at
all, but a mollusk,
related to squids and
octopuses.

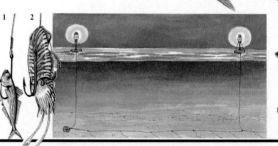

28

Trawling was introduced by the Italians in the 1950's. Trawlers usually work the tides for three days at a time, catching red mullet by day and prawns by night.

Trawl lines

Danleno ball

Bottom cable with bobbins

Panels

Wing

Top cable with floats

Bottom of net

CRYSTAL PRAWN
A "Lessepsian" species.

TRAWLING
The net sweeps through the depths, held open by two pieces of wood and metal. The fish, terrified by the cable which drags along the sea bed, take refuge in the bottom of the net.

HORSE MACKEREL
Caught with trawl and drawnets.

RED MULLET
This brilliantly colored fish is a very popular dish.

NILE MULLET
Another "Lessepsian" species, with a characteristic yellow band along its body.

1 The net is cast in the form of an open pouch.

2 The seine is then drawn in.

STREEP DASSIE OR ZEBRA
Rocky coastlines are the favorite haunt of this highly prized fish.

SEINES OR DRAWNETS
Seiners are between 36 and 43 feet long. In summer these brightly lit boats, known as lamparos, fish at night for sardines. During the rest of the year they catch the smaller members of the tuna family (bonito) and amberjack.

SARDINE
Sardines are the most heavily fished. They thrive in Israel's coastal waters, enriched by sediment from the Nile.

DUSKY SEA PERCH OR DUSKY GROUPER
The dusky grouper, the most highly prized catch, can grow to lengths of around 4 feet.

ATLANTIC, OR BELTED, BONITO
This migratory species feeds on small fish such as sardines and mackerel. It is caught using a draw net.

GRAY MULLET
Fishermen surround shoals with nets. They then create a disturbance to frighten the fish which become entangled in the nets.

COMMERSON'S BARRED SPANISH MACKEREL
This bonito-mackerel has recently arrived from the Red Sea ▲ *178* via the Suez Canal.

29

MEDITERRANEAN BELT

Short-toed eagle

The Mediterranean belt, originally covered predominantly with oak forests, was badly damaged by Neolithic Man. The trees were gradually replaced by a wide variety of different types of shrubs that formed a scrub-like vegetation known as garrigue (limestone regions) or maquis (siliceous terrain). The desert influence of the Negev and the Jordan Valley has produced a number of unusual plant combinations, some of which are found nowhere else in the Mediterranean Basin.

The wide variety of flora found in the hills around Jerusalem is endemic to the Mediterranean Basin.

Greek tortoise   Hermann's tortoise

GREEK TORTOISE
This tortoise is a common sight in European zoos. It prefers the dry conditions of the garrigue.

BUTTERFLY ORCHID
The butterfly orchid grows in chalky or slightly acid soil and flowers from March to May.

HAIRY CALICOTOME
In spring the hillsides are covered with the yellow flowers of the hairy calicotome, a close relative of broom.

ITALIAN GLADIOLUS
This gladiolus flowers from March to June in cultivated soil by the roadside, on hillsides and on the garrigue.

SAGE-LEAVED ROCK ROSE
The sage-leaved rock rose grows in large, dense colonies on the hills around Jerusalem.

RED-RUMPED SWALLOW
Large numbers of these swallows nest under bridges and on low cliffs, especially in Galilee.

LESSER KESTREL
The lesser kestrel lives in colonies, nesting on cliffs or in old buildings.

SARDINIAN WARBLER
These birds are found in large numbers in the garrigue around Jerusalem. Their grating calls can be heard in early spring.

GOLDFINCH
Flocks of these brightly colored, gregarious birds brighten up the winter landscape of the garrigue.

YELLOW-VENTED BULBUL
This bird is a common sight in orchards and parks. It is never far from human habitation and can be heard in the early hours of the morning.

Helichrysum sanguineum

Wild oats

Galilee orchis

Hairy flax

Asiatic buttercup

LAUGHING DOVE
This bird is frequently seen in Galilee, on the coastal plains, in towns and their wooded environs.

EGYPTIAN MONGOOSE (PHARAOH'S RAT)
The Egyptian mongoose can be seen at dusk or early in the morning, mainly on the coastal plain near Tel Aviv.

Some plants on the garrigue have a highly developed root system while others have waxy or downy leaves for greater water retention. All have adapted to the poor soil and the hot, dry Mediterranean climate.

31

■ IRRIGATION

Roman aqueducts – like the one in Caesarea (right) – were early examples of irrigation in the Holy Land.

Water – whether for consumption or irrigation – is a rare commodity in the Holy Land, where the arid climate makes distribution difficult. Drilling was carried out for the first time in the early 20th century when more land was given over to agriculture. Water wheels were gradually replaced by motorized pumps, and ancient irrigation channels by mechanized watering systems. Drilling (to depths of several hundred feet), the development of vertical pumping and the construction of a complex distribution system soon made it possible to irrigate the Negev. The trickle-watering technique, developed in the 1970's, was the next stage in a more rational use of water for agriculture.

— National Water Carrier
—— Secondary water-supply network

WATER SUPPLY

The National Water Carrier, completed in 1964, is Israel's largest irrigation project. This network of canals, reservoirs and pumping stations covers the southern and central regions of the Holy Land and provides 13,500 million cubic feet of water per year for irrigation and consumption.

The Jordan Canal, one of the main canals in the water-supply network, was built as part of the National Water Carrier. It runs from the Sea of Galilee and covers a distance of 10 miles. Its trapezoidal cross section measures 39 feet at ground level at its widest point. The sides are fenced off to reduce the risk of pollution caused by man and animals.

Rotating spray systems were widely used during the 1970's. Today these are often replaced by a trickle-watering system.

Crops grown under cloches, to reduce evaporation, and irrigated by trickle-watering are increasingly widespread in Israel.

Salt water pumped from beneath the desert is used to irrigate the land. Wells as deep as 3,280 and even 7,545 feet have been sunk in the Arava Valley.

Computers are an important "fertigation" aid to farmers, enabling them to supply the exact amounts of water and fertilizer necessary for trickle watering.

Plant

Distributor

Area of high humidity

Area of humidity

1

TRICKLE WATERING. By using a device which "drip feeds" water, it is possible to maintain an area of humidity adapted to the particular needs of the plants being grown.

In a well-prepared, fine-grained soil (**1**) capillarity creates a hemispherical area of humidity. In an unprepared, stony and compacted soil the area of humidity is random (**2**). This is even more pronounced in a coarse-grained soil (**3**) where gravity detracts from the efficiency of the process.

Tomatoes watered with salt water have a characteristically sweet flavor.

The distributor is a spiral tube which reduces pressure by extending distance. The water is trickle fed at the base of the plant through a wide hole less likely to become blocked.

Irrigation techniques used on the arid lands of Israel have been exported to the desert regions of South Africa, the US and Australia.

"Thou visitest the earth, and waterest it:
thou greatly enrichest it with the river of God,
which is full of water: thou preparest them corn,
when thou hast so provided for it.
Thou waterest the ridges thereof abundantly:
thou settlest the furrows thereof:
thou makest it soft with showers:
thou blessest the springing thereof.
Thou crownest the year with thy goodness;
and thy paths drop fatness.
They drop upon the pastures of the wilderness:
and the little hills rejoice on every side."
PSALM 65 (64)

FRUITS AND VEGETABLES

Hothouse strawberries are often grown vertically to save space.

The cultivation of fruits and vegetables in the Holy Land is the result of intensive research carried out by the Israelis. It is based on the crossing of local and imported varieties of citrus fruits, vegetables and subtropical fruits. The farming methods used by the *moshavim* ● 132 of northern Israel and the Negev are very labor-intensive, whereas the kibbutzim are mechanized and use modern techniques. In Samaria, Judea and the Gaza Strip, the Palestinians use traditional methods to cultivate small market gardens.

WATERMELON
This refreshing fruit is grown in Samaria by Palestinians.

MELON
Melons are produced by the *moshavim* and kibbutzim of the Negev and Arava Valley.

GRAPEFRUIT
Around 80 percent of this (yellow or pink) citrus fruit is produced for export.

ORANGE
Intensive research has been carried out to produce new varieties of orange.

GRAPES
The vineyards of Rehovot supply a booming wine industry. The fruit is also produced as a dessert grape.

Yellow peach   White peach

PEACHES
There are several varieties of peach. Most of the peaches produced come from northern Negev.

APPLE
The many varieties of apple that require a period of cold are grown in Upper Galilee and Golan.

PEPPER
Peppers are red, yellow, green or orange and are mainly grown on the kibbutzim of southern Israel.

EGGPLANT (AUBERGINE)
Grown by *moshavim* in the Arava and Jordan Valleys.

CUCUMBER
Cucumbers are grown in the north, in lower Galilee and especially in the Arab villages of central Israel.

TOMATO
Most of the tomatoes grown (mainly under glass) are used in the processing industry.

AVOCADO
Several varieties of this fruit are grown on plantations in northern and central Israel.

HISTORY

CHRONOLOGY, *36*
THE LAND OF CANAAN, *44*
THE KINGDOM OF DAVID
AND SOLOMON, *46*
THE HASMONEAN DYNASTY, *48*
ROMAN RULE, *50*
MUSLIM PALESTINE, *52*
THE KINGDOM OF JERUSALEM, *54*
1948, *56*
LANGUAGES, *58*

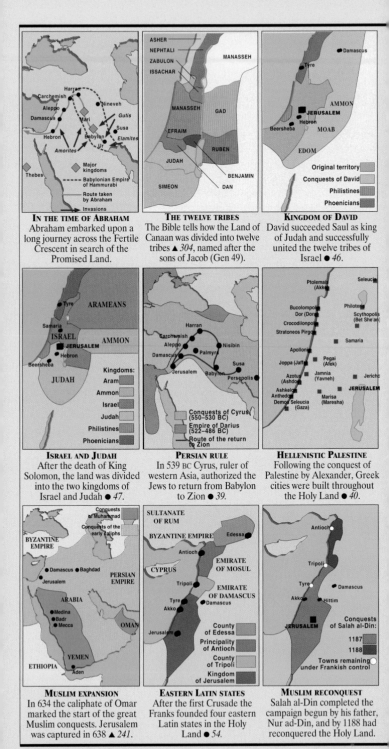

IN THE TIME OF ABRAHAM
Abraham embarked upon a long journey across the Fertile Crescent in search of the Promised Land.

THE TWELVE TRIBES
The Bible tells how the Land of Canaan was divided into twelve tribes ▲ *304*, named after the sons of Jacob (Gen 49).

KINGDOM OF DAVID
David succeeded Saul as king of Judah and successfully united the twelve tribes of Israel ● *46*.

ISRAEL AND JUDAH
After the death of King Solomon, the land was divided into the two kingdoms of Israel and Judah ● *47*.

PERSIAN RULE
In 539 BC Cyrus, ruler of western Asia, authorized the Jews to return from Babylon to Zion ● *39*.

HELLENISTIC PALESTINE
Following the conquest of Palestine by Alexander, Greek cities were built throughout the Holy Land ● *40*.

MUSLIM EXPANSION
In 634 the caliphate of Omar marked the start of the great Muslim conquests. Jerusalem was captured in 638 ▲ *241*.

EASTERN LATIN STATES
After the first Crusade the Franks founded four eastern Latin states in the Holy Land ● *54*.

MUSLIM RECONQUEST
Salah al-Din completed the campaign begun by his father, Nur ad-Din, and by 1188 had reconquered the Holy Land.

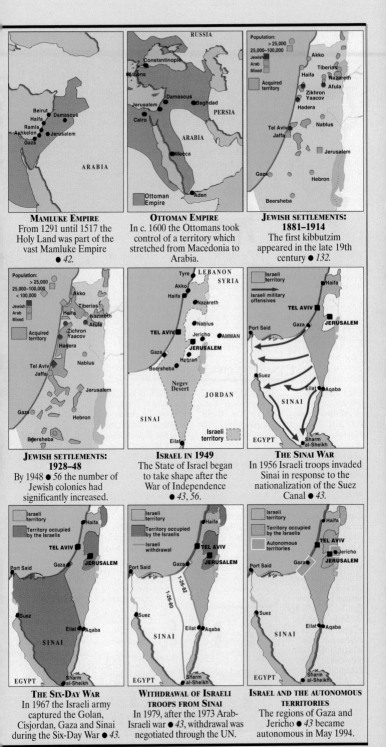

MAMLUKE EMPIRE
From 1291 until 1517 the Holy Land was part of the vast Mamluke Empire ● *42*.

OTTOMAN EMPIRE
In c. 1600 the Ottomans took control of a territory which stretched from Macedonia to Arabia.

JEWISH SETTLEMENTS: 1881–1914
The first kibbutzim appeared in the late 19th century ● *132*.

JEWISH SETTLEMENTS: 1928–48
By 1948 ● *56* the number of Jewish colonies had significantly increased.

ISRAEL IN 1949
The State of Israel began to take shape after the War of Independence ● *43, 56*.

THE SINAI WAR
In 1956 Israeli troops invaded Sinai in response to the nationalization of the Suez Canal ● *43*.

THE SIX-DAY WAR
In 1967 the Israeli army captured the Golan, Cisjordan, Gaza and Sinai during the Six-Day War ● *43*.

WITHDRAWAL OF ISRAELI TROOPS FROM SINAI
In 1979, after the 1973 Arab-Israeli war ● *43*, withdrawal was negotiated through the UN.

ISRAEL AND THE AUTONOMOUS TERRITORIES
The regions of Gaza and Jericho ● *43* became autonomous in May 1994.

37

| 10,000–8200 BC | | 3200 BC | 1200–1000 B |
| Natufian | | Canaanites | Judges |

| 16,000 BC | 12,000 BC | 8000 BC | 6000 BC | 4000 BC | 2000 BC | 1000 |

| 750,000–16,000 BC | 16,000–8000 BC | 8200–4000 BC | | 4000–3200 BC | 3200–1200 BC | 1200–587 BC |
| Paleolithic | Mesolithic | Neolithic | | Chalcolithic | Bronze Age | Iron Age |

PREHISTORY

There is evidence suggesting a human presence in Palestine, which lay on the overland route between Africa and Asia ● 44, during the Lower Paleolithic and probably even earlier. In c. 100,000 BC the so-called Proto-CroMagnon, the direct ancestor of the Upper Paleolithic European populations, lived in Galilee and Carmel ▲ 364. Between 40,000 and 16,000 BC the number of human settlements increased

and, during the Mesolithic, stone tools became smaller. A general warming of the climate was accompanied by the formation of sedentary communities of hunter-gatherers.

This occurred earlier in Palestine (c. 10,000 BC) than elsewhere with the first Natufian troglodyte villages of Ein Mallaha a Einan. Two thousand years later, the introduction of agriculture and livestock heralded the arrival of the Neolithic age. Villages became more widespread, forms of artistic and religious expression increased and the often circular architecture became more elaborate ● 118. The Holy Land was at the forefront of the cultural development of man. In c. 5600 BC it was superseded by a Mesopotamian

civilization in which pottery had already been developed. However Palestinian innovation came to the fore once again during the Chalcolithic when the use of copper ▲ 185 became widespread, especially around Beersheba (Beer Sheva), Tel Aviv and in the Lower Jordan Valley. This is known as the Ghassulian civilization.

CANAANITE CIVILIZATION

The Canaanite civilization was established during the Early Bronze Age with the birth of the first city-states ● 44 which, for reasons that are still unclear, disappeared in c. 2200 BC. For almost two hundred years Palestine was occupied by nomadic shepherds. It was not until the beginning of the Middle Bronze Age, under the influence of the Egyptian Middle Kingdom (2040–1786 BC), that the first Canaanite villages were re-established. The exact nature of the relations between Palestine and Egypt is not known, but several Canaanite principalities are mentioned in Egyptian texts of the 19th century BC

as having opposed the pharaoh. Their towns, e.g. Hatzor ▲ 403, which at the time was the capital of an important kingdom, were strongly fortified ● 118. In c. 1550 BC the pharaoh Ahmose I captured Avaris, the Hyksos capital in the Nile Delta, and pursued the Hyksos into southern Palestine. The whole of Palestine came under Egyptian control when, in

c. 1468–1436 BC, the armies of Thutmose III conquered its principalities as far as the Euphrates. For the next three hundred years Palestine was the Egyptian province of Canaan and, although the kings of the city-states of Ashkelon, Jaffa, Gezer, Jerusalem, Shechem, Megiddo and Akko may have vied with each other, they nevertheless recognized the sovereignty of the pharaoh and carried out his orders

under the watchful eye of a high-ranking Egyptian official living in Gaza ▲ 336. However, economic exploitation by Egypt and the insecurity brought about by the campaigns associated with the wars between the Canaanite city-states gradually led to the depopulation of central Cisjordan.

JUDGES

The Canaanite civilization came to an end under the combined effect of the Philistine ● 44 (the so-called Sea Peoples) and Israelite (semi-nomadic shepherds from Transjordan ● 78) invasions. The Israelites were divided into two tribes, the Bene Jacob of Aramean origin and the Yahwist Bene Israel from the eastern Nile Delta who made their way into central Cisjordan where, together with the Gibeonites, they succeeded in driving back the Canaanite-Egyptian army in the Valley of Ayalon ▲ 330. The Bene Israel settled between Jerusalem and Shechem (Nablus) ▲ 312 and, by joining forces with the Bene Jacob, laid the foundations of the Israelite tribal confederation. The kinship group known collectively as Bene Jacob was scattered into different areas (see, for example, Judges 5). Part of the group spent time in Egypt, others remained in Palestine. A more permanent cooperation was only achieved after the period of the Judges, when the kinship components (parts of which were brought in by covenant agreements) made the Israelite tribal confederation effective.

KINGS

Saul's successors, David and Solomon, united the kingdom ● 46 and enabled Israel to establish itself as a regional power. However in 931 BC the kingdom broke up ● 46. Following a coup (841 BC) in the land of Israel, to the north, Jehu established a new dynasty in Samaria, initially marked by Aramean domination. In c. 790–750 BC Jeroboam II achieved a political and economic revival. However in 720 BC Sargon II made Samaria ● 46 a province of Assyria and scattered its population ▲ 332. In 701 BC the kingdom of Judah, to the south, suffered the destructive campaign of the Neo-Assyrian king, Sennacherib, and became part of the Neo-Assyrian empire until 605 BC when it passed under Neo-Babylonian control. The two conquests of Jerusalem by Nebuchadnezzar, in 597 and 587 BC, marked the beginning of the Exile.

PERSIAN PERIOD

In 539 BC, following Cyrus' conquest of the Babylonian empire, Palestine became part of the vast Persian empire. However Cyrus granted the population (assembled in Babylon) the right to return to their lands and re-establish their own form of worship, with the result that some of the Exiles returned to Jerusalem, rebuilt the Temple and, under the direction of Nehemiah, reconstructed the walls. The provinces of Judah and Samaria were administered by governors, usually Jewish or Samaritan ▲ 313 notables, while the western coast came partly under Phoenician control. The conquest of Alexander the Great put an end to Persian domination in Judea.

EXILE
The relative freedom enjoyed by the exiles in Babylon enabled them to rebuild their community. The Judeans, captives within a pagan empire, were granted the right to assemble for prayer and meditation. Priests and prophets were thus able to maintain the Jewish culture ● 58 and religion.

| 285–200 BC | 200 BC | 167–142 BC | 142–63 BC | 63 BC | 30 BC | 66–73 AD |
| Ptolemaic rule | Seleucid rule | Maccabean rebellion | Hasmoneans | Pompey in Jerusalem | Death of Christ | First Jewish Revolt |

| 300 BC | 200 BC | 100 BC | 0 | AD 100 |

| 323–281 BC | 280–63 BC | 66–62 BC | 31 BC |
| Wars of the Diadochi | Hellenistic kingdoms | Pompey campaigns in the East | Augustus sole master of Rome |

HELLENISTIC PERIOD

Following the siege of Gaza and the suppression of the Samaritan rebellion ▲ *334*, Alexander forced Palestine to swear an oath of allegiance in 332 BC. His death in 323 BC was followed by a period of wars between his successors, the Diadochi. In c. 285 BC the kingdom, which lay on the route of many Greek armies, came under the control of the Alexandrian Ptolemies and, in 200 BC, of the Seleucids of Antioch. The towns became veritable Greek cities and were given such new names as Ptolemais ▲ *368*, Scythopolis ▲ *397* and Marisa ▲ *332*. In 167 BC the anti-Israelite decrees of King Antiochus IV Epiphanes provoked the Maccabean rebellion ● *48* (167–142 BC) which resulted in the foundation of the Hasmonean ● *48* dynasty. The Jewish sovereigns managed to extend their power to such an extent that, on the death of Alexander Jannaeus in 76 BC, the Hasmonean kingdom, placed under the regency of his wife Alexandra (76–67 BC), included a large part of Cisjordan and Transjordan. In 67 BC the power struggle between their two sons Hyrcanus II and Aristobulus II provoked the intervention of the Romans and in 63 BC Pompey entered the Temple of Jerusalem to re-establish Hyrcanus II as ruler.

THE HERODIAN DYNASTY UNDER ROMAN RULE

Hyrcanus II was exiled to Babylon at the time of the Parthian invasion in 40 BC. Meanwhile Herod, son of Antipater, the governor of Galilee, had the Roman Senate recognize him as king ● *50* before he conquered Judea with the help of the Roman legions. In 37 BC he extended his control to Samaria, Galilee and most of the coastal region. On his death the kingdom was divided between his three sons, Archelaus, Philip and Herod Antipas. Archelaus kept the largest part (including Judea, Samaria and Idumea) for himself but was overthrown by the Romans, exiled and replaced in AD 6 by a prefect. This was the beginning of Rome's direct administration of the kingdom. Only Herod Agrippa I, descended from both Herod and the Hasmoneans, succeeded in re-establishing a semblance of Jewish independence (AD 41–44) and, with the help of Caligula and then Claudius, regaining control of the territory ruled by his grandfather.

THE SANHEDRIN
The Sanhedrin, the Jewish High Court, exercised religious and legal authority over all Jews within the limits determined by Rome. Its seventy-one members were laymen from noble families, priests, high priests and doctors of the Law ● *49* – scribes who were often Pharisees themselves, though some supported the more conservative Sadducees.

132–135	361-363	Circa 400	614	626
Second Jewish Revolt	Julian rebuilds the Temple	Completion of the "Jerusalem" Talmud	Jerusalem captured by the Persians	Jerusalem captured by the Byzantines

| AD 200 | AD 300 | AD 400 | AD 500 | AD 600 |

| 7–138 ign of drian | 293 Diocletian organizes the Tetrarchy | 313 Edict of Milan | 324–337 Reign of Constantine | 476 Fall of the western Roman Empire | 527–565 Reign of Justinian |

JUDEA, A ROMAN PROVINCE

On the death of Agrippa I, Palestine was administered by procurators whose political ineptitudes provoked the first Jewish Revolt in AD 66. The uprising was quelled by the Romans in AD 70 ● 50 and a depopulated Judea became a Roman province, controlled by the 10th Legion based in Jerusalem, before being attached to the province of Syria-Palestine after the second Jewish Revolt in AD 132–5 ● 50. Antoninus Pius (AD 138–61) authorized the Jews to carry out circumcision once again. The Sanhedrin was established in Galilee and its president recognized by the Romans as the representative of the Jewish community. Alongside the Samaritans and Christians ▲ 313, a large proportion of the population adopted the Graeco-Roman "pagan" religion, especially in Caesarea and the towns on the coastal plain. In c. AD 293 Diocletian reorganized the vast Roman Empire and appointed two "emperors" (who bore the title Augustus), one in the west and one in the east, to ensure better government. In AD 313 the western emperor, Constantine, put an end to persecution of the Christians with the Edict of Milan, which guaranteed freedom of worship and reparation for damages suffered. In AD 324 he defeated his pagan rival, Licinius, in the East and became sole ruler of the entire Roman Empire.

BYZANTINE PERIOD

After the first Council of Nicea (325), Constantine (324–37) began to build churches on the traditional Christian sites. These included the Church of the Holy Sepulcher ▲ 272 in Jerusalem. In c. 351 anti-Jewish laws led to a rebellion against Gallus, sent to the East by Constantine. The emperor Julian, Constantine's successor, made every effort to re-establish pagan worship and allowed the Jews to rebuild the Temple, but his premature death thwarted this attempt at restoration. Under Theodosius I the Great (379–95) Christianity became the official state religion. At the time Palestine was divided into three provinces: Prima with its capital at Caesarea, Secunda with its capital at Scythopolis (Bet She'an) ▲ 397, and Salutaris with its capital at Eleutheropolis (Bet Guvrin) ▲ 331. Although the western Roman Empire came to an end in 476, its eastern counterpart – with its developing Graeco-Christian civilization – was flourishing. Farms, convents and churches sprang up throughout Palestine, which experienced an unprecedented population increase. The civilization reached its height during the reign of the emperor Justinian who harshly repressed the Samaritan rebellion. At the dawn of the 7th century, the Byzantine empire was unable to resist the might of Persia and, in 614, Chosroes II invaded Palestine and destroyed many places of Christian worship before being stopped in 626 by the emperor Heraclius. Ten years later, the arrival of the Arabs ● 52 marked the end of the Byzantine civilization.

638
Arabs capture
Jerusalem

877–905
Dynasty of Ahmad
Ibn Tulun

1099–1187
Latin kingdom
of Jerusalem

600   800   1000   1200

622
Hegira: beginning
of the Muslim era

641–750
Umayyad
dynasty

750–1258
Abbasid dynasty

973–1171
Fatimid
dynasty

1096–1099
First
Crusade

1171–1250
Ayyubid
dynasty

A THRICE-HOLY LAND

The universal message bequeathed by the prophet Muhammad led the Arab nations to embark on a series of

great conquests in the name of the *jihad* ● *52*. In 638 the caliph Umar I captured Jerusalem, where the proclamation of Mu'awiya as caliph in 661 marked the beginning of the Umayyad dynasty. The Umayyads were soon replaced by the Abbasids, who made Baghdad their capital ● *53* and tended to neglect Palestine. In 877 the governor of Egypt, Ahmad

Ibn Tulun, brought the territory under Egyptian control until 905 when the Abbasids re-established their authority over Egypt. At the end of the 10th century Egypt and Palestine were conquered by the Fatimids from North Africa. Between 1070 and 1087 the Seljuq Turks took possession of Syria and Jerusalem. In 1095 the period of Crusades began, which included Crusades to the Near East. Crusaders landed in the Holy Land in 1099 and founded the Latin kingdom of Jerusalem ● *54* which lasted for the next two hundred years. The Mamlukes, victorious at St John of Akko in 1291, put an end to the Frankish presence and governed Palestine until 1517,

when their defeat by the troops of the sultan Selim I marked the beginning of four centuries of Ottoman domination. After the reign of Suleyman the Magnificent ▲ *224* (1520–66), who made some splendid contributions to Jerusalem's architecture, the kingdom was increasingly neglected by its Ottoman governors and gradually declined. In 1799 Napoleon Bonaparte attempted to capture Syria as part of his Egyptian campaign, but withdrew after his defeat at St John of Akko. The viceroy of Egypt, Mehmet Ali (1805–48), tried to assert Egypt's independence in the face of the Ottoman threat and in 1831 his son, Ibrahim Pasha, captured Palestine with the help of the French. Ten years later he was forced to relinquish it to the British. During the second half of the 19th century, partly as a result of pogroms, Russian Jews began to settle in Palestine and,

1897, Theodor Herzl chaired the first Zionist congress in Basel ● *56*. In 1917 Britain's General Allenby captured Jerusalem and forced the Turks, who were allies of Germany, to surrender ▲ *251*.

THE BRITISH MANDATE

The Balfour Declaration (1917) in favor of a "Jewish home in Palestine" led to increased Jewish immigration ● *56* into a country placed under British mandate by the League of Nations in 1922. From 1933 there were riots as more and more Jews arrived from central Europe as a result of Hitler's

anti-Semitic campaign. In 1939 the measures designed to limit this immigration and published in the British "blue book" provoked an outbreak of Zionist protests which intensified after 1945 and ended, in 1947, with the United Nations partition plan and the departure of the British.

1291	1517–1917	1799	1948	1994
The Mamlukes capture Akko	Palestine under Ottoman rule	Napoleon in Palestine	Creation of the State of Israel	Mutual recognition of Israel and the PLO

| 1400 | | 1600 | | 1800 | | 1994 |

1250–1517	1453	1520–1566		1939–45
Mamluke kingdom	Capture of Constantinople	Suleyman the Magnificent		World War Two

ISRAEL AND PALESTINE

On May 14, 1948 David Ben-Gurion, head of the Jewish Agency ● 56, proclaimed the creation of the State of Israel, which immediately had to confront the claims of its Arab neighbors: the first Arab-Israeli war ● 56 broke out on the same day. The truce signed in 1949 put an end to the war for a time. Although it was favorable to the Israelis, the Arab contingent of King Abdullah of Jordan managed to maintain a firm hold on Cisjordan while the Gaza Strip remained

regimes. Palestinians in Gaza were governed by Egypt, those in Cisjordan became Jordanian subjects and the Palestinians in Galilee and the Negev were granted Israeli citizenship. In 1956 the nationalization of the Suez Canal by President Nasser of Egypt provoked French and British intervention and gave rise to the second Arab-Israeli war, this time in Sinai. Under the combined pressure of the UN and the US, Israel withdrew from the conquered territories. On June 5, 1967, the Israeli army responded to the closing of the Strait of Tiran by capturing Golan, Cisjordan, Gaza and Sinai during the Six Day War. On October 6, 1973 – Yom Kippur (the Day of Atonement) ● 80 – Egyptian troops retaliated by crossing the Suez Canal, while the Syrians attacked Golan. When they had recovered from the surprise, the Israeli army drove both armies back and mounted a counterattack. An agreement, signed in 1974

by the warring countries under the auspices of the UN, stipulated the Israeli withdrawal to the east of the Suez Canal which would from then on be policed by the UN. Israel retained Gaza and the West Bank (the occupied territories) from 1967. When Menachem Begin, the candidate for the Israeli right-wing (Herut) party, won the elections in May 1977, he immediately encouraged the establishment of Jewish settlements in the occupied territories. The Camp David agreements, signed between Egypt and Israel on March 16, 1979, led to the restoration of the Sinai Peninsula to Egypt on April 25, 1982. In May 1994, after seven years of Intifada ("uprising", often called "war of stones"), Israel accepted the autonomy of the regions of Gaza and Jericho under the control of Yasir Arafat, President of the PLO (Palestine Liberation Organization). This recognition was followed by the signing of a peace treaty between Jordan and Israel on October 26, 1994.

STATUTE OF JERUSALEM

On December 9, 1917, the troops of General Allenby entered Jerusalem and martial law was declared. It stipulated that "all sacred buildings, monuments, holy places, sanctuaries, traditional sites, foundations, charitable bequests and habitual places of worship [would be] maintained" and would be open to members of the three religions.

under Egyptian control. Some Palestinians fled and those who remained were subject to three different

● THE LAND OF CANAAN

A civilization known as the Canaanite flourished in the 2nd millennium BC. It was based on a system of city-states in which sedentary farmers lived alongside semi-nomadic shepherds. By the Middle Bronze Age, fortified towns – which first appeared during the Early Bronze Age – were made up of strong ramparts, palaces and temples. This was the golden age of the Canaanite civilization. During the Late Bronze Age the Land of Canaan became part of the Egyptian empire and was incorporated into the trade network of the countries of the Levant and eastern Mediterranean. Centuries of coastal raids by "peoples of the sea" culminated in more permanent settlement by Philistines from 1200 BC onward.

Canaan is situated at the end of the Fertile Crescent, at the intersection of the great civilizations of Egypt and Mesopotamia.

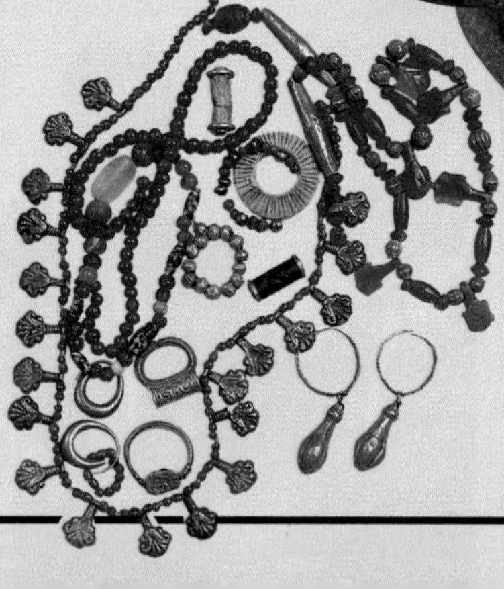

MEDITERRANEAN SEA
SYRIA
ASSYRIA
PHOENICIA
MESOPOTAMIA
CANAAN
BABYLONIA
EGYPT
ARABIAN DESERT
RED SEA
PERSIAN GULF

THE FIRST URBAN CIVILIZATION
The geographical division of the country led to the formation in the third millennium BC of city-states: small, autonomous political organizations centered around a fortified town. The Canaanites were both a military and a commercial people who exported luxury products, oil and wine to the Mediterranean basin.

THE ISRAELITES

Around AD 1200 the Israelites, originally from Canaan and Sinai, emigrated to Samaria and Judea, where the pottery (below) was found.

CANAANITES AND AMORITES

The Bible uses the term "Canaanites" to refer to the peoples who settled between the Dead Sea and the coast before the arrival of the Israelites. The term "Amorites" is used to refer more generally to the western Semites and includes the Canaanites. Canaanite vase in the form of a head (below).

CANAANITE GODS

The Canaanites worshipped anthropomorphic divinities who personified the forces of nature and were represented by stelae, statues and figurines (above). Baal and Astarte (Ashtoreth) were the principal figures in the Canaanite pantheon. Their beliefs and legends are in the Ugaritic (Ras Shamra) texts.

THE PHILISTINES

The Philistines, from Crete and the Aegean, are hard to describe, even after their settlement on the coast – little evidence survives. Their sarcophagi were decorated with human figures (left).

45

THE KINGDOM OF DAVID AND SOLOMON

Map of the twelve tribes of Israel at the time of Saul (1010–1006 BC)

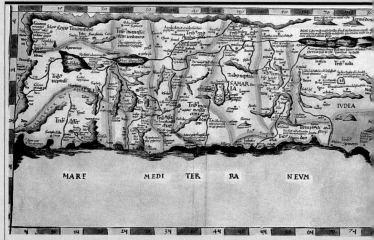

Saul, the first King of Israel, was succeeded by David, who united the twelve tribes into a single kingdom. His military and political success continued by his son Solomon, marked the golden age. When Solomon died, the northern tribes reverted to their traditional independence, resulting in the division of the kingdom into two: Judah in the south, with Jerusalem as its capital, and Israel in the north, which, although richer, suffered from political and religious instability. It fell easy prey to the Assyrians and in 722 BC Samaria was captured and part of its population deported. Judah held out until the Siege of Jerusalem by Nebuchadnezzar in 587 BC, which marked the beginning of the Babylonian Exile.

Model representing Solomon's Temple

GOLDEN AGE OF THE KINGDOM OF DAVID AND SOLOMON
David (right) was the first to unite the kingdom of Israel and extend its borders. Solomon ruled by diplomacy rather than force and improved the administrative system.

SOLOMON BUILDS A TEMPLE TO YAHWEH
Solomon actually built the temple planned by David to house the Ark of the Covenant. He imposed forced labor ▲ 243 on his people, particularly for the quarrying and transport of the stone.

SCHISM: THE KINGDOMS OF ISRAEL AND JUDAH

In 931 BC the Israelites gathered in Shechem ▲ 312 to appoint Solomon's successor. His son, Rehoboam, was not acceptable to the northern tribes as he wanted to increase taxes and the amount of forced labor, which had already caused discontent toward the end of his father's reign. His kingdom was limited to Judah and Benjamin, while Jeroboam was placed at the head of the ten northern tribes which formed the kingdom of Israel. Seal (below) of one of the servants of Jeroboam II.

THE FALL OF JUDAH

The kingdom of Judah inherited the prestige of Jerusalem and of Solomon's Temple. During the late 8th century BC its population was subjected to Assyrian and then Neo-Babylonian sovereignty before rebelling. In 587 BC Nebuchadnezzar burned the Temple, captured the holy city and deported its inhabitants to Babylon ● 39.

CONQUEST OF SAMARIA

From the time of the Omri dynasty (881–841 BC), the kingdom of Israel had to confront the expansion of the Neo-Assyrian empire. After periods of resistance and submission, Samaria ● 39 was captured in 722 BC and its inhabitants either deported or assimilated by other conquered peoples. The second register of the Black Obelisk shows Jehu, King of Israel, paying tribute to Assyria.

After the Exile, Jerusalem was eventually rebuilt under Ezra and Nehemiah, and the Temple became the dominant authority. In 198 BC Seleucid Syria established its domination over Judea. A Hellenizing party emerged in conflict with vital commands in the Torah. Antiochus IV (Epiphanes, manifestation of Zeus) established a garrison in Jerusalem and sought to introduce recognition of his sovereignty in the Temple. This provoked a rebellion led by Judas Maccabeus, son of Mattathias, of the Hasmon family, hence the successful Maccabean revolt and ensuing Hasmonean dynasty, a period of independence remembered with pride to this day.

SELEUCID DOMINATION. Following the Seleucid victory (elephant from the military campaign, left), Antiochus III confirmed the validity of the Jewish Law. However, Syria's pressing financial needs led its kings to appoint high priests who were open to Greek influence and prepared to accept increased tributes.

ꟽACHABEORꟽ

MACCABEAN REBELLION

In 167 BC King Antiochus IV Epiphanes embarked upon a policy of enforced Hellenization. Mattathias, a priest from the village of Modeen, organized a rural rebellion. His son, Judas (nicknamed Maccabeus), recaptured the Temple in 164 BC and restored the pure form of worship. The rebellion became known as the Maccabean rebellion.

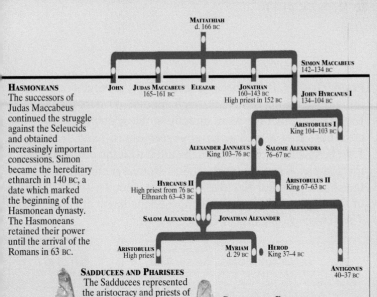

MATTATHIAH
d. 166 BC

SIMON MACCABEUS
142–134 BC

JOHN **JUDAS MACCABEUS** **ELEAZAR** **JONATHAN**
165–161 BC 160–143 BC
High priest in 152 BC

JOHN HYRCANUS I
134–104 BC

ARISTOBULUS I
King 104–103 BC

ALEXANDER JANNAEUS **SALOME ALEXANDRA**
King 103–76 BC 76–67 BC

HYRCANUS II **ARISTOBULUS II**
High priest from 76 BC King 67–63 BC
Ethnarch 63–43 BC

SALOM ALEXANDRA **JONATHAN ALEXANDER**

ARISTOBULUS **MYRIAM** **HEROD**
High priest d. 29 BC King 37–4 BC

ANTIGONUS
40–37 BC

HASMONEANS

The successors of Judas Maccabeus continued the struggle against the Seleucids and obtained increasingly important concessions. Simon became the hereditary ethnarch in 140 BC, a date which marked the beginning of the Hasmonean dynasty. The Hasmoneans retained their power until the arrival of the Romans in 63 BC.

SADDUCEES AND PHARISEES

The Sadducees represented the aristocracy and priests of the Temple, while the Pharisees were more closely associated with the common people. They opposed or supported the Hasmonean dynasty at various points throughout history.

SADDUCCEES, PHARISEES AND SECTARIANS

These forms of Judaism emerged at this time. Sadducees adhered to the Torah as written, applying it strictly. Pharisees allowed interpretation, leading to the Oral Torah (and to Mishnah and Talmud), and to such new beliefs as resurrection and life after death. The Sectarians, who aspired to a greater purity while awaiting the end of time, existed on the margins of these two groups ● *212*.

JUDAISATION

John Hyrcanus extended the territory regained from the Seleucids toward the Mediterranean and Red Sea and had coins struck. Alexander Jannaeus continued these conquests, extending the Jewish kingdom to include Judea, Samaria, Galilee, the coast between Mount Carmel and Rafah, and part of the right bank of the Jordan from Golan to the Dead Sea.

49

● ROMAN RULE

From 63 BC on, Rome became increasingly dominant in Judea, initially exercising control through appointed rulers such as King Herod and then more directly by the appointment of governors after AD 6. The latter's excesses provoked the first Jewish Revolt (AD 66–70), which ended with the destruction of the Temple. A second revolt against Roman domination, led by the charismatic Bar Kochba (AD 132–5), ended with the victory of the emperor Hadrian, who imposed the name of Palestine. The Jewish people fled to Galilee.

THE KINGDOM OF HEROD, VASSAL OF ROME
Herod (below) came to power under the aegis of Rome. He was a great admirer of the Graeco-Roman civilization and was seen as a usurper by many Jews. With the support of Rome, he maintained a reign of terror – and his throne – for almost a quarter of a century. Herod was a great builder ▲ 229 and undertook such projects as the reconstruction of the second Temple, whose western enclosure wall (the so-called "Wailing Wall") can still be seen today.

"JUDAEA CAPTA"
Under Roman domination Judea was initially a province governed by a *praefectus* (the title of Pontius Pilate) and then by a procurator dependent on the governor of Syria.

THE FIRST JEWISH REVOLT (66–73). The so-called Great Revolt was instigated by two religious movements opposed to the Roman presence: the Sicarii captured Masada ▲ 202 and the Zealots launched a rebellion in Jerusalem. Vespasian, the general sent by Nero, subjugated Galilee and part of Judea. He was proclaimed emperor in AD 69 and left for Rome, leaving his son Titus (right) to end the war.

COINS
During the Jewish Revolts coins dated Year 1 (to mark the beginning of the revolt and the "redemption of Israel") were struck and distributed throughout the kingdom. Bar Kochba coins (above).

THE BURNING OF THE TEMPLE BY TITUS
Since Jerusalem was protected by thick walls and a plentiful supply of water, Titus decided to besiege the city and starve it into submission. He captured the Antonia Fortress and set fire to the Temple ▲ 260 where a section of the population had taken refuge (AD 70). The city was laid waste and the leaders of the revolt sent to Rome. The last pocket of resistance, Masada ▲ 209, fell in AD 73.

YAVNEH BECOMES THE CENTER OF JEWISH LIFE
From AD 70 the liturgy of the Temple ceased to exist and the Sanhedrin ● 40 disappeared. Jewish life, based on study and prayer, reconverged around the town of Yavneh (Yibna), on the coastal plain, where the foundations of rabbinic (rabbi means master or teacher) Judaism were laid. The *tannaim* collated the Pharisaic oral traditions of the Mishna which forms the basis of the Talmud ● 78.

HADRIAN AND THE BAR KOCHBA REVOLT (132–135)
Hadrian's decision to rebuild Jerusalem as the pagan city of Aelia Capitolina provoked the second anti-Roman revolt, led by Bar Kochba ("son of the star"), in which hundreds of thousands of people died. The Jewish people fled from a devastated Judea to become Diaspora (Dispersion) Judaism; those in Palestine and Babylon included the *amoraim*, who continued to work on the Talmud.

Standard symbolizing the Prophet's military power

Shortly after the death of the Prophet Muhammad (632), Arab and Muslim expansion reached the Byzantine provinces of Syria and Palestine. Jerusalem (Muslim name al-Quds, the Holy Place) was besieged in 638 and acquired privileged status in the Islamic tradition. Under the Umayyad (661–750) and Abbasid (750–1258) dynasties the language of the conquerors gradually replaced Greek and Syriac and an Arabic system of administration was introduced. Sunni Islam became the dominant religion and, although Jewish and Christian communities continued to exist, they became part of the commercial network established by the Arabs.

THE "JIHAD"
Jihad means "effort": it may be making an effort for God internally (by moral improvement, the Greater Jihad) or by war which can only be defensive (the Lesser Jihad), when Islam is attacked.

JERUSALEM, HOLY CITY OF ISLAM
Following the conquest of Jerusalem by the caliph Umar I in 638, Mu'awiya, founder of the Umayyad dynasty, consecrated the city by having himself proclaimed caliph there in 661 ● *94*. It became the *bayt al-Maqdis* (house of Holiness) and an important place of pilgrimage. The Umayyads used architecture to demonstrate the fulfillment of God's purpose in Islam, building the Dome of the Rock on the former Temple esplanade (believed to be the site of the Prophet's ▲ *284* miraculous Night Journey), in 692, and the Al-Aqsa Mosque ▲ *286* in 715.

STATUS OF JEWS AND CHRISTIANS
Jews and Christians were granted a form of
protection (*dhimma*) which guaranteed their
public and private rights, provided they paid taxes
and accepted Muslim authority. As a result there
were no coerced conversions. Islamization took
place within the context of the social relations
established between the Muslim aristocracy and a
population which wanted to avoid paying taxes.

PALESTINE, A COMMERCIAL CENTER
With the arrival of Islam commerce was
extended to all sections of the
population, whether Muslims, Jews or
Christians. Palestine became an
important trading center. The caravans
sometimes followed the pilgrim routes to
Mecca ● *91*, from Damascus via the Gulf
of Aqaba ▲ *182*.

A CENTRALIZED POLITICAL SYSTEM
Under the Umayyad dynasty Palestine
became an administrative and military district
attached to the capital, Damascus. Under the
Abbasids the center of gravity of the Muslim
empire shifted toward Baghdad, in Iraq. Plan
of 16th-century Baghdad (above).

The First Crusade ended with the capture of Jerusalem (1099) and the founding of four Latin states, including the Kingdom of Jerusalem. The Muslim retaliation began in 1128 under Zengi, Lord of Mosul. It was continued by his son Nur ad-Din, who enlisted the support of Syria and Egypt, and furthered by the victory of Salah al-Din (Saladin) who recaptured Jerusalem in 1187. From then on, although they maintained a presence in the Holy Land until the end of the 13th century, the Crusaders ceased to be a threat to Islam. They were finally driven out by the Mamlukes in 1292.

THE CAPTURE OF JERUSALEM

The Crusaders reached Jerusalem in June 1099 and launched their final attack on July 15. A Frankish chronicler described the horrific scenes of carnage: "Our soldiers boiled pagan adults in cooking pots, speared children and roasted them on spits."

NUR AD-DIN AND MUSLIM RETALIATION (1146–1172)

Nur ad-Din led the struggle against the Franks in the name – and spreading the ideology – of the jihad ● 54. Efficient administrative and financial management enabled him to unite Syria and take control of Egypt in 1164.

FOUNDATION

After the capture of Jerusalem the Crusaders chose Godfrey of Bouillon (above) as their leader. His successors Baldwin I and Baldwin II founded a monarchy and extended the frontiers of the kingdom as far as Beirut and beyond the Dead Sea. In the early 12th century the kingdom of Jerusalem, allied to the emirate of Damascus, was an influential force in the Holy Land.

SALAH AL-DIN

Saladin brought the campaign begun by Nur ad-Din to a successful conclusion. Such was his loyalty, courage and generosity that even the Franks saw him as the embodiment of the ideal Muslim knight.

HORNS OF HITTIM

Lured onto the battleground chosen by Salah al-Din, the Franks, overwhelmed by the heat and short of water, sought refuge high up on the Horns of Hittim ● *384* where they were slaughtered on July 4, 1187. Three months later the Muslims recaptured Jerusalem.

FINAL FRANKISH EFFORTS IN THE HOLY LAND

After the defeat of 1187, Richard the Lionheart succeeded in ensuring the continued existence of the Latin states in the Holy Land for the next hundred years. Saladin's successors, the Ayyubids (1171–1250), agreed to tolerate the Frankish presence in order to avoid another Crusade. However, in 1248, Saint Louis (Louis IX) set out for the Holy Land where, in spite of the strength of his army, he was stopped and captured near El-Mansura as he retreated.

When Saint Louis set out on the Sixth Crusade his sights were set on Cairo, which he considered to be the key to Jerusalem.

Following the first Zionist congress, held in Basel in 1897, Theodor Herzl pressed for the foundation of a Jewish state. During the first half of the 20th century increasing numbers of Jewish immigrants arrived in Palestine. Their settlement in the Holy Land, seen as an injustice by the Arabs, was carried out under the British Mandate in a climate of growing violence. On May 14, 1948, the State of Israel was officially proclaimed and the first Arab-Israeli war was declared. Although the rapid victory (1949) of the new state put an end to the statelessness of the Jewish people, it also created a new category of exiles: the Palestinians.

THEODOR HERZL (1860–1904)
At the end of the 19th century Theodor Herzl ▲ *302*, a liberal Jew deeply concerned by the climate of growing anti-Semitism, brought the concept of the "return to Zion" – which has always been deeply rooted in the Jewish consciousness – into the political arena. He founded the Zionist Organization in 1897 and undertook a number of diplomatic initiatives.

THE PIONEERS
The foundations of the State of Israel were laid by the victims of the Russian pogroms who, inspired by a deep-rooted sense of patriotism, emigrated to Palestine in the 1880's.

In 1917 the Balfour Declaration in favor of the establishment of a "Jewish home in Palestine" angered the Palestinians.

UN PARTITION PLAN (1947)

- ☐ Territory allotted to the Jews
- ▨ Territory allotted to the Palestinians
- ☐ International zone
- ☐ Demilitarized zone

AFTER 1949:

- ☐ Territory taken by the Israeli army

BIRTH OF A STATE
On May 14, 1948 David Ben-Gurion issued the announcement of Israeli independence. The newly formed state was soon recognized by the US as well as the then USSR, which gave Israel its military support.

JEWISH IMMIGRANTS
The re-establishment of a Jewish territory enabled the Jewish people scattered throughout the world to be reunited. The first arrivals – survivors from the concentration camps – were soon joined by some 300,000 Jews whose future in the Islamic countries had become uncertain.

A COUNTRY AT WAR
Following the Arab rejection of the partition of Palestine proposed by the UN on November 29, 1947, the entire country was soon at war. By the end of April the Israeli army controlled most of the territory allotted to Israel by the UN. At dawn on May 15, 1948, 24,000 men from five Arab countries (Syria, Iraq, Jordan, Lebanon and Egypt) crossed the border into Palestine. The peace agreements signed in 1949 left Israel with more territory than it had been allotted by the partition plan.

PALESTINIAN EXODUS
The war provoked an exodus of 700,000 Palestinian refugees – some fleeing, others expelled by the Jewish army – who settled on the borders of Israel, in Syria, Lebanon, Gaza and on the banks of the Jordan ● 43. The poorest went into refugee camps. All cherished the hope of one day returning to Palestine, a cause championed by the new organizations (such as Yasir Arafat's Fatah) created in the 1960's.

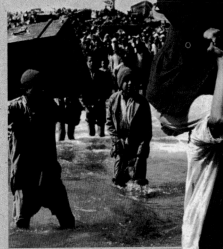

BIBLICAL HEBREW

The sacred status of Biblical Hebrew has meant that it has survived where other languages might well have perished. The Hebrew used in the oldest Biblical works was the language of the kingdom of Judah ● 46, the language of most of the inscriptions found to date. A few traces of the language of the kingdom of Israel ● 46 have survived on Samarian *ostraca* and are believed to appear in the manuscripts of the prophet Hoshea. The Hebrew that has survived to the present day is, therefore, essentially "Judean". Since Aramean was the official language of Babylonia and Persia at the time of the Babylonian Exile ● 39, the Judeans assimilated many of its terms and became familiar with the Aramean style of writing the alphabet, which was considered more elegant than the ancient Hebraic script. When they returned to Jerusalem they found that the peasants "were no longer able to speak Judean", so they undertook to revive their national language. All that remains of the vast body of literature of the "postexilic" period are the writings included in the Biblical canon. They show a concern on the part of the authors to imitate the style of "pre-exilic" Hebrew, although the spoken language must have changed considerably over the years. The language of the Mishna, written c. AD 200, bears the marks of all these influences. After the destruction of the second Temple in AD 70 ● 50, Hebrew was used throughout the Diaspora as a liturgical and literary language, while Biblical Hebrew was reserved for poetry.

The language of the Mishna was used for rabbinic treatises and scholarly correspondence. Although Hebrew continued to be written, spoken Hebrew was replaced by various local dialects which, over the years, have taken on a characteristically Jewish form: Judeo-Arabic, Judeo-Persian, Judeo-Spanish and Yiddish ● 60.

ISRAELI HEBREW

The project to revive Hebrew as a spoken language was instigated by a Lithuanian Jew,

Eliezer Ben Yehudah, who settled in Jerusalem in 1881. This ideal became a reality since Hebrew proved to be the common cultural basis shared by the Jews from different countries who had settled in the rural communities ● 132.

In 1890 Ben Yehudah founded a language committee, the forerunner of the Hebrew Academy. It provided the new Hebrew-speaking generation with lists of newly created words. With the British mandate ● 42, Hebrew was recognized as an official language alongside English and Arabic. At the Technion (the university college founded in 1924) and the Hebrew University established in 1925 ▲ 302, courses were taught in Hebrew. As the country welcomed increasing numbers of immigrants, a new policy was developed: *Ivri, daber ivrit* (Hebrew, speak Hebrew). The *Ulpan* (crash course in Hebrew) became obligatory for all new arrivals. Today, *Ivrit* (modern Hebrew) is spoken by almost five million people. Although it is becoming increasingly distinct from Biblical Hebrew, due to the natural development of a spoken language, it still retains some basic similarities and Israeli schoolchildren can understand a Biblical text of average complexity. Israelis returning to Israel after spending some time abroad will find that new words have been introduced by the Hebrew Academy and new slang expressions, different from the ones they used in the army or on the kibbutz, have been coined. Today *Ivrit* in its revived form shows every sign of being a dynamic language. This is confirmed by the existence of a press with a wide circulation ◆ 420 and a rich body of Hebrew literature.

"THUS WE HAVE REVEALED IT, A DECISIVE UTTERANCE IN ARABIC."

SÛRAH XIII

ARABIC

Arabic is the language of revelation (that is, of the Qur'an), and as such is deeply revered. The Qur'an cannot be translated into another language but only paraphrased. Spoken Arabic exists in many dialects and became increasingly distinct from written Arabic. All Arabic-speaking countries underwent this "diglotic" experience whereby a spoken form of the language existed alongside literary Arabic, the religious, scholarly form of the language learned in school. In the Holy Land a number of Arabic dialects were imported by Jews from the Maghreb and the Near and Middle East and coexisted with the Palestinian dialect spoken in a particular region by both the Arabs born in Palestine and the Jews who settled there before 1948. These Arab dialects include the Maghrebi and the Near Eastern dialects. Those in the second group (including Jordano-Palestinian Arabic) use expressions similar to those used in modern literary (or standard) Arabic, the intermediate form of the language between classical Arabic and the Syro-Lebanese and Palestinian dialects.

PALESTINIAN ARABIC

Although the Palestinian dialect is very similar to the Syrian and Lebanese dialects, there are several variations due to a greater Christian, and especially Jewish, presence in the Holy Land than in other Arabic countries. This has led to differences between the Christian and Muslim dialects spoken within the same region, for example southern Palestine. As in all Arabic-speaking communities, a spoken form of Arabic – more open to external influences than a written language – has developed alongside classical Arabic. Linguistics has demonstrated that the spoken forms of a language are never pure, and this is especially true of Arabic dialects. Thus Judeo-Arabic is a mixture of Hebrew and Arabic. The development of the Palestinian dialect shows signs of English and Hebrew influence, while at the same time remaining close to the Syrian and Lebanese dialects. It is not spoken in a uniform manner from one end of the country to the other. In the towns the *qâf* ("q"), a "k" exploded in the throat, is not pronounced and has been replaced by the vocalic attack of the *hamza*. In rural areas and on the desert borders the *qâf* is pronounced as a hard "g", while the Druzes ● 94 pronounce it as a "k" exploded in the throat. The variations in the pronunciation of the *qâf* are not limited to Palestine, and the similarities between theoretically very different dialects are sometimes perplexing. Thus several dialects from the Gulf of Aqaba, Egypt and the Maghreb (such as the dialect spoken by the Ulâd Brahim of Saïda) have points in common with the Bedouin dialects of northern Israel.

ALPHABETS
Arabic and Hebrew are both Semitic languages. They are written from right to left.

● LANGUAGES

FOREIGN LANGUAGES IN THE HOLY LAND

As the ancestral land opened up to the Jews of the Diaspora, Israel has become a land of many languages, where you can hear Amharic, Ethiopian or Finnish and now-declining tongues such as Yiddish or Ladino, spoken by the descendants of the Jews expelled from Spain in 1492. In the 20th century Hebrew has tended to promote cultural unity at the expense of the individual heritage of each community. However, the use of foreign languages continues in the Holy Land because Jewish immigrants have preserved the culture that sustained them during the Diaspora. There are also pockets of linguistic resistance, for example the German Jews who arrived in the 1930's. They still speak German today in the streets, on café terraces and

on the beaches of Haifa ▲ 364. However, Israel maintains close ties with the outside

world and most Israelis learn several languages: English, Arabic, French, Russian, German and even Hungarian, Polish and Chinese.

ENGLISH
English is widely used in everyday life in Israel, to some extent as the inheritance of the British mandate ● 42 but mainly because it is an international language. It is compulsory in schools from the age of ten and is a condition of university entrance.

FRENCH
As a reaction against British colonialism, French became

Israel's third official language, after Hebrew and Arabic, in 1948. However it was gradually replaced by English as a result of the political changes that occurred after the Six-Day War ● 43. Today, with the immigrants from North Africa and the French cultural centers established in the Holy Land, Israel has a French-speaking community – in Netanya, Jerusalem, Bat Yam and Ashkelon – of around 600,000 people.

RUSSIAN
Israel's Russian-speaking community, which originally consisted of the early Zionists, was significantly increased by the massive influx of immigrants from the USSR in the 1970's and the former USSR in the early

1990's. Today the population of about 700,000 people is concentrated in the cities of northern and central Israel and towns built for new arrivals, such as Carmiel, Nazrat Ilit and Arad.

SPANISH
Spanish is spoken by several tens of thousands of South American immigrants, a community which includes some ultra-orthodox religious figures and members of the left who fled the military regimes of Latin America. They settled in the kibbutzim as well as in new urban developments (Carmiel and Ashkelon) and Tel Aviv.

YIDDISH
Yiddish appeared in central Europe in the Middle Ages and combines Germanic with Hebraic and Slavic elements. Although it began to disappear as a result of the extermination of the Jewish communities of Eastern Europe during World War Two, the language was preserved by the few survivors who emigrated to Israel and by the ultra-orthodox communities from Poland, Russia, the Baltic countries and Rumania. Today Yiddish language and literature are taught in universities.

ARTS AND TRADITION

POTTERY, *62*
OIL LAMPS, *64*
PALESTINIAN EMBROIDERY, *66*
JEWELRY, *68*
ARAB AND JEWISH MUSIC, *70*
ARAB AND JEWISH DANCES, *72*
FOOD: BREAD, *74*
OLIVES, *76*

Pottery is an ancient Palestinian tradition mentioned several times in the Bible. It developed as populations became more sedentary and had to devise a means of preserving food that was adapted to their new way of life. The Holy Land boasts a wide variety of domestic, religious and artistic pottery, both hand-made and turned, produced and decorated according to the customs of each particular region.

PHILISTINE BEER PITCHER
This Iron Age ● *38* pitcher has a filter.

The so-called pilgrim's bottle (right) was used by travelers and soldiers during Biblical times. The narrow neck made it easy to seal. Iron Age ● *38* terracotta weight (below).

MAKING POTTERY
First the clay is mixed with water. If it is too rich and likely to crack during firing, the potter makes it more pliable by adding quartz and sand or, in rural areas, pieces of terracotta or basalt, fine straw or goats' hair. It is then worked on the wheel (above) or by hand.

PALESTINIAN COIL TECHNIQUE

Rural pottery is made by adding coils. Once the basic shape of the container has been created, its sides are smoothed by hand and then dried. Any cracks that appear as it dries are sealed over using a wet stone. The coils are then added to produce the final shape.

BIBLICAL POTTERY

In Biblical times pottery played an important part in everyday life. Discoveries have included kitchen utensils; large earthenware jars and pitchers for carrying oil, wine and water and for storing documents ▲ 214 (below); oil lamps ● 64; and decorative items. Ordinary pottery was made of brown or gray earthenware, while luxury items were polished, painted or engraved before being fired.

ARAB POTTERY

Once it has been shaped, the earthenware pottery is coated with red clay, decorated with geometric designs and colored using a dye obtained from a decoction of tree bark. It is sometimes fired by burning dried animal dung in a ditch. The relatively porous pottery allows water to evaporate and keeps liquids at constantly cool temperatures.

● OIL LAMPS

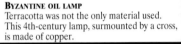

BYZANTINE OIL LAMP
Terracotta was not the only material used. This 4th-century lamp, surmounted by a cross, is made of copper.

Oil lamps first appeared in the Holy Land during the Neolithic Age. Over the centuries their shape changed as potters produced increasingly elaborate designs. The body became longer and flatter until the Hellenistic period when the lamps (which looked like a small bowl) assumed their definitive form. From then on they consisted of a burner which held the wick and a round container pierced with a hole for replenishing the oil. The first decorative motifs appeared at about the same time.

NEOLITHIC OIL LAMP
The black marks found on several Neolithic bowls indicate that they were used as lamps. A single wick was steeped in the oil and rested against the side of the bowl.

CHALCOLITHIC OIL LAMP
The bowl is less rounded and shallower. Its sloping sides are slightly pinched at each of the four points where the wick was placed.

EARLY BRONZE AGE OIL LAMP
This lamp is deeper and more enclosed. Its four symmetrical burners (they were becoming increasingly pronounced) and slightly flattened base give it a flower-like appearance.

MIDDLE BRONZE AGE OIL LAMP
The shell-like bowl has a single burner. This new type of lamp is a fine example of the originality of Canaanite art ● *44*.

LAMP FROM THE PERSIAN PERIOD
The edges of the deep, cup-shaped bowl are joined together. The lamp has two openings, one for the wick and the other for the oil.

IRON AGE OIL LAMP
This lamp is very similar to the Middle Bronze Age lamp, but its sides have a narrow border. During the Late Iron Age some lamps stood on a base.

HELLENISTIC LAMP
From this point on the neck was distinct from the body and more elongated. Molded or engraved geometric designs appeared for the first time on the body and around the burner.

ROMAN OIL LAMP
Roman lamps were flatter than Herodian lamps and often richly decorated. On the body of this lamp (1st century BC), a fisherman is sorting his catch in a shallow bowl.

HERODIAN OIL LAMP
During the Roman period lamps became more rounded and were often decorated with symbolic motifs, such as divinities. The distinctive Herodian lamp can be distinguished from the Roman lamp by its soberness, its shorter, triangular burner and its smaller, more rounded body.

BYZANTINE OIL LAMP
The decoration on this elongated, pear-shaped lamp combines various motifs – religious symbols and Greek inscriptions (above) – with geometric figures.

CLASSIC ARAB OIL LAMP
The motifs on this classic lamp are typical of the Umayyad and Abbasid dynasties. The burner is incorporated into the body of the lamp.

PENTAGONAL ARAB OIL LAMP
This lamp (probably 11th-century) is a pentagonal version of the classic Arab lamp. The burner has a narrow opening.

OIL LAMP FROM THE TIME OF THE CRUSADES
This type of lamp could be found throughout Palestine between the 11th and 13th centuries. Its pure lines are reminiscent of the Herodian lamp, but it is deeper and has a handle.

65

Embroidery, one of the most important crafts practiced by Bedouin and Palestinian women, is handed down from mother to daughter. In towns and villages alike, the women embroider their everyday clothes, trousseaus, bridal and ceremonial dresses. Although the technique used is more or less the same throughout the country, each region has its own distinctive color and its own style of embroidery characterized by a particular stitch. The costumes worn by the members of the same tribe are an indication of their region of origin. Although traditional geometric motifs are widely used, costumes are sometimes decorated with floral designs and arabesques which are the result of western influence.

STITCHES
Embroidery is executed on hand-woven linen or coarse cotton which makes it easier to count the stitches. The most widely used stitch is the *fallahi* (peasant woman) stitch, while the "satin stitch" used in Galilee and the "couching stitch" of Jerusalem are equally distinctive.

JAFFA EMBROIDERY
Jaffa embroidery is famous for its fineness and precision as the stitches are small and the designs extremely complex. The basic color of embroidery in the Jaffa region is the purplish red used on this dress (left), embroidered in 1890.

BEDOUIN HEADDRESS
Embroidered in c. 1930, this headdress belonged to a Bedouin woman from southern Palestine. The train is decorated with Ottoman coins and ends with a row of plastic buttons (instead of the usual shells) sewn onto the material.

Palestinian women in ceremonial dress, showing off their embroidery on the Haram el-Sharif ▲ 282.

HEBRON EMBROIDERY
The Hebron region is famous for its embroidery ▲ 220 which uses multicolored cross stitch and a variety of designs. The cotton garments are dyed violet blue before being embroidered.

RAMALLAH EMBROIDERY
Summer garments are made of embroidered natural white linen ▲ 310 and winter garments of a black-dyed cloth. The threads are carefully counted so that the stitches are equal.

EMBROIDERED CUSHIONS FROM HEBRON
Bridal trousseaus used to include between four and twelve embroidered cushions.

GAZA EMBROIDERY
The garments worn in the villages of the Gaza region are edged with *Janna Wa Nar*, bands of green and magenta-striped silk which, according to tradition, symbolize hell and heaven.

67

The jewelry designed and created by the Palestinians and Yemenite, Iranian, Asian, North African and central European Jews is a fine example of the wealth of different cultural influences in the Holy Land. It is worn on ceremonial occasions, such as weddings, and is an indication of membership of a social group as well as a means of amassing wealth. The different types of jewelry are as varied as the materials used and, for the Palestinians and North African Jews, sometimes assume a protective value. In this case form and color, invested with magical properties, are more important than authenticity of the materials used.

FILIGREE

Filigree, with its fine gold openwork patterns, is a technique developed by Jews from North Africa, the Yemen and Iran. It makes it possible to produce extremely elaborate designs, such as the fine arabesques on this necklace.

The fine gold threads are cut, twisted and then soldered.

YEMENITE JEWELRY

On the occasion of important Jewish festivals Yemenite women adorn themselves with the sumptuous jewelry for which Yemenite jewelers are famous. The young bride (below) is wearing no fewer than eight rings, a silver bracelet, a headdress made from bands decorated with silver, a choker and a neckpiece consisting of six rows of filigree beads.

STONES

Jewish and Palestinian goldsmiths and craftsmen use all kinds of precious and semi-precious stones: amber, coral, agate, turquoise, cornelian and mother-of-pearl. Bedouin necklaces are sometimes made of unusual materials: glass, wood, clay and even cloves!

NORTH AFRICAN-JEWISH JEWELRY

This Tunisian-Jewish necklace (19th century) is made of coral beads, gold coins and hands of Fatima, believed to ward off the Evil Eye and protect the wearer.

BEDOUIN JEWELRY

Bedouin women wear two items of jewelry not worn by their Palestinian counterparts: nose ornaments and a type of face veil made from a piece of material decorated with embroidery, beads and silver.

BOKHARAN-JEWISH JEWELRY

Bokharan jewelers tend to use precious rather than semi-precious stones. These earrings are set with emeralds and baroque pearls.

PALESTINIAN JEWELRY

This typically Palestinian necklace comes from the Bethlehem region. Clusters of chains set with cornelian, coins, glass beads and small pieces of metal decorated with fine, twisted threads have been soldered onto the interlaced metal choker.

IRANIAN-JEWISH JEWELRY

Iranian jewelry, used as a way of amassing wealth, is made of precious stones and metals. When it is valued, its weight is as important as the craftsmanship. These extremely fine filigree (an Iranian specialty) earrings are made of solid gold.

The many different styles of Jewish musical heritage reflect the artistic influence of the countries in which the Jewish communities lived before emigrating to Israel. This diversity has been very much in evidence in both religious and Jewish and Israeli folk music since the creation of the State of Israel. Arab music can be divided into two main categories: traditional music, with its extensive repertoire of rural folk music performed by poet-musicians, and the more erudite music found mainly in the cities.

"KLEZMER"
The small musical groups known as *klezmer* ("instrumentalists") first appeared in central Europe during the 17th century. They do not use any form of written music and play violins, double-basses, drums and clarinets.

ARAB MUSIC
Important occasions in rural communities are marked by traditional Arab folk songs, characterized by a surprisingly wide variety of poetic genres. The poet-musicians, celebrated for their ability to improvise, are central to these musical gatherings, while the assembled company joins in the responses. A more erudite type of music, performed mainly in such northern cities as Haifa and Nazareth, tends to follow the fashion set by Lebanon and Egypt.

"SHOFAR"

The *Shofar* (first mentioned in Exodus 19.16) is a ram's horn blown to announce the New Year and (often) the end of the Day of Atonement – Maimonides says "to rouse you from sleep, to examine your deeds, to turn in repentance and to remember your Creator".

"OUD"

The *oud* is the ancestor of the lute and the key instrument in Arab music. The musician plucks the strings with a small piece of wood known as a plectrum.

"QANUN" AND "ARGHUL"

The *qanun* is a trapezoidal instrument with seventy-two strings. The *arghul* is a type of double clarinet used to accompany Arab dances.

ISRAELI FOLK MUSIC

Israeli folk music is a compilation of the music that has survived from the rich heritage developed over the centuries by the communities of the Diaspora, and the new repertoire of popular songs built up since the creation of the State of Israel.

RELIGIOUS MUSIC

The sung part of the liturgy became important during the 6th century when religious poetry (*piyyutim*) was presented and performed by professional singers. With the exception of the synagogues of the Reform Movement, where instruments were introduced in the 19th century, synagogue music is always sung.

71

● ARAB AND JEWISH DANCES

Among the sources that have influenced Israeli popular dances are the refined Yemenite-Jewish dances, the vibrant Hasidic dances and the Arab and Druze dance known as the *debka*. Yemenite dances, accompanied by singing and drums, highlight the skills of individual dancers, while Hasidic dances, accompanied by singing and sometimes *klezmer*, are collective. The *debka*, a vigorous dance characterized by a rhythmic stamping of the feet, is performed in Arab villages to the sound of the *arghul*. Finally a form of ecstatic, religious dance is performed by certain mystic Muslim orders.

DANCE IN BIBLICAL TIMES
In Biblical times dance was a way of expressing joy in the worship of God. This was why the Hebrews began to dance in the desert when they set up the image of the Golden Calf at the foot of Mount Sinai (Exodus 32). There is no record of choreography or technical details and, unlike other ancient civilizations, the folk dancing of Biblical times was not an integral part of religious worship.

YEMENITE DANCING
Yemenite dancing represents the most refined and sophisticated tradition of the Diaspora. The dances performed by the women are simpler and more reserved than those of the men, where two, and sometimes three or more dancers execute extremely complex steps and movements within a limited space. Israeli popular dances were inspired by this.

HASIDIC DANCING
For the Hasidim ● *82*, dancing is a means of achieving a state of religious ecstasy and spiritual elevation. Hasidic dancing is spontaneous, individual or collective, frenzied and often acrobatic. It can be seen on the Shabbat, festivals and at weddings.

"DEBKA"
This is an energetic, vigorous dance. The closely formed line of dancers, holding each other by the shoulders, performs various movements accompanied by stamping and jumping. The order and series of movements are decided by the leader at the front of the line. He waves a scarf to indicate changes of movement.

ISRAELI POPULAR DANCES
Initially Israeli popular dances placed the emphasis on collective, "socialist" dancing. Today they are a mixture of various influences, incorporating elements from central European, Hasidic, Yemenite and even Arab dances (such as the *debka*).

ECSTATIC DANCING
Ecstatic dancing is part of the religious practice of some Sufi (left) orders. Mystical union is its ultimate aim, achieved by dance and respiratory techniques executed at a frenetic pace to the accompaniment of religious songs and sometimes musical instruments.

There are few books in the Bible that do not mention bread (the "staff of life") – always an important part of meals in the Holy Land. Even today meals do not begin until the pitta has been served. This edible "spoon" is used for eating *falafel*, filled with balls of garbanzo beans. *Challah* is a plaited leavened bread, the so-called "priest's share" sometimes made as an offering. It is eaten on the Shabbat and festivals.

INGREDIENTS FOR TWELVE PITTAS:
1 rounded tbs dried yeast, 1 rounded tbs salt, 2 rounded tbs honey and 5–5½ cups plain flour.

1. Mix the yeast, honey and ¼ pint water in a bowl and leave to stand for 10 mins. Measure out 3¼ cups flour and add the yeast mixture and 1 pint warm water.

2. Beat the mixture for 2 mins, add the salt and remainder of the flour and beat again. Knead the dough on a floured board for 10 mins and then place in a greased bowl.

3. Leave the dough to rise for 1 hour in a warm, draft-free place (it will double in volume). Pre-heat the oven to 230°C (445°F) and divide the dough into twelve portions.

4. Roll each portion into a ball and then flatten into rounds about 2¼–2½ inches thick. Allow to rise before cooking. Cook for 10 mins and then raise the temperature so that they brown.

INGREDIENTS FOR THREE "CHALLAHS":

½ rounded tbs dried yeast, 1 tsp sugar, 3 eggs, ¾ cup sugar, ¼ pint vegetable oil, pinch of salt, 2¼ lb or 7 cups flour.

1. Mix the yeast, ¼ pint warm water and 1 tsp sugar in a bowl. Add ¾ pint warm water, the oil, salt and the remaining sugar. Then add ¾ of the flour.

2. Knead the dough on a floured board for 10 mins, adding the remainder of the flour.

3. Place the dough in a greased bowl and cover with a damp cloth. Leave to rise for 1 hour (it will double in volume).

4. Divide the dough into three and roll each portion into an elongated "sausage".

5. Plait each "sausage" into a figure-of-eight. Avoid compressing the dough to allow it room to double in size.

6. Brush the challahs with a mixture of the beaten eggs and water and sprinkle with sesame or poppy seeds. Cook for 15 mins until golden brown. If they sound hollow when you tap them, they are ready.

75

● OLIVES

The olive tree celebrated in the Bible is a symbol of beauty, wealth and fertility.

Crushing and pressing the olives and separating the oil from the residue are the three stages in the production of olive oil, a process which has been carried on in the Holy Land for the last five thousand years. In fact, wild and cultivated olives – still part of the region's staple diet – and their oil (the main source of light) have been extensively produced since the Iron Age. Over the centuries oil-extracting techniques have been improved and the number of presses has increased.

BEAM-PRESS
The typically Iron Age beam-press consists of two presses operated by a beam-lever, a crushing vat (in which the olives are no longer trampled with wooden shoes but crushed with a roller), a press-bed, a separation vat and a lateral collection vat. During the Hellenistic period, the crushing process was greatly improved by the introduction of the wheel.

Wild olives can be distinguished from cultivated olives (*Olea europaea*) by the size of their stone. Olives have been traded since classical times.

SCREW-PRESS
During the Byzantine period the screw-press appeared in towns, making mass production possible. In the predominantly rural regions of the Upper Galilee, Samaria and Judea it was used alongside the lever-press.

CRUSHED OLIVES
The traditional Palestinian method of producing olive oil by crushing the fruit is still used today. The olives are crushed in earthenware or wicker containers pierced with holes to allow the liquid to drain out. Although only small amounts of pure olive oil are produced by this method (6 percent), the quality is extremely high.

RELIGIONS

ORIGINS AND HISTORY
OF JUDAISM, *78*
JEWISH FESTIVALS, *80*
JUDAISM IN THE HOLY LAND, *82*
ORIGINS AND HISTORY
OF CHRISTIANITY, *84*
CHRISTIAN FESTIVALS, *86*
CHRISTIANITY IN THE
HOLY LAND, *88*
ORIGINS AND HISTORY
OF ISLAM, *90*
MUSLIM FESTIVALS, *92*
ISLAM IN THE HOLY LAND, *94*
CALENDARS, *96*

● ORIGINS AND HISTORY OF JUDAISM

Judaism is based on belief in one God and on the covenant between Him and His people which began with Noah, and continued with Abraham, Isaac and Jacob, supremely with Moses on Sinai, and also with David. Every aspect of Judaism – cultural, ritual, religious and national – is founded on the Bible (Tanach means T-orah, guidance and law, N-ebiim, prophets, and Ch-etubim, Writings). Application to life (supremely in Torah shebeʻal peh, oral Torah, transmitted by word of mouth, gathered in Mishnah and Talmuds) continues to the present.

THE LAW OF THE COVENANT

Moses received the Ten Commandments from God on Mount Sinai ▲ *170* and gave them to the Israelites. The Commandments formed the basis of the Covenant between God and His people: "Thou shalt have no other gods before me. Thou shalt not make unto thee any graven image . . . Thou shalt not take the name of the Lord thy God in vain... Remember the Sabbath day, to keep it holy . . . Honor thy father and thy mother... Thou shalt not kill. Thou shalt not commit adultery. Thou shalt not steal. Thou shalt not bear false witness against thy neighbor. Thou shalt not covet . . . any thing that is thy neighbor's." (Exodus 20, 3–17)

THE FIRST COVENANT

The first covenant was made with Noah and embraces all people, so that Gentiles are in that basic universal covenant and do not necessarily have to convert. God commanded Abram to leave Ur of Chaldaea and go to a new land where, as Abraham, he would become the father of a people with whom God would establish a particular covenant, to make them a holy people, demonstrating obedience to God until the knowledge of God shall cover the earth as the waters cover the sea.

THE TORAH

The scrolls of the Torah (guidance including Law), known as the Pentateuch, bring together the first five books of the Bible – Genesis, Exodus, Leviticus, Numbers and Deuteronomy. They tell of creation, of the evils of disobedience and of God's work of repair culminating in Moses.

THE KETUVIM (WRITINGS)

The third part of the Tanach is made up of the Writings, thirteen books including the Five Scrolls (Megillot), Song of Songs, Ruth, Lamentations, Ecclesiastes and Esther, which are read at particular festivals.

THE ORAL LAW

Oral law, also believed to have been revealed on Sinai, is, with the Tanach, the foundation of the great codes of law in the Middle Ages, especially that of Joseph Caro, the *Shulhan Aruch*.

THE NEVIÍM (PROPHETS)

The Prophets are those who set forth the word and the will of God, either in narrative (the Former Prophets, Joshua, Judges, Samuel and Kings) or in oracles (the Latter Prophets, for example Isaiah, Jeremiah, Ezekiel): "But his word was in mine heart as a burning fire shut up in my bones." (Jeremiah 20)

The bitter herbs eaten at the *seder* on Passover symbolize the "bitter life" of the Hebrews in Egypt.

The Jewish calendar is punctuated with dates commemorating the events that have determined the course of Jewish history. Festivals symbolically aim to remind the Jewish people o these events, relate them to current situations and discover their relevance to other places and times. There are two types of festivals: those traditionally involving an annual pilgrimage to the Temple of Jerusalem, and those commemorating the elimination of threats to the continued physical and spiritual existence of the Jewish people. Shabbat (Sabbath) is a day of rest on which no work is permitted, lasting from sunset on Friday to nightfall on Saturday.

SUKKOT
The Feast of Tabernacles commemorates the nomadic life ▲ 174 of the Hebrews during their forty years in the desert. Symbolic booths are built in every district to celebrate the return of the Jewish people to their homeland. Throughout the week-long festival Jewish families eat their meals in the booths. The palm branch, myrtle (left), willow and citron (the "four kinds") are used during prayers over Sukkot. The last day, Simchat Torah, marks the end of the annual cycle of the reading of the Torah and the beginning of the next one.

PURIM
Purim commemorates Esther's deliverance of the Jews from Persian domination ● 39. It is celebrated by children dressing up in costume, and parades.

YOM HAATSMAUT

Yom Haatsmaut ("Independence Day") is the anniversary of the creation of the State of Israel in 1948 ● 56. It marks the end of the Diaspora for the Jewish people and is celebrated with military parades on the beaches of Tel Aviv and firework displays throughout the country.

ROSH HASHANAH AND YOM KIPPUR

Rosh Hashanah (the Jewish New Year) symbolizes God's sovereignty on earth and marks the beginning of the religious year. It begins a period of repentance and prayer, culminating in Yom Kippur (the Day of Atonement) when the fate of every Jew is sealed for another year.

HANUKKAH

During the eight-day Festival of Lights a candle is lit on each of the seven branches of the *menorah* to commemorate the inauguration of the purified Temple, after the Maccabean victory ● 48.

SHAVUOT

Shavuot (Pentecost) is a harvest festival seven weeks after Pesach marked by the offering of first fruits at the Temple. It also marks God's gift of the Torah to the Jewish people ● 78.

PESACH. Pesach (Passover) celebrates the Exodus of the Israelites from Egypt ▲ 168. At the festive meal or *seder*, the head of the family carries out God's command to Moses to "tell the children of Israel" (Exodus 19: 3–4) by reading the story of the departure from Egypt as recounted in the Haggadah.

Judaism has always included a variety of different ways of being Jewish, all of them unified by their endeavor to interpret the Torah according to the will of God, and to fulfill the obligations of the Covenant. During the period of the 2nd Temple, for example, there were Sadducees, Pharisees, Sectarians. There are now other and different variations. Some may not regard others as adhering to the covenant, but most coexist at least for the sake of Israel as the promised land. Some extreme Orthodox do not support Zionism, since there will be no return to the Land until the Messiah comes.

ORTHODOX JEWS
Orthodox male Jews can be recognized by their *kipa* (skullcap). Modern Orthodox Jews often wear a crocheted *kipa*, and participate in the country's economic, scientific and artistic life as well as serving time in the army.

Hasidism appeared in central Europe during the 18th century. The majority of Hasidim (the Pious) recognize the sanctity of the land in which they live, but not the political authority of the State. Nor do they see Zionism within the context of an explicit relationship with God. They invest their rabbi (*rebbe*) with an hereditary function as the intermediary between themselves and God. For Hasidic Jews prayer, study, and fervent dancing ● *72* are the means of achieving a state of religious ecstasy. Their style of dress is characteristic of the regions of central Europe where their respective rabbinic dynasties originated.

REFORM JEWS (liberals)
This form of Judaism emerged in the 19th century, in a non-Jewish environment, to facilitate religious practices such as observance of the Shabbat and *kashrut* (Jewish dietary laws). The liberal communities in the Holy Land are attempting to introduce into Judaism the precepts of western society, such as the improved status of women.

SECULAR ZIONISTS
The pioneers of the creation of a Jewish State were secular Zionists. A significant proportion of the Jewish population of Israel today considers religious practice to be redundant. However, they speak the language of the Bible quite naturally, celebrate Jewish festivals as national holidays, and the majority eat kosher food.

Jesus, a Jewish teacher, believed the condition of the covenant with God was not simply Torah but the faith that God has power to renew the world and human life. This power (which Jesus emphasized came from the Father) was mediate[d] through Jesus in word, healing and action, so tha[t] his disciples believed that "he and the Father are one", and that he was the awaited Messiah (Greek *Christos*, i.e. Christ). The authorities crucified him, but his disciples met him alive after death, and he continued to empower them through his presence in bread and wine as his body and blood. The renewing of life is now offered to all, and on this basis Christianity becam[e] a new religion.

JESUS. Jesus was born in Bethlehem ▲ *226* around 7–5 BC and lived in Nazareth ▲ *388*, completing his mission on earth between AD 28 and 30. He traveled through Galilee and visited Jerusalem with his followers. In AD 30 he was arrested, judged and condemned to death.

THE GOSPELS
The first three Gospels were written in AD 70–80, and the fourth in c. 100 by Matthew, Mark, Luke and John, the disciples who witnessed the acts and words of Jesus. They sought to guide the spiritual quest of early Christians.

THE EARLY CHURCH
The death and resurrection of Jesus extended to the whole world the healing and forgiveness which Jesus had mediated to those he met during his lifetime. This universalizing of the good gifts of God led to the mission of the Church throughout the world.

"YESHUAH"
The word *Yeshuah* ("God the savior") is engraved here on an ossuary. It is the Hebrew form of the Greek name Jesus.

PAUL, "THE APOSTLE TO THE GENTILES"
Paul was the only Apostle not to have known Jesus during his lifetime. He was a Hellenized Jew from Tarsus, in Cilicia, who had been a persecutor of the early Church before his conversion on the road to Damascus and subsequent opening up of Christianity to the Gentiles. His epistles, addressed to the new churches founded by him in Asia Minor, Greece and Macedonia during his three missionary journeys, contain remarkable pages on the salvation brought by Christ, as well as laying foundations for Christian doctrine.

4TH–6TH CENTURY PILGRIMAGES
The measures taken by Constantine to promote Christianity ensured the triumph of the Church. The impressive sanctuaries built on the site of holy places were visited by pilgrims for the next two hundred years. Jerusalem was the site of the advent of Salvation, as shown on this 6th-century map discovered at Madaba.

THE CRUSADES
The eight Crusades in the Holy Land marked the beginning of a Christian period that lasted from July 15, 1099 to October 2, 1187. The first Crusade in particular represented a spiritual quest which took the form of a collective pilgrimage to unite Christendom.

By normalizing the relationship between the Holy See and the State of Israel in 1993, Pope John Paul II confirmed the decisions of the Vatican Council II of 1965, which lifted the age-old anathema against the Jewish people.

"Christianity" was in origin a form of Judaism – an interpretation of what the covenant (Latin *testamentum*) with God should mean, hence New Testament. The break from Judaism did not mean that God's dealings with Judaism were repudiated, but they were developed to incorporate Gentiles to the point that the Torah-based covenant seemed to have been displaced. Christian festivals follow Judaism in celebrating the acts of God, but now more particularly the life of Jesus and the founding of the Church; they also celebrate exemplary Christians (especially saints, martyrs and teachers). The Church as the Body of Christ is meant to be a living manifestation of *agape*, unselfish love.

CHRISTMAS
Western Christians celebrate the Nativity, or birth, of Christ with a midnight Mass held in Bethlehem, in the Church of the Nativity. Twelve days later Eastern (Orthodox) Christians celebrate Epiphany, the manifestation of the Messiah in Jesus: the adoration of the Magi, the baptism in the Jordan and the marriage in Cana.

EASTER

The Easter period commemorates the "passage" of Jesus from death to life, and of the Christian from the death of sin to life in Christ. It marks the end of Holy Week (the Last Supper on Maundy Thursday, the Crucifixion on Good Friday) and is preceded by the forty days of Lent. This period of penitence evokes the forty years of the Exodus ▲ *168* and Jesus' forty days of fasting after he was baptized by John ▲ *406*. On Good Friday, Christians follow the Procession of the Cross along the Via Dolorosa ▲ *268* (above, left). For Orthodox Christians Easter is an extremely festive and joyful occasion. For a month they light candles (above, right), embrace and greet one another with the phrase: "Christ is risen!"

ASSUMPTION OF THE VIRGIN

The feast of the Assumption commemorates the doctrine (affirmed since the 7th century) that the body and soul of Mary were assumed into heaven when her earthly life was ended. The Church sees in her the image of perfect Redemption. On August 15 an Orthodox procession carries an icon of the Virgin from the Patriarchate to the Tomb of the Virgin.

ASCENSION

The Franciscans celebrate the Ascension (Christ's ascent into heaven forty days after Easter) by gathering to pray at the Chapel of the Ascension on the Mount of Olives.

PENTECOST

The Latin Patriarchate of Jerusalem presides at the Dormition Church on Pentecost (fifty days after Easter) to commemorate the descent of the Holy Spirit on the Apostles who were gathered with Mary. The event marked the birth of the Church and, on that day, each member of the assembled crowd heard the news proclaimed in their own tongue, and the proclamation went to the ends of the earth.

TRANSFIGURATION

The Eastern Church celebrates the Transfiguration by a solemn Mass held in the basilica of Mount Tabor. This important festival demonstrates the unity of the humanity and divinity of the Messiah (on "an high mountain" the man Jesus appeared in all his divine glory ▲ 390), as well as the unity of the Old and New Testaments.

CHRISTIANITY IN THE HOLY LAND

Seventeen churches in Jerusalem serve the city's Christian minority. The successive schisms were the result of theological disputes and the widening gulf between East and West. Following the Council of Chalcedon's assertion, in 451, of the dual nature (human and divine) of Christ, the Monophysites (Armenians, Copts, Syrian Jacobites and Ethiopians) seceded. In 1054 the Eastern Churches refused to recognize papal authority or the addition by the Western Church of the *Filioque* (and the Son) to the Creed. In the 16th century some Monophysites (the Uniat Churches – Armenians, Copts, Syrians and Greek Catholics) realigned with Rome, while retaining their own liturgy. The Reformation led to a split with Rome and the birth of the Protestant Church.

LATINS
Western pilgrims arrived in the Holy Land in the early centuries AD and built monasteries, churches and hospices. The Crusaders established a Latin Patriarch in Jerusalem. In 1342, just over one hundred years after the journey of Saint Francis to the Holy Land, the Pope gave the Franciscans (below) the task of watching over the holy places. The Patriarchate was restored in 1847 and religious communities were established in Jerusalem. In 1988 an Arab was set at the head of the western Catholic Patriarchate for the first time.

ARMENIANS
The Armenian nation, which was the first to subscribe to Christian Monophysitism, formed a Catholic church in the mid-eighteenth century. Today the Armenian Patriarchate in Jerusalem, which depends on the "catholicos" of the Armenian community living in Etchmiadzin, has around 2,500 members (monks and laymen) centered on the Armenian Convent of St James.

COPTS
There has been a Coptic Patriarchate in Jerusalem since 1899. The Copts are Egyptian Christians whose name is derived from the Greek word *aegyptos.* They were made famous by Saint Anthony and Saint Pachom (the Desert Fathers) and the founding fathers of Monachism, Athanasius and Cyril of Alexandria.

GREEK ORTHODOX

The Greek Orthodox community is the largest of all the Orthodox Churches in Jerusalem. It is governed by a Patriarch assisted by a synod of bishops, archimandrites and celibate priests, all of Greek nationality. Pastoral care, however, is entrusted to married, Arab priests.

ETHIOPIANS

According to tradition the Ethiopians are the descendants of the Queen of Sheba and King Solomon. They were converted to Christianity in the 6th century and adopted the Monophysitic doctrine. The Ethiopian Church in Jerusalem is governed by an archbishop. Ceremonial processions are held in the Ethiopian Monastery on the roof above the Armenian Chapel of St Helena in the Church of the Holy Sepulcher.

PROTESTANTS

Lutherans (Church of the Redeemer ▲ 277, near the Holy Sepulcher), Anglicans (St George's Anglican Cathedral ▲ 394) and Baptists are all represented in Jerusalem, as well as several national Churches such as the Churches of Scotland and Denmark.

MARONITES

The Maronite community is of Syrian origin and was founded by St Maro in 410. The Maronites remained faithful to Rome during the Nestorian crisis and account for most of the Christians in Lebanon. There are around six thousand Maronites in the Holy Land.

THE ANGEL GABRIEL
Visited the Prophet
on Mount Hira.

Islam is a monotheistic religion within the tradition of the Holy Scriptures. It requires obedience to Allah's eternal will and his absolute transcendence and to the holy word (the Qur'an) the sacred Message revealed by the Angel Gabriel to the Prophet Muhammad. The letters p.b.u.h. abbreviate the blessing "peace be upon him", invoked by Muslims whenever his name is spoken or written. Based on Qur'an and sunna (below), Islam is made manifest in the five pillars: faith (*shahada*), prayer (*salat*), charity (*zakat*), the fast of Ramadan (*sawm*) and the pilgrimage to Mecca (*hajj*).

THE DIVINE REVELATION
One night in the year 610, Muhammad was sleeping in a cave on Mount Hira (Mountain of Light), northwest of Mecca, Arabia. He was awakened by the voice of the Angel Gabriel announcing that he had been chosen as the apostle of God (Allah) to reveal religion to mankind.

THE QUR'AN
Revealed through the angel Gabriel/Jibrail (1st revealed verse above right), the Qur'an was collect under Uthman ● *94* and consists of 114 chapters (*sûrah*) divided into 6,243 verses (*ayat*). The openin (al-Fatihah) *sûrah* is followed by longest to shortes

IN THE TRADITION OF THE PROPHETS
The Apostle of God, Muhammad, was the last of the line of Prophets, beginning with Adam and continuing through Noah, Abraham (*Ibrahim*), Moses (*Musa*), Lot, David, Solomon, Jonah, Elijah, Job, Isaac, Jacob, Joseph, John and Jesus (*Isa*). Islam considers Abraham and his son Ishmael, borne to him by Hagar, as the Muslim patriarchs. He is therefore known as al-Khatim, the "Seal" of the Prophets.

"Read: in the name of thy Lord who createth, Createth man from a clot. Read: and thy Lord is the Most Bounteous, Who teacheth by the pen, Teacheth man that which he knew not." Sûrah XCVI

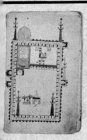

THE HIJRA
Persecuted in Mecca, Muhammad left for Medina with Abu Bakr in 622. This is Year 1, the beginning of the Muslim era, hence dates are called A.H., After the Hijra (exodus) to Madina, where Muhammad formed the first Muslim community.

TRADITIONAL ISLAMIC LAW
The *Sunna* gathers Hadith, narrations of the words, actions and silences of Muhammad and his Companions. These were later gathered and written down by the great collectors (six collections have authority, especially al-Bukhari) and now inform Muslim life by showing how Qur'an was first applied in life.

PRAYER
Prayers are said five times a day, after the performance of ritual ablutions, facing Mecca.

PROFESSION OF FAITH
The profession of faith (*shahada*) is the assertion of the belief that "There is no god but God (Allah): Muhammad is the apostle of God." The *shahada* (above) is repeated three times and is the formula for conversion to Islam.

PILGRIMAGE, OR "HAJJ"
The fifth pillar of Islam requires Muslims to make the pilgrimage to Mecca at least once in their lifetime. Pilgrims are dressed in white and must complete the ritual of the *hajj*. This involves walking round the Kaaba and making the ritual journey between the two hills of Safa and Marwa, near Mecca, seven times.

● MUSLIM FESTIVALS

Giant calligraphy of one of the ninety-nine names of Allah.

Among a larger number of festivals, five are of particular importance, when Muslims are called together to commemorate the great events in the life of the Prophet, to celebrate the effort required to accomplish the two most difficult – in time and space – of the five pillars of Islam (the fast of Ramadan and the pilgrimage to Mecca), and to remember – by offering their own sacrifice – the sacrifice of Abraham, forefather of the Faithful. Together with Friday prayer, these occasions are the most obvious examples of the collective nature of Islam.

MAWLID AN-NABI
Mawlid is the anniversary of the Prophet's birthday, traditionally celebrated on Monday 12 or 13 of the month of Rabia al-awal (a date which coincides with his death). On this occasion the Faithful gather in the mosque (Dome of the Rock, right) to intone his praises.

RAS ES-SANA
Some sources claim that on his arrival in Medina, Muhammad instituted a ten-day fast which marks the beginning of the Muslim calendar (left).

RAMADAN

The ninth lunar month, Ramadan, during which the Prophet received the Revelation, is observed as a fast when Muslims eat nothing from dawn to dusk.

ID AL-FITR

The first day of Shawal ● *96* ends the fast of the month of Ramadan, the month of sacrifice and the test of true faith.

In the evening Muslims eat dried apricot paste (*amar ed-din*) in accordance with a ritual established by the Prophet in Medina when, after the ceremony of prayer, he ordered alms (*zakat* – wheat, barley, dates and raisins) to be dispensed to mark the breaking of the fast.

"MIRAJ"

The twenty-seventh day of the month of Rajab ● *96* commemorates the Prophet's Night Journey (*isra*) from Mecca to Jerusalem, after which he ascended to heaven (*Miraj*). It is marked by the reading of the *surah* of the ascension in the Al-Aqsa Mosque.

ID AL-ADHA

Held on the tenth day of the month of Zul Hijja to commemorate Abraham's sacrifice. Every Muslim family sacrifices a sheep.

Muslims living in the Holy Land belong either to Sunni or Shiah Islam. These are the two main branches of Islam which emerged as a result of the conflict between Ali and the governor of Syria, twenty-five years after the death of Muhammad. As in most Muslim countries, the Sunnis are in the majority, although they represent only one-seventh of the population of the Holy Land. The Druzes are not recognized by Sunnis as true Muslims: they have secret doctrines and initiation, and are a small minority.

SCHISM

Following the assassination of Uthman, in 656, the caliphate of Ali was challenged by Mu'awiya, governor of Syria who was also related to Uthman. In 657, after a terrible battle at Siffin, Iraq,

a split occurred within the Muslim community when Ali agreed to the arbitration proposed by his adversary: the Shi'ites, who were followers of Ali, believed that he was the only legitimate successor to Muhammad, while the Sunnis recognized the authority of the first four caliphs.

SUCCESSION OF MUHAMMAD

On the death of Muhammad, in 632, Abu Bakr was appointed first caliph by the community of Medina. In 634 Umar, another of the Prophet's fathers-in-law, proclaimed himself "emir of the Faithful". He was assassinated in 644 and succeeded as caliph by Uthman.

THE DRUZES

The Shi'ites, who refer to imams rather than caliphs, are divided: some recognize twelve imams as the legitimate successors of Ali, while for the Ismailis and Druzes (in the Holy Land, right) there are only seven in the line of descendancy. The Druzes, who settled in Palestine in 1000, are not recognized by Sunnis as true Muslims: they have secret doctrines and initiation, and are a small minority.

"THE BEST FORM OF ISLAM INVOLVES GIVING FOOD TO
THE HUNGRY AND SALVATION TO THOSE YOU KNOW
AND ALSO TO THOSE YOU DO NOT KNOW."

HADITH

SUNNIS

Sunnis attach great importance to the legal aspects of Islam: the Law of Islam (*Sharia*) and Muslim law (*fiqh*). They belong to one of four schools of law: Malakite, Shafi'ite, Hanafite and Hanbalite. Palestinian Muslims belong to the Shafi'ite and Hanafite schools.

THE SHI'ITE COMMUNITY

The Shi'ites (above) are fewer in number than the Sunnis and are characterized by their attachment to the Prophet's cousin Ali. They believe that only Ali and his sons, Hasan and Husain, received the Prophet's "testament".

The Jewish and Muslim festivals are calculated according to the lunar calendar whereas the Christian festivals follow the solar calendar. Only Easter, based on the Jewish festival of Pesach (Passover), moves as it remains linked to the lunar cycle.

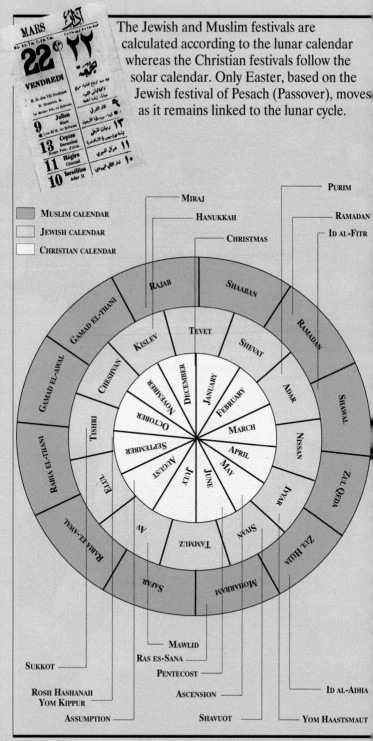

MUSLIM CALENDAR
JEWISH CALENDAR
CHRISTIAN CALENDAR

PURIM
RAMADAN
ID AL-FITR
MIRAJ
HANUKKAH
CHRISTMAS

RAJAB
SHAABAN
GAMAD EL-THANI
KISLEV
TEVET
SHEVAT
RAMADAN
GAMAD EL-AWAL
CHESHVAN
ADAR
SHAWAL
TISHRI
DECEMBER
JANUARY
FEBRUARY
NISSAN
RABIA EL-THANI
NOVEMBER
OCTOBER
MARCH
ZUL QEDA
ELUL
SEPTEMBER
APRIL
AUGUST
MAY
IYAR
RABIA EL-AWAL
AV
JULY
JUNE
SIVAN
ZUL HIJJA
TAMMUZ
SAFAR
MOHARRAM

MAWLID
RAS ES-SANA
PENTECOST
ASCENSION
SHAVUOT
YOM HAASTSMAUT
ID AL-ADHA

SUKKOT
ROSH HASHANAH
YOM KIPPUR
ASSUMPTION

GLOSSARY

◆ A ◆

Abu (M): (meaning "father of") is followed by the name of the eldest son of the father in question. Many Arabs and Muslims use this patronymic which earns them respect and admiration as the father of a first-born, male child.

Adhan (M): call to prayer issued by the *muezzin* from the top of the minaret. In Sunni Islam it is expressed in seven formulae.

Adventist (C): known as the "Church of the Seventh-Day Adventists". They await the return of Christ (Advent), who has promised to appear at the end of time.

Aga Khan (M): title of the imam of the Nizari Ismaili Shi'ites, who live mainly in East Africa and Persia.

Ahl al-Kitab (M): ("people of the Book") the name given, according to Muslim tradition, to the practicing members of another revealed religion – primarily Judaism and Christianity – who enjoy the status of *dhimmi* (protected people) ● 52.

Alawites (M): an Arab minority of Shi'ite origin, found mainly present in Syria where, in spite of a predominantly Sunni population, Hafiz al-Asad, the head of state, is an Alawite.

Alim (M): the singular of *ulamâ* (ulema), a body of Muslim scholars, exegetes, jurists and theologians who, as the custodians of knowledge (*ilm*), are the guardians of Muslim Tradition, the five "pillars" of Sunni Islam, and the representatives of the *consensus omnium* (*ijma*) of the religious community.

Aliyah (J): literally "going up" to the Holy Land ● 157. In modern parlance it refers to emigration to Israel. It can also mean "going up" to the reading of the Law in synagogue.

Allah (M): *the* God – that which is God beyond the conflicting claims of polytheists in Mecca, or of divided religions.

Altar: originally a mound or stone tablet used for sacrifices. By extension, the table on which Mass is celebrated ● 110.

Anglican (C): that part of the Church which does not recognize the jurisdiction of the Pope, but (locally) recognizes the sovereign as the governor of the Church under Christ.

Apocalypse (J): attributed to the apostle John. It evokes the struggle of the Church against the forces of Evil and announces the final victory of the kingdom of God.

Apocrypha (J and C): Jewish and Christian writings, similar to those of the Bible but not included in the Scriptures.

Archimandrite (C): head of certain monasteries in the Greek Church.

Ark of the Covenant (J): see *Aron hakodesh*.

Arkan (M): the five "pillars" of Islam: profession of faith, prayer, charity, fasting and pilgrimage ● 90.

Armenian Church (C): adopted the Monophysitic doctrine in the 6th century. During the course of its history the Church was divided into two Patriarchates, with Jerusalem retaining the greater prestige. Today there are Catholic and non-Catholic (Gregorians) Armenians, the latter being Monophysites ● 88.

Aron hakodesh (J): "holy ark" in Hebrew. Originally referred to the Ark of the Covenant containing the two tablets of the Law given by Yahveh to Moses on Mount Sinai ▲ 168. Today it designates the niche in every synagogue, containing the scrolls of the Torah ● 78.

Ashkenazim (J): Jews from Germany, Poland and, more generally, central and eastern Europe.

Ashura (M): festival marking the tenth day of the Muslim lunar year. For Shi'ites it is a festival of contrition to commemorate the martyrdom of the Prophet's grandson, Husain. For the Sunnis it is an occasion for joyful celebration.

Assyrians (C): name of an ancient Mesopotamian civilization. In the 19th century it was attributed to the Nestorian Christians, living mainly in Iraq and Turkey, whose mother tongue and liturgy were Aramean (the language spoken by Christ). The Chaldeans were the branch that decided to align themselves with Rome.

Ayat (M): (meaning "sign" or "miracle") is primarily used to designate the verses of the Qur'an ● 90.

◆ B ◆

Baptist (C): a sect, created in the 19th century, constituting the largest branch of the Protestant Church and characterized by believer's baptism and the authority of the Bible.

Baptistry (C): a round or polygonal structure, next to or inside the church, where baptisms (by immersion on the part of Baptists) are carried out.

Bar Mitzvah (J): "son of the commandment". Jewish religious ceremony during which a thirteen-year-old boy symbolically attains his religious majority and joins the ranks of the adult community ▲ 262.

Basilica (C): religious building including between three and five naves and often built above the tomb of a saint ● 124.

Bat Mitzvah (J): girls' equivalent of the *bar mitzvah*, except that girls are considered to have

reached their majority at the age of twelve.

Baya (M): oath of allegiance sworn by the Faithful to the Prophet or his successor.

Bet hamidrash (J): room in a synagogue devoted to the study of the Torah. Its sacred character is due to the importance attached to study by rabbinic Judaism.

Bey (or beg) (M): a Turkish title which means "lord" and which has a wide range of practical applications.

Bible (J): comes from the Greek word *biblia* meaning "books". It is the foundation of the Jewish people ● 78 and consists of three elements: the Torah, the Prophets and the Hagiographa (Writings).

Bible (C): consists of the Old Testament (the Jewish Bible) and the New Testament, written during the 1st century AD and comprising the four Gospels, the Acts of the Apostles, the Epistles and the Apocalypse.

Bishops (C): successors of the Apostles and overseers (Greek *episcopoi*) of the churches.

Bull (C): a formal document or mandate issued by the Pope, sealed with a leaden *bulla* (seal) and dealing with weighty matters.

◆ C ◆

Cadi (or kadi) (M): judge whose judicial competence is exercised in accordance with Muslim religious law and deals with religion and associated matters, such as (theoretically) penal and civil law.

Caliph (M): an Arabic word (*khalifa*) meaning "successor" of the Prophet (*khalifa* is the office) and used to designate the head of a Muslim community ● 93. Throughout its history the caliphate was challenged and divided between rival powers. It was suppressed in 1 924 by the Turkish president Mustafa Kemal.

Calvinism (C): a form of Protestantism developed by the Frenchman John Calvin, who converted to the Reformed Church in 1533 and gave it a more humanistic interpretation.

Cara (J): a Hebrew term denoting an individual who reads and interprets the holy texts without referring to the commentaries.

Cardinals (C): responsible for electing the Pope and also act as his chief counsellors.

Censer (C): a sort of incense-burner suspended on chains.

Cham (M): a term used to encompass the geographical entity of Syria – Lebanon – Palestine. *Bilad .-Cham* refers to Syria in its broadest historical and geographical sense.

Cherubim (J and C): winged beings who appear as the servants of Yahweh.

Chi-Rho (C): monogram for Christ formed by two, intertwined Greek letters and often accompanied by alpha and omega ● *110*.

Chrismation (C): orthodox ritual performed during the christening service whereby the priest anoints certain parts of the body of the baptized with sacramental oil.

Christ (C): from the Greek meaning "messiah". For Christians this means Jesus, son of God, who came to earth in human form to save humankind through his Passion, death and resurrection.

Ciborium (C): sacred vessel containing the consecrated Host used in Holy Communion.

Circumcision (or brit milah) (J): (meaning the "covenant of circumcision") the ritual removal of the foreskin, considered to be a sign of allegiance to God.

Codex sinaiticus (C): 4th-century manuscript containing the whole of the New Testament, discovered in St Catherine's Monastery and today housed in the British Museum, London.

Confraternities (or brotherhoods) (M): encourage popular religious practices and beliefs, such as the worship of local saints (*marabouts*).

Conservative Judaism (J): a religious movement that appeared in the United States in the late 19th century and has spread to other countries. A moderate form of modernism lying midway between rigid traditionalism and radical reform.

Coptic Church (C): Egyptian Christians converted in the 1st and 2nd centuries. They opposed the Council of Chalcedon (see *Monophysitism*) by a large majority. Today there is only one Coptic bishop in the Holy Land (in Jerusalem) and a community of one hundred or so families ● *88*.

Council of Chalcedon (C): see *Monophysitism*.

Council of Ephesus (C): see *Nestorians*.

Councils (C): see *Bishops*.

Crypt (C): an area usually built beneath the center of the church and originally intended to house the remains of a saint ▲ *272*.

♦ D ♦

Deacon (C): an minister ordained second grade in the hierarchy of holy orders, who ranks below a priest (see *Priest*).

Decalogue (J): the Ten Commandments ● *78* (from the Greek meaning "ten words"). According to Jewish and Christian tradition these were the ten commandments given by God to Moses on Mount Sinai ▲ *168*.

Devshirme (M): under the 15th- and 16th-century Ottoman Empire, the levying of Christian children to be trained as janissaries or to work in the Ottoman administration or Palace.

Dhikr (M): the "call" or invocation of the Name of God and, in the mystic brotherhoods, the collective quest for ecstasy.

Dhimmi (M): ● *52*.

Diaspora (J): dispersal of the Jewish people throughout the world, dating (symbolically) from AD 135, the date of the final defeat of the Jews by the Romans. The creation of the State of Israel has led to the so-called Palestinian Diaspora.

Djinn (M): an Islamic spirit or demon.

Dormition (C): in iconography, the last sleep of the Virgin.

Druzes (M): an Arab minority of Shi'ite origin who settled mainly in Lebanon, Syria and Golan, the territory annexed by Israel. Their esoteric religion seems to be a syncretism of Islam and Greek and Indian philosophies ● *95*.

♦ E ♦

Ecumenical councils (C): convened the bishops of all regional Churches and reflected the linguistic, cultural and religious diversity of the early Christian communities.

Efendi (M): an honorific Ottoman title used primarily for high-ranking, civil and religious officials.

Elohim (J): lit. "gods", but in Hebrew "God above gods".

Emancipation (J): abolition of the legal disadvantages imposed on the Jews.

Epiphany (C): (meaning "manifestation") a Christian festival commemorating the recognition of the Messiah in the newly born child, Jesus, by the three Magi ● *86*.

Episcopate (C): bishops collectively.

Epistles (C): letters sent by ministers of the Church to their communities to offer support and guidance in the practice of their faith.

Essenes (J): Jewish religious sect of the 1st centuries BC and AD ▲ *212*.

Ethiopian Church (C): Ethiopians converted in the 4th century and who later adopted *Monophysitism*. There is an Ethiopian bishop in Jerusalem ● *88*.

Ethnarch (J): title assumed by the Hasmonean sovereigns and, later, under Roman rule, by hereditary Jewish leaders.

Etrog (J): citron, one of the "four kinds" of plants used during prayers on *Sukkot* (Tabernacles) ● *80*.

Eucharist (C): from the Greek meaning "act of grace". The sacrament of the Eucharist commemorates Christ's sacrifice and the Last Supper by the sharing of bread and wine ("the body and blood of Christ") ● *110* during Mass.

Exilarch (J): hereditary leader of the Jews during the Babylonian Exile.

♦ F ♦

Falashas (J): Black Ethiopian Jews said to be the descendants of the Jerusalem notables who accompanied Menelik, heir of Solomon and the Queen of Sheba ▲ *292*.

Fast: a religious practice undertaken for a given period, in the three great

99

monotheistic religions: the Muslim fast of Ramadan (one of the five pillars of Islam), the Christian period of Lent, and the Jewish fasts which include Yom Kippur.

Fiqh (M): jurisprudence, the science of the religious law of Islam. It is traditionally divided into principles (*usul*) and practical rules.

Fish (C): The Greek word *ichthus* is formed from the initial letters of the Greek words meaning "Jesus Christ Son of God the Saviour". By extension the fish became the symbol of the early Christians ● 84.

Franciscans (C): order founded by Saint Francis of Assisi and which attaches great importance to the vow of poverty ● 88.

♦ G ♦

Genizah (J): room (or cupboard) in a synagogue for storing sacred books and objects that are no longer used but which it is forbidden to discard. The most famous of these is the genizah in the synagogue in Old Cairo.

Gentile (J): term used from the end of the period of the Second Temple to designate non-Jews (all pagans). It was used by Christians to designate pagans.

Ghazi (M): a Muslim warrior in the fight against the Infidels, used particularly during the Turkish period.

Gnosticism (J): complex religious movement which exerted a major influence on orthodox Judaism and Christianity.

Goi (J): non-Jew.

Gospels (C): The four Gospels (from the Greek meaning "good news") were compiled from the testimonies of four of the disciples and destined for the Church. They form the main part of the New

Testament ● 84.

Greek Catholic Church (C): Arabic-speaking Christians of the Byzantine rite (also known as Melkites), made up of Orthodox and Uniats (*q.v.*), in the patriarchates of Antioch, Jerusalem and Alexandria who accept Chalcedon.

Greek Orthodox Church (C): independent part of the Orthodox Church found mainly in Greece; ● 88.

♦ H ♦

Haftarah (J): a reading from the Prophets which follows the reading of the Torah during morning service on the *Shabbat* and Jewish festivals.

Haggadah (J): the book that is read during the seder (ritual supper) on Passover. Families gather to read and discuss the account of the Exodus from Egypt ● 81, ▲ 170.

Hajj (M): the pilgrimage to the holy places in and around Mecca.

Halacha (J): the body of legal and moral laws which bind all members of the Jewish faith.

Hametz (J): any yeast-based substance forbidden by Jewish Law during *Pesach* (Passover) ● 81.

Hanafites (M): one of the four schools of Sunni Islam characterized by the importance it attaches to the personal judgment of scholars in the interpretation of the Law ● 95.

Hanbalites (M): one of the four schools of Sunni Islam which advocates basic respect for Tradition according to the Qur'an and the Prophets.

Hanif (M): adherent of a monotheistic religion.

Hanukkah (J): Feast of Lights ● 80.

Haram (M): that which is sacred, forbidden. It has given rise to the term harem

which designates the women's quarters ● 114.

Hashishi (M): 11th-century Ismaili sect reputed to take hashish to heighten bravery in conflict.

Haskalah (J): movement of Enlightenment within the Jewish world, founded in Germany in the 18th century by Moses Mendelssohn. It subsequently spread to Poland and Russia where its adherents, known as *Maskilim*, were violently opposed to the Hasidim.

Hasidism (J): a religious revival movement which first appeared in Poland in the 18th century (although the term is older). Its members are grouped around a *rebbe* or *tzaddik* ● 82 believed to have spiritual powers.

Hatzot (J): midnight.

Havdalah (J): (meaning "Separation") a prayer recited at the end of the *Shabbat* and festivals to mark a distinction between holy days and weekdays.

Hebrews (J): term used for the ancient eastern Semitic people, descended from Abraham and his lineage, whose story is told in the Old Testament and ends with the destruction of Jerusalem in AD 70 ● 51.

Hegira (M): derived from the Arabic word *hijra*, meaning "emigration". It refers to Muhammad's departure from Mecca for Medina ● 90.

Herem (J): the most official form of excommunication, rarely practiced today.

Heresy (C): a doctrine which does not conform to the dogma established by a particular Church as the basic truth.

Hijab (M): the veil. For some Muslims the controversial wearing of the veil is not compulsory, either in practice or with reference to the Qur'an, but modesty is.

Hilal (M): the crescent, the emblem of Islam, became the official emblem of Turkey and Tunisia at the beginning of the 19th century.

Holocaust (J): In modern history this refers to the genocide of six million Jews, killed in concentration camps by the Nazis in World War Two.

Huppah (J): the canopy symbolizing the bridal chamber beneath which the marriage ceremony is performed.

♦ I ♦

Iconostasis (C): a screen, pierced by three doors and decorated with icons, separating the sanctuary (*bema*) and the nave in the Eastern Church ● 110.

Ijma (M): see *alim*.

Ijtihad (M): the "effort" of making a personal interpretation of Muslim Law, currently opposed to the unreserved submission to Tradition or *taqlid* ("imitation").

Imam (M): communal prayer leader. For the Shi'ites imams are particularly important as they are the representatives of God among the Faithful while awaiting the return of the (12th) "hidden imam".

Indulgences (C): common practice among Roman Catholics prior to Vatican Council II. Some types of indulgence (prayers, fasts and even payments to the Church) helped to alleviate suffering in the hereafter.

Islam (M): a term designating "submission" and "abandonment" to God. The new religion took its name from the Qur'an ● 90.

♦ J ♦

Jabr (M): a theological term signifying the all-powerfulness of God over Man. The word algebra is derived from the Arabic *al-jabr*.

Jacobite Church (C): name given to the Syriac Christians who refused to abide by the Council of Chalcedon and do not recognize papal authority. They have an orthodox Syriac Patriarchate in Antioch ● 88.

Jahannam (M): Hell, *Gehenna*.

Jihad (M): means "effort toward a specified goal" but is often only associated with the latter part of this definition – the "holy war", or struggle to defend Islam (lesser jihad). The greater jihad is the personal effort required to achieve moral and religious perfection ● 52, 91.

Judaism (J): Jewish religion and way of life. Its beliefs, practices and rituals are based on Scripture (Tanach ● 79), above all the Torah, which contains *mitzvot* (commandments) for life ● 82.

◆ K ◆

Kaaba (M): the cubical, gray stone building (also known as the "House of God") in the courtyard of the mosque in Mecca into which the basalt meteorite that Muslim pilgrims come to venerate ● 90, known as the black stone, has been built.

Kabbalah (J): an essentially esoteric, 12th-century religious tradition based on a mystical and allegorical interpretation of the Bible. It influenced Christianity greatly during the Renaissance.

Kaddish (J): (meaning "Sanctification") a prayer recited at the end of the main passages of the liturgy.

Karaite sect (J): a religious movement that rejected the rabbinic tradition

(Oral Law, that is the Mishna and Talmud) in favor of strict adherence to the Bible (Written Law).

Kashrut (J): "kosherness", the state of being kosher (*q.v.*).

Ketubah (J): marriage contract specifying the husband's obligations toward his wife.

Kharijites (M): those who believe that the leader of a religious community should be chosen by the Faithful, regardless of race or dynasty.

Khutba (M): the Friday sermon delivered first by the leader of the Muslim community and then by his representative.

Kiddush (J): a sanctification prayer said over wine on *Shabbat* and festivals.

Kipa (J): the skullcap worn by Jewish men as a symbol of their obedience to God.

Kitab (M): any form of written document, especially a contract, letter, book and also the revealed Scripture (of the three great monotheistic religions).

Koran (M): see Qur'an.

Kosher (J): a Hebrew term used to describe food that conforms to Jewish dietary laws.

Kotel (J): the Jewish name for the remains of the Temple of Jerusalem – the Western Wall. The Christian name (the "Wailing Wall") is rejected by the Jews ▲ 258.

Kuttab (M): Qur'anic school.

◆ L ◆

Last Supper (C): the last meal that Jesus shared with his disciples ● 238.

Latins (C): name given in certain parts of the East to – French, Italian, etc. – Roman Catholics ● 88.

Lazarus (Order of St) (C): a chivalric order established in

Jerusalem in the late 11th century with the object of assisting lepers, whose patron was Saint Lazarus. The order still exists in France today as the Hospitaliers de St-Lazare.

Liberals (J): members of a branch of Judaism whose beliefs are best defined as "reformed", a term used mainly in western Europe.

Liturgy (C): the body of symbols, gestures and rituals which form the public service.

Lovers of Zion (J): name given to the group, formed in the 1830's, by Jewish immigrants from Eastern Europe who settled in Palestine.

Lubavitch (J): a major branch of the Hasidic movement, inspired by the works of Shneur Zalman from Ladi (Russia), founder of the Lubavitch dynasty ▲ 262.

Lulav (J): a palm branch. One of the "four kinds" used during prayers on *Sukkot* (Tabernacles).

◆ M ◆

Maariv (J): evening prayer; also the name of one of the leading Israeli evening newspapers.

Maccabean (J): ● 50.

Madrasa (M): college, school, religious teaching establishment ▲ 283.

Maghreb (M): (meaning the "place where the sun sets") a term used to designate the West and, in particular, the Muslim West.

Magus (M): Magi was the name given to the Zoroastrians. In western Islam it was used to designate the Normans.

Mahdi (M): "the guided one" (that is, guided by God). The name applied, particularly in Shiah Islam, to the awaited Imam who will reinstate the reign of justice and pure Islam at the end of time.

Maksura (M): wooden panel in a mosque separating the imam or sultan from the congregation.

Malak (M): angel.

Malakites (M): one of the four schools of Sunni Islam ● 95.

Malik (M): is most widely used in its secular sense, meaning "king".

Marabout (M): a holy hermit, an Islamic saint, whose tomb is often a place of pilgrimage.

Maronites (C): a Christian community from Syria, founded in the 5th century by Saint Maro ● 88. They have retained the Syriac liturgy and remained faithful to Rome. Most of the Christians in Lebanon are Maronites.

Marranos (J): a pejorative term applied to Spanish and Portuguese *crypto* (Jews), people who were forcibly converted to Christianity, but who secretly continued to maintain their Jewish faith.

Mashriq (M): (meaning the "place where the sun rises") a term used to designate the East and, in particular, the Muslim East in medieval Arabian geography.

Matza (J): the unleavened bread eaten during Passover in remembrance of the "bread of affliction" eaten by the Hebrews on their departure from Egypt ▲ 168.

Melammed (J): teacher of young children.

Mendicant orders (C): the Franciscan and Dominican religious orders first appeared in the early 13th century and were active in the Holy Land, living by alms and preaching.

Menorah (J): Hebrew name for the seven-branched candelabrum which stood in the Temple of Jerusalem. A symbolic object in the Jewish religion ● 106.

Mental restriction (M): an attitude practiced by the Shi'ites and Druzes. It involves answering a question in the manner expected by the questioner while replying mentally in accordance with their own beliefs.

Messiah: For Jews, the awaited "anointed one" (*mashiach*) of David's line, who will inaugurate God's kingdom. For Christians, this is Jesus (Christ means Messiah). Messianism is a belief in the coming of a messiah who is descended from David.

Methodism (C): a Christian movement founded by John Wesley and derived from the Anglican Church. Its name probably comes from the methodical nature of its teaching and life.

Metropolitan (C): in most Eastern Churches, an archbishop.

Mezuzah (J): ▲ 291.

Mihrab (M): decorated niche in a mosque indicating the direction (qibla) of Mecca ● 114.

Minaret (M): tower of a mosque from where the Faithful are called to prayer ● 116.

Minbar (M): the pulpit in a mosque ● 114.

Minha (J): an offering. Afternoon prayer.

Mishnah (J): (Oral Law) is exclusive to Judaism and consists of commentaries on the Torah. After the destruction of the Temple of Jerusalem by the Romans it was recorded in a written form known as the *Mishna*.

Mitnaggedim (J): the "Opponents" of the Hasidim of Eastern Europe denounced, in particular, the latter's naive belief in the special powers of the *rebbe* or *tzaddik*.

Mitzvah (J): commandment or religious duty. The Torah contains 613 *mitzvot*.

Mohel (J): the person who performs the rite of circumcision.

Monophysites (C): Christians who, in the 5th century, asserted their belief in the single, divine, nature of Christ. They were considered heretics and condemned by the Council of Chalcedon in 451. The Jacobites (see *Jacobite Church*) – the most famous of the communities established as a result – founded the Church of Syria in the 6th century ● 88.

Mormon (C): a member of the Church of Jesus Christ of Latter-day Saints. Mormons believe that Christ will return at the end of time and reign for one thousand years. Their extremely strict regime of day-to-day living is regulated by the Bible.

Mosaic Law (J): Jewish doctrine based on the Law given to Moses by God and which attaches great importance to the study of this Law.

Muezzin (M): the official of a mosque who issues the call to prayer.

Mufti (M): an expert who gives advice (*fatwa*) on a point of Muslim law. The use of the *fatwa* is, theoretically, strictly controlled.

Muhajirun (M): the companions of Muhammad who joined his exodus from Mecca to Medina.

Mullah (or Mollah) (M): an honorific Iranian title given to religious figures, notably Shi'ite Doctors of the Law who are the mouthpiece and interpreters of the thoughts of the "hidden imam".

Mutazilite (M): member of a classic school of Islam, characterized by its strongly rationalist tendencies.

◆ **N** ◆

Nabi (M): prophet (or patriarch).

Nasi (J): prince, patriarch or exilarch.

Ner tamid (J): light which shines permanently in a synagogue above the holy ark containing the scrolls of the Law ● 106.

Nestorians (C): Christians who, in the 5th century, professed their belief in the two distinct persons (human and divine) of Christ and thereby denied that Mary was the mother of God. Condemned by the Council of Ephesus in 431.

◆ **O** ◆

Orthodox Church (C): European Christians who did not support the Bishop of Rome, in the 11th century, in his decision to institute a judicial power (his own) over all Christian communities. Orthodox means "right-thinking", that is, remaining faithful to the dogmas established by the ecumenical councils. Orthodox Churches worldwide recognize the honorary primacy of the Patriarchate of "Constantinople" ● 88, 110.

Orthodox Jews (J): the branch of Judaism which conserves the observance of the Torah as elaborated through the ages. Ultra-orthodox are strict traditionalists ● 82.

◆ **P** ◆

Paraclete (C): a mediator or advocate. Name given by Christians to the Holy Ghost.

Parochet (J): Hebrew word for the curtain hanging in front of the holy ark in Akenazi synagogues.

Pasha (M): the most honorific Turkish title, usually given to provincial governors and ministers of the Ottoman Empire.

Patriarch (C): in the Old Testament, the name given to the early heads of a family or tribe. From the 6th century, a title given to the bishops of the five principle ancient sees: Rome, Constantinople, Alexandria, Antioch and Jerusalem. Today only non-Latin Churches (with very few exceptions) have a patriarch ● 88.

Patriarchate (C): regional churches at the time of the early Christian communities who recognized the Church of Jerusalem, and, later, Rome ● 88, as the common center of the primacy of love.

Peyot (J): the earlocks worn by Hasidic and Yemenite Jews.

Pentecostalism (C): The ten or so Pentecostal movements are rooted in Methodism and attach great importance to the agency of the Holy Ghost.

Pharisees (J): "separated" or "interpreters", Jews (from 2nd century BC) who encouraged interpretation of the Torah, thus helping ordinary people to keep it. They were forerunners of rabbinic Judaism. Christians used the term for those who are excessively concerned with law (a use also found in later Jewish sources).

Pogrom (J): a Russian term designating the wave of violence against the Jewish communities in Tsarist Russia in the late 19th and early 20th centuries.

Pope (C): (1) the bishop of Rome (claimed to be successor of Peter the Apostle) and head of the Roman Catholic Church. (2) a priest in the Slavonic Orthodox Church.

Priest (C): a minister of religion who has been ordained third grade in the hierarchy of holy orders in the Roman Catholic and Eastern Churches.

Prophet (C): an individual inspired to speak in the name of God, whose words are then preserved in the Bible and Qur'an.

Protestantism (C): see *Reformation*.

◆ Q ◆

Qanun (M): law, code.
Qibla (M):
● *114.*
Qiyas (M):
reasoning by analogy based on the Qur'an and the *Sunna:* one of the basic processes of classic Muslim law.
Qubba (M):
in general, a cupola or dome and, specifically, a building containing the tomb of an important person or saint in Arab countries.
Qur'an (or Koran) (M): (literally meaning "recitation") the sacred book of Islam revealed by the Angel Gabriel to Muhammad, who delivered all of it (in sections) during his years of prophetic ministry.

◆ R ◆

Rabbi (J):
(1) the Aramean word for "teacher". Title given to doctors of the Law in post-Biblical texts. Christ is sometimes referred to as Rabbi in the Gospels.
(2) doctor of the Law or spiritual guide qualified to commentate Biblical and Talmudic texts. Today, a Jewish minister of religion who officiates during services and teaches children and adults. The Chief Rabbi represents the Jewish community before the civil authorities of a country.
Rakaa (M):
series of ritual gestures (recitation, prostration) accompanying Muslim prayer.
Rasul (M): apostle, messenger. *Rasul Allah* means Apostle of God, that is, Muhammad.
Reconstructionism (J): religious movement which appeared in the United States. It combines a naturalistic theology with the idea that Judaism is a civilization invested

with a religious value.
Reformation (C):
16th-century schism within the Catholic Church; the result of the criticisms leveled at the Catholic hierarchy by their contesters, the Protestants.
Reform Judaism (J): The Reform Movement first appeared in Germany in the 19th century. It aimed to bring Jewish tradition into line with modern life.
Roman Catholic Church (C):
Christians from western Europe who, in the 11th century, supported the Bishop of Rome (the Pope) in his decision to commute his "primacy of love", recognized by all Christian communities, to a judicial primacy that he would exercise over these communities. "Catholic" means "all-inclusive, universal"
● *88.*

◆ S ◆

Sabra (J):
the Hebrew word for the fruit of the prickly pear (soft beneath its prickly exterior) and a metaphor for the Jews born in Israel.
Sacraments (C):
a recurring feature of Christian life, from birth to death. They assume a ritualistic significance by sanctifying certain events and presenting the tangible symbols of the Spirit of God. Two sacraments are dominical (i.e. from the Lord); five others are recognized by many, but not all, Christians.
Salafism (M): from the term *salafi* (traditional). A 19th-century system of thought which preaches the revival of Islam by a return to the essential spirit of its source: the Qur'an.
Samaritans (J):
descendants of the northern tribes, recognizing only the Torah. Two small communities remain. Mt. Gerizim is their

holiest place. They converted to Judaism but retained the worship of their idols and were considered heretics by the Jews ● *313.*
Sanhedrin (J):
● *40.*The Supreme Jewish Council in ancient Jerusalem, with religious, political and judicial powers.
Sawm (M):
ritual fast during the month of Ramadan and one of the five pillars of Islam ● *90.*
Sayyid (or saïd) (M): a general term for "leader" and a modern honorific title (Sir).
Seder (J):
see *Haggadah.*
Sefer Torah (J):
("Scroll of the Law") copy of the text of the Bible, handwritten on sheets of parchment which are stuck and sewn end to end and rolled around two wooden handles
● *160.*
Semites: from the name of Shem (or Sem), Noah's eldest son. According to Biblical tradition Shem is the eponym of the Semites, a Near-Eastern people who spoke non Indo-European languages. The term "anti-Semitism" was first coined in the 19th century by the German journalist Wilhem Marr.
Sephardim (J):
Jews from the Mediterranean Basin (especially Spanish, Portuguese and North African). The term is used in Israel to designate non-Ashkenazim.
Seven-branched candelabrum (J):
see *menorah.*
Shabbat (J): the Jewish Sabbath which lasts from dusk on Friday to nightfall on Saturday. It serves as a reminder that after the Creation, God rested on the seventh day and that humankind should also take time off from material creation.
Sharia (M): religious law ◆ *95.*
Sharif (or shereef) (M): usually designates the descendants of the

Prophet through his daughter Fatima.
Shaytan (or Shaitan) (M): leader of the demons (Satan).
Shi'ites (M): a minority branch of Islam which reserves the imamate for a descendant of Ali and Fatima, the Prophet's daughter ● *94.*
Shirk (M):
polytheism, the "act of associating" other divinities with God.
Shofar (J): a musical horn, made from a ram's horn as a reminder of the animal sacrificed by Abraham in place of his son. It is usually blown by the officiant during the New Year service and at the end of Yom Kippur.
● *70, 81.*
Shtibel (J):
place of prayer used by Ashkenazim and, in particular, Hasidim.
Simchat Torah (J):
festival marking the end of the annual cycle of the reading of the Law.
Sira (M): biography of the Prophet Muhammad, chronicling his words, acts and gestures, and constituting one of the basic sections of the Sunna.
Star of David (Magen David, shield of David) (J): six-pointed star (two triangles interlocking), an ancient symbol, but in the 19th century associated by Zionism with Jewish identity
● *106.*
Streimel (J):
the fur hat worn by Hasidim.
Sufis (M): Muslim mystics, who first appeared in the 8th century and were named after their rough-homespun (*suf*) robes. Their various religious practices include a litany and sacred dances. The most famous Sufis are the so-called "dancing dervishes".
Sujud (M):
prostration, one of the basic gestures accompanying Muslim prayer.
Sultan (M):
originally meant "power" or "authority". By extension it was

used to designate the holder of acquired power, as opposed to the inherited power of the caliphs (*khalifa*). The Ottoman emperor was a sultan.

Sunna (M): the customs and traditions of the Prophet ● 90.

Sunnis (M): the largest Muslim community, accounting for almost 90 percent of all Arab and non-Arab Muslims worldwide. The basic principle of their faith is respect for the *Sunna* ● 90.

Synagogue (J): from the Greek word meaning "assembly". A building dedicated to Jewish worship which today often includes educational and social facilities ● 106.

Syriacs (C): Arabic-speaking, eastern Christians who are sub-divided into the Catholic Syriacs who, although they have retained their patriarch and forms of service, recognize papal authority, and the Orthodox Syriacs (or Jacobites).

Tabernacle (C): meaning "tent". In the Christian religion a small, locked cupboard containing the "sacrament of the Eucharist". A small light shining beside it indicates the "real presence" of God.

Talit (J): white and black or blue striped shawl, with fringes at each corner, worn by Jewish men during prayer. They sometimes use it to cover their heads during religious ceremonies.

Talmud (J): A compilation, in Hebrew or Aramean, of the teachings and debates of the ancient rabbis on a wide range of subjects. It is also referred to as the Oral Law ● 78. Although disputed by the Karaites and the Reform Movement, it remains the basis of teaching in the yeshivot. The Talmud

comprises the Mishna (dealing with the application of the Torah), the Gemara and the Kabbalah (or "Tradition") which is a more or less esoteric interpretation of the Law.

Tashbih (M): anthropomorphism. One of the gravest heresies in the eyes of Islam.

Tefillin (J): small leather boxes containing Biblical verses copied onto strips of parchment. They are attached by straps to the forehead and left arm of Jewish men during morning prayer.

Templars (C): a military religious order founded by a French nobleman in 1125 and established within the Temple of Jerusalem to defend Christian interests. On their return to France they were persecuted and finally dissolved in the 14th century.

Theophany (C): or "manifestation of God". Commemoration by orthodox Christians of Christ's baptism in the Jordan.

Torah (J): ● 78. In its broader sense, the Jewish Law given by God to the Jewish people through Moses. In the stricter sense, the five books of Moses (or Pentateuch – Genesis, Exodus, Leviticus, Numbers and Deuteronomy) which tell the story of the Hebrew people, from the beginning to the death of Moses.

Transfiguration (C): marked with great ceremony in the Eastern Churches. It symbolizes unity in God and the unity of the Old and New Testaments ● 87.

Tzitzit (J): ritual fringes decorating the corners of the *talit* and symbolizing the holy commandments.

Ulema (M): see *Alim*.
Umma (M): community of the Faithful.

Umrah (M): rite observed by Muslim pilgrims to Mecca ● 90.

Uniat Churches (C): Disparaging name given by Orthodox Christians to Eastern (-rite) Catholics, that is, those in communion with Rome but retaining, among other things, their own customs and canon law ● 88.

UNRWA: United Nations Relief and Works Agency for Palestinian Refugees in the Near East.

Urf (M): custom, as distinct from Sharia.

Vizier (M): in classic Islam, the supreme head of administration and, later, chief minister.

Vulgate (C): the 4th-century, Latin version of the Bible, compiled mainly by Saint Jerome.

◆ **W** ◆

Wailing Wall (J): see Kotel ▲ 260.
Wali (M): benefactor, protector or friend. In religious terms, the saint whose worship is a feature of certain brotherhoods.
Waqf (M): a religious foundation.

◆ **Y** ◆

Yad (J): the "reading hand" used by Jews when reading the Bible to avoid damaging or marking the sacred Book ● 107.

Yahweh (J): According to tradition Yahweh means "I am that I am" (Exodus 3) and thus confirms the absolute existence of God whose name may be neither pronounced nor written in full.

Yehudi (J): Hebrew word meaning "Judean" (land of Judah). It was also used to designate the inhabitants of Samaria as well as all those who practiced the Jewish religion after the Babylonian Exile.

Yeshiva (J): a traditional Talmudic school whose curriculum may also include subjects other than the Talmud. Today it also refers to Jewish denominational secondary schools.

Yiddish (J): Medieval German dialect written with Hebrew characters. It became the vernacular language of the Eastern European Jews and subsequently spread to other parts of the world ● 60.

Yishuv (J): collective term for the Israelites who returned to live in Israel, as opposed to galut (those who did not).

Yom Kippur (J): ● 81.

◆ **Z** ◆

Zakat (M): (charity or almsgiving) one of the five pillars of Islamic law and a duty that each Muslim must perform ● 90.

Zealots (J): name given to a group of Jews who opposed the Romans. They advocated strict observance of the Law and an all-out struggle against the Roman enemy ● 50.

Zikr (M): see Dhikr.

Zohar (J): ("Splendor") one of the texts of the Kabbalah whose central element (criticized by the rabbis) is a mystic commentary of the Torah, written in Aramean, in the late 12th century, collected by Moses de Leon.

ARCHITECTURE

SYNAGOGUES, *106*
ROMAN AND BYZANTINE
SYNAGOGUES, *108*
CHURCHES, *110*
CHURCHES IN THE HOLY LAND, *112*
MOSQUES, *114*
MOSQUES IN THE HOLY LAND, *116*
EARLY ARCHITECTURE, *118*
HERODIAN ARCHITECTURE, *120*
ROMAN ARCHITECTURE, *122*
BYZANTINE ARCHITECTURE, *124*
ISLAMIC ARCHITECTURE, *126*
CRUSADER ARCHITECTURE, *128*
TRADITIONAL PALESTINIAN
VILLAGES, *130*
KIBBUTZIM AND MOSHAVIM, *132*
NOMADS' TENTS, *134*

● SYNAGOGUES

The *magen David* (shield of David, often called the star of David), religious symbol of the medieval Jewish communities of central and Eastern Europe, assumed a national significance in the 19th century.

The *Bet knesset* ("house of assembly" or synagogue) is the center of Jewish religious life in Israel and the Diaspora. Its origins are probably linked to the Babylonian Exile when the destruction of the Temple (the only authorized place of worship) led religious officials to establish an alternative place of worship. The synagogue became a most important part of Jewish life. Its roles as a place of meeting, of learning and study, and of prayer, were reinforced by the destruction of the second Temple in AD 70. A synagogue's level of orthodoxy today depends on the type of Judaism practiced.

THE HOLY ARK
The large, elaborately decorated cupboard containing the scrolls of the Torah symbolizes the Ark of the Covenant. The ark is concealed behind richly embroidered velvet hangings. It usually stands against the eastern wall of the synagogue.

"NER TAMID"
Above the holy ark is the *ner tamid* (eternal lamp) which is kept permanently lit as a symbol of the divine presence: Yahweh appeared to Moses from the midst of a burning bush ▲ *168* and, during the Exodus, He led or followed the Hebrew people ▲ *169* in the form of a pillar of fire.

FURNITURE

106

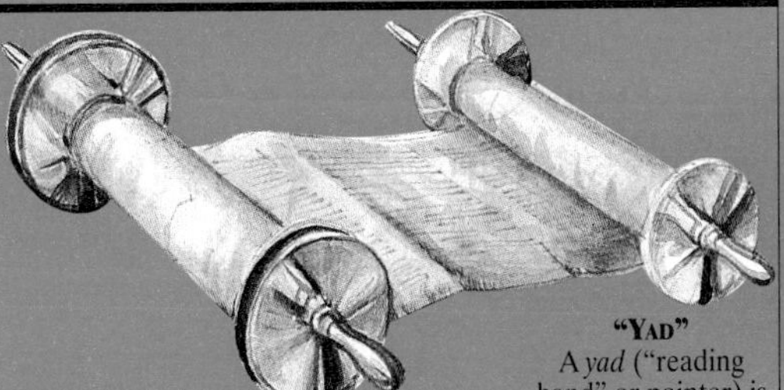

"SEFER TORAH"

During services the *sefer Torah* (scrolls of the Torah) is taken out of the holy ark, carried in procession, and placed on the platform to be read. It takes over a year to copy the text of the Pentateuch by hand onto sheets of parchment sewn end to end and rolled onto two wooden handles.

"YAD"

A *yad* ("reading hand" or pointer) is used to follow the sacred text so that the parchment is not damaged by continual handling. At the end of the service the *yad* is attached to a fine chain above the scroll.

The scrolls are wrapped in an embroidered cloth cover and decorated with ritual silver objects.

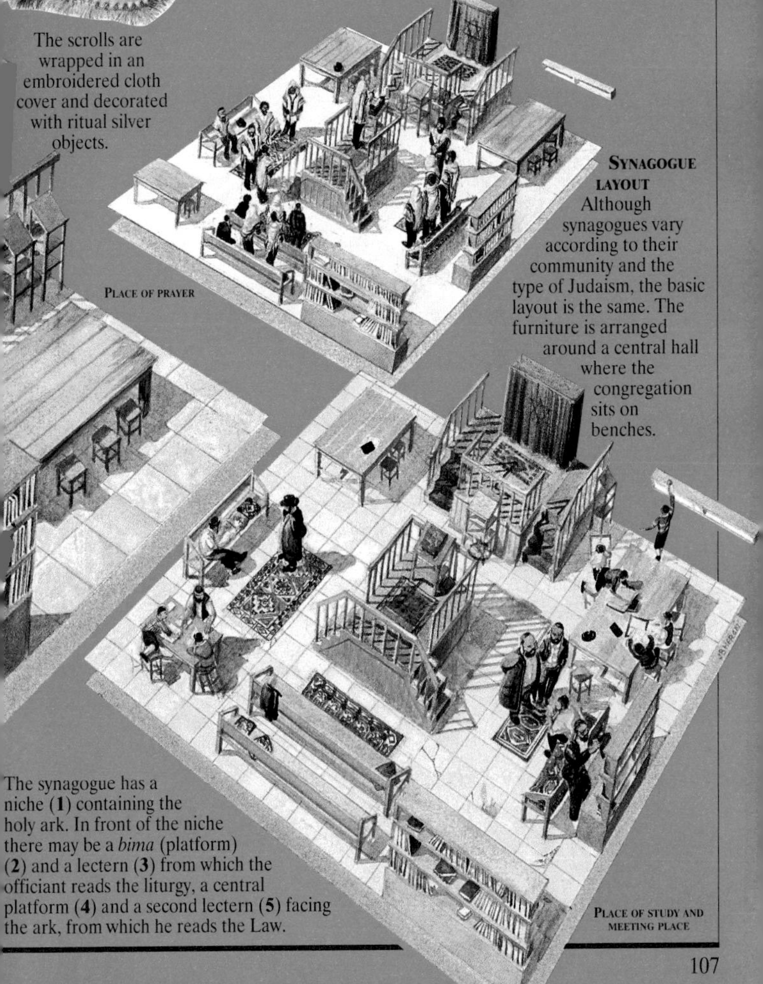

PLACE OF PRAYER

SYNAGOGUE LAYOUT

Although synagogues vary according to their community and the type of Judaism, the basic layout is the same. The furniture is arranged around a central hall where the congregation sits on benches.

The synagogue has a niche (**1**) containing the holy ark. In front of the niche there may be a *bima* (platform) (**2**) and a lectern (**3**) from which the officiant reads the liturgy, a central platform (**4**) and a second lectern (**5**) facing the ark, from which he reads the Law.

PLACE OF STUDY AND MEETING PLACE

The variations in layout and construction of the Roman and Byzantine synagogues discovered in the Holy Land led researchers to draw up a chronological classification based on types of decorative elements, the presence or absence of mosaic floors, interior design and orientation. However, recent discoveries forced them to abandon this conventional symbolism and concede that no general rules can be applied. Differences in design within the same region were the result of the many religious traditions that coexisted, as well as economic, political and cultural influences.

Although the Arab and Jewish interdict and Byzantine iconoclasm often led to the destruction of human and animal images after the 8th century AD, the images of Ma'on, in Galilee, have survived.

PRAYER HALL
The rectangular prayer hall included a colonnade and had benches lining the walls. The wall at the far end faced Jerusalem as, for example, at Masada ▲ 202.

FLOORS
The floor of the prayer hall was decorated with mosaics. The mosaics of Bet Alpha ▲ 397 combine geometric and floral motifs (in accordance with the Biblical interdict on human images) with Jewish and pagan religious representations of the Byzantine period.

ZODIACAL WHEEL
Figurative images, Biblical scenes and Jewish and pagan motifs such as the ark, the menorah, the binding of Isaac ▲ 236 or the zodiacal wheel of the mosaics of Bet Alpha, appear to have been tolerated in synagogues from between the 3rd and 8th centuries AD.

"BASILICAN" SYNAGOGUE
The "basilican" synagogue had a monumental-style, porticoed façade in finely worked, hewn stone, facing Jerusalem. The prayer hall, as in the synagogue of Kefar Bir'am (right), was arranged around a central area divided by columns into a broad nave and two wings.

CAPITALS
Capitals were decorated with acanthus leaves and religious symbols (above, Ein Nashut).

GENERAL LAYOUT
A courtyard and vestibule opened onto the prayer hall where, above a platform reached via three steps, a niche contained the holy ark ● 106, usually in the wall facing Jerusalem. The walls opposite and at the far end were lined with benches, while the central area was decorated with mosaics.

The menorah, either a mosaic design or carved in the stone, was one of the most widely used Jewish motifs in the decoration of synagogues.

The many different crosses reflect different ways of understanding Christ on the cross, from suffering servant to hero conquering death.

The interiors of churches tend to vary according to local traditions. Churches always face the east, the direction of the rising sun from which Christ will come on Judgment Day, and are divided into two main areas: the sanctuary, reserved for the clergy, and the nave, for the congregation. The position of the choir is different in Orthodox, Catholic and Protestant churches. The Eastern Church is characterized by the physical separation of the sanctuary from the nave, whereas the Catholic Church insists (since the reform of the Vatican Council II) that these two areas communicate.

CROSS OF JERUSALEM
This cross symbolizes Christian presence in the Holy Land. Today the Franciscan, Greek Orthodox and Armenian communities all have a role in watching over the holy places.

THE HOLY WORD
While the Scriptures present the Word of God in a visible (written) form, the shape of this Ethiopian gospel-book acts as a reminder of the incarnation of the Word of God in Jesus Christ.

THE HOLY PRESENCE
The flame of this Byzantine lamp, decorated with the "Chi-Rho", is the traditional symbol of the "real presence" of God in the Holy Sacraments of the Eucharist.

IN THE WESTERN CHURCH:
THE ALTAR IS OPEN TO THE FAITHFUL.
The Western Church commemorates the Last Supper by making table around which the celebrant and faithful crucifix and candles are placed on the altar, th communicants are placed nearby and, in front the lectern or "ambo" for proclaiming the Wo

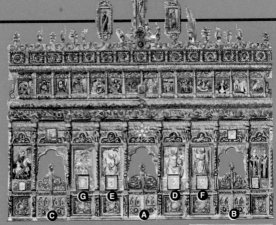

IN THE ORTHODOX CHURCH:

THE ALTAR IS CONCEALED FROM THE FAITHFUL. The choir is the representation of a tradition that considers the altar as the place of the offered sacrifice. It is a holy place, reserved for the clergy and concealed behind the iconostasis (a partition decorated with icons ▲ 268) separating the sanctuary and the nave. In its most elaborate form the iconostasis comprises five rows of panels and three doors. In front of the central door is the *solea* (platform) from which the Word of God is proclaimed and where the Faithful make their communion. A lectern stood on this spot.

A. Holy door, reserved for the officiant
B. South door or entrance to the sanctuary
C. North door or exit from the sanctuary
D. Icon of Christ, Wisdom of God
E. Icon of the church's patron saint
F. Icon of John the Baptist
G. Communion given to the Apostles

Icon of the mother of God, Gate of Heaven

ORTHODOX SANCTUARY

In the Orthodox Church the sanctuary, which is separated from the nave by the iconostasis, comprises:
1. The altar, sometimes beneath a canopy
2. The raised throne or bishop's seat
3. The priests' seat
4. The prothesis for the preparation of the offerings of the Divine Liturgy
5. The "diaconicon", where the ministers put on their robes.

ETHIOPIAN CROSS

The Greek-style, Ethiopian cross (below) is an important part of the Ethiopian liturgy. It is carried on a staff and has two openings through which a piece of precious cloth is threaded.

● CHURCHES IN THE HOLY LAND

Stained-glass window in the neo-Gothic cathedral (completed in 1872) of the Latin Patriarchate in Jerusalem.

The preaching of Christ's early disciples led to a rapid increase in the number of monasteries, holy places and hospices in the Holy Land during the Byzantine period, although many of these were abandoned during the Islamic invasion ● 52. Despite their short-lived presence, the Crusaders managed to build a number of sanctuaries, but the Christians did not build again in the Holy Land until the 19th century. The Christian communities were strongly attached to their national heritage and built churches in the style of their country. It is not uncommon to find several different styles of church on the same site.

BASILICA OF THE ANNUNCIATION
The conical dome, built immediately above the site of the Incarnation, looks like the inverted calyx of a lily ▲ 388.

ST GEORGE'S ANGLICAN CATHEDRAL
The bell tower (left), completed in 1911, is typical of the neo-Roman and neo-Gothic styles in England.

ITALIAN HOSPITAL
The "medieval Italian"-style hospital was built by the Italian community in Jerusalem during World War One. It is reminiscent of the Palazzio Vecchio in Florence and the public buildings of Siena.

ST ANNE'S CHURCH
The pure Romanesque style of the Church (attached in the 12th century to a convent of enclosed nuns ▲ 266) is reminiscent of Cistercian churches.

SEVEN ARCHES OF THE VIRGIN
The name of the double row of columns to the north of the Catholicon inside the Church of the Holy Sepulcher ▲ 272 refers to the northern colonnade of the Byzantine courtyard, which runs parallel to the supporting pillars of the transept.

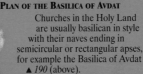

PLAN OF THE BASILICA OF AVDAT
Churches in the Holy Land are usually basilican in style with their naves ending in semicircular or rectangular apses, for example the Basilica of Avdat ▲ 190 (above).

The early Christians met in private houses. The House of St Peter in Capernaum ▲ 383 is an example of one of these early domus ecclesiae ("church houses").

CHURCH OF ST MARY MAGDALENE AT GETHSEMANE
The golden domes of the Church of St Mary Magdalene, which symbolize the Mount of Olives, were inspired by the domes of the Russian Church of the Holy Trinity ▲ 291. The basilica, built and consecrated in 1888 by Tsar Alexander III, is reminiscent of 16th- and 17th-century Muscovite religious architecture, the Ostankino Church in particular.

The mosque (*masjid* in Arabic) is the Muslim place of worship. Its style of architecture, which is remarkably homogeneous throughout the Muslim world, was inspired by Muhammad's house of exile in Medina. Today's hypostyle domes were originally a piece of cloth attached to the branches of a palm tree. Although mosques are the most elaborate expression of Muslim esthetics, above all they meet the religious requirements of Islam and represent the dedication of art to the rules of everyday living as decreed by the Prophet.

The prayer hall, the central area of the mosque, is wider than it is long in accordance with the tenet that during prayers the Faithful must form parallel rows facing Mecca. This vast hypostyle hall (supported by columns) opens – especially in the larger mosques – onto a courtyard which can also

"HARAM"
accommodate worshipers if necessary. The *qibli* wall (from *qibla* meaning "direction of Mecca") at the end of the haram

houses the most sacred, and therefore the most lavishly decorated, architectural elements in the mosque: the *minbar* and *mihrab*.

In the early stages of Islam, the haram was not used solely as a place of worship. Like the Greek agora and the Roman forum, it was a place to meet, debate or hold a court of law.

ARABIC CALLIGRAPHY Calligraphy was developed to celebrate Allah and the Qur'an as the final revelation. Its abstract and artistic qualities gave it an essentially decorative value.

"MINBAR"

The *minbar* (pulpit) from which the *imam* delivers the Friday sermon stands against the *qibli* wall. It is thought to have developed as a result of an incident that occurred in the Prophet's life: by 628 the crowds coming to listen to his sermons in the courtyard of his house in Medina had become so great that his companions built him a raised platform.

"MIHRAB"

The niche in the *qibli* wall, indicating the direction of Mecca, has a religious and decorative function. It was introduced in 706 during the reconstruction of the Prophet's house in Medina by the caliph Al-Walid I.

"MIHRAB" IN THE AL-JAZZAR MOSQUE

The mosque was built in Akko in 1781 by Jazzar Pasha. This typical example of developed Ottoman art is lavishly decorated with ceramics and marble inlaid with blue and brown.

ABLUTIONS FOUNTAIN

The Faithful have to perform ritual ablutions before entering the *haram.* There are always fountains and basins near the entrance to mosques. The fountain (above) of the Al-Jazzar Mosque in Akko ▲ *372.*

MINARETS ● *116*

The *adhan* (call to prayer) is issued by the *muezzin* from the top of the minaret, the tower at the corner of all Muslim religious buildings.

MOSQUE OF ABU GOSH

This partly Muslim village ▲ *328* has a modest mosque whose simplicity embodies the essence of Muslim architecture.

● Mosques in the Holy Land

The *muezzin* issues the call to prayer from the top of the minaret, a stone tower at the corner of the mosque. The tower consists of several sections: the (often square) base is surmounted by the stories, each distinguished by a particular architectural decoration in relief, or by the tower's general plan, whether cylindrical, square, octagonal or hexagonal. At the top is the *muezzin*'s gallery, supported by a simple or elaborately decorated cornice, and always surmounted by a lantern with the characteristic *alam*. The minaret is the key to the style and period in which the mosque was built.

MINARET OF BETHLEHEM
The minaret is crowned by a domed lantern with an *alam*, a metal ridge spike bearing the Muslim crescent (a decoration found on all mosques).

AL-QALA MINARET
The cylindrical minaret in the Citadel of David, built in 1532, is typically Ottoman in style ▲ *252*.

AL-GHADIRIYEH MINARET
The Mamluke style of the circular minaret, which stands on a square base, is particularly unusual.

MINARET (JAFFA)
The octagonal body of this 12th-century minaret is topped by a cylindrical upper section, a combination rare in Palestine.

MINARET (CAESAREA)
This 19th-century, cylindrical Ottoman tower stands on two massive, square sections ▲ *358*.

MINARET (HEBRON)
The minaret was added to the Tomb of the Patriarchs ▲ *221* by Salah al-Din. The typically Syrian, square tower reflects the pastiche of styles used by the Ottomans.

AL-OMARIYEH MINARET
This octagonal, Mamluke minaret has five stories, each marked by a characteristic band of pink and white stone and highlighted by small ogives ▲ *335*.

AL-JAZZAR MINARET
The Al-Jazzar Mosque, consecrated in 1781, has a distinctive minaret: its fine, pencil-like tower stands on a bulbous base ▲ *372*.

AL-GHAWANIMA MINARET
This Mamluke minaret, built – in the square, Syrian style – in 1298, stands at the northwestern end of the Haram al-Sharif ▲ *282*. The stories of the tower, surmounted by the muezzin's gallery, are decorated with *muqarna* (sculpted stone stalactites).

MINARET (JERICHO)
This modern, cylindrical minaret has five stories. The slender tower stands on a square base.

The limited resources of the period before the monarchy meant that princes were unable to undertake large-scale architectural projects. Compared with the public buildings, palaces and temples of Mesopotamia and Egypt, those in the Holy Land were modest, like the political institutions they represented. Fortifications were occasionally the only exception: the powerful ramparts of the 3rd millennium BC, strengthened in the 2nd by huge, earth glacis and enhanced with complex monumental gateways, constituted some of the most impressive defensive architecture in the ancient Near East. Superstructures were in mudbrick, while rough stone and quarry stone were used for the bases of walls and foundations.

RECTANGULAR HOUSES
Rectangular houses, inspired by the lightweight materials used for huts and tents, appeared in the chalcolithic period. They formed the nucleus of domestic communities consisting of several structures grouped within an enclosed space. The temple of Ein Gedi ▲ 210, the oldest religious building in the Holy Land, is an example of this type of domestic setup.

ROUND HOUSES
Round houses, often built partly below ground level, were the earliest form of shelter. They appeared during the epi-Paleolithic, the transitional period between the Paleolithic and Neolithic, during which hunter-gatherers became more sedentary. They were built up until the Late Byzantine period by the semi-nomadic herdsmen from the semi-desert regions of the Negev and Sinai. The roofs of the more elaborate round houses were made from large stone slabs.

ISRAELITE HOUSES
The most developed form of the pillared Israelite houses consisted of a transverse room preceded by three longitudinal areas (two rooms leading off a central courtyard and separated from it by stone pillars). The more elaborate houses had an upper story reserved for living quarters, while the first floor was used as a reception area, for carrying out domestic activities and for providing shelter for the livestock.

INCENSE ALTARS

Incense altars, usually a monolith decorated with horns, were widely used by the Israelites in both a religious and domestic context. It was an indispensable part of Israelite worship and an important feature of the desert tabernacle and the Temple of Jerusalem ▲ 260.

TEMPLE OF SOLOMON

Although nothing remains of Solomon's Temple of Jerusalem ● 46, archeological discoveries and the detailed description given in the Bible have enabled its reconstruction.

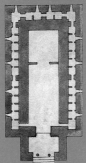

TEMPLE LAYOUT

The layout of the Temple – the vestibule (*ulam*), rectangular hall (*hechal*) and Holy of Holies (*devir*) lying along the same axis – is similar to that of Syro-Palestinian temples of the same period (Tel Atchana, in Syria, and Nablus ▲ 312).

FORTIFICATIONS

One of the most elaborate city gates is the (10th-century BC) gate of Megiddo ▲ 396, often attributed to Solomon. It was flanked by two towers and included four pairs of interior pillars that defined a series of four passages, each 13½ feet wide. In the 9th century an outer gate was added, linked to an angled ramp which was also fortified. As the seat of the assembly of the Elders, the city gates played an important part in everyday life.

● HERODIAN ARCHITECTURE

Herod the Great was made King of Judea by the Romans, who ruled Palestine in the 1st century BC. He adopted both Roman and Hellenistic cultures, imposing them on the population, and undertook an extensive program of construction characterized by vast scale and spectacular sites which gave rise to some remarkable technical achievements. By combining Roman innovations and aspects of eastern Hellenistic civilization with local traditions, Herod developed an unprecedented architectural style in which the structures blended with the landscape.

ROMAN DECORATIONS
Herod used two typically Augustan decorative techniques: the *opus reticulatum*, a diagonal stone decoration which gave the impression that the building was covered with a net, and the *opus quadratum*, where the stones were arranged in regular layers, like bricks (cement was not widely used in the East). These techniques tend to suggest that Roman architects were used to train the local work force.

QUARRYING THE STONE
The stone was cut in uniform, and often very large, blocks so that they presented a flattened boss on the façade decoration. The quarryman began the extraction process by tracing the outline of the blocks, of the shape and size required by the architect, on the rock face with his pick.

THE HERODION ▲ 229
The Herodion is a fine example of Herod's plan for his buildings to blend in with their surroundings. While the Romans flattened or filled in their sites before building, Herod respected the relief of the terrain and, when he built the vast Herodion, he gave it the appearance of one of the surrounding hills.

CAPITALS
Columns were surmounted by Corinthian capital carved with acanth and palm leaves.

WINTER PALACE IN THE JUDEAN DESERT
Water was supplied to the Herodian palaces of Jericho (built in three stages) by aqueducts. The most remarkable of the palaces was built on either side of the Wadi Qelt. In winter, the residents enjoyed the benefit of the water from the wadi which also filled the pools in the garden on the south bank.

CISTERNS AND WATER COLLECTION
Herod installed a system for collecting and storing rainwater from the wadis in the fortress of Masada, on top of a promontory in the Judean Desert. Two aqueducts, built into the northwest face of the fortress, channeled the water into twelve cisterns, with a capacity of 1,057,000 gallons.

Large reservoirs were built at the highest point of the fortress of Masada ▲ *202* to store water for everyday use as well as for the many baths in the thermae (public baths) and palaces.

In the upper part of each cistern were two openings: one linked to a flight of steps for drawing water and another, lower down, through which the water was channeled.

A GRANDIOSE SITE
Herod built the "North Palace" of Masada ▲ *205* on three natural terraces overlooking the Dead Sea. He ensured that his luxurious reception rooms, each of which was perched on a rocky outcrop, enjoyed a magnificent view of the surrounding countryside.

ROMAN ARCHITECTURE

Palestine was under Roman control from 63 BC until the Muslim capture of Jerusalem in 638. In 324 Constantine moved the capital from Rome to Constantinople, and Palestine was called "the Holy Land". The government of Rome played an active part in the founding of cities, the construction of public buildings and aqueducts, and the organization of a vast road network. These projects were facilitated by new construction techniques, notably the arch and vault, and the use of concrete.

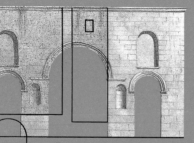

ROMAN ARCH
Although Roman arches were usually erected to celebrate events of historical or military importance, they were also used by Roman architects to conceal irregularities in the alignment of streets. One such example is the arch of *Ecce Homo* (above), part of which can still be seen on the Via Dolorosa.

ROMAN THEATERS
These doubled as places of entertainment and the venue for public meetings. They were built as a semicircular arena with several levels of tiered seating (*cavea*) (**1**) separated by a semicircular corridor (*praecincto*) (**2**), an enclosure reserved for important spectators, a raised stage (*pulpitum*) (**3**) and a stage front (*scaenae frons*) (**4**) representing a richly decorated façade with three doors flanked by tiered columns and niches.

The stage front of the Bet She'an theater, built at the end of the 2nd century AD, is similar to those of theaters built in the western Roman Empire.

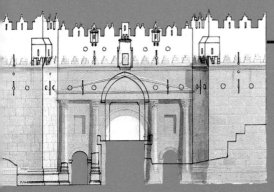

ROMAN CITIES
Roman cities were built according to a grid system of parallel and perpendicular streets. Two wider, main avenues – the *cardo* running north-south and the *decumanus* running east-west – were often bordered by colonnades and lined with shops. However this layout was not rigidly observed and was adapted to suit local conditions. In Jerusalem the ruins of the Temple of Herod forced Hadrian's architects to modify the standard layout by dividing the *cardo*.

CITY GATES
The Neapolis Gate, discovered beneath the Damascus Gate ▲ 244, marked the entrance to the city at the end of the *cardo* ▲ 255. Its triple-arched structure, the columns supporting the entablature and the niches above the lateral gates, are similar to the triple-arched Roman triumphal arches built during the 2nd and 3rd centuries.

MILESTONES
The Latin inscription named the emperor who commissioned the road and the date, while the Greek script gave the distance from the town to which the road led ▲ 326.

In the 4th century AD the victory of the Christian emperor
Constantine and the establishment of Christianity as a
legitimate religion within the Roman Empire marked the
beginning of the Byzantine period. Palestine, where Christ was
born and died, became a holy land and place of pilgrimage.
The population grew and towns and villages expanded.
Commemorative churches were built in the holy places, while
the conversion of a large section of the population led to the
building of many others in the towns and villages. The most
widely found were the basilica-type structures (in the form of
a tripartite rectangle) which were ideally suited to the new
religion. The circular, polygonal or cruciform churches were
based on a centralized layout and were less common. They
fulfilled an essentially commemorative role.

Remains dating from the
reign of Constantine revealed
a large octagon adjoining the
basilica and built above the
cave of the Nativity. The
floor was decorated with
a beautiful
mosaic.

"CARDO"
The
Byzantines
continued to use
the colonnaded
Roman streets in
many eastern
Mediterranean cities,
and even built new
colonnades along the
same lines. In
Jerusalem the Roman
cardo ● *123*, ▲ *255*
from the Neapolis
Gate ● *123* was
extended southward
to link the Nea
Church ▲ *255* and the
Church of the Holy
Sepulcher ▲ *272*.

BASILICAS
The rectangular
hall of basilica-
type churches is divided into a central
nave (**1**), usually surmounted by high wooden
beams, and two side-aisles (**2**) – lower, narrower,
lateral areas with flat ceilings – defined by colonnades (**3**).
The altar (**4**) stands at the eastern end of the church, the direction
of the rising sun, in the niche formed by the apse. The layout was
inspired by the Roman basilica, designed for legal and public
meetings, but the religious architecture was enhanced by such new
elements as the colonnaded courtyard (atrium) and the wide corridor
(narthex) (**5**) in front of the entrance to the main prayer hall.

This mosaic of 6th-century Jerusalem, on the floor of the Church of Madaba (Jordan), shows Roman architectural elements – the divided *cardo*, the Neapolis Gate, the arch of *Ecce Homo* – as well as many Byzantine churches and buildings.

MOSAICS
Religious elements are rarely found in the mosaic floors of churches, which are composed of floral, geometric and/or symbolic motifs. In 427 an imperial decree forbade the representation of religious images on floors to prevent them from being trampled underfoot.

SCULPTED DECORATIONS
Although partly obscured by later constructions, the Byzantine decoration on the Double Gate of the Herodian Temple ▲ 244 is still visible on the south wall of the esplanade facing the Ophel and above the Al-Aqsa Mosque.

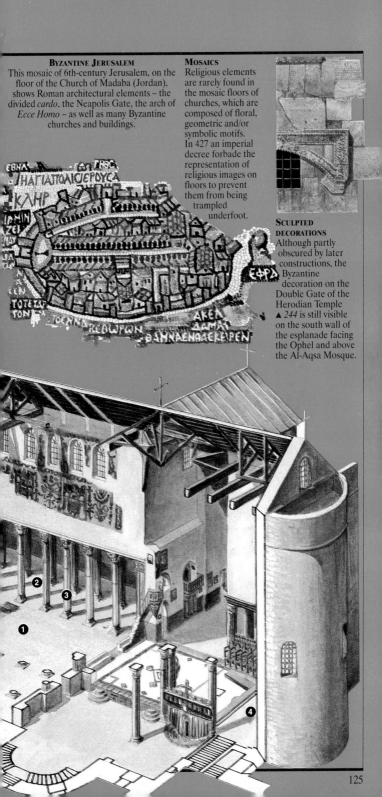

● ISLAMIC ARCHITECTURE

Less than twenty years after the Prophet's death, the Islamization of the religious and cultural melting pot that was the Holy Land was signaled by the great masterpieces of Muslim architecture. Umayyads, Mamlukes and later Persians and Ottomans all left their mark. From the early sanctuaries of emerging and eventually conquering Islam to the madrasas, mausolea, fountains and bath houses (the jewels in the crown of a triumphant culture), Islamic art developed its repertoire of styles and forms.

"ABLAQ"
Ablaq are a typical feature of Mamluke exterior decoration. They consist of red and yellow or, more rarely, black and white stones arranged in geometric designs.

"MUQARNA"
The niche above the entrance porch of the Al-Kilaniyya *turba* is a fine example of the "stalactite" decorations that reached their height with the Mamlukes.

"TURBA"
Mausolea (*turba* in Arabic) usually consist of a single chamber surmounted by a dome, for example the Al-Abughdi *turba* built in the Mamilla gardens in Jerusalem. The tomb is in a crypt beneath the *turba*.

AL-KILANIYYA "TURBA"
On the first floor of the *turba*, large windows fitted with heavy iron grilles open onto the street.

The mausoleum has several rooms, each surmounted by a dome. It is easily recognized in the Street of the Chain (Shari' al-Silsila) ▲ 255 by its porch and windows surmounted by projecting, carved stone decorations.

QAITBAY FOUNTAIN

The fountain, which is capped by a stone dome and sculpted with arabesques, is surrounded by a band of calligraphy telling the story of its construction. It also bears excerpts from the Qur'anic *sûrah* and is decorated with red and yellow *ablaq* and *muqarna*.

TURCO-MUSLIM DECORATION

In the 19th century the Jews flattered the Ottoman authorities by entrusting the design of the Ben Zakkai synagogue to Turkish architects who combined Turco-Muslim and Jewish influences.

OTTOMAN CALLIGRAPHY

This inscription glorifying Suleyman the Magnificent ▲ *244* is inscribed in the wall that the Ottoman sovereign had built around the old city between 1536 and 1541.

"SABIL"

In 1536 the emperor Suleyman the Magnificent built six public fountains or *sabil* to fulfill the dual function of ensuring a supply of drinking water for the local inhabitants and providing places for the Faithful to perform ritual ablutions on their way to the Haram al-Sharif. The most beautiful of these *sabil*, known as the Fountain of Sultan Suleyman, is located near the Gate of the Chain (Bab al-Silsila) on the route most frequented by Muslim pilgrims.

MAMLUKE WHEEL

The windows, façades and porticos of Mamluke buildings were decorated with these finely worked marble inlays. They may have been seals identifying the owner or person who commissioned the work.

MAMLUKE HOUSES

The windows overlooking the street were small and only found on the upper floors. This was because large interior courtyards let light and air into the house.

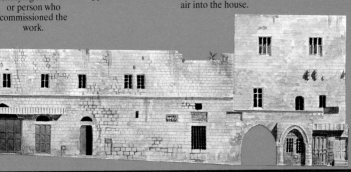

127

During their time in the Holy Land the Crusaders were indefatigable builders, constructing churches, monasteries, manors and fortresses, all in the space of a few years. Although little remains of the civil buildings, the many ruined fortresses provide examples of Crusader military architecture. The most beautiful remains are the religious buildings. The Basilica of the Holy Sepulcher, St Anne's Church and the Church of Abu Ghosh are fine examples of an expertise which combined western with local architectural techniques.

LOOPHOLE: FORTRESS OF BELVOIR

The loophole is remarkable for its black (basalt) and white (limestone) stone bonding. In the East loopholes were generally built below a niche and not in a simple embrasure. This technique did not become widespread in the West until the 13th century.

GLACIS
To counter the effects of earthquakes and artillery fire, the Crusaders developed the "sloping masonry" technique. The slope incorporated a vaulted gallery with loopholes that made it easier to change position and keep the moat under close surveillance.

St Mary of the Germans
The cross-section of the complex, built in 1128 by the German Knights of the Hospitallers Order, shows the church (center), the hospital (right) with the reception room on the upper floor, and the hospice (left) which is today part of the living quarters.

Church of St John the Baptist
The Church of St John the Baptist, undoubtedly the oldest church in Jerusalem and the seat of the Order of the Knights of the Hospital of St John, was renovated by the Crusaders who retained the original trefoil design (left). The trilobate façade and the vestibule were added later.

Angled colonnette
Capitals were supported by the short, straight – single or double (Abu Ghosh ▲ 328, above) – colonnettes that were characteristic of the eastern influence on western architecture.

Façade of the Holy Sepulcher
On two stories the double portal is echoed by a double window. The slightly pointed, surrounding arches are decorated with the gadrooned voussoirs that characterize Arab architecture.

Capitals
The single-leaf decoration on the capital above is typical of Romanesque architecture overseas.

Fortresses
The simple, rectangular layout of the Fortress of Belvoir, uncommon in the Holy Land, was not the result of Roman or Byzantine influence. It followed the relief of the terrain, a plateau overlooking the Jordan Valley ▲ 397, and consisted of two concentric outer walls, with angle towers and oblong salients, surrounding a central keep.

The majority of Palestinian villages were found in the mountains of central Palestine which were divided into twenty-one chieftaincies, each governed by a sheik. Each chieftaincy had several villages gathered around a central complex where the sheik resided and which reflected his power. As an assertion of this power and a symbol of their wealth, the sheiks (and the richest families in the village) added urban architectural elements to their rural dwellings. Villages were divided into districts, each inhabited by a particular tribe, opening onto the center of the village on one side, and onto the fields on the other.

TRADITIONAL PALESTINIAN HOUSES

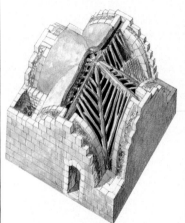

Traditional Palestinian houses were built on three levels. The first, *qa el-beit* (stable), housed the animals and agricultural implements. The second level, *el-mastabah* (dwelling), was where the family lived. It comprised a bedroom (during the day the mattresses were stored in a large niche or *qaws*), a living room, a kitchen and a dining room centered around a whitewashed hearth (*mawqaq*). A huge, earthen chest, used for storing food, separated the living area from the third level, *er-rawieh* (attic), where the harvest and clay were stored: produce was dried on the roof in the sun and then dropped into the attic through a hole. Typical Palestinian houses were topped by a groined vault (left) symbolizing the unity between the *fallah*, the earth and nature.

LAYOUT
The typically tripartite layout of Palestinian houses or *dar* (a word used to designate the family living area, a group of houses arranged around a central courtyard or even a tribal district) had many local variations. Some houses were "L" shaped, with the living area flanked by the stable and the attics.

"QASR"

The *qasr* or *mantarah* was the only structure permitted on agricultural land. It was made of irregularly shaped stones, carefully arranged to form a dry-stone, two-story building. The lower level was used as a storage area, while the upper level was covered with branches and served as a lookout post.

MAIN ENTRANCE OF PALESTINIAN HOUSES

The main entrance of a Palestinian house (its size, the richness of the stone decoration and the detail of the carved wooden leaves of the door) is an important decorative element, and a reflection of the social status of the owners. The richly decorated keystones on the door arches of the houses belonging to the sheik and the wealthy families of the village have recurrent floral, geometric and spiral motifs. The huge, finely carved wooden doors have a smaller opening (*khokhah*) for everyday use. Thus crossing the threshold of the main entrance, which marks the transition between public and private space, means bending down as a sign of respect.

"AREISHEH"

The *areisheh* was a small structure made of mudbrick and dried branches adjoining the stone (the basic material in mountain regions) house. It had an important social function as it enabled the family to gather together on summer days and evenings.

KIBBUTZIM AND "MOSHAVIM"

Kibbutzim and *moshavim* are two kinds of Israeli rural community. These model agricultural ventures represent a way of life which has led to the development of a particular type of architecture. Kibbutzim are based on the principle of collective production and consumption, the pooling of income and the equality of their members. *Moshavim* are an offshoot of the kibbutzim and are a form of cooperative in which families work their own land while sharing collective ownership of production methods and services.

KIBBUTZIM

Originally buildings occupied an enclosed, rectangular area with a single entrance (**1**). The central living area (**2**), comprising the refectory, common rooms, children's accommodation (**4**), dormitories (**4**) and common service areas (**5**), were arranged around a central courtyard (**3**). During the 1930's the previously centralized activity areas (**6**) and residential districts became separate.

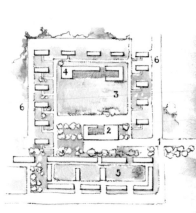

MATERIALS

Under the British mandate the early kibbutzim consisted of a group of flimsy wooden huts surrounded by a palisade and guarded by a watchtower. The structural elements (beams, wall and palisade sections, doors and windows) were made secretly in a neighboring kibbutz and assembled overnight: an Ottoman law still in force prohibited any structure albeit illegal from being destroyed.

"MOSHAVIM"

Moshavim do not have a standardized layout, but the areas of land allocated to families by the cooperative are usually of equal size and quality, and near where they live. In 1910 Nahalal (opposite), the first *moshav* founded in the Holy Land, was designed by Richard Kaufman according to a circular layout: the inner circle is made up of common services, while the second is formed by individual houses and the third by cultivated land.

WATCHTOWER
The watchtower is the first structure to be erected on a kibbutz so that a watch may be kept on the surrounding area. Watchtowers played a vital role when the first colonies were founded in isolated areas, and made kibbutzim strategically important during the early years of the newly created State of Israel ● 43.

The tent is perfectly adapted to the seasonal lifestyle of nomadic shepherds and its low, compact outline can still be seen in the deserts of the Holy Land today. Nomadic dwellings – tents made of woven black wool in winter, and solid huts for protection against sandstorms in summer – are ideally suited to the extremes and frequent changes of the desert climate. The tents are easy to erect and extremely light once dismantled and packed up. They constitute the main item of Bedouin wealth and symbolize the freedom of their nomadic lifestyle.

The Bible refers to these summer "tents" as *sukkot*. The Hebrews used them during the forty years of their Exodus. The festival of Sukkot ● *80* commemorates this episode in the Scriptures.

SUMMER TENTS
The high summer temperatures slow the pace of nomadic migration and the need for dwellings to be easy to dismantle is outweighed by the need for protection against sandstorms and heat. Bedouins erect semipermanent huts made of branches held together with mud and supported by upright poles.

WEAVING THE TENT
The dark-colored (heat-absorbent) cloth used for winter tents is woven by the women after the men have shorn the sheep. The wool is washed and spun by hand using a wooden spindle with a metal hook. It is then dyed using natural colorants such as indigo and decoctions made from tree roots and pomegranate skins. The women weave the cloth on a horizontal hand loom placed on the ground.

STRUCTURE AND LAYOUT
The wool and hair of the sheep and goats of Sinai tends to swell when wet and thus provides complete protection against the torrential winter rains. Tents are made from strips (over 33 feet long) of cloth, sewn together and supported by a ridge pole. The supporting uprights divide the tent into two equal sections: the men's area and the women's quarters. Carpets – the famous *kilims* made by Muslim nomads from the Caucasus to Sinai – and cushions ensure the comfort of the occupants.

The Holy Land as
seen by artists

The artists attracted by the Holy Land discovered a lyrical and exotic people whose traditions allowed them to test new esthetic theories. In 1893 the English artist Sir Frank Brangwyn (1867–1956) used the stalls of the *Orange Market in Jaffa* (**1**) to conduct research on the simplification of form and the optimal use of color in graphics.

"IN SHORT, THE POPULATION OF JERUSALEM IS ONE OF THE MOST COSMOPOLITAN, BUT IT IS A POPULATION DIVIDED: BY RELIGION, CUSTOMS, RACE."

CHARLES LALLEMAND

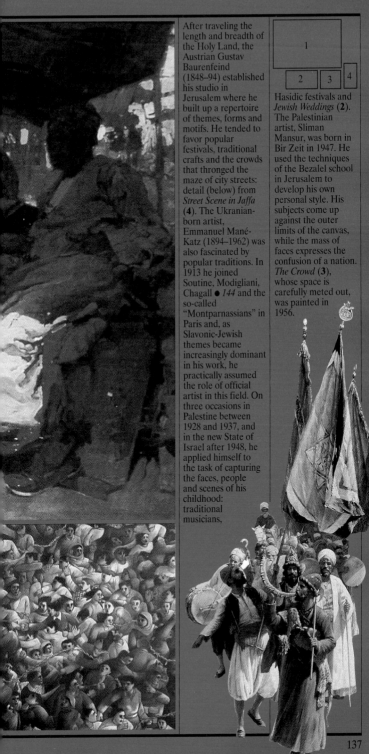

After traveling the length and breadth of the Holy Land, the Austrian Gustav Baurenfeind (1848–94) established his studio in Jerusalem where he built up a repertoire of themes, forms and motifs. He tended to favor popular festivals, traditional crafts and the crowds that thronged the maze of city streets: detail (below) from *Street Scene in Jaffa* (**4**). The Ukranian-born artist, Emmanuel Mané-Katz (1894–1962) was also fascinated by popular traditions. In 1913 he joined Soutine, Modigliani, Chagall ● *144* and the so-called "Montparnassians" in Paris and, as Slavonic-Jewish themes became increasingly dominant in his work, he practically assumed the role of official artist in this field. On three occasions in Palestine between 1928 and 1937, and in the new State of Israel after 1948, he applied himself to the task of capturing the faces, people and scenes of his childhood: traditional musicians,

Hasidic festivals and *Jewish Weddings* (**2**). The Palestinian artist, Sliman Mansur, was born in Bir Zeit in 1947. He used the techniques of the Bezalel school in Jerusalem to develop his own personal style. His subjects come up against the outer limits of the canvas, while the mass of faces expresses the confusion of a nation. *The Crowd* (**3**), whose space is carefully meted out, was painted in 1956.

Nachum Gutman (1898–1980) was the pupil of Abel Pann and Boris Shatz, who founded the Bezalel school in 1906. Along with Reuvin Rubin and Anna Ticho, he was one of the so-called "pioneer" artists who fled Nazism and settled in the Holy Land, introducing the new European trends associated with Expressionism, Dadaism and the Bauhaus ▲ 343. These influences produced several avant-garde groups, for example the "New Horizon" with Yossef Zaritsky ▲ 408, and the "synthetist" movement with Miron Sima, Moshe Castel, Mordechai Ardon ● 140 and Marcel Janco. Imbued with Jewish symbolism, Nachum Gutman drew upon his poetic expressionism to develop an artistic vocabulary to convey the Jewishness of place. For example, according to a *midrash* that inverts the apocalyptic Christian vision, his terrestrial Jerusalem was echoed by a celestial one, and watched over by various ritual objects: *menorah*, *shofar*, and so on.

Jerusalem is the incarnation of prophetic and Messianic dreams, the "center of the world" mentioned 656 times in the Old Testament and 140 times in the New Testament, and the "throne of Allah" in the Qur'an. Jerusalem in all its glory, whether idealized, symbolic or real, is a fertile ground for all imaginations and the subject of innumerable representations. The anonymous artist of a 15th-century manuscript (**1**) depicts it as a two-dimensional square, surrounded by walls and guarded by the twelve Apostles. Mantegna's (1431–1506) imaginary city in *Jesus in the Garden of Olives* (**3**) is grandiose and awesome, illuminated by flashes of apocalyptic light. For Mordechai Ardon (1896–1992), Jerusalem initially symbolized the enchantment of the East until he entered its gates and saw the symbols, letters and *sefirots* that form the mystery of the inexpressible (**2**).

"AND I SAW A NEW HEAVEN AND A NEW EARTH: FOR THE FIRST HEAVEN AND THE FIRST EARTH WERE PASSED AWAY; AND THERE WAS NO MORE SEA. AND I JOHN SAW THE HOLY CITY, NEW JERUSALEM, COMING DOWN FROM GOD OUT OF HEAVEN."   REVELATION 21

Many western artists (Gustav Baurenfeind, Bresdin, Dadd, Dauzats, Gleyre, Hunt, David Roberts, Loubon, Tissot, Wilkie) have frequented the paths which, punctuated by prayers, recitatives and chants, led to the sites of the Passion – of all passions – and set up their easels before the monuments and stones that, in this land, provide a framework for prayer. Jean-Léon Gérôme (1842–1904) (**4**) was fascinated by the Jews who addressed their prophetic dreams to the *Western Wall* (**1**). On one of his visits to Jerusalem Carl Haag (1820–1915) painted *The Sacred Rock* (**2**) in the Dome of the Rock, the Muslim monument erected as the first geographical center of prayer. The *Basilica of the Nativity in Bethlehem* (**3**), by the Italian artist Hermann Corrodi (1844–1905), is characterized by the same religious fervor.

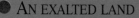

Faces, people and animals fill the world of Marc Chagall (1887–1985) with visual and poetic metaphors. His esthetic vocabulary, initially influenced by Expressionism and Cubism and later by a form of lyrical surrealism, combines familiar scenes and childhood memories. The Jewish people and their history are the leitmotif of a prolific artistic production in which the laws of gravity have been abolished and the traditional concept of perspective ignored. In the world of Chagall there is no place for classical dogma. He brings the Bible, history and current events together with a joyous disregard for the unities of place, time and action, creating areas of intense color in which a kaleidoscope of figures revolves around the central theme: here *King David*.

PILGRIMS AND HOLY PLACES

CALVARY, AD 724

At the age of twenty-two, an English monk, St Willibald (700?–786), went on a ten-year pilgrimage to Rome and the Holy Land. During his travels he visited "The Place of Calvary".

❝From there he came on to Jerusalem, to the place where the Lord's Holy Cross was found. That place is called 'The Place of Calvary' and there is now a church there: in earlier times it was outside Jerusalem, but Helena put the place inside Jerusalem when she found the Cross. Now there are three wooden crosses standing there outside the church, on the east of it near the wall, to commemorate the Holy Cross of the Lord, and those of the others who were crucified with him. Nowadays they are not indoors, inside the church, but stand out of doors under a roof outside the church. And near there is the garden in which was the Saviour's tomb. The tomb had been carved out of rock, and the rock stands up out of the ground: at the bottom it is square, but it is pointed on top. The tomb is now surmounted by a cross, and there is now a remarkable building over it. On the east of the tomb, in the actual rock, a door has been made, through which people enter the tomb for prayers. And inside there is a shelf on which the Lord's body lay. Fifteen golden bowls stand on the shelf. They are filled with oil, and burn day and night. The shelf on which the Lord's body lay is inside the tomb on the north side, that is, on the right side as one enters the tomb to pray. And there also, in front of the tomb door, is a large square stone, like the original stone which the angel rolled away from the tomb door.**❞**

IN *JERUSALEM PILGRIMS BEFORE THE CRUSADES*
TRANS. JOHN WILKINSON, PUB. AVIS & PHILIPS LTD.
QUOTED IN ERIC NEWBY, *A BOOK OF TRAVELLERS' TALES*
PUB. COLLINS, LONDON, 1985

A SPRING NEAR CANA

Edward Daniel Clarke (1769–1848) visited the holy sites during his extensive travels. Here he describes a peaceful pause at Cana.

❝It is difficult to ascertain [Cana's] exact distance from Nazareth. Our horses were never out of a foot's pace, and we arrived there at half past seven. About a quarter of a mile before we entered the village, is a spring of delicious limpid water, close to the road, whence all the water is taken for the supply of the village. Pilgrims of course halt at this spring, as the source of the water which our Saviour, by his first miracle, converted into wine. At such places it is usual to meet, either shepherds reposing with their flocks, or caravans halting to drink. A few olive-trees being near to the spot, travellers alight, spread their carpets beneath these trees, and, having filled their pipes, generally smoke tobacco and take some coffee; always preferring repose in these places, to the accommodations which are offered in the villages. Such has been the custom of the country from time immemorial.
We entered Cana, and halted at a small *Greek* chapel, in the court of which we all rested, while our breakfast was spread upon the ground. This grateful meal consisted of about a bushel of cucumbers; some white mulberries, a very insipid fruit, gathered from the trees reared to feed silk-worms; hot cakes of unleavened bread, fried in honey and butter; and, as usual, plenty of fowls.**❞**

EDWARD DANIEL CLARKE,
*TRAVELS IN VARIOUS COUNTRIES
OF EUROPE, ASIA AND AFRICA,*
PUB. T. CADELL AND W. DAVIES, 1817

> "THOSE WHO GAZE ON THE DOME OF THE ROCK,
> COVERED FOR THE MOST PART IN GOLD, ARE DAZZLED BY ITS
> BRILLIANCE, NOW GLOWING LIKE A MASS OF LIGHT,
> NOW FLASHING LIKE LIGHTNING." IBN BATTUTA

A SICKENING CHEAT

The well-traveled American writer Herman Melville (1819–91) kept a journal during his visit to the Holy Land. In idiosyncratic fashion, he describes his disappointing experience of the Holy Sepulcher.

❝ /The Holy Sepulchre /No Jew allowed in Church of H.S./ – ruined dome – confused & half-ruinous pile. – Laberithys {Labyrinths} & terraces of mouldy grottos, tombs, & shrines. Smells like a dead-house. dingy light. – At the entrance, in a sort of grotto in the wall a divan for Turkish policemen, where they sit crosslegged & smoking, scornfully observing the continuous troops of pilgrims entering & prostrating themselves before the anointing-stone of Christ, which veined with streaks of a mouldy red looks like a butcher's slab. Near by is a blind stair of worn marble ascending to the reputed Calvary where among other things the showman point show you by the smoky light of old pawnbrokers lamp of dirty gold, the hole in which the cross was fixed & & through a narrow grating as over a cole-cellar, point out the rent in the rock! On the same level, near by is a kind of gallery, railed with marble, overlooking the entrance of the church; and here almost every day I would hang, looking down upon the specatle [spectacle] of the scornful Turks on the divan, & the scorned pilgrims kissing the stone of the anointing. – The door of the church is like that of a jail – a grated window in it. – The main body of the church is that overhung by the lofty & ruinous dome whose fallen plastering reveals the meagre skeleton of beams & laths a sort of plague-stricken splendor reigns in the painted & mildewed walls around. In the midst of all, stands the Sepulchre; a church in a church. It is of marbles, richly sculpted in parts & bearing the faded aspect of age. From its porch, issue a garish stream of light, upon the faces of the pilgrims who crowd for admittance into a space which will hold but four or five at a time. First passing a wee vestibule where is shown the stone on which the angel sat, you enter the tomb. It is like entering a lighted lanthorn. Wedged & half-dazzled, you stare for a moment on the ineloquence of the bedizened slab, and glad to come out, wipe your brow glad to excape as from the heat & jam of a show-box.

All is glitter & nothing is gold. A sickening cheat. The countenances of the poorest & most ignorant pilgrims would seem tacitly to confess it as well as your own.**99**
HERMAN MELVILLE,
JOURNAL OF A VISIT TO EUROPE AND THE LEVANT,
PUB. PRINCETON UNIVERSITY PRESS, PRINCETON, 1955

GUARDIANS OF THE HOLY SEPULCHER
French novelist Gustave Flaubert (1821–80) reveals a similar disgust at the way the Holy Sepulcher is looked after.

66The Holy Sepulchre is the agglomeration of all possible execrations. Within this tiny space, four churches: Armenian, Greek, Latin, and Coptic. All heartily insulting and cursing one another, each quarrelling with its neighbors over candlesticks, rugs, pictures – and what pictures! It's the Turkish Pasha who keeps the keys to the Holy Sepulchre. When you want to visit it, you must get them from him. I find that quite striking. On the other hand, it's the most humane solution. If the Holy Sepulchre were given over to the Christians, they would unfailingly massacre each other. Such cases have been known.**99**
GUSTAVE FLAUBERT,
THE LETTERS OF GUSTAVE FLAUBERT 1830–57,
SELECTED, ED. AND TRANS. BY FRANCIS STEEGMULLER,
PUB. HARVARD UNIVERSITY PRESS, BOSTON, 1979

MIRACLE WINE JARS
English novelist, biographer and travel writer Evelyn Waugh (1903–66) displays a similarly cynical attitude to Cana and other holy sites.

66We went to Cana of Galilee, where a little girl was offering wine jars for sale. They were the authentic ones used in the miracle. If they were too big she had a smaller size indoors; yes, the small ones were authentic, too. Then we drove on to Tiberias, a small fishing village of cubic houses on the Sea of Galilee. There were the ruins of some kind of fort and a white domed public bath of steaming mineral water. We were led into this bath. In the courtyard a kind of picnic was going on; an Arab family sitting on the ground and eating bread and raisins. It was almost dark in the bath; the naked bathers lay about in the steam undisturbed by our intrusion. We lunched at Nazareth in an hotel managed by Germans, and ate omelettes, rissoles, and pork, and drank an uncommendable wine called Jaffa Gold. During luncheon the rain stopped. We went to visit the holy places. Mary's Well, in the central square of the town, is the most likely of these to be genuine. It is a communal fountain of obvious antiquity and traditional design; the present fabric may not date from the beginning of the Christian era, but there is a strong probability that a well of similar design has always occupied the same spot. The villagers coming to draw water must bear a strong resemblance to those of two thousand years ago, except that, instead of the earthenware ewers depicted by Mr. Harold Copping, they now carry petrol tins on their heads. The Church of Annunciation is of modern construction and meagre design, but it is approached through a pretty courtyard containing fragments of early erections. We were shown the site of the Annunciation and Joseph's Workshop; both these were caves. A cheerful Irish monk with a red beard opened the gates for us. He was as sceptical as ourselves about the troglodytic inclinations of the Holy Family.**99**
EVELYN WAUGH, *LABELS – A MEDITERRANEAN JOURNEY*,
PUB. DUCKWORTH, LONDON, 1930

NATURE

A MONITOR IN THE DESERT

Fifteenth-century traveler Bertrandon de la Brocquière (fl. 1432) describes a surprising encounter in Gaza with a monitor lizard.

❝We thus travelled two days in the desert, absolutely without seeing any thing deserving to be related. Only one morning I saw, before sunrise, an animal running on four legs, about three feet long, but scarcely a palm in height. The Arabians fled at the sight of it, and the animal hastened to hide itself in a bush hard by. Sir Andrew and Pierre de Vaudrei dismounted, and pursued it sword in hand, when it began to cry like a cat on the approach of a dog. Pierre de Vaudrei struck it on the back with the point of his sword, but did it no harm, from its being covered with scales like a sturgeon. It sprung at Sir Andrew, who, with a blow from his sword, cut the neck partly through, and flung it on its back, with its feet in the air, and killed it. The head resembled that of a large hare; the feet were like the hands of a young child, with a pretty long tail, like that of the large green lizard. Our Arabs and interpreter told us it was very dangerous.❞

FROM *EARLY TRAVELS IN PALESTINE*, ED. THOMAS WRIGHT, PUB. HENRY G. BOHN, LONDON, 1848

THE TROUBLE WITH CAMELS

Artist, traveler, and writer, Edward Lear (1812–63) gives us a humorous picture of the camel – the desert's most reliable beast of burden – and the natural history of the Moab Mountains during a journey to Petra.

❝We are all moving long before daybreak. Myriads of gay little grasshoppers jump up and spray from the grass at each footfall as I walk. The camels appear good, a matter of great import for such a journey. Mine is a very handsome and young one, and behaves himself tranquilly. Giorgio's looks as if he had been boiled or shaved, but is spare and active. Then there is a huge white Hubblebubble who is evidently a *piece de résistance* for all the goods the others decline to carry; one for Abdel, one for the Sheikh Salah, the chief guide (who is called the brother of Abou Daôuk), and one more for luggage, complete the tale of six. But this last individual turns out to be a violent party, and refuses to be loaded, particularly opposing all attempts to make him carry the cage of poultry, as an uncamel-like and undignified burden. Altogether the din of snarling, growling, screaming, and guggling was considerable; and the lean Jehaleen attendants, of whom there are fifteen, seem a very filthy and incapable lot by way of escort. But it is useless to complain; the Petra journey is to be made now, so be it made as best it may.

At length we started. A walk over the South Downs from Lewes to Brighton would give a fairly correct idea of the general forms of the rolling hill scenery intersected with smooth dales, through which we passed; but here there is much more rock and much less verdure, though certain portions of the land are pretty profusely tufted with herbs. I always hate camel-riding, and walked on for more than an hour, finding a constant pleasure in the exquisite carpets of lilac hepatica and pale asphodel spread over the most level ground, and the knots of sage, broom, and other shrubs which vary the hill-sides.

The pleasant progress of the morning was frequently delayed by the wicked camel utterly refusing to go on; for whenever one of the cocks in the cage, from a cheerful sympathy with nature in general, or a wish to make an audible comment on his own particular elevation, gave way to crowing – that moment the huge beast abandoned himself to extreme spasms of terror, shaking, screaming, and kicking till all the *roba*, including the guilty fowls, was on the ground. A long cord, passed through the handles of boxes and round baskets, prevented the complete separation of the baggage, and the vexed Ship of the Desert could not disengage himself from his miseries, but dashed hither and thither with a long chain of goods; a curious performance to see, but not altogether conducive to the safety of the articles in motion. After this had occurred three times, the awkward Jehaleen wasting much time in the reloading, the cheerful fowls were transferred to the huge Hubblebubble, whose gravity all the crowing in the world hardly seems likely to move. **99**

FROM *EDWARD LEAR'S JOURNALS, A SELECTION*,
ED. HERBERT VAN THAL, PUB. ARTHUR BAKER LTD., LONDON, 1952

A WALK TO AIN TULMA

British archeologist and travel writer Gertrude Bell (1868–1926) traveled widely in the Middle East. Here she describes a pleasant walk with a friend after a period of heavy rain.

66Charlotte and I put on short skirts and thick boots and went for a long walk to a lovely spring she knew of. We walked down a deep valley which as long as we have known it has been as dry as a bone and where to our surprise we found a deep swift stream. Ain Tulma, our

"TWO SHADOWS . . . STARED DOWN AT THE CITY'S NIGHT. IN THE CORNER A SUITCASE OF CLOTHES, SOUVENIRS FROM THE HOLY LAND – HIS BLUE EYES STRETCHED LIKE SAD LAKES. HE LOVED JERUSALEM; SHE WAS HIS MYSTICAL LOVER."

FADWA TUQAN

object, was on the other side and as there are no bridges in this country (there being no rivers as a rule) there was nothing for it but to take off our shoes and stockings and wade. The water came above our knees. The other side was too lovely – the banks of the river were carpeted with red anemones, a sheet of them, and to walk by the side of a rushing stream is an unrivalled experience in this country. When we got to Ain Tulma we found the whole place covered with cyclamen and orchis and a white sort of garlic, very pretty, and the rocks out of which the water comes were draped in maidenhair. There were a lot of small boys, most amiable young gentlemen, who helped us to pick cyclamen, and when I explained that I had no money they said it was a bakshish to me – the flowers. We had a very scrambly walk back, waded the stream again and when we got to a little village at the foot of the hill, we hired some small boys to carry our flowers home for us.

GERTRUDE BELL,
THE LETTERS OF GERTRUDE BELL,
PUB. PENGUIN TRAVEL LIBRARY, LONDON, 1987

SCENTS OF CHILDHOOD

In his novel "Past Continuous", Israeli novelist Yaakov Shabtai (1934–81) gives a nostalgic account, tinged with regret, of a garden of the Holy Land.

Goldman . . . succeeded in transferring his sadness to Israel, together with a sense of the hopelessness and pointlessness of everything, as well as his great weariness, and the persistent, monotonous chirping of the crickets, which sounded as if it would go on forever, went on rising from the empty courtyard, together with the summer scents so familiar to Israel from the days of his childhood which he had spent in this same courtyard, on the lawn and under the tall-topped poinsettia regia and the Persian lilac and the jacaranda trees and in the secret recesses of the giant, evergreen ficus, and the shade of the dense fir trees, in games of hide-and-seek and catch, and ball games, and all kinds of entertaining and impudent exploits and mischief, and in the soft, dewy summer nights he had been initiated here into the pleasurable secrets of sex by means of stories and rude jokes and rumors and the mutual masturbation in which the boys would sometimes secretly indulge and which gave rise to excitement and unendurable pleasure mixed with fear and feelings of guilt, and the calm voices of people and the sound of music would come floating down from the windows and balconies, and black bats would emerge from the darkness in sudden, aimless flights, diving like stones and rising again, and they all kept on warning each other to be careful not to let the bats get into their hair, because if they did they would never let go, and Israel felt himself growing old as he sat in this room, and again he stole an involuntary glance at Goldman and said nothing.

YAAKOV SHABTAI, *PAST CONTINUOUS,*
TRANS. DALYA BILU.
PUB. THE JEWISH PUBLICATION
SOCIETY OF AMERICA,
PHILADELPHIA, 1985

THE HOLY CITY

THE CONQUERED CITY OF THE CROSS

British traveler Robert Curzon (1810–73) has left us a vivid picture of Jerusalem in the 19th century.

66Jerusalem has been described as a deserted and melancholy ruin, filling the mind with images of desolation and decay, but it did not strike me as such. It is still a compact city, as it is described in Scripture; the Saracenic walls have a stately, magnificent appearance; they are built of large and massive stones. The square towers, which are seen at intervals, are handsome and in good repair; and there is an imposing dignity in the appearance of the grim old citadel, which rises in the centre of the line of walls and towers, with its batteries and terraces one above another, surmounted with the crimson flag of Turkey floating heavily over the conquered city of the cross.99

ROBERT CURZON,
VISIT TO THE MONASTERIES OF THE LEVANT,
PUB. JOHN MURRAY, LONDON, 1849

THE KNOBBIEST TOWN IN THE WORLD

Mark Twain (1835–1910) visited Palestine in 1867. Here, in his own inimicable way, he gives a fascinating sketch of the Holy City.

66A fast walker could go outside the walls of Jerusalem and walk entirely around the city in an hour. I do not know how else to make one understand how small it is. The appearance of the city is peculiar. It is as knobby with countless little domes as a prison door is with bolt-heads. Every house has from one to half a dozen of these white plastered domes of stone, broad and low, sitting in the centre of, or in a cluster upon, the flat roof. Wherefore, when one looks down from an eminence, upon the compact mass of houses (so closely crowded together, in fact, that there is no appearance of streets at all, and so the city looks solid,) he sees the knobbiest town in the world, except Constantinople. It looks as if it might be roofed, from centre to circumference, with inverted saucers. The monotony of the view is interrupted only by the great Mosque of Omar, the Tower of Hippicus, and one or two other buildings that rise into commanding prominence.

The houses are generally two stories high, built strongly of masonry, whitewashed or plastered outside, and have a cage of wooden lattice-work projecting in front of

"THE LORD DOTH BUILD UP JERUSALEM:
HE GATHERETH TOGETHER THE OUTCASTS OF ISRAEL."

PSALMS 147

every window. To reproduce a Jerusalem street, it would only be necessary to up-end a chicken-coop and hang it before each window in an alley of American houses.

The streets are roughly and badly paved with stone, and are tolerably crooked – enough so to make each street appear to close together constantly and come to an end about a hundred yards ahead of a pilgrim as long as he chooses to walk in it. Projecting from the top of the lower story of many of the houses is a very narrow porch-roof or shed, without supports from below; and I have several times seen cats jump across the street from one shed to the other when they were out calling. The cats could have jumped double the distance without extraordinary exertion. I mention these things to give an idea of how narrow the streets are. Since a cat can jump across them without the least inconvenience, it is hardly necessary to state that such streets are too narrow for carriages. These vehicles can not navigate the Holy City."

MARK TWAIN, *THE INNOCENTS ABROAD* OR *THE NEW PILGRIMS' PROGRESS,*
PUB. AMERICAN PUBLISHING COMPANY, HARTFORD, 1875

AN ASTONISHING PLACE

Eric Gill (1882–1940), British sculptor, engraver, writer and typographer, describes the Holy City through the eyes of an artist.

"It is an astonishing place. Words fail me. I can't begin to describe it. There is a mad balance (preserved by Brit. Govt.) between ancient & utter loveliness & mod. bestial commercial enterprise – in fact they cancel out. There is also a mad confusion of religions, all worshipping & scrapping at same shrines. . . . Jerusalem is a city of stone & as there are no streets wide enough for wheeled traffic (except a few hundred yards by the Jaffa gate & the Bab Siti Miriam) there is no noise save that of human voices & footsteps &, inside the walls, there is a complete absence (except in the cheap factory stuff & tinned foods which they sell in their little shops – or in some of them) of our filthy western life & none of its filthy apparatus. And, in the midst, the Holy Sepulchre (which, whatever one may say about the silly squabbles of the rival caretakers, Catholic, Greek & Copt etc., is a palpably holy place) and, occupying all one corner, the Haram el Sheraf (called by us 'the Temple Area'), than which nothing, nothing, nothing could be lovelier, holier, more dignified, more humane or more grand. Thank God I got a permit from the Grand Mufti to go in and out every day ('cept Fridays, when it is reserved for Moslems exclusively & jealously). I did a few drawings sitting on the roof of a house in the via Dolorosa. Which, whatever the valuelessness of the drawings, was a fine way of staying put & thus really soaking up the scene."

ERIC GILL,
THE LETTERS OF ERIC GILL,
ED. WALTER SHEWRING,
PUB. JONATHAN CAPE,
LONDON, 1947

A WALK THROUGH THE OLD CITY
Canadian-born American novelist and Nobel Prize-winner Saul Bellow (b. 1915) published a personal account of his visit to the Holy City. In this description of his search for a Hamam, he captures the atmosphere of the old city and the characteristics of its inhabitants.

❝Kahn insists on showing me some ancient baths at the lower end of the Old City and we ask our way through endless lanes, where kids ride donkeys, kick rubber balls, scream, fall from wagons, and build small fires in buckets to warm their fingers, for the weather is cold. A freezing east wind blows above the arches of the covered streets. The ancient stone is very cold. The sun does not often get into these streets. A gang of black Sudanese boys shout frantic advice at a driver backing his truck into a narrow lane, scraping the Arabic inscription of a plugged fountain, the gift of some eleventh-century sultan, I imagine. Kahn asks again for his Turkish baths. A candy seller, cutting up one of his large flat sticky cakes, a kind of honeyed millstone, appears indignant. His business is to sell cakes, not to give directions. We get into an arcade where a money changer in a turtleneck tells us to retrace our steps and turn left. He offers to pay me two pounds on the dollar over the official rate. I take the trouble to tell him how virtuous I feel about this sort of thing, and he cannot conceal his opinion, which is that I am very stupid. True. If I were *thinking*, I wouldn't say such things to a man whose trade is money. But there you are – the fellow with the dollars is frequently foolish. . . . We make our way out of the arcade and inquire of a stout, unshaven storekeeper in Arab headdress and busted shoes who deals in chipped green glassware. He lights up at our question. Yes, of course, *he* knows. Engaging us in conversation, he offers us coffee. Next he submits to our admiring inspection a crumpled snapshot in color of his son who is studying medicine in Chicago. I tell him that I am from Chicago. He is enchanted. The photograph, smudged by loving thumbprints, passes from hand to hand. So now we are bound together in friendship. The small dead end where we stand has the customary fallout of orange peel and excrement, eggshells and bottle tops.

Almost embracing us with his guiding arms, the shopkeeper escorts us to the Hamam. And here is the place itself at the corner, down a salmon-colored plaster passage that bulges asymmetrically. If this is Ladies' Day, we will have to turn back. Respectful of ladies' modesty, our friend opens the door cautiously and holds up a hand in warning. He inquires, shouting into hollow spaces, and then waves us forward. We enter a vast, domed, circular room that is perhaps a thousand years old – one thousand four hundred, our guide insists. For reasons of self-respect I am obliged to cut him down by a few centuries. But who can care for long about the dates. The little idiocy of skeptical revision passes off. I find myself to my joy in an ancient, beautiful, hot, sour-smelling chamber. Divans made up with clouts and old sheets are ranged against the walls for the relaxing clients. Tattered towels hang drying on lines overhead. These lines crisscross up, up, up into dim galleries. An Arab woman, very old, is resting on a divan. One of her short legs is extended. She

"JERUSALEM THE GOLDEN
WITH MILK AND HONEY BLESSED
BENEATH THY CONTEMPLATION,
SINK HEART AND VOICE OPPRESSED."

THE RHYTHM OF BERNARD
DE MORLAIX, 12TH CENTURY

makes a gesture of Oriental courtesy. In this towel-bannered chamber people rest from the fatigues of bathing. We go through several steaming rooms, now empty. Our Arab friend says, 'You spend a whole night here, you will be a very different man.' I can well believe it. An attendant is scrubbing the floors with a stiff brush. He must be the husband of the ancient odalisque. He is stout, low, bandy-legged, and round-backed. He is so bent that if his deep-brown eyes, the eyes of a walrus, are to meet yours he must look upward. The white stubble and his color – the high color of a man of heat and vapor – are agreeable. 'This is not the place I had in mind. The one I wanted to show you is much older,' says Kahn. But I rejoice greatly in this one and ask for nothing better. **99**

SAUL BELLOW, *TO JERUSALEM AND BACK*,
PUB. SECKER & WARBURG, LONDON, 1976

THE WAILING WALL

*American author and journalist John Gunther (1901–80) describes one of Jerusalem's
most famous landmarks.*

66 Jerusalem does, however, give out a decided Oriental flavor even in its western quarters. Ben Yehuda Street and Jaffa Road, two of the main thoroughfares, look more like streets in Baghdad than in New York. There are stalls selling *gazoz*, a raspberry-flavored carbonated water, and open sheds displaying trays of *felafel*, a kind of vegetarian meatball made of chick-peas and peppers. Arabs wearing the kaffiyeh, or white headdress bound with black rope, are to be encountered frequently, and at regular intervals five times a day the muezzin, or call for prayer toward Mecca, may be heard from a nearby mosque. . . . The foremost of the ancient sights is, to my mind, the Mount of Olives, and after this the Wailing Wall. A large Jewish cemetery, the most sacrosanct in Zion, covered part of the Mount of Olives; the Arabs destroyed this, and used the tombstones for paving blocks on the roads nearby. This the Jews will never forgive, if only because this is the place where they believe that the resurrection will occur. The Wailing Wall is larger, heavier, more massive than I had remembered, but short in length. Built as part of the wall surrounding the Temple area within the Old City, it is this relic, more than anything else, that tells Jews that they are veritably living in the City of God. No site in the world, the Jews say, has absorbed so much agony; no monument has ever given a people such collective strength. 'Millions of Arabs surround us, but we have no fear,' is a watchword enhanced by the Wall. The square stones near the top are smaller than those below; they were put there by Sir Moses Montefiore, the nineteenth-century Anglo-Jewish philanthropist, to keep the edge from crumbling. Filaments of barbed wire, a surviving element of the British occupation, keep Arab ragamuffins from tossing rocks down on the Jews praying below. More than a hundred thousand Jews, half the population of the city, visited the Wall in one day on the first anniversary of victory in the June war. We watched some worshipers, while gangs of children played about, and saw that letters, messages, supplications, had been stuffed into interstices in the blocks of stone, next to projecting tufts of green moss or grass. **99**

JOHN GUNTHER, *TWELVE CITIES*, PUB. HAMISH HAMILTON, LONDON, 1969

CROWDED STREETS

Scottish novelist Muriel Spark (b. 1918) captures the hustle and bustle of the Old City in her novel "The Mandelbaum Gate".

66 To arrive here, a mile from the outskirts of Jerusalem on the Jordan side, Freddy had jostled his way from the guardhouse at the Mandelbaum Gate, through the Old City's network of alleys, past the Damascus Gate. It had been too hot to take a crowded bus, and not for one moment was he tempted by a taxi. Sometimes Joanna could manage to meet him with her car, but Freddy was just as well pleased when she couldn't. Past the Damascus Gate, towards the Holy Sepulchre and down to the Via Dolorosa, plodded Freddy, dodging the loaded donkeys and stick-wielding boys who in turn were constantly dodging the vast wide motor-cars that hooted with rage and frustration down the lanes; these cars were filled with hooded Arabs of substance and their emancipated wives. Freddy and numerous tourists had to flatten themselves hastily against a wall or a tangy-breathed donkey whenever the fanfare of a motor horn heralded one of these feudal-minded carloads. At the Via Dolorosa he ran into the huge Friday pilgrimage headed by the praying Franciscans, who moved from station to station, on the route from the Pillar of the Flagellation to Calvary. Freddy, with a large number of the English Colony, had followed a much larger procession than this, last Easter, along the Way of the Cross; he had found it religiously moving, but it had exhausted his capacity for any further experience of the sort. 99

MURIEL SPARK, *THE MANDELBAUM GATE*
PUB. THE REPRINT SOCIETY, LONDON, 196●

THE DOME OF THE ROCK

British travel writer Eric Newby (b. 1919) captures the majesty and gives an account of the history of Jerusalem's foremost Muslim site, the Dome of the Rock.

66 Dominating everything from up here, rising into the air from its platform opposite the Mount of Olives like some exotic space vehicle waiting to take off, is the Qubbat es-Sakhra, the Dome of the Rock, the masterpiece of the Umayyad

שמש אור החיים

Caliph Abd el-Malik, one of a dynasty which ruled from its capital, Damascus, from AD 661–750. He built it in about 691, at a cost of what was said to be the equivalent of seven years' revenue from Egypt, in order to attract Umayyad pilgrims who could not make the pilgrimage to Mecca because at that time they were being refused admission to the Kaaba (the most sacred Muslim pilgrim shrine into which is built the black stone believed to have been given by the Archangel Gabriel to Abraham, in the direction of which muslims turn when they are praying). He also built it in order to outdo the dome of the Emperor Constantine's original church, which had been raised over the Holy Sepulchre in the fourth century. The walled platform on which it stands is known to Muslims as the Haram es-Sherif, the Place of the Temple. It conceals within it the Holy Rock on which David erected his altar, having bought the threshing floor on which it was to stand and the oxen to make his first sacrifice for fifty shekels of silver. And it is the site of Solomon's Temple, and the Second Temple built when the Jews returned from Babylon to find Solomon's Temple destroyed, and of the Third and last Temple, built by Herod.

According to the Talmud, the main authoritative compilation of ancient Jewish law and tradition, the Rock covers the entrance to the Abyss in which the waters of Noah's flood can be heard roaring. It is also the Centre of the World, a title it shares with a point in the nave of the Greek Cathedral in the Church of the Holy Sepulchre, the place where Abraham was about to slay Isaac, the Rock anointed by Jacob, and the Stone of the Foundation, the *eben shatyâ*, on which the Ark of the Covenant stood and beneath which Jeremiah concealed it at the destruction of Jerusalem, where it still lies buried. It was also the Rock on which was written the great and unspeakable name of God (*shem*) which, once Jesus was able to read it, allowed him to perform his miracles.

According to Muslims the Rock is without support except for a palm watered by a river of Paradise, which hangs in the air above the Bir el-Arwah, the Well of Souls, where the dead assemble to pray weekly. Others say it is the Mouth of Hell.

It was Mohammed, who prayed here before being carried away to heaven on his mare, al-Burak, who said that one prayer here was worth a thousand anywhere else; and in the underside (the ceiling) of the Rock there is the impression made by his head and the handprint of the Archangel Gabriel, who managed to hold on to it and prevent it from following the Prophet to Paradise. **99**

ERIC NEWBY, *ON THE SHORES OF THE MEDITERRANEAN*,
PUB. HARVILL PRESS, LONDON, 1984

● THE HOLY LAND AS SEEN BY WRITERS

YEARS OF CONFLICT

WHAT ENTANGLEMENT IN THIS SMALL COUNTRY

Israeli poet Yehuda Amichai (1948–1994) gives an eloquent impression of the tension and violence which permeated the lives of Israelis during the decades of conflict after the founding of the Jewish State.

❝What entanglement in this small country,
What confusion! 'The second son of the first husband
Goes out to his third war, the Second Temple
Of the first God gets destroyed every year.'
My doctor treats the guts
Of the cobbler who repairs the shoes of the man
Who defended me in my fourth trial.
In my comb strange hair, in my handkerchief strange sweat,
Memories of others stick to me
Like dogs, by the smell,
And I must drive them off
Scolding, with a stick.

All are contaminated by each other,
All touch each other,
Leave fingerprints, and the Angel of Death
Must be an expert detective
To tell them apart.❞

YEHUDA AMICHAI, FROM *A LIFE OF POETRY 1948–94*,
TRANS. BENJAMIN AND BARBARA HARSHAV, PUB. HARPERCOLLINS, NEW YORK, 1994

THE LAND, THE PEOPLE, THE THREAT

In his novel "A Perfect Peace", award-winning Israeli novelist Amos Oz (b. 1939) deals with the contemporary themes of guilt and persecution. In this passage, set in 1965, he describes the optimistic mood of the new Jewish settlers, an optimism tempered with continual reminders of the conflict and danger still present.

❝All around him, as if every minute were precious, settlers were digging into the flat, sandy strip of coast flanked by rocky mountains. Heavy equipment moved huge mounds of earth so that concrete foundations could be laid. Hilltops were being leveled every morning. Fields of weeds were being cleared, virgin brushland plowed, roads paved from village to village. Metals were being melted down to be cast in foundries. And all this while hordes of people were buying and selling, changing addresses and fortunes, scouting the lay of the land, searching for new opportunities. Apartments passed from hand to hand. Crafty maxims were rife. Strike while the iron is hot. Live by your wits. Don't look a gift horse in the mouth. The people on the bus were reading newspapers in many languages besides Hebrew. Even the bus driver struck Yolek as being a recent immigrant, from Iraq probably, who had already managed to get ahead in life. All these desperate refugees, he thought. We gathered them here from the four corners of the earth. It's up to us to impart our dream to them and make it sing in their bones. Let not the warm but weary heart grow chill in these good times that we dreamed of through all those harsh years. Eshkol was right to have chosen last night to talk about the Ta'anach region. In this urban sprawl along the coast, building plots are selling like hotcakes. When the whole state of Israel seems on the verge of overflowing, why not the weary heart too? We still haven't said our last word. And that's how I'll begin today at the meeting. Without denying the dangers, without overlooking all that's wrong, I'll tell the party to open its eyes, to take a good look all about it, and rejoice. We've had enough gloom and doom.

> **"In Israel, in order to be a realist, you must believe in miracles."**
>
> David Ben-Gurion

> Yet on these winter nights winds sometimes swept up the wadis and through the crevices of the mountains until you heard them break into a desperate howl right outside your window, as if they had been driven all the way from the snowy steppes of the Ukraine and still had found no peace. And right before dawn a formation of jets would sometimes shoot with savage furor across the low canopy of sky like a pack of hounds in heat.**"**
>
> Amos Oz, *A Perfect Peace,* trans. Hillel Halkin,
> pub. Chatto & Windus, London, 1984

IDENTITY CARD

Palestinian poet Mahmoud Darwish (b. 1941) expresses the bitterness felt by Israel's Arab population.

> **"**Write down
> I am an Arab
> & my I.D. card number is 50,000
> & my children are eight in number
> & the ninth
>   arrives next summer.
> Does this bother you?
>
> Write down
> I am an Arab
> & I work with comrades in a stone quarry
> & my children are eight in number.
> For them I hack out
>   a loaf of bread
>   clothing
>   a school exercise-book
> from the rocks
> rather than begging for alms
>   at your door
> rather than making myself small
>   at your doorsteps.
> Does this bother you?
>
> Write down
> I am an Arab.
> I am a name without a family-name.
> I am patient in a country where everything
> lives by the eruption of anger.
> My roots
>   gripped down before time began
>   before the blossoming of ages
>   before cypress trees & olive trees
>   . . . before grass sprouted.
> My father
>   is from the family of the plough
>   not from a noble line
> & my grandfather
>   was a peasant
>   without nobility without genealogy!
> & my house
>   is a crop-warden's shack
>   built of sticks & reeds.
> Does my social status satisfy you?
> I am a name without a family name.

159

Write down
I am an Arab
& colour of hair: jet black
& colour of eyes: brown
distinguishing features:
    on my head a camel-hair headband
    over a *keffiyeh*
    & my palm is solid as rock
    scratching whoever touches it
    & to me the most delicious food
    is olive oil & thyme.
Address:
    I come from a remote forgotten village.
    Its streets are nameless
    & all its men in the fields & the quarry
    love communism!
Does this bother you?

Write down
I am an Arab.
You usurped my grandfather's vineyards
& the plot of land I used to plough
I & all my children
& you left us
    & all my grandchildren
nothing but these rocks . . . so
your government
will it take them too as rumour has it?
So be it.
    Write down at the top of the first page:
    I do not hate people.
    I steal from no-one.
However
    If I am hungry
    I will eat the flesh of my usurper.
Beware beware of my hunger
& of my anger. 〞

MAHMOUD DARWISH,
FROM *LEAVES OF THE OLIVE TREE*,
TRANS. I. WEDDE AND F. TIRQAN,
PUB. CARCANET PRESS, 1973

ITINERARIES
IN THE HOLY LAND

SINAI, *167*
EILAT, *181*
BEERSHEBA, *193*
JERUSALEM, *231*
TEL AVIV, *337*
TIBERIAS, *375*

▼ The Dome of the Rock on Haram al-Sharif at nightfall

▼ Jerusalem in the snow

The Jewish cemetery on the Mount of Olives ▲

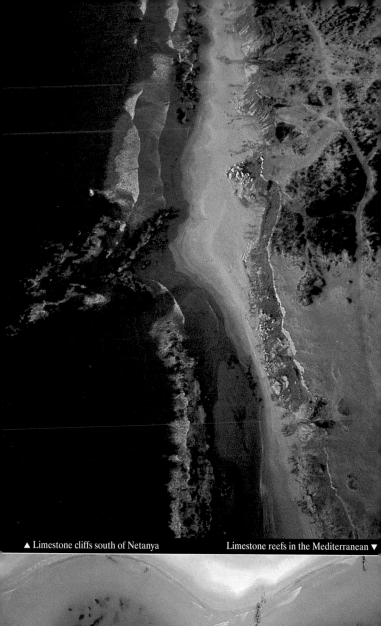

▲ Limestone cliffs south of Netanya

Limestone reefs in the Mediterranean ▼

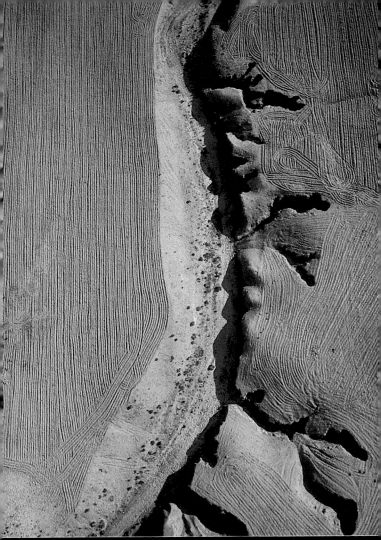

▲ A dried-out wadi in the north Negev   Algae on the surface of the Dead Sea ▼

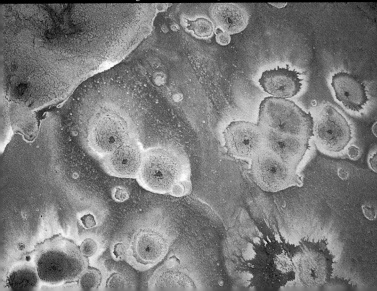

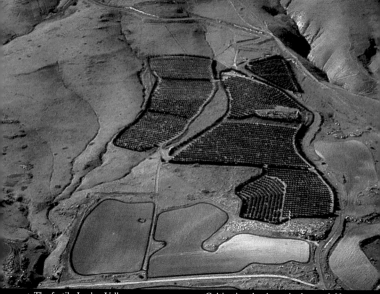

▲ The fertile Jordan Valley   Cultivating the desert in the north Negev ▼

▼ Salt accretions on the surface of the Dead Sea

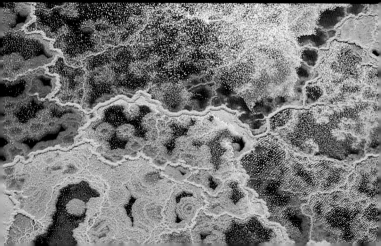

SINAI

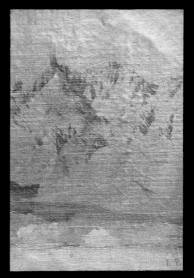

THE HOLY SCRIPTURES,
EXODUS FROM EGYPT, *168*
ST CATHERINE'S MONASTERY, *174*
TOWARD SUEZ, *177*
SHARM AL-SHEIKH, *178*
TABA, *180*

Decisive in the forming of the Jewish people is the Exodus. Once the Hebrews had been liberated from slavery Moses led them out of Egypt through the Red Sea and across the Jordan to the Promised Land. Three important events take place in this story: crossing the Red Sea, which marks the end of oppression in Egypt; receiving the Ten Commandments at Sinai, the covenant that sets forth the demands of true freedom; and the forty years in the desert which were an apprenticeship to living with that covenant.

THE ISRAELITES UNDER PHARAOH
"Now there arose up a new king over Egypt, which knew not Joseph . . . And the Egyptians made the children of Israel to serve with rigour: And they made their lives bitter with hard bondage, in mortar, and in brick, and in all manner of service in the field." (Exodus 1)

THE CALL
"And the angel of the Lord appeared unto him in a flame of fire out of the midst of a bush: and he looked, and, behold, the bush burned with fire, and the bush was not consumed . . . God called unto him . . . Moses, Moses. And he said Here am I. And He said, Draw not nigh hither: put off thy shoes from off thy feet, for the place whereon thou standest is holy ground. Moreover he said, I am the God of thy father, the God of Abraham, the God of Isaac, and the God of Jacob." (Exodus 3)

> "I AM COME DOWN TO DELIVER THEM OUT OF THE HAND OF THE EYPTIANS, AND TO BRING THEM . . . TO A LAND FLOWING WITH MILK AND HONEY." EXODUS 3

AARON AS MOSES' INTERPRETER

"And Moses said before the Lord, Behold, I am of uncircumcised lips, and how shall Pharaoh hearken unto me? And the Lord said unto Moses, See, I have made thee a god to Pharaoh: and Aaron thy brother shall be thy prophet. Thou shalt speak all that I command thee: and Aaron thy brother shall speak unto Pharaoh, that he send the children of Israel out of his land." (Exodus 6)

THE SIGN OF THE CHOSEN

"And the Lord spake unto Moses and Aaron in the land of Egypt . . . In the tenth day of this month they shall take to them every man a lamb . . . until the fourteenth day of the same month: and the whole assembly of the congregation of Israel shall kill it in the evening. And they shall take of the blood, and strike it on the two side posts and on the upper door post . . . for a token upon the houses where ye are: and when I see the blood, I will pass over you." (Exodus 12)

GOD'S PEOPLE LEAVE

"at midnight the Lord smote all the firstborn in the land of Egypt . . . And [Pharaoh] called for Moses and Aaron by night, and said, Rise up, and get you forth from among my people, both ye and the children of Israel . . . And the people took their dough before it was leavened, their kneadingtroughs being bound up in their clothes upon their shoulders." (Exodus 12)

CROSSING THE RED SEA

"And Moses stretched out his hand over the sea; and the Lord caused the sea to go back by a strong east wind all that night, and made the sea dry land, and the waters were divided. And the children of Israel went into the midst of the sea upon the dry ground . . . and the waters returned, and covered the chariots, and the horsemen, and all the host of Pharaoh that came into the sea after them . . . Thus the Lord saved Israel that day out of the hand of the Egyptians." (Exodus 14)

THE HOLY MOUNT

"... in the morning, that there were thunders and lightnings, and a thick cloud upon the mount, and the voice of the trumpet exceeding loud; so that all the people that was in the camp trembled ... And mount Sinai was altogether on a smoke, because the Lord descended upon it in fire ... And when the voice of the trumpet sounded long, and waxed louder and louder, Moses spake, and God answered him by a voice." (Exodus 19)

GOD GIVES MOSES THE TABLETS OF THE LAW

"And the glory of the Lord abode upon mount Sinai, and the cloud covered it six days; and the seventh day he called unto Moses ... and Moses was in the mount forty days and forty nights ... he gave unto Moses ... two tables of testimony [● 78], tables of stone, written with the finger of God." (Exodus 24, 31)

THE ISRAELITES BETRAY THE GOD OF ABRAHAM, ISAAC AND JACOB

"And the Lord said ... they have made them a molten calf, and have worshipped it ... and Moses turned, and went down from the mount, and the two tables of testimony were in his hand ... as soon as he came nigh unto the camp, that he saw the calf, and the dancing: and Moses' anger waxed hot, and he cast the tables out of his hands, and brake them beneath the mount." (Exodus 32)

THE TEST OF THIRST

"And Moses and Aaron gathered the congregation together before the rock . . . and Moses lifted up his hand, and with his rod he smote the rock twice: and the water came out abundantly . . . because the children of Israel strove with the Lord, and he was sanctified in them." (Numbers 20)

THE TEST OF HUNGER

"At even the quails came up, and covered the camp: and in the morning . . . when the dew that lay was gone up, behold, upon the face of the wilderness there lay a small round thing, as small as the hoar frost on the ground . . . And Moses said unto [the Israelites], This is the bread which the Lord hath given you to eat." (Exodus 16)

171

THE BEDOUINS
The majority of the Sinai Peninsula's 200,000 inhabitants are Bedouins. Each particular tribe follows its own traditional customs, regulating both economic and social affairs. Today the Bedouins are mostly sedentary and are becoming marginalized by new economic trends. Although their nomadic lifestyle may be disappearing, traditional activities are still maintained.

The Sinai Peninsula covers about 24,000 square miles between Asia and Africa with the Mediterranean to the north, the Gulf of Suez to the west, and the Gulf of Aqaba to the east. The northern coastal plain, where most of the people of the Sinai live, stretches from the Suez Canal to the Gaza Strip. In the south it gradually gives way to a limestone plateau, the Al-Tih Desert. Even farther south, the mountains Sinai, a huge crystalline mass, with peaks over 6,5 high, shelter wadis in their valleys, and many oase traditional methods of agriculture and are still used. The Red Sea lies at the farthest ti the peninsula. Its turquoise waters are famous for great variety of fish. The Gulf of Aqaba is warm round, whereas the coastal region to the north ubject to the influence of the Mediterranean and be s from winter rainfall which is markedly greater tha e regional average, as well as cooler temperatures. Arid constant in the vast desert stretches of the Sinai, and is st acute on the central plateau, whereas the mountains of Sinai can be battered by torrents of destructive rain i e autumn and early spring. In winter, the highest peaks ar en covered in snow.

LAND OF CONFR TION OR UNION? The peninsula was taken by force during raeli counteroffensive that followed the Egyptian attac 67. Central to the 1979 Camp David Accords, it was ned by Israel bit by bit between 1981 and 1982. Since the Sinai has been the focus of many development p as much touristic as agricultural or industrial. Egy rds this huge area as a potential solution to its problem crowding. It is hoped that the Al-Salam Canal, a water ntly being built to link the Nile and North Sinai, w 420,000 acres, illustrating the desire to populate and ductive a region which has until

1. ST CATHERINE'S MONASTERY
2. ST CATHERINE'S MOUNT
3. WADI AL-SHEIKH
4. FEIRAN
5. UYUN MUSA
6. DAHAB
7. WADI NASB
8. SHURA AL-MANQUATA
9. RAS NASRANI
10. SHARM AL-SHEIKH
11. RAS MUHAMMAD
12. NUWEIBA
13. CORAL ISLAND
14. COLORED CANYON
15. TABA
16. SUEZ
17. EILAT
18. AQABA
19. MT SINAI

MEDITERRANEAN SEA

ISRAEL

JORDAN

EGYPT

EGYPT

AL-TIH DESERT

SAUDI ARABIA

GULF OF SUEZ

GULF OF AQABA

now been neglected, because it was vulnerable to invasion. Peace in the region should restore the peninsula to its traditional position as a link between Africa and the Levant.

🚗 300 miles
🕐 Six days

THE ROUTE OF THE EXODUS
Reconstructing the route of the exodus from the Biblical account has not proved easy. Some propose a direct route, others a northern route. Both agree on the finishing point in southern Palestine, at the springs of Kadesh.

▲ ST CATHERINE'S MONASTERY

 The first thing you see on approaching the monastery, situated more than 5,000 feet above sea level at the foot of Mount Horeb, on the site of the "Burning Bush", are its gardens surrounded by cypress trees, and imposing walls. Built between 527 and 565 on the orders of Justinian, it is named after Saint Catherine, an Alexandrian martyr who died in 395. Her body was said to have been carried away by angels, and was found five centuries later at the top of the mountain that now bears her name. The monastery's interior reflects different periods and even boasts a 10th-century mosque built as a sign of allegiance to the Muslim powers that undertook its protection.

THE LIBRARY

Over 4,500 works in Greek, as well as in Arabic, Syriac and Egyptian are held here, including some of the world's most important manuscripts. Many are illustrated with priceless miniatures. Although the monks no longer allow access to these gems, either in the museum or in the library, the manuscripts can be viewed on microfilm.

THE COMMUNITY. The monastery was built at the request of the Fathers of the Sinai when monasticism was developing around Mount Horeb. It has its own abbot under the Greek Orthodox Patriarch of Jerusalem.

At the heart of the smallest diocese in the world, the monks devote themselves to the life of the spirit through asceticism.

ICONS
In the Byzantine-style Church of the Transfiguration, a beautiful collection of icons from different periods gives a glimpse of the monastery's riches. But this is a mere fraction of the 2,000 preserved icons, the oldest being painted using the rare encaustic technique.

175

THE JEBALIYE (GEBEL MUSA)
These "mountain people" are the descendants of two hundred Wallachian and Bosnian families sent by the Emperor Justinian to defend the monastery at its establishment in 527. They have remained a cohesive group and do not mix with people from other tribes.

ST CATHERINE'S MONASTERY AND ITS ENVIRONS

The alpine aura of St Catherine, a village with stone-built houses, is startling against the backdrop of its desert surroundings. Almost four hundred people live in the village today, mostly Bedouins of the Jebaliye ("mountain") tribe.

GOD'S MOUNTAIN ★. Mount Sinai or the Mountain of Moses is the "smoking mountain" where Moses received the Ten Commandments from God. It rises 7,500 feet above sea level to the south of the monastery. It can be reached by following a route to the east of the walls (two and a half to three hours to the top), or via three thousand steps carved into the rock to the south. Both lead to an amphitheater, said to be that of the "Seventy Elders of Israel", recalling the assembly of sages and learned men who accompanied Moses on to God's mountain (Exodus 24), where St Stephen's Hermitage can be found, surrounded by a garden. Some 750 steps take you to the summit where a chapel built in 1934 evokes the original built in 363, then rebuilt by Justinian in 527. The view from the chapel is exceptional; on a clear day you can see the Gulf of Aqaba and the coast of Saudi Arabia.

ST CATHERINE'S MOUNT (GEBEL KATERIN) ★. Four miles south of the Monastery, it takes about five hours to reach the highest point on the Sinai peninsula (8,650 feet). Your starting point should be at the south of the village, but permission from the village police should first be obtained. A small chapel marks the spot where Saint Catherine's body is said to have been found.

> "AND MOUNT SINAI WAS ALTOGETHER ON A SMOKE, BECAUSE THE LORD DESCENDED UPON IT IN FIRE . . . THE LORD CAME DOWN UPON MOUNT SINAI, AT THE TOP OF THE MOUNT . . . AND MOSES WENT UP ."
>
> EXODUS 19

FROM ST CATHERINE TO SUEZ

The northeast route crosses the magnificent granite corridor of Wadi al-Sheikh on its way to intersect with Nabi Saleh. To the left you will see the mausoleum of Sheikh Nabi Saleh, where the local Bedouins celebrate the festival of Mawlid, the anniversary of the birth of the prophet Muhammad.

WADI AL-SHEIKH. About 9½ miles from St Catherine, the road passes a natural opening in a chain of granite mountains known as the Watia col. Just a few miles further on it rejoins Tarfat Kurdreen, an oasis with fresh water wells, luxuriant orchards and a small Bedouin village.

THE FEIRAN OASIS. Tel Feiran extends into the western part of the oasis. An exposed pass begins at the small monastery at the foot of the hill which sheltered a bishopric founded in the year 400, and leads to the top of this archeological tumulus and the remains of a great Byzantine church dating from the 5th century AD.

ALONG THE GULF OF SUEZ. The route crosses Wadi Feiran and joins the road to Suez 30 miles on. It then meets the village of Uyun Musa ("Moses' Springs"), 75 miles to the north. It was here that Moses tamed the bitter waters by throwing a piece of wood into them (Exodus 15), which is how the oasis came to be called Mara ("bitter" in Hebrew). A well whose waters reach 104°F feeds the oasis which is planted today with palm trees, mimosa and tamarisk (see below).

About 37 miles from St Catherine, the road opens onto the large oasis of Feiran and a 4½-mile palm grove. It has magnificent orchards and market gardens as well as a Bedouin village.

ST CATHERINE TO SHARM AL-SHEIKH

NASB WADI ★. The road down to Dahab runs through the great Wadi Rayeb, an unpaved corridor cut through the granite, and comes out 22 miles later at the crossroads of the Wadi Rayeb to rejoin the asphalt road. The great canyon of Wadi Nasb opens out to the right. With a four-wheel drive vehicle you can take one of the most beautiful routes in southern Sinai all the way along this wadi to St Catherine's Monastery. You will come across superb gorges incorporating a natural pool, then the spring of Moyet Kara and a succession of gardens, orchards and pure water wells in the high part of the Nasb Canyon. Just before you reach St Catherine you come across the fantastic forms sculpted in stone by the wind. At least five hours are needed to cover the 53 miles of this unforgettable journey.

THE GULF OF AQABA. Another 6 miles down the main road is Dahab, a Bedouin village of the Muzeina tribe, which has become the most important resort on this coast. The village is divided into three areas, each retaining its particular charm: a complex of luxury hotels borders a lagoon to the south; in the center a string of Bedouin and Egyptian cafés stretches along a bay enclosed by a coral reef; and the Bedouin fishermen's village lies to the north. A track follows the coast from Dahab to the north as far as "Blue Hole". This is the most popular spot in the Gulf of Aqaba for scuba diving. A natural hole in the coral reef which goes straight down to a depth of 295 feet below sea level provides a rare treat for the experienced diver, but should not be attempted by anyone who does not have extensive deep-water diving experience.

The camel, the pre-eminent symbol of Bedouin nomadism, is increasingly giving way to the motor vehicle, although some caravans still cross the Al-Tih Desert and the wadis of the Sinai mountains to reach the coastal village of Dahab (see below).

SHAIRA COL. The road to Sharm al-Sheikh runs along the vast valley of Gany al-Rayan ("well-watered snake") and emerges on the Shaira col ("Naqh Shaira"). An old track formed by the explosions of the Israeli army during the Sinai campaign begins there and continues into the mountainside. On the other side of the col, the road penetrates the granite valley of Wadi Milhag, continuing for 12½ miles to the intersection of Wadi Milhag and Wadi Kid. Turning left here you can abandon the asphalt road and continue instead on a manageable desert track which leads to the sea. This gives access to RAS NASRANI – an observation point from where the islands of TIRAN and SANAPHIR can be viewed – and ends at Sharm al-Sheikh airport from where you can rejoin the main road.

SHARM AL-SHEIKH. Situated on a coral reef visible today above two magnificent bays of deep blue water, Sharm al-Sheikh has become the most popular tourist attraction in the Gulf of Aqaba, particularly for scuba diving enthusiasts. Since the return of the Sinai to Egypt in 1982, following the Israel-Egypt peace treaty, many luxury hotels with restaurants and cafés have appeared along the two bays which surround the village. International diving clubs can be found here renting out diving suits, tanks and boats as well as giving diving lessons. Dragnet fishing is another popular and rewarding activity due to the abundance of reef sharks and barracuda in these waters ■ 26.

RAS MUHAMMAD. Since 1989 the southernmost tip of the peninsula has been a national park whose aim is to protect the ecosystem both on land and at sea. The 295 feet of vertical reefs, among the most beautiful in the world, are home to hundreds of different types of fish. Foxes, gazelles and caracals have been reintroduced on land and the park is an ornithologist's paradise because migratory birds regularly stop there on their cross-continental journeys as they do in Eilat ▲ 182.

SHURA AL-MANQUATA
The Strait of Tiran at Shura is bordered by vegetation found on the coast of East Africa, unusual in this region: an *Abyssinia* type mangrove. Here plants and trees, but above all mangroves growing in the very salty sea water, direct some of their roots up toward the sky to seek oxygen.

TOURISM
The traditional lifestyle of the peninsula's inhabitants often suffers as a result of Egypt's attempts to develop the region's tourist potential. These people are becoming more and more marginalized although some benefit from tourism by offering their services to visitors. The fishermen on the coast whose income is usually minimal are very glad to take tourists out in their traditional vessels.

CORAL ISLAND
This small granite formation is also known by its Arabic name, "Marsa Murah". It is about 330 yards from the coast and is dominated by Salah al-Din's castle. The fortress was built by the Muslims in the 12th century to prevent the Crusades from reaching the Sinai, and restored in the 19th century.

"The depths of the water are more various in colors ... than a field covered in primroses. As for the color on the surface of the sea, all possible shades float by, shimmer, break up and merge into one another, from chocolate to amethyst, from pink to lapis lazuli and the palest green. It is remarkable."

Flaubert,
Notes

In 1868 seven artists led by the painter Jean-Léon Gérôme captured the spirit of the place in words and sketches during a five-month tour.

ST CATHERINE TO TABA

After rejoining the asphalt road the steep descent of the Saada valley brings you to Nuweiba, a village which boasts a myriad of nautical activities and luxury hotels, as well as the largest population of Bedouins of the Tarabin and Muzeina tribes. The port offers a ferry service to Aqaba. It is also worth traveling to Ein al-Fourtaga, a small oasis 10½ miles from Nuweiba. A track turns off to the right at the entrance to the oasis, which follows the valley floor for some 8 miles before reaching a plateau which overlooks the Colored Canyon. The Bedouins who live there are willing to accompany tourists wanting to see the superbly colored limestone and sandstone formations of the gorges.

The road continues north from Nuweiba, through the breathtaking gulf coast where the spectacular coral reefs at RAS-BURKAR and BIR-SUUVEIR can be seen, as well as a deep bay surrounded by granite cliffs, just 2½ miles from Coral Island.

TABA. A stumbling block in Egypt-Israel relations for six years, Taba was returned to Egypt in 1989, following international negotiation. Major development projects are under consideration to turn it into a true coastal resort at the gateway to Israel. The wealthiest casino anywhere in the region is found in Taba.

EILAT

EILAT, *182*
THE MOUNTAINS OF EILAT, *184*
THE ARAVA VALLEY, *186*
THE NABATEANS, *188*
NABATEO–BYZANTINE CITIES
OF THE NEGEV, *190*
SDEH BOKER, *192*

> **"**The general impression is pink but it is as if it is marked down the middle by an infinitely long band which is almost black through being so intensely blue, and which must be painted with pure Prussian blue lightly striped with emerald green. This band is the sea, the incomparable sea at Aqaba.**"**
>
> Pierre Loti,
> *Le Désert*

As Jewish kingdoms succeeded one another through the ages, ancient Eilat changed hands amid raids and wars. The town is situated at the end of the Gulf of Aqaba, its history marked by the famous travelers who passed through it: Moses and the Jewish people at the time of the Exodus, and the Queen of Sheba en route to Jerusalem where Solomon awaited her. The city was turned into a main trading port called Etzion Geber by Solomon, and the

MOUNTAINS OF EILAT

⑩

④

③

①

②

riches of *Arabia felix* and Ethiopia passed through it. In 1949 when Tzahal, the Israeli army, occupied Eilat it was a sleepy town with a population of two hundred, having lost its role as exporter to neighboring Aqaba. The State of Israel took advantage of Eilat's climate by turning it into a seaside resort. Today the town offers visitors beautiful beaches and stunning marine life.

Canthigaster Solandri (below), and the red or tropical grouper, *Cephalopholis miniatus* (right).

UNDERWATER LIFE. The waters of the Gulf of Eilat are shallow and clear, ensuring exceptional visibility for the amateur diver equipped only with mask and snorkel. For the more seasoned diver there are numerous diving schools and people renting out sophisticated equipment. Coral collecting is strictly forbidden in order to protect the various species. The less adventurous tourist can take to the water in a glass-bottomed boat called the *Jules Verne* in which you can admire the reefs without getting wet.

THE UNDERWATER OBSERVATORY
A huge complex to the south of Coral Beach allows you to observe the bay's glorious marine life at close quarters. A jetty, about 100 yards from the shore, leads to an observatory with transparent walls plunging about 30 feet below water level. A visit beforehand to the oceanographic museum on the coast will enable you to name the

THE INTERNATIONAL BIRDWATCHING CENTER.
Eilat is a true crossroads for birds migrating from tropical Africa. Their breeding grounds are anywhere between Eastern Europe and the open plains of central Asia, and the task of the International Birdwatching Center is to inform and increase awareness regarding the protection of these species. Storks and herons, sandpipers, plovers and glareoles can all be spotted in the migrating flocks. The salt marshes of Eilat are internationally renowned for harboring these birds, which are regularly joined by pink flamingoes. Ornithologists can observe the birds undisturbed and without upsetting them from a marked out path. The canal that runs along the main access path is a migratory site frequented by numerous small sparrows from humid climes, while to the north of the salt marshes, the melon, tomato and alfalfa fields of a kibbutz are staging posts for the pipits and wagtails returning to East Africa in early spring. The superb eastern bee-eater also nests there, its brilliant colors aglow in the acacia trees from which it flies in search of insects. The males of many species lose their beautiful courtship plumage during the fall, although in Eilat you can still see huge gatherings of birds of prey, particularly eagles from the steppes.

creatures you see from the observatory. The complex has a miniature submarine that takes tourists on board.

THE MODERN PORT
As Israel's open door to Asia and East Africa, Eilat plays an important part in transporting goods in and out of the country. This means the bay is frequently filled with large numbers of tankers and cargo.

▲ EILAT TO BEERSHEBA

🚐 175 miles
🕐 Six days

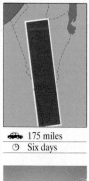

The pillars of Amram.

THE MUSHROOM
This sandstone
monolith rises some
15 feet above the
ground. Its sculptural
outline is natural: the
aggregation of chalky
particles were denser
at the bottom than at
the top. At its widest
point its diameter is
around 15 feet while
it is no greater than
7 feet at its base.

THE MOUNTAINS OF EILAT

The topography of the deep south region of the Negev ■ 16 i
deeply marked by the great Syrian-African rift ■ 18, and
provides an ideal opportunity to observe the ever-changing
faces of the tremendous rift valleys in the desert. Wadis ■ 22
formed in this way provide channels for the low amount of
rainfall needed by the oases. Avoid walking in the desert
♦ 431 after mid-morning during the summer, and always take
water with you. The water you come across along the way is
often stagnant and unsuitable for drinking. Collecting plants
or rocks in this area is strictly forbidden and may incur fines.

SOLOMON'S GORGES. Three miles to the west, this canyon is
easily accessible from the seaside resort. Nahal Shlomo
("river of Solomon") runs through gorges providing the little
humidity needed by the acacia trees ■ 18 typical of the region
The path is marked out and the trip takes just over four
hours.

EIN NETAFIM. Six miles to the northwest of Eilat, this place is
a haven for birds and mammals because it is the only
permanent spring to be found in this dry region. It should be
approached in silence to avoid scaring the animals that come
there to drink. A magnificent view over the gulf and the Sinai
can be seen from the top of YOASH Mountain just to the south
of the oasis. Ein Netafim is an open border post with Egypt,
as are Taba ▲ 180 and Rafah ▲ 336.

THE PILLARS OF AMRAM ★. This canyon owes the brilliance of
its colors to the oxidization of metallic particles in the rocks.
If you follow Nahal Shani through the pillars and into a gorge
you will be met by a dazzling spectacle of ochers and the
brightest reds, the blue of the sky becoming a mere vertical
strip stretching out about 100 feet above the river. The
softness of the sandstone made it particularly susceptible to
erosion and over the years created a deep and narrow gorge.
The canyon proper is no wider than 1,000 feet, but the
richness of its shapes and colors more than justify the two or
three hours on foot.

4. ARAVA VALLEY 5. MITZPEH RAMON 6. MAKHTESH RAMON 7. LODZ 8. MOUNT RAMON 9. AVDAT 10. SHIVTA 11. NITZANA 12. HALUTZA 13. MAMASHIT 14. EIN AVDAT 15. SDEH BOKER 16. YEROHAM 17. DIMONA 18. **BEERSHEBA**

MEDITERRANEAN SEA

JUDEA

NEGEV

THE NATURE RESERVE AT TIMNA ★.

This copper mine known to the Egyptians since the 15th century BC is the oldest in the world. It was worked by Solomon ● 46, then the Nabateans ▲ 188 and the Romans ● 50. A wall surrounding the mines prevented the escape of the many slaves who worked it from Egyptian times. Lower down are the remains of a TEMPLE dedicated to the Goddess Hathor, miners' dwellings, equipment, ovens, and labyrinthine tunnels deep into the mountainside. But the site's natural beauty is also of great interest: man's excavations and erosion caused by the wind have, between them, created a mineral decor of majestic and incongruous shapes pressed against the foot of a carmine-red escarpment (see for example the MUSHROOM and the PILLARS OF SOLOMON). You can visit the reserve by car, by bicycle, or on foot between 7am and sunset.

185

THE ARAVA VALLEY

PANTHERA LEO
A symbol of the power to protect in the Bible, the lion once lived in forests of the valley of the River Jordan. Smaller than its African cousin, the Asian lion, whose habitat once stretched from the Ganges Valley to Sinai, survives today only in the forest of Gir in India.

The Yotvata Oasis in the heart of the Arava Valley was referred to in the Bible as Jotbath (Numbers 33) and known as "a region of running brooks" (Deuteronomy 10). It was rediscovered by Jewish immigrants in 1951 who set up a kibbutz there. With the assistance of the area's abundant springs these determined pioneers made good agricultural use of the land. Fruits, vegetables ■ *34* and flowers grown here today are distributed throughout the country and even exported to Europe. The fertility of the oasis makes it an attractive stop on the way to Beersheba ▲ *196*.

"The wolf also shall dwell with the lamb, and the leopard shall lie down with the kid; and the calf and the young lion and the fatling together; and a little child shall lead them. And the cow and the bear shall feed; their young ones shall lie down together; and the lion shall eat straw like the ox. And the suckling child shall play on the hole of the asp, and the weaned child shall put his hand on the cockatrice's den."
Isaiah 11

THE HAI BAR NATURE RESERVE. The reserve was created in 1968 to act as a conservatory for biblical fauna threatened with extinction and was not opened to the public until 1977. The main work of the reserve today is still concerned with reproduction, using the most up-to-date genetic science. The animals are free to roam, and observing them requires both luck and patience. Three particular herbivores are the pride of Hai Bar. The first, the WHITE ORYX, is one of the world's most threatened animals; it has almost disappeared from its traditional habitat which originally extended from Persia to the Sinai, and is now limited to the steppes of Oman. Seen in profile, this imposing antelope appears to have only one horn and may therefore account for the unicorn legend. It is remarkably well adapted to life in an arid climate and can survive without water for months on end. The DESERT IBEX is the second, and survives today only in Israel. Cliffs and rocky escarpments are the desert ibex's preferred territory where its astounding agility allows it to escape from predators. Finally there is the WILD DONKEY OF SOMALIA which owes its presence here to, of all things, the quality of the Carmel wines. Extinct in the Negev since the beginning of the 19th century, this ancestor of the domesticated donkey was reintroduced into the Arava Valley through an East African breed, which was exchanged for some Israeli wine. In addition the reserve shelters carnivores, the biggest being the WOLF and the CARACAL, as well as many different birds, rodents and reptiles. The park's management also protects flora typical of the region by trying to recreate the countryside as it was in biblical times. The reserve may only be visited on official tours, run at specific times throughout the day.

MITZPEH RAMON ★

The new town of Mitzpeh Ramon is right in the heart of the Negev plateau and 80 miles from Eilat. It extends to the rim of Makhtesh Ramon (Wadi Ruman) ■ 20, one of the biggest craters in the world. Twenty-five miles long and 5 miles wide, it reaches a depth of 1,300 feet. The origins of its formation are still shrouded in mystery: its elongated shape tends to disprove the theory that it was caused by a fallen asteroid, and scientists generally believe that it is the result of an unusual amount of erosion on the mountains of the central Negev. It is also possible that a collapse following a series of subterranean tremors ■ 16 hollowed out the peak of the mountain. The site is breathtakingly beautiful and the national park that surrounds it is the largest in the country. The view from the summit of Mount Ramon, accessible from Borot Lodz to the western extremity of the crater, takes in the whole length of the fault. The central plain shelters varied flora and fauna, although the wild leopards that live there are not easy to spot. A tourist information center at the entrance to the new town offers invaluable data on exploring the crater, as well as the services of a guide. Do not miss the fossil exhibit: the sedimentary rocks of the crater are nothing short of an open-air museum. Staff at the center will also tell you about trips, on foot or by car, within the grounds of the park. The road which goes north to Beersheba leads to the foot of the Avdat acropolis some 25 miles beyond the park.

BOROT LODZ
This small village at the entrance to a huge military training zone is one of the region's forestation centers. Those who are called up contribute logistical help to the center.

THE DROMEDARY
This tamed animal of the camel family can be found from India to West Africa. It is a beast of burden which also carries people, and has been used since ancient times for military purposes. The Arabs took advantage of its speed and endurance during times of invasion at the beginning of Islam.

▲ THE NABATEANS

The Nabateans (nomads originally from northern Arabia) flourished from the 4th century BC to AD 106 from the caravan trade of myrrh and spices from southern Arabia to Gaza, Alexandria and Damascus. Their capital, Petra, whence came their God Dusares ("He of Shara"), has left impressive ruins. At the start of the Christian era, Nabateans dominated the lands of Edom and Moab the oasis northwest of Arabia and the Sinai, the south of Hauran and the Negev Desert. Following a decline in caravan traffic, rou toward Egypt by the Romans, they became sedentary and develo agriculture. Nabatean civilization survived after the Roman annexation, by Trajan in AD 105, and disappeared in the 4th century with the arrival of the Byzantine Empire.

A CHRONOLOGY OF THE NABATEAN KINGS

Like the coins used by the Seleucids and the Ptolemies, bronze and silver Nabatean coins, struck in Petra, reveal the chronology of the Nabatean kings, from Aretas II to Rabel II: on the obverse these coins bear the image of the king, then the royal couple and on the reverse, a symbol such as a monogram.

NABATEAN INSCRIPTIONS
The Nabateans adopted Aramaic from Persian times, as can be seen from the many religious and funerary inscriptions and graffiti carved on the rock walls, the steles of Petra, in the caravan centers and also on the Nabatean papyrus found in the caves of the Dead Sea. The language was arabized only after the Roman annexation.

The Nabateans built many cisterns (left and right) and dams to feed towns and to hold the rain water on the hills and slopes of the wadis in order to cultivate cereals, vines, olive and pomegranate trees and vegetables in desert conditions.

Nabatean tombs were hollowed out of sandstone façades, as with the classical style at Petra (El-Khazneh, above), or the eastern style at Medain Saleh.

The oblique marks on the stone and the horn-shaped capitals are typical of the architecture which also developed a classical urbanism in the towns of the Negev and Harran.

SANCTUARIES

In addition to the temples, open-air sanctuaries were built in the 1st century AD. They had stelae carved out of the sandstone façades and were arranged according to cult needs for banquets.

NABATEAN POTTERY

Based on Hellenistic models, Nabatean pottery was either rather crudely made, or painted with rolled or printed decorations. The first pieces would have appeared from the 1st century BC, but the most characteristic (such as cups and small perfume bottles) and the most highly worked (red or ocher in color and decorated with dark red or brown naturalistic motifs) date from the 1st to 2nd centuries AD.

CITADELS
Forming a defense system aimed at the Bedouins from the south, the citadels, like the one at Avdat (above), were reinforced in Byzantine times.

THE NABATEO-BYZANTINE CITIES OF THE NEGEV

In Ancient Nabatea, between the 4th and 2nd centuries BC, the caravan peoples settled in the central Negev and founded three towns – Elusa, Oboda and Nessana – which were abandoned around 100–30 BC after Gaza was taken by the Hasmoneans ● *48*. They were restored in the Middle Nabatean period (between 30–25 BC and AD 50–70) then replaced by Sobata, Mampsis and Ruheibeh. Real urban centers with temples, theaters and forts then developed. The Nabateo-Byzantine period, between AD 350 and AD 650 which saw the spread of Christianity in the Negev, is characterized by the building of churches in the center of cities and the extending of the wine-producing areas. The decline of the Negev began after the Muslim conquest.

AVDAT. Avdat (Oboda), forty miles south of Beersheba, was the oldest stage on the caravan route between Petra and Gaza. It owes its name to the Nabatean king Oboda I ▲ *188*, and is the most impressive city in the Negev. On its vast

LEOPARD
The Hellenistic art of Alexandria is evoked by the style of this Nabatean bronze encrusted with a colored paste, dug up at Avdat. It shows the richness and refinement of the Nabatean caravan travelers.

acropolis, which dominates the remains of the Nabatean lower town and the ancient Roman camp, there is a citadel, enlarged in Roman and Byzantine times following raids by Bedouins. It included temples dedicated to Dusares and al-'Uzza (equated with Zeus and Aphrodite) and Oboda I. The northern and southern monoapsidal churches, which today are in ruins, were built after the earthquake of 502 on the spot of the old Nabatean temple. Below, baths, a pottery oven, a wine-making area and stables dating from the time of Rabel II have been uncovered.

SHIVTA. Further west are the remains of Sobata (Shivta), a city built during the middle Nabatean period, along a wadi whose waters were held in the large double reservoir to the north which supplied the town. Stables and buildings for wine-making show that agriculture was the main resource of these nomads who had become sedentary by the end of the 1st century AD ▲ *188*. The mosque, baptistry and bishop's residence in the southern church reveal the harmonious coexistence of Christians and Muslims after the conquest of the town. To the north is a T-shaped sanctuary. It has two adjacent apses, an arrangement undertaken to accommodate the growing number of the Faithful linked to the cult of the martyrs in the Negev.

NIZANA. The site, ten miles southeast of Shivta, reached its apogee in Byzantine times with the headquarters of a permanent garrison in the upper town and a pilgrimage center in the lower town. The traces of the city that remain include a basilica with one apse which has a floor of multicolored marble, the domestic buildings of a monastery where Greek papyruses have

been found and a more recent church, with a triapsidal layout, to the west. The many tombs bear witness to the terrible bubonic plague epidemic that struck Egypt in the 6th century.

HALUTZA. On the road to Gaza are the remains of the place which was, in the 1st century BC, the main Nabatean town of the Negev. Built on a sandy plain, Elusa (Halutza) prospered, and became the capital of the province of Palestina Tertia. At that time, it had a huge cathedral, a theater and a necropolis. The site revealed the oldest of known Nabatean inscriptions, written around 170 BC.

MAMSHIT (KURNUB). On the old road from Hebron to Aila, Mampsis (Mamshit), "the Oriental Woman", guarded the pass to the Arava Valley where the Romans dug the "way of the Scorpions". Not having any springs, Mampsis was provided with water by three barrages straddling the wadi, linked to a series of pipes which served public and private cisterns as well as Roman baths. Imposing buildings, built completely out of stone and with stables, reveal its prosperity; one of these houses is decorated with frescos representing Eros and Psyche. The cathedral (to the east) and the western church were inserted, not without difficulty, into a saturated urban network, limited by a wall built around 300. The church is decorated with mosaics which are the most beautiful uncovered in the Negev to date. There is a camel ranch offering camel safaris to visitors.

THE CULT OF THE MARTYRS
From 324, when Constantine became head of the Roman Empire, the martyrs' cult grew. Local Christian communities gathered around the tomb or relics of the martyr placed in churches, inside niches built for this purpose (above at Shivta), on the anniversary of his death.

BAPTISTRY
This cruciform baptistry with steps for the exclusive use of adults comes from the southern church of Shivta.

BEN-GURION
Born in Poland in 1886, he emigrated to Palestine in 1906, to one of the early Jewish settlements in Galilee. He was the first prime minister of the State of Israel, a position he held intermittently until his retirement in 1964.

EIN AVDAT ★. The spring of Ein Avdat lies 2½ miles to the north of the Nabatean city, tucked away at the bottom of a gorge. The turquoise green of its basin sets off the ocher of the sides that contain it. Its ample water supply favors the survival of luxuriant tropical vegetation and ibex ■ *22*, which, sadly, are rare.

SDEH BOKER. The establishment of a prosperous agricultural development 25 miles south of Beersheba ▲ *196*, in the heart of the most arid desert in Israel, almost defies belief. However, in 1952 a handful of idealists rose to the challenge, joined in 1953 by David Ben-Gurion ● *57*. He was convinced that the development of the Negev was crucial to Israel's survival. Today the kibbutz ● *132* is thriving and has become a genuine artificial oasis, some of whose produce ■ *34* is exported. The development doubles as a study center, part of Ben-Gurion University, which focuses on the science of cultivating crops in arid regions ■ *32*. Irrigation, genetic engineering of vegetables, and treatment of brackish and saline water are the main branches of research there. The agronomists who work there have become archeologists in deference to the cultivation methods used by the Nabateans ▲ *188*, who achieved perfect mastery of irrigation. Researchers have also reestablished some of the varieties of fruit, vegetables and even flowers that are able thrive in the strong salinity of the water from the Dead Sea, thus avoiding costly water treatment. The university welcomes visitors and any questions they may have about its research. The graves of Ben-Gurion and that of his wife, Paula, are on the campus. His home, in the center of the village, is now a museum dedicated to his life and work.

YEROHAM. The road to Beersheba crosses a bare steppe ■ *20* before reaching the new town of Yeroham, whose pride is the iris for which it is named. When the flowers bloom between February and March, a pink carpet covers the stony stretches of the reserve created especially for this plant. Just before reaching Beersheba, the road crosses the new town of DIMONA, founded in 1955 by immigrants from North Africa where French is still the most common language used. The town draws most of its wealth from its industrial potteries.

BEERSHEBA

THE HOLY SCRIPTURES, *194*
BEERSHEBA, *196*
BEERSHEBA TO JERUSALEM
VIA THE DEAD SEA, *198*
MASADA, *202*
QUMRAN, A SECTARIAN
"MONASTERY" *212*
THE HOLY SCRIPTURES, *216*
BEERSHEBA TO JERUSALEM
VIA HEBRON AND BETHLEHEM, *218*
ARCHITECTURE AND WATER, *224*

Centuries before the Exodus, Abraham, recognized by Jews, Christians and Muslims alike as the first to enter into a relationship of faith with one God, settled in Beersheba with his wife Sarah, his nephew Lot and his people. Soon the land of Beersheba ("Seven Wells", a symbol of the divine word) was no longer big enough for the whole community and Lot chose to settle with his shepherds in the fertile plain of the Jordan Valley. The tents of his people extended as far as the city of Sodom, long before God destroyed it.

ONE LAND, ONE LINE OF DESCENT
"Lift up now thine eyes, and look . . . For all the land which thou seest, to thee will I give it, and to thy seed forever. And I will make thy seed as the dust of the earth: so that if a man can number the dust of the earth, then shall thy seed also be numbered."
(Genesis 13)

ABRAHAM'S VOCATION
"Get thee out of thy country, and from thy kindre and from thy father's house, unto a land that I wi show thee. And I will make of thee a great nation and I will bless thee, and make thy name great; and thou shalt be a blessing." (Genesis 12)

THE WELL, SYMBOL OF DIVINE PRESENCE
"Hagar . . . wandered in the wilderness of Beer-sh And the water was spent in the bottle, and she cas child under one of the shrubs . . . and sat her down against him . . . and lift up her voice, and wept. A God heard the voice of the lad . . . And God ope her eyes, and she saw a well of water." (Genesis

MARRIAGE AT THE WELL

"[The servant of Abraham] . . . made his camels to kneel down without the city by a well of water at the time of the evening, even the time that women go out to draw water . . . And the damsel was very fair . . . and when she had done giving him drink, she said, I will draw water for thy camels also . . . and the servant took Rebekah, and went his way." (Genesis 24)

ABRAM [ABRAHAM] AND LOT SEPARATE

"And Abram said unto Lot . . . separate thyself, I pray thee, from me: if thou wilt take the left hand, then I will go to the right; or if thou depart to the right hand, then I will go to the left . . . Then Lot chose him all the plain of Jordan; and Lot journeyed east: and they separated themselves the one from the other. Abram dwelled in the land of Canaan and Lot dwelled in the cities of the plain." (Genesis 13)

SODOM IS DESTROYED

"And the Lord said, Because the cry of Sodom and Gomorrah is great, and because their sin is very grievous; I will go down now, and see whether they have done altogether according to the cry of it, which is come unto me; and if not, I will know . . . Then the Lord rained upon Sodom and Gomorrah brimstone and fire . . . And he overthrew those cities, and all the plain, and all the inhabitants of the cities, and that which grew upon the ground . . . God remembered Abraham and sent Lot out of the midst of the overthrow."
(Genesis 18, 19)

🚗 106 miles
🕐 Three days

BEERSHEBA (BE'ER SHEVA)

Semi-nomads occupied the area from the 4th millennium BC (see Tel Arad ▲ *199*). An Israelite town was built c. 1100 BC at Tel Sheva/Tel Be'er Sheba ▲ *197*, four miles east of the present town. Beersheba was a garrison town until it was largely

abandoned in the Middle Ages. The Turks made it the administrative center for the Bedouins of the Negev c. 1900, building a new town (the present Old Town) in 1907. The mosque (now Negev Museum ▲ *198*) and a railway were built to supply troops. The town was captured by Allenby in 1915. After Independence (1948), it grew rapidly to about 130,000 inhabitants, undertaking to make "the desert . . . blossom as the rose" (Isaiah 35). Worth a visit are the market (south, at the corner of Derekh Elat and Hevron) and the Museum (in Ha'atzmaut Street; at the southeast end is Abraham's Well, with a restaurant round a recent construction).

MODERN BEERSHEBA
Built very quickly, the town, which began life as an experimental architectural development site, is full of futuristic buildings. Beersheba's long airy avenues are punctuated with modern white apartment blocks perfectly adapted to life in the desert. The architects of this city were awarded an international architecture prize by the American Institute of Architecture in 1976.

THE BEDOUIN MARKET ♦ *446.* Thursday morning is when the Bedouins arrive at the souk (market) south of the town, to sell their crafts: jewels ● *68,* carpets,

ISRAEL

DEAD SEA

JORDAN

traditional clothes and containers made from beaten copper. The first few hours are the most interesting, both for the atmosphere and to avoid the sudden rise in prices when groups of tourists come in the late morning.

THE NEGEV MUSEUM (MUNICIPAL MUSEUM). A visit to the museum provides a fine introduction to exploring Tel Beersheba ▲ *198.* The history of the town and the Negev ▲ *186,* Bedouin culture ● *68* and architectural remains dating from Byzantine times are all exhibited with scholarly concern. From the top of the museum minaret ● *116* there is a striking view over the town and the edge of the desert. To the northern end of Beersheba, you will see the NEGEV MONUMENT (Negev Brigade Memorial): take the Hebron Road and soon after crossing the railway, turn left.

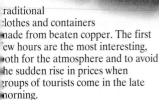

Between 1963 and 1968 the sculptor Dani Karavan worked on the Negev Monument in homage to the Palmach brigade who defended the kibbutzim and their vital water pipeline during the War of Independence.

197

"COFFEA ARABICA"
Coffee, originally from the high Abyssinian plateaux, was grown by Arabs in the Yemen in the 14th century. A flourishing trade began with its export to the Near East and Europe from the port of Al-Mukha (which gave its name to a type of coffee). From the 15th century, coffee consumption spread throughout the Arab world. Its long, highly ritualized preparation by the Bedouins is symbolic of the slow pace of life.

TEL BEERSHEBA (TEL SHEVA)

About 2½ miles to the east of the modern town, the remains of a number of different cities can be found. A society of nomads who became sedentary settled on this raised ground around 4000 BC. When Abraham settled there ▲ *194*, the town was occupied by a group related to the "Philistines from Caphtor" (Amos 9). Their king, Abimelech, allowed the Patriarch to use a well and "that is why this place is called Beersheba", in Hebrew "the well of the covenant" – "because there they sware both of them" (Genesis 21). Isaac and Jacob passed through the area, the latter obeying God's command to settle in Egypt to find his son Joseph (Genesis 46). After the Exodus ▲ *168*, Beersheba became the southern boundary of the land of Israel, a crossroads on trade routes, and a border town open to outside influences. There is a small museum on site on the theme "Man in the Desert".

Excavations carried out at the beginning of the 20th century by a French team show that people lived there in the chalcolithic age, and the items dug up are preserved in the Louvre museum in Paris. The oldest dwellings consisted of underground rooms, excavated from the thick mud of the wadi, which protected man and beast from extreme changes in temperature and sand storms. The village was made up of a group of caves centered around a large communal underground room all linked by a network of tunnels; these troglodyte dwellings were a solution to the shortages of timber and the extreme climatic conditions. At the time of the Patriarchs, shepherds built houses of sun-dried brick ● *118* on stone foundations. Their remains are still visible today. Furniture, crockery and other domestic items found on the site are displayed in the Negev Museum in Beersheba ▲ *197*.

THE MUSEUM OF BEDOUIN CULTURE
The need to preserve popular Bedouin arts and traditions has been made more urgent by the fact that so many tribes are becoming sedentary. The museum, located in Kibbutz Lahav about 12 miles north of Beersheba, houses a remarkable collection of Bedouin jewels and textiles, as well as an audio-visual presentation tracing their history. The library is open to all researchers.

TEL ARAD

This tell ▲ *394*, 6 miles to the west of the new town, is the Negev's richest biblical archeological site.

Twelve towns are built on top of one another, the oldest dating from the first chalcolithic era (3rd millennium BC). Of the three Canaanite towns (up to 1500 BC) ● *44*, only the walls and towers still exist. The remains of houses, a palace and a cult center ● *44* provide a real sense of urbanism, which is further demonstrated by the size of the town (22 acres). The first dwellings were troglodyte, following the model of Tel Beersheba. In the 10th century BC Jewish and Canaanite tribes fought for control of

Arad. As a result, the town became part of the Kingdom of Judah ● *46* and Solomon built a fortress there which was rebuilt six times between then and the Roman era. Walls and doors survive as well as a very important Jewish temple – the only one of its kind so far excavated – containing an altar and stele. Their cult use conforms with that of the Temple in Jerusalem ▲ *260*. But after the return

from Babylon ● *39*, King Josiah demanded strict application of the law of Moses, restricting cult practices to the Temple of Jerusalem, and he probably razed the sanctuary to the ground (2 Kings 23). The town remained important as a trading center, being abandoned only after the Islamic conquest, 7th century AD. A large number of pottery pieces were dug up during excavations; some of them were Egyptian in origin, illustrating the town's role as a place of trade. Most of them are preserved today in the MUSEUM of the new town of Arad. Finally, two more recent constructions have been uncovered on the site of the Jewish citadel: a Hellenist tower 40 feet wide and a fortress dating from the 1st century AD which made it possible for the Romans to watch the border before Nabatea was annexed ▲ *188*. Restoration work on the site began in 1976 in order to protect the ruins and make them more accessible to visitors. The walls of the Jewish citadel have also been rebuilt.

EXCAVATIONS
The discovery of the tell of Arad dates only from 1962 and the main part of the site was not uncovered until 1980.

THE BRASS SERPENT
God punished his people with "fiery serpents" for complaining during their wanderings in the desert. Moses interceded and made a brass serpent which he fixed on top of a staff; whoever had been bitten and looked upon the staff survived.

Numbers 21

SODOM (SEDOM)

At 1,300 feet below sea level, the plain of Sodom (the lowest inhabited point in the world) is the center of the phosphate extraction industry which draws on the evaporation fields that run the length of the Dead Sea. Nothing remains of the town destroyed by God's wrath unless you can picture the city of sin covered with stones fallen from the skies ▲ *195* by looking at the mountainous mass which runs to the west of the salt marshes. This collection of crumbling rocks contains countless caves and labyrinthine tunnels through which you can walk, with a torch to light your way. Above a salt cave near Sodom is a pillar of salt said to be Lot's wife who, turning back one last time toward Sodom despite the angel's prohibition, was transformed into this pillar. Fantastically shaped salty accretions ▲ *166* litter the banks of the Dead Sea. The Arabs have given poetic names to the most evocative ones.

Extraction of the Dead Sea phosphates which are regularly tested for the levels of salt concentration is crucial to the Israeli economy. The need to buy almost all its energy from abroad, however, means that the young state has a trade deficit.

THE BANKS OF THE DEAD SEA (YAM HAMELACH, BAHR LUT, THE SEA OF LOT) ★

This extraordinary body of water, at 1,286 feet below sea level, is the lowest point on the earth's surface, and fills a natural basin formed by the Syrian-African fault ■ *16*. The vast salty lake is fed by water which springs from the Anti-Lebanon mountains and is swollen by the streams of water in the hills that border it to the east and west. It is 47 miles long and covers 385 square miles. Its depth varies from 130 feet in the northern part to some 30 feet in the south. In the summer the water level is lowered by heavy evaporation and can go down by several feet in just a few months. The waters of the Dead Sea are ten times saltier than the Mediterranean's, and as such prevent the existence of any complex ecosystem ■ *32*. It was long

"And he overthrew those cities . . . and all the inhabitants of the cities, and that which grew upon the ground. But [Lot's] wife looked back from behind him, and she became a pillar of salt." (Genesis 19)

Visitors covered in the famous Dead Sea mud.

thought that the Dead Sea harbored no life at all, and in the Bible it is a symbol of sterility and misfortune. The Prophet Ezekiel evokes the coming of the Messiah with the vision of water springing from the Temple in Jerusalem and running into the Dead Sea to purify it: "Every living thing that liveth whithersoever the rivers shall come, shall live: and there shall be a very great multitude of fish because these waters shall come thither; and the water of the sea shall be healed (Ezekiel 47) ▲ 236. In fact, micro-organisms have long since become acclimatized to these living conditions and today they proliferate at the bottom of the lake.

NEVEH ZOHAR (NEWE ZOHAR). Six miles to the north of Sodom the road, which runs along the banks of the Dead Sea, crosses the spa of Neveh Zohar whose waters are famous for their rich sulfur content. The kibbutz has devoted a small museum (Bet Hayozer) to methods of exploiting the wealth of minerals and hot springs in the Dead Sea. A track about 2 miles long leads from the village to the ruins of a Hasmonean citadel, rebuilt by the Romans and later occupied by a Byzantine religious community. From the top of the fortress the view over the landscape of the salt marshes and the Moab mountains is worth the climb. Note also the fine views from the road to Arad.

EIN BOKEK (EN BOQEQ). The road that leads to Ein Bokek is littered with signposts to bathing areas. Since the water here can be caustic, it is a good idea to take advantage of the showers that have been installed in these areas and to rinse well after each dip. You are also strongly advised not to put your head under water. Ein Bokek boasts many luxury hotel complexes linked to hydropathic establishments. The international center for the treatment of psoriasis is there. The famous Dead Sea mud – sedimentary and full of micro-organisms – is used for therapeutic purposes. North of the town are the remains of Mezad Boqeq, an ancient fort. A short excursion up Wadi Bokek leads to a luxuriant oasis set among gorges. This mini-paradise has the advantage of being less frequented by tourists than Ein Gedi ▲ 210. After about twenty minutes of traveling along the winding road to the north, you will see the spur of Masada ● 120, ▲ 202, recognizable because its prow is shaped like the huge staircase which sheltered Herod's palace.

It is unusual to get sunstroke in this area since at 1,300 feet below sea level the ultra-violet rays are weak.

❝Vespasian went there to see and he threw in people who did not know how to swim and who had their hands tied behind their backs; but what happened was that they all swam.❞
Flavius Josephus

▲ MASADA

He
palac
perchec
the north
of the rock of
Masada ● *120*.

The rock of Masada rises 1,300 feet above the west bank of the Dead Sea at the edge of the Judean Desert. The summit, a plateau 1,900 feet long and 650 feet wide, can be reached, albeit with difficulty, from the east face via the "snake path", rediscovered in 1867. From the western side, initially very steep, you can still see the access ramp built by the Romans to conquer the citadel. Masada, a significant landmark in Jewish history, became a place of cultural pilgrimage for Israeli youth in the 1940's before the cable car made it accessible to tourists.

ACCESS
Climbing the "snake path" takes a good hour. The Roman slope, which is less steep, can only be reached by a road coming straight from Arad. The site is open from 6.30am to 4pm (the cable car operates from 8am).

POTTERY SHARDS
Found *in situ*, these pott
shards bearing names w
in ink must have been u
draw lots before the ma
suicide.

▲ MASADA

Masada was made into a Roman garrison in AD 6, and ca
in 66 by the Sicarii, fanatical nationalists, providing the fi
indications of the forthcoming revolt against Rome. Elea
Yair's son, commanded the stronghold from 67 to 73. In t
spring of 73, the Roman general Flavius Silva established
camp at the northeast corner of Masada. He made a dirt
embankment on which he put a platform made of large s
On this stood a helepole, a war machine designed to thro
objects. In April 73, the assault began.

A pile of burnt
arrows and traces of
the fire lit by the last
survivors illustrate
Josephus' narrative
concerning the end
of Masada. Twenty-
five human skeletons
have also been
uncovered, some
with their armor,
sandals or women's
plaited hair at their
sides.

These bronze scales
found at Masada
were sewn to overlap
on a thick cloth to
make an effective
breastplate.

AN ENDURING MYTH
Although it has recently been thrown into
question, the myth of Masada remains a
powerful symbol of resistance for Israelis.
Every year armored unit recruits pledge from
atop the mount that "Masada will never fall
again".

> "WE DECIDED A LONG TIME AGO, BRAVE SOLDIERS THAT WE ARE, NOT TO BE THE SLAVES OF THE ROMANS OR OF ANY PERSON OTHER THAN GOD: FOR HE ALONE IS THE TRUE AND JUST MASTER OF MEN." FLAVIUS JOSEPHUS

1. WESTERN PORTAL
2. WESTERN PALACE
3. BYZANTINE ENTRANCE
4. MANUSCRIPT ROOM
5. SYNAGOGUE
6. BUILDING NO. VII
7. WATER GATE
8. PUBLIC BATHS
9. NORTHERN PALACE
10. LUXURIOUS BATHS
11. STOREHOUSES
12. SUMPTUOUS DWELLING
13. QUARRY
14. GATE TO THE SNAKE PATH
15. EASTERN WALL AND ZEALOTS' QUARTER
16. BYZANTINE CAVES
17. OPEN CISTERN
18. SOUTHEAST WALL
19. COLUMBARIUM
20. CISTERN
21. SOUTHERN FORTRESS
22. LARGE SWIMMING POOL
23. WESTERN WALL
24. BUILDING NO. XIII

HEROD THE BUILDER

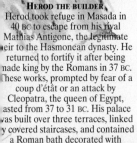

Herod took refuge in Masada in 40 BC to escape from his rival Mathias Antigone, the legitimate heir to the Hasmonean dynasty. He returned to fortify it after being made king by the Romans in 37 BC. These works, prompted by fear of a coup d'état or an attack by Cleopatra, the queen of Egypt, lasted from 37 to 31 BC. His palace was built over three terraces, linked by covered staircases, and contained a Roman bath decorated with remarkable mosaics, a place to rest

THE EXCAVATIONS

It was not until 1838 that the ruins of Sabba were identified with those of the famous fortress of Masada. The peak was excavated in the course of two expeditions (December 1963 to May 1964 and December 1964 to April 1965) led by the famous Israeli archeologist Yigal Yadin. Research has made it possible to identify many buildings dating from Herodian times: a villa-palace on three levels ● 120, another official palace, hot public baths, storehouses, a synagogue ● 106 and a fortifying wall surrounding the whole plateau except for the northern tip.

with columns, and apartments opening out onto the desert through a large semicircular portico.

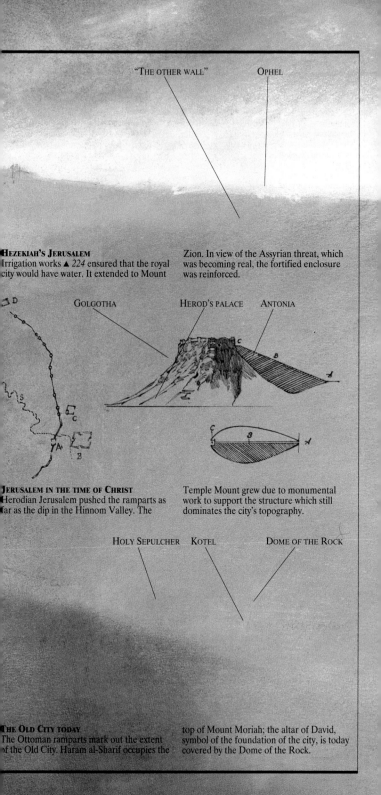

"THE OTHER WALL"   OPHEL

HEZEKIAH'S JERUSALEM
Irrigation works ▲ 224 ensured that the royal city would have water. It extended to Mount Zion. In view of the Assyrian threat, which was becoming real, the fortified enclosure was reinforced.

GOLGOTHA   HEROD'S PALACE   ANTONIA

JERUSALEM IN THE TIME OF CHRIST
Herodian Jerusalem pushed the ramparts as far as the dip in the Hinnom Valley. The Temple Mount grew due to monumental work to support the structure which still dominates the city's topography.

HOLY SEPULCHER   KOTEL   DOME OF THE ROCK

THE OLD CITY TODAY
The Ottoman ramparts mark out the extent of the Old City. Haram al-Sharif occupies the top of Mount Moriah; the altar of David, symbol of the foundation of the city, is today covered by the Dome of the Rock.

NAHAL DAVID
This river, which originates in the summits of the Judean Hills, is where the future King David sought refuge from the jealous King Saul. The latter, informed that "David [was] in the wilderness of En-gedi. Then Saul took three thousand chosen men out of all Israel, and went to seek David and his men upon the rocks of the wild goats." (1 Samuel 24). Ein Gedi exemplifies in Song of Songs (1:14) a place of great beauty.

EIN GEDI, EN GEDI (THE GOATS' SPRING) ★

THE NATIONAL PARK. The reserve, which is situated at the edge of the Dead Sea, close to the fortress of Masada, is made up of wadis and plateaus. It forms an oasis for flora and fauna due to the springs whose water streams down through the gorges of Nahal David to the north and Nahal Arugot to the south. The flora here is extremely rich, and desert,

tropical ■ 22 and aquatic plants grow together. Among the most remarkable of these are the moringa with its pale pink flowers, and acacias which recall the African savannah. The reserve is also home to a number of mammals such as the ibex ■ 22, or wild goat of Nubia, which bounds across the narrow ledges of the steep hillsides, and the rock coney ■ 22, which has the appearance of a huge rodent. Ein Gedi's gem, however, remains without doubt the panther. Birds add color to the area, among them the black Tristram's Grackle ■ 22 (cousin of the European starling) which unfolds its orange wings in flight, while crows with short tails found almost nowhere else in the world soar high above. At the entrance to the reserve the information center ♦ 446 provides maps and suggested routes from between one and a half to seven hours long for walkers of all abilities. One suggestion is to climb NAHAL DAVID first, as far as the waterfalls, more than 590 feet high, and then to go left following a path that leads to the CAVE OF THE SHULEMITE, then to the remains of a CHALCOLITHIC TEMPLE, an oasis inhabited since the 4th millennium BC. At Nahal Mishmar, 7½ miles south of Ein Gedi, ivory carvings and heads probably from the temple, have been found; at Nahal Hever, 3 miles south, letters and a settlement from the Bar Kochba revolt (132–5) have been found, including, in the

Cave of Horrors, the remains of refugees. Excavations carried out there revealed that the oasis has been inhabited since the 3rd millennium BC. At NAHAL MISHMAR, 7½ miles south of Ein Gedi, a large quantity of copper objects were found, which almost certainly belonged to the cult. The path then leads to the SPRING OF EIN GEDI on the right, and to TEL GOREM on the left which shelters Roman baths and a Byzantine synagogue ● 124, the most significant archeological remains of the park. Its floor is decorated with a remarkably preserved mosaic. Parallel to Nahal David, but about 1 mile to the south, flows NAHAL ARUGOT. These gorges, as spectacular as their neighbors to the north, are less frequently visited and therefore better for observing the fauna. A path links Nahal David to Nahal Arugot passing the Chalcolithic temple and Ein Gedi spring. The two rivers flow into the Dead Sea. At the edge of the sea is the kibbutz ● 132, founded in 1953, which runs a famous hydropathic establishment. Its waters are particularly recommended as therapy for sufferers of asthma, rheumatism and arthritis.

MITZPEH SHALEM. This kibbutz, founded in 1969, is a pioneer in the cultivation of winter produce. Its palm grove produces some of the best dates in the country. The kibbutz also boasts a laboratory which produces a range of cosmetics made from the natural resources of the Dead Sea. Finally the kibbutz has created an information center, METZOKEH DRAGOT, situated some miles to the north in the middle of the desert. The center arranges for parties to explore the desert, to climb, or walk ◆ 430 in the Judean hills which rise up between the dip of the Dead Sea and Jerusalem. These excursions are worthwhile as much for the quality of the accompanying guides as for the beauty of the surrounding countryside. The center also offers lodgings at a reasonable price.

PANTHERA PARDUS
Of all the great felines the panther or leopard is the one with the most extensive habitat, from the Malay Jungle to southern Africa. However the characteristics of the species vary according to its habitat: the Negev panther is markedly smaller than the African leopard, and is not a danger to man. It dwells in trees and hauls its prey up to raised branches where it can screen it from vultures and feed off it for many days. It hunts at night and rests in the hot hours of the day, making it difficult to observe its movements.

Excavations at Qumran (Khirbet Qumran) have uncovered a succession of settlements from c. 150 BC to AD 68, when the last settlement was destroyed by Romans during the Jewish revolt. It is usually assumed that the Scrolls found nearby (▲ 214) express the beliefs of the sect(s) that lived there (though some may have simply been collected by them); if so, the sect resembled the Sectarians, an ascetic group described by Josephus and Pliny the Elder, but it also differed from them. Qumran seems to have been a refuge for those displeased with those in control of the temple of Jerusalem (for example, Hasmonaeans or Herodians), and it thus received diverse viewpoints. It was a target for the Romans because of its austerely resistant outlook. The word "monastery" may be misleading, since no sleeping accommodation has been found.

LEVEL 0
The 8th-century building uncovered on the site is mentioned in the book of Joshua among the small forts of the eastern border of Judah, under its old name of *Sekakah.* This name appears many times in the list of hiding places in the copper scroll found in cave no. 3. The name *Qumran* came from a mistake in locality, through a deformation of the Biblical Gomorrah.

LEVEL IA
The settlement of the first Sectarians exiled voluntarily in 152 BC was not great and only lasted for a short time. The date of the end of this first period of occupation is controversial: historians place it in 143 BC or 134 BC, corresponding to the deaths of Jonathan and Simon ● *48.*

THE DINING ROOM
The Sectarians, dressed in spotless garments, began their communal meals with a ritual blessing.

> OU HAVE TO ADMIRE . . . THEIR APPLICATION OF JUSTICE . . . THEIR
> POSSESSIONS ARE ALL FOR COMMUNAL USE, AND THE RICH MAN
> MAKES NO GREATER USE OF HIS FORTUNE THAN
> WHO HAS NOTHING." FLAVIUS JOSEPHUS, *ANTIQUITIES*

THE RULES OF THE COMMUNITY
Rules for living had to be adapted to the increasing complexity of the growing community. A legal system that revolved around a chief of justice dealt with hierarchical and ritual organization.

A LIFE OF SELF-GOVERNMENT
The self-sufficient community cultivated the irrigated land around the spring of Ein Feshka, where many agricultural implements have been found. Rearing cattle assured sufficient food as well as the main material for manuscripts. This community also included potters, dyers, tanners and blacksmiths.

LEVEL IB
The grouping of communal type buildings marks the apogee of the settlement of the Sectarian community until 31 BC. Hasmonean policies survived under John Hyrcanus I ● *48*.

LEVELS II AND III
Soon after the earthquake of AD 31 the Sectarians reorganized and consolidated the settlement. Soldiers of the 10th Fretensis Legion destroyed it toward the end of June 68, during the first Revolt ● *50*. The surviving Sectarians finally left Qumran; a squad of Roman soldiers restored some parts of the ruins.

RITUAL ABLUTIONS
The *mikveh* was a ritual bath fed by an aqueduct whose water came down from the hills. It was used several times a day by the "pious" to purify themselves according to Mosaic law in a religious ceremony which prepared them for prayer.

THE "SCRIPTORIUM"
Identified by a long table and by the ink wells which were found there, this room harbored the activities of the Sectarian scribes. Large scrolls (between 10 and 12 inches high) for communal use and pocket scrolls for the hermits were found there. A cave dug under the scriptorium housed the main library.

Many bits of exercises by Qumran scribes have been found on pottery shards and scraps of leather.

Between 1947 and 1956 thousands of fragments of manuscripts (and some almost complete) were found, stored in pots, in caves to the north of Qumran. In all probability, this is the "library" of the Qumran community (▲ 213). Among these manuscripts, with paleographic dating extending over roughly three centuries (from 250 BC to AD 50) are all the Biblical books except for Esther, the non-Canonical books and Sectarian writings. Most of the texts, written on scrolls (leather, papyrus or copper), were copied at Qumran by scribes; the oldest scrolls, dating from the 3rd century BC, were brought in. Nearly all the manuscripts are preserved in Jerusalem in the Israel and Rockefeller museums.

THE CAVES
Of the forty-one caves that have been explored, twenty-five show evidence of occupation at the time of Qumran. The caves hollowed out of the marl cliffs would have been dwellings before being used as hiding places for the library when the arrival of the Romans was announced. The natural caves of the limestone cliffs, which are more difficult to enter, would have served as hiding places, like cave no. 1 (above), in which a Bedouin found an earthen jar in 1947 containing seven manuscripts, broken or empty jars and the remains of seventy-four more manuscripts.

PRESENTATION OF A SCROLL

The scrolls were kept rolled up by a leather thong. This was fixed around the middle of the right side of the first column, often with no epigraph and sometimes bearing the title at the end of the volume. Often the reader did not roll up the scroll after using it, so that in many cases the end has completely disappeared. It may be that a papyrus scroll reinforced the back of a scroll in leather, normally written on the "hairy side". The sizes of the scrolls vary according to the content and/or completeness of the work.

THE EARTHEN JARS

The manuscripts were discovered in earthern jars. They were wrapped in linen and placed there by the inhabitants.

THE NAME OF GOD

In texts in Aramaic, the four-letter (Tetragrammaton) name of God, Yhwh, was written in Hebrew to underline the sacred nature of the divine name, for example in the scroll of Psalms from cave no. 11.

SURVIVAL

The manuscripts are seen as rolls of papyrus and copper. The best preserved were written on leather (sheep or goat skins). Those which were discovered loose suffered from gnawing and rotting, and are now in fragments.

DECIPHERMENT

The languages of these texts span many centuries and are not uniform: the most commonly used languages are Hebrew for the Biblical texts and Qumran works, Aramaic for the Biblical books and translations of Biblical books and the non-Canonical works (recopied pre-Qumran works), and Greek for translations of the Torah, the Prophets and Job. Hebrew is generally written in the Aramaic script of the time, but sometimes in Hebrew letters (especially the Pentateuch).

WRITING MATERIALS

The copper manuscripts were engraved or pushed out with a burin. Those on papyrus and leather were written with ink using a sharpened reed pen. The ink, usually black, red, and sometimes bluish, was made of vegetable matter or from animal matter in the case of the black ink.

It was in Hebron, near the oak of Mamre, that Abraham received word from God about a line of descendants. It was the first land which Abraham owned in Canaan, and the place he chose for his wife Sarah's grave, as well as those of his family. Eight centuries later David was anointed king in this same town. He was part of the family of Jesse of Bethlehem, a modest village already known at the time of the patriarchs. Indeed, it was there that the remains of Rachel, the wife of Abraham's grandson, were buried, and where the meeting between Ruth the Moabitess and Boaz, Abraham's descendant, took place. Finally, it was at Bethlehem, with the birth of Jesus, that the promise of the coming of the Messiah was fulfilled for Christians.

THE PROMISE OF DESCENDANTS
"And God said, Sarah thy wife shall bear thee a son indeed; and thou shalt call his name Isaac: and I will establish my covenant with him for an everlasting covenant, and with his seed after him."
(Genesis 17)

DAVID ANOINTED KING AT HEBRON
"And the men of Judah came, and there they anointed David king over the house of Judah ... So all the elders of Israel came to the king to Hebron; and king David made a league with them in Hebron before the Lord: and they anointed David king over Israel."
(2 Samuel 2)

BOAZ MARRIES RUTH

"Now this was the manner in former time in Israel concerning redeeming and concerning changing, for to confirm all things; a man plucked off his shoe, and gave it to his neighbour . . . Therefore, the kinsman said unto Boaz, Buy it for thee. So he drew off his shoe . . . So Boaz took Ruth, and she was his wife." (Ruth 4)

THE BIRTH OF JESUS

"And the angel said unto them, Fear not: for, behold, I bring you good tidings of great joy, which shall be to all people. For unto you is born this day in the city of David a Saviour, which is Christ the Lord. And this shall be a sign unto you; Ye shall find the babe wrapped in swaddling clothes, lying in a manger." (Luke 2)

HEROD'S MESSENGERS GO TO BETHLEHEM

"[the wise men] departed; and lo, the star which they saw in the east, went before them, till it came and stood over where the young child was . . . And when they were come into the house, they saw the young child with Mary his mother, and fell down, and worshipped him: and when they had opened their treasures, they presented unto him gifts; gold, and frankincense, and myrrh." (Matthew 2)

Above Beersheba, the Tatraite plain stretches out to the north as far as the hills of Hebron. Since the Arab conquest in the 7th century, the region has been populated by Bedouin tribes who follow the nomadic traditions and pastoralism of their ancestors from the Arabian peninsula. Following the establishment of the State of Israel in 1948 ● *43*, kibbutzim ● *132* were established in the region, so that two radically different worlds coexist here more or less successfully. The road crosses stark countryside where the stone reflects every nuance of gray according to the light and the intensity of the wind.

THE "GREEN LINE". Leaving the Tatraite plain, some 17 miles to the south of Dahariyeh, Israeli army road blocks mark the frontier which separates the State of Israel from the territories occupied in 1967 ● *43* (Trans-Jordan and the Gaza Strip ▲ *334*). It corresponds to the old armistice line recognized on August 11, 1949 by the Security Council of the United Nations.

THE HISTADRUT
This trade union, motivated by Golda Meir and David Ben-Gurion ▲ *192*, was a powerful factor in the absorption of Jewish immigrants and in organizing the first kibbutzim, particularly those around Hebron.

NEGEV

🚗 53 miles
🕐 Four days

WADI AL-KHALIL. Once you have crossed the "green line", the road goes into Wadi al-Khalil, or the "Valley of Hebron", where the ground once again becomes suited to cultivation ■ *34*. Today the valley is populated by Qais and Yamans, two tribes originally from the Arabian Peninsula but sedentary since their invasion of the valley during the pre-Islamic era; their population is composed equally of Christians and Muslims. Wadi al-Khalil also harbors a number of refugee camps for those who fled the State of Israel in 1948. At the entrance to the valley of Hebron is Dahariyeh, a city built on the ruins of a Canaanite town, Jocheme, "the town which is difficult to cross", in contrast to the plain of Beersheba which is favorable to migration. Dahariyeh's fifteen thousand inhabitants are mostly of Qais origin. Further north is the

Arab village of Samoa which appears in the Old Testament under its Canaanite name of *Eshtemoa*, meaning "heard", a symbol of its obedience to God. Juttah, a Qais village with a population of about five

thousand, lies close to Hebron, built on the spot of the old Juttah ("plain" or "stretch" in Canaanite). Juttah is mentioned in the Bible for many reasons: the high priest Zacharias lived there and his son John the Baptist was born there. Some sources say that the virgin Mary, at the time of her visit to Elizabeth, John the Baptist's mother, spoke the magnificat there, the address to God who singled her out from among all women, although tradition identifies this event with Ain Karim.

The old rivalry between Qais and Yamans, encouraged by the Umayyads and the Ottomans making use of the "divide and rule" principle, hardly exists today, although it is still the butt of many jokes among the region's inhabitants.

DOURA
The tomb of Noah, recognized also by Muslims as a prophet (Nuha), was

built at the heart of this ancient Canaanite city. The myth of the flood recurs in cosmogonies in the Fertile Crescent and beyond.

The homes of important Palestinians had characteristic groined vaults ● 130. More modest houses were protected by a layer of clay, which was not always watertight.

HEBRON (HEVRON, AL-KHALIL)

The Bible (Numbers 13, 17 to 24) tells us that Hebron was built by the Canaanites on the hill of Rumeida seven years before Zoan (Tanis) in Egypt, that is, in about 5500 BC. The town was known as Kiryat Arba ("Town of the Four" or " Four Clans"), and the tribes that lived there were relatively self-sufficient. With the development of urban civilization, it was called Hevron, then Hebron which comes from the word *chever* (association) after nomadic society was replaced by a more complex social system. The town was the most important one for an ancient people, the Anakim. The Hebrews, on their way out of Egypt, feared this bellicose people: "And all the people that we saw in it are men of a great stature. And there we saw the giants, the sons of Anak, which come of the giants: and we were in our own sight as grasshoppers, and so we were in their sight " (Numbers 13). Since the Mamluke occupation in the 12th century, Hebron has been known by its Arabic name Al-Khalil ("the friend"), in homage to Abraham/Ibrahim (al-Khalil ar Rahman "friend of God") ● 78. These Bedouins are particularly generous and hospitable, but visitors should respect tribal laws and avoid wearing short or scanty clothing (shorts, short sleeves and open necklines). Hebron is about 30 miles from Beersheba and about 24 miles from Jerusalem.

THE TOMB OF THE PATRIARCHS ▲ *216*. Abraham was leading a nomadic life around Hebron when in 1805 BC he bought from Ephron the Hittite a field and a cave (the cave of Machpelah), opposite the hill of Rumeida, in which to bury his wife. This cave later became Abraham's burial place and that of his descendants down to Jacob. The present construction, called in Arabic Haram al-Khalil ("the sanctuary of the friend"), was built on the cave of Machpelah with a number of later additions. Herod began the building to

please his Jewish subjects: the huge outer wall forming a rectangle of 180 feet by 112, gives the appearance of a real fortress, each wall's thickness measuring 8½ feet. A long flight of steps takes you to the main entrance of the sanctuary. Two irregular hollows above the sixth step, opposite the traditional entrance to the cave, mark the spot where, for centuries, Jewish pilgrims came to pray. They were not allowed to go further up the steps. The Israeli occupation of 1967 gave them access to the sanctuary while a part of the mosque was turned into a synagogue. Passing through the medieval portal, the visitor reaches the CENTRAL COURTYARD where two polygonal mausoleums dating from the 9th century AD can be seen, one on each side. According to tradition, the one on the right contains Abraham's cenotaph while his wife Sarah lies in the other. The door between the two tombs opens onto a BYZANTINE CHURCH, which has a multicolored veneer. It contains the graves of Rebekah and Isaac ▲ 216, Abraham's son. This church was added to the building during the Crusaders' occupation of the town around AD 1115, when Hebron was raised to a bishopric. In 1187, the year of the Muslim reconquest, the church was converted into a mosque; Salah ud-Din (Saladin) was carried there in a remarkably well preserved carved wooden seat known as a *minbar* ● 114. Next to the *minbar* and completely hidden by old wooden flooring you will find, below, the CAVE OF THE PATRIARCHS to which entry is forbidden. Only an opening in the wall of the mosque allows the visitor to appreciate the depth of the cave under the floor. Opposite Abraham's cenotaph is the new SYNAGOGUE, which houses the tombs of Jacob and Leah. In the WOMEN'S MOSQUE, to the left of the central courtyard, a flagstone protects a footprint said to be Adam's.

THE OAK OF MAMRE
To the north of town, this venerable tree marks the spot where Abraham made camp. It was here that he received God's promise of a line of descendants
(Genesis 18).

The patriarchal figure of Abraham has inspired the seventh art: in 1966 John Huston gave us the Hollywood version with his film *The Bible*.

THE CASBAH. Winding alleys lead from the tomb of the patriarchs to Haret al-Yahoud ("the Jewish quarter") – mostly inhabited by new immigrants from America – where Arabs are not welcome. The old town has picturesque features, like Haret al-Qittun ("the tanners' quarter"), and the souk, whose stalls are filled with the widely admired Hebronite handicrafts. The production of blue-colored glass began in the Middle Ages and for centuries its manufacture has remained the jealously guarded secret of one family. Pottery has been produced there since Canaanite times ● *44*. Embroidery and the manufacture of mats and woollen coverings are also crafts for which the area is renowned. The MUNICIPAL MUSEUM, to the north of the town, exhibits old and valuable examples of local craftsmanship, as well as some sculpture; this collection will form the basis of the future Palestinian archeological museum. Beit Ilanim (2½ miles north, ¼ mile east of the Jerusalem road) was regarded by Christians as the home of Abraham. There are remains of Herodian buildings, destroyed by Titus in AD 70.

PALESTINIAN EMBROIDERY
The *jellaya*, the typical festive garment, was embroidered all over and made from linen except for the sleeves: as women had to raise their arms to clap long and loud at marriages, they preferred to make the sleeves out of a lighter cotton.

TEL ROUMEÏDA. The hill of Rumeida is located immediately to the south of the Jewish quarter in the same place as the original town. It is a fascinating archeological site, as ruins from various eras are found on top of one another: the city of the giants mentioned in the Bible (Numbers 13), Hasmonean walls (c. 130 BC) and Byzantine remains.

THE JUDEAN HILLS

BANI NAIM. Dominating the Judean Desert and the Dead Sea this village (3 miles east) built by the Canaanites was originally called Kfir Brik. Today's name dates from the time of the Nameans, a tribe which settled there in the 13th century BC. It contains a mosque built over a Byzantine church, which, according to local tradition, contains the tomb of Lot ▲ *195*. He was protected by Abraham from divine anger at the time of the destruction of Sodom.

TAFFOAH. This village (5 miles west) is mentioned in the Bible (Joshua 15:53) as Beth-Tappuah. A Byzantine church was discovered in the valley in 1946.

The name, taken to mean "House of Apples", reflects the fertility of these hills in earlier times.

HALHOUL. The town mosque is said to have been built on Jonah's tomb. Jonah was ordered by God to preach to the people of Ninevah, but fled on a boat instead. He was swallowed by a marine monster during a storm and lived in its stomach for three days and three nights, giving him time to reflect on the obedience he owed God (Jonah 5).

AL-KHADER. Coming from Hebron, you reach the village of Al-Khader via the St George Gate (Bab al-Khader in Arabic), dating from the time of the Crusades. According to legend, St George hid in a Greek Orthodox Church in this village. Rings in the walls of the church courtyard are a reminder of the ancient practice of holding lunatics so that they could be healed by the saint's intervention, a belief shared by both the Christian and Muslim communities of the region. For this reason, perhaps, the only psychiatric hospital in Palestine was built on a hill facing Al-Khader.

ARTAS. This little village nesting below the pools of Solomon, just 1½ miles to the right of the road between Hebron and Bethlehem, sheltered the "garden of King Solomon", celebrated in Song of Songs : "I am come into my garden, my sister, my spouse: I have gathered my myrrh with my spice; I have eaten my honeycomb with my honey; I have drunk my wine with my milk." Artas, from the Latin *hortus* ("garden"), is still famous for the quality of its vegetables, which benefit from the area's excellent irrigation.

KING SOLOMON'S POOLS ★. These three reservoirs, each located on a different level, were probably cut into the rock in Herodian times. They collect water from rainfall and from nearby springs to supply Jerusalem, which is 2½ miles away. The site, which is very pleasant, is planted with palms and pines. Near the road is QALAAT AL-BOURAK, a fortified Turkish castle and caravanserai of the 17th century.

Since the 2nd millennium BC, fruit – particularly strikingly large grapes – and various Mediterranean vegetables and cereals have been grown around Hebron. No doubt the altitude (3,300 feet) contributes to the area's fertility, renowned for four millennia.

Red remains the base dye for the clothes of those living in the Judean Hills, having been the distinctive and privileged color of the Qais tribes since pre-Islamic times.

Aqueduct at Caesarea

In a region where since antiquity water has been the most
fiercely disputed commodity, the Israelite architects and later
the Hasmoneans managed to achieve a mastery of irrigation
unrivaled at the time. The rugged terrain required new methods
of conserving the precious resource. A complex system of
tunnels allowed water from the hills of Judea to reach
Jerusalem.

During periods
drought, the po
Solomon, posit
upstream of th
irrigation syste
regulated the f
the canal from
Hebron to the
Temple.

**THE POOLS OF
SOLOMON**
The three basins
which embrace the
terrain's topography
were originally dug at
the spot where today
the rock has been
leveled (**1**) then
surrounded by
embankments (**2**) to
give the pools a flat
bottom.

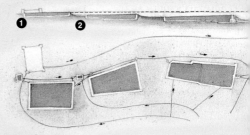

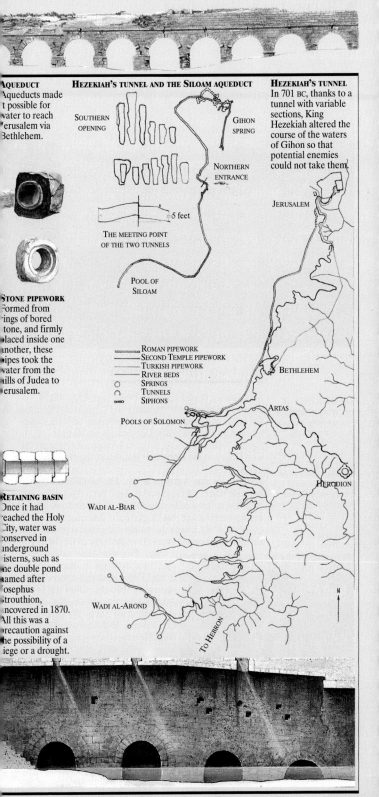

AQUEDUCT
Aqueducts made it possible for water to reach Jerusalem via Bethlehem.

STONE PIPEWORK
Formed from rings of bored stone, and firmly placed inside one another, these pipes took the water from the hills of Judea to Jerusalem.

RETAINING BASIN
Once it had reached the Holy City, water was conserved in underground cisterns, such as the double pond named after Josephus Strouthion, uncovered in 1870. All this was a precaution against the possibility of a siege or a drought.

HEZEKIAH'S TUNNEL AND THE SILOAM AQUEDUCT

SOUTHERN OPENING

GIHON SPRING

NORTHERN ENTRANCE

5 feet

THE MEETING POINT OF THE TWO TUNNELS

POOL OF SILOAM

⎯⎯ ROMAN PIPEWORK
⎯⎯ SECOND TEMPLE PIPEWORK
⎯⎯ TURKISH PIPEWORK
⎯⎯ RIVER BEDS
○ SPRINGS
∩ TUNNELS
∞ SIPHONS

POOLS OF SOLOMON

WADI AL-BIAR

WADI AL-AROND

TO HEBRON

HEZEKIAH'S TUNNEL
In 701 BC, thanks to a tunnel with variable sections, King Hezekiah altered the course of the waters of Gihon so that potential enemies could not take them.

JERUSALEM

BETHLEHEM

ARTAS

HERODION

N

▲ Beersheba to Jerusalem, via Hebron and Bethlehem

Bethlehem,
19th century

BETHLEHEM (HOUSE OF BREAD)
BEIT LAHM (HOUSE OF MEAT)

THE SLAUGHTER OF THE HOLY INNOCENTS
Having been alerted to the impending arrival of the Messiah, Herod demanded that the wise men tell him the exact place of his birth. But warned in a dream, they returned home without obeying him. In the Christian story, "Herod . . . was exceeding wroth, and sent forth and slew all

the children that were in Bethlehem, and in all the coasts thereof, from two years old and under"
(Matthew 2).
Herod was ruthless, but no trace of this episode has been found elsewhere.

Six miles south of Jerusalem, Bethlehem has a mixed population of (mainly) Muslims and Christians. Pilgrimage to the home of David's father and birthplace of Jesus makes tourism its main industry. Life centers on Manger Square/Nativity Square, with the Mosque of Omar on the west side, and the Church or Basilica of the Nativity on the east side.

BASILICA OF THE NATIVITY ● *124*. The basilica was built above the cave where Christ is said to have been born. Poor Bethlehem families traditionally used the rocky hollows of the region as stables or dwellings. So the 2nd-century Christian tradition which places the nativity in a cave is plausible, even though the Evangelists mention the birth of Christ in a manger. Protochristians in the area continued to honor the spot, even though in AD 135 the Roman emperor Hadrian had established the cult of the god Adonis-Tammuz. The original sanctuary was built in AD 323 by the Emperor Constantine, at the behest of his mother, Saint Helena, who even came to supervise the work in AD 326. Nothing remains of this first building except the nave with its four rows of columns. Under Justinian in AD 540 three projecting apsides were added to the apse by Christians. The basilica is reached through a small paved courtyard, which was once the site of the original atrium; reservoirs collect the rainwater needed for ritual ablutions. The remains of an Armenian door with carved wood panels, dating from 1277, gives access to the basilica. The total length of the sanctuary is 177 feet. It is divided into five symmetrical naves of 66 feet each, separated by four rows of columns. You may find the interior of the

226

basilica disconcerting because of the juxtaposition of chapels and places of worship associated with different branches of Christianity. The Byzantine church, until now used by the Greek Orthodox church, is decorated with remarkable mosaics representing Christ's ancestors on a gold background; there are only seven figures with gold haloes whose names appear in Latin. The Cave of the Nativity may disappoint some pilgrims who imagine it to be plainer and barer. It is a crypt 39 feet long, 10 feet wide and 10 feet high, with a vaulted masonry roof. To the east you will find an apsidal chapel decorated with a damaged mosaic which covers the altar of the birth of Christ. Immediately below there is a vermilion star bearing the following inscription: *Hic de Virgine Maria Jesus Christus Natus est* (Here Jesus Christ was born of the Virgin Mary). *1717*. During the general restoration of the cave a mosaic of the Nativity dating from 1160 was discovered. Walking through the crypt, it is possible to visit the network of underground caves which emerge at the Franciscan Church of St Catherine. The first of these caves, held up by a column shaft, is dedicated to the Holy Innocents.

THE CAVE OF MILK. Southeast of the basilica (5 minutes' walk) is the Cave (converted into a Chapel) where, according to tradition, the Holy Family hid before the flight into Egypt, and where a drop of Mary's milk turned the stone white. The walls were thus believed to make suckling easier. In the 19th century a Franciscan church was built on the remains of the earlier chapel.

THE MEDIEVAL FRESCOS
Images of saints with their names written in Latin or Greek figure on the limestone columns in the central nave (below is Saint Brasius).

THE DOORS OF HUMILITY
These low doors, only 4 feet high, may have been installed to prevent Muslim cavalry from entering the church on horseback, or possibly to oblige pilgrims to bow down on entering this holy place.

227

THE "SHATWA"

The traditional headdress of the elegant women of Bethlehem, this hat, shaped like a truncated cone and decorated with gold and silver coins or coral, was an essential part of the bride's costume. If she did not own one, she would have to borrow one for the duration of the wedding festivities. Celibate girls did not have the right to wear one. During periods of mourning the *shatwa* was covered by a black veil in order to hide its riches and colors.

It could also be covered with a linen or silk embroidered shawl called a *tarbi*.

THE CASBAH. From the highest point in the center of town – accessible via an alleyway of steps which climbs immediately to the west of the basilica – the old town houses the CENTRAL MARKET where local crafts are bought and sold: mother-of-pearl work and items made from olive wood ● 76 and copper, as well as the famous local embroidery ● 66. These crafts are the town's main source of income. The MUSEUM OF OLD BETHLEHEM is a short distance northwest of the Mosque of Omar. Opened in 1972, it is kept by the Union of Palestinian Women, and displays very beautiful embroidery as well as furniture, documents and objects evoking life in Bethlehem in the 19th century. David's Well is west of Manger Road, near St Joseph's Church, a cistern cut from rock.

BET-SAHOUR. A field here is (traditionally) the one in which Boaz saw Ruth (▲ 217) reaping, and another (Shepherds' Field, about half a mile to the east) the one in which the shepherds saw the angels (Luke 2:1); hence the village is called "Shepherds Village". From Shepherds' Field is a view of the ruins of a Byzantine monastery built on top of important military relics from the Herodian period.

MONASTERY OF ST ELIAS (ELIJAH). One mile north, on the right of the road to Jerusalem, this monastery (6th century, rebuilt in the 11th and 17th centuries) offers a fine view of Bethlehem.

HERODION (HERODEION) ★

This is a 12½-acre architectural complex designed to serve as palace, fortress and mausoleum for Herod the Great. The Herodion is 6 miles southeast of Bethlehem at the top of Jabal Foureidis or the Franks' Mount (2,560 feet), the place of an important victory by the king over the Hasmoneans. The magnificent fortified complex is on two levels: the palace-fortress at the top and the town at the bottom. Archeological excavations have revealed a number of gardens surrounding a large basin in which the foundations of a circular building are found. The gardens were surrounded by colonnades, and some ruins in the Ionic style remain visible. The palace, storehouses and baths in typically Roman style, were all set around the gardens and fed by water from Tarbas ▲ 223.

A five-minute climb on foot along a steep slope brings you to an exceptional panorama which extends from the Dead Sea to Jerusalem. At the summit of this gigantic rocky cone, the ruins of the summer palace appear quite modest in light of the astounding luxury of the actual building, finished shortly before Herod's death ● 50. The palace was divided into two parts: a large peristyle courtyard at the foot of the eastern tower and, to the west, the residential wing with apartments, reception rooms and baths fed by water from four huge tanks. The excavations which unearthed these reservoirs carved out of the hillside about 50 feet below the palace give the summit of Jabal Foureidis the appearance of a crater. Surrounded by a double wall with four towers situated at points of a compass, the Herodion was accessible by an underground passage which appears to have been sealed after Herod's death. His grave has never been found. Nine and a half miles southwest of the Herodion you will find the archeological site of TEGOAH, or Khirbet Tegoah. Excavations there have uncovered the ancient city of *Tekoa*, which was fortified by Solomon's son, King Rehoboam ● 46. The remains of a Byzantine church have also been preserved.

HEROD THE GREAT
Flavius Josephus says of him in his *Jewish Antiquities*, "As Herod was hungry for glory and this passion dominated him completely, he was inclined to munificence every time he hoped that someone would remember him in the future or that someone would praise him there and then." Herod's building was prodigious (whole towns, parks, fortresses, above all the restoration of the Temple in Jerusalem), and extended far beyond Palestine. Many of the most important archeological sites derive from his reign.

SAINT SABAS
Born in AD 439 in Cesarea in Cappadocia (Kayseri), Sabas left his native Turkey at the age of eighteen to settle in a cave in the Sidron Valley. His reputation for piety drew a group of disciples, and a monastery was set up *de facto*. Its church, the current St Nicholas, was ordained (unusual for hermits) in 490. At the age of fifty-three, Sabas was appointed head of the group of hermits in the desert.

MAR SABA ★

Eleven miles from Bethlehem, Mar Saba (Greek *Megiste Laura*, the Great Laura) clings to cliffs peppered with caves (early used as cells) in the Kidron Valley. For more than 1,500 years, it has been home to one of the oldest monastic organizations with a particularly austere way of life. Established at the end of the 5th century by Saint Sabas, the community imposed upon itself strict rules which have hardly been relaxed in the intervening years. It is difficult to gain access to Mar Saba for the most part, and completely impossible during Lent ● *86* or vespers. The effort of climbing the gorge to the monastery is, however, justified by the beauty of the site itself as well as by the vision of the irregular overlapping cupolas and the walls which have risen anarchically over the centuries. The interior courtyard houses the tomb of Saint Sabas, opposite which is the main church, completely destroyed several times by the Persians or earthquakes, and always rebuilt. The present building dates from the reconstruction following the 1834 earthquake. The church of Saint Nicholas is obscured by its own shadow on the site of a cave which held the first chapel of the monastery. The monks will lead visitors to the cell of Saint John the Damascene and to the cave of Saint Sabas to which the founder withdrew on his arrival in the valley. At the foot of Saint Simeon Tower a path leads to the right, meandering to the other side of the valley, where the view over all the buildings is particularly impressive. To enter the monastery itself, all you can do is ring at the door and hope for someone to open it. Only men may enter the monastery, but women may enter the tower on the hill to the right, which has a good view.

THE LAURAS (OR LAVRAS, GREEK FOR "STREET")
The first Greek monastic organization, the Lauras appeared in Palestine during the 4th century. Hermits lived in separate cells (huts or caves) but under a single abbot. The escarpments and caves of the Judean Desert where the monks withdrew for prayer and meditation were perfectly suited to a hermetic ideal.

JERUSALEM

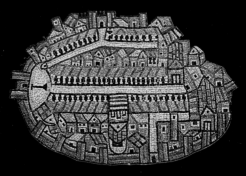

JERUSALEM FROM ITS ORIGINS
TO THE PRESENT DAY, 232
THE HOLY SCRIPTURES, 234
WALLS AND GATES, 244
THE CITADEL MUSEUM, 252
THE JEWISH QUARTER, 254
TEMPLE MOUNT, 260
HASIDIC COSTUMES, 262
THE ARMENIAN QUARTER, 264
THE CHRISTIAN QUARTER, 266
THE VIA DOLOROSA, 268
THE HOLY SEPULCHER, 272
THE MUSLIM QUARTER, 280
THE DOME OF THE ROCK, 284
AL-AQSA MOSQUE, 286
MODERN JERUSALEM, 290
THE ISRAEL MUSEUM, 298
HADASSAH SYNAGOGUE, 304
EAST JERUSALEM, 306

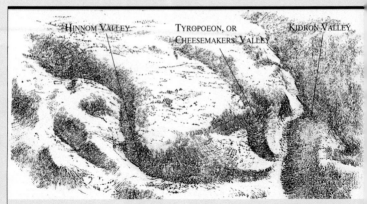

HINNOM VALLEY   TYROPOEON, OR CHEESEMAKERS' VALLEY   KIDRON VALLEY

The topography of Jerusalem is punctuated with sudden dips forming the three valleys which surrounded the ancient city. Between the Kidron Valley and the Cheesemakers' Valley, the Hill of Ophel extends to the north, via Mount Moriah, or the Temple Mount.

SILOAM CISTERN   CISTERN OF THE KING

JEBUS, CITY OF DAVID
Conquered from the Jebusites, the city was proclaimed the capital by King David, who also made it the religious center of the kingdom. An altar was erected on Mount Moriah, to hold the Ark of the Covenant.

ROYAL PALACE   TEMPLE   MOUNT OF SCANDAL

SOLOMON'S JERUSALEM
Under the reign of David's successor, the city grew to the north and received new fortifications. The first Temple was built on the top of Mount Moriah which, to this day, is the spiritual heart of the city.

"THE OTHER WALL"   OPHEL

HEZEKIAH'S JERUSALEM
Irrigation works ▲ 224 ensured that the royal city would have water. It extended to Mount Zion. In view of the Assyrian threat, which was becoming real, the fortified enclosure was reinforced.

GOLGOTHA   HEROD'S PALACE   ANTONIA

JERUSALEM IN THE TIME OF CHRIST
Herodian Jerusalem pushed the ramparts as far as the dip in the Hinnom Valley. The Temple Mount grew due to monumental work to support the structure which still dominates the city's topography.

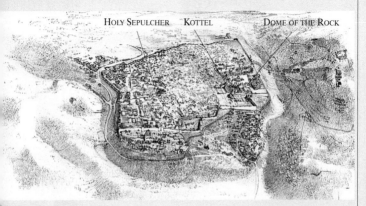

HOLY SEPULCHER   KOTTEL   DOME OF THE ROCK

THE OLD CITY TODAY
The Ottoman ramparts mark out the extent of the Old City. Haram el-Sharif occupies the top of Mount Moriah; the altar of David, symbol of the foundation of the city, is today covered by the Dome of the Rock.

233

If David achieved the political unity of a kingdom with Jerusalem as its capital, he established the importance of the city even more by moving the Ark of the Covenant from Kiryat Yearim to Jerusalem, to make it God's chosen city. In the Biblical universe, the holy city then became the axis of the world at its center, the Temple Rock, on the top of Mount Moriah, is the place of the meeting with God. Furthermore, temporal Jerusalem is a symbol of the world to come: heavenly Jerusalem, where all the Faithful are gathered together in peace around the Messiah.

JERUSALEM, THE POLITICAL CENTER

"[David] and his men went to Jerusalem unto the Jebusites, the inhabitants of the land . . . David took the strong hold of Zion: the same is the city of David."
(2 Samuel 5)

THE TEMPLE IS BUILT IN JERUSALEM

"So Hiram [king of Tyre], gave Solomon cedar trees and fir trees according to all his desire. And Solomon gave Hiram twenty thousand measures of wheat for food to his household, and twenty measures of pure oil . . . And king Solomon raised a levy out of all Israel . . . And the king commanded, and they brought great stones, costly stones, and hewed stones, to lay the foundation of the house. And Solomon's builders and Hiram's builders did hew them . . . so they prepared timber and stones to build the house."
(1 Kings 5)

THE ARK OF THE COVENANT IN JERUSALEM

"David and all the house of Israel brought up the ark of the Lord with shouting, and with the sound of the trumpet . . . And they brought in the ark of the Lord, and set it in his place, in the midst of the tabernacle that David had pitched for it: and David offered burnt offerings and peace offerings before the Lord." (2 Samuel 6)

> "IN THAT DAY SHALL THE LORD DEFEND THE INHABITANTS OF JERUSALEM; AND HE THAT IS FEEBLE AMONG THEM AT THAT DAY SHALL BE DAVID."
>
> ZECHARIAH 12

HARVEST

"Thou shalt take of the first of all the fruit of the earth, which thou shalt bring of thy land, that the Lord thy God giveth thee, and shalt put it in a basket, and shalt go unto the place which the Lord thy God shall choose to place his name there."
(Deuteronomy 26)

AT THE CENTER OF HOPE, JERUSALEM TO COME

"For brass I will bring gold, and for iron I will bring silver, and for wood brass, and for stones iron: I will also make thy officers peace, and thine exactors righteousness. Violence shall be no more heard in thy land, wasting nor destruction within thy borders; but thou shalt call thy walls Salvation, and thy gates Praise."
(Isaiah 60)

235

COVENANT FORMED WITH ABRAHAM

"Take now thy son, thi
only son Isaac, whom
lovest, and get thee in
the land of Moriah, ar
offer him then for a b
offering upon one of t
mountains which I wil
thee of . . . And Abrah
stretched forth his har
and took the knife to s
his son. And the ange
the Lord called unto h
out of heaven, and sai
Abraham, Abraham: a
he said, Here am I. Ar
he said, Lay not thine
hand upon the lad, ne
do thou any thing unto
him: for now I know t
fearest God, seeing th
hast not withheld thy s
thine only son from m

Genes

"Because thou . . . hast not withheld thy son, thine only son: That in blessing
I will bless thee, and . . . I will multiply thy seed as the stars of the heaven . . .
And in thy seed shall all the nations of the earth be blessed." Genesis 22

THE GLORY OF GOD

"As for the likeness of the living creatures, their appearance was like burning coals of fire, and like the appearance of lamps: it went up and down among the living creatures; and the fire was bright, and out of the fire went forth lightning . . . behold one wheel upon the earth by the living creatures, with his four faces. The appearance of the wheels and their work was like unto the colour of a beryl . . . And above the firmament that was over their heads was the likeness of a throne, as the appearance of a sapphire stone: and upon the likeness of the throne was the likeness as the appearance of a man above upon it . . . and it had brightness round about. As the appearance of the bow that is in the cloud in the day of rain, so was the appearance of the brightness round about. This was the appearance of the likeness of the glory of the Lord."   Ezekiel 1

THE VISION OF THE FOUR LIVING CREATURES

"And every one had four faces, and every one had four wings . . . And they had the hands of a man under their wings . . . they four had the face of a man, and the face of a lion, on the right side: and they four had the face of an ox on the left side; they four also had the face of an eagle."   Ezekiel 1

THE COVENANT RENEWED WITH JACOB

"and behold a ladder set up on the earth, and the top of it reached to heaven: and behold the angels of God ascending and descending on it. And, behold, the Lord stood above it, and said, I am the Lord God of Abraham thy father, and the God of Isaac: the land whereon thou liest, to thee will I give it, and to thy seed."   Genesis 28

PILGRIMAGE TO JERUSALEM

"And when he was twelve years old, they went up to Jerusalem after the custom of the feast . . . Jesus tarried behind in Jerusalem; and Joseph and his mother knew not of it . . . they found him in the temple . . . And he said unto them, How is it that ye sought me? wist ye not that I must be about my Father's business? And they understood not the saying which he spake unto them." (Luke 2)

JESUS IS "THE LIGHT OF THE WORLD". "[A man which was blind from his birth] answered and said, A man that is called Jesus made clay, and anointed mine eyes, and said unto me, Go to the pool of Siloam, and wash: and I went and washed, and I received sight. Then said they unto him, Where is he? He said, I know not." (John 9)

THE PEOPLE ARE DIVIDED ABOUT JESUS

"And it was the sabbath day when Jesus made the clay . . . Therefore said some of the Pharisees, This man is not of God, because he keepeth not the sabbath day. Others said, How can a man that is a sinner do such miracles? And there was a division among them." (John 9)

MESSIANIC ENTRANCE

"unto the mount of Olives . . . [the disciples] brought the ass, and the colt, and put on them their clothes, and they set [Jesus] thereon. And a very great multitude spread their garments in the way . . . And the multitudes that went before, and that followed, cried, saying . . . Blessed is he that cometh in the name of the Lord . . . And when he was come into Jerusalem, all the city was moved." (Matthew 21)

THE LAST SUPPER

"Jesus took bread, and blessed, and brake it, and gave to them, and said, Take, eat. This is my body. And he took the cup, and when he had given thanks, he gave it to them; and they all drank of it. And he said unto them, This is my blood of the new testament, which is shed for many." (Mark 14)

JESUS REVIVED FROM THE DEAD

"[Mary Magdalene] seeth two angels in white sitting . . . where the body of Jesus had lain . . . supposing him to be the gardener . . . Jesus saith unto her, Touch me not; for I am not yet ascended to my Father: but go to my brethren, and say unto them, I ascend unto my Father and your Father; and to my God and your God." (John 20)

HEAVENLY JERUSALEM

"And I saw a new heaven and a new earth; for the first heaven and the first earth were passed away; and there was no more sea. And I, John, saw the holy city, new Jerusalem, coming down from God out of heaven, prepared as a bride adorned for her husband." (Revelations 21)

MELCHIZEDEK AND ABRAM
Early on, Jerusalem was identified by Jewish tradition with the town of Salem whose king, Melchizedek, met Abram and offered him bread and wine (Genesis 14).

BEGINNINGS. In 3500 BC there were settlements on the edge of the Judean Desert at the spring of Gihon. Between the 14th and 18th centuries BC the Jebusites, a Canaanite people, built a 10-foot-thick wall which protected it until the 8th century BC. They called the place Urushalim, after their God Shalem.

JERUSALEM, THE CITY OF DAVID AND SOLOMON. Around 1000 BC ● *46*, King David (left) took the town and fortified it: Jerusalem, from then on called the "city of David", became the capital of the kingdoms of Judah and Israel. Solomon gave it its political and religious dimensions by building a royal palace and the Temple ● *46*. At his death in around 931 BC the kingdom of Israel separated from the Davidic dynasty; Jerusalem, which then became a small capital of the kingdom of Judah ● *47*, was successively besieged by the kings of Samaria, Assyrian sovereigns and then the neo-Babylonians ● *37*. In 587 BC it fell into the hands of Nebuchadnezzar, the Temple was destroyed and the population dispersed in different directions ● *47*.

RECONSTRUCTION. After the fall of Babylon in 539 BC, Cyrus allowed exiles to return to Jerusalem ● *41*. The Temple was rebuilt in 515 BC under Zerubabel and Joshua. Then, from 445 BC under Nehemiah, the walls were rebuilt and the town repopulated. After Alexander's conquest in the 4th century BC, Jerusalem came by turns under the rule of the Ptolemies, then the Seleucids and became a Hellenistic *polis*. In 167 BC, Antiochus IV dedicated the Temple to Zeus Olympian after he had destroyed its walls ● *48* and installed a garrison in the Akra fortress, actions which

provoked the Maccabees' revolt ● 48; Jerusalem then remained under Hasmonean rule until 63 BC, the year Pompey entered the town ● 42.

HEROD'S TIME AND ROMAN RULE. In 37 BC Herod succeeded in overcoming the town ● 42. The new king immediately undertook rebuilding it in a systematic manner: temple, palace, theater, amphitheater and walls were built, renovated and embellished. Jerusalem became one of the most beautiful towns of the Levant. Herod Agrippa I (41–44) began to build a third wall north of Jerusalem. Completed some twenty years later, the ramparts were not enough to protect the town: in AD 70, Titus burned the Temple and took Jerusalem ● 50. When in 130 the emperor Hadrian decided to rebuild the town under the name of Aelia Capitolina and to erect, on the holy site of the Temple, a sanctuary dedicated to Roman divinities, he provoked Bar Kochba's revolt ● 50: Jerusalem was forbidden to the Jews.

CHRISTIAN JERUSALEM. In 324, Constantine, now Emperor of the Holy Roman Empire, renamed Aelia Capitolina "Jerusalem" and built the Holy Sepulcher in 335 ▲ 272 at the place of the Capitol, thus marking the beginning of a period of construction; monasteries, churches and hospices were built throughout the town to receive pilgrims from everywhere ● 88.

MUSLIM JERUSALEM. The tradition of Muhammad's Night Journey ● 90 means that Jerusalem (usually known as al-Quds, the Holy Place) is a city venerated by the Muslims. In 638, the town was conquered by Caliph Umar ● 52. The Umayyads built two great edifices, the Dome of the Rock (Qubbat as-Sakhrah), piously but wrongly also called "the Mosque of Umar" ▲ 284, and al-Masjid al-Aqsa, the Aqsa Mosque ▲ 286: Jerusalem became the third holy city of Islam ● 52. From 750, under the Abbasids, then the Fatimids of Egypt, the city lost its prestige: it even witnessed the destruction of its churches under Caliph al-Hakim (996–1021). In 1070, the Seljuq Turks, rulers of the city, persecuted Jews and Christians. In the west the Franks were preparing to regain the holy city: this was the first Crusade.

HELENA
In 325, Constantine (above, left) sent his mother, Empress Helena (middle), to Jerusalem to identify the holy places where Christ lived.

More alive than historic Jerusalem is an imaginary Jerusalem where heroes roam. It was in the holy city that the young Ben Hur, ardent defender of the Jewish people, triumphed over Messala, for whom the power of Rome was paramount, at the time of the chariot race made famous by William Wyler's 1959 film.

Suleyman the Magnificent, above. The Crusades represented Jerusalem, below, as a perfect circle (1170); the lower part depicts the victory of a knight over an infidel.

WILHELM II
The Kaiser came to Jerusalem in 1898 to reinforce German presence in the Holy Land.

THE CRUSADES. In 1099 Godfrey of Bouillon entered Jerusalem, which soon became the capital of a Latin kingdom ● *54*. The town now met with great changes: the large population (about thirty thousand inhabitants) was comprised of mostly French-speaking Christians; pilgrimages began again; new churches were built or renovated, like St Anne ▲ *266* and the Holy Sepulcher, and mosques were turned into Christian sanctuaries. This move was reversed in 1187 when Salah al-Din retook Jerusalem ● *55* and restored the Dome of the Rock and Al-Aqsa Mosque.

MAMLUKE AND OTTOMAN TIMES. In 1260 the holy city was taken by the Mamlukes; even though it then underwent an economic and demographic decline (to about ten thousand inhabitants) it became a center for Muslim scholarship; its architecture benefited from the influence of its new occupants. At this time, many Sephardic Jews settled in Jerusalem and built one of the first synagogues in the present-day Jewish quarter, Rambam Synagogue ▲ *256*. Under Ottoman rule (1517–1917) Suleyman the Magnificent undertook considerable building works, particularly reconstructing the fortifications (1537–41) which can still be seen today. However, those who succeeded him let this fall into decay.

OUTSIDE THE WALLS, MODERN JERUSALEM. Toward the middle of the 19th century a growing population living under increasingly difficult conditions led the Jewish inhabitants to settle outside the city walls. Mishkenot Sha'ananim, Mea Shearim and Nahalat Shiva were some of the new quarters. It was also at this time that the Ottomans liberalized the purchase of land, allowing the Great Powers to gain access to the holy city through various buildings (hospitals, churches, monasteries, consulates, embassies, schools and houses). Then the European "colonies" began to appear, the German ● *294*, British ● *294*, Russian ● *214* and so on.

> "JERUSALEM THE HOLY, THREE TIMES HOLY. FOUR HUNDRED MILLION CHRISTIANS, MUSLIMS AND JEWS, TURN THEIR GAZE TO THE PRODIGIOUS CITY, RUINED TWENTY TIMES AND STILL STANDING." CHARLES LALLEMAND

JERUSALEM DIVIDED
From 1948 to 1967, the city was divided by a wall which was not always enough to protect the inhabitants on either side from gunfire. However in spite of this division the population continued to grow due to the influx of Palestinian refugees in the east, and the arrival of new immigrants in the west. In June 1967, the battle between Israelis and Jordanians for Jerusalem lasted three days and two nights and ended in a victory for the Jewish state, which immediately pulled down the wall.

GENERAL ALLENBY
General Allenby served at first in Africa before being sent to France in 1914. In June 1917 he was placed at the head of British forces in Palestine.

FROM THE BRITISH MANDATE TO THE PRESENT DAY. In 1917, General Allenby entered Jerusalem and inaugurated the era of the British Mandate ● 56. His campaign against the Ottomans took him to Jerusalem, Damascus, Aleppo and Megiddo where he won a definitive victory on October 30, 1918. Thus Count Allenby of Felixstowe also became Count of Megiddo. On arrival in Jerusalem he issued an edict in many languages announcing his intention to respect the triple sanctity of Jerusalem ● 43. The British installed an urban infrastructure (schools, administrative and military buildings, the sanitization of pipes and sewers). They also fixed the norms of construction (the use of the characteristic white "Jerusalem" stone). The 1948 war ● 57 left Jerusalem split by a wall: part of the town reverted to Jordan, while West Jerusalem became the capital of the State of Israel. The Mandelbaum Gate was then the only point of passage between East and West. It was pulled down in 1967 by Israeli troops ● 57 in the eastern part, although the city is still divided today. The thrice-holy city has however known a period of unparalleled growth, partly under the direction of Teddy Kollek, mayor from 1965 to 1993. The city has expanded both to the west and the east, and the apartment blocks perched on hillsides are now part of the landscape.

An impressive wall defines the Old City of Jerusalem. Its master builder, Sultan-Caliph Suleyman the Legislator, known in the west as "the Magnificent", built it between 1520 and 1566 on the lines of the Roman fortifications. The ramparts were intended to protect Jerusalem from later Bedouin raids or a Crusader offensive; at between 39 and 49 feet high, and roughly 5,330 yards long, with eight gates, they gave the city the shape of an irregular trapezium. In nearly five centuries, these fortifications have not changed significantly.

SULEYMAN THE MAGNIFICENT

Suleyman's (1494–1566) achievements were not limited to military conquests. The sovereign organized the vast Ottoman Empire and was raised to the rank of *Qanuni* (Legislator).

In a centralized state, where taxes were regularly collected, the immense resources on which Suleyman could draw allowed him to maintain a permanent army, and also to undertake works on a grand scale.

Along its whole length, t crenellated ramparts are pierced with embrasures.

FOUNDATIONS

The wall of Jerusalem was built on medieval foundations, themselves erected on the ruins of Herodian ramparts. Near Damascus Gate (**2**), you can make out two different strata: the perfectly jointed stone blocks with slight projections and joint lines (weighing several tons), of the 2nd century BC, and, above, Ottoman construction.

EASTERN WALL (D–A)

Exposed to the desert wind, the stone of the southern (**C–D**) and eastern (**D–A**) parts of the fortifications has a more golden appearance than the ramparts to the north and west.

A

NORTH WALL (A–B)

The fortifications boast monumental, massive gates, opening onto the main traffic routes [out]side, and flanked by [t]owers and bastions [w]ith projections and [r]ecesses. The north [w]all links the eastern (**D–A**) part of the [r]amparts to the Stork Tower, a square [to]wer recognizable by its carved seal in relief (below).

HEROD'S GATE (1)

Bab el-Sahireh ("the Gate which watches"), or Bab el-Zahireh ("flower gate"), is also called Herod's Gate. Convinced that the house next to this gate belonged to Herod Antipas, pilgrims gave it the name of this king. In the middle of the last century Ibrahim Pasha, the son of the Khedive of Egypt, partially bricked it up.

WESTERN WALL (B–C)

The western part of the fortifications, closing the city at Jaffa Road ▲ *339*, formed the section which was most exposed to attack. It encompasses "the citadel" Al Qads, restored by the Ottoman sovereign who was anxious to install his garrison there. He took care to preserve its autonomous systems of defense.

SOUTHERN WALL (C–D)

[Or]iginally this wall [wa]s to have been [bu]ilt further south: [Su]leyman the [Ma]gnificent was obsessed by the one idea of including all the holy places within the enclosure, and had thus planned to enclose Mount Zion in the quadrilateral. Lacking sufficient funds, however, notably from Franciscans, he was forced to move the wall further north.

ZION GATE (5)

Like Jaffa Gate and the Lion Gate, its layout makes you turn inside the outer gate, the idea being that assailants who penetrated the first gates would not be able to break through the second because they could not go back far enough. Arabs call this gate Bab el-Nabi Dahoud, "David's Gate", after the prophet. The original gate, built in 1540 still bears the marks of shells dating from 1948.

DAMASCUS GATE (2)

Bab el-Amud ("Gate of the Column") ● 122 is called Damascus Gate ▲ 280 since it gives onto the road which led to the Syrian capital. It was built between 1537 and 1538.

B

MAGHREB GATE (DUNG GATE) (6)

It owes its name to the community from the Maghreb, which settled below Haram el-Sharif at the end of the 12th century. It leads to the esplanade, opened up in 1967 and to Haram el-Sharif.

JAFFA GATE (4)

This gate was built in 1538 and faces onto the road to Hebron. The Arabs therefore call it Bab el-Khalil ("Gate of the Friend") ▲ 220. It was called the Jaffa Gate in the last century because it opens onto the road to the town of that name ▲ 220.

D

GOLDEN GATE (7)

The Golden Gate has been bricked up for more than a millennium because a Muslim tradition holds that one day a conqueror will enter through this gate to destroy the city. Another Muslim belief is that the double opening (one is called Bab el-Tawba or "Gate of Repentance" and the other Bab el-Rahma or "Gate of Mercy") will be the first to open before the Messiah on the day of the Resurrection.

DISCOVERING JERUSALEM

...salem "buried in ...mountains", ...ounded "by a ...rinth of shifting ...", reveals itself to ...traveler at the ...last moment. ...an initial ...ression of its ...y facets, it is ...th climbing the ...s that surround ...city, or walking in ...valleys at the foot ...ts walls. From the ...nt of Olives, ...nt Scopus or ...from the Kidron ...ey, the panorama ...arvelous. In 1830 ...d Roberts (right) ...ted the city. To

convey its nebulous quality he chose to paint it from the hills to the valleys: Jerusalem seen from the south (top); Jerusalem from the north (above, left); Jerusalem seen from the village of Bethany (above, right); and Jerusalem seen from the Kidron Valley (left).

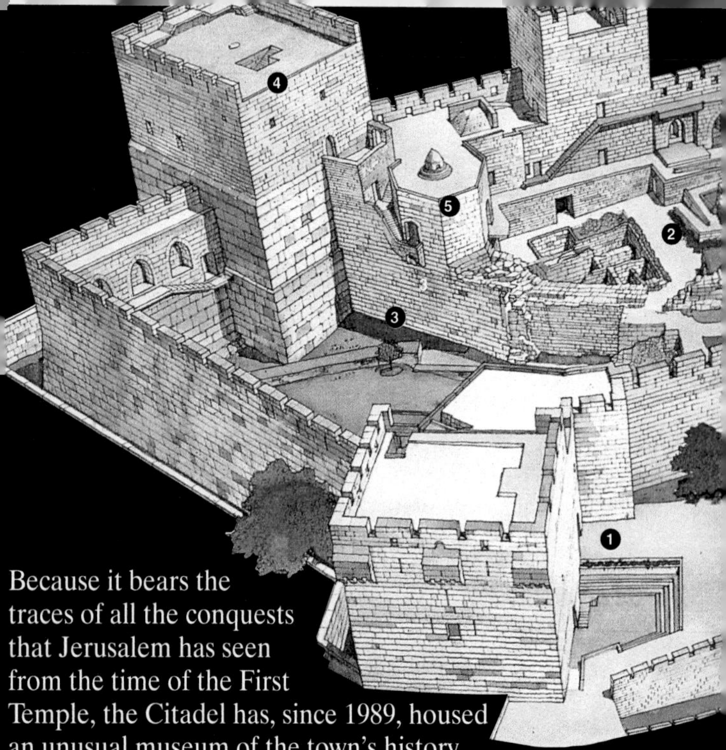

Because it bears the
traces of all the conquests
that Jerusalem has seen
from the time of the First
Temple, the Citadel has, since 1989, housed
an unusual museum of the town's history,
the Tower of David. Its name, however, owes nothing to King
David: this is the result of a faulty interpretation of the writings
of Flavius Josephus.

URBAN EVOLUTION
The museum does not
display authentic
items or documents,
but retells the
history of
Jerusalem. This
diorama is a
reconstruction
of Jerusalem
at the time of
King David
in the 10th
century BC.
The ramparts
that protected
the city marked
out an area that no
longer corresponds to
the Old City of today
▲ 232.

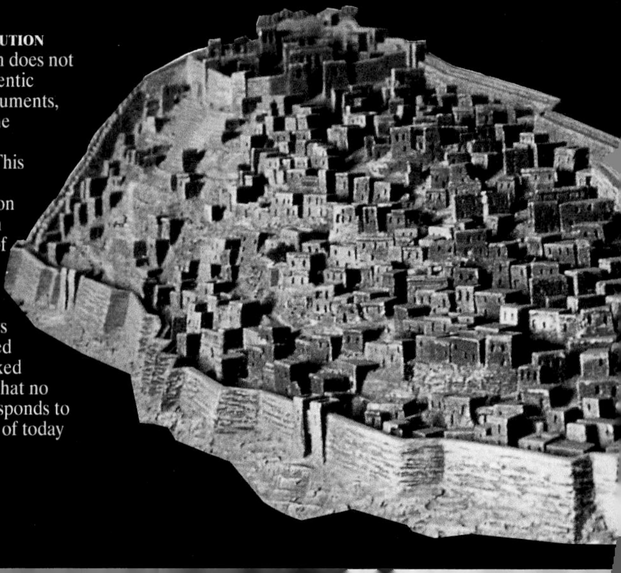

6

RELIGION

The museum traces the history of Jerusalem through models of places of worship built by adherents of the three religions: the Herodian Temple (above), the Holy Sepulcher and the Dome of the Rock.

1. MUSEUM ENTRANCE
2. ARCHEOLOGICAL GARDEN
3. REMAINS OF THE HASMONEAN WALLS
4. PHASAEL'S TOWER (HERODIAN ERA)
5. BASE OF AN ANCIENT MUSLIM TOWER
6. TOWER OF DAVID

CITY LIFE

It is easy to imagine the life of Jerusalemites in centuries past: pilgrims, monks and inhabitants of the 19th century crowd round a fountain at Haram al-Sharif.

HISTORY

The museum's animated movies show how the city was marked by different conquerors. The Church of St Anne (shown in the diorama above) was built during the Crusades and was turned into a *medresa* (school) by the Ottomans.

ARCHITECTURE

The architectural development of the city is shown by restoring buildings to their original state. This model is the only representation of the Holy Sepulcher ▲ 272 in the 4th century.

The photographic studio of Palestinian artist Khalil Raad at the beginning of the century at the Jaffa Gate.

JAFFA GATE
Almost a month after landing in the Holy Land, Lamartine ● *150* arrived at the Jaffa Gate, which, because of the plague, was shut: "The gate to Bethlehem, dominated by two towers crowned with Gothic crenellations, but deserted and silent like those gates of abandoned castles, was opened before us. We stayed still for some minutes, looking at it." Almost seventy years later in 1898, a gap nearly 40 feet wide was made between Jaffa Gate and the Citadel to allow Kaiser Wilhelm II ▲ *242* to enter the old city in an automobile.

Dominated by the Citadel ▲ *252*, the JAFFA GATE, which today opens onto an area dotted with little cafés and souvenir stores, was once the end of the road from the port of Jaffa ▲ *339* to Jerusalem. At the end of the last century, the vast square, the vibrant heart of the city, held establishments intended to house travelers and pilgrims ● *88*, who were increasing in number. Thus the NEW IMPERIAL HOTEL was built by the Greek Orthodox church in 1889. PETRA HOTEL nearby, the first modern hotel in the Old City, houses the offices of the Christian Information Center. The first Anglican buildings in Palestine (CHRIST CHURCH and its neo-Gothic guest quarters) rose up around a paved courtyard. When they were built, it was necessary to import from London the pieces needed

for the basic structure because there was not enough wood in Jerusalem. From Jaffa Gate the Street of the Chain, which crosses the old city from west to east, opens onto the four picturesque quarters of the Armenian, Christian, Muslim, and Jewish communities.

THE JEWISH QUARTER

This is a veritable network of alleyways full of synagogues, Yeshivot, small interior courtyards, archeological ruins from which, here and there, bell towers and minarets rise proudly. Exploration of the Jewish quarter culminates in the open space in front of the *Kotel* ("Western Wall") ▲ 260. Severely tested during the fighting in 1948, this small area suffered much destruction and was then deserted by its inhabitants when the city was partitioned. In 1967, the Israeli government undertook to renovate it, taking great care to preserve its historical remains.

THE CARDO ● 124. From the Street of the Chain, Habad road leads to the Cardo, built in the 5th century by the Byzantines, at the time when they undertook to reconstruct the whole city according to the Roman model of *Aelia Capitolina ● 51*. The old artery appears on the Madaba map, which has been reproduced on one of the walls of the covered part of the Cardo. The Roman-Byzantine axis, 72 feet wide, probably went from the Zion Gate ▲ 244 to the Damascus Gate ▲ 280. It can be best explored from the foot of the marvelously preserved columns at the level of the city at the time. Only a part of the Cardo has been restored. Through glass screens between various shops you can see the remains of fortifications from the time of the First Temple and of the Hasmoneans ● 48. Farther along the Cardo, right to the south of the present-day Jewish quarter, was the NEA (NEW) CHURCH, or the "New Church of Saint Mary", built by Emperor Justinian in 543. Destroyed by an earthquake, the Byzantine building was uncovered in 1967. Nothing remains of the church except for a few traces of one of its apsidal chapels preserved *in situ* and which you can see at the foot of the walls, to the east of the Zion Gate.

THE CONTRASTS OF THE OLD CITY
A maze of narrow roads, lined by small stalls which give the city its oriental atmosphere, begins on both sides of the Cardo, an alley marked by western influences.

EVERYDAY BUSINESS
Before the city spread beyond its walls, the Jaffa Gate was the meeting point for merchants from east and west: today, as in the 19th century, it is a street of commerce with banks, hotels, travel agencies and many stores.

MUSEUM OF THE OLD YISHUV
Retraces the life of the people of the Jewish quarter in the 19th century. Reconstructed interiors make it possible to compare Sephardic and Ashkenazic ways of life.

SYNAGOGUES. Most of the synagogues in the Jewish quarter were destroyed during the 1948–9 War of Independence ● 57, but those which could be saved have been restored. The RAMBAN SYNAGOGUE is so-called from its founder in 1267, *Rabbi Moshe ben Nachman*(ides) (initials = Ramban). He was forced to flee Spain because he had been the victor in a religious *disputatio* with Christian theologians, and had settled in the Holy Land in 1267. The synagogue was almost certainly built on the foundations of a Crusader church but its ceiling rests on four very old Byzantine pillars. For many centuries it was the only place of Jewish worship in the city, so the core of the Jewish community formed around the building. Nearby you will find the HURVA SYNAGOGUE ★. The stone arch, which is all that remains, justifies its name: in Hebrew, *hurva* means "ruins". It was established in 1700 by Rabbi Yehuda Hanassi and his disciples, immigrants from Poland who bought land from the Muslims. The adjoining minaret was put up shortly after by the Ottomans, who were anxious to assert the rule of Islam in the Jewish city.

The "Hurva" only took its final form in the 19th century when Moses Montefiore acquired the land and built a splendid synagogue. Then it served all the Ashkenazic inhabitants ● 82 of Jerusalem, its dome dominating the whole Jewish quarter until it was destroyed in 1948. The complex of SEPHARDIC SYNAGOGUES was built from the 16th century onward, by Jews expelled from Spain. Renovations began in 1969, and the four buildings, today joined into one, are below ground because, at the time they were built, Ottomans required that synagogues must not be on the same level as mosques. Finally, the KARAITE SYNAGOGUE was built in the 15th century, when the members of the sect bearing the same name settled in the Jewish quarter. The Karaites split off from rabbinic Judaism in the 8th century to form a sect because they only respected the written law and did not accept the validity of the Talmud ● 78 or the Mishna ● 78. Adjoining the synagogue is a small museum devoted to them.

THE BATTEI MAHASSEH. This is the name of the organization which in the 19th century raised money to build this group of dwellings for the poor of the Old City. The building financed by Wolf Rothschild in 1871 is certainly the most remarkable in the complex. It has beautiful regular arches on three different levels.

THE HERODIAN QUARTER. Excavations carried out in the 1970's revealed a large number of dwellings from Herodian times. Today they make up a museum. The small rooms of the houses, decorated with paintings, stucco work and remarkably restored mosaics, reveal the Roman influence on Jewish dwellings at the time of the Second Temple. However, the *mikvehs* ▲ *213* (ritual baths) were built strictly according to the tenets of Jewish law.

THE BURNT HOUSE. After 1967, archeologists uncovered many houses burned down by the Romans in AD 70 when they destroyed the Second Temple and the residential quarter of Jerusalem, then situated in the upper town. The house which is now called the Burnt House belonged to the Kathros family. This rich abode had no fewer than seven rooms. The many items found there – ink pots, cooking utensils, prayer objects, money and weights – are displayed, and a short film traces their history.

SEPHARDIC SYNAGOGUES
These paintings recreate the atmosphere which must have prevailed inside the four synagogues of the Sephardic complex ● *82*. The first bears the name of Rabbi Johanan ben Zakkai, the scholarly founder of the center of Yavneh ● *51* after the fall of the second Temple; it is worth noting because of its holy double ark which houses the Ten Commandments ● *49* in marble, imported from Livorno. The synagogue of Elijah, the oldest of the four, houses a chair where the prophet is said to have sat one Yom Kippur ● *80*, before disappearing. The central synagogue, the smallest of the four was, it is said, linked by a tunnel to the tomb of King David. Lastly the Istambuli Synagogue, where Turkish Jews came to pray, stands out because of its Spanish windows and its Italian furniture.

The last remains of the Temple have always been called the "Western Wall" in Hebrew; but, because the people of Israel shed so many tears there, Christians in the Middle Ages called it the "Wailing Wall". Jews believe that the Shechina (Divine Presence) soars above it. The dew drops that cover the branches of hyssop and wild caper growing between the rocks are likened to tears shed by the wall for the sorrows of Israel. It was the tears of men and women, though, that moved Loti when he went to Jerusalem in 1895: "Against the wall of the Temple, against the last debris of its past splendor," he wrote, "are the lamentations of Jeremiah which they all repeat . . . 'Because of the Temple which is destroyed,' cries the Rabbi. 'We sit alone and we weep!' replies the crowd. 'Because of our walls which are fallen,' 'We sit alone and we weep!' 'Because of our majesty which has passed, because of our great men who are no longer alive.' 'We sit alone and we weep!'" The wall has become a symbol of hope, and men and women slip pieces of paper on which their prayers are written between the stones.

THE WESTERN WALL (HA-KOTEL HA-MA'ARAVI)

This is the last vestige of the western part of the ramparts that surrounded the holy Temple of the Jews, built by Solomon and destroyed by Nebuchadnezzar ● 46, rebuilt by the Babylonian exiles and by Herod, and then burned down by Titus ● 50. From the day after the destruction of the sanctuary, Jews gathered to weep and pray on these ruins. They later had to pay the Romans for right of access. But when the cupola of the Dome of the Rock ▲ 284 covered them, there only remained one side of the holy structure that had once housed the Holy of Holies: the *Kotel* then became a symbol of the Jewish people.

Most of the wall's huge stones, which rise 50 feet above the ground, come from the Second Temple, while the foundations date from the time of Solomon. In 1967 a large number of buildings and houses were destroyed to free the land and the Jews, who had not had access to the Old City since 1948, were once again able to gather at the *Kotel*. Since then lamentations, murmurs and whispers are heard there daily. The *Kotel* is especially busy at the beginning of Shabbat and on the High Holy Days. Each year on the 9th of Av (July–August), the anniversary of the destruction of the Temple, at least ten thousand people gather at the *Kotel* to say prayers of mourning.

PRAYER
Two places where portions of the Torah are read every day around desks and chairs have been laid out at the foot of the *Kotel*, one strictly for men, the other for women.

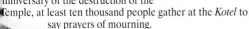

Herod, who wanted to win the Jews' favor, decided to rebuild their sanctuary. On Mount Moriah, the site of Solomon's First Temple, he completely razed the structures which had been put up by the Babylonian exiles. To enlarge the holy enclosure, he banked up the hill and made deep foundations: the mount – which today is the site of the Haram al-Sharif – was once home to the Second Temple, which was very grand with its columns of white marble and its gates of silver and gold; the western wall is a part of its immense retaining walls.

GREEK INSCRIPTION
Inside the first enclosure this inscription forbade Gentiles to cross, under pain of death, the edge of the holy area which enclosed the Holy of Holies.

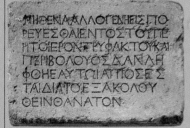

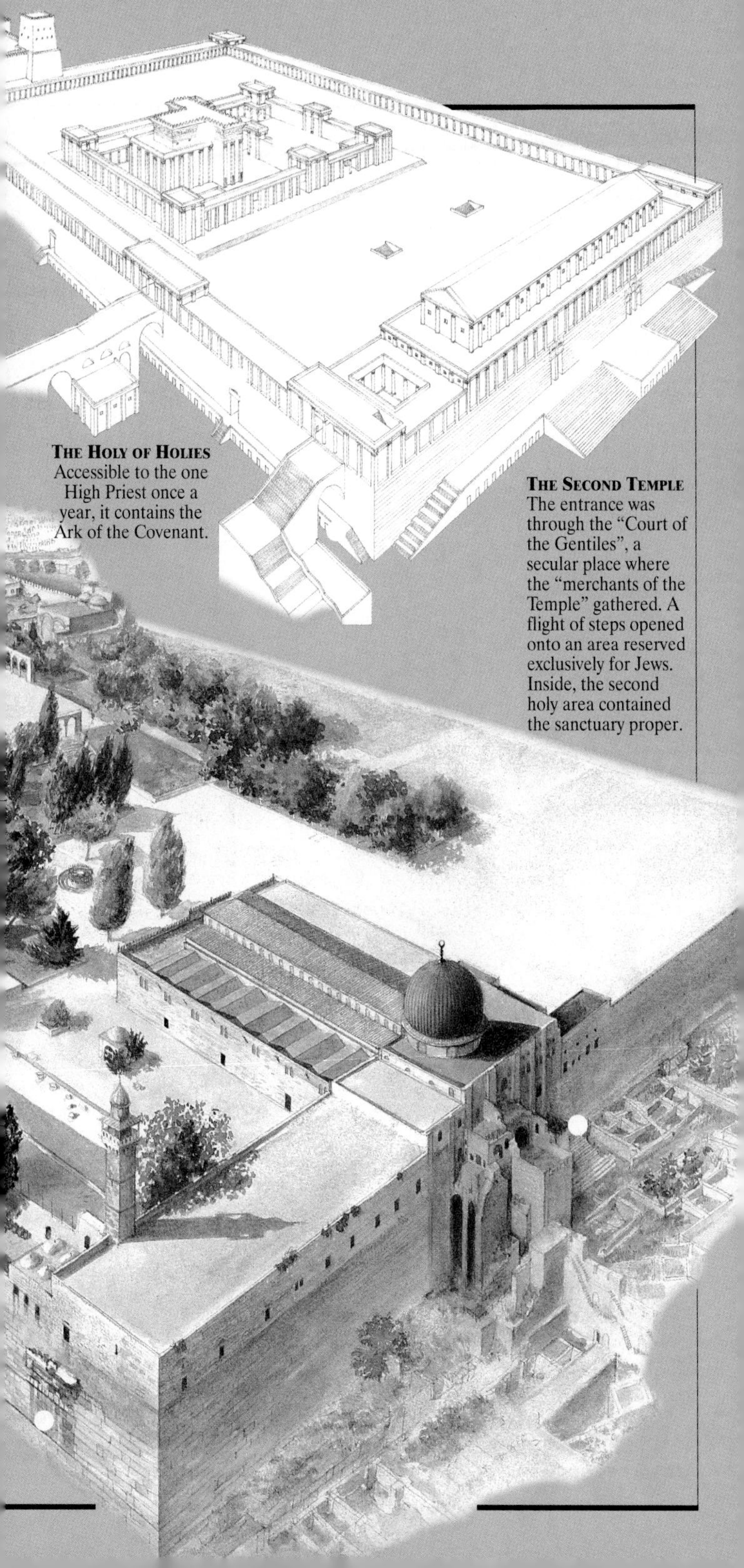

THE HOLY OF HOLIES
Accessible to the one
High Priest once a
year, it contains the
Ark of the Covenant.

THE SECOND TEMPLE
The entrance was
through the "Court of
the Gentiles", a
secular place where
the "merchants of the
Temple" gathered. A
flight of steps opened
onto an area reserved
exclusively for Jews.
Inside, the second
holy area contained
the sanctuary proper.

Hasidic costumes tend to mirror the style of dress of 19th-century Eastern Europe. The religious sect of Hasidism encompasses communities from many different regions, each with its own ideas and customs. Men's and women's costumes vary according to their age, family situation, and the particular sect to which they belong. After his bar mitzvah, the hat is a sign that the young boy has been initiated into the religious community. Festive clothes are generally worn on the eve of Shabbat, when many Hasidim may be found at the *Kotel*.

A married Jerusalemite woman covers her hair with a white scarf ready for the Shabbat.

THE HASIDIC JERUSALEMITE WOMAN
She can be identified by thick, dark-colored tights and her headscarf.

This Jerusalemite is wearing his Shabbat clothes, a striped, satin coat with a round collar.

THE YOUNG BOY
Before his bar mitzvah he wears shorts and *tsitsit*. His *peyot* are not cut.

For Shabbat and festivals the women wear colored dresses, thick light-colored tights, and, if married, a white headscarf.

HASID FROM TOLDOT AHARONA
He does not wear a hat but a *kipa*. His stockings cover his calves.

HASID FROM GUR
Dressed for Shabbat, he sports the *spidic streimel*, a hat with a fur border.

A YOUNG LITHUANIAN
Renowned for his concern for elegance, the young Lithuanian pushes his *peyot* behind his ears.

HASID FROM SATMAR (HUNGARY)
His hat, stockings which reach to his knees, and his *peyot* cut in line with the chin, indicate his origins.

YOUNG GIRL
Until sixteen years of age Hasidic girls keep their hair braided in two plaits.

HASID FROM BELGIUM
His brown coat and black stockings and his *spidic streimel* are characteristic.

Hasidim from Toldot Aharona can be identified by their white *kipot* (right).

LUBAVITCH
He wears trousers and a long coat.

HASID FROM GUR
This man (right) belonging to the Gur movement of Poland is married. This is evident from his hat and trousers which reach to his calves. Like the child (left) he leaves his *peyot* outside his head-covering.

263

▲ THE ARMENIAN QUARTER

MOUNT ARARAT
This mountain range on the border of the Armenian Republic, Turkey and Iran, at the heart of historic Armenia, is the traditional site where Noah's ark came to rest after the flood. It has a sacred value for the Armenian people. The characteristic hood of the Armenian monks recalls

the shape of this volcanic cone.

The Armenian codex in the National Library shows that the Armenian Church of Jerusalem in the 5th century used a calendar setting out all the events in the liturgical year. This unique document has made it possible for

us to become familiar with the holy days celebrated at the dawn of Christianity, as well as the places of worship. Saint Thonos' chapel contains four thousand Armenian manuscripts of great historical value. Many date from the Middle Ages.

The Armenian quarter is in the southwest part of the Old City, between Jaffa Gate and Zion Gate, near the Citadel of David. The Armenian presence in the Holy Land dates back to the 4th century when, after AD 301, the small kingdom of the Caucasus foothills adopted Christianity as the state religion. Pilgrims have come in successive waves (especially after the Massacre of 1915). By the 7th century there were already seventy Armenian monasteries in the Holy Land, founded and maintained by princely families. At the time of the Crusades the Armenian kingdom of Cilicia (now in southern Turkey) kept close links with the Crusader kingdoms, giving rise to dynastic, cultural and economic relations which continued until the fall of the Cilician kingdom in the 14th century. At that time, Armenians in Jerusalem were so important that special codes relating to their population were integrated into the law books.

Written sources from Crusader times reveal the existence of an Armenian quarter and there, the Cathedral of St James. Under Ottoman rule the number of Armenian pilgrims kept increasing. Ottoman generosity, plus the need for additional housing, contributed to the expansion of the Armenian quarter. In the 19th century the Patriarchate benefited from the dynamism of some patriarchs who assured

its economic stability through the acquisition and development of land outside the city walls which provided regular income. Today the Armenian community of Jerusalem consists of about three thousand people, mainly craftsmen, potters or goldsmiths.

THE CATHEDRAL OF ST JAMES. The cathedral was the first building to have been built in the Armenian quarter (in the year 430) and houses the tomb of Saint James the Greater, the first apostle martyr, brother of Saint John the Evangelist (his apostolate in Spain, which gave birth to the belief that his body was buried at St John of Compostella, stems from a later story). Tradition holds that the tomb of Saint James the Minor, Christ's cousin and the first bishop of Jerusalem, is under the main altar. Contemporary with Judeo-Christianity, the cathedral holds the tombs of the Fathers of the Church, like Saint Macarius, bishop of Jerusalem. In the northern part of the cathedral, where the architecture is essentially medieval, there are two 5th-century chapels with barrel vaults which escaped the destruction following the Persian invasion in 614. The church was originally oriented to the north, with its main entrance in the south; you can still see the traces of three arched transepts. The cathedral, built in Byzantine times, was enlarged during the Crusades, but its structure has not been modified in over 850 years. The ornamentation dates from different periods, mostly later than the 15th century. The church, always lit by 350 silver lamps given by different Armenian villages, has no seating, conforming to ancient practice. You will find beautiful examples of marquetry – carved wood from the 17th century – particularly the altar and the pulpit which has wooden panels encrusted with pearls, tortoiseshell and ivory. The walls are covered with hundreds of scenes from the Old and New Testaments, and dozens of carved votive crosses, called *khatchbar*. The oldest, dating from the 12th century, are on the western wall. In the Armenian quarter there are other places of worship like the CHURCH OF THE ARCHANGELS, surrounded by a convent in a medieval building, which according to tradition was the first of Christ's prisons. Covered by a chapel with Byzantine foundations, the HOUSE OF CAIAPHAS sheltered the high priest who delivered Jesus to Pontius Pilate; in its courtyard, Peter three times denied Christ (John 18); it is near the ARMENIAN CEMETERY.

The walls of the cathedral are decorated with thousands of white faience tiles from Kutaba. In the 18th century Armenian craftsmen from this town were sent to decorate the Dome of the Rock in Jerusalem where they profited from their stay by embellishing many Armenian churches with the fruits of their talent.

THE SEMINARY
The interior courtyards in many of the buildings are the most striking characteristic of the architecture in the Armenian quarter. The present-day Seminary (above), founded in 1975, is on the site of Herod's palace. The old theological seminary, dating from 1853, has since been transformed into a museum for the history of the Armenian people.

ST STEPHEN'S GATE
Also known as the
"Lions' Gate" as it
shows two lions, the
emblem of Sultan
Baybars.

POOLS OF BETHESDA
Water was used in the
Temple not only for
daily needs, but also
at ceremonial times.
Ablutions were
prescribed by the
laws of purity for the
officiant and also to
purify holy
containers, clothes
and sullied people.
According to
Christian tradition,
it was by the Pool of
Bethesda that Jesus
cured a man of
paralysis
(John 5:1-13).

THE HOLY SEPULCHER

In the northwest part of the Old City, the Christian quarter
developed around sites linked to the life and death of Jesus:
the Via Dolorosa and the Holy Sepulcher. Diverse
Christian communities ● 88 own many convents and
churches there, and inns have been open to
pilgrims for centuries.

THE CHURCH OF ST ANNE. Given by the
Ottoman sultan to France in 1856 for taking
part in the Crimean War, this church was
built by the Franks on a spot charged with
Biblical associations. Two cisterns for
holding rain water were dug there in the 7th
and 3rd centuries BC in order to fulfill the
needs of the Temple. Linked by an aqueduct
to one large reservoir near the temple, in the
time of Herod the Great, they preserved
their holy character and the *mikvehs* (Jewish
ritual baths) ▲ 213 took the name of the
POOLS OF BETHESDA. The house of Anne and
Joachim in which Mary is said to have grown up,
was reputedly on this site, as the remains excavated
below the current church show. After 135 the Romans
filled in the cisterns and built a temple to Asclepios ● 50 on
the ruins of which the Byzantines built a large basilica in the
5th century dedicated to the Virgin, and destroyed in 1009 by
Caliph Al-Hakim. It was on this site that the Crusaders built a
large and beautiful Romanesque church which is still admired
today. In 1192 when Salah al-Din took Jerusalem, the church
and convent next to it (of which fragments of the décor of the
cloister remain) was turned into a Qur'anic school ▲ 252,
then gradually abandoned. Given to the White Fathers in
1856, the church has been restored. Excavations have been
carried out and a museum opened.

THE "ANTONIA". This fortress, of which nothing remains, was
built from 37 to 35 BC by Herod the Great. Its name comes
from Mark Antony, who, after his victory at the Battle of
Philippi, received the task of governing the Near East
conquered by Rome. The *Antonia* covered a large space which
spilled onto the current Via Dolorosa to the right and the left
▲ 268. At the place where the present-day Omariyeh College
is, the fortress protected the northwest angle of the Temple of
Herod. In AD 70 Titus' troops besieged the fortress ● 50 and
destroyed it.

HEROD'S FORTRESS
"He had this rock encrusted with marble from top to bottom, as much for the beauty as to make it so slippery that you could neither go up it nor down. Although it was so strong on the outside, inside there were so many living quarters, baths and rooms which could hold a large number of people that it could pass for a superb palace and the offices were so beautiful and so comfortable that you could have mistaken it for a small town." This is how *Antonia*, shown above, was described by Flavius Josephus in his *Wars of the Jews against the Romans*, 5, 238 ff.

CONVENT OF FLAGELLATION. According to Christian tradition, it was here that Jesus was flogged. The convent, built by the Franciscans (who were present at holy sites from the 13th century) contains a Museum of Archeology and History.

ECCE HOMO ● *122.* The arch of Ecce Homo frames the Via Dolorosa and overhangs the road. Probably dating from AD 37–44, the right side of the pillar and the small arch to the north are visible in the chapel of the Convent of the Sisters of Zion.

THE STATIONS OF THE CROSS. The first pilgrims to visit the places of the Passion were traditionally the women who surrounded Christ and some of his disciples, who began to commemorate these places when news of the Resurrection spread. It was during the Middle Ages that it became an object of veneration. Its starting point was fixed in the 13th century at the *Antonia*, where the Roman governor, Pontius Pilate, was based, particularly at the time of Passover. (Today it seems more likely that Pilate's praetorium was situated at the royal palace.) It ends at the Calvary (Golgotha), the place of executions, which in Jesus' time stretched out above the ramparts ▲ *244.* The route does not follow an established historical course: the siting of the fourteen stations is arbitrary, and Jesus' three falls, like his encounter with Veronica, do not actually figure in the Gospels. In addition, the ground of the Via Dolorosa was later raised several feet when Hadrian built a temple to Roman divinities.

Some have claimed that patterns traced on the paving stones were carved by Roman soldiers – those who were guarding Jesus – as part of a game. This interpretation is, however, contradicted by archeology which shows that the slabs date from the 2nd century AD.

The Arch of Ecce Homo, Via Dolorosa.

▲ THE VIA DOLOROSA

Jesus was crucified close to Jerusalem. The date is uncertain (perhaps AD 30, perhaps AD 33). The death of this man, little noticed at the time, changed the course of history. For Christians the "Son of God" began a radically different era with his sacrifice that day announcing freedom from sin and death by his resurrection. In memory of Jesus, "the Christ", Christian pilgrims from the whole world travel the Via Dolorosa from Antonia, the praetorium which may have been Pontius Pilate's seat of government, to the basilica of the Holy Sepulcher, built on Golgotha, the "hill of the Skull". The route commemorates the Passion of the Son of God, announced by the prophets, but it is also a route symbolizing the bearing of the cross with Christ.

THE ART OF THE ICON Icons frequently appear in churches, in the decoration of ceilings and walls, and particularly on the iconostasis, the screen separating the sanctuary from the congregation. They usually depict Christ, saints or scenes from religious history. Icons are believed to contain some essence of the saint or mystery depicted and are therefore venerated. Some are said to be endowed with miraculous powers. The very creation of the icon is itself a religious procedure, often preceded by a time of prayer and fasting.

> **"THIS ROAD OF SORROW . . . THE MYSTERY OF THE SHADOWS TRANSFIGURES IT; ITS NAME ALONE, WHICH I SAY TO MYSELF, IS HOLY MUSIC; THE GREAT MEMORY SEEMS TO SING EVERYWHERE IN THE STONES . . ."**
> PIERRE LOTI

«VIA DOLOROSA»

THIRTEENTH STATION

JESUS, DESCENDED FROM THE CROSS, IS PLACED IN HIS MOTHER'S ARMS. Mary was told, "Thou shalt bring forth a son . . . God shall give unto him the throne of his father David . . . and of his kingdom there shall be no end."

FOURTEENTH STATION

JESUS IS PLACED IN THE TOMB Passover began at sunset on this day. A tomb was nearby. Its owner, Joseph of Arimathea, offered it and, with the permission of Pilate, the body of Jesus was placed in it. The stone was rolled on top.

In the face of total human defeat, she whom the church designates by the name of the Blessed Virgin knows the Scriptures: "Love is strong like death."

CRUCIFIXION

Later Saint John wrote, "They crucified him, and two others with him, on either side one, and Jesus in the midst. And Pilate wrote a title, and put it on the cross. And the writing was, Jesus of Nazareth the King of the Jews. This title then read many of the Jews; for the place where Jesus was crucified was nigh to the city; and it was written in Hebrew, and Greek, and Latin."

Position of the Via Dolorosa, inside the Old City of Jerusalem.

NINTH STATION
JESUS FALLS FOR THE THIRD TIME
"So that I could achieve this flight to the divine I had to fly so much, that I lost myself from sight, and despite everything in

this feat, in full flight I weakened, but love made him so high . . . When I went higher, my eyes were dazzled and my strength over-come, which happened in the dark, but love gave spring of a blind man and with a jump I was so high, so high . . . However much higher I came, from this so sublime flight, even lower and exhausted and shattered I found myself, I said nothing could attain it, and I threw down myself so low, so low, that was so high, so high . . . In a strange way, a thousand flights I made from one flight, for the hope of heaven, so much obtains as is hoped, I only wished for this flight and there was no failure in hope, for I was so high so high."
St John of the Cross

TENTH STATION
JESUS IS DEPRIVED OF HIS CLOTHES
The son of God speaks to his father through the words of

the psalmist – at this moment he speaks with his whole body – "You wanted neither sacrifice nor oblation, you gave me one body, you did not agree on either holocaust or sacrifice, so I said, 'Here I am I come . . .' in order that thy will be done O Lord."

ELEVENTH STATION
JESUS IS PUT ON THE CROSS
Jesus' words resound: "And I, raised from the earth, will draw all men to me."

In these words he indicated the manner of his death. For a Christian believer, the whole world enters through these words into the reality of the crucifixion.

TWELFTH STATION
JESUS DIES
The last testimony of he who had said "the father and I are one" gave forth this terrible cry: "My God, my God, why hast thou forsaken me?" Then "Jesus cried with a loud voice, and gave up the ghost." The apostle Paul was to say, "Jesus, of divine condition . . . becoming like men . . . and having behaved like a man, humbled himself even more, obedient until death on a cross."

GREEK CHOIR (14)

The raised wall between the pillars of the Catholicon, an old church of the 12th century, and the iconostases built for the needs of the Greek Orthodox have changed the sobriety of the Romanesque choir. The high partitions and bricked up windows of the chapels of the ambulatory have finally managed to stifle the interior of the church.

The Holy Sepulcher today (**D**)

The Holy Sepulcher has private and communal areas. The former are given to each of the seven communities who share the church and its maintenance. The communal parts are under the authority of the Armenian, Greek Orthodox, and Latin churches.

POSSESSIONS

- ETHIOPIANS
- ARMENIANS
- COPTS
- GREEKS
- LATINS
- MUSLIMS
- COMMUNAL AREAS

CLOISTER OF THE CANONS (22)

Outside the church there was a cloister linked to the Romanesque ambulatory by a direct passage. The area, used as a terrace for the chapel of St Helena, is occupied by a community of Ethiopian monks.

INVENTION OF THE CROSS (21)

In a quarry dug in a ditch parallel to the ramparts of the Jewish city, the empress Helena built the chapel (**20**) which bears her name. The crypt, situated in a deeper spot, was called the chapel of the Invention of the Cross because Saint Helena was said to have found a pile of "wood of torment" thrown into the quarry on the eve of Good Friday (an incident which the Church celebrates with the name of the Invention of the Holy Cross).

THE ETHIOPIAN ORTHODOX MONASTERY.

Opening onto the terrace of the Holy Sepulcher, a door decorated with an Ethiopian inscription gives access to a long chapel, then to a collection of small houses built inside the ruins of the Crusader cloisters, from where you can see the beginnings of the arches. In the middle of the "village", the crypt of St Helena is lit by a skylight around which the Ethiopian monks circulate on the night of Good Friday to commemorate the search for Christ's body.

THE MURISTAN.

South of the Holy Sepulcher, at the spot where the buildings of the souvenir market were built in the beginning of the 20th century, Charlemagne obtained permission from the caliph Haroun al-Rashid to build a lodging place for pilgrims from Latin lands, a consecrated church and a library. Destroyed by the caliph al-Hakim in 1009, this set of buildings was restored from 1063 by merchants from Amalfi who added three churches and their hospitals: St Mary the Latin (now the CHURCH OF THE REDEMPTION) was for men, ST MARY THE LITTLE, reserved for women, was at the spot of the current fountain. The church of St John the Baptist, administered by Benedictine monks and nuns, welcomed the poor. In 1099 several knights wounded when the city was captured were cared for at the Church of St John the Baptist, the oldest church in Jerusalem ● *112.* Some of them stayed to devote their lives to the sick; they are the founders of the Knights of the Order of the Hospital of St John, which became the military order of the Hospitallers.

ETHIOPIAN PRIEST
The presence of the Ethiopian Orthodox in Jerusalem is long-standing. This country, with Armenia, was the first to adopt Christianity as the religion of the state ● *84.*

THE HOSPITALLERS IN MURISTAN
Having taken Jerusalem, Salah al-Din accepted in 1187 that ten Hospitallers should stay near the remaining sick. Thanks to a nephew of the Kurdish chief, part of the premises continued to function as a hospice. In the 16th century, the hospital complex being completely destroyed, Suleyman the Magnificent reused the stones to build the city wall. The Muristan quarter (right) remained in a state of ruin until the beginning of the 20th century.

THE CHRISTIAN QUARTER ▲

TOWARD THE MOUNT OF OLIVES ★

This long "plateau" lies to the east of the Old City, from which it is separated by the Kidron Valley. For a long time it has been both a point of passage and a burial place. Graves were dug there from the time of the Jebusites in the 2nd millennium BC. Then, having captured the city from them, the Judeans placed their dead there in collective "cave-tombs". Today the Jewish cemetery has been greatly enlarged. According to the tenets of Christianity, Judaism and Islam, this will be the place of the Last Judgment.

TOMB OF THE VIRGIN. Steps on either side of the TOMB OF 15TH-CENTURY ARAB HISTORIAN MUJIR AL-DIN, lead to the terrace on which the door giving access to the tomb of Mary,

THE GOLDEN GATE
This Byzantine edifice decorated with sculpture can be seen from the Mount of Olives (above). It is a replica of the Golden Gate in Constantinople, built on the spot of the Gate of Susa, the sacred entrance of the Jews to the city.

THE JEWISH CEMETERY
This necropolis (left) contains Jewish remains in addition to Jebusite and Judean tombs. Until 135 Christians who were Jewish in origin could be buried there.

mother of Jesus, opens. There, according to Christian tradition, the body of the Virgin was placed – not buried – during her Dormition, until her Assumption. It was only in 451 that the site was reserved for this "Dormition". At the end of the 6th century a church was said by pilgrims to exist on this spot. Then in 670 the pilgrim Arculf described a church whose lower level was covered by a rounded stone vault, just like the upper level. This last was destroyed and rebuilt several times. The CRYPT, partly dug out of the rock, served both as a necropolis for some members of the families of the Latin kings of Jerusalem, including Queen Melisande, who died in 1161.

GETHSEMANE. It was in this garden planted with olive trees that Jesus spent the last moments before his arrest. The first Christians were already holding regular gatherings there, when a church was built between 379 and 384. This church was destroyed by an earthquake. The Crusaders later built an oratory on the site, then a church with three apses which touched the "ROCK OF THE AGONY". The Crusader building was abandoned around 1345 and subsequently fell into ruins. It was not until the beginning of the 20th century that the present basilica was built. It covers and protects the rock, as well as the remains of BYZANTINE MOSAICS and some elements of Crusader architecture.

GETHSEMANE
It was in this garden (below) that Christ, wracked with doubt and the anguish of the coming torment, suffered the agony of finally accepting his Passion and his death. The kiss of Judas, identifying Jesus to those seeking him, was to mark the true beginning of his way to the Cross.

277

CHURCH OF ST MARY MAGDALENE. The old path with stone steps leading to the top probably ran close to this charming building with bulbous cupolas, erected at the end of the 19th century by the Russian Orthodox. It lends an element of fantasy to the severe hillside of the Mount of Olives.

"DOMINUS FLEVIT". Close to this place where Jesus cried for Jerusalem, the Franciscans built a small chapel in 1881. Excavations in 1954 revealed the traces of a 5th-century monastery as well as those of a cemetery used by the Jebusites from 1600 to 1300 BC. The present-day church was built in 1955 on the layout of the Byzantine chapel. Some of the mosaic fragments of this chapel have been preserved.

MOSQUE-CHURCH OF THE ASCENSION. Christ's rise to the heavens was celebrated from the 4th century on the Mount of Olives. The first church was built before 392 in the shape of a rotunda around a rock where Christ's feet left their imprint. The building was converted into a mosque in 1198.

PATER NOSTER. Above the cave where Jesus taught the Lord's Prayer to his disciples, Queen Helena (Constantine's mother) built a church, destroyed by the Persians in 614. A Crusader oratory followed and versions of the Lord's Prayer in Hebrew, Greek and Latin carved into the stone have been found. In 1868 the Princess of the Tour d'Auvergne bought the land and built a Carmelite convent there. In 1910 excavations uncovered the Byzantine building, which was restored and partly rebuilt, resulting in a beautiful church open to the skies. The Lord's Prayer appears in sixty-two languages on the walls of a cloister.

THE CHURCH OF ST MARY MAGADALENE
Founded by Alexander III, this church evokes its 15th- and 16th-century Russian sisters. A great Orthodox power, Tsarist Russia maintained a strong presence in Jerusalem, where pilgrims arrived in droves. It built a vast complex of buildings – the Russian Compound – to house them.

THE PALM BRANCHES
Egeria, who stayed in Jerusalem from 381 to 383, described the procession: "Thus, at the seventh hour, everyone goes up to the Mount of Olives (...) Everyone walks before the bishop to the song of hymns and antiphons (...) crossing the whole city, everyone on foot, even the ladies, even the illustrious persons, they all escort the bishop (..); they progress in this way very slowly (...) so as not to tire the crowd already fallen when they arrive at the Anastasis. Once there (...) the people are sent away."

THE KIDRON VALLEY

To the east, the Kidron separates the Old City from the Mount of Olives and its meeting to the south with the Tyropoeon, or Cheesemakers' Valley, marks out the extent of the hill of the Ophel. At the bottom of the Kidron Valley some half-built tombs remain which, like Absalom's, date from the 1st century.

ABSALOM'S TOMB. Also called the "pillar of Absalom", this structure is from the 1st century AD. The isolated part of the rock is formed, as far as the rock ledge, by the rock itself. Its upper part, in the shape of a cone with curved walls, was built on. Behind it eight mortuary chambers were dug out of the rock.

ZACHARIAH'S TOMB. This monument was built in the 2nd century BC with a roof in the shape of a pyramid. It is associated with a series of tombs dug into the rock. A Hebrew inscription on the architrave indicates that they belonged to the Bene Khezirs, a family of priests.

THE TOMB OF ABSALOM
This funerary building constructed on a catacomb dates from ten centuries after the death of the rebellious son of David.

MOUNT ZION

This hill close to the Zion Gate was definitively placed outside the Old City by Suleyman the Magnificent's wall ▲ 244. A Byzantine church and a Crusader building were successively built on the ROOM OF THE LAST SUPPER ▲ 238. In the same building you will find DAVID'S CENOTAPH. At the spot of the CHURCH OF ST PETER IN GALLICANTE, the Apostle three times denied Jesus (who had just been arrested) before the cock's crow. Remains from Herodian times (37 BC to AD 70) were discovered under the present building. At the top of the hill, near the Zion Gate, DORMITION ABBEY was built in 1900 by German Catholics in a Romanesque Carolingian style.

WILHELM II IN JERUSALEM
The Germany of Bismarck and Wilhelm II was the most active of the powers present in Jerusalem in matters of building. The emperor went there in 1898 and built Dormition Abbey which, through its architecture, expresses a national affirmation. German Protestants are distinguished by the importance of their social and educational activities. Among them are the Templars, a sect born in southern Germany in 1854; these "rural people" built many houses still standing in the German colony. Suppliers to the Kaiser's armies, in 1917, they had to suffer the victory of the British who exiled them to Egypt.

Unlike Jesus who chased away the "temple merchants", Muhammad honored the profession of the merchant. He himself was active as one

before he received the revelation. Provided it is exercised with honesty, the occupation of merchant is highly esteemed under Islam. One need only consider the doctrinal vocabulary of Islam to measure its exemplary character. Thus, the religion is called *din*, or "debt", and the day of the last judgment is *Yom al-Din*, or "day of reckoning". That is why the Qur'an pities the man who sells his existence in heaven for the price of his life on earth! This passion for bargaining is so strong that a *hadith* ● 91, or word of the prophet, promises that in eternal paradise the elect will continue to go to a daily market made for him. Thus the Haram al-Sharif (the Noble Sanctuary) which is the third holy place of Islam, is today surrounded by all sorts of stores, stalls and street vendors. And Friday, the day of collective prayer, is of course the day of the souk, when goods are bought and sold in a pious frenzy.

The old Arab city of Jerusalem stretched out over a long plateau with a network of ravines at the foot of the Temple Mount, the Noble Sanctuary, which, six centuries after Titus ● 50, Islam restored as a place of prayer. Jerusalem "the holy", al-Quds in Arabic, was the first stage of Muslim pilgrimage from the 8th century. There an inextricable maze of alleyways begins, where more than a thousand years ago the first Muslim pilgrims settled, and where others, en route to Mecca, rested after prayer, while merchants conducted their business.

THE SOUK

Start at Bab al-Amud (Gate of the Columns) or DAMASCUS GATE, where a money-changer is installed behind the imposing opening. Here the air is full of all the smells of the East, thanks to a spice vendor. You can buy cardamom, without which Arab coffee is no more than a blackish liquid, "dark and insipid like death". And cloves, cumin, Alba wood, musk and amber, with which the believer going to the mosque covers his beard and coat, are all sold here. Typically local crafts with religious themes, made from olive wood and copper, are on sale – everything the pilgrim needs. The Christian pilgrim may be tempted by a "Holy Family's Flight to Egypt" carved in wood, the Last Supper engraved on copper, or the Virgin on a china plate. For the Jewish or Muslim collector there is the name of God or a depiction of Jerusalem on various different materials. The most luxurious of the religious crafts are the reading stands, caskets or mother-of-pearl bindings of the Bible or the Qur'an. Lastly there is "peace"; the word appears everywhere, on postcards, cups, and T-shirts – the motto of this thrice-holy city. Going down Al-Wad Road, the pedestrian crosses a series of little stores and popular restaurants, almost like beads on a rosary. The display of all imaginable kinds of wares on the roadside includes delicious falafels to stimulate the appetites of passersby. Further on, behind a cart crowned with a pyramid of oranges, the vendor extols the virtues of his carrot juice, while in the stores of the covered market pastries are piled high on copper trays.

"THOSE THAT GIVE AWAY THEIR WEALTH FROM A DESIRE TO PLEASE GOD ARE LIKE A GARDEN ON A HILLSIDE: IF A SHOWER FALLS UPON IT, IT YIELDS UP TWICE ITS NORMAL PRODUCE; AND IF NO RAIN FALLS IT IS WATERED BY THE DEW." SÙRAH II

"Many a time have We seen you turn your face towards heaven. We will make you turn towards a qibla that will please you. Turn your face towards the Holy Mosque; wherever you be, turn your faces towards it. Those to whom the Scriptures were given know this to be the truth from their Lord."

Sûrah II

The fountain of Al-Qads.

MINBAR BURHAN AL-DIN
Built near the Dome of the Rock, in the 8th century, in order to serve as a tribune for the Imam for the sermon delivered on holy days and the days when the prayer for rain is said.

HARAM AL-SHARIF

Covering about a sixth of enclosed Jerusalem, the Haram al-Sharif, the Noble Sanctuary or the Temple Mount, is a concentration of architecture as sumptuous as it is holy. From the southeast of the Old City, dominating the Kidron Valley (*Wadi Sitt Maryam*), the adjoining parts of the church of Our Lady Mary, Haram al-Sharif (in Arabic) present the shape of a huge trapezoid. Entrance is via one of fifteen gates, including the Maghreb Gate (Dung Gate), the only opening in the immediate vicinity of the Kotel Hama'aravi, the Western or "Wailing" Wall, a holy place for Jews ▲ 258. The gate's name still recalls the quarter founded here in the 12th century by an Algerian saint from the west to house pilgrims from the Maghreb who ended up settling there. The quarter was demolished the day after the occupation of East Jerusalem in June 1967, in order to open up the esplanade of the Western Wall ▲ 260. Haram al-Sharif is bordered on its east and west sides by an Ottoman wall, like the enclosure protecting the thrice-holy city, entirely built by Suleyman the Magnificent between 1520 and 1566. Almost in the center of the esplanade, opposite the Aqsa Mosque, is the majestic DOME OF THE ROCK ▲ 284 (*Qubbat al-Sakhra*), on a platform specially raised above the Biblical Mount Moriah ▲ 236 where Abraham prepared to sacrifice his son. As well as the fountains, Haram al-Sharif houses many small buildings. Opposite the entrance to the

AN INDIVISIBLE MOSQUE
Al-Aqsa Mosque (below), which is considered quite complete, like one *masjid*, an indivisible mosque with all non-Muslims forbidden to enter at the time of prayer, rises on Haram al-Sharif to the south. The Faithful prostrate themselves from one end to the other of the esplanade, whose many *mihrabs,* or niches, indicate the direction of Mecca, toward which every Muslim should turn when he prays, lest his act of faith be nullified.

Dome of the Rock is the DOME OF THE CHAIN (*Qubbat al-Silsila*). It owes its name to the chain which, according to legend Solomon ● *46* (whom Islam treats as a prophet set apart) suspended between heaven and hell. Only the righteous man could grasp it in order to avoid falling into hell on the day of the Last Judgment which would take place on the Haram, as Muslim tradition requires. Not far from there, you can see the small building of BAIT AL-MAL, the "treasury" dating from Umayyad times (665–750), where the printed budget was kept. To the northwest of the Dome of the Rock, the DOME OF THE ASCENSION (*Qubbat al-Miraj*), commemorates the night journey of the Prophet from Mecca to Jerusalem, and his ascension to the holy rock ▲ *284*. It dates from the 12th century. Hidden between the two, the DOME OF THE PROPHET (*Qubbat al-Nabi*) boasts a lead-covered dome resting on a polygonal arcature. Haram al-Sharif was soon transformed into a Christian

sanctuary by the Crusaders, who turned the Dome of the Rock into a Temple topped by an enormous cross. Since its return to Islam by Salah al-Din in 1187, it has been the object of extraordinary building zeal. Many people, from caliph, sultan and emir to imam, helped build the most important madrasa destined to consolidate the orthodox Muslim character of the place. Thus there is the splendid MADRASA OTHMANIYA, on the western side of the esplanade, built in 1437 by Isfahan Shah, a noble lady from Asia Minor, or the ACHRABIYA, the theological school opened in 1482 by the Mamluke sultan Al-Malek al-Ashraf Qait Bey, the same man who lent his name to the graceful fountain still standing in the Haram. In the southern part of the quadrilateral, near Al-Aqsa Mosque, is the MUSEUM OF ISLAMIC ART, the first in the country. It houses manuscripts, brocade banners, and coins and pottery. At the entrance to the museum are T-shirts, jerseys, trousers and shirts stained with blood, the blood of the "martyrs", men, women and children killed on October 22, 1990, on the Haram esplanade where the holy mosque itself is.

Fragments of doors made from cedar on display in the Museum of Islamic Art.

The Dome of the Rock, in Arabic "Qubbat as-Sakhra", the emblematic jewel of the Holy Land, casts the glory of its golden dome all over Jerusalem; no place in the world can lay claim to such an ancient holiness, recognized by three religions, nor such liveliness attested to by the pilgrims who have flocked there for more than a millennium. An inestimable sign of the architecture of nascent Islam and its first masterpiece, this "Noble Sanctuary" enchants visitors of all religions.

EXTERNAL DECORATION
The external mosaics have been restored many times but are nonetheless faithful to the original plan of Abd al-Malik; Suleyman replaced the Umayyad and Ayyubid pottery with Persian. These gave way in 1964 to glazed tiles of Armenian manufacture, surmounted by a frieze with verses from the Qur'an.

THE ROCK
The rock in the middle of the dome, where Abraham prepared to sacrifice his son Isaac (Genesis 22) in the founding act of monotheism, symbolizes the center of the world in Muslim geography. The Faithful can make out the footprint of the Prophet, as well as the handprint of the archangel Gabriel. The cave under the rock is called the well of souls, because of a tradition which maintains that the souls of the dead linger there before disappearing.

THE DOME

The dome is formed by two superposed cupolas, between which a space was worked in to protect the decoration from the rigors of the climate. It is home to a sublime mosaic in gold and glass with mainly Greco-Roman motifs. An epigraphic strip 262 yards long, to the glory of Jesus, a prophet according to Islam, runs round the drum.

LAYOUT OF THE BUILDING

The Dome of the Rock is octagonal, superimposed on two squares offset by an angle of 45°, and as such it is a miracle of balance and harmony. Its layout, subject to complex and symbolic laws of geometry (the three concentric ambulatories evoke the passage from the secular world to the holy) has made it a model for later Islamic architecture.

This marble paneling runs round the outside of the octagon up to the height of its windows.

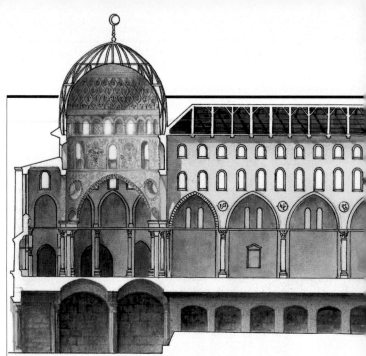

The Al-Aqsa Mosque, built between 705 and 715 at the southern extremity of the Haram al-Sharif, is the largest in Jerusalem. The building was destroyed several times by earthquakes and now has only a few of the elements of its original Umayyad structure. The main part of the present building is the work of the Fatimid caliph of Egypt Al-Zahir, who restored the mosque in 1035. The Crusaders and then the Ayyubids worked on beautifying it, making Al-Aqsa a mixture of architectural styles which is rare in Islamic architecture.

THE "HARAM"
Caliph Umar ● *52* initially simply covered the ruins of the royal portico of the Herodian Temple with a roof. This construction was, however, a temporary measure, and from 705, the caliph Al-Walid ordered the construction of a prestigious monument, and granted the project to artisans from Egypt. On this occasion the arcades of a mosque were for the first time oriented perpendicularly rather than parallel to the *qibla* wall ● *11*, an arrangement which has since been generally adopted.

AL-AQSA MOSQUE ▲

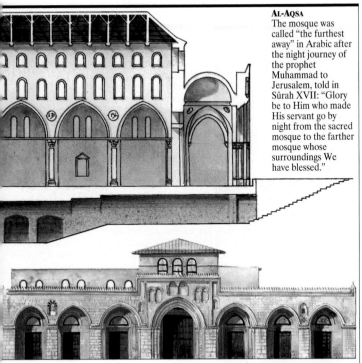

AL-AQSA
The mosque was
called "the furthest
away" in Arabic after
the night journey of
the prophet
Muhammad to
Jerusalem, told in
Sûrah XVII: "Glory
be to Him who made
His servant go by
night from the sacred
mosque to the farther
mosque whose
surroundings We
have blessed."

The modern
window, a
perforated, fixed
screen in stucco set
with glass,
hermetically seals
one of the bays of
the façade of the
mosque. Its refined
tracery is inspired
by Ottoman art.

THE NORTHERN FAÇADE
Islam accepted from its beginnings that it was
wise to startle the eye to win the soul. The
need to counterbalance the prestige of the
Byzantine masterpieces, particularly the Holy
Sepulcher, was all-important in the building
of this monumental mosque. The seven arches
of the portico from Ayyubid times
nevertheless echo the seven parts of the
layout of the basilica.

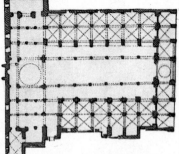

LATER CHANGES
After the Crusader
conquest the mosque
became the seat of
the Order of the
Templars. The
oratory of Zachariah,
the old chapel of the
Templars originally
next to the west wall
of the building, was
reintegrated into the
Muslim building by
order of Salah al-
Din. The materials of
other crusader

additions were used
to remake the
building of the
Haram al-Sharif.
Under Ottoman rule,
the mosaics of the
cupola were renewed
and the exterior
pulpit of the mosque
restored. Lastly the
ceiling was
redecorated in 1939
thanks to a gift from
the former King of
Egypt, Farouk.

PILLARS
The dozens of pillars,
more than any other
feature, sum up the
mix of styles which
make up the building;
rare Umayyad traces,
Romanesque columns

from Crusader times,
Ayyubid and
Ottoman additions,
and even pillars in
Carrera marble (gifts
from the King of
Italy) unite to hold
up the roof of the
many-pillared *haram*.

The pendant of the Robinson Arch, under which are cisterns carved out of the rock (above, top), is Wilson's Arch (above) situated to the east of the *Kotel*.

THE ARCHEOLOGICAL GARDENS

OPHEL. The rock of Ophel, southwest of the Temple Mount, supported the first walls of the city, those of the Jebusites ▲ *240*. Thus excavations carried out between 1968 and 1984 revealed nearly twenty-five strata of different civilizations between the 1st millennium BC and the Ottoman period. The most impressive remains on the site are those of the time of the Second Temple. The Robinson Arch was part of the steps which linked the upper town to the Temple Mount. The steps of the HULDA STAIRS, which also led to the Mount ▲ *260*, are lined with *mikvehs* ▲ *257* where pilgrims purified themselves before entering the sanctuary enclosure. The two TRIPLE DOORS also date from Herodian times.

THE CITY OF DAVID. Situated outside the walls of the Old City, it is the oldest part of Jerusalem; there you will find the ruins of a Canaanite citadel as well as the remains of David's fortress. WARREN'S SHAFT (named after the British archeologist who excavated the site in 1870) is in fact a tunnel which was first dug by the Canaanites in order to reach the level of the spring of Gihon ▲ *240*. In 701 BC King Hezekiah extended it by 1,760 feet in order to divert the water to the Pool of Siloam which was below in the Kidron Valley where the city is at its most vulnerable. This is why the basin was protected by two parallel walls flanked by a tower.

ARAB VILLAGES

Outside East Jerusalem, some villages, situated to the south of the city, have remained Arab: this is the case with Beit Sahur, Sur Bahir and also Um Tubas. SILWAN (a deformation of the Hebrew word Shiloah) is found in the extension of the city of David: underground pipework laid in the 8th century BC by Hezekiah stretched that far. At that time pagan altars were erected here, so that the hill where the village is was called "the mount of offenses". It was at Silwan that the notables of the town were buried during the reigns of the kings of Judah and tombs were dug out of the rock. Badly deteriorated by Roman-Byzantine times, they were incorporated into the structures of the village houses and can still be seen today.

RACHEL'S TOMB

In south Jerusalem Kibbutz Ramat Rachel, near Bethlehem ● 224, is named after Jacob's favorite wife, who is said to be buried there: "Rachel died, and was buried in the way to Ephrath, which is Bethlehem" (Genesis 35). The small white-domed sanctuary which can be seen today shelters only a cenotaph; it probably dates from the Mamluke period, but has been restored several times since then, and in 1841 Moses Montefiore ● 296 opened the arcades through which access is gained. Venerated by both Jews and Muslims alike, the tomb is an important place of pilgrimage.

JUST OUTSIDE THE WALLS

THE MONTEFIORE WINDMILL
Built in Yemin Moshe in 1858, this building did in fact serve less as a windmill than as an observation post during the 1948–9 war. Today it houses a small museum dedicated to Montefiore.

BEN YEHUDA
Ben Yehuda Street owes its name to the "father of modern Hebrew" ● 58.

From 1860 Jerusalem began to extend beyond its walls ▲ 242. The first buildings put up at the foot of the ramparts formed the core from which the town developed west and then north of the Old City. These new areas were relatively scattered to begin with, but slowly spread to form a single entity: modern Jerusalem.

MISHKENOT SHA'ANANIM. Shocked by living conditions inside the Old City, the English Jewish philanthropist Moses Montefiore had the idea of building outside the walls. He obtained the sultan's permission to acquire land and in 1860 MISHKENOT SHA'ANANIM ("the Homes of the Blessed") was established. The homes here today house the "villa Medici" c Jerusalem.

YEMIN MOSHE. The Yemin Moshe quarter developed out of this building program of 1892. It acted as a bridgehead during the War of Independence, was deserted when the city was divided, and then renovated after 1967. Today Yemin Moshe is mainly inhabited by artists and the rich bourgeoisie of Jerusalem and is one of the most exclusive residential areas o the city. Opposite Yemin Moshe is the LIBERTY BELL PARK, inaugurated on the occasion of the bicentennial of the independence of the United States, and the BLOOMFIELD GARDEN, which is said to contain the tomb of Herod's family ● 57.

NAHALAT SHIVA. Following in Moses Montefiore's footsteps, Rabbi Joseph Rivlin joined with six other Jews from the Old City to build what is now called *Nahalat Shiva*, "the domain of the seven". Renovation of the quarter, which was pedestrianized in the 1980's, has made it possible to appreciate the originality of its architecture with its low houses, wells, interior courtyards and wrought-iron balconies. Since then artists and night owls have chosen to live there. The bars, restaurants and discotheques of Nahalat Shiva form, with Ben Yehuda Street (also paved over and lined with cafés), one of the liveliest parts of the city. At the heart of all this is ZION SQUARE, a popular meeting place for Jerusalemites.

THE RUSSIAN COMPOUND. By the sultan's decree the Russians obtained land outside the walls and undertook to build a vast complex of buildings ▲ 243 in 1857, forming their own miniature colony. At the end of the last century, this little village had a consulate, an imposing cathedral, the HOLY TRINITY CHURCH ★, a hospital, hostelries and a large caravanserai to welcome Russian pilgrims. In the same period SERGEI HOUSE was built, with a Renaissance-style tower, and consecrated by the son of the tsar. Today this ancient hospice has become the Society for the Protection of Nature ◆ 430. In 1950 all the buildings except the church were bought by the Israeli government which set up its own offices there. The old building of the British prison was turned into a Museum of Heroism, devoted to the clandestine Jewish struggle against the British.

THE STREET OF THE PROPHETS. This street links DAVIDKA SQUARE to Damascus Gate. It is also called Consulate Road because at the turn of the last century the Ottomans and the Westerners installed offices there. The beginning of the road is marked by the Anglican school, recognizable by its green shutters, which was built in 1896. Further on, at number 58 is TABOR HOUSE which was built in 1882 and now houses the Swedish theological seminary.

TABOR HOUSE
The self-taught architect Conrad Schick (1822–1901) rejected academism to such an extent that he built his house by mixing western, eastern and archeological elements. This work was nicknamed the "House of Dreams".

THE JERUSALEM POST
The offices of the national daily newspaper in the small Harav Kook Street which runs off the Street of the Prophets.

THE RUSSIAN CHURCH
Its bells were the first in Jerusalem because the Turks had forbidden their use.

THE ETHIOPIAN QUARTER ★. The charming Street of the Ethiopians, which begins in the Street of the Prophets, leads to the Church and monastery bearing the same name. Probably built by Conrad Schick ▲ 297 at the end of the last century, it is round in shape, inspired by Ethiopian churches, conceived, it is said, to defy Satan who could hide in corners. On the church pediment, the Lion of Judah ● 47, emblem of the Ethiopian kingdom, recalls the spiritual links of Ethiopia with King Solomon's Jerusalem. Immediately opposite is the house where Ben Yehuda ● 58 lived for some years. From there Harav Kook Street ▲ 297 leads to TICHO HOUSE. This place which belonged to the artist Anna Ticho has been renovated and turned into a café by the municipality. Taking the Street of the Prophets once again, you will come to the Morasha quarter. Here, the Mandelbaum Gate once marked the border with East Jerusalem ▲ 306.

THE FALASHAS
Ethiopian Jews settled in the Holy Land, the "falashas" ("stranger" in Ethiopian) are said to be the descendants of the Queen of Sheba and King Solomon ● 46.

IN MEA SHEARIM
"Why do they dress like that?" asks one of the characters in a Harry Kemelman novel: "Strictly speaking, through pure conservatism.

MEA SHEARIM, AN AREA BEYOND TIME. To escape the temptations of secularism and the modern world, orthodox Jews who came from Poland and Lithuania decided in 1874 to move away to a new area, now to the north of the Street of the Prophets. Mea Shearim, organized like a sort of fortress by Conrad Schick ▲ 297, is a town within a town where time seems to have stood still. Its name is derived from its founders' goal to build a hundred houses at the same time. All the strands of Hassidism are gathered here even if they do not always get on well with each other. Specialists will recognize the adherents of different groups by their hats, long coats and even sometimes the length of the *peyot* which distinguish one from the other ▲ 262. The best times for a

It was the costume of rich Polish and Russian merchants in the 18th century, probably worn by the Ba'al Shem Tov, founder of the Hassidic movement; in memory of this rebbe they continue to wear this garb."

times for a walk in the area are Friday afternoon, when people are preparing for Shabbat, and Saturday, when prayers

and litanies emanate from synagogues and talmudic schools.

THE BOKHARAN QUARTER. In the 19th century, the rich founders of this quarter sought to recreate the atmosphere of central Asia where they came from. The regular intervals between roads, their width, and the grandeur of the huge houses, such as DAVIDOFF HOUSE (above) soon made the Bokharan quarter into one of the most beautiful parts of Jerusalem. After the Russian Revolution, when other Bokharan Jews immigrated, it was necessary to divide the living space of the quarter into several parts. Today even if somewhat run down with time, the area has kept much of its charm.

SANHEDRIA QUARTER. This 1920's suburb to the north of the new town is now inhabited by orthodox Jews. It owes its name to the tombs of the seventy-one members of the Sanhedrin, the ancient assembly of doctors of the Law ● *40*, which are in the gardens of the quarter. The entrance to the catacombs, Greek in inspiration, is carved with acanthus leaves, fruits and geometric designs in bas-relief. Inside, the tombs are pushed back on different levels in a cave hollowed out in the rock.

AROUND SANHEDRIA. Less than a mile west of Sanhedria, the unique BIBLICAL ZOO is home to all the types of animal (reptiles, birds and wild animals) mentioned in the Old Testament. On the other side, east of the quarter, is AMMUNITION HILL, where one of the fiercest battles of the 1967 ● *43* war took place. The trenches, fortifications and tanks in the park have remained as the soldiers left them at the end of the conflict.

"YAD FATIMA"
The *yad Fatima*, or *al-kaff*, is a charm and symbol in Islam (and other religions) of power over disorder, and often adorns Arab houses and those of Jews who have come from oriental communities.

General Allenby
entered Jerusalem on
December 9, 1917.

THE YMCA
When they undertook
to reorganize
Jerusalem, the British
recognized that it was
a place of many
communities,
historical and
religious. The YMCA
was built between
1928 and 1933 by
Jews and Arabs, and
mixed elements of
Roman, Moorish and
Islamic architecture.
The building, with its
impressive tower, has
become one of the
city's landmarks. It
was designed by Q.L.
Harmon, who also
designed the Empire
State Building.
Immediately opposite
the YMCA is the
King David Hotel,
whose guests have
included Jimmy
Carter, Anwar Sadat,
Henry Kissinger and
Menachem Begin. It
is one of the most
prestigious hotels
in Jerusalem. A
true witness to
the history of
the city, the
hotel was the
target of an
attack in 1945 by
the clandestine
Zionist
organization
Etzel, when it
housed the
General
Quarters of the
British police.

THE HINNOM VALLEY

According to the Biblical account, it
was in the valley of Hinnom (that is,
Ge-Hinnom), at the foot of the
walls, that Manasseh, king of Judah,
built a sanctuary devoted to Moloch,
the Canaanite god eager for human
sacrifices. From this, Gehinnom
(Greek *Gehanna*) became a name
for hell. In this valley there are many
tombs, in particular a Karaite
cemetery, which you can see from the
Cinematheque terrace, a spot favored
by locals. At the foot of Yemin Moshe,
the SULTAN'S POOL is an old water
reservoir designed to collect the waters
which flowed toward the Dead Sea.
Suleyman, who beautified it, gave it his
name. Today, it is an open-air stage,
used mainly in spring and summer. If
one escapes toward Hebron, one
takes Kedoshei Saloniki
Road, arriving at the Haas Promenade, where
there is a magnificent view of the city. If you
choose David Remez street, part of the Valley
of Gehenna, you emerge at the station and
the Khan. This ancient Mameluke
caravanserai was a silk factory in the
19th century, then a beer cellar for the
German Colony before being turned into
a cultural center in 1972. Its theater puts
on folklore spectacles among other
entertainments.

THE BRITISH ITINERARY

Between 1917 and 1949 the whole of
the new city was marked by the mandate,
and it is interesting to follow the
footsteps of the British. Thus the
Scottish church, ST ANDREW, admirably
sober, next to the Khan, was built in
1927 in memory of Scottish soldiers
who died in 1917 "to liberate Jerusalem".
At the end of Hebron Road ▲ *220*
above the Haas Promenade, the
old GOVERNOR'S PALACE
houses the offices of the
UN observers. But the
most "British" quarter in
Jerusalem is still the
quarter between Jaffa Road,
King David Street and King
George Street. There you will
find the center of the modern
city where there are offices,
banks, businesses and the
big hotels.

The station has hardly changed since the Ottomans inaugurated the first railway line in Palestine in 1892.

KING DAVID STREET. On this main road the outlines of the two most famous hotels in the city face one another: the King David, a palace in the 1930's, and the YMCA, a building constructed at the initiative of the Young Men's Christian Association, an association interested in promoting peace. Above King David Street, Agron Street leads to INDEPENDENCE PARK where Jerusalemites congregate on Saturdays.

JAFFA ROAD. This 2-mile long road makes use of the old route from Jaffa to Jerusalem. It was paved over in 1898 for the arrival of Kaiser Wilhelm II in the Holy Land, and today it is lined with businesses, banks, offices and restaurants. It is animated day and night and is especially attractive near Mahaneh Yehuda, the biggest covered market in the city. Its colorful displays of fruit and vegetables, its stalls packed with all sorts of spices, and its small cafés and disordered streets in the middle of the modern city give off a powerful and exotic whiff of the Orient.

MAHANEH YEHUDA MARKET
"Rabbi Small," writes Harry Kemelman, "followed twisting streets and suddenly found himself in an open market with rows of stalls where mainly fruits and vegetables were displayed, but also fish and meat stalls, as well as, here and there, cloth and clothes. The traders, Arabs, bearded Jews or gossipy women, shouted, traded, gesticulated and praised their goods, each one better than the last. There were also stalls . . . where you could buy combs, diaries, packets of needles, tissues and even coats."

295

THE HEBREW UNIVERSITY OF JERUSALEM

The idea of building a Hebrew University was put forward in

1882 by the Zionist Z.H. Shapiro, but it was only in 1918 that the first stone was set in place. The first buildings were inaugurated in 1925 (above) in the presence of Lord Balfour and Chaim Weizmann, who later became the first President of Israel ▲ 360. From 1967, the university, which has undergone a vast extension and modernization program, has become one of the leading faculties in the country.

MOUNT SCOPUS

At 2,755 feet Mount Scopus is the focal point of Jerusalem. Its name is a Greek translation of the Hebrew words *Har Hatsofim*, meaning "mountain of the Warriors"; its summit, 980 feet above the Old City, overlooks the whole of the city where the hills of the Judean Desert peter out. The British made a cemetery there for the soldiers who died when Jerusalem was taken during World War One. It was here that in 1925, the first buildings of the Hebrew University were constructed as well as the buildings of the Hadassah Hospital. At the time of the 1948–9 war ● 56, Mount Scopus, cut off from Jerusalem, became an Israeli enclave under the auspices of the UN: but medical and university services had to be removed to the western part of the city. This is how the Hadassah Hospital ▲ 304 in Ein Kerem ▲ 303 and a new university in Givat Ram came to be.

TO THE WEST OF JERUSALEM

Talbieh, reached by way of Jabotinsky Street, is one of the prettiest residential parts of the modern city. It slopes gently toward the Valley of the Cross, to the west of which is the administrative heart of Jerusalem. Number 9 Smolenski Street is the RESIDENCE OF THE PRESIDENT OF THE REPUBLIC. It was built in 1938 by a rich Egyptian Jewish merchant. Close by is the INSTITUTE OF ISLAMIC ART which, since 1973, has held a magnificent collection of Muslim art. Some yards away the JERUSALEM THEATER puts on plays, dance, and classical and modern music. Next to it the verdant quarter of REHAVIA was built at the beginning of the British Mandate by pioneering Jews who refused to live in the conditions prevailing in the religious areas. The radically different spirit soon seduced a number of white-collar workers and intellectuals who had their own houses built by well-known architects in an international style.

THE "MENORAH"
Given by the British
government in 1956, it
is decorated with bas-
reliefs evoking the
history of the Jewish
people.

THE VALLEY OF THE CROSS

The Valley of the Cross,
stretching out at the foot of
Rehavia, is home to the city's
main cultural and political bodies.
It takes its name from the Greek
Orthodox monastery constructed like a
fortress by Georgians from the Caucasus.

THE MONASTERY OF THE CROSS. According to
tradition, it was built in the heart of the forest where
the tree grew from which wood for the Crucifixion
cross was taken. It unites different types of
architecture which have followed one another since its
inception in the 11th century: the wall and monastic
buildings date from the
monastery's beginnings, but the
buttresses at the back and its neo-
baroque bell tower were added in the
19th century. Today only one monk
looks after the monastery, which
belongs to the Greek Orthodox church
of Jerusalem.

PARLIAMENT
The legislative body
consists of 120 elected
members.

THE ADMINISTRATIVE PART OF THE CITY.
In the 1960's the Israeli government
decided to unite all the branches of
government in one place. The seat of
parliament was built in 1966, and was
called the KNESSET in memory of the
central legislative body of Israel at the
time of the Second Temple. Its
architecture, a modern version of old
classical buildings, recalls the
Parthenon in Athens. The Gobelins
tapestry in the entrance hall is by
Chagall ▲ *304* and depicts the history
of the Jewish people. THE ROSE GARDEN opposite, used for
diplomatic receptions as well as demonstrations, has no fewer
than four hundred varieties of roses from all over the world.
It is there that the imposing menorah (nearly 17 feet high) by
the sculptor Beno Elkan can be found. In 1992 the SUPREME
COURT was inaugurated. It is linked to the Knesset by a
corridor. On the other side of Ruppin Road you will find a
cluster of museums which includes the BIBLE LANDS MUSEUM,
the SCIENCE MUSEUM and the ISRAEL MUSEUM, a
veritable masterpiece of futuristic architecture.

CERAMICS
The architects of the
rich Arab houses of
Talbieh used highly
colored mosaics and
ceramics to decorate
the façades of the
houses as well as the
floors.

Like an acropolis dominating an ancient city, the Israel Museum, a large cultural center founded in 1965, overlooks Jerusalem. Famous for the Shrine of the Book which holds the Dead Sea Scrolls, the museum also has an archeological section, a fine art department, one of the biggest collections of Jewish art in the world and the Billy Rose Sculpture Garden, a modern sculpture park.

HEBREW MANUSCRIPTS
The collection of Hebrew manuscripts in the Jewish art section boasts exceptional pieces. The Rothschild manuscript (1470–80) has more than two hundred very beautiful illuminated miniatures.

THE DEPARTMENT OF ARCHEOLOGY
It sets out chronologically the culture of the peoples of the Holy Land in all its forms (art, architecture, daily life and so on) from Prehistory to the Muslim conquest. The scepter in the shape of an ibex discovered in a cave in the Judean Desert is a remarkable piece from the Chalcolithic age ● 38.

JEWISH ART
This piece of linen (18th century) used during a circumcision, was painted and decorated before being given to the child at the time of his first visit to synagogue.

CANAANITE ART
This bronze mirror, showing the art of the Canaanite era (14th to 13th centuries BC) was discovered in a perfect state in a tomb in Akko. The design was inspired by craftsmanship from Egypt, where many similar objects have been found. The gold pendant, which has survived intact, shows the goddess Hathor.

SENNACHERIB'S PRISM
This prism is one of the writing props used to describe Sennacherib's third campaign which established Assyrian rule in Syria and the Land of Canaan ● *39*.

MODERN AND CONTEMPORARY ART
The fine art galleries display a large collection of Impressionist, modern and contemporary works. Some galleries are devoted to Israeli art (young talent and established artists). To the right is an urban scene by Egon Schiele (1890–1918).

A SCULPTURE GARDEN IN THE OPEN AIR

The garden, designed by Isamu Nogushi, is built on a hill with paved terraces and structured courtyards. It mingles Japanese and European traditions. All the modern and contemporary sculptures are linked to the space by a natural or artificial element. The mobile (right) by Calder (1898–1976) moves with the wind. Henry Moore's (1898–1986) *Vertebrae* are centered on the infinity of the sky while Emile Bourdelle's (1861–1929) *Warrior* has a more intimate relationship with the Jerusalem stone (below).

THE GREAT PENELOPE

Bourdelle studied at the School of Fine Arts in Toulouse and then in Paris where he became one of Auguste Rodin's favorite assistants. This monumental sculpture displayed in the Billy Rose Sculpture Garden is inspired by the great master but also by ancient Greek art.

THE OPEN SPACES OF THE SCULPTURE GARDEN

Nogushi conceived a series of outdoor galleries adapted to sculptures. Geometrical elements in stone are arranged to heighten the appreciation of works whose smaller size demands a more intimate rapport with the environment. From left to right, *Girl skipping* (1954) by the Italian Luciano Minguzzi, Aristide Maillol's *Harmony* (1842) and *Young Girl with Shirt* by the Englishman Reg Butler.

"ASCENSION"
A monumental work
by Otto Frendlich
(1878–1943), one of
the youngest of the
generation of
abstract art pioneers.

DER JUDEN STAAT.
THEODOR HERZL

THEODOR HERZL
Theodor Herzl, a fashionable playwright and writer, born in Budapest in 1860 into an assimilated family steeped in German culture, could not have been a less likely candidate to be the founder of a movement that would radically change the future of the Jewish people. However, the growth of anti-Semitism led him to formulate a revolutionary response. In his renowned work *Der Judenstaat* (*The Jewish State*), which appeared in 1896, he proposed the creation of a State that would guarantee dignity and security to Jews from all over the world.

MOUNT HERZL

To the west of the Knesset, above the university campus of Givat Ram, you will find Mount Herzl.

CEMETERY AND HERZL MUSEUM. Theodor Herzl's ashes ● 56 were moved to Jerusalem in 1949, in accordance with the wishes of the author of *The Jewish State* to be buried in the Jewish fatherland which he had helped bring into being. His family and other leaders of the Zionist movement lie at his side in the cemetery on the hill. In the same place the small museum devoted to him contains a reconstruction of his Viennese study, some documents, photographs and works related to his life and works.

YAD VASHEM. Since the opening of the Yad Vashem holocaust memorial here, Mount Herzl has also been called "Hill of Remembrance". This vast complex, dedicated to the memory of Holocaust victims, houses: archives; a MUSEUM OF HOLOCAUST HISTORY; an ART MUSEUM where works which were completed in the camps are exhibited, as well as many sculptures inspired by the theme of deportation; a MAUSOLEUM; and a SYNAGOGUE. The CHILDREN'S MEMORIAL is, without a doubt, the most

YAD VASHEM
This haunting sculpture at the Memorial of Yad Vashem symbolizes the horror of the concentration camps.

disturbing; here, in long, dark corridors, the names of the young victims are lit by candlelight. The Yad Vashem Memorial is both moving and shocking. More than just a museum, it is a true sanctuary of remembrance.

EIN KAREM ★

A VILLAGE IN TOWN. From Mount Herzl, a road winds its way down to Ein Karem (2½ miles). This village owes its name to the many vines which grow there, as well as to the spring (*ain* in Arabic) where Mary is said to have drunk: it is the "spring of Our Lady Mary". Ein Karem is situated in a sea of greenery, and has, since 1948, been transformed into a residential area of Jerusalem populated mainly by artists, men of letters and journalists. It is a pleasure to wander through its little alleyways and to discover galleries and artists' studios alongside churches and convents. According to Christian tradition the parents of John the Baptist, Elisabeth and Zacharias, lived here.

EIN KAREM CHURCHES. "Blessed art thou among women," exclaimed Elizabeth when she received her cousin Mary after the announcement made by the Archangel Gabriel (Luke 1). The Virgin replied with a hymn to the glory of God. So the *Magnificat* appears in several languages in the exterior courtyard of the Church of St John the Baptist. This was built in 1674 by Franciscans on the site which would have been the home of the prophet's parents: it contains the cave where he is said to have been born and the remains of a Byzantine mosaic. Constructed on the hill which overlooks the spring, the Church of the Visitation was conceived by the architect Barluzzi in 1955. On its façade a mosaic depicts Mary perched on a donkey, going from Nazareth to Jerusalem. Inside, a cavity would have been dug out by Elisabeth to hide John the Baptist at the time of the massacre of the Innocents (Matthew 2). Right next door is the Moscovite church of St John: the building of a second church was interrupted by the Bolshevik revolution. Opposite, the convent of the Sisters of Zion was established at the end of the 19th century by Ratisbonne, a French Jew who converted to Christianity.

CONVENT OF THE MOSCOVITE CHURCH
Kept by sisters of the Russian Orthodox church, the buildings of the convent of the Moscovite church are on different levels on the hillside, and form a completely separate quarter, the Laura, or convent.

ST JOHN OF THE DESERT
This monastery can be reached via Ein Karem. It was built in the heart of the Jerusalem Forest, where Saint John the Baptist is said to have withdrawn before leaving for the Jordan to perform baptisms. A Greek Melkite community runs the church and monastery. The town's expansion means the monastery is less and less in the desert (as its name suggests), but it is still on a marvelous site, on the side of the Sorek Valley ▲ 326.

These stained glass windows are "the modest present which I give to the Jewish people who have always dreamed of love, friendship and peace among peoples". These were the words spoken by Marc Chagall at the inauguration of the synagogue in the Hadassah Hospital. The hospital was founded in 1962 by an American Zionist women's organization of the same name. The windows depict the twelve tribes of Israel (the sons of Jacob) as evoked in the blessing spoken by the patriarch before his death (Genesis 49). The colors are inspired by the precious stones on the breastplate of the High Priest, described in the Bible (Deuteronomy 33) and the motifs which decorated the flag of each tribe.

THE TWELVE TRIBES OF ISRAEL

Each of the twelve tribes of Israel was assigned a symbol in the Bible, a precious stone and a function, reproduced here by Chagall. Reuven (ruby) embodies material creativity; Simeon (topaz), knowledge and instruction; Levi (emerald), priesthood and service of the Tabernacle; Judah (sapphire) kept spiritual and temporal power – this is also King David's tribe; Zevulun (light emerald) rules over commerce and international relations; Issachar (carbuncle) has scientific knowledge; Dan (jacinth) is the tribe of judges and jurisprudence; Gad (agate) is attributed with both war and agriculture; Joseph (onyx) is responsible for the historical accomplishment of Israel; lastly, Benjamin (jasper), like Gad assured the defense of the people.

THE TRIBE OF NAPHTALI

"Naphtali is a hind let loose: he giveth goodly words" (Genesis 49). The stained glass, which shows Naphtali, whose precious stone is amethyst, is dominated by shades of violet and yellow. This tribe, which ensures communication between peoples, has as its emblem a hind, the bearer of messages. Chagall has shown it at rest but the whole window has a sense of movement.

THE TRIBE OF ASHER

"Out of Asher his bread shall be fat, and he shall yield royal dainties" (Genesis 49:20). Asher is endowed with all the activities of transformation. The dominant color in the window, inspired by beryl, the tribe's stone, is olive-green. An impression of abundance flows from the whole where Chagall has represented symbolic birds, a dove and a peacock, as well as a menorah.

ATTRIBUTES

All the tribes are endowed with an attribute: Reuven's is the rising sun; Benjamin's is the wolf; Judah's is the lion; Zevulun's is the ship, and so on. Here the dove holds in its beak an olive branch, symbol of the tribe of Asher.

CHAGALL'S TECHNIQUE

Rather than using traditional techniques which consisted of separating each piece of colored glass, Chagall and his assistant C. Marq perfected a process of laying the painting directly onto the material while adapting it for natural light.

Between 1948 and 1967, Morasha marked the border with East Jerusalem. The quarter was built in the last century by Palestinian Christians, and after the first Arab-Israeli conflict ● *56* it was inhabited by Jews who had emigrated from North Africa. For almost twenty years MANDELBAUM GATE, opened at the time of the partition of the city in the wall which divided it in two ▲ *243*, was the only point of passage between East and West Jerusalem. Today the wall no longer exists, but the city remains divided in reality; on the old demarcation line there is now a motorway. East Jerusalem has its own banks, station, and newspapers, and its mostly Muslim inhabitants live in accordance with the Hegiran calendar ● *96*.

DAMASCUS GATE. Palestinians called it Bab al-Amud, or "Gate of the Column", because in the 7th century, in the time of Muslim Palestine, an ancient pillar dating from the time of Aelia Capitolina ● *50* stood in its place. In 1537 Suleyman the Magnificent made it into the grandest entrance into the city ▲ *244*. The gate is raised on the junction of two Muslim quarters of Jerusalem (one inside the Old City, the other outside the walls) and has become the meeting point for the Muslim community. It overlooks a lively square where street vendors spread out a variety of goods, clothes, perfume, postcards, fresh drinks and so on. Damascus Gate opens on to Nablus Road, one of East Jerusalem's main thoroughfares.

THE QUARRIES SAID TO BE SOLOMON'S. To the right of Damascus Gate an escarpment marks the entrance to Solomon's quarries. In these immense underground galleries the Jewish king had great blocks extracted for use in building the Temple and palaces in Jerusalem ● *46*. These quarries also bear the name of Zedekiah, the last king of Judah; he hid there when Jerusalem was taken by Nebuchadnezzar in 587 BC ● *47*.

THE GARDEN TOMB. In 1883 the British general Charles Gordon, using Jewish tradition as his reference point, decided that Jesus could not have been buried inside the walls of the Old City. Instead he identified this site as the tomb of Jesus. The skull-shaped rock in which a grave was dug recalled Golgotha ▲ *268*, as it is described in the Gospels. Many accepted this interpretation but then abandoned it in the absence of any firm archeological proof to back it up.

THE "KEFFIYEH"
This Arabic word designating the head covering of the Bedouins comes from the Latin word *cofea* – perhaps "coif" – which may be linked to the word *kipa* ▲ *266* (the Jewish skullcap). The *keffiyeh*, a sort of shawl, is formed from a square of material folded into a triangle and held in place by a binding called *agal*. Belonging to the Arab orient, the *keffiyeh* with black, red or violet squares has become a nationalist symbol for the Palestinian resistance as was the *fez* in Turkey before the time of Ataturk.

THE FESTIVAL OF THE SHEEP
At Eid al-Adha ● *93*, ("Feast of Sacrifice", commemorating Abraham's willingness to sacrifice his son), Muslims gather at Damascus Gate. Sheep are sacrificed there.

THE PRECINCTS OF THE DOMINICANS.

From very early on this site was venerated as the place of the stoning of Stephen, the first Christian martyr. In 460 Empress Eudoxia built a basilica and monastery there. The buildings were destroyed by the Persians in 634 and replaced by St Stephen's Church, built by the patriarch Sophronius in 638, then restored by the Crusaders. In 1890 the Dominican Father Lagrange (below) chose this place to found the Biblical College. This institute of archeological and Biblical research was the first in the Holy Land to link exegesis with a concrete knowledge of the land of the Bible. In 1920 it became a French school of archeology whose many students are taught in French and English. The school directs digs in Israel and Jordan.

A huge library there contains works of reference on archeology, religion and history.

THE BISHOPRIC OF ST GEORGE.

Further north on the Nablus Road, this bishopric is home to an Anglican Arab community.

The Garden Tomb, a French possession, is a haven of peace and freshness in the heart of Jerusalem.

JERUSALEM STONE

The centuries-old tradition of extracting stone in Jerusalem dates back a long time as is testified by the so-called Solomon's quarries. In the 19th century, when the city was spreading outside the walls the stone cutters (below) had to extract large amounts of it. Its systematic and compulsory use from the beginning of the 20th century has allowed an architectural unity to develop throughout the city.

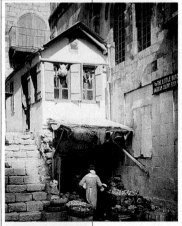

THE TOMB OF THE KINGS. At the crossroads of Nablus Road and Saladin Street, the French flag flies over a small patch of grass – the Tomb of the Kings – which has been placed under French authority. This necropolis, long attributed to the ancient kings of Jerusalem, was built by the royal family of Adiabene, a kingdom in Asia Minor, which, after embracing the Jewish religion, settled in Jerusalem in the 1st century AD. The tombs are reached by the portal cut in the cliff, then a cave, a sort of ante-chamber lined with benches. The sepulchral chambers, closed by large stone doors pivoting on hinges, recall the tomb of Christ, dug in the same period.

ORIENT HOUSE. The building situated just behind the Tomb of the Kings is becoming more and more well-known in its capacity as headquarters for the PLO in Jerusalem ● *43*. This beautiful late 19th-century Arab residence belonged to the great Husseini family. It is now decorated with a Palestinian flag and has become a compulsory stop for political delegations visiting from abroad.

THE AMERICAN COLONY. The American Colony, opposite Orient House, is, after the King David ▲ *295*, the most elegant hotel in the holy city. It is the place for informal meetings between Jewish and Arab intelligentsia, as well as the preferred stopover for journalists from the international press. It is in the old palace built between 1865 and 1876 by the rich merchant Rabah al-Husseini, who lived there until 1890 with his four wives and a large number of servants. The American colony of Jerusalem settled there in 1895 and in the 1950's the residence was turned into a luxury hotel. Further north is the quarter of SHEIKH JARRAH and its beautiful small mosque with a graceful minaret of uncut stone. About 220 yards from there is a tomb in a cave. It is the tomb of a doctor of the Law, Simon the Just.

AMERICAN COLONY
Horatio and Anna Spafford decided to leave Chicago to settle in the Holy Land after an accident which cost them the lives of their daughters. Accompanied by some of their friends, they settled in a house near the Damascus Gate. The place soon became too small and they had to find another one. The Spaffords bought the richly decorated palace (the mosaic, above, is a detail) of the merchant Al-Husseini, who had just died without an heir. And so the colony developed around the great house. Above, at the top, is a butcher of the quarter in 1919.

SALADIN STREET. It is here that you will find Jeremiah's cave. The Bible tells how this prophet was thrown there for having predicted the fall of Jerusalem before Nebuchadnezzar in 587 BC ● *47*: "[The princes] took Jeremiah, and cast him into the dungeon of Malchiah, the son of the king, that was in the court of the prison: and they let down Jeremiah with cords. And in the dungeon there was no water, but mire: so Jeremiah sunk in the mire" (Jeremiah 38). Saladin Street leads to the Gate of the Small Plain (*Bab al-Sahireh*) or Herod's Gate. It was given this name in the 16th century because there was a house there which was identified with the house of Herod Antipas, son of Herod the Great.

THE ROCKEFELLER MUSEUM. This museum was built northeast of the Old City, and was founded in 1937 during the Mandate at the instigation of the British, thanks to the gift of the wealthy American oil magnate John D. Rockefeller. The building was conceived by the architect Austin St Barbe Harrison and subtly mixes the old (the white stone characteristic of Jerusalem ▲ *307*) and the modern (reinforced concrete), as well as both western and eastern elements – one of the internal courtyards is reminiscent of the Alhambra in Granada. Since 1967 the entire building has been administered by the Israel Museum ▲ *300*. The museum, one of the most important archeological museums in the Middle East, is dedicated to the civilizations in Palestine from prehistory to the 16th century. The periods predating Roman rule as well as the Byzantine and Muslim periods are especially well represented by a large number of assorted items: coins, jewels, sculptures, pottery and ceramics and funerary steles. Among the most remarkable objects are: a portrait modeled on a skull found in Jericho ▲ *316* (around 6000 BC); a vase with a human head from Canaanite times; a Bull's head (left) dating from the Bronze Age (1500–1200 BC); the lintels of the Holy Sepulcher ▲ *272*; carved plasterwork and sculptures from the palace of the Umayyad caliph Hisham ▲ *318* (including several anthropomorphic representations and an incised stucco cupola which covered the hammam); wood panels from the Al-Aqsa Mosque ▲ *286*; several sculptures from the time of the Crusades; and a number of works dating from the Ottoman period (right, the head of a 14th-century knight).

THE PAINTED HOUSES OF EAST JERUSALEM
A popular tradition, belonging to the Orient, demands that on every return from the pilgrimage to Mecca, the happy *Hadji* should paint the outside of his house with a fresco depicting his spiritual journey step by step. It usually incorporates a boat or a plane, according to the chosen mode of transport, the *Kaaba* of Mecca, the green dome of the mosque at Medina – tomb of the prophet – and lastly, the Dome of the Rock ▲ *284*, the last stage of this fifth pillar of Islam, the pilgrimage.

▲ JERUSALEM TO JERICHO

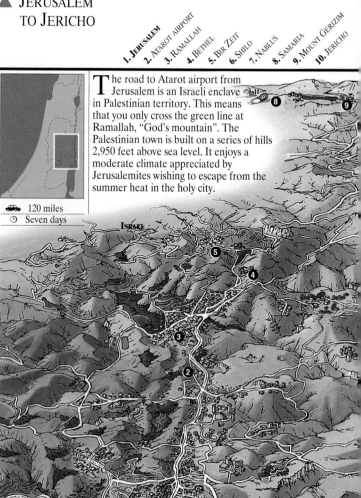

The road to Atarot airport from Jerusalem is an Israeli enclave in Palestinian territory. This means that you only cross the green line at Ramallah, "God's mountain". The Palestinian town is built on a series of hills 2,950 feet above sea level. It enjoys a moderate climate appreciated by Jerusalemites wishing to escape from the summer heat in the holy city.

🚌 120 miles
⏱ Seven days

The first archeological digs show that the site has been occupied since the Bronze Age. Ramallah became an important economic center at the end of the 19th century, but went into decline in 1967 ● 43. The town has nonetheless remained the area's administrative center and since the 1980's has seen the creation of women's groups wanting to preserve their Palestinian cultural heritage, including such local crafts as pottery and embroidery. About 4 miles north of Ramallah is the old city of Beth El, the ancient

11. KHIRBET AL-MAFJAR
12. MOUNT OF THE TEMPTATION
13. HEROD'S PALACE
14. ST GEORGE'S MONASTERY
15. NABI MUSA

SAMARIA

JORDAN

JORDAN VALLEY

ISRAEL

BETHEL ("house of God"). This was where Jacob dreamed of the ladder descending from heaven, marking the land which God had chosen (Genesis 28). The town became one of the most important cultural centers of the northern kingdoms after King Solomon's death ● 47.
BIR ZEIT, on the road to Nablus, boasts a prestigious Palestinian university. Before crossing Jabal Batin, a little road to the right leads to the site of SHILOH (SEILUN), Israel's ancient religious capital, of which nothing remains. However, the town received the ark of the covenant on the return from the Exodus (Joshua 18) and was the center of the Jewish faith for two centuries. Defeated by the Philistines, who seized the ark, the town was abandoned around 1000 BC (1 Samuel 4).

Local tradition dictates that men pick the olives in the groves of Samaria.

JENIN
The city is the gateway to Samaria from the Jezreel Plain, called in the book of Joshua Ein Ganim ("garden spring") because of its astonishing fertility. Jenin was the scene of a famous miracle performed by Christ, who cured ten lepers there (Luke 17), and is home today to a large Christian Arab community. It is a symbol of Palestinian nationalism, and its prosperity comes from its orchards.

Lamartine's first impression of Jericho after crossing the Judean Desert: "We rushed at a gallop on our horses, drawn by the novelty of the sight, and by the attraction of the freshness, humidity and shade which filled this valley: there were the greenest of green lawns everywhere, and they were full of clumps of rushes in flower scattered here and there."

JERICHO (YERIHO, AR-RIHA) ★

Ar-Riha, the modern Arab town which stretches out about a mile east of the tell of ancient Jericho, is only the last link in a chain which has seen a succession of changing civilizations over ten thousand years. This biblical city is most famous for the fall of its walls, caused by the holy ram's horn trumpets blown by Joshua's priests. Jericho was the first city conquered by the Hebrews after the Exodus, and was razed to the ground and cursed (Joshua 6). It was rebuilt by Ahab in the 9th century BC and then fortified by the Maccabees. Jesus passed through it several times in the course of his ministry, including the time when he cured two people's blindness. It was there also that the tax collector Zacchaeus promised to return fourfold the sums that he had extorted (Luke 19). Like Mesopotamia, the oasis of Jericho was not a place which encouraged the growth and even less the conservation, of monumental architecture. Dried-out bricks made of earth, dung and straw, were, until the recent advent of breeze blocks, the main building materials used, which explains the almost complete disappearance of traditional architecture. Today the town displays a broken-down urban network devoid of any guiding principles of town planning. The luxuriant tropical vegetation of the site, however, is a pleasing note in the otherwise muddled, graceless

rchitectural mass of this
illennia-old city. Today, the
dest town in the world, and
s youngest capital, has no
ore than seventeen
ousand inhabitants.
s in Gaza, you will find many
efugees who fled Israel in
948, both in town, where they
ork in business, and particularly in
e camp of Aqabat al-Jar to the south
f the oasis. The region's participation
the intifada ▲ 335 has remained
iscreet, because tourism, vital to the municipal economy,
at the mercy of the slightest curfew. Jericho, a city
ugged by a sacred river, is home to a mixed African and
rab population and has a laid-back atmosphere accentuated
y its tropical vegetation; the village of Abu Diuk, pressed
gainst the side of the Mount of Temptation, houses a black
frican population. The population professes Islam,
ut also honors the Evangelist and has a small Christian
ommunity. The community is made up mostly of the original
alestinian refugees who are Greek and Russian Orthodox
nd Catholics. The two parishes and a brand new mosque
reet you at the entrance to the conglomeration. Apart from
s calm and the hospitality of its inhabitants, the town has
ttle to offer travelers. The morning markets, in the center,
ith stalls overflowing with bananas, dates or pomegranates,
st manage to rouse the sleepy town. You will enjoy exploring
e area.

LISHA'S SPRING. The secret of the town's prosperity lies
idden in the direction of the huge mound of old Jericho:
lisha's spring. Now known by its Arabic name of Ein al-
ultan ("Sultan's spring"), it was purified, according to
gend, by this prophet, who threw a handful of salt into it
2 Kings 2). The resurgence of this vast supply of
nderground water is still vital to the agriculture of the whole
region: an ingenious system of irrigation
begins there, distributing the precious
resource to the very edges of the
plain. The ancient town was built
on the hill
opposite the
spring. It is
accessible on
foot from
the town
center. North
of Elisha's
spring is Hisham's
Palace (Qirbat al-
Mafyar) ▲ 318).

THE ALLENBY BRIDGE
The strategic
importance of this
bridge is
disproportionate to
its structural
simplicity. Officially
the Jordanians do not
regard it as a border
post, for they have
never accepted the
annexation of Trans-
jordan, while the
Israelis have put an
important garrison
there. The tension in
the area is palpable.

THE TREE OF HELL
This thorny tree,
indigenous to this
area, produces a fruit
which the Koran
suggests as rations for
miscreants who will
meet the fires of
Gehenna (hell).
The pits from its fruit
yield a bitter oil used
in the treatment
of rheumatism.

315

▲ THE TELL OF JERICHO

The tell is an artificial hill formed from archeological debris ▲ 394.

The oldest city ever discovered is situated near the modern city of Jericho, more than 60 feet below ground level, under a pile of rocks, earth and the superposed ruins of the many cities which followed it. Built almost ten thousand years ago, the first Jericho has yielded a primitive private dwelling, public works and a whole set of archeological artifacts teaching us about the civilization of its different occupants.

FORTIFICATIONS
The ability of a community to undertake the construction of public buildings marks its passage to the status of an urban society. The discovery of a wall (above) dating from the 13th century BC flanked by a defensive tower (right), makes Jericho the oldest city in the world. This 6 ½-foot-thick wall with solid foundations anchored in the rock was erected on a base of tightly placed stones. Later civilizations did not achieve such an accomplished mastery of masonry.

SKULLS
Archeologists still puzzle over the meaning of these skulls covered in clay from neolithic times, almost certainly linked to Sumerian and Canaanite myths about man's creation from dust.

RECTANGULAR DWELLINGS
Following the circular shelters in 7000 BC, these houses mark a symbolic turning point: for the first time a building built by man follows a geometric plan, the rectangle, a human invention different from the curve, which appears in nature.

Discovered on the north bank of Wadi Nueima in 1935, the *qasr*, or "palace" of Hisham, named after the eighth Omayyad caliph, would have been built during his reign, between 724 and 743, but does not seem to have been inhabited except by his heir, El-Malik II, who made it his winter residence. The palace was considered to be one of the best examples of Islamic art and architecture of the earliest times, but was destroyed by an earthquake in 747. The site, then abandoned, was called Khirbet el-Mafjar: the "ruins of Mafjar".

The square palace flanked by round towers was arranged around a central courtyard lined with arcaded galleries in the middle of which the decorated lintel (above) of a window could be seen.

1. CENTRAL COURTYARD
2. SMALL MOSQUE
3. COLD ROOM
4. LARGE MOSQUE
5. RECEPTION ROOM
6. "FRIGIDARIUM"
7. "DIWAN"
8. POOL
9. RAMPARTS

THE RESIDENCE
The stairs situated at the two opposite angles of the courtyard made it possible to reach the rooms on the first floor, which were decorated with painted murals. The ground floor was reserved for guests, servants and storage.

THE MOSQUE
The mosque was identified thanks to its *mihrab*, and was built according to a rectangular plan. Its roof was supported by a double row of three arches, each one resting on pillars which are still visible.

THE BATHS

In the northern part of the palace the baths included a reception room, a series of small bathrooms and latrines. The *frigidarium*, the main room of the part set aside for ablutions, measured 35 square yards and its roof rose into a central dome.

The floor of the *frigidarium*, the baths and the *diwan* was paved with mosaics of colored stone.

The *diwan* was a room furnished with cushions. It included an apsidal platform in its northern end. Benches lined the walls of the room with eight windows.

The main entrance to the baths to the east was formed by a high dome-covered arcade. The dome rested on a cylindrical drum lit by fourteen niches containing plaster statues. The interior of the porch was covered with artistically sculpted stucco. In addition, four small rooms off the *frigidaruim* have been found. Two of these rooms had a refreshing atmosphere, while the other two were heated by furnaces whose pipes hidden in the thick walls spread the heat.

DECORATION

The architects used a large spread of floral motifs like palm and vine leaves, pine cones, and rosettes, but the dominant decorative element was the acanthus leaf, symbol of paradise. Carved on the capitals and the colonnades, it was painted red and blue or gilded with gold leaf.

The rose dome with acanthus leaves of the *iwan*, typical of Corinthian style, served as a setting for six busts grouped around a blooming flower in the middle.

UMAYYAD STATUARY
The plaster statues found in the entrance to the palace corridors and under the porch of the bath room represented the full-size forms of men and women, and animals crouched down below the niches.

The architecture and decoration of the palace were influenced by Christian, Byzantine and Sassanid traditions. For the first time in Palestine, stucco – a glue-based coating which imitates marble – was mainly used as an ornament and base material in the construction of windows, balustrades and corbelling where human, animal, floral and geometric motifs of Sassanid inspiration appeared.

Although the archeologists named it the "mosaic of the tree of Life" the floor of what was the *diwan*

▲ *318*

of the palace has strictly profane motifs. Its beauty is a testimony to the perfection of the work of

the Umayyad artisans whose remarkably preserved works also decorate the floor of the *frigidarium*.

AROUND JERICHO

THE MOUNT OF TEMPTATION. After his baptism, "Jesus was led into the desert by the Holy Ghost to be tempted by the Devil" (Matthew 4). Jesus fasted there for forty days and forty nights before being tempted three times by Satan: "Again, the devil taketh him up into an exceeding high mountain, and sheweth him all the kingdoms of the world, and the glory of them; and saith unto him, All these things will I give thee, if thou wilt fall down and worship me" (Matthew 4). According to lore, a mountain to the west of Jericho is the one on which Christ finally triumphed over the tempter. Crusaders called it the "Mount of the Forty" (*Deir el-Qarantal* in Arabic) and since this time it has been a hill frequented by Christian pilgrims. At its peak is a GREEK ORTHODOX MONASTERY, restored in the 19th century on the ruins of a Byzantine church. Its foundations contain the cave in which Jesus stayed for forty days.

HEROD'S PALACE ● *120*. Built on both sides of Wadi Qelt, next to the Hasmonean buildings which it includes, the palace of Jericho was where King Herod took refuge from the harsh Jerusalem winters. Even today it can still give you an idea of its former glory. Its luxurious baths on the north side, linked to the gardens and palace of the south side by a bridge, are, perhaps, the most striking feature of the Herodian period. The splendid basins were decorated with precious mosaics, and surrounded by walls covered with frescos. The baths are accessible through a gigantic reception hall surrounded by marble and gold columns, similar to the entrance to the Temple in Jerusalem.

Herod's impending death gave rise to a struggle for influence among his children over his succession, which he cruelly curbed. The monarch died in the palace and is said to be buried near there, but his grave has never been found ▲ *229*.

ST GEORGE'S MONASTERY ★.

Clinging to the escarpments of Wadi Qelt, the narrow canyon which links Jerusalem to Jericho, the blue domes of one of the oldest monastic communities of the Holy Land pierce the monochromatic landscape. Since the beginning of Christianity, these cliffs full of caves were the refuge of hermits, later of the Lauras ▲ *230*, when those communities developed. The present buildings date from the 19th century, but the site has been occupied since the 5th century, and demolition and reconstruction have often taken place since then. For the most part the monks admit visitors and will willingly act as guides. The most spectacular attractions of the monastery are the 6th-century mosaic set in the floor of the Church of St John, and the funerary niches of the martyred monks (including Saint George of Koziba, who gave his name to the community). Brave travelers can walk from Jerusalem to Jericho following the bed of Wadi Qelt, but should be in good physical shape and have plenty of water for the trek through the desert which takes over five hours.

NABI MUSA. The last lines of *Deuteronomy* recount how Moses died on the top of Mount Nebo in present-day Jordan. Its peak, about 18½ miles away, is visible from Nabi Musa. "He buried him in a valley in the land of Moab, over against Beth-Peor; but no man knoweth of his sepulchre unto this day." In order to make up for this loss, Allah showed Salah al-Din in a dream the spot where the Prophet should be venerated. A cenotaph was erected there, then a mosque was built on top by Baybar in 1269. Popular enthusiasm soon promoted the cenotaph into the actual place of burial. At the beginning of the 19th century the Turks even instituted an annual pilgrimage which drew a fervent crowd all the way from Jerusalem. The British mandate put an end to this practice, claiming it was too disruptive to public order. Non-Muslims are allowed into the mosque if suitably dressed.

ST GEORGE'S MONASTERY
Since the monastery's reconstruction in 1878, St George has been occupied by Greek Orthodox monks.

New interest in the hermetic way of life has turned the caves of Wadi Qelt, empty for centuries, into retreats for modern hermits.

PILGRIMAGE TO NABI MUSA
Tens of thousands of pilgrims coming on

foot from Jerusalem camped for a week at the foot of the tomb.

The Shephelah describes the hills which run along the mountains of Judea as far as the coastal plain. The valley of Ayalon and the cliff that dominates it have been the scene of great battles for control of the land through the ages, in particular against the Philistines. Samson, whose deeds will lead us to Gaza, and the misfortunes of the Ark of the Covenant, are symbols of this rivalry. This road which links Jerusalem to the sea, was also traveled by the Evangelist's disciples.

SAMSON AGAINST THE PHILISTINES, IN THE TEMPLE OF DAGON
"And Samson took hold of the two middle pillars upon which the house stood, and on which it was borne up, of the one with his right hand, and of the other with his left. And Samson said, Let me die with the Philistines. And he bowed himself with all his might; and the house fell upon the lords and upon all the people that were therein. So the dead which he slew at his death were more than they which he slew in his life." (Judges 16)

THE ARK OF THE COVENANT FALLS INTO PHILISTINE HANDS
"The Philistines fought and Israel was smitten, and they fled every man into his tent: and there was a very great slaughter; for there fell of Israel thirty thousand footmen. And the ark of God was taken; and the two sons of Eli, Hophni and Phinehas, were slain." (1 Samuel 4)

THE DISCIPLES AT EMMAUS MEET JESUS

"And it came to pass, as he sat at meat with them, he took bread, and blessed it, and brake, and gave to them. And their eyes were opened, and they knew him; and he vanished out of their sight." (Luke 24)

PHILIP BAPTIZES A EUNUCH

"And the eunuch said, See, here is water; what doth hinder me to be baptized? . . . they went down, both into the water, both Philip and the eunuch, and he baptized him. And when they were come out of the water, the Spirit of the Lord caught away Philip, that the eunuch saw him no more." (Acts 8)

THE ARK OF THE COVENANT IS MOVED TO JERUSALEM

"And David arose, and went with all the people that were with him from Baale of Judah, to bring up from thence the ark of God . . . And they set the ark of God upon a new cart . . . And David and all the house of Israel played before the Lord on all manner of instruments . . . even on harps, and on psalteries, and on timbrels, and on cornets, and on cymbals." (2 Samuel 6)

THE BATTLE OF AYALON

"And it came to pass, while Saul talked unto the priest, that the noise that was in the host of the Philistines went on and increased: and Saul said unto the priest, Withdraw thine hand. And Saul and all the people that were with him assembled themselves, and they came to the battle: and behold, every man's sword was against his fellow . . . So the Lord saved Israel that day." (1 Samuel 14)

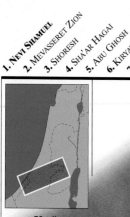

75 miles
Four days

The west way out of Jerusalem is overlooked by the hill of Nevi Shamuel, which has a Crusader church at its summit. It was occupied by the Premonstrants from 1157 and turned into a mosque in the 17th century. The excavations around it, completed in 1994, have made it possible to identify objects dating from the time of the First Temple to the Crusades. This site is perhaps the high place of Gibeon, the ancient Canaanite town where Solomon asked for wisdom (1 Kings 3:4-15), but, contrary to what has traditionally been held since the 6th century, Samuel's burial place is not there but at Ramah (1 Samuel 25:1). The Crusaders first caught sight of Jerusalem from this high vantage point and called it Montjoie.

THE BAB EL-OUED PASS. After passing through Motza and Mevasseret Zion you come across the ruins of the Arab village of Castel above you to the left. The military head of the Palestinian resistance, El-Husayni, was killed here in 1948, during a battle that was crucial to the success of the Zionist offensive. At the Shoresh crossroads, there is a monument to the memory of the combatants who died in the battle for control of the only road giving access to Jerusalem. This is where the Bab el-Oued pass (Sha'ar Hagai in Hebrew) starts: the shells of army lorries at the side of the road are tragic evidence of Israel's fight for independence during the spring of 1948. Arab fighters attacked supply convoys en route from Tel Aviv for Jerusalem, driving at night without lights. These ambushes often resulted in the deaths of dozens of men and the loss of provisions. The men of the Haganah therefore carved out another route further south. This was the "ßirmania route", open to the fire of the Jordanian legion. At the end of the motorway to Abu Ghosh you will find Ein Hemed National Park. This site was the Romans' *Aqua Bella* where Titus' soldiers came to relax; later, the Crusaders built a

THE TENTH ROMAN LEGION
An inscription in the crypt of the Crusader church reveals the presence of a detachment of the tenth Roman legion in Abu Ghosh, in the reign of Vespasian (1st century AD). A vast Roman reservoir collects water from the spring. Travelers to Nicopolis, in the plain, or to Jerusalem stopped in the area. In the 7th century, after the Muslim conquest, caliphs used the Roman road between Jerusalem and Rame.

JERUSALEM TO GAZA

country house there. The ruins of the medieval building amid the trees and the small river running through create a romantic setting.

ABU GHOSH

The old road crosses Abu Ghosh, a busy Arab village built on the hillside. It was known in the past as Kiryat el-Anab ("town of grapes") and, with its 8th-century caravanserai, was long confused with Kiryat Yearim ("town of forests"). This was where, according to the Bible, the Ark of the Covenant stayed for twenty years before David took it to Jerusalem (2 Samuel 7). The large 19th-century statue of Mary holding the baby Jesus, above Abu Ghosh near the Church of Our Lady of the Ark of the Covenant, celebrates this connection. "At Kiryat el-Anab we saw a spring coming out of a rock and the water tasted delicious," wrote the Persian traveler, Nassiri Khosrau, in 1047. The Crusaders decided that this water flowed from the spring at Emmaus. Anxious to leave their mark on siting episodes from the New Testament, the Crusaders named this site as the scene of Christ's appearance to two of his disciples during a famous meal. They built one of the most beautiful Romanesque buildings of Palestine there, the Church of the Resurrection, above the holy spring. Offered to Napoleon III by the sultan the church was acquired in 1900 by the French state. In the meantime, a line of sheikhs gave their name to the village which became Abu Ghosh.

MEETING ABU GHOSH
Chateaubriand revived the tradition of pilgrimage to the Holy Land, and after visiting Jerusalem, met the Arab chief whose patronym was Abu Ghosh: "We found, at the bottom of the valley of Terebinth, the Arab chiefs of Jeremy, Abu Ghosh and Jaber: they were expecting us. We arrived at Jeremy around midnight: we had to eat a lamb which Abu Ghosh had prepared for us. I wanted to give him some money, but he refused it and asked me only to send him two chests of Damietta rice."

327

The spring bubbling from the rock (an ancient holy place of the cult of Baal) and its proximity to Jerusalem (8 miles) made Abu Ghosh both a holy and a strategic spot. In the 1st century the Romans built a staging post there with two cisterns. Then in the 7th century the caliphs built a *khan* there, before the Crusades; the Crusader church was built around 1142. Thereafter the site was alternately abandoned and restored, and finally given to the French government in 1873; today it is inhabited by Benedictine monks and nuns of the order of Mount-Olivet.

To the left of the entrance to the crypt is a Roman inscription of the 10th Fretensis Legion.

THE CRUSADER CHURCH
The Crusaders raised the walls of the old Roman cistern anchored in the rock in order to build the choir facing the west ● *110*, the nave and the side aisles of their church. The great unity of the space is apparent in the inside of a structure which is both pure and austere and which, from the outside, does not reveal its purpose.

THE COURSE OF THE WATER
The spring was linked to the caravanserai by a clever arrangement of basins and pipes making their way through the rock.

Souls in Abraham's bosom and the faces of Abel and Jacob (above) appear from now on. The discoveries of French 19th-century archeologists (above, top) made it possible to undertake restoration.

RESTORING THE CHURCH FRESCOS

In spite of having suffered at the hand of man and from the passage of time, a glimmer of the original splendor of the Romanesque frescoes which decorate the inside of the church can still be made out. They have been stoned and beaten with hammers by Muslims for whom human representation was equated with idolatry, and covered with calcite by humidity from the water coming up through the thick walls of the old reservoir. Their preservation was becoming a matter of great urgency. This has now been done: at the end of a period of restoration, the screen of calcite has disappeared and the layer of paint is fixed. The restoration has been undertaken by reconstructing what could have been there using removable pigments.

MONKS AND NUNS
The brothers and sisters of the monastery pray together, according to a tradition dating back to the 15th century. The community in this Israeli-Palestinian village includes men and women from France, Africa, Russia and America.

THE CRYPT
From the end of the nave, a staircase leads to the crypt. It is there, between the pillars which support the floor of the upper church, that the spring bubbles up.

THE JERUSALEM–TEL AVIV TRAIN
The railway track goes through the Sorek Valley, once full of forts used by the Philistines in their attacks against King David's Jerusalem.

LATRUN WINE
Trappist monks originally brought stocks of black and white grapes here from France. The vineyard developed quickly and in 1917, Turkish officers emptied the casks so as to deprive their British adversaries of the pleasure of tasting the contents which already enjoyed a good reputation. Latrun won first prize for dry wines at the Jaffa exhibition of 1927. The monks, devoted to the French tradition of wine-making, now produce more than 300,000 bottles of wine annually, 80 percent of which are dry.

LATRUN

The Cistercian Abbey of Latrun, famous for the quality of its wines, was founded in 1890 by Trappist monks from Burgundy. It was built on a hill dominated by the remains of a Crusader castle where Richard the Lionheart took refuge. From its position at the crossroads on the plain, the abbey witnessed battles between the British and the Germans and Turks in 1917, and between Jews and Arabs in 1948. About half a mile northeast you will find the ancient Amwas, where the Maccabees confronted the Syrian Hellenists in the 2nd century BC. The town which was here in the Roman era was identified by the Byzantines as the village of Emmaus, where Jesus made himself known to two of his disciples after the resurrection (Luke 24). In a property owned by the French community of the Beatitudes you can visit the central apside of a church and an interesting cruciform baptistry, both from the 5th century. The Arab village of Imwas, razed to the ground in 1967, has given way to "Canada Park", with its view of the whole plain of Ayalon.

TEL GEZER

This flattened hill, situated in the middle of the plain of Esdrelon, once controlled the routes linking the empires of Egypt and Assyria (the semitic root GZR means "to cut"). Inhabited since the year 3000 BC, fortified fourteen centuries later, it is cited among the conquests of Thutmose III. Tel Gezer was taken by the Assyrian Teglat Phalashar III, and destroyed by Sheshonq. Tel Gezer regained its strategic role during the revolt of the

Maccabees ● *48*, and became the personal property of the Hasmoneans. The site was excavated in 1902 having been forgotten since the 12th century. Archeologists discovered a palace, stelae, a hydraulic system recalling the one at Megiddo, and one of the oldest known Hebrew agricultural calendars (950 BC).

THE PLAIN OF SHEPHELAH

This large valley is a transitional point between the Judean Hills, the Tel Aviv–Jaffa coastal plain to the south, and the Negev Desert. In its chalky subsoil (*kirton*) covered by a layer of enriched limestone (*nari*) astonishing underground cavities have been carved out. The Canaanite towns there were conquered by the Philistines, who came from the central Mediterranean in the 12th century BC. They stamped the region with their mark of a mixed Semitic-Mycenian civilization, whose temples and pottery initially decorated in "monochrome" and then in "bichrome" are typical. In the 6th century BC, the Edomites from Jordan settled in the Shephelah, following the First Jewish Exile to Babylon, creating Idumea. Following the revolt of 70 crushed by Hadrian, the Romans did not use the name Judea, and then westerners called the Holy Land by its Hellenized name of Philistia, or Palestine.

BET SHEMESH

Bet Shemesh ("house of the sun"), a Judean border town, is above all famous for having received the Ark of the Covenant from the Philistines (1 Sam 6:9–20). Near the rapidly expanding modern town, excavations have uncovered decorated Philistine pottery from the First Iron Age (1200–1000 BC).

BET GUVRIN

Here you are in the heart of Idumea, in countryside full of fields and vines. Coming from Jerusalem, the Roman road is marked by many carved milestones. Nearby Tel Goded hides tunnels and underground rooms where the memory of the refugees from the Jewish revolt led by Bar Kochba ● *50* lives on. At Bet Guvrin in the year 200 Septimus Severus created Eleutheropolis ("Free Town"), on which a vast region depended. An amphitheater, a rare structure in the Roman Orient, revealed in 1980, could accommodate five thousand spectators. Several church mosaics and the inscribed lintel of an inn reveal the dynamism of the Byzantine town which, ravaged by the Arabs, was partially rebuilt by King Fulk of Jerusalem in 1136.

THE GEZER CALENDAR
Carved on a stele (left), the months appear with the cycles of sowing and harvesting.

DAVID AND GOLIATH
The valley where tradition sites the fight between David and Goliath (1 Sam 17:12–58) ends at Ha Ela junction. Today it leads to the memorial to French Jews who were deported during the Vichy years. A scene from the American film of King David, made in 1985 is below.

Discovered in the plain of Shephelah, this Jewish tomb made with rounded stone, dates from the 1st century AD.

331

THE CAPTURE OF LACHISH BY SENNACHERIB
The Assyrian king decorated his palace of Nineveh with a bas-relief, preserved in the British Museum, London, which illustrated the capture of Lachish as a way of indicating its importance. The detail opposite shows an assault on a defence tower. Around the Judean fortified palace which dominates the tell, excavations have uncovered 850 arrow tips, another sign of the fighting. Access to the fortified gate of the town, the Assyrian assault ramp (246 x 197 feet) and the Judean counter-ramp are being restored.

THE ROMAN AGORA
The Ashkelon National Park is extended by a vast rectangular esplanade enclosed by a low wall. Between palm trees and cedars there are colonnades with richly decorated capitals which were erected during the four centuries of Roman occupation.

MARESHA

This town belonged to the tribe of Judah (Joshua 15:44) and later became the thriving capital of Hellenistic Idumea. It was conquered by John Hyrcanus of Judea around 112 BC, and was restored by Pompey only to be destroyed by the Parthians in 40 BC (1 Macc 65-66; Jewish Antiquities XIII, XIV). Supplanted by Bet Guvrin, it was never rebuilt and the ruins of the ancient town center and the fortifications are in the best state of any Hellenistic town of the Levant. The below-ground areas of the lower town, filled with cisterns, have revealed oil presses and houses built of kirton "bricks" which have provided a rich variety of household items.

LACHISH

Built on one of the biggest tells of the Holy Land, Lachish flourished under the Canaanites. Archives from Tel Amarna in Egypt name three of its 14th-century kings. Fortifications and temples have yielded Egyptian items, the effigy of a gold-plated Canaanite goddess and the oldest known Canaanite

text written on shards. Lachish was the second town of Jewish Judea, Lachish was destroyed by Sennacherib in 701 BC (2 Chronicles 11:9 and 32:9). The discovery in 1937 of eighteen letters written on *ostraca* (pottery shards) by the governor of Jerusalem to the governor of Lachish not long before its destruction by the Babylonians in 586 BC shows that the Hebrew language at the time was identical to biblical Hebrew ● 58. Further east are the caves

of Hazan, containing old oil presses put together again for the refugees from Bar Kochba's revolt. To the west, toward Ashkelon, you cross the town of Kiryat Gat, where integration of Jewish immigrants from Morocco, Ethiopia and Russia is taking place. Its name is borrowed from one of the five main towns of the Philistine region. Gat was one, and the others were Ashkelon, Ashdod, Ekron and Gaza (Joshua 13:3). At the edge of the coastal valley, you can dip into the hot, sulphurous springs of Hamei Yoav.

ASHKELON

The ancient tell of Ashkelon is in the Yigal Yadin park, buried in the modern town. The southernmost town in Israel, it is as famous for its mellow lifestyle due to the temperate climate year round, as for its garden city appearance. Ashkelon is shaped like a huge bowl, and sheltered some twenty towns between 3500 BC and AD 1500. Divided by the sea, the strata are visible from the beach where excavations are being carried out. To the north, the rampart of earth and sun-dried bricks dating from the Middle Bronze Age (2000–1550) dwarfs the tourist with its 82-foot-high walls. Below, the temple of the small "silver calf", sheltered in its sanctuary of baked clay, welcomed the visitor (Hosea 13:1–2). Ashkelon became one of the five Philistine towns often attacked by the Hebrews around 1175 BC. Samson carried out his legendary massacre here (Judges 14:19). In 604, Nebuchadnezzar destroyed the town and exiled the Philistines. In the 6th century, the Persians made Ashkelon "a daughter of Tyre" of Lebanon when they accused the Phoenicians of exploiting the coast from Acre to Gaza. They have left us a spectacular cemetery of seven hundred dogs. Their divinity, Astarté-Phanebal of the doves, was still venerated in Roman times. The pillars of a civil basilica with effigies of Victory and Isis still adorn the park. In Byzantine times, the town was famous for its wines. Ashkelon produced a perfumed onion, later known in Europe as the shallot. THE CHURCH OF ST MARY THE GREEN, which leans against Richard the Lionheart's walls, taken down by Salah al-Din, bears witness to the fact that the Crusaders passed through.

A LACHISH CAT
This 14th–13th century BC object in carved ivory from the temple of Lachish, escaped the fire and has preserved its natural color.

EXCAVATIONS AT ASHKELON
The excavation site (above) is in the National Park where remains of the many portside businesses from the Canaanites to the Ottomans lie on top of one another, dominated by the Crusader wall which crowns the outline of these imposing ruins to form a sort of belvedere. Among the many statues that have been uncovered are an Isis with Harpocrates leaning on her shoulder, and two famous representations of the goddess Nike, one of which is reproduced left.

PHILISTINE SARCOPHAGI AT DEIR EL-BALAH
The Philistines were an Indo-European people brought by the migration of the sea people and stopped at its ports by Egypt in the 12th century. They were more advanced than the Hebrews, and knew about fire. They settled in the Holy Land at the time when the Jews were conquering it from the east. Even vanquished they were a formidable neighbor for Israel.

This center, situated in the south of the Holy Land, about 2 ½ miles from the coast, has been known since earliest times. It was a stage on the Via Maris between Mesopotamia and Egypt, and the scene of successive invasions. This city, with its history of rebellions, still proclaims its desire to control its own destiny.

HISTORY OF THE TOWN. Gaza, at the gateway to Egypt, was conquered by the pharaoh Thutmose III in 1468, then coveted by the Assyrians and the Persians. Alexander the Great took it, reducing the population to slavery after two months of siege. However, the Roman period was calm and prosperous, and the fame of Gaza wine reached as far as Western Europe. The town became a center of rhetoric with the temples of Apollo, Athena and Marna, the Cretan god, guard it. It was only in 330 that Christianity reached Maioumas, the port of Gaza. In 363 Emperor Julian allowed the violence against Christians to escalate. In the 5th century, Bishop Porphyrus, with the help of Eudoxia, empress of the east, tackled paganism: eight temples were razed to the ground and new churches were built, one of which was dedicated to Eudoxia. When the Arabs crushed the Byzantines, sixty soldiers refused to convert, choosing rather to die. The memory of these "martyrs of the faith" is perpetuated. The Crusaders were not unaware of the strategic importance of the town which, for one hundred years, was part of the Latin states. In 1244, it was once again attacked and destroyed, as the Crusades to the east came to an end. In 1517 the Mameluks presided over the destiny of the town, which had become the center of the district. Then in 1799 Gaza once again fell victim to a conqueror. This time it was Napoleon Bonaparte. But the town was flourishing and, preferring commerce to combat, it opened its doors to the exhausted French troops. During World War One, Gaza

JEWISH MOSAICS
The remains of a synagogue have been revealed in Rashid Street in south Gaza. Fragments of a 4th-century mosaic floor (above) have survived. They portray animals lodging in vine branches and, very unusually, a human figure, that of King David with a harp.

was one of the bases used by the Germans and Turks. The English lost more than ten thousand men in order to open the road to Jerusalem. Gaza then became a part of Palestine under the British mandate. After the 1948 war the area around the city, known as the "Gaza Strip" (196 square miles), was administered from Cairo without being annexed by Egypt. The first direct confrontations between Israelis and Palestinians after 1949 took place there at the time of the Israeli occupation following the 1956 Suez conflict. Troops were withdrawn in 1957, and while Fatah structured itself and infused Palestinian nationalism with new life, the Gaza Strip was once again occupied in 1967 after the Six-day War ● *43*. Twenty-seven years of military occupation followed, with the landscape punctuated with barbed wire around isolated refugee camps and army control points. Radical resistance was organized from the start, but was met with fierce measures. The movement nonetheless continued, finding its apogee between May and June 1979, when Egypt and Israel had just signed the Camp David Accords. However, it was the Intifada of 1987 that brought the world's attention to the problem. The revolt which began in Gaza, in the refugee camp of Jabaliya, was "not terrorism ... it was a people rising up" (Y. Smilanski). Following the Oslo Accords between Israel and the Palestine Liberation Organization, Gaza became autonomous on May 4, 1994.

THE INTIFADA
This Palestinian uprising in the occupied territories stunned the world by its audacity and length and forced the Israeli government to negotiate with the PLO. In the camps (above) of Lebanon, Jordan and Syria, Palestinians are still waiting to be allowed to return.

A FATAH POSTER
The Palestinian organization makes clear (above) the demands of a people for rights to its land.

The Towns, a painting by the Palestinian artist Tayseer Barakat, a native of Deir el-Balah.

The Great Mosque, or Ahmed's mosque, in Gaza, 1914.

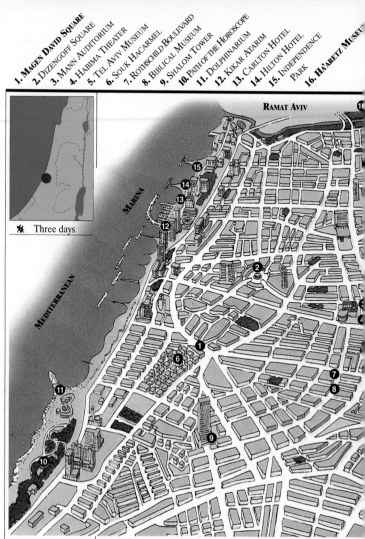

1. MAGEN DAVID SQUARE
2. DIZENGOFF SQUARE
3. MANN AUDITORIUM
4. HABIMA THEATER
5. TEL AVIV MUSEUM
6. SOUK HACARMEL
7. ROTHSCHILD BOULEVARD
8. BIBLICAL MUSEUM
9. SHALOM TOWER
10. PATH OF THE HOROSCOPE
11. DOLPHINARIUM
12. KIKAR ATARIM
13. CARLTON HOTEL
14. HILTON HOTEL
15. INDEPENDENCE PARK
16. HA'ARETZ MUSEUM

RAMAT AVIV

MARINA

MEDITERRANEAN

✳ Three days

"[Jaffa] is a very prosperous town, well built in squared stone, of a richness and comfort which surprise when you arrive from Egypt, and it is surrounded by old ramparts which form a double enclosure on land. The roads are so steep that neither horses not mules can climb them, and this slope means that you see the sea with the slightest turn, often from vaulted passages which seem to date from the crusades."
Thomas Seddon,
Memoir and Letters

Tel Aviv is the economic and cultural center of Israel, the city of leisure and night life, but also the center for business, newspapers and publishing. Banks have their head offices there, and more than half the big companies as well as a quarter of the active population of Israel work there. Today, greater Tel Aviv, that is the city and its suburbs (Ramat Gan, Ramat Aviv, Bat Yam and Holan Givatayim) has about one million inhabitants. Its history began in 1909 when a group of Jewish immigrants in Jaffa bought some desert dunes from the Turks who then ruled Palestine. They built (for the first time in two thousand years in the Holy Land) a Jewish town, a modern city situated on the periphery of one of the oldest ports in the world. In fact the origins of Jaffa have been traced as far back as the Flood.

JAFFA

A TOWN OF LEGENDS. *Yafo* (the beautiful one) for the Hebrews, *Joppeh* for the Greeks, *Joppa* for the Romans, *Yafa* for the Arabs, *Yopheh* for the Crusaders, Jaffa was, according to legend, created by Japhet, the son of Noah. The first fortified city on the hill of Jaffa dates from 1800 BC. Papyruses

EXHIBITION PARK

have conveyed to us the history of the soldiers of the Pharaoh Thutmose III who conquered the town in the 15th century BC by entering hidden in jars. Jaffa next underwent the rule of the Philistines, Phoenicians and Persians. According to the Bible, it was at Jaffa that the cedars from present-day Lebanon were unloaded for the Second Temple built by Solomon. In 322 BC the city fell into the hands of Alexander the Great. When it became Roman it was given to Cleopatra by Mark Anthony, then returned to Herod. It fell into decline when he preferred Caesarea.

THE PORT OF PILGRIMS. The arrival of the Crusaders in 1091 made Jaffa the "port of Jerusalem". It was taken back by Salah al-Din in 1187, then by Richard the Lionheart four years later. After 1291 Jaffa was ruled for two centuries by Mamelukes and for four years by Turks. This last period was interrupted by the conquest of Napoleon Bonaparte, who became famous in Jaffa for having his own soldiers, sick with plague, shot. The decline of Acre after 1840 was exploited by Jaffa, which once again attracted pilgrims, travelers and immigrants.

UNDER THE BRITISH MANDATE. Jaffa was conquered by General Allenby in 1917, and its proximity to Tel Aviv exacerbated conflicts between Jews (who, in the face of riots, left the old city in large numbers in 1929) and Arabs. In 1948 the Jewish minority again found refuge in Tel Aviv, from where Zionist organizations started attacks against the Palestinian population of Jaffa. Many of the 70,000 people left the place and in 1950 Jaffa was incorporated administratively into Tel Aviv.

RESTORATION. In 1960 the Israeli government and the municipality of Tel Aviv decided to reconstruct the old town. Today the restored houses on the top of the hill are home to a community of artists.

JONAH AND THE WHALE
According to the Bible, it was at Jaffa that Jonah embarked, abandoning the mission to Nineveh which God had sent him on.

"We have just dropped anchor in Jaffa, the town being to our south-east, and the minaret of the mosque is to the east south-east"
Chateaubriand in the Holy Land.

JAFFA SEEN FROM THE SEA
On a hill facing the sea, Jaffa is flanked by two natural and fairly shallow bays to the north and south, a position encouraging to very early settlements as well as providing an excellent harbor from the time of Antiquity. The port was founded by Simon Maccabee in 142 BC.

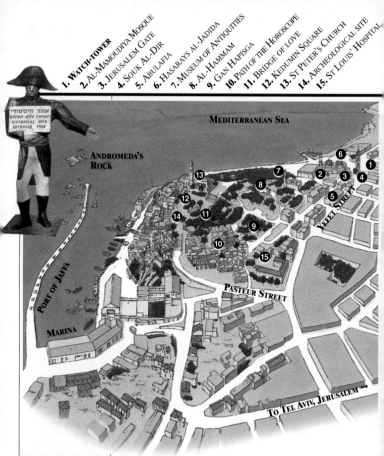

1. WATCH-TOWER
2. AL-MAMOUDIYA MOSQUE
3. JERUSALEM GATE
4. SOUK AL-DIR
5. ABULAFIA
6. HASARAYS AL-JADIDA
7. MUSEUM OF ANTIQUITIES
8. AL-HAMMAM
9. GAN HAPISGA
10. PATH OF THE HOROSCOPE
11. BRIDGE OF LOVE
12. KEDUMIM SQUARE
13. ST PETER'S CHURCH
14. ARCHEOLOGICAL SITE
15. ST LOUIS' HOSPITAL

MEDITERRANEAN SEA

ANDROMEDA'S ROCK

PORT OF JAFFA

MARINA

YEFET STREET

PASTEUR STREET

TO TEL AVIV, JERUSALEM →

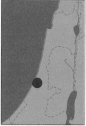

✖ One day

STATUE OF NAPOLEON
This statue in Kedumim Square indicates the entrance to the underground museum.

OLD JAFFA

Jaffa today is a wonderful place in which to wander. You will find many craftsmen's quarters, boutiques, restaurants, and a flea market – all open on Saturday.

AROUND THE CLOCK TOWER. Built in 1906 by Sultan Abdul Hamid II for the thirtieth anniversary of his reign, this tower marks the entrance to the old town. The buildings which surround it, on Haganah Square, date from Ottoman times. To the west of this square is the mosque of AL-MAMOUDIYEH constructed from the ruins of Ashkelon and Caesarea. It was built in 1812, like the neighboring Suleyman's fountain, by the Turkish governor Mahmud whose despotism earned him a nickname meaning the giver of blows. The Abulafia bakery, a veritable institution in Jaffa, is at Yefet Street, near the SOUK HAPISHPESHIM (flea market). Antique shops abound in the alleyways, next to Yehuda Ragousi Street, which boasts beautiful Ottoman houses, many still in ruins.

THE MUSEUM OF ANTIQUITIES AND ITS SURROUNDINGS.
It occupies the palace of the governor Mahmud and its collections of objects from neolithic to Byzantine times, come from excavations on the hill of Jaffa. Ancient Turkish baths nearby are now the site of the Aladani Restaurant. The museum is surrounded by stepped gardens (GAN HAPISGA) which include an amphitheater and a "bridge of love", with a view over the whole of Tel Aviv, on which newlyweds have their pictures taken. Below, a huge door has been found which is part of the façade of a citadel dating from the time of Ramses II.

NEAR KEDUMIM SQUARE. On Mifratz Shlomo Street, the Franciscan church of St Peter, built in 1650, is linked by a set of steps to Kedumim Square, in the center of which walls from the time of Ramses II and traces of the Roman town of Flavia Joppa have been found. In the paved alleys nearby you will find the old religious hostelries, which once sheltered pilgrims.

THE ARAB QUARTER. ST GEORGE near Pasteur Road is the main Greek Orthodox church. The Saint Louis French Hospital is at the corner where this road joins Yefet Street. On the right, going up to an Arab quarter (both Muslim and Christian) is the Church of St Anthony. A detour toward the sea allows you to see some beautiful houses as well as the Maronite church on Dolphin Road.

THE PORT

You can get to the lighthouse by walking through the alleyways of the old town.
Behind it is the house of Simon the Tanner, where the Apostle Peter resuscitated Tabitha (Acts 9:40). The port of Jaffa, where all the conceivable methods of catching fish are practiced, is surrounded by old warehouses containing restaurants with enchanting marine décor that tend to be very busy on Saturdays.

ANDROMEDA'S ROCK. To enter the port, trawlers use a channel between two rocks; one of them bears the name of Andromeda: Cassiopeia's daughter was chained there to appease the anger of a sea monster sent by Poseidon, and saved *in extremis* by Perseus. Near the sea, in the direction of Tel Aviv, past the Armenian church and ST NICHOLAS' MONASTERY (Haster Harmonium) is JIAMAH AL-BAHAR, a mosque which used to serve the sailors as a landmark.

THE PATH OF THE HOROSCOPE ★
The alleyways of this picturesque quarter of the old city bear the names of the signs of the zodiac (above).

The Church of St Peter, Kedumim Square

THE JAFFA ORANGE
This fruit, produced on fertile soil which stretches to the east of the town, owes its initial fame to Palestinian peasants. They were initiated into the techniques of grafting citrus fruits by the German Templars in 1869. Palestinian production was mostly exported, and only equalled in 1948 by Jewish farmers.

THE "HILL OF SPRING"

The creation of Tel Aviv was declared on the dunes in 1908. Building of the city was immediately organized and from 1920 the first communal vehicles ran on its asphalt-covered roads.

LE-SOL JUIF
RENAÎT

ITS CREATION

Architects from all over Europe found in Tel Aviv an opportunity to apply principles learned from modern masters such as Walter Gropius and Le Corbusier. They adapted them to the demands of the local climate. The new avant-garde architecture immediately won over the developers with its rationality and the socialist pioneers with its proud, egalitarian appearance.

TEL AVIV

In 1909, a group of Jewish immigrants from Jaffa acquired some desert dunes from the Turks who then ruled Palestine. These were situated to the north of the town which was called Tel Aviv, "the hill of spring", after the hill of the same name where the Babylonian exiles settled.

BIRTH OF A METROPOLIS. Tel Aviv began life as a canvas camping ground but grew between 1920 and 1936 under the guidance of its first mayor, Meir Dizengoff. The first solid building there was a school, the HERZLIYA GYMNASIUM. The town developed with the arrival of money from the Diaspora. It obtained municipal autonomy from the British, and a 1923 statute authorized the creation of its own police force to combat Palestinian rebellion. Arab riots did not stop, however, and in 1929 the Jews of Jaffa left the old town for the new city. In 1936 the great Palestinian strike blocked the port of Jaffa and the youth of Tel Aviv dug a new port in twenty-four hours. However, it could receive only light cargo. From that time the city developed its commercial side.

A TEMPORARY CAPITAL. Jews fleeing Nazi Germany came to swell the population of Tel Aviv, which grew from 15,000 to 220,000 inhabitants between 1915 and 1947. The city was bombarded by Italian and French planes during World War Two. The political center of the Jewish population, chosen by Ben Gurion to proclaim the creation of Israel in 1948, Tel Aviv was to be the temporary capital of the new state for a year. It was built by immigrants who reproduced and adapted European models and the city forms an unusual architectural whole: neo-classical houses built in the 1920's are juxtaposed with International Style buildings, which were built in the 1930's under the influence of the German Bauhaus and Le Corbusier.

> "PLAIN WHITE FAÇADES, WITHOUT SOCIALLY OSTENTATIOUS DISTINGUISHING MARKS, AIRY PILES SUPPORTING THE BUILDINGS, FLAT ROOFS AND AN APPEARANCE OF A STEAMER OR TURBINE CHARACTERIZES THIS NEW ARCHITECTURE." C. WEILL-ROCHANT

BAUHAUS STYLE

Natives of Tel Aviv call the style of the apartment blocks built between 1930 and 1948 "Bauhaus". Usually called the International Style, this architecture was born of the debates and experiments conducted in the 1920's, particularly in the famous German art and design school of the Bauhaus. Around Dizengoff Square and Rothschild Boulevard there are some four thousand buildings in the International Style. It was at the beginning of the 1930's at the time when the city was undergoing enormous expansion that the International Style really took over under the architect Arieh Sharon, a former Bauhaus pupil. Basic shapes made of concrete, plain white façades without any ostentatious ornamentation, airy supporting piles, roof terraces and the appearance of a steamer or turbine characterize this new architecture.

DIZENGOFF SQUARE
Dizengoff Square in the heart of Tel Aviv was the symbol of the new spirit of the city in the 1930's. Its layout was drawn up in the master plan of the Scottish town planner Sir Patrick Geddes, inspired by English garden cities. But his architecture, like that of all the blocks built at this time, is inspired by the International Style. The square is the work of Genia Averbuch (above) and other architects like Arieh Sharon and Yehuda Magidovitz. It was for a competition in 1934 that Genia Averbuch conceived the plan for the square and the architectural project.

THE CENTER OF TEL AVIV

The main roads of Tel Aviv linking Jaffa to the northern part of the city meet at MAGEN DAVID SQUARE. As its shape suggests (star of David with six points), this square is the meeting point for six avenues: Sheinkin Street, lined with boutiques and cafés, where Tel Aviv's young people gather, Allenby Road which joins, from the coast, the old central station and lastly George Hamelech Street, which leads to DIZENGOFF SQUARE. In the middle of this square that bears the name of the first mayor of Tel Aviv, is the MODERN FOUNTAIN "FIRE AND WATER", conceived in 1986 by the Israeli artist Yaacov Agam. Here the pedestrian part of Dizengoff Street starts and with it a concentration of restaurants and cafés. Some, such as Kassit, have had Frank Sinatra, among other celebrities, as customers.

THE CULTURAL CENTER. Its entrance on Dizengoff Street is marked by the MANN AUDITORIUM (from the name of a wealthy American), the largest concert hall in Israel, where the national Philharmonic Orchestra plays. Behind the building facing Habima Square are the CAMERI and HABIMA THEATERS, where the first plays in modern Hebrew were staged. Finally, at the corner of Tarsat Street is the HELENA RUBINSTEIN PAVILION, an annex of the ART MUSEUM OF TEL AVIV which displays works of modern art by Israeli, Palestinian and foreign artists. Dizengoff Street then crosses the most important commercial center of Tel Aviv – set out on several levels, it has boutiques, cafés and cinemas – and rejoins BIALIK STREET full of residences (open to the public) which belonged to a number of famous figures. Number 14 is the residence of the Israeli painter Reuven Rubin. Number 22, flanked by a small tower and a façade similar to the Doge's Palace in Venice, was the home (now a museum) of the Israeli poet Haim Nahman Bialik, a militant writer in favor of the rebirth of Hebrew. Number 27 is occupied by the HISTORICAL MUSEUM of Tel Aviv and Jaffa, founded in 1956, where written documents, maps and photographs are preserved.

SOUK HACARMEL ★. The Eastern atmosphere of this market, where fruits and spices flood in every day, contrasts with the modernity of the quasi-European city. Next to the market the YEMENITE QUARTER, one of the most picturesque in the city, attracts tourists as well as the souk vendors and natives of Tel Aviv.

THE MUSEUMS OF ROTHSCHILD BOULEVARD.
Running through a dried-out wadi, this road brings you to number 23, the MUSEUM OF THE HAGANAH, devoted to the history of Tzahal ▲ *374*. At the entrance to Nahalat Binyamin Road is the monument to the founders of the city, created in 1950 by the sculptor Aharon Priver. The old HOUSE

OF MEIR DIZENGOFF at number 16, where David Ben-Gurion announced the Declaration of Independence of Israel on May 14, 1948 ● *56,* houses an art museum. Rare copies of the Scriptures are displayed there; in 1973 it became the BIBLE MUSEUM.

SHALOM TOWER. Built in 1979 on Herzl Street on the site of the old Herzliya Gymnasium ▲ *342* (the first solid building of Tel Aviv) the Shalom Tower, the highest building in the city, forms the heart of the business center. It houses offices, boutiques, a wax museum and, from the top of its thirty-seven floors, offers a panoramic view of Tel Aviv and its environs.

SOUK HACARMEL
The souks of Tel Aviv begin at Allenby Street, each one more or less indistinguishable from the last. In Hacarmel Street the businesses established by corporations offer fruits, vegetables, cooking utensils, clothes and material on their shaded stalls. In the adjacent alleys are basket makers and small shops selling spices, olives and dried fruit.

HABIMA THEATER
The theater is the shrine of dramatic art where both classical and contemporary pieces are staged. At the time of Tel Aviv in Spring and the Festival of Music and Theater of Israel ◆ *411,* the theater's stage is graced by troupes from all over the world.

"Bursa"
The largest center in the world for transforming and dealing in diamonds occupies two large towers in Hatzionut Square in Ramat Gan, the eastern suburb of Tel Aviv. The diamond industry here was founded before World War One by Jewish immigrants. After 1945 Palestine became the foremost center in the world for diamond cutting.

BESIDE THE SEA

The beach of white sand stretches out for nearly 4 miles along the Mediterranean coast, lined with luxury hotels reached from Jaffa by Hayarkon Road. This last bears the name of the Yarkon River which, before David and Solomon, marked the border between the territories of two of the twelve tribes, Dan and Ephraim. Today it separates Tel Aviv from the suburbs of Ramat Gan and Ramat Aviv.

THE PROMENADE. It begins in the CHARLES CLORE GARDEN, an immense area of greenery where ice-cream sellers and café terraces invite you to pause a while. Here, around the dolphinarium which is at the end of the park, you will find many skateboarders, skilful in a sport which is very fashionable in Tel Aviv. Continuing northward the promenade comes out on Gordon Road, the "street of galleries" where the works of Picasso and Chagall ● *144* are displayed as well as those of Israeli artists such as Nahum Guttman ● *140* ★. Toward Ramat Aviv, KIKAR ATARIM, a vast, open-air concrete commercial complex displays its exuberant colors. Overlooking the Tel Aviv marina to the south, this 1960's complex rises at the beginning of Ben Gurion Boulevard where the one-time residence of the Israeli Prime Minister, at number 17, has been turned into a museum. Once past the marina, where you can hire boats, surfboards and other equipment for nautical sports, are the Carlton and Hilton hotels next to one another, opposite a swimming pool with sea water maintained at a constant temperature of around 75°F. The Hilton, conceived by the Israeli architect

Yaacov Rechter, rises up in the middle of
INDEPENDENCE PARK. Further on you will
see the port of Tel Aviv. Nowadays the
traffic has slowed, as the shallow waters
which force ships to anchor at sea has
hampered its expansion.

RAMAT AVIV

Along the banks of the river, HAYARKON
PARK, highly valued by the natives of Tel
Aviv, stretches out to the edge of Ramat
Aviv. In the heart of this luxuriant haven
of peace, a path leads to a tropical garden
and an open-air amphitheater where
concerts are held. The suburb is also
home to the Exhibition Park of Tel Aviv,
located on both sides of the Ayalon
highway. Since 1956 the university of Tel
Aviv has been on the north side of the
Yarkon River at Ramat Aviv. In this area
arranged around the archeological site of
TEL QASILE ▲ 348, are the two largest
museums in the city : HA'ARETZ ▲ 348, a complex with no
fewer than eleven departments, and the Diaspora Museum or
"BET HATEFUTSOT" ▲ 350. The excavations undertaken on
the tell have shown occupation of these places by twelve
successive civilizations from neolithic times to the 15th
century AD. The archeological material which it yielded is
mostly preserved in three of the Ha'aretz
Museum's pavilions.

"KIKAR LEVANA" ★
This environmental
sculpture by the
Israeli artist Dani
Karavan, *Kikar
Levana* (White
Square) crowns
Wolfson Park from its
place at the summit
of a hill which
dominates the city. A
belvedere tower
allows you to take in
the panorama: the
sea which borders the
city to the west, and

the hills of Judea to
the east. The pyramid
symbolizes a tent, in
homage to the
pioneers who built
the city. The
geometric shapes in
white concrete are
enlivened by natural
or ephemeral
elements: rays of
light, lines of water,
the sound of the wind
blowing through the
pipes, a line of grass
across the sculpture,
an olive tree inside
the open dome.

The 1948 excavations of the tell of Qasile, to the north of the city, revealed a dozen archeological layers, from the 13th century BC to the 15th century AD. When Walter Moses offered his collection of ancient glass to the city of Tel Aviv, the idea was born of starting an archeological, anthropological and historical museum dedicated to ha-'Aretz Israel, the land of Israel, on the hill of Tel Qasile. The collections of the Ha'aretz Museum, opened in 1953, are presented in eleven pavilions devoted to glass, ceramics, the alphabet and numismatics.

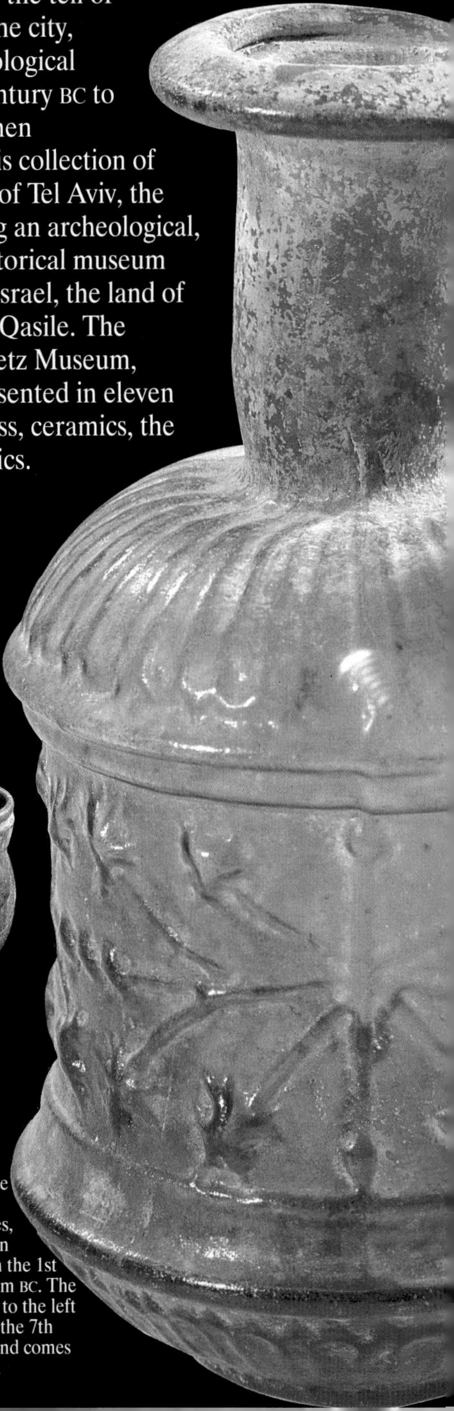

THE CERAMICS PAVILION
Objects found here make it possible to retrace the history of ceramics in Palestine, in the ancient Orient (below) and also in Central America.

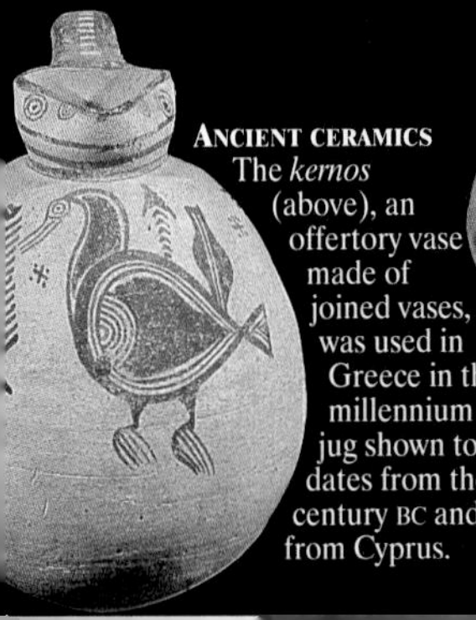

ANCIENT CERAMICS
The *kernos* (above), an offertory vase made of joined vases, was used in Greece in the 1st millennium BC. The jug shown to the left dates from the 7th century BC and comes from Cyprus.

ETHNOLOGY AND FOLKLORE
This pavilion displays popular Jewish objects relating to ritual and art from the Diaspora, as well as the finds of the excavations at Tel Qasile: it was there that this 11th-century BC cylindrical support with human forms was found.

THE GLASS PAVILION
The collection of ancient glass includes Mediterranean pieces from the Old Bronze Age to Islamic times: it is one of the most comprehensive in the world. To the left is a molded glass jug dating from the 1st century AD.

NUMISMATICS
The museum has almost eight thousand coins struck in the Holy Land. Above is a coin of Bar Kochba ● *51*.

AN ATHLETE THROWING THE JAVELIN
This *kylix*, a cup with slightly curved horizontal handles, is representative of Classical Greek art (5th century BC).

Conceived to strengthen the links between the Jews of Israel and those who are dispersed throughout the rest of the world, the Diaspora Museum (*Bet Hatefutsot*) retraces two thousand years of Jewish history from the destruction of the Second Temple in AD 70. It offers in addition an ethnographic vision of the future of Israel and emphasizes what has allowed the Jewish people to survive through the centuries. *Bet Hatefutsot* is made up of six departments devoted to the family, community, spirituality, creativity, relations with the surrounding milieu and the return to Israel. This Museum, open to the public since 1978, contains collections of objects that are the fruits of reconstruction or the product of artists' imaginations, guided by men of science who specialize in Judaism and the civilization of the Jewish people.

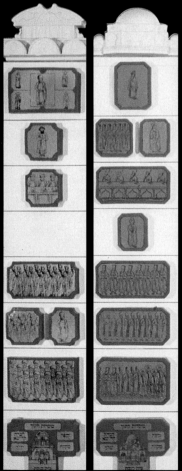

THE COMMUNITY
The "institution" of community, a gathering together of families, has made it possible for the Jewish people to survive in the Diaspora, maintaining their identity while steeping themselves in outside influences. The thousands of Jewish communities across the world are represented here in schematic form, enabling the constants in their organization to emerge.

BELIEF
Belief, for the Jew, is the dedication of an effort acquired through study and behavior. It expresses itself in the synagogue, represented here by thirty models from around the world.

CREATIVITY
The Text and culture which the Jews of the Diaspora encountered form the two sources of their creativity. The manuscripts gathered here are testimony to this attachment to the written word and to study in general.

THE FAMILY

The place and role of each member of the family, the duties of the parents who run it, and the events which punctuate traditional Jewish family life, are themes touched on with the aid of scenography.

AMONG THE NATIONS

To live in the Diaspora is to live under the eye of other nations and, while this was often beneficial, it sometimes ended in the destruction of centuries of communal life by the massacre or banishment of the Jews.

RETURN

The nostalgic aspiration of the Jews to return, symbolized by the *menorah* ● *109* and turned into an ideology by Theodor Herzl, culminated in the creation of the State of Israel ● *43* in 1948. The exiled peoples gathered in Israel were defined by a cultural pluralism which is illustrated by a large collection of photographs.

351

The south of Tel Aviv was one of the first areas to be invested in by the Jewish pioneers of the first Aliyah ● *157* who at the end of the 19th century, founded Rishon Lezion and Rehovot. Here Ramla is one of the few Palestinian villages to have kept its Arab identity.

RAMLA (RAMLEH)

Built in 716 on the dunes (*ramle*) by the Umayyad caliph Suleyman Abd al-Malek, the city swiftly became an important stage on the caravan route between Syria and Egypt. Having been laid waste by war and earthquakes, Ramla was entirely reconstructed by the Mamlukes who took it in 1267. Its convent was built in the 16th century, dedicated to those who buried Christ, Joseph of Arimathea and Nicomedes. It was there that Bonaparte stayed during the Syrian campaign. Since 1948 Ramla has become an important town for immigrants and one where Palestinians coexist with the Jewish population. In the heart of the souk, which has kept all its authenticity, the GREAT MOSQUE has imposing Crusader vaults and pillars decorated with capitals ● *128* of the old medieval cathedral of St John, one of the best preserved in Palestine.

THE MAIN SQUARE. The town's two most important buildings, the SQUARE TOWER and the WHITE MOSQUE, stand opposite each other on the main square. Here on the Thursday after Easter ● *86* festivities in honor of Nebi Saleh (the Muslim prophet of Ramla) take place. Suleyman, the founder of the village, dug three immense CISTERNS of 8,250 cubic yards. Two of them, known as *Al-Anzia* by the Arabs, are accessible from Haganah Road.

THE SQUARE TOWER AND THE WHITE MOSQUE
The Square Tower (above) was built in 1318 by the Mamluke sultan Kalun Salah. It combines the religious function of a minaret with an observation tower: its summit dominates the vast countryside which extends in the west as far as the Mediterranean Sea, and in the east to the foot of the mountains of Judea and Samaria. At almost 100 feet high, the building now overlooks the desolate ruins of the White Mosque, a complex created by Suleyman in the 8th century. In the earliest days of Muslim rule ● *52*, it housed the government and religious administrators of the region. Only one minaret remains of this complex which collapsed in the 18th century.

> **"GO THY WAY, EAT THY BREAD WITH JOY, AND DRINK THY WINE WITH A MERRY HEART: FOR GOD NOW ACCEPTETH THY WORKS."**
> (ECCLESIASTES 9)

REHOVOT

Rehovot was founded by farmers in 1880 on lands bought by a Zionist organization. The viticultural area, soon planted with almond trees, was transformed into a vast orange grove. One of the largest centers for scientific research in the country, the WEIZMANN INSTITUTE, is in Rehovot. The institute, founded in 1934, which today uses close to two thousand researchers, biologists, chemists, physicists and mathematicians, has acquired an international reputation. Its buildings, which include a particle accelerator, cover some 250 acres of lawn and gardens. At the eastern edge of the campus CHAIM WEIZMANN'S HOUSE (a fine example of architecture heralding the International Style) was designed by Eric Mendelsohn in 1937.

RISHON LEZION

In 1882 one of the three colonies of the first Aliyah ● *152* (seventeen families originally from Russia) founded the agricultural village baptized Rishon Lezion ("the first in Zion"). Five years later Baron Edmond de Rothschild subsidized the kibbutz ● *132* there to develop viticulture. Rishon Lezion today is one of the biggest towns in Israel.
DISCOVERING RISHON LEZION. A yellow band painted on the surface of roads in the town leads the visitor to the museum, where historical documents and objects from everyday life from the time of the pioneers are on display. The museum's buildings were built by the founders of the city, and include the first synagogue in Palestine built by Zionist pioneers and the first Hebrew-speaking playground for children.
THE CELLARS OF EASTERN CARMEL. These very sophisticated cellars were conceived by the German architect Shumacher in 1897. They produce the wine ▲ *354* which is now the most famous in the country: from the end of the 19th century, viticultural properties in the region could cultivate the stock of Bourgogne and Bordeaux, using the advice of the French agronomists sent by Baron de Rothschild.

It was in 1885 at Rishon Lezion that a Jewish flag was unfurled for the first time. On the occasion of the third anniversary of the colony the pioneers used the prayer shawl of its founder, Zeev Abramovitch, as a banner: they embroidered a star of David ● *106* on it in the same shade of blue as its stripes.

CHAIM WEIZMANN (1874–1952)
Born in Motol in Russia, Chaim Weizmann studied chemistry in Europe before running laboratories for the British Admiralty in 1914 where he achieved the synthesis of acetone, a product indispensable to the manufacture of munitions. In 1920 he settled in Rehovot, where he founded a scientific institute in 1934. Ten years later this became the Weizmann Institute. A committed Zionist and a militant of the worldwide Zionist Organization, Chaim Weizmann became the first president of the State of Israel in 1949.

▲ WINE

Wine is mentioned in the Old and New Testaments and is an essential element in Jewish and Christian rituals. It plays a big role in the history of a millennium in the Holy Land, and although viticulture was interrupted by the settlement of Muslims in Palestine, some vineyards placed under Christian auspices were still properly maintained. At the end of the 19th century the vine was reborn, under the impetus of Baron de Rothschild. Today, some twenty sites produce characteristic white, rosé and red wines as well as kosher wines developed under the watchful eye of rabbis.

THE DISTRIBUTION OF WINE PRODUCTION

Wines are placed in five main classifications, each of which corresponds roughly to a region:
1. *Galil*: Upper and Lower Galilee, Golan plateau (Meron);
2. *Shomron*: Mount Carmel, coastal plain (Zichron Yaacov);

3. *Shimson*: Shephaleh Valley and Ayalon Valley (Ashkelon, Latrun, Rishon Lezion;)
4. *Harei Yehuda*: hills of Judea (Hebron, Bethlehem, Jerusalem);
5. *Negev*: Negev (Beersheba)

BARON EDMOND DE ROTHSCHILD
It was he who financed the construction of the Rishon Lezion ▲ 353 and Zichron Yaacov cellars which today put out 75 percent of production. After an outbreak of phylloxera in 1890, he taught the wine growers to plant vines grafted from American stock.

354

KOSHER WINE

The laws of *kashrut* are applied to every stage of production, from growing the vine to bottling the wine. No gentile is allowed to take part in the wine-making process.

PRODUCTION

Israel's latitude places it in a zone naturally adapted to the growth of *vitis vinifera*, made of Cabernet Sauvignon, Merlot and Chardonnay. Today, with the help of artificial irrigation, wine-growers can grow grapes in the Negev. The process of vinification is classic (harvest, fermentation, conservation and ageing), except for kosher wines.

WINE, JUDAISM AND CHRISTIANITY

Wine is associated with times of great religious Jewish occasions and ceremonies. At the start of Shabbat, the head of the family blesses the wine (this is *kiddush*). It is customary to drink four cups at the *seder* on Pesach ● *80*, two at a wedding and one to celebrate a circumcision. For Christians bread and wine are directly involved in the mystery of transubstantiation. This is what Jesus proclaimed when he said, "He that eateth my flesh, and drinketh my blood, dwelleth in me, and I in him" (John 6).

PACKAGING

The labels on the most sought-after bottles of wine generally give the following information: region (Shimshon), grape (Cabernet Sauvignon), color of the wine (red), cellar (Carmel), year, and when necessary, the kosher stamp. Less prestigious wines are often made with grapes from more than one stock.

From Tel Aviv to Haifa and as far as the large bay which leads to Akko, the Romans used the *via maris*, which linked Assyria to Egypt. This route is now a highway, and Crusader fortresses which dot the coast, ancient ports and immense beaches all invite travelers to stop and take a look around.

THE VINES OF ZICHRON YAACOV
A vineyard developed here thanks to Edmond de Rothschild, and the vines imported from France. The cellars are open to visitors all year round and a wine festival has been held every September since 1992.

HERZLIYA. This city, which was founded in 1924 by American immigrants who developed flourishing agriculture here, now has more than 65,000 inhabitants, and has become a coastal resort frequented by the cream of Israeli society and the intelligentsia. The elegant quarter of Herzliya Pituah is home to movie studios.

NETANYA. This coastal resort is very popular among French Jewish tourists who savor a familiar atmosphere because of the presence of many pieds-noirs there. With more than 100,000 inhabitants, Netanya lives principally on income from the hotel trade, citrus fruits, and diamond-cutting. The diamond industry was introduced in the 1930's by Belgian and Dutch immigrants and is currently among the foremost export activities of the country. To the north of the town, at Ayihayil, the MUSEUM OF THE JEWISH LEGION houses the archives of this group who fought with the Allies during World War Two. In the HASHARON MUSEUM, named after the valley which surrounds Netanya, is the *moshav* of Kefar Monash where archeological pieces, works of art and regional treasures are on display.

ZICHRON YAACOV. This is a residential town which was founded in 1882 by Romanian Jews near the ancient Arab Zammarine. Zichron Yaacov ("the memory of Jacob") is situated in the heart of a rich viticultural land.

EMPEROR HADRIAN
In Caesarea, you can see the red porphyry statue of the man who repressed the great revolt of AD 132.

TANTURA-DOR. The beach of the present-day Kibbutz Nahsholim ("the waves") is protected from the swell by four little islets. This site which already served as a refuge for ships in the 17th century BC was called Dora by the Phoenicians who

1. TEL AVIV 2. HERZLIYA 3. RAANANA 4. KFAR SABA 5. NETANYA 6. HADERA 7. TULKARM 8. CAESAREA 9. DOR 10. ZICHRON YAACOV 11. ATLIT 12. HAIFA 13. KIRYAT BIALIK 14. AKKO 15. ROSH HANIKRA

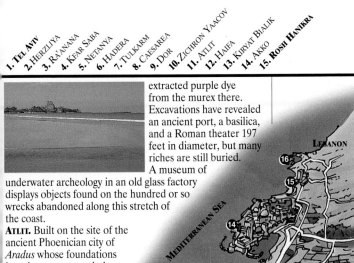

extracted purple dye from the murex there. Excavations have revealed an ancient port, a basilica, and a Roman theater 197 feet in diameter, but many riches are still buried. A museum of underwater archeology in an old glass factory displays objects found on the hundred or so wrecks abandoned along this stretch of the coast.

ATLIT. Built on the site of the ancient Phoenician city of *Aradus* whose foundations have been uncovered, the fortress of Atlit was the last Crusader stronghold to resist the Mamlukes until 1291. The "Castle of Pilgrims",

LEBANON

MEDITERRANEAN SEA

🚗 80 miles
🕐 Seven days

as it is called, protected a port which for a long time constituted the first access route, after Akko, for westerners traveling to Palestine.

Between the old salt marshes and the beach, Atlit fortress (above) served as a refuge for the Jewish resistance group Nili (an abbreviation of "the victory of Israel shall not be denied") during World War One, and as a prison for illegal immigrants before independence.

357

THE PRAISES OF FLAVIUS JOSEPHUS
The 1st-century Jewish historian who admired Caesarea wrote: "While the site was completely at odds with him, Herod got to grips with the difficulties so successfully that the solidity of his buildings revealed themselves completely to the test of the sea and their beauty shone forth."

AN IMPORTANT CHRISTIAN RELIGIOUS PLACE
At the time of his last voyage to Jerusalem in 58 the apostle Paul was arrested by the Jewish authorities, and saved from death by the Romans: "Keep ready to depart for Caesarea, at the third hour of the night, two hundred soldiers, seventy knights and two hundred men at arms. Let there also be horses to carry Paul and take him safe and sound to Governor Felix," ordered the tribune of Jerusalem. Paul was detained in Caesarea for two years and then transferred to Rome.

CAESAREA

Halfway between Tel Aviv and Haifa is an ancient Crusader site which was forgotten after the 13th century. Archeologists began to uncover it in the 1950's. Today the port city imagined and created haphazardly by Herod, king of the Jews from 37 to 4 BC, appears in all its glory.

THE CAPITAL OF JUDEA, A ROMAN PROVINCE. Caesarea was built on the site of a Phoenician port whose tower was kept by the Greeks. It is named after Caesar Augustus: in 30 BC Octavius, the grandson of Julius Caesar and the future Roman Emperor, gave Herod the site on which the town would be built. The king, a talented builder, made it into the biggest port of the east and, in twelve years, enlarged the city to an area of 370 acres within the ramparts, with roads, a theater, aqueducts, irrigation and drainage systems. Judea became a Roman province in AD 6 and Caesarea its capital, the seat of the procurators. The Acts of the Apostles tells us that Saint Paul was imprisoned there in 58 and 59. The Jewish minority of Caesarea, whose population was then mostly Greco-Syrian, was massacred for taking part in the revolt of 66–70 ● 50.

It was at Caesarea that the leaders of the revolt of 131 were put to death. Peace ensued and Christians were authorized to hold a Council there in 195.

AN INTELLECTUAL CENTER IN BYZANTINE TIMES. The Archbishop of Caesarea, Eusebius (264–340) wrote the *Onomastikon* in Greek there. It is the first geography of Palestine. In the 5th century, Christians of the East lived in the town which, until its capture by the Persians in 612 and then by the Arabs in 640, was proud of its library, the largest in the East after that of Alexandria.

THE CRUSADES. After taking Caesarea in 1101 and massacring its population, the Crusaders built their own town on a much smaller area. Forced to abandon it to Salah al-Din in 1187, they reconquered it in 1228 and Saint Louis built the impressive fortifications in 1251. These were not sufficient, however, to prevent the Mameluke Baybars from capturing the city in 1265. It then fell into oblivion.

THE RENAISSANCE OF CAESAREA. In 1878, the Ottoman government settled a Muslim community from Bosnia in Caesarea. They created a village of fishermen (it was destroyed in 1948). In 1940 the kibbutz of Kissaria (or Sdot Yam) was founded nearby, at the start of the first

excavations of the site.
Archeologists then followed, and
discoveries multiplied.

CAESAREA SAVED FROM THE SAND

Herod sent to Rome for the most exclusive building
materials and the excavations, between the Roman theater
and the Crusader fortifications, have again uncovered new
buildings, like Herod's palace, with a basin dug in the rock
which was once fed by soft water. The Roman hippodrome
built by Herod has only been partially excavated. At 1,050
feet long and 265 feet wide it was reserved for chariot
races and could hold twenty thousand people. Not far on,
along the "Byzantine Road" are
two statues. One in red
porphyry represents the
emperor Hadrian.

THE CRUSADER TOWN.
Entrance to the town is
gained via a postern with
two right angles typical of
the architecture imported
by the Latins, who found
among the ancient ruins
good quality materials
(the streets are of Carrera
marble) which accounts
for the remarkable state
of preservation of the
walls. Inside you can
still see traces of a
road protected by
arcades and those
of the church of St
Paul, which remained
unfinished. These
ruins are on the high
stone platform
which supported the
temple dedicated
to Augustus in
Herodian times.

The porticoes of the
Crusader fortress
(above) and the
carved marble foot
found in the Roman
theater in Caesarea
(left)

Hidden under the sea and swallowed by sands, Caesarea was discovered by fishermen in 1940 before being explored by workers from the kibbutz of Sdot Yam, and then mainly by Italian archeologists over a period of more than twenty years. They uncovered the very large Roman theater open to the sea – one of the most beautiful in the East – and took part in the restoration of the powerful Latin Gothic buildings. From the time of Antiquity, glass was manufactured in the region of Akko, and many vases and bottles have been dug up. In 1959 a jar filled with gold jewelry of the 12th and 13th centuries was found, and the site has not yet revealed all its secrets.

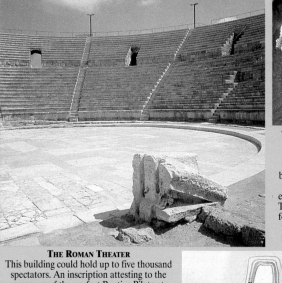

THE ENTRANCE TO THE CRUSADER FORTRESS
These Gothic buildings withstood the devastating earthquake of 1837. The Crusaders built for eternity because they believed they might see it again.

THE ROMAN THEATER
This building could hold up to five thousand spectators. An inscription attesting to the presence of the prefect Pontius Pilate at Caesarea at the time of Christ and a mosaic representing the masks of Comedy (below) and Tragedy have been discovered.

PALACE

BYZANTINE WALL

SECOND AVENI

ROMAN THEATER

← TO SDOT YAM

GLASS
These objects found in Caesarea are typical of the glass containers, or their remains, which archeologists uncovered in stratigraphic layers dating back to Roman times. A carafe, a bowl and a cosmetic bottle are seen here (left).

RESEARCH
It has made possible an appreciation of the vast scale of the Herodian work: walls and jetties were erected on a base of enormous submerged blocks.

AERIAL VIEW OF THE PORT
It was, according to Flavius Josephus, larger than Piraeus in Athens.

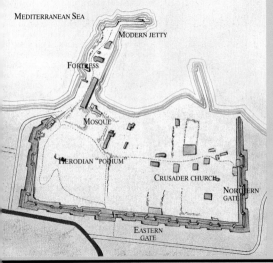

MEDITERRANEAN SEA

MODERN JETTY

FORTRESS

MOSQUE

HERODIAN "PODIUM"

CRUSADER CHURCH

NORTHERN GATE

EASTERN GATE

THE PORT
The port originally dedicated to Augustus by Herod is now full of boutiques, restaurants and cafés. Trips to sea allow you to view the ancient submerged remains of the fortress itself, often Roman columns. To the north of the enclosure built by the Crusaders, a path (not recommended for cars) crosses the place of the old Jewish quarter and runs along the beach as far as the aqueducts.

Mount Carmel, which overlooks the Mediterranean, is linked to the figure of Elijah, the first of the great prophets of Israel. In the face of corrupt and idolatrous royal rule, this exceptional figure represented fidelity to the covenant. A man of prayer whose beliefs were formed in the solitude of the mountain stream of Kerith, he could defy the powerful on earth. On Mount Carmel, he provoked the priests of Baal. Pursued by the vengeful Queen Jezebel, he sought in the Sinai the experience of prayer. His disappearance on a chariot of fire indicates, visually, the hold of the living God over the prophet's existence.

THE CHALLENGE TO IDOLS

"So Ahab sent unto all the children of Isra and gathered the prophets together unto Mount Carmel. And Elijah came unto a the people, and said, How long halt ye between two opinions? if the Lord be God follow him: but if Baal, then follow him. [...] and Elijah said unto the prophets of Baal, choose you on bullock for yourselves, and dress it first: for ye are many: and call on th name of your gods, but put no fire under. And they took the bullock which was given them, and they dressed it, and called on the name Baal from morning even until noon saying, O Baal, hear us. But there w no voice, nor any that answered [...] And it came to pass at the time of the offering of the evening sacrifice, that Elijah the prophet came near and said [...] Hear me, O Lord, hear me, that t people may know that thou art the Lo God [...] then the fire of the Lord fell, and consumed the burnt sacrifice and the wood." (1 Kings 18)

ELIJAH FED BY AN ANGEL IN THE DESERT
"But he himself went a day's journey into the wilderness, and came and sat down under a juniper tree: and he requested for himself that he might die; and said, it is enough; now O Lord, take away my life; for I am not better than my fathers. And as he lay and slept under a juniper tree, behold, then an angel touched him, and said unto him, Arise and eat. And he looked, and, behold, there was a cake baken on the coals, and a cruse of water at his head. And he did eat and drink, and laid him down again. And the angel of the Lord came again the second time, and touched him, and said, Arise and eat; because the journey is too great for thee. And he arose, and did eat and drink, and went in strength of that meat forty days and forty nights unto Horeb the mount of God."
(1 Kings 19)

THE RAISING OF ELIJAH ON A CHARIOT OF FIRE
"And fifty men of the sons of the prophets went, and stood to view afar off: and they two stood by Jordan. And Elijah took his mantle, and wrapped it together, and smote the waters, and they were divided hither and thither, so that they two went over dry ground; and it came to pass, when they were gone over, that Elijah said unto Elisha, Ask what I shall do for thee before I be taken away from thee. And Elisha said, I pray thee, let a double portion of thy spirit be upon me. And he said, Thou has asked a hard thing: nevertheless, if thou see me when I am taken from thee, it shall be so unto thee; but if not, it shall not be so. And it came to pass, as they still went on, and talked, that, behold, there appeared a chariot of fire, and horses of fire, and parted them both asunder; and Elijah went up by a whirlwind into heaven. And Elisha saw it and cried, My father, my father, the chariot of Israel, and the horsemen thereof. And he saw him no more and he took hold of his own clothes and rent them in two pieces. He took up also the mantle of Elijah that fell from him, and stood by the bank of the Jordan." (2 Kings 2)

HAIFA

THE CARMELITE MONASTERY
Also called *Stella Maris*, this monastery was built in the 19th century on the western tip of Mount Carmel, on top of ruins of older religious buildings. The interior of the church of Our Lady of Mount Carmel is covered in marble, and frescos illustrate episodes in the life of the prophet Elijah whose cave, which is the object of pilgrimages, is situated at the foot of the promontory.

When Chateaubriand saw Carmel from the sea his emotions were marked by "something both religious and august at the same time". The holy mountain which overshadows the site of Haifa, and is revered by adherents of the three religions of the Bible ▲ *362*, inspired him. The author could not follow in the footsteps of the Crusaders in the Holy Land without conveying this feeling in his writings, but the old city which he discovered was only a small town. Nobody could have predicted the renaissance which in the course of the 20th century has made Haifa Israel's prime industrial center. From the port to the nearby working-class district, the city has spread to the slopes of Mount Carmel, where you will find the business area and higher up, the residential quarter.

VERY ANCIENT ORIGINS. The remains of a human dwelling more than 100,000 years old have been discovered in Haifa and, according to the Bible, the prophet Elijah found refuge in a cave on Carmel to fight worshippers of Baal, in the 9th century BC. At the foot of Mount Carmel, on the site of an ancient Phoenician village, the old *Shiqmona* developed in the 4th century BC. This Hellenist, and later Byzantine, city was destroyed in 662 by Arabs.

> "MOUNT CARMEL, A RAISED CHAIN OF MOUNTAINS WHICH STARTS
> FROM THE JORDAN RIVER AND SUDDENLY STOPS AT THE SEA . . .
> ITS LINE OF DARK GREEN STANDS OUT ON A SKY OF DARK BLUE
> FULL OF WAVES OF WARM MISTS."
>   LAMARTINE

THE CRUSADES. The Latins took Haifa in 1099 when it was called Cayphas and was a Jewish and Muslim town. When they finally withdrew from it in 1265, the order of Carmel abandoned the slopes of the mountain which saw its birth, and Haifa, from where the Mamlukes were chased by the Turks in the 16th century, fell into a state of decay until the 18th century. The Bedouin Sheikh Daher al-Omar, master of Akko, extended his power to Haifa, rebuilding its walls and the port. In 1775, Al-Jazzar, his successor, allowed the Carmelites to return to Haifa.

THE DRUZES
The villages of Isfiya and Dalyat al-Carmel are inhabited mainly

by Druzes. This Isma'ili community, also found in Syria and Lebanon, enjoys special status in Israel: the Druzes serve in the army and have their own religious tribunals.

A TOWN OF IMMIGRANTS. The town's population fell to just eight thousand in 1890, but Haifa soon became a hub of communications: Turks built the railway which links Haifa to Damascus in 1904 and the port was enlarged in 1910. After World War One, the English established the railway link with Cairo. Haifa welcomed many new immigrants, and by 1931 its population had once again swelled to 100,000.

CARMEL

The *Carmelit*, a funicular railway, takes you to central Carmel. Mount Carmel, which was once covered in vines, rises 1,640 feet above sea level with escarpments of 985 feet facing the sea. Today it houses a residential quarter with sumptuous villas and luxury hotels which enjoy a panoramic view over the bay of Haifa. GAN HAEM PARK which runs along Panorama Road is a popular place among the town's inhabitants. There is a zoo there, and BET PINCHAS MUSEUM, dedicated to the prehistory and fauna of Carmel and the northern region. The national park of Mount Carmel offers a wide range of excursions across its 22,240 acres, which form the largest forest reserve in the country. THE UNIVERSITY OF HAIFA, whose buildings bear Oscar Niemeyer's signature, dominates the bay and the Galilee. It is home to the REUBEN

CARMEL WINE
Much care has been lavished on the vines of the slopes of Mount Carmel.

AND EDITH HECHT ARCHEOLOGICAL MUSEUM,
created to provide information about the
country, the land and the people of Israel, through
a wealth of archeological collections.

HAIFA TODAY. Haifa's rebirth came about through the
German Protestants (who settled in the areas of Kiryat
Eliyahu and Moshava Germanit), the French Catholics
(on the present-day French Carmel), Palestinians in
search of work (at the end of the 19th century), and
Jewish immigrants (in the 1930's). Many of its 250,000

**NATIONAL
MARITIME MUSEUM**
The Maritime
Museum was founded
in 1953 by the officer
of the Israeli
Marines, Arieh L.
Ben Ali, in the city of
Haifa. The museum is
a true study center,
devoted to five
thousand years of the
history of navigation
in the Mediterranean,
the Red Sea and the
Indian Ocean. Often
rare collections of old
sea maps, models of
boats and navigation
instruments are on
display, as well as
original engravings
depicting Haifa. An
old ship's bronze
beak, found in Atlit,
indicates the museum
entrance.

**"AN OPEN WINDOW
ON HAIFA"**
A gouache on panels
(above, right; private
collection) by the
Russian painter
Emmanuel Mané-
Katz (b. 1894). A
museum has been
founded in his house
in Haifa where he
lived until 1962. Many
artists arrange
exhibitions here.

inhabitants today have houses that overlook the blue waters
of the Mediterranean. Both a workers' town (the Histadrut
trade union was founded there in 1920) and a university town,
rich in cultural institutions and many museums, Haifa is also a
tolerant community where the different religious groups
(Jewish, Muslim, Druze, Christian and Bahai) live together in
harmony. It is a cosmopolitan town, more emancipated than
others from religious supervision, and buses run there on
Saturdays.

"HADAR HACARMEL"

This quarter whose Hebrew name means "glory of Carmel" is
situated above the port, halfway up the mountain. It is a
commercial, cultural and administrative center whose

activities revolve around Herzl Street, the Hadar's main road.

HAIFA MUSEUM. The museum has many sections: modern art, ethnology, and ancient art. The latter has a carefully set out collection of objects from the excavations at Caesarea, Shiqmona and Mount Carmel. One part is dedicated to the extraction of purple dye and another to women's hairstyles in Antiquity.

THE BAHAI TEMPLE ★. The golden dome which emerges halfway up Mount Carmel marks this sanctuary of the Bab ("Gate of Faith", a name taken by Mirza Ali Muhammad, the founder of the Bahai religion, executed in Persia in 1850) where the Faithful come on pilgrimage. The building is made of Chiampo stone and features Western architecture and Eastern decoration. The gardens, which overlook the bay and incorporate motifs inspired by Persian carpets, are a fascinating place in which to wander.

THE PORT AND ITS BASIN

The bay of Haifa offers natural shelter close to the port which continues to grow with the town and the industrial zone it has generated. It is around the port that you will find the oldest parts of the town. Dagon Tower, a grain silo and an example of beautiful industrial architecture, has a Wheat Museum housed in it. At the mouth of the River Kishon, the Shemen oil factory, one of Haifa's foremost industries, has a small museum on the manufacture of olive oil ● 76 from Antiquity.

MUSEUM OF CLANDESTINE IMMIGRATION. This museum, situated opposite Elijah's cave, is dedicated to a tragic period in the history of Haifa, when the British White Paper of 1939 authorized the mandate power to return or imprison Jewish immigrants over the quota of fifteen thousand people a year. It was then that the drama of immigrants who were turned away began as well as the era of blockade runners. Perhaps the best known of these events is the tragedy of the *Exodus*: on July 10, 1947, a steamer left Sete with five hundred Holocaust survivors on board. They were rejected by the British at Haifa and a confrontation resulted in five dead and many wounded. The passengers were taken back to France where they refused to step on dry land, and then to Hamburg. The museum displays many documents relating to this period, as well as the history of the Israeli navy since 1948.

AKKO (ACRE)

The town has been known since biblical times, and until the 19th century was a maritime port coveted by Syria and Persia. The Crusaders called it Acre and made it into an important base for two centuries, as the only sure refuge against storms on the Palestinian coast. Akko 's port – so important in the eastern Mediterranean for twenty-five centuries – was eventually deposed by Haifa ▲ *364*, which was more accessible to steamships.

HELLENISTIC PTOLEMAIS. After the conquests of Alexander the Great, Akko developed and took the name of Ptolemais. Its Jewish inhabitants did not regard it as an integral part of the land of Israel (it had not been conquered by Joshua) so they buried their dead 15 miles away on the slopes of Mount Carmel. It became the port of Damascus after its conquest by the Arabs in 636, and fell into Crusader hands in 1104. The knights of the order of the Hospital of St John had their general quarters there, and Saint John of Akko was to be at the head of the Christian kingdom for a hundred years after the loss of Jerusalem in 1192.

THE CAPITAL OF JAZZAR PASHA. Destroyed in 1291 by Al-Ashraf, leader of the Mamlukes, Akko was partially restored in 1750 by the Bedouin sheikh Daher al-Omar, whose work was followed by Al-Jazzar (the Butcher), a Turkish pasha of Albanian origin known for his ferocity.

"The sleeping town did not show itself except by its crenellated walls, square towers and tin domes of its mosques, indicated from afar by a sole minaret. Apart from this Muslim detail you can still dream of the feudal city of the Templars, the last rampart of the crusades."

Gérard de Nerval

He was also the town's master builder and its victorious defender against Bonaparte in 1799. After 1840 the port was silted up and Akko had no more than eight thousand inhabitants when it was conquered by the British ● 42. The English reduced its role to that of a fortress-prison.

THE CLOSED TOWN

The present-day old town was built in the 18th century on the ruins of the Crusader city, now underground. A walk along the walls which surrounded it (built by Daher al-Omar and Al-Jazzar) will give you a sense of the urban topography.

THE CITADEL. Today the Ottoman citadel which dominates the old town is a psychiatric hospital. There, the Turks imprisoned Baha Ullah, one of the founders of the Bahai religion, and the English imprisoned many Arab and Jewish nationalists. Many of its rooms now house the MUSEUM OF HEROISM, where documents relating to Zionist resistance to the British are on display.

THE UNDERGROUND TOWN ★. The citadel rests on the ruins of the medieval castle and a series of large interconnecting rooms which form the UNDERGROUND CITADEL of the Crusaders, a trace of the town which once had fifty thousand inhabitants. The crypt which served both as a church and refectory for the knights remains the central element in a veritable warren of underground corridors, not to be missed.

THE PORT. The port was created by the Persians in the 6th century BC and enlarged by the Arabs. Under Crusader rule it could hold up to sixty Western ships in search of goods from the East which came by caravan. Today a small fishing and pleasure port remain as well as the FLY TOWER.

CRUSADER RELIQUARY This 14th-century object was supposed to contain a holy thorn.

THE TEMPLARS The hospital orders, the knights of St John, and the Teutonic knights, often rivals, seized power in Akko with the Templars. Both monks and soldiers, these last (below) constituted a force whose independence was feared by kings.

The Hammam was developed from Roman baths, and fills the requirements of the purification rituals set down by the Qur'an; it also plays an important social role. It was constructed by Al-Jazzar following the architectural model of the Cairo Central Hammam, and the building in the enclosed town of Akko has served as a public bath for centuries. This is proven by the heating system discovered below the building, dating from Roman and Crusader times. The Akko Hammam, which has well-preserved mosaics, has housed a museum of Islamic arts and traditions since 1953, although the collections are currently not in the building as it is undergoing restoration.

LIGHTING
The light in these steam baths filters through small round pieces of thick glass shaped like bottle ends and encrusted into the dome. This makes the light spread ou in fine rays.

THE HYPOCAUST
Modeled on Roman baths, the channels of an underground furnace spread the heat under the floor of the *caldarium* (hot bath room) and its neighboring rooms.

"STEAM BATHS"
The Hammam where women take off their veils – a variation on the Venus theme – was a
constant source of inspiration for the Orientalist painters. Gérôme ● *143* himself painted
many bath scenes and legend recalls how he had to undress to sketch the room.

The floor of the
rooms is decorated
with geometric

Opening onto the
small garden (**1**), the
frigidarium (**2**) was used
in summer as a hallway or
resting area. The *tepidarium* (**3**)
allowed you to adapt gradually
to the heat before reaching
the *caldarium* (**4**) where the
temperature was greatest.

mosaics made with
different colored
marble from Tyre
and Caesaria.

THE PRAYER ROOM
The interior of
Al-Jazzar Mosque
is decorated with
ceramic murals,
colored marble and
quotations from
the Qur'an ● *90*
inscribed in beautiful
calligraphy.

THE MOSQUE
As in every Muslim
place of worship, it is
the place where the
Faithful gather and
where prayers are
said ● *114*. So the
marble pulpit is to the
right of the *mihrab*
(a niche in the wall
indicating the
direction of Mecca).
Oriental carpets are
spread out on the
floor on which the
Faithful gather.
Upstairs, the gallery
is reserved for
women. Legend has it
that the strong box
which is there
contains hairs from
the Prophet
Muhammad's beard
● *90*. The inhabitants
of Akko may
sometimes be found
in the mosque
discussing, resting or
refreshing themselves
or receiving some
instruction for
although the *haram* is
a place of prayer, it is
also open to all other
religious activities of
the Muslim
community.

THE AL-JAZZAR MOSQUE. "It ill becomes
idolaters to visit the mosques of God, for they
are self-confessed unbelievers. Vain shall be
their works, and in the Fire they shall abide for
ever. None should visit the mosques of God
except those who believe in God and the Last
Day, attend to their prayers and render the
alms levy and fear none but God" (Qur'an,
Sûrah IX: 17). Despite these Koranic
prescriptions, Al-Jazzar Mosque, together
with the Dome of the Rock, is one of the only
Muslim places of worship in the Holy Land
open to a non-Muslim public. Next to the
entrance gate is the fountain of ablutions
which no longer works. Here secular visitors
prepare themselves by putting on large tunics
before entering the grounds of the sanctuary.
Surrounded by arcades with granite and
porphyry columns which were brought from
the sites of Caesarea and Tyre in Lebanon, it
was built in 1781 by Al-Jazzar. According to
legend the cruel pasha buried alive workers
who made mistakes in building. All around
the rectangular courtyard, rooms sheltered
pilgrims and the servants of the mosque. The
Faithful finish the usual rites of purification by
washing their feet, hands and mouth before
taking off their shoes near the fountain of
ablutions, in the center of the patio. The
remains of Al-Jazzar and his successor
Suleyman Pasha rest inside mausoleums in
white marble which are next to the sundial.
Next to the mosque is the minaret to the top
of which the *muezzin* ● *102* (replaced today by
a loud speaker) climbed to call people to
prayer. The mosque is on the site of an old

Byzantine church which the Arabs replaced with a Muslim sanctuary after conquering the town in 636. This was destroyed by the Crusaders in 1104. The Church of St John was then built: the cisterns, which are under the courtyard, date from this time. They were built to hold the rain water in order to supply the inhabitants of the town during periods of siege, when the water distributed by the aqueduct could not reach the town.

THE SOUKS. Akko is no longer today the great commercial port it once was. However its markets are still very lively and form the vibrant heart of the town. The SOUK AL ABIAD ("white bazaar") was built around 1750 by Dahar al-Omar and reconstructed by Suleyman Pasha in 1818. This long alley covered with domes is lined on each side by narrow and deep shops. The old Turkish market which remained buried for a long time was excavated by archeologists before being restored and then reopened to trade. However, the most frequented center of the enclosed town is not one of the Eastern souks but the STREET MARKET which begins at Farhi Square and leads to the port. The town's inhabitants flock here to buy their meat, fish and vegetables, and a large number of artists have settled here.

THE KHANS. In the past, the caravanserais welcomed visitors and their mounts. The first khans in the Holy Land were built by the Mamlukes on the site of Christian buildings. On the ground floor the galleries divided into cells held animals. Upstairs, the guests were housed in rooms. Today the khans, no longer serve to provide shelter, and are

sometimes occupied by stores. Akko has three, all built by Al-Jazzar at the end of the 18th century to receive the traders of the Mediterranean. The khan al Umdan (below), or "inn of pillars", a square courtyard enclosed by a series of arcades, is the best preserved of them all. A "clock tower" was added to it in 1906 to celebrate, in just the same way as in Jaffa, the thirty years of the reign of Sultan Abdul Hamid II. Today, it serves as a stage during the festival of street theater which takes place every year in September (◆ 411). Going along the town walls to the east, you cross the khan al Shawarda where boats are still made. Hidden in the midst of a labyrinth of alleyways, khan al Afranj (the khan of the Francs) was constructed on the former site of a Franciscan convent.

"The sight is among the most picturesque: the skewers of kebab . . . turn above sweet-smelling embers, the honey *qalua* and the blocks of pressed dates, other multicolored titbits are enough to make any child's mouth water. It is the season of fresh vegetables . . . Rays of sunlight make blueish tracks in the dust and the floating mists, provoking lively plays of light on the movements of the heaving crowd."
The Marquis of Vogue

The khans sheltered travelers until the end of the 19th century. Chateaubriand wrote: "We sleep in caravanserai or under the night sky sheltered by trees . . . I enjoy everything; I savor the sky, the stones, the sea and the ruins."

Along the border you will find many Palestinian Christian villages.

NAHARIYA

The small town of Nahariya was founded in 1934 by German Jews from Bavaria and was the first Jewish colony in the Galilee. In 1947 a Canaanite temple from the 2nd millennium BC and a four-thousand-year-old Phoenician temple dedicated to Astarté, the goddess of love and fecundity, were discovered here on the BEACH OF GALEI GALIL. The statue is now preserved in the Israel Museum ▲ 298 in Jerusalem. Nahariya has become a much sought-after place for honeymooners! Its beautiful sandy beaches, the shady parks and gardens, its nautical sports facilities and equestrian clubs make it into one of the most valued of coastal resorts in the country. The small river of Gaton runs through the town center and is lined with cafés and restaurants. On the fifth floor of the town hall, the MUNICIPAL MUSEUM has archeological pieces dug up in the region, shells, and modern paintings and also houses an exhibition on the history of the town. On the road to Rosh Hanikra, the AKHZIV NATIONAL PARK contains the remains of an ancient Phoenician port.

ROSH HANIKRA

Situated to the north of Israel on the border with Lebanon, the spotless cliffs of Rosh Hanikra plunge into the deep blue of the Mediterranean. Battered for thousands of years by the waves the limestone caves, accessible by funicular railway, are made up of impressive labyrinths, where the sounds of the waves reign in semidarkness. The tunnel (now condemned) which held the railway linking Haifa to Beirut can still be seen next to these caves. The border post attributed to Israel in 1949 is reserved for soldiers of the UN and the military police.

MILITARY BERETS
The Israeli army is a constant presence in Rosh Hanikra. As in the rest of the country, the berets of the soldiers of the Haganah allow you to identify their owner's military unit. From top to bottom: Parachutists, Army, Givati Brigade, Army (novices), Border Guard, Military Engineering, Navy, Golani Brigade, Army (*Nahal*: pioneering youth), Intelligence, Air Force.

TIBERIAS AND THE SURROUNDING AREA

THE HOLY SCRIPTURES, 376
TIBERIAS, 378
AROUND THE LAKE, 382
LOWER GALILEE, 384
THE HOLY SCRIPTURES, 386
NAZARETH, 388
THE HOLY SCRIPTURES, 390
THE TELL, 394
UPPER GALILEE AND GOLAN, 398
THE JORDAN, 406

It was on the shores of the Sea of Galilee that Jesus called his first disciples and began his ministry and a new era in the authority of his word. Was he, with the cures and "miracles" he performed, the Messiah the Jews awaited? He called himself, not Messiah, but the son of man, one who has to die but will be rescued by God. He would not allow any political interpretation to be attached to his mission. After his death and resurrection, the disciples returned to the Sea of Galilee, where the profound nature of their experience then appeared to them in a new light.

JESUS CURES A MAN SICK WITH PALSY
"And they come unto him, bringing one sick of the palsy, which was borne of four . . . But that ye may know that the Son of man hath power on earth to forgive sins, (he saith to the sick of palsy,) I say unto thee, Arise, and take up thy bed, and go thy way into thine house. And immediately he arose, took up the bed, and went forth before them all." (Mark 2)

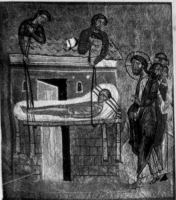

JESUS' FIRST DISCIPLES
"Now as he walked by the sea of Galilee, he saw Simon and Andrew . . . casting a net into the sea: for they were fishers. And Jesus said unto them, Come ye after me, and I will make you to become fishers of men . . . And when he had gone a little further thence, he saw James . . . and John . . . who also were in the ship mending their nets. And straightway he called them: and they left . . . and went after him." (Mark 1)

THE MIRACULOUS CATCH
"He said unto Simon, Launch out into the deep, and let down your nets for a draught. And Simon answering said unto him, Master we have toiled all the night, and have taken nothing: nevertheless at thy word I will let down the net. And when they had this done, they inclosed a great multitude of fishes: and their net brake." (Luke 5)

THE SERMON ON THE MOUNT

"And he opened his mouth, and taught them, saying . . . Ye are the salt of the earth: but if the salt have lost his savor, wherewith shall it be salted? . . . Ye are the light of the world . . . Let your light so shine before men, that they may see your good works, and glorify your father which is in heaven." (Matthew 5)

JESUS REAPPEARS

"Jesus shewed himself again to the disciples at the sea of Tiberias . . . Jesus saith unto them, Children, have ye any meat? . . . Cast the net on the right side of the ship, and ye shall find . . . Therefore that disciple whom Jesus loved saith unto Peter, It is the Lord. Now when Simon Peter heard that it was the Lord, he girt his fisher's coat unto him . . . and did cast himself into the sea." (John 21)

THE MIRACLE OF THE LOAVES

"[Jesus] took the five loaves, and the two fishes, and looking up to heaven, he blessed, and brake, and gave the loaves to his disciples, and the disciples to the multitude . . . And they that had eaten were about five thousand men, beside women and children." (Matthew 14)

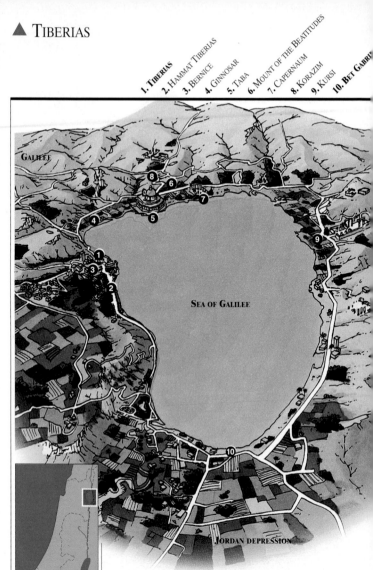

⏷ 30 miles
⏱ Four days

Lake Tiberias is also called the Sea of Kinneret, from the Hebrew *kinnor* ("lyre") since the lake is in the shape of that instrument. It was renamed the Sea of Galilee at the time of the Gospels, then later it was referred to in the Talmud as "the Eye of God". It is 13 miles long from north to south, and 7½ miles across at its widest point.

At the time of the kingdom of Israel lower Galilee was the ancient territory of the tribes of Dan and Naphtali ▲ *304*. It was the first region to fall into the hands of the Assyrians, from 730 BC. Some of its Jewish population was deported and pagans took their place. During the Hasmonean era ● *48*, benefiting from the area's relative distance from the center of power, Aristobulus made Galilee into an independent Jewish kingdom, which it remained, despite Roman and Seleucid invasions, until the time of Herod the Great, who made it part of his lands in 37 BC. At the tyrant's death, the kingdom was divided and lower Galilee fell to Herod Antipas, who reigned from 4 BC to AD 39 and founded Tiberias. The town, built around the edge of the lake bearing its name, acted as the capital of a rich, densely populated region. This is how Lamartine ● *150* recalled it when on a pilgrimage to the heart of the small region that saw the birth of Christianity, a place where "almost always an intelligent eye discovers a secret and profound analogy between the land and the great man, between the scenery and the actor, between nature and the genius formed and inspired by it."

Land of the Gospels *par excellence,* the banks of Lake Tiberias offer a remarkable number of sites holy to both Christians and Jews, as well as many spots evocative of the history of the Holy Land from the time of the first Canaanite ● *44* occupation to the birth of the State of Israel.

TIBERIAS (TEVERYA)

The town was built on the ruins of an old Jewish cemetery, and was founded by Herod Antipas around AD 19 in homage to the Roman Emperor Tiberius. Originally it was shunned by the non-Romanized part of the population, which explains why it is not often mentioned in the Gospels. The move by the Sanhedrin ● *40* (the Jewish supreme council both in religious and legal matters) from Yavneh to Tiberias in AD 135 marked the beginning of a real Jewish presence in the town. Part of the Jerusalem Talmud was written down here, and it was here also that the Massoretes – from *massore* ("transmission") – who were accomplished in the study of the Hebrew Bible, established the vocalization of the biblical text with a new system of punctuation ● *58.* From the 4th century, the town became one of Judaism's four holy cities. It is also famed for its hot springs (up to 140°F) with medicinal properties at Hammat Tiberias to the south of the town. These luxurious establishments, built when the town was first founded, were designed to attract a population reluctant to settle there. Today the remains are on display in a small museum surrounded by hotels which use the springs as tourist attractions. About a hundred yards to the north, on the banks of the lake, the remains of the Byzantine SYNAGOGUE OF SEVERUS were found. The mosaic on the floor, one of the most beautiful in the country, depicts the signs of the Zodiac and elements of the liturgy from the Temple in Jerusalem ● *260.* The mausoleum of the famous 2nd-century Rabbi

THE SYMBOLISM OF WATER
Each of the four holy towns of Judaism is associated with one of the four basic elements: air in Safed, fire in Jerusalem, earth in Hebron and water in Tiberias. Water which originates in the mountains, traditionally known as the home of the gods, is the symbol of divine life granted to the believer.

"A land which a great man lived in and liked best, during his time on earth, has always appeared to me the most certain and articulate relic of him; a sort of material manifestation of his genius, a silent revelation of part of his soul . . .**"**
Alphonse de Lamartine

OLAN

THE SYNAGOGUE OF SEVERUS
The integration of profane ornamental motifs, after Hellenization in the Holy Land, was followed in the 5th century by a return to purely religious symbolism in synagogue decor. Animal and human figures were obliterated in favor of the *menorah* and the Ark of the Covenant. Only synagogues which were already secularized escaped this iconoclastic tendency and later revealed mosaics and lintels in the Greco-Roman style.

❝I then went to the town of Tabariah. It was once a large and important town, but now there are only a few simple remains, which however show its past grandeur and importance. There you will find marvelous baths which have two separate quarters, one for men and the other for women. The water in these baths is very warm.❞
Ibn Battuta

Meir Ba'al ha-Nes ("the worker of miracles") was dug on the hillsides, set back from the banks. Further north, people venerate the tomb of Rabbi Akiba. The immaculate mausoleum surrounded by luxuriant vegetation honors this illustrious doctor of the Jewish tradition, who supported the second Jewish revolt against the Romans in AD 132–5. It was he who granted messianic privileges to Bar Kochba ● 50, the rebellion's instigator. He was, however, unlucky and was burned alive on Yom Kippur ● 80 after being arrested and taken to Caesarea ▲ 358. Moses ben Maimon (Maimonides), philosopher and theologian, asked to be buried on this very same hill, in the heart of the old town. Legend has it that after his death in Cairo, his body was put on a camel's back, but when the camel reached Tiberias, it refused to go any further. The tomb must have been dug at the very spot chosen by the camel. If it seems more likely that it is only a cenotaph, the fervor with which it is maintained and the prayers addressed to "the doctor of Cordoba" are not affected. Maimonides, who was a broad-minded and tolerant man, is venerated by Jews and Muslims alike. Alongside the tomb is that of Yohanan ben Zakkai. He was high priest at the time of the first Jewish revolt and obtained permission from Titus to open a religious school at Yavneh ● 51. Archeologists have just uncovered a quarter called Berenice, above the lower town, named in memory of Agrippa II's sister who harbored an illicit love for her brother, as mentioned in the Acts of the Apostles (Acts 25) as well as by Josephus. During the Jewish war, she had a stormy liaison with Titus, as reported by Tacitus and Suetonius. The excavations, which were interrupted in 1990, revealed beneath thick alluvial layers a Roman theater with a seating capacity of five thousand, built around the 2nd and 3rd centuries AD.

The construction has not been completely uncovered, but archeologists already have a substantial amount of information about it. It faced north, so that spectators would not be disturbed by the sun's rays; also the size of the stage (about 145 feet) shows its importance. Its existence also seems to indicate that the population of Tiberias, although mostly Jewish, had integrated and accepted the Roman culture of the time. A Byzantine church, surrounded by ramparts from the time of Justinian, was also uncovered at the top of Mount Bernice. Restored at the beginning of the 9th century, the new building followed the layout of a basilica; its walls were decorated with frescos, and its floor with mosaics. It was used until the end of the Crusades, when the Franks reinforced the walls. An excavation soon to be undertaken will, it is hoped, make possible the discovery of the foundations of the original church and its remains. From the top of Mount Bernice the view over the lake is marvelous. Lower down you can still see parts of the wall built by Guy de Lasignan's Crusaders, who could not prevent the town from being taken by Salah al-Din in 1187. In their attempts to save the town, the Crusaders fell into the trap of the Horns of Hittim ● *54*, ▲ *394*. The area around the port is very pleasant; St Peter's Church there with its prow-shaped apside is reminiscent of a boat, the emblem of the first of the popes.

AROUND THE LAKE

Ginnosar, Genesereth in the Gospels, has given its name to the major kibbutz in the fertile plain that borders the lake, where an important archeological discovery was made. The inhabitants found a boat in the mud when the water level was exceptionally low. Experts have dated it as 1st century, and it is at present undergoing treatment aimed at preventing its decomposition. A short movie retracing all the stages in its discovery and its identification is shown in the kibbutz museum. The village is surrounded by prolific banana groves whose cultivation is made possible by the subtropical climate of this depression in the Syrian-African fault ■ *16*. The fruits are picked before they have ripened, then preserved in a refrigerated atmosphere for many weeks. They are then made to ripen through a sudden rise in temperature, as dictated by the needs of the marketplace.

TABGHA. An Arabic deformation of the Greek name *Heptapegon*, which means "the seven springs", this small village houses the CHURCH OF THE MULTIPLICATION OF THE LOAVES, rebuilt in 1982 on the model of a 5th-century Byzantine basilica ● *124*.

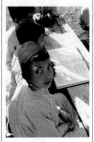

THE TALMUD
A vast work containing the teachings of the Rabbis (Amoraim) of Palestine and Babylon, as a commentary on the Mishnah.

MAIMONIDES
This Jewish philosopher and Talmudist was born in Andalusia in 1135, but was driven out by persecution under the Almohad dynasty. Settling in Fez, then in Palestine and Egypt, Maimonides became the personal doctor to the Ayyubid kings. Apart from his medical treatises, his work includes a monumental commentary on the Mishnah; the *Guide for the Perplexed*, a work of religious philosophy inspired by Aristotle and written in Arabic; and, above all, the *Mishne Torah*, a great code of Jewish law.

381

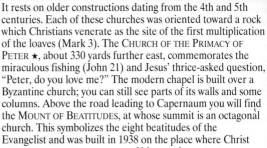

The famous mosaic found in Tabgha only shows four loaves, in place of the five mentioned in the Evangelist's text: "When he had taken the five loaves and the two fishes, he looked up to heaven and gave them to his disciples to set before

It rests on older constructions dating from the 4th and 5th centuries. Each of these churches was oriented toward a rock which Christians venerate as the site of the first multiplication of the loaves (Mark 3). The CHURCH OF THE PRIMACY OF PETER ★, about 330 yards further east, commemorates the miraculous fishing (John 21) and Jesus' thrice-asked question, "Peter, do you love me?" The modern chapel is built over a Byzantine church; you can still see parts of its walls and some columns. Above the road leading to Capernaum you will find the MOUNT OF BEATITUDES, at whose summit is an octagonal church. This symbolizes the eight beatitudes of the Evangelist and was built in 1938 on the place where Christ gave one of his most important sermons (Matthew 5).

CAPERNAUM. This, according to Matthew, was Christ's own town. The lake and the *Via maris* ▲ *356*, which crosses it, assured this border post thriving trade and business. The HOUSE OF SAINT PETER, in which Jesus lived while his apostle was lodged by his in-laws at Bethsaide, is now covered by a church with basalt walls which still show the 1st-century ruins. One room in

the people. And the two fishes divided he among them all. And they did all eat, and were filled. And they took up twelve baskets full of the fragments, and of the fishes" (Mark 6). The fifth was symbolized by the bread of the eucharist to be found on the church altar. In fact, this miracle prefigures the miracle of the Last Supper and the celebration of the portion of bread.

particular is worth a careful look: its walls were decorated and surrounded by later constructions, a sign of special attention which proves that it was venerated from the earliest days of Christianity. Graffiti declaring devotion to Jesus by the Judeo-Christians have also been found there. In the 4th century they built an important place of worship, demolished a century later by the Byzantines, whose octagonal basilica is decorated with mosaics still visible at the side of the present building. About 100 yards from there a large white limestone synagogue is said to have echoed with the words of the Bread of Life, which Jesus addressed to the Jews.

This religious edifice was built in the 4th century, later than the rest of the city, but rests on the foundations of an older synagogue. You can still see the black basalt foundations ● 108 of the older building.

KORAZIM. This 12-acre site was the subject of a lamentation by Jesus, who reproached its inhabitants for not converting to the call of one of God's messengers (Matthew 11). A black basalt synagogue and some houses which have been reconstructed by archeologists can be found here.

This representation from the 4th century AD found in the ruins of the synagogue at Capernaum is not the Ark of the Covenant, always held aloft by poles carried by Levites, but rather the synagogue chest containing the scrolls of the Torah.

KURSI. An important monastic complex from Byzantine times has been discovered on this site which was pagan at the time of the Gospels. It was built here to commemorate the expulsion of demons embodied in pigs that Jesus had caused to be drowned in the lake (Mark 5). This was Jesus' only visit to the pagans, who begged him to return home to the land of the Jews. All the buildings here are of black basalt. A grill on the ground on the south side forms the entrance to a crypt. A large part of its floor is still covered in mosaics with varied motifs such as fruits, vegetables, flowers, animals and everyday and cult objects. The southern apside has a baptistry bearing a Greek inscription.

At the side of the northern lateral nave an oil press has been preserved. In the eastern tradition this provision ● 76 had many liturgical uses. The people of the Mediterranean always attribute the origin of the olive to a divine presence, and the Talmud taught that only the oil of this blessed fruit was worthy of providing the light for Jewish worship. Christian tradition followed, and it was laid down that the "holy oils" used in everything from baptism to extreme unction had to be extracted from the produce of the olive tree, by papal decree.

BET GABRIEL. This cultural center, which was founded by Gitta Sherover in memory of her son Gabriel, hosts a variety of art events (including concerts, plays, ballets, painting and sculpture exhibitions) as well as political conferences and rallies. The style of this attractive building is a pure, modern architecture which combines glass, stone and steel. The extensive gardens which stretch out in front of the terrace offer a magnificent view over the lake.

THE SYNAGOGUE
This building in Greco-Roman style was erected at the end of the 3rd century. It is rectangular, 78 by 52 feet, and half pointing toward Jerusalem. Uncovered in 1905, its richly decorated façade mixes profane representations of eagles, gryphons and lions with religious motifs ● 108.

SAINT PETER
Simon was renamed Peter by Jesus – from the Greek *petros*, a translation of the Aramean *Kepha* – in order to indicate the apostle's pre-eminence in the new Christian church hierarchy. Simon-Peter, who died in Rome between 64 and 67, is looked on as the first pope.

FROM TIBERIAS TO NAZARETH

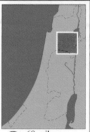

🚗 60 miles

🕐 Three days

ARBEL. This agricultural *moshav* ● *132* gives access to the old town bearing the same name. An important residence and a beautiful Byzantine synagogue (5th century) have been found there. The synagogue dominates the plain of Ginnosar, the most fertile near the Sea of Galilee. Flavius Josephus describes it thus: "The most idle man discovers in himself the vocation of farmer because the plain is so fertile and gives harvest every month of the year." To one side you will notice the ruins of a large castle from Crusader times which was occupied until the end of the Mameluke dominion.

THE HORNS OF HITTIM. To the west is a vast sanctuary, Nabi Shueib, where the tomb of Moses' father-in-law, Jethro, is located, venerated by the Druze. Returning to Nazareth, you will come across the Horns of Hittim (*Karnei Hittim*). This crater from an old volcano, visible from the surrounding hills, acted as a camp during the

HADJAR AL-NASSARA
This *moshav* ● *132* was founded in 1908 by immigrants of Russian origin, fleeing the pogroms. The new collective was installed on the site of the Arab village of Hadjar al-Nassara, the "Rock of Christians".

8. MOUNT TABOR 9. NAIM 10. MOUNT HAMOR 11. AFULA 12. MOUNT GILBOA 13. MEGIDDO 14. BET ALPHA 15. BET SHE'AN 16. **BELVOIR**

SEA OF GALILEE

JORDAN VALLEY

Crusades at the time of a decisive battle ● *54*, which marked
the end of the Frankish kingdom in Palestine on July 4,
1187. Salah al-Din's victory confined the Franks to the
coast. During this battle, the Muslims tore the "True
Cross" from the knights. This relic was supposed to
contain a piece of the wood on which Jesus was
crucified, and the Crusaders saw the loss of such a sacred
object as a sign of ineluctable defeat and it dealt a mortal
blow to the morale of the troops.

CANA. The small town of Cana is now a suburb of Nazareth.
Two churches, one with eastern and the other Latin rites
● *88*, rest on top of Byzantine ruins. They preserve the
memory of the miracles of the Evangelist – water changed
into wine (John 2) and the distant cure of the
nobleman's son by Christ (John 4) ▲ *384* – but the true
site for these is probably farther north and not easily
accessible.

▲ THE HOLY SCRIPTURES, AROUND NAZARETH

Nazareth plays a part in Jesus' hidden life. In this small village, which is not mentioned in the Old Testament, Mary received from the archangel Gabriel the announcement that she was to bear a son to be called Jesus and "son of the Highest". Jesus grew up in the tranquility of Nazareth, raised in the Jewish tradition and with respect for the Scriptures. He later returned to the town of his childhood to unveil his mission. According to the gospel of Saint John, Jesus took part in village weddings in Galilee.

THE CHILDHOOD OF JESUS THE NAZARENE
"He turned aside unto the parts of Galilee and he came and he dwelt in a city called Nazareth: that it might be fulfilled, which was spoken by the prophets, He shall be called a Nazarene." (Matthew 2)

THE WEDDING AT CANA
"The mother of Jesus saith unto him, They have no wine . . . Jesus saith unto them, Fill the waterpots with water . . . Draw out now, and bear unto the governor of the feast . . . When the ruler of the feast had tasted the water that was made wine, and knew not whence it was: (but the servants which drew the water knew.)" (John 2)

HE SETS OUT HIS MISSION AT NAZARETH
"And there was delivered unto him the book of the prophet Esaias . . . he found the place where it was written, The Spirit of the Lord is upon me, because he hath anointed me to preach the gospel to the poor; he hath sent me to heal the broken-hearted, to preach deliverance to the captives, and recovering of sight to the blind . . . And he began to say unto them, this day is this scripture fulfilled in your ears." (Luke 4)

THE ANNUNCIATION. "And the angel said unto her, Fear not, Mary: for thou hast found favor with God. And, behold, thou shalt conceive in thy womb, and bring forth a son, and shalt call his name Jesus. He shall be great, and shall be called the Son of the Highest: and the Lord God shall give unto him the throne of his father David. And he shall reign over the house of Jacob forever: and of his kingdom there shall be no end." (Luke 1)

387

Until the beginning of the 20th century the women of Nazareth wore the *Qumbaz*, a festive coat of embroidered silk, under which they wore a long cotton shirt. They wore billowing trousers gathered at the ankle, Ottoman style. The headdress, called *semadi*, comprised a fringed skull cap with gold and silver coins hanging from it. Nazareth's was the first among traditional Palestinian costumes to disappear because of the rapid westernization of the town under the influence of pilgrims and mission schools.

TOBACCO
Traditional cultivation of tobacco was increased at the beginning of the 1940's, driven by the industrialization of Palestinian society.

NAZARETH

Today, Nazareth is home to the largest Arab community in the State of Israel. During the 1950's, however, the town saw its population swollen by a massive influx of Jews, who were concentrated in the new quarter of Nazareth Illit. The old village, tucked away in a natural basin, is almost entirely covered by the sanctuaries which protect archeological treasures. The main cupola, in the form of a tent, is easily spotted. Nazareth is first mentioned in the Bible at the time of the Annunciation ▲ *385*, described thus by Luke: "The angel Gabriel was sent from God unto a city of Galilee, named Nazareth, to a virgin espoused to a man whose name was Joseph, of the house of David; and the virgin's name was Mary." Nazareth does not appear in the Old Testament.

THE BASILICA OF THE ANNUNCIATION ● *112*.
The Franciscan church dating from 1730 was destroyed in 1955 to give way to a new building, completed in 1969. The construction allowed the site to be excavated, the results of which are on view in the FRANCISCAN MUSEUM within the walls of the basilica. Its layout is superposed onto the old Crusader church which was razed to the ground by Baybar in 1263. Only its north wall survives and is still visible. The church choir was built on the apside of the Byzantine church, which is below, and its mosaics were found to be remarkably well preserved. The cave, which is frequently rearranged to allow pilgrims to pray, opens out under the basilica's central choir. It must have been an annex to the virgin's house. These cavities were often used as additional rooms in constructions which had floors on different parts of a slope. To the left of the cave, a small sanctuary is dedicated to Conon, a 3rd-century martyr originally from Nazareth, and a member of Jesus' family. The graffiti found there have made it easier to understand the Judeo-Christians, Jesus' first disciples. The community existed until Byzantine times when it mysteriously disappeared. The sanctuaries of these first Christians are the most authentic and provide an early glimpse of Christian religious life.

The choir of the Basilica of the Annunciation

The words *Ave Maria* ("Rejoice, Mary") inscribed in stone are proof of the long history of devotion to the Virgin. Its outline has been preserved in the Franciscan Museum, where you will also see the magnificent carved capitals, made for a Crusader church. These were hidden before being installed in order to escape the destruction which followed Salah al-Din's victory ● *54*. They have therefore been marvelously preserved. The highly ornate upper basilica is used as a place of worship for the large Latin Christian community of Nazareth. ST JOSEPH'S CHURCH, known as the "Church of Nutrition" in deference to Christ's father, is situated to the north of the old village. Below ground-level an important Judeo-Christian baptismal basin is preserved. Its black and white coarsely shaped stones symbolize the passage from darkness to light. The CONVENT OF THE SISTERS OF NAZARETH rests on the old cemetery and has a tomb sealed by a movable stone. Visits are only possible by prior arrangement. The church, presented as the synagogue of Jesus' village, where he gave an important sermon to a population guilty in his eyes of a lack of fervor toward him (Luke 4), is located outside the old perimeter and probably not authentic. Nazareth is a bustling town. The "Temple Merchants" have taken it over and the souk has many souvenirs for tourists and pilgrims. Silence and tranquility may be found at the Little Sisters of Jesus and the Poor Clares. They commemorate the memory of Father Foucauld, the French explorer, who lived in Nazareth from 1897 to 1900 before his ordination as a priest.

ZIPPORI ★. Three miles northwest of Nazareth, the home of Mary's parents is famous for its ruins of a Roman town. They include a collection of patrician houses and a theater. The large Byzantine town, just below, contains a masterpiece: a mosaic called the "BIRTH OF THE NILE", representing the festivities which accompanied the flooding of the river, as well as beautifully depicted hunting scenes ◆ *428*. The Italian Sisters maintain the church dedicated to saints Anne and Joachim, the virgin's parents. Mount Carmel was the scene of many confrontations between the kingdoms of the north and south, at the Megiddo Pass. According to the Apocalypse of Saint John, it will be on the heights of Megiddo that the forces of evil will gather at the end of the world. On the other side of the Valley of Jezreel rises Mount Tabor, a sacred spot since Canaanite times, where Christian tradition places the episode of the Transfiguration.

THE NAZARETH DONKEY
An indispensable companion to the wandering merchant, the donkey was domesticated during the Neolithic era and remains a valuable pack animal.

MOUNT TABOR
This mountain is one of two (the other is Mount Hermon) which lays claim to being the Mount of the Transfiguration. It was climbed by Jesus with Peter, James and John. "And was transfigured before them: and his face did shine as the sun, and his raiment was white as the light. And, behold, there appeared unto them Moses and Elias talking with him. Then answered Peter, and said unto Jesus, Lord, it is good for us to be here: if thou wilt, let us make here three tabernacles; one for thee, and one for Moses, and one for Elias. While he yet spake, behold, a bright cloud overshadowed them: and behold a voice out of the cloud, which said, This is my beloved Son, in whom I am pleased; hear ye him." (Matthew 17)

389

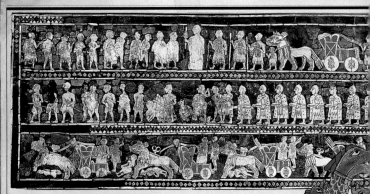

Mount Carmel, which blocks the *Via Maris*, the north–south coastal route, was the scene of many confrontations between the kingdoms of the north and south at the Megiddo Pass and the waters of Tamas. According to the Apocalypse of Saint John, it will be on the heights of Megiddo that the forces of evil will gather at the end of the world. On the other side of the fertile valley of Jezreel – the grain-producing area of the Holy Land – rises Mount Tabor. This has been a sacred place since Canaanite times and is where Christian tradition places the Transfiguration when Jesus revealed to his disciples the presence within him in order to strengthen them before the test of the Passion.

THE SEVEN SCOURGES OF THE SEVEN VIALS
"And I heard a great voice out of the temple saying to the seven angels, Go your ways, and pour out the vials of the wrath of God upon the earth . . . He gathered them together into a place called in the Hebrew tongue Armageddon." (Revelations 16)

EGYPT AND SYRIA IN THE PLAIN OF MEGIDDO
"Necho, king of Egypt, came up to fight against Charchemish by Euphrates . . . Nevertheless, Josiah would not turn his face from him, but disguised himself, that he might fight with him, and harkened not unto the words of Necho from the mouth of God, and came to fight in the valley of Megiddo." (2 Chronicles 35)

ISRAEL AND CANAAN FIGHT AT MOUNT TABOR. "[Deborah] sent and called Barak . . . and said unto him, Hath not the Lord God of Israel commanded, saying, Go and draw toward mount Tabor, and take with thee ten thousand men of the children of Naphtali and of the children of Zebulun? And I will draw unto thee to the river Kishon Sisera, the captain of Jabin's army, with his chariots and his multitude; and I will deliver him into thine hand . . . So God subdued on that day Jabin the king of Canaan before the children of Israel." (Judges 4)

MISEREMINI·MEI·SALTEM
VOS·AMICI·MEI·

THE TRANSFIGURATION

"Jesus taketh with him Peter, and James, and John, and leadeth them up into an high mountain . . . and he was transfigured before them . . . And there appeared unto them Elias with Moses: and they were talking with Jesus. . . . And there was a cloud that overshadowed them: and a voice came out of the cloud, saying, This is my beloved son: hear him." (Mark 9)

THE VALLEY OF JEZREEL

The Valley of Jezreel is a vast alluvial plain that runs from northwest to southeast, bordered by Mount Carmel to the south and Mounts Tabor ▲ 329, Hamor, and Gilboa to the north. It symbolizes the efforts of Jewish immigrants to transform a barren ancestral land into a flourishing garden ■ 34. From the heights which surround it on all sides, the view is striking: straight-edged fields and plantations follow one another to create an abstract and beautiful effect. But a price had to be paid for the valley's irrigation: a canal from the Sea of Galilee ▲ 382 and a diversion of the reserves of water in South Lebanon. The result is that the verdant Valley of Jezreel may be considered the greatest success of Israeli agriculture today.

MOUNT TABOR

THE FIRST KIBBUTZIM
Inspired by the idealism of young Eastern European settlers in Palestine at the end of the 19th century, the kibbutz ● 132 is an original experiment in community organization. The first kibbutzim were in Galilee and the Valley of Jezreel, and until the early 1960's their rise assured the young state a degree of self-sufficiency. The movement is not growing, however, as it conflicts with the realities of the market economy.

This mountain rises 1,970 feet from the plain of Jezreel which was the scene of fighting between the Israelites and Canaanites in the 12th century ● 44 (Judges 4–5), and later of the resistance of Josephus, who, with his troops, endured a siege by the Roman army. More recently the hill was the site of Bonaparte and Kleber's victorious battle against the Turks in 1799. This mountain is the sanctuary of the Transfiguration of Jesus whereby he revealed to his disciples the divine presence within him in order to strengthen them before the test of the Passion. The mountain shelters on its sides two churches which commemorate this episode in the Gospels. The Latin church is the most welcoming: it dates back to 1924, but was built on the remains of Byzantine and Crusader basilicas. Its terraces mostly open out onto the plain and offer a sumptuous panorama over the whole valley as far as the summit of Mount Carmel ▲ 364.

NAIM AND MOUNT HAMOR

Strategically located and valued as a lookout, this small mountainous mass (Givat Hamoreh) was the scene of numerous battles at the time of the Judges and Saul. Nein (the old Naim), to the north of the summit, is frequented by Christian pilgrims who commemorate there Jesus' resurrection of the only son of a widow (Luke 7). The small town of Afula, a traditional crossroads of the trade routes to the heart of the Valley of Jezreel, was nicknamed "the bean" by the Crusaders because it was perched on a small patch of rugged land. Today the town has few attractions. One of the only sights worth visiting here is the ruins of the fort, once a Templar stronghold, which fell beneath Salah al-Din's blows in 1187.

MOUNT GILBOA ★

A pretty road leads out from Nurit, about 6 miles southwest of Afula, and winds its way through the foothills of the mountain range of Gilboa, to the top of this small chain. The view from there is over the whole valley, from Bet Shean in the east to Mount Tabor and the hills of Nazareth and of Givat Hamoreh in the north, Carmel in the west, and the mountains of Samaria in the south. There is an information point near a lookout tower which is easy to find. Irises cover the mountainside in spring, and paths have been made through them so that people can enjoy but not spoil them. The descent via Ma'ale Gilboa leads you to a magnificent

THE GARDEN OF ISRAEL
The marshes, which formed the main part of the valley floor, were dried out and the hillsides planted with trees, thanks to the kibbutzim and the Society for the Protection of Nature. The planting of trees which has a religious significance has become symbolic for many immigrants and visitors. The result is spectacular, particularly in the Balfour Forest, 3 miles southwest of Nazareth.

park laid out beside three springs (in Hebrew *Gan Hashlosha*), which is a perfect place to stop for a dip and a siesta. You should be aware that the "green line" goes almost exactly through the middle of this mountain peak: the south side is in Transjordan.

JEZREEL

Major excavations have been undertaken to reveal the second capital of the kingdom of Israel ● *46*. Mentioned several times in the Old Testament, the town was the seat of King Ahab and his sadly famous wife Jezebel. They were an impious couple who devoted themselves to the worship of the god Baal until the prophet Elijah realized this and they were delivered to the dogs (2 Kings 9). The tell ▲ *394* which still covers most of the site has not been completely removed and those traces which have been found, whether in the form of architectural remains or everyday objects, are not displayed.

"Bring health to the Valley of Jezreel", is the inscription in Hebrew, Yiddish and Polish on the poster of this Jewish national foundation. Very much around in Poland in the 1930's, a country rocked by growing antisemitism, this propaganda poster helped build the population of the Galilee. The work to improve the valley dates from this time.

From neolithic times some privileged sites have remained inhabited continually for many millennia. Once in ruins, their buildings have been flattened and covered over by new buildings. As these operations recurred many times over the centuries, the superposed ruins finally formed strata several feet high. These artificial mounds, formed from archeological debris, are called tells (in Hebrew, *tel*).

VESSEL IN THE SHAPE OF A FISH
This cup is one of the best preserved examples of a ceramic style which appeared at the beginning of the 2nd millennium, known as the "style of Tel al-Yahudiyeh". The object was discovered at the time of the excavation of Tel Poleg, south of Netanya.

THE GODDESS HATHOR
This delicate ivory figure of the 2nd millennium was found during excavations of the tell of Megiddo ▲ 396.

A CHRONOLOGY
The relative dating of levels of construction is determined by the archeological artifacts they contain, mainly pottery shards. Every era is characterized by ceramics of specific shapes and decoration. The chronology of changes of Palestinian pottery now being well known, the main types of vases can be dated with satisfying precision, which means that it is possible to establish correspondences with historic events.

FRAGMENTS OF A CANAANITE JAR
This painting of a person is one of the rare remains of Canaanite plastic art. Dating from the 13th century BC it was found at the tell of Bet She'an.

THE STRATIFICATION OF A TELL

The archeologist's task consists of recognizing a tell's stratification, that is, the succession of ruins and archeological layers which make it up, then uncovering them in an order inverse to their formation. The levels of construction are generally numbered from top to bottom, from the most recent to the oldest.

THE SERPENT CENSER

This style of pottery with a serpent motif is characteristic of pieces from the recent Canaanite era. This example was discovered during the excavations of Tel Bet She'an ▲ 396.

JEWELRY BOX

This precious box, finely carved from a single block of ivory, was uncovered in the tell of Megiddo ▲ 396. It dates from the 13th or 14th century BC and the style of these reliefs recalls Hittite statuary.

Ivory woman's head in the Egyptian-Canaanite style.

THE "HILL OF BATTLES"
Megiddo saw its history marked by wars and mourning; King Josiah was killed there in 609 BC (2 Kings 23), while Saint John's Revelations places the final combat of Good over Evil there, with Jesus emerging as victor through his death and resurrection.

THE MEGIDDO ALTARS
A large Canaanite altar, made from a monolith 32 feet in diameter, was discovered in the middle of a holy area dating from the 2nd millennium. An altar with four horns was dug up ● 118 dating from the kingdom of Israel and is now on display at the Israel Museum in Jerusalem.

The hillsides of the Gilboa mountains around Bet Alpha.

MEGIDDO

In addressing themselves to the exploration of the tell of Megiddo, the archeologists of the beginning of the 20th century identified twenty towns on top of one another. However the empirical and not very rigorous methods of the first excavators broke the strata and considerably altered the appearance of the places. From afar, the artificial mound which strategically commanded the Jezreel Valley appears to be cut by a long trench which allows direct access (in complete disaccord with today's methods for this type of excavation ▲ 394) to the oldest strata. A visit to the museum before beginning an exploration of the site is therefore strongly recommended. Its educational presentation is indispensable to understanding the history of the tell and the excavations carried out there. Access to the site is via an old ramp and the door with triple tenailles, from the Canaanite era (18th century BC) ● 118. Hardly anything of the palaces and fortifications of Solomon's garrison remains except for a vast grain silo with a perfectly preserved double staircase.

A cult area from the 4th millennium was discovered below; it seems that the sacred character of this land was preserved: around the Canaanite altar, archeologists later uncovered Jewish sanctuaries. Next come the stables of Solomon's fortress, mentioned in the Bible (1 Kings 9). The visit ends with a spectacular descent into an underground system for removing water dug by the Canaanites. An iron staircase leads to the tunnel which stretches out for nearly 330 feet ending up outside the old wall.

BET ALPHA

In 1928, members of the Kibbutz of Hefzi Bah discovered the ruins of a 6th-century synagogue when they were digging an irrigation channel. They uncovered the mosaic decorating the nave of the building, a masterpiece of Byzantine art broken up into three tableaux: the binding of Isaac by Abraham (Genesis 22) to the right; the chariot of the sun and the signs

of the Zodiac in the middle; the heavenly liturgy revealed by Moses on the panel to the left ● 78. The walls which remain teach us about the layout of the building: the apse faced toward Jerusalem, and had a niche in which the Ark containing the scrolls of the Torah was to be found.

BET SHE'AN

The ancient fortress, whose ramparts exposed King Saul's plunder (1 Samuel 31), had *Scythopolis*, one of the most beautiful Hellenistic cities of Palestine, built at its foot in the 1st century AD. This "town of the Scythians" must have been so named as a reminder that mercenaries from these people of the steppes formed the garrison. It was dedicated to the Greek god Dionysus, whose wet nurse Nysa was buried on the hill according to Pliny the Elder. The Roman theater of Bet She'an, completely excavated in 1963 after three years of work, is the best preserved of the Holy Land. With the capacity to seat eight thousand, the building was formed of stepped layers, backing on to a chalky escarpment. Only the lower floor of this remains. Some blocks of the upper floor were recovered in the Byzantine baths, where they had been reused. One must also see the remains of the basilica, the main road with columns and the Byzantine and Roman odeons, typical of a Roman town with sophisticated urban planning.

BELVOIR

On one of the summits on which a fire was lit to announce the appearance of the new moon (the announcement of the festival of Neomenia was sent from Jerusalem to outlying communities) the Crusaders constructed one of their most beautiful fortresses in 1140. The three concentric enclosures of the castle ● 128 which dominated the valleys of the Jordan and the Yarmuk withstood all of Salah al-Din's attacks, but finally capitulated in 1191, after the defeat of the Horns of Hittim ● 54.

THE VALLEY ROAD
A large avenue lined with columns led from the temple of Dionysus to the Roman baths.

This mosaic, the work of a father and his son, as a Greek inscription on the site proclaims, is composed of squares of semi-precious stones in addition to cubes of colored glass in places.

FULK OF JERUSALEM
From a long dynasty of sovereign counts of Anjou, Fulk V, called the Young, became king of Jerusalem in 1131, at the age of thirty-six. Under him, the kingdom acquired many fortified castles, of which Belvoir is without doubt the masterpiece. His son, Geoffrey Plantagenet, was to found the longest dynasty of the kingdom of England.

The road from Tiberias to Kiryat Shmona turns north from the banks of the lake, toward Taba ▲ *383*, and runs along the west side of the Mount of Beatitudes ▲ *383*. Once you have crossed the first hills, you are in the Upper Galilee, a rugged and mountainous region where alpine flora mingles with Mediterranean species as the altitude increases. The harshness of the region and its prayer-inducing atmosphere help explain why it has kept its character as a haven for the Jewish population who remained in Palestine after it became Muslim. From the constantly twisting road which climbs to bare peaks, you can see from the Sea of Galilee to the Golan plateau ▲ *404*. Nine and a half miles beyond Taba, the road splits in two: the main branch goes north toward the Hula Valley and Kiryat Shmona, while a 3-mile ride along the left branch takes you to Safed. Just beyond this crossroad is the old village of Rosh Pinah, "the corner stone", built at the end of the 19th century by the first Jewish immigrants from Eastern Europe. A verse from Psalm 118, cited by Jesus as an epilogue to the parable of the murderous vine growers (Matthew 21) gave the village its name: "The stone which the builders refused is become the head stone of the corner. This is the Lord's doing; it is marvellous in our eyes." From Rosh Pinah the road climbs up toward Safed through which it passes before reaching the summit of Mount Kenaan, the highest point in the town, where the old "British" police station is located.

SAFED

Safed (Safad in Arabic) is a holy town, perched on the summit of a hill 2,950 feet above sea level. Since the 15th century it has been the center for the study of holy texts in the Holy Land. Before the Spanish Reconquest, Andalusia was the seat of a flourishing and brilliant Jewish culture, but the fall of the caliphate of Grenada in 1492 gave the Catholic Inquisition the signal to begin. Soon after it expelled the Jews from the Spanish kingdom. A small number found refuge in the Upper Galilee, taking with them memories of four centuries of theological and philosophical reflection developed through contact with the Arab writers of al-Andalus. Then the region became a hotbed of poets, commentators and rabbis and the center of Kabbalistic studies. The *Zohar* was discovered here, largely written by Moses of Leon at Guadalajara

SAFED SILKS
Festive coats (above) were worn until the beginning of the century in the villages around Safed. The cotton cloth was dyed indigo and then decorated with silk taffeta. This was imported from Lebanon, but the dyeing was done on the spot. The lower part of the coat was embroidered as was the front, and had geometric decorations which resembled patchwork.

THE JEWISH CEMETERY
For four centuries this small plot has been surrounded by an almost holy aura, because it is home to the graves of the greatest masters of the Kabbalah. Some anonymous graves hold just a Torah – the scrolls of the Law also had a right to a burial place as they had a soul.

1. TIBERIAS 2. KIRYAT SHIMONA 3. ROSH PINAH 4. SAFED 5. HATZOR 6. LAKE HULA 7. TEL DAN 8. BANYAS 9. MOUNT HERMON 10. NIMROD'S FORTRESS 11. MAJDAL SHAMS 12. KATZRIN 13. GAMLA

GOLAN

UPPER GALILEE

SEA OF GALILEE

🚗 190 miles
🕐 Five days

at the end of the 13th century: this "Book of Splendors", a major work of Jewish mysticism, seeks to promote a direct link between the divine one and the faithful, through fideist and esoteric experience. Fed by the Spanish Kabbalah, in the 16th century Safed founded an original school: first of all Moses Cordovero synthesized the Italian tradition, tinged with neo-Platonism, and the Spanish tradition, in his work *Pardes Rimonim*, "Garden of Pomegranates", then his successor Isaac Luria Ashkenazi founded his own school insisting on the esoteric nature of his teaching. By the end of the 16th century, Safed Kabbalism was spreading toward Europe, to such centers of scholarship as Salonica and Venice, where it exercised considerable influence on Jewish and Christian thought. The graves of these Kabbalistic rabbis, sanctified

YOSSEF ZARITSKY
The painter Yossef Zaritsky was born in the Ukraine in 1891 and settled in Palestine in 1923. He lived in the Galilee and painted *Safed* (right) in 1924 in his enthusiasm for the Promised Land. In 1942 Zaritsky founded the group "New Horizons" and became the leading exponent of lyrical abstract art in Israel.

**THE ARTISTS'
QUARTER ★**
Since the 1930's the old Muslim quarter, at the foot of the citadel ramparts, has attracted painters and designers seduced by the purity of the light and the city's calm. The quarter houses art galleries and ateliers where you can see works inspired by Jewish mysticism and sacred symbolism.

by posterity, are constantly visited by crowds of pilgrims who come to collect their thoughts and to address requests to the graves in the belief that they are endowed with miraculous powers. As one looks also at the city's many synagogues, it is not hard to sense an atmosphere of great devotion to God in the midst of a modern city. It is reinforced by the long history of rabbis at prayer and by the murmurs which rise from the synagogue quarter, where most of the schools of religion can be found. At the heart of the city, MEDINIM SQUARE is a perfect starting point for fascinating walks through the labyrinthine streets of the old city. THE SYNAGOGUE OF ISAAC LURIA ★, dating from the 16th century, is one of the most venerated of the city's synagogues. It is decorated with wall paintings incorporating Kabbalistic motifs, and contains valuable bibliographical treasures including old handwritten scrolls of the Law. THE SYNAGOGUES OF ISAAC ABUHAV, RABBI HABANNAI AND JOSEPH CARO are also holy and worth visiting. A climb up the tall slopes of the hill leads you to the old Muslim quarter, today the chosen spot of Jewish painters and sculptors charmed by the town's ambience. Dominating the hill higher up is the ancient Crusader fortress of King Fulk of Jerusalem ▲ *128*, surrounded by gardens. This is a focal point for the town's inhabitants. This fortress offers a spectacular unbroken view of the Upper Galilee. Safed was home to the first printing press on the Asiatic continent, imported at the end of the 16th century to facilitate the spread of the Kabbalah to Europe. In the middle of the artists' quarter the Association of Book Craftsmen has created a HEBREW MUSEUM OF PRINTING ART which has a number of *incunabula* and which retraces the history of Hebrew writing through the ages and the story of the spread of printing in the Holy Land. The craftsmen associated with the Museum revitalize old printing methods and the results are on display to visitors.

AROUND MOUNT MERON

The village of Meron, which is home to the famous tomb of Rabbi Simon Bar-Yochai, is about 6 miles west of Safed and gives onto the MOUNT MERON NATURE RESERVE, the largest in the Galilee. It is a good idea to obtain a topographical map before venturing onto one of the pedestrian paths which snake away among the gorges, crossing vast areas planted with olive trees, pines and eucalyptus. South of Mount Meron is the deep AMUD VALLEY, another national park whose paths stretch as far as the Sea of Galilee. From the village of SASA, an agricultural colony founded in 1949 by American pioneers, a track crosses a green oak plantation to reach a camping ground. From here a small path marked for 330 yards leads to an observation point. At some 3,960 feet above sea level you will see on the horizon the peaks of Mount Hermon, the Lebanese mountains, the now dry Hula Valley, the Golan plateau and, further south, the Sea of Galilee. From Mount Meron, a twisting road, which you are advised to approach with care, runs near the Israeli-Lebanese border before rejoining the GOREN NATIONAL PARK. To the south, a track leads through a forest of oak trees to a promontory which overlooks the fertile Kriv Valley, where the striking MONTFORT CASTLE stands. This was owned by the Order of the German Knights until it was destroyed by Baybars.

HATZOR

Its 190 acres form the most extensive archeological site in Israel. Mentioned by the Egyptians from the 19th century BC, the town of Hatzor was destroyed by the Hebrews when they arrived in Canaan, then taken back by Solomon who built a fortress and garrison with the mission of supervising the northern border of the kingdom. In the 8th century BC, the Assyrian conquest ● 46 overthrew it, a blow from which it never recovered. The archeological site is divided into two parts: the ACROPOLIS of which the fortifications and the citadel remain, and the ENTRENCHED CAMP which housed the temples and dwellings. The Canaanite fortifications of the acropolis, which extends over 24 acres, recall those of Jericho. Archeologists have found traces of four fortresses on which an Assyrian camp has been built. The entrenched camp covers the remains of successive towns, each one yielding treasures, such as the immense Canaanite altar or the temple arranged like the Temple in Jerusalem ▲ 260.

PEKI'IN
On the southwest side of Mount Meron the villages neighboring Peki'in ★ and Beth Dagan are home to members of the small Druze and Christian communities of Israel ● 96. Of all the Muslim minorities the Druze are certainly the best integrated into the life of the young state. They are the only ones to do military service and these redoubtable fighters join elite units.

TEL HATZOR
Kibbutz Ayelet Hashahar, on the other side of the road opposite the entrance to the archeological site, has a marvelous exhibition on the history of Hatzor, as well as remains from Canaanite times found in the acropolis.

401

▲ Upper Galilee

CASPIAN TORTOISE
You can admire this aquatic tortoise when it sunbathes perched on stumps emerging from the edges of the banks of papyrus.

TEL DAN
At the foot of Mount Hermon, the ruins of ancient Leshem stretch out, renamed Dan after the settlement of the tribe bearing the same name. It used to mark the northern limit of the kingdom of Israel, "from Dan to Beersheba". The site has only been partially excavated.

WATER BUFFALO
It used to live here in the wild and has now been successfully reintroduced into the reserve.

LAKE HULA RESERVE

Bordered to the east by the Golan, and to the west by the Anti-Lebanon mountains, the depression of the upper Jordan shelters Lake Hula, which probably corresponds to the place known as "the waters of Merom" in the Bible. It was there that Joshua defied Jabin, the Canaanite king of Hatzor (Joshua 11). This once marshy plain collects the waters of the Jordan which spring up in Jabal al-Sheikh ("old man's mount", the Arab name for Mount Hermon) and extends 290 yards upstream of the Sea of Galilee. The valley forms a natural corridor between Asia and the Syria-Palestine coast, which means it has long been an indispensable route for caravans traveling from Damascus to Cairo. Hula was the traditional fiefdom of the Arab tribe, Ghawarina, and at the end of the last century it filled with many Jewish immigrants from central Europe. Like the Jordan Valley, Hula is rich in subtropical vegetation unusual in this dry eastern land, including the Egypt papyrus, giant waterlilies, rushes and reeds over 13 feet high. In particular, rice, cotton and indigo are grown there, as well as sugar cane. The discovery of this astonished the Crusaders. An ambitious project to dry out the lake would be a veritable ecological disaster and the small reserve gives you an idea of the flora and fauna that lived in this lost paradise. Earth paths, routes raised on posts, running through the banks of papyrus, and observation towers allow you to discover the depths of the marshes in peace. Here you may find nesting herons, pelicans (stopping off on their migration route), many types of duck, including the shovelduck and teal, and the rough-footed spotted eagle which frequents the lake in winter. Reeds and papyrus give homes to countless sparrows which fill the air with their song. Mammals such as the water buffalo or the coypu can be observed in the grounds of the reserve.

MARBLED DUCK
Some pairs of this uncommon species nest in the banks of papyrus.

> "MAY GOD PROTECT IT! THIS CITY, A BORDER POST OF THE LAND OF THE MUSLIMS, IS SMALL, WITH A CITADEL SURROUNDED BY A MOAT."
>
> IBN JOBAIR

BANYAS

At the foot of Mount Hermon, 1,700 feet above the Sea of Galilee, is Banyas. It occupies a cool valley where the water, which is plentiful, maintains luxuriant vegetation. The quality of lemons, rice and cotton here has been praised by more than one classical Arabic writer. Its name, Banyas in Arabic and Paneas in Greek, dates back to Hellenist times, when the cave which is there was dedicated to Pan, the Greek god of music. In front of this site, King Herod the Great built a temple in honor of Augustus. His son, Philip Herod, beautified the place before renaming it Caesarea Philippi. It was there that Jesus addressed to the apostle Paul the famous injunction, "Thou art Peter, and upon this rock I will build my church" (Matthew 16). The town was Christianized relatively early and became a bishopric of the Antioch patriarchate in the 4th century. It served Heracluis' army during the Muslim conquest. The Umayyid Caliphate of Damascus was the chief town of the district of Al-Jawlan (Golan). In the Middle Ages it fell into Crusader hands. They made it into an advanced post against the Sultan of Damascus, as is shown by the fortress of Al-Subayba, also called Nimrod's fortress, which still dominates it. Banyas then played the role of meeting place between the lands of Islam and those of the Christian Crusaders; the two groups eventually peacefully divided the use of this fertile plain, according to the eyewitness account of the great 12th-century North African traveler, Ibn Jobair. At the foot of a limestone rock which rises steeply above the village (destroyed the day after the Israeli occupation of the Golan in June 1967) you will find the main source of the Jordan River. Nahar Banyas, which flows into Lake Hula, runs from here. On a rock ledge is a little sanctuary dedicated to al-Khader, the "green one", a Muslim saint often identified with the Prophet Elijah or Saint George.

THE BANKS OF PAPYRUS
Tropical in origin, papyrus is found in Hula at the northern edge of its grounds. Here it takes on a brownish color because of the cooler climate. The high-pitched, trilling call of the wood kingfisher of Smyrna comes from the branches of trees. It feeds equally on small fish as on lizards. As for the gray night heron, it nests in large numbers in the large papyrus banks which border the north side of the lake.

MOUNT HERMON ★

With reference to the snows that adorn it, the Arabs call Hermon "old man's mount". The 18½-mile-long chain has three towering peaks. The highest (9,200 feet) overlooks the Lebanese Bekaa valley to the north. The second, 330 feet south of the first, dominates the Damascus plain. The third, the only one visible from the Golan, watches over the Jordan Valley from its height of 7,300 feet. There is a ski center open from January to March ◆ 431.

THE ASSASSINS

The name of this Ismaili sect, whose castle of Nimrod was a shrine, comes from hashish, a substance they are said to have used to gain courage at the time of battle. Begun in 1090, the sect preached absolute submission to the religious leader and for them violence was a ritual and political necessity.

THE GOLAN HEIGHTS

Above Wadi Saara, in the direction of Banyas, is the small Syrian village of AIN QUNIYA which still has a Druze population. At the side of the hill, the road rejoins MASAADA, a verdant Druze township, then continues in the direction of Jabal al-Sheikh, whose peak, snow-covered until the start of summer, dominates the horizon. The wine-producing land on the Golan Heights, on Mount Hermon's foothills, produces the best wine in the country. Founded in 1983, the wine-making establishment here has invested a great deal of money, using the most modern equipment in the world. The methods as well as the vines used come from California, ensuring pleasant, light and fruity wines. Of course, the wines are strictly kosher, and non-practicing wine-makers are not allowed to touch the equipment after the treading of the grapes. The property belongs to a cooperative of eight kibbutzim ▲ 132.

NIMROD'S FORTRESS ★. East of Banyas, Nimrod's fortress rises proudly on a mountain which is part of the Hermon chain. Overlooking the neighboring plain from a height of 985 feet, this prime strategic position was occupied since earliest times. But the parts of the fortress that are still visible today date mainly from the defensive architecture of the Arabs and Franks at the time of the Crusades. The fort of Al-Subaya was, from 1126, run by Ismaeli Shi'ites with the agreement of the Atabeg of Damascus. It became a refuge for the fearsome sect of the Hashishin, or "Assassins". Opposed by Sunni Muslims, the sect finally gave up the place to the Crusaders in 1130, who established the Banyas bishopric. Taken back by Nur ad-Din in 1164, the Atabeg of Aleppo, the site remained the property of Islam after a fruitless attempt at reconquest by Saint Louis in 1253.

MAJDAL SHAMS. Clinging to the east side of Mount Hermon and dominating the plateau from its height of 3,940 feet, Majdal Shams is on the cease-fire line drawn up by Israel and Syria in 1974. It is opposite the Syrian border-post of Hadar, and not a day passes without one half of a family, refugees in the interior of the country, coming to talk, with the aid of a megaphone and telescope, to the other half who did not relocate before the June

1967 partition date and who have been separated from their relations ever since. The "Sun Tower" gives the impression of land at the end of the earth, forgotten, strange and impenetrable. Above Majdal Shams, Mount Hermon stands at more than 8,860 feet. From the summit, which can be reached via a pretty road and a chairlift built for the ski resort also situated there, a stunning panorama over southern Lebanon, the Galilee and the whole of the Golan as far as Damascus ★ can be seen.

THE ROUTE TO THE SOUTH. The road crosses the bare plateau of the central Golan, running along the demilitarized zone which separates the Golan under Israeli occupation from Syria. Its monotony is sometimes broken by the appearance of the truncated cone of an extinct volcano. Uncertainty over the region's future means that some villages abandoned by the Syrian population have not been re-inhabited. This has not, however, detracted from the land's fertility. Going down to the Jordan depression, the road reaches the village of KATZRIN, a regional capital and the only major Jewish presence in the area. Founded in 1977, it has become the industrial capital of the Golan. From the west side of the town as far as the banks of the Sea of Galilee, a forest of oak trees, with paths running through, extends for about 9½ miles, sheltering the YA'AR YEHUDIYA NATURE RESERVE which is riddled with numerous streams and waterfalls. Apart from the oaks, there are jujube trees, pistachio trees and white poplars ■ 22. The forest is dominated by the fortified village of GAMLA, the "Masada of the north" ▲ 202 where more than five thousand fighters, women and children, threw themselves into oblivion rather than face defeat and the Roman yoke in AD 67.

THE VINE
Held in the highest esteem since Canaanite times, in the Bible the vine symbolizes the power of God to bring to fruition or to destroy. So Israel is God's vineyard in Isaiah. Jesus presented himself as the true vine whose fruits would not disappoint the grower (John 15).

MAJDAL SHAMS
The "Sun Tower" is the most important agglomeration in the Golan. It is considered to be a bastion of Syrian nationalism. Largely Druze, the population overwhelmingly rejected the offer of naturalization suggested by the Jewish state shortly after annexation in 1981. Since 1987 the statue of Sultan al-Atrach (left) has reigned from the town square. He was a national hero who fought the French mandate of Syria at the beginning of the century.

405

▲ THE JORDAN

A mosaic found at
Madaba showing the
crossing of the Jordan.

THE BAPTISM
"Then cometh Jesus
from Galilee to
Jordan unto John, to
be baptized of him . . .
And Jesus, when he
was baptized, went up
straightway out of the
water: and lo, the
heavens were opened
unto him, and he saw
the Spirit of God
descending like a dove
and lighting on him.
And lo, a voice from
heaven, saying, This is
my beloved son, in
whom I am well
pleased" (Matthew 3).
The identification of
the place of baptism is
controversial. Two sites
fight for the honor,
one in the northern
part of the river, the
other not far from
Jericho. The Gospels
do not settle the
matter, but tradition
favors the southern
site.

Although far more modest in size than the Euphrates, the
Tigris or the Nile, the Jordan River has nonetheless
played an important role in religious history. The name of
Jordan (*ha Yarden* in Hebrew and *Al Urdun* in Arabic), comes
from the Semitic root *yrd,* meaning "descend", "expedite" or
"reject". In Arabic it is also commonly called *Al Sharia al-
Kabira*, "the large watering place". The river is born of the
meeting of three waterways which begin in Mount Hermon:
the Hasbani, which crosses southern Lebanon, the Banyas,
which begins in the Syrian part of the Golan (annexed by
Israel) and the Dan, which springs up in the extreme north of
Israel. All three run into the Hula Basin before flowing
toward Lake Tiberias. For the 60-odd miles which separate
the mouth of the lake from the Dead Sea, in which the river
comes to an end, the slope of the land is so slight that the
water waltzes along twisting every which way for more than
185 miles. For most of its length, the Jordan now forms
the border between Jordan and Israel and the
occupied territories. In fact throughout the
course of the history of the Hebrew kingdoms,
the river has always been a border between the
Promised Land and the enemy. Abraham
crossed it to reach

Canaan, but on the return from exile, Moses was forbidden by God to cross it and had to contemplate the promised land from the summit of Mount Nebo, now in Jordan. Some days after his death, the miraculous crossing of the river ended forty years of wandering. In 1967, at the start of the Six-Day War, the Jordan once again became the border of the Israeli State.

FROM LAKE TIBERIAS TO JERICHO

About 6½ miles south of the lake, the Jordan meets its main affluent, the Yarmuk, coming from the Syrian Haran and whose deep and narrow valley now separates Jordan from the Golan. The mountains of Gilead, whose beauty Solomon celebrated in the *Song of Songs*, rise on the other side of the river whose valley, until it reaches Transjordan, is kept to the dimensions of a large gorge. The fertility of the depression of Lake Tiberias is followed by the aridity of the Hills of Samaria. Despite uncertainty over the region's future, planting begun by Jewish pioneers has lasted to the beginning of the 1990's. It has significantly altered the landscape: irrigation, reforestation and development of agriculture have made it possible to profit from a land traditionally neglected. Unusually for the Holy Land you can cross the many miles from Bet She'an ▲ *396* to Jericho ▲ *314* without coming across the least site of archeological or historical interest – as if the land wished to allow the traveler to appreciate the beauty of the landscape at his leisure. At the entrance to the Jericho oasis, Samaria gives way to Judea. Three miles to the south of the ALLENBY BRIDGE which, level with Jericho, crosses the Jordan at the place called AL-MAGHTAS, is the ford the Israelites are said to have crossed to reach the Promised Land on their return from Exodus, not far one of the sites where Jesus may have been baptized. Two churches,

❝And as they that bare the Ark were come unto Jordan, and the feet of the priests that bare the ark were dipped in the brim of the water, (for Jordan overfloweth all his banks all the time of harvest) that the waters which came down from above stood and rose up upon an heap very far from the city . . . and those that came down towards the sea of the plain, even the salt sea, failed, and were cut off; and the people passed over right against Jericho.❞ (Joshua 3)

The water of the Jordan River, because of its associations, is bottled here by Americans, forming the basis of a vast trade.

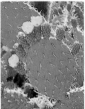

PHOENIX DACTYLIFERA
The palm tree not only provides the highly nutritious date, but also raw material for crafts. It is a basic resource of the oases, which it protects from the ravages of the sun and wind.

the Qasr al-Yahud and Qasr Hajila, commemorate this baptism.

BLUE GOLD. The water from the river naturally contains a saline residue of calcium chloride, soda, sulfuric acid and magnesium. It irrigates a valley covered in subtropical vegetation where the flora is as plentiful as it is diverse. Of the 162 types of plants, 35 also grow in Europe and 135 in Africa or India. Among the plant species that flourish there are the Egyptian papyrus, tamarisk, banana palm, orange and bitter orange trees, acacia, bamboo and jujube. The latter, called *Ziziphus Spinachristi* (*dom* or *baak* in Arabic), would have been used to make the crown of thorns which inflicted on Jesus an additional mortification at the time of the Passion. The *myrobalanum* (*zaqum* in Arabic), very common in the region, is the tree whose bitter fruit will, according to the Qur'an, serve as a terrible ration for those condemned to Hell. In a region marked by aridity, the river sharpens jealousies, not least because the natural reserves of soft water in the seven countries of the Middle East (including Israel and Jordan) are insufficient for their needs. Israel has decreed that the water of Transjordan is a strategic resource under military control. Distribution of the waters of the Jordan, which accounts for about 35 percent of Israel's water supply (the occupied territories included) is a central issue in the ongoing peace negotiations with Jordan. Syria is uneasy about eventual Israeli control over the waters of Mount Hermon, as the Damascus plain badly needs this precious resource too. The huge importance of the control of the rivers and aquifers of Samaria to both Arabs and Israelis will be a major issue in the future of the peace process in the Middle East.

PRACTICAL
INFORMATION

USEFUL INFORMATION, *410*
TRAVELING TO THE
HOLY LAND, *414*
LOCAL TRANSPORT, *416*
BY CAR, *418*
MAIL AND TELEPHONE, *419*
LIVING IN THE HOLY LAND, *420*
JEWISH PILGRIMAGE, *422*
CHRISTIAN PILGRIMAGE, *424*
IN THE FOOTSTEPS OF . . . , *426*
ARCHEOLOGY
IN THE HOLY LAND, *428*
NATURE, SPORTS
AND NATURAL REMEDIES, *430*
JERUSALEM IN THREE DAYS, *432*
MAP OF THE OLD CITY
OF JERUSALEM, *434*
THE HOLY LAND
IN A WEEK, *436*
THE HOLY LAND
IN THREE WEEKS, *438*

◆ USEFUL INFORMATION

For over one thousand years, the Holy Land has welcomed a constant and ever-increasing stream of visitors: pilgrims in search of their God; archeologists in search of past history; nature lovers inspired by a landscape of deserts, hills and seashores; vacationers in search of sun and the mysteries of the Orient. These visitors and their widely varied aspirations are the tangible expression of the richness of this unique land which has nurtured the three related monotheistic religions of this region.

FORMALITIES

If you are traveling from the US or the EU, all you need to visit Israel is a passport valid for at least six months. You will be authorized to remain in the country for three months from the date of your arrival. To extend your stay, apply to the Israeli Ministry of the Interior. If you want to work in Israel, you will need a special visa, obtained in advance from the Israeli Ministry of the Interior by your employer. If you intend to visit an Arab country subsequently, it is worth ensuring that the customs stamp appears on a separate form. You don't need an international license to drive in Israel ◆ 418.

CUSTOMS

Declare any video equipment, personal computers and diving gear at Israeli customs as you will be required to pay a security deposit which is refunded when you leave the country. Expect to be questioned for security reasons, briefly or at length, by Israeli police officials and don't be surprised if this questioning assumes the proportions of an interrogation. Don't panic and reply in a direct manner. Remember this is only a routine check. It is advisable to keep to the check-in time before flights (usually about three hours).

N.B. Your boarding card should have the same number of stickers as you have pieces of luggage. You can avoid problems with customs by leaving the country with the same number of cases and bags as when you arrived.

If you don't, Israeli customs police may begin to wonder what has happened to one of your bags during your stay.

HEALTH

Make sure you pack a good pair of sunglasses, a sun hat and a high-protection sun cream. A drinking bottle is also a good idea as it is important to maintain your liquid intake and stay hydrated when you are out and

about in the hot, dry climate of the Holy Land.

RECOMMENDED VACCINATIONS

Hepatitis A
Tetanus
Typhoid
Polio

INSURANCE

Some bankers' cards (American Express, Visa Premier International) offer additional services such as medical insurance and repatriation. Ask for information to avoid over-insuring yourself. If you reserve a "package holiday" through a tour operator, insurance is not always included in the price. Take out additional insurance to cover loss of luggage, repatriation, third party liability, etc. A cancellation insurance, even for your air ticket, means you will automatically get your money back if you have to cancel your flight. In the US contact International SOS Assistance Tel. (800) 523 8930 Travel Assistance International Tel. (800) 821 2828

ISRAEL GOVERNMENT TOURIST BOARD

In the US: Tel. (800) 596 1199
In the UK: Tel. 0171 434 3651
For other useful addresses see ◆ 444

WHEN TO GO

Although you can visit the Holy Land all year round, it has different things to offer at different times of year. In spring the hills of the Galilee, barren for most of the year, are swathed in grass and wild flowers. Before Easter the Christian processions along the Way of the Cross are joined by many pilgrims and tourists. Shortly afterward Jews celebrate Pesach, while the Muslim fast of Ramadan has already ended. In summer, when it is humid in Tel Aviv and scorchingly hot on the shores of the Dead Sea, cool winds blow on the shores of the Sea of Galilee and dispel the heat haze. In August the Eilat jazz festival attracts its share of music lovers. Toward the end of summer the number of tourists begins to decrease at a time when several festivals are held in the gentler September sun. In winter you may be lucky enough to visit Jerusalem in the snow or ski on the slopes of Mount Hermon, while the Red and Dead seas continue to welcome sun-seekers. At Christmas the Nativity gives rise to some original events. Finally a hot, dry, desert wind (*khamsin*) blows across the Holy Land for several days every year.

SELECTION OF FESTIVALS IN ISRAEL
JERUSALEM FILM FESTIVAL
FOLK-DANCE FESTIVAL – CARMIEL
July
FESTIVAL OF ISRAEL – JERUSALEM
May to June
Classical music, pop music, rock
INTERNATIONAL JAZZ FESTIVAL – EILAT
August

ISLAMIC FESTIVALS IN THE 1990's ● 92

GREGORIAN CALENDAR	MUSLIM CALENDAR (HIJRA)	RAS ES-SANA	BEGINNING OF RAMADAN	AÏD AL-ADHA (AL-KEBIR)	MOULOUD
1997	1418	MAY 9	JANUARY 10	APRIL 18	JULY 17
1998	1419	APRIL 28	JANUARY 1	APRIL 7	JULY 6
1999	1420	APRIL 17	DECEMBER 20	MARCH 27	JUNE 25

JEWISH FESTIVALS IN THE 1990's ● 80

GREGORIAN CALENDAR	JEWISH CALENDAR	PURIM	BEGINNING OF PESACH	SHAVUOT	ROSH HASHANAH	YOM KIPPUR	BEGINNING OF SUKKOT	BEGINNING OF HANUKKAH
1997	5757	MARCH 23	APRIL 28	JUNE 11	OCT. 2	OCT. 11	OCT. 16	DEC. 24
1998	5758	MARCH 12	APRIL 11	MAY 31	SEP. 21	SEP. 30	OCT. 5	DEC. 14
1999	5759	MARCH 2	APRIL 1	MAY 21	SEP. 11	SEP. 20	SEP. 25	DEC. 4

PROTESTANT AND CATHOLIC FESTIVALS IN THE 1990's ● 86

GREGORIAN CALENDAR	EASTER	ASCENSION	WHITSUN	ASSUMPTION	ALL SAINTS	CHRISTMAS
1997	MARCH 30	MAY 8	MAY 18	AUGUST 15	NOVEMBER 1	DECEMBER 25
1998	APRIL 12	MAY 21	MAY 31	AUGUST 15	NOVEMBER 1	DECEMBER 25
1999	APRIL 4	MAY 13	MAY 23	AUGUST 15	NOVEMBER 1	DECEMBER 25

ORTHODOX* FESTIVALS IN THE 1990's ● 86

GREGORIAN CALENDAR	EASTER	ASCENSION	WHITSUN	TRANSFIGURATION	CHRISTMAS (THEOPHANY)
1997	APRIL 14	JUNE 5	JUNE 15	AUGUST 6	JANUARY 5–6
1998	APRIL 19	MAY 28	JUNE 7	AUGUST 6	JANUARY 5–6
1999	APRIL 11	MAY 20	MAY 30	AUGUST 6	JANUARY 5–6

* celebrated on the dates given by most Orthodox churches

CHOOSING YOUR SEASON

JAN.	FEB.	MARCH	APRIL	MAY	JUNE	JULY	AUGUST	SEP.	OCT.	NOV.	DEC.

☀ Dry season   🌧 Rainy season   ☁ Intermediate season   🚶 Tourist numbers

◆ PREPARATIONS

MAPS
A detailed road map of Israel is essential. Make sure the road and junction numbers are marked ◆418.

WHAT TO PACK
CLOTHES

Between April and October, take lightweight clothing but pack a sweater for air-conditioned buildings and evenings in the mountains or the desert. From November to March, pack warm and waterproof clothing.

PHOTOS

You can buy film in the large towns and on most of the tourist sites, but it tends to be more expensive than in Europe or the US. Keep film with you at the airport so that it is not fogged by X-rays. As the light is extremely bright, use film with a low light-sensitivity (100 or 200 ASA) and don't leave cameras and film exposed to heat or sandstorms (use a special brush to clean your camera). Observe notices prohibiting the use of cameras in certain places, such as military zones, and in certain districts, especially during religious festivals.

USEFUL ITEMS

Women will find a scarf an extremely useful – and versatile – accessory in the Holy Land. As well as providing protection against the sun and sandstorms, it is essential for visiting holy places.
A pair of binoculars adds to the enjoyment of a walk in the country.

FOR YOUNG PEOPLE

INTERNATIONAL STUDENT IDENTITY CARD
The card entitles you to discounts on museum and movie-theater admissions and bus travel. You may well need one if you intend to stay in youth hostels. The card costs $16.

INFORMATION
Council Travel (a subsidiary of Council on International Educational Exchange), 16th floor 205 East 42nd St New York, NY 10017 Tel. (212) 661 1414

YOUTH HOSTEL
These are the cheapest form of accommodation. You may be asked for your membership card.
INFORMATION
In the US: The American Youth Hostel Association Tel. (800) 825 9399
In the UK: Tel. 01727 855215

BUDGETING FOR ISRAEL

A LOW-BUDGET WEEK
A double room for seven nights will cost between 300 and 400 shekels per person in a youth hostel, hospice or low-budget hotel. For 55 shekels per day you can buy a good breakfast, a light lunch and a substantial dish in a restaurant in the evening. A one-week Egged Israbus travel card ◆ 416 costs 217 shekels. Allow approximately 1,000 shekels for a low-budget week in Israel.

A MIDDLE-BUDGET WEEK
A double room for seven nights in a reasonably comfortable, good category hotel or kibbutz-hotel will cost around 1,400 shekels per person. Allow 150 shekels per day for a good breakfast, a hot lunch and an evening meal in a good restaurant. Car rental costs between 550 and 1,350 shekels for a 7-day (unlimited mileage) package ◆ 418. Your week's budget will therefore be around 3,000 shekels.

TOURIST INFORMATION

You can obtain further information from the Tourist Office at Ben-Gurion Airport on arrival or, during your stay, from Tourist Offices in the large towns and coastal resorts. There are also free English-language publications such as *This Week in Jerusalem* or *This Week in Tel Aviv* and *The Jerusalem Times, Tourist Guide*, distributed by the Palestinian Chamber of Commerce in Europe. Before you leave you can also consult the Israeli Tourist Office in your own country.

TIME DIFFERENCES

There is a 7-hour time difference between New York and Israel and a 2-hour difference with the UK.

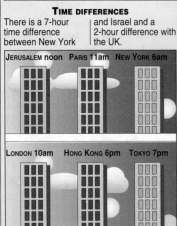

JERUSALEM noon   PARIS 11am   NEW YORK 6am

LONDON 10am   HONG KONG 6pm   TOKYO 7pm

The national unit of currency in Israel is the shekel. But beware: the exchange rate is extremely unstable and it is not advisable to change large sums of money at a time. Take a supply of dollars in small denominations since many places accept American currency and goods are often priced in dollars. And a transaction in dollars may well prove to be a better deal than one in shekels.

CURRENCY

The national unit of currency is the shekel (New Israeli Shekel or NIS) which is divided into 100 agorot (Ag). Notes are in denominations of 10, 20, 50 and 100 shekels while coins are 5 and 10 agorot, and ½, 1, 5 and 10 shekels.

Dollars and travelers' checks are also accepted. You can draw cash from most banks with Visa, Master Card, Access, Eurocard and American Express cards.

CHANGING AND DRAWING MONEY

Banks are open from Sunday to Thursday, between 8.30am and 12.30pm, and on Sundays, Tuesdays and Thursdays,

BANK HAPOALIM

between 4pm and 6pm. On Fridays and the eve of public holidays they close at 12pm. Leumi and Hapoalim are the two main Israeli banks.

In the street, Arab moneychangers offer shekels at a favorable exchange rate, but keep your wits about you. In May 1997 the exchange rate was 3.36 shekels to the US dollar and 5.18 shekels to the UK pound. Dollars can also be changed in most hotels and automatic teller machines are fairly widespread.

bank leumi בנק לאומי

TAXES AND INVOICES

Some items and services (accommodation, organized tours, car rental and internal flights) are VAT-free if paid for in cash, while all items and services invoiced in Eilat are exempt. Tourists spending over $50 in stores recommended by the Ministry of Tourism benefit from a 5 percent reduction and a VAT refund. Ask for an invoice and keep it somewhere safe. Your purchase and a copy of the invoice are then placed in a sealed, transparent plastic bag which must not, under any circumstances, be opened before you leave. The VAT will be refunded by the Bank Leumi at Ben Gurion Airport or the Port of Haifa, after the contents of the bag have been checked.

TIPPING

Tips are nearly always included in hotel and restaurant prices, unless otherwise indicated: in which case allow for a gratuity of around 15 percent. Taxi drivers do not automatically expect a tip.

◆ Traveling to the Holy Land

By Air

From the UK:
◆ British Airways
Tel. 0181 759 5511
Daily flights to Tel Aviv from Gatwick and Heathrow. Return fare £387 (economy), £346 (apex); £924 (business).
◆ El Al Israel Airlines
Tel. 0171 437 9255 for information
Daily flights to Tel Aviv from

Heathrow (4½-hour flight); twice a week from Manchester (Mon. and Thur.) From £249 return. Eilat twice a week in winter.

From the US:
There are three airlines that offer direct flights from New York to Tel Aviv:
◆ El Al Israel Airlines
Tel. (800) 223 6700

Nonstop flights from New York (JFK or Newark), daily (except Fri.). Coach fares range from $1,015–1,322 (flights are generally cheaper from Newark than JFK). Flights from Chicago, usually nonstop during the summer, Mon. and Wed. $1,056–1,209. Flights from Los Angeles, with a stop in either Chicago or New York, Mon. and Wed., $1,319–1,719.
◆ Tower Air
Tel. (718) 553 8500
Nonstop flights from New York, $999–1,399. Flights from Los Angeles with a stop in New York, $1,287–1,667.
◆ Trans World Airlines
Tel. (800) 892 4141
Nonstop flights from New York, $979–1,000. Flights from Chicago with a stop in JFK, $1,021–1,263. Flights from Los Angeles with a stop in JFK, $1,287–1,452.

London
Paris
Marseilles
Algiers   TUN
ALGERIA

Road links
Air links
Sea links

On arrival at Tel Aviv Airport

The international Ben Gurion Airport is situated approximately 11 miles from Tel Aviv. A "United Tours" bus (no. 222) leaves for the city center every hour and runs from Sunday to Thursday between 4am and midnight. There is no service between 8pm on Friday and 1pm on Saturday. The bus leaves from the El Al terminal and drops passengers in Arlosorov Street

(railway station) or at the Dan Panorama Hotel in Hayarkon Street.

An Egged bus runs to Tel Aviv, Jerusalem and Haifa every 20 minutes. To reach Jerusalem direct you can always take a Nesher company ◆ *433 sherut* (shared) taxi. The main car rental firms have offices at the airport (open 24 hours) but it is advisable to reserve in advance ◆ *418*.

Internal flights
Internal flights – to Eilat, for example – leave from Sdeh Dov Airport, about 1 mile north of Tel Aviv. Take a no. 26 bus from Ben Gurion Airport to the central bus station in Tel Aviv and then a no. 475 bus to Sdeh Dov. Alternatively take a taxi.

By boat
Boat services from Italy and Greece to Israel (Haifa) take 5–6 days and sometimes include an overnight stop in Piraeus. The cost of the crossing (separate tickets) varies between $150 (deck, off-peak season) and $650 (luxury cabin, peak season). Departures are from Brindisi, Bari and Ancona. Cunard operate cruises in the eastern Mediterranean starting from Venice, then sailing to Alexandria, stopping at Ashdod and Haifa, then up to Athens. Prices for 15 nights are from £2,375.
Tel. 01703 634166

Venice • Vienna
Rome • Brindisi • GREECE
Athens • Heraklion • *Black Sea*
Istanbul • Ankara
Rhodes • TURKEY
Larnaca • CYPRUS • SYRIA
Damascus
Beirut • Jerusalem
Mediterranean Sea • ISRAEL
Tripoli • Port Said • Amman
Alexandria • Tel Aviv
Suez • SINAI
Cairo
LIBYA • EGYPT
SAHARA • Luxor • Aswan • *Nile*

BORDER POSTS

◆ ISRAEL–EGYPT
The border is open at Rafah, to the south-west of Ashkelon, from 9am to 5pm every day, and at Taba, south of Eilat, 24 hours. These times should be checked as they may vary. Border posts are closed for Yom Kippur ● 80 and the festival of Aïd el-Adha. You can cross the border in a private car but not in a rented vehicle.

◆ JORDAN–ISRAEL
The border crossing at Allenby Bridge, 25 miles from Jerusalem, is closed on Sat. and for festivals. It may not be crossed by private vehicles, bicycles or pedestrians. It has recently become

BY ROAD

possible to cross via Eilat and Aqaba, but only by public transport. In addition to the Allenby Bridge you can use the Sheikh (King) Hussein Crossing in the north. You can also return to Israel from Jordan without having to go through your country of origin, but there is a tax to leave Israel.

VISAS
When crossing from Egypt or Jordan into Israel the formalities are the same as when entering Israel direct from any other country.

FROM ISRAEL TO EGYPT
You can obtain an Egyptian visa, free of charge, at the border provided:
– you are not staying

in Egypt for more than seven days;
– you are only visiting Sinai;
– you enter and leave Egypt via the border post at Taba. If you do not fulfil all three conditions, you have to obtain a visa from the Egyptian consulate in Israel or, preferably, your country of origin. The visa is valid from the date of issue and not the date of entry into Egypt. Allow about 2½ hours for formalities at the border.

FROM ISRAEL TO JORDAN
Tourists entering Jordan from Israel must have a Jordanian visa. Once in Jordan, you can only return to Israel via your country of origin.

BY ROAD FROM ISRAEL TO EGYPT
BUS
Sinai buses operate a return service between Cairo and Tel Aviv Mondays and Wednesdays, payable in Egyptian pounds (£E). Egged Tours operates daily Cairo–Tel Aviv and Cairo–Sharm el-Sheikh–Eilat services, while Galilee Tours runs a Cairo–Tel Aviv–Cairo service twice a week. The Cairo–Tel Aviv journey takes between 7 and 9 hours, excluding border formalities.
SHARED TAXIS
A shared taxi from Sharm el-Sheikh to Taba (where you can take the bus) costs only a fraction more and is a lot more comfortable.

Israel is a fairly small country with an excellent road and rail infrastructure servicing the entire territory. Roads are usually good, even though, in some areas, they are more akin to tracks than surfaced roads. Buses are the most widely used form of public transport. Travel by train between the major towns is slow but picturesque and inexpensive. To get from one end of the country to the other as quickly as possible, it is well worth taking an internal flight. Finally taxis are ideal for urban travel, while the suburbs are serviced by *sherut* (shared) taxis – an Israeli specialty, ideal if you want to travel further afield, more cheaply, and in small groups.

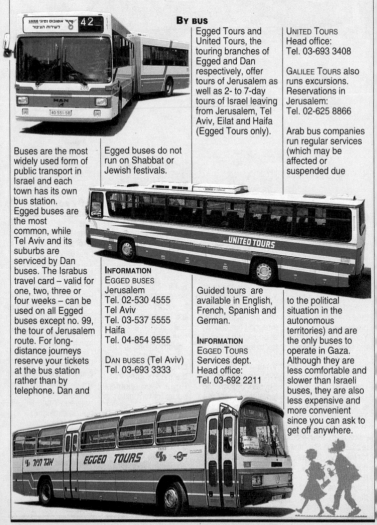

BY BUS

Egged Tours and United Tours, the touring branches of Egged and Dan respectively, offer tours of Jerusalem as well as 2- to 7-day tours of Israel leaving from Jerusalem, Tel Aviv, Eilat and Haifa (Egged Tours only).

UNITED TOURS
Head office:
Tel. 03-693 3408

GALILEE TOURS also runs excursions. Reservations in Jerusalem:
Tel. 02-625 8866

Arab bus companies run regular services (which may be affected or suspended due

Buses are the most widely used form of public transport in Israel and each town has its own bus station. Egged buses are the most common, while Tel Aviv and its suburbs are serviced by Dan buses. The Israbus travel card – valid for one, two, three or four weeks – can be used on all Egged buses except no. 99, the tour of Jerusalem route. For long-distance journeys reserve your tickets at the bus station rather than by telephone. Dan and

Egged buses do not run on Shabbat or Jewish festivals.

INFORMATION
EGGED BUSES
Jerusalem
Tel. 02-530 4555
Tel Aviv
Tel. 03-537 5555
Haifa
Tel. 04-854 9555

DAN BUSES (Tel Aviv)
Tel. 03-693 3333

Guided tours are available in English, French, Spanish and German.

INFORMATION
EGGED TOURS
Services dept.
Head office:
Tel. 03-692 2211

to the political situation in the autonomous territories) and are the only buses to operate in Gaza. Although they are less comfortable and slower than Israeli buses, they are also less expensive and more convenient since you can ask to get off anywhere.

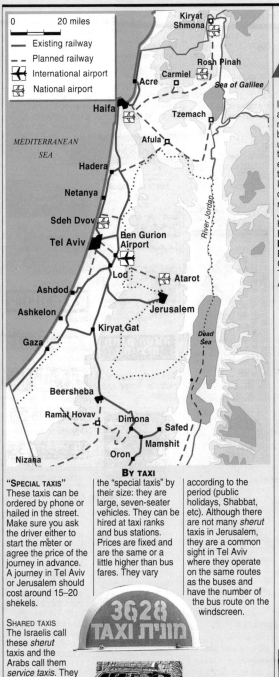

```
0        20 miles

──────  Existing railway
- - - -  Planned railway
✈       International airport
✈       National airport
```

Kiryat Shmona

Rosh Pinah

Carmiel

Acre

Sea of Galilee

Haifa

Tzemach

Afula

MEDITERRANEAN SEA

Hadera

Netanya

River Jordan

Sdeh Dvov

Ben Gurion Airport

Tel Aviv

Lod

Atarot

Ashdod

Jerusalem

Ashkelon

Kiryat Gat

Dead Sea

Gaza

Beersheba

Ramat Hovav

Dimona

Safed

Mamshit

Oron

Nizana

BY PLANE

In Israel distances are short and there is no real advantage to be gained by flying, unless you are traveling from one end of the country to the other. Arkia, Israel's internal airline company, operates regular flights from Jerusalem, Tel Aviv, Haifa, Beersheba, Eilat and Rosh Pinah.

INFORMATION
Ben Gurion Airport
General reservations:
Tel. 03-971 0111
Arkia: 03-690 3333

BY TRAIN

The rail network is limited and stations are often some distance from the city center. But traveling by train is cheaper and more picturesque than by bus, especially between Tel Aviv and Jerusalem. There are few trains on Fridays and none on festivals and Shabbat. Tickets cost between 2.5 and 26 shekels.

INFORMATION
Tel. 03-565 2200
or 03-693 7515

"SPECIAL TAXIS"

These taxis can be ordered by phone or hailed in the street. Make sure you ask the driver either to start the meter or agree the price of the journey in advance. A journey in Tel Aviv or Jerusalem should cost around 15–20 shekels.

SHARED TAXIS
The Israelis call these *sherut* taxis and the Arabs call them *service taxis*. They run between towns and cities and can only be distinguished from

BY TAXI

the "special taxis" by their size: they are large, seven-seater vehicles. They can be hired at taxi ranks and bus stations. Prices are fixed and are the same or a little higher than bus fares. They vary

according to the period (public holidays, Shabbat, etc). Although there are not many *sherut* taxis in Jerusalem, they are a common sight in Tel Aviv where they operate on the same routes as the buses and have the number of the bus route on the windscreen.

417

DRIVING IN ISRAEL
HIGHWAY CODE

The highway code is the same as in the US and Europe, but there are a few points to remember. Cars travel on the right and speed limits are: 90km (56 miles) per hour on roads, 110km (68 miles) per hour on freeways and 60km (37 miles) per hour in built-up areas. Seat belts are compulsory. From November 1 to March 30, headlights are used even in daylight on main roads.

SAFETY

Safety is often a matter of common sense and diplomacy: in the autonomous territories, rent a car with a blue (Palestinian) number plate rather than an Israeli one.

PARKING CARD

Scratch off the date and time of arrival on the parking card and display it behind the windscreen. A one-hour parking card costs 3.5 shekels and can be bought from kiosks, post offices and bazaars, as well as where you pay your parking fines, a penalty from which tourists are not exempt.

CAR RENTAL

Some local companies and the main international car-rental agencies are represented in the major towns and cities and at Ben Gurion Airport. To rent a car you need to be over twenty-one and to have held a driving license for at least one year. You can make your reservation from your country of origin. Some travel agencies and car-rental companies offer special rental packages.

FREEWAYS
AND ROAD SIGNS

BEWARE: On freeways the best way of not reaching your destination (unless it is a large town or city) is to look for it on the road signs.

When you look at the map, don't look for the name of the place you are going to but the name or number of the intersection that gives access to it. A detailed road map is invaluable ◆ 412.

SHAPPIRIM — מחלף
INTERCHANGE 1 שפירים

MISCELLANEOUS SIGNS

Bus stop and sign indicating that military hitchhikers have priority.

תחנת הסעה
לחיילים

Tourist signs are in Hebrew, Arabic and English.

מצדה
MASADA →

עין גדי
EN GEDI →

עין צוקים
EN ZUQIM →

The blue and white lines mean there is a charge for parking.

NUMBER PLATES

47-301-04
Israeli

מ-31-074
Police

Military

CC72-098-22
Diplomatic corps

35-552-33
Palestinian, autonomous territories

VISITING GAZA

There are two ways of visiting the Gaza Strip: by rental car or by taxi. Either way you will have to change vehicles at the border post of Erez. No driver of a vehicle registered in Israel – with its easily identifiable, yellow number plate – will cross into the Gaza Strip. You would therefore be well advised to arrange for a Gaza ▲ 334 taxi to meet you at Erez. The ideal rendezvous is the PAZ gas station about 100 yards from the check point, on the right. Gaza taxi drivers are used to tourists and have a reputation for being adept guides. The day should cost you around $100.

RENTAL RATES

For a small, Group A type car	
AVIS	1 day, 155 miles max.: 260 sh
	1 wk, unlimited mileage: 1,750 sh
HERTZ	1 day, 60 miles: 210 sh
	1 wk, unlimited mileage: 1,600 sh
BUDGET	1 day, 60 miles max.: 210 sh
	1 wk, unlimited mileage: 1,295 sh

Mail and telephone services in Israel are managed by two separate departments. As central telephone points are becoming obsolete, it is well worth investing in a phone card – it will come in useful sooner or later. Israel has a unique *poste restante* system – in the street. Banks of tiny mail boxes are a common sight in towns and cities. Box holders collect their mail which has been carefully preserved on the public highway.

MAIL

Main post offices are open from Sunday to Thursday, between 8am to 6pm (except Wednesdays: 8am to 1.30pm), and on Fridays the day before public holidays from 8am to 12pm. Central post offices all have poste restante facilities. Minor post offices are closed between 12.30pm and 3.30pm. When addressing mail, remember that zip codes vary within the same town and that the address alone is not always enough – the zip code is essential. There is also a more reliable express service:

for example, a letter takes 5 days to reach the US and 2–3 days to Europe. Mail boxes are in two colors: yellow for letters sent within the same region and red for letters sent to other regions or abroad. Stamps are sold in post offices and at hotel reception desks.

RATES FOR POSTCARDS AND LETTERS
Israel: 0.85 NIS
Europe: 1 and 1.3 NIS
Canada and the US: 1 and 1.8 NIS

DELIVERY TIME FOR MAIL
National: 1–2 days
International: approx. 1 week

TELEPHONE

Telephone booths take magnetic phone cards which are sold in post offices and kiosks. They are in units of 10, 20, 50, 120 or 240 and cost between 6 and 88 shekels. A local company, Solan Telecommunications and Computers Ltd, open around the clock, 7 days a week, sells and

rents portable phones, with discounts on international calls.

Ask for information as there are some interesting offers.

TELEPHONING IN ISRAEL
Telephone numbers have five, six or seven digits. To call Israel from the US, dial 011 972, or from the UK 00 972, followed by the code for the region (without the 0) and the number you are calling. For calls made within the same region, you can dial the number you are calling direct. If you are calling another region, don't forget to dial 0 before the regional code.

TELEPHONING ABROAD FROM ISRAEL
Dial 00 (international) and then the code for the country you are calling:

US: 1
Canada: 1
UK: 44

CODES
06 SAFED
Kiryat Shmona
Tiberias
Nazareth
04 HAIFA
09 NETANYA
Ra'anana
03 TEL AVIV – JAFFA
(and immediate environs)
08 ASHOD
Lod
02 JERUSALEM
Bethlehem
07 ASHKELON
Eilat
057 BEERSHEBA
Dead Sea

COST OF A TELEPHONE CALL

CALLS WITHIN ISRAEL

Local — 29 Ag. for each 72 seconds

Regional — 29 Ag. for each 24 seconds

Reduced rates: 1pm to 8pm; 8pm to 10pm and 10pm to 8am

CALLS TO EUROPE AND THE US

3.67 sh per minute

Reduced rates: 10pm to 1am (2.75 sh.) anmd 1am to 8am (1.84 sh.)

DIRECTORY ENQUIRIES
IN ISRAEL :
National: 144
IN THE UK:
International: 155
IN THE US:
International: 411

◆ LIVING IN THE HOLY LAND

"MEET THE ISRAELI AT HOME"
Meet Israelis in their own homes and exchange views on a wide range of subjects over refreshments. Ask at the nearest Tourist Information Office.

The Holy Land, situated at the crossroads of Africa, Asia and Europe, is the birthplace of the three related monotheistic religions of the region. Since the end of the 19th century it has been the point of convergence for Jews from all over the world, who have brought a wide diversity of cultures to all aspects of everyday life. This diversity is reflected in the vast range of culinary specialties and the many different types of tourist accommodation that represent a very particular way of life. An extremely varied press also plays an important role in a region suffering from constant political tension.

PRESS AND MEDIA

NEWSPAPERS
The only English-language daily is the *Jerusalem Post* (which also has a French edition). The other major dailies are in Hebrew: *Yediot Achronot*, *Maariv* and the more liberal *Ha'aretz*. Foreign language newspapers are sold in kiosks and bookstores in the large towns.

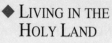

RADIO
Channel A broadcasts the news in English and French. Music lovers can listen to pop and jazz on Channel C or classical music on the Voice of Music. However one of the best radio stations is Galei Tzahal (originally an army station) which today offers a varied program of music, comedy sketches, news and interviews. The national station is the Voice of Israel. Radio frequencies and programs are published in the daily newspapers.

TELEVISION
The pro-government programs broadcast on Channel 1 are usually in English with subtitles in Hebrew and Arabic. The news is presented in English at 8pm, from Sunday to Thursday, and at 7.15pm on Fridays and Saturdays. Channel 2 is very similar, while cable TV gives access to programs from a number of countries.

SHOPPING

OPENING HOURS
Stores are open from 8.30am–1pm and 4–7pm.

DAYS OF REST AND FESTIVALS
Jewish festivals and *Shabbat* (Sabbath) ● *80*, begin at nightfall on the previous evening: on Fridays and the day before festivals, stores close in the early afternoon. Friday and Sunday are the Muslim and Christian days of rest. Although some stores and restaurants stay open throughout the week, in Nazareth they are closed on Sundays and on Wednesdays after 2pm.

HEALTH
Medical services are on a par with those in Europe. In an emergency or if you need medical advice, call 101, the Magen David Adom (equivalent of the Red Cross), who will give you the address of the nearest doctor or hospital. You will find a list of duty pharmacies and emergency services in the *Jerusalem Post*.

There are two main types of traditional cuisine: the "eastern" cuisine based on the culinary specialties of the Sephardic Jews and Palestinians, and the "Western" cuisine of Russia and central Europe introduced by the Ashkenazim.

RESTAURANTS
There are also numerous American snack-bars and French, Italian and Chinese restaurants. Menus are printed in Hebrew and English.

KOSHER FOOD
Although many restaurants, hotels and food stores observe Jewish dietary laws (*kashrut*), there are also many non-kosher restaurants and stores, particularly outside Jerusalem.

RESTAURANT CATEGORIES
1) 3-course menu
2) Average price of a dish
* (one-star)
1) 40 shekels
2) 20 shekels
** (two-star)
1) 40–60 shekels
2) 30–40 shekels
*** (three-star)
1) 100 shekels
2) 60–70 shekels

ELECTRICITY
The current is 220 volts and three-pin plugs are the norm. You may need a transformer for 110v appliances (electric razors, travel irons, hairdriers etc).

ACCOMMODATION

From religious hospices to vacation villages, and dormitories in youth hostels to luxury hotels, accommodation in the Holy Land is adapted to suit every need. Hotel prices are in dollars or shekels (VAT not included).

HOTEL CATEGORIES (PRICE PER NIGHT FOR A DOUBLE ROOM)
* (one-star)
20–40 shekels
** (two-star)
80–130 shekels
*** (three-star)
< 130 shekels

HOTELS
Hotels are not classified by stars, but there is an official list which indicates their category. All the big hotels have a synagogue, while luxury hotels such as the American Colony offer economy-class rooms at affordable prices.

INFORMATION
Israel Hotel Association
29 Hameret St.
Tel Aviv
Tel. 03-517 01 31
Fax 03-510 01 97

KIBBUTZ HOTELS
Some kibbutzim have opened comfortable hotels, enabling visitors to experience kibbutz life at first hand and attend information evenings. Allow between 50 and 160 shekels for a double room (including breakfast).
INFORMATION
Kibbutz Hotels
90 Ben Yehuda St.
64437 Tel Aviv
Tel. 03-524 61 61

KIBBUTZ HOTELS CHAIN

GUEST ROOMS
Some kibbutzim and *moshavim* ▲ 132 have reasonably priced guest rooms. Ask at the local Tourist Office. In Jerusalem you can combine a visit to the city and a stay with a local family where you will be given a room or an adjoining apartment.
INFORMATION
Good Morning Jerusalem
1 Shazar Bd
PO Box 6001
Jerusalem
Tel. 02-51 12 70
Fax 02-51 12 72

CHRISTIAN HOSPICES
Christian hospices offer reasonably priced rooms and dormitories, but some are reserved for pilgrims. Although some impose strict rules, notably going to bed by 10pm, most are fairly accommodating. Prices vary between 15 shekels for a dormitory and 50–120 shekels for a double room.
INFORMATION
Department for the promotion of pilgrimages
Israeli Ministry of Tourism
23 Hillel St
92262 Jerusalem
Tel. 02-24 79 62
Fax 02-25 34 07

YOUTH HOSTELS
Most (more than 30) youth hostels are affiliated to the Israeli Youth Hostel Association (IYHA) and are found throughout Israel, often near tourist sites. They also offer packages (1 week to 1 month) which include half-board, a travel card for unlimited travel on the Egged network and entrance tickets for various national parks. These can be reserved through tour operators in your country of origin or in Israel ◆ 412.
INFORMATION
IYHA
3 Dorot Rishonim St
Jerusalem 94625
Tel. 02-25 27 06
Fax 02-25 06 76

CAMPING
Campsites rent out tents, caravans and chalets. They also offer 2-week (16 nights) packages and car rental facilities.
INFORMATION
The Israel Camping Organization
Nahariya 22100
Tel. 04-925 392

SOME PRICES

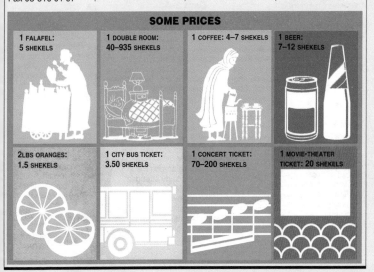

1 FALAFEL:
5 SHEKELS

1 DOUBLE ROOM:
40–935 SHEKELS

1 COFFEE: 4–7 SHEKELS

1 BEER:
7–12 SHEKELS

2LBS ORANGES:
1.5 SHEKELS

1 CITY BUS TICKET:
3.50 SHEKELS

1 CONCERT TICKET:
70–200 SHEKELS

1 MOVIE-THEATER TICKET: 20 SHEKELS

◆ JEWISH PILGRIMAGE

After the Romans crushed the final Jewish revolt (AD 135), Jews were dispersed (Greek, *Diaspora*) throughout the world, and could no longer perform the Temple rituals. Equivalent ways of devotion were developed, but always the hope and prayer has been for the return to Jerusalem. This longing has been anticipated through the ages in pilgrimage. Today the State of Israel welcomes pilgrims who come to pray at Judaism's most sacred sites, mostly associated with the Old Testament, but sometimes with recent rabbis and theologians.

Day 1

SAFED
The town of Safed, formerly one of the main centers of Jewish mysticism and Kabbalism in the Holy Land, has remained an important center for Talmudic study. From Ben Gurion Airport, highway no. 2 takes you to Akko from where highway no. 85 runs direct to Safed. Places of pilgrimage: the synagogue district ▲ *400* and the tomb of Haari Ashkenazi ▲ *399*.

Day 2

TIBERIAS
Morning: half an hour away by road (highways no. 89 and 90) are the much frequented memorials of Tiberias where two of the greatest Jewish theologians are buried. Places of pilgrimage: the tombs of Maimonides ▲ *380* and Rabbi Meir Ba'al Haness ▲ *380*.

NABLUS
Afternoon: Nablus, where Yahweh gave Abraham the Land of Israel, is reached via highways no. 77 (to Nazareth) and no. 60. Places of pilgrimage: the Tomb of Joseph and Mount Gerizim, the holy mountain of the Samaritans ▲ *312*.

Praying at the Wailing Wall.

Days 3–5

JERUSALEM
Throughout the Diaspora, Jerusalem was the ultimate symbol of the return to the Promised Land. Today it is the highlight of any pilgrimage to Israel. Arrive mid-morning after an hour by road (highway no. 60). Places of pilgrimage: the Western Wall ▲ *258*, Yad Vashem (Holocaust memorial) ▲ *302*, the Tomb of David ▲ *257* and the Ramban Synagogue ▲ *256*.

DAY 6

HEBRON
Hebron, one of the holy cities of Judaism (Al Khalil in Arabic), houses the Tomb of the Patriarchs, where Abraham, Isaac and Jacob are buried. From Jerusalem, head south along highway no. 60 toward Hebron, where you will arrive in the late morning. Places of pilgrimage: Tomb of the Patriarchs ▲ *217* and Abraham's Oak ▲ *216*.

BEERSHEBA
Continue along highway no. 60, arriving in Beersheba in the afternoon. Place of pilgrimage: Abraham's Well ▲ *194*.

DAY 7

If you stay overnight in Beersheba you can take highway no. 40 to Ben Gurion Airport the next morning. For those who prefer to stay in Tel Aviv, visit the Diaspora Museum ▲ *350* (which offers an insight into the history and diversity of the Jewish communities scattered throughout the world) before leaving for the airport.

SAFETY
Anti-Jewish feeling among the Palestinians is particularly strong in Nablus and Hebron. Visiting these towns in a car with a Jewish number plate is out of the question. If the political situation is tense during your stay, avoid the occupied territories.

On the eve of Shabbat, Orthodox Jews from Mea Shearim ▲ 262 gather at the Wailing Wall. This is the best time to admire (but don't photograph) their traditional costumes.

LEARNING HEBREW

For some European and American Jews, a visit to the Holy Land in search of their roots offers an opportunity to learn the official language of the State of Israel. Some *ulpanin* (language schools) are also open to non-Jews. The main centers for learning modern Hebrew (*Ivrit*) are Jerusalem, Tel Aviv and Netanya. Some kibbutzim also offer practical language courses with special accommodation for students, but these are longer and run for a minimum of one month.

SHOPPING

Copies of the Torah, bound in leather or cloth, make ideal souvenirs, even for "gentiles" who will appreciate the quality of the calligraphy. The Jaffa Road, leading to the Jaffa Gate, is one of the main streets and the commercial center of the new city of Jerusalem. The choice of goods is overwhelming and you will find some really beautiful *kipot* (skullcaps) and *talitot* (prayer shawls). High-quality craft products can also be found in Arts and Crafts Lane, a delightful street that runs through the Mitchell Gardens at the foot of the ramparts. The artists' district, at the foot of the Citadel ramparts, is an Aladdin's cave of (often very expensive) souvenirs, with its art galleries and workshops whose works of art are inspired by Jewish mysticism and religious symbolism.

LEBANON

Sea of Galilee

Haifa

MEDITERRANEAN SEA

Tel Aviv

Jerusalem

Gaza

Beersheba

ISRAEL

Dead Sea

JORDAN

EGYPT

Eilat

Aqaba

30 miles

GALILEE — Safed

Haifa

Tiberias

Sea of Galilee

Nazareth

Afula

65

60

Hadera

4

SAMARIA

Netanya

Nablus

River Jordan

MEDITERRANEAN SEA

Tel Aviv — Ben Gurion Airport

Ramallah

Jericho

Jerusalem

Bethlehem

JUDEA

40

Gaza

Hebron

60

Dead Sea

Beersheba

0   6   12   18 miles

423

A Christian pilgrimage in the Holy Land offers an opportunity to visit the sites of the ministry of Jesus, who was born and lived there until his Ascension into heaven. The route suggested enables you to cover – in seven days – the scenes of the main events described in the Gospels, starting in Galilee and ending in Judea and Jerusalem.

MOUNT OF BEATITUDES

It was on this mountain, overlooking the Sea of Galilee, that Jesus gave the Sermon on the Mount. A Franciscan sanctuary and hospice welcome pilgrims ▲ 382.

EN SHEVA (SPRING OF SEVEN)

The village of Tabgha is said to be the scene of the multiplication of the five loaves and two fishes. A Byzantine church, decorated with beautiful 5th-century mosaics, commemorates the miracle ▲ 382.

CANA

The church commemorating the marriage at Cana, where Christ turned water into wine ▲ 386, stands in what is today the small village of Kefar Cana.

NAZARETH

Nazareth, Jesus' home up to the time of his ministry and departure from Galilee, is one of the oldest Christian cities. Its Christian churches include the Basilica of the Annunciation, the largest church in the Near East ▲ 388.

MOUNT TABOR

Mount Tabor is a traditional place of pilgrimage. The Church of the Transfiguration, incorporating the chapels of Moses and Elijah, stands on the summit ▲ 392.

NAIM

The tiny village has a Franciscan church commemorating the resurrection of the widow's son.

SYCHAR

One of the oldest Biblical cities, where Abraham entered the Promised Land. Jacob's Well, where Jesus received water from the Samaritan woman, is still in use. Today it lies within the precincts of an orthodox church ▲ 313.

JESUS' BAPTISM

The Greek Monastery of St John the Baptist (Qasr el-Yehud), overlooking the River Jordan, commemorates Christ's baptism ▲ 406.

MOUNT OF TEMPTATION

A monastery stands on the summit of the Mount of Temptation (Deir al-Qarantal) which rises above Jericho. This was where Christ endured the forty days of temptation that followed his baptism (Matthew 4) ▲ 322.

JERUSALEM

The most venerated churches in Christendom are found in the ancient city of Jerusalem, where the Via Dolorosa and the Church of the Holy Sepulcher ▲ 266–7 provide a fitting end to a pilgrimage.

BETHANY

A modern church built on the ruins of Byzantine churches commemorates the resurrection of Lazarus.

BETHLEHEM

The Church of the Nativity, the supposed site of Jesus' birth, is one of the principal shrines of Christianity and one of the high spots of all pilgrimages ▲ 226.

EMMAUS

The location of Emmaus has been the subject of much controversy, and the village of Abu Ghosh is one of several sites recognized as the town where Jesus first appeared after the Resurrection. Two churches welcome pilgrims, especially the Crusader church ▲ 226.

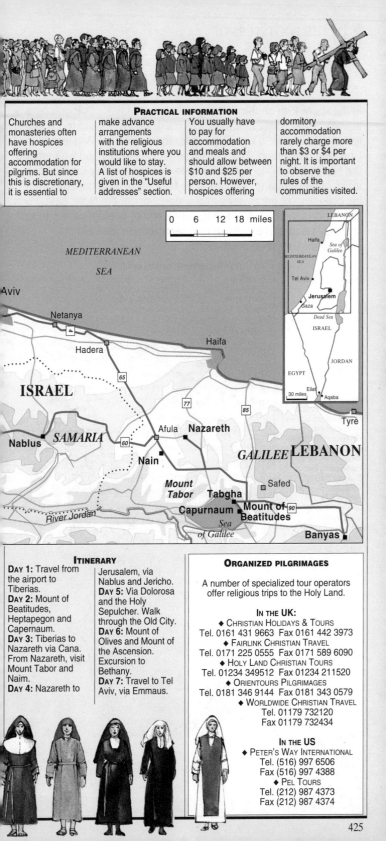

PRACTICAL INFORMATION

Churches and monasteries often have hospices offering accommodation for pilgrims. But since this is discretionary, it is essential to make advance arrangements with the religious institutions where you would like to stay. A list of hospices is given in the "Useful addresses" section. You usually have to pay for accommodation and meals and should allow between $10 and $25 per person. However, hospices offering dormitory accommodation rarely charge more than $3 or $4 per night. It is important to observe the rules of the communities visited.

ITINERARY

DAY 1: Travel from the airport to Tiberias.
DAY 2: Mount of Beatitudes, Heptapegon and Capernaum.
DAY 3: Tiberias to Nazareth via Cana. From Nazareth, visit Mount Tabor and Naim.
DAY 4: Nazareth to Jerusalem, via Nablus and Jericho.
DAY 5: Via Dolorosa and the Holy Sepulcher. Walk through the Old City.
DAY 6: Mount of Olives and Mount of the Ascension. Excursion to Bethany.
DAY 7: Travel to Tel Aviv, via Emmaus.

ORGANIZED PILGRIMAGES

A number of specialized tour operators offer religious trips to the Holy Land.

IN THE UK:
◆ CHRISTIAN HOLIDAYS & TOURS
Tel. 0161 431 9663 Fax 0161 442 3973
◆ FAIRLINK CHRISTIAN TRAVEL
Tel. 0171 225 0555 Fax 0171 589 6090
◆ HOLY LAND CHRISTIAN TOURS
Tel. 01234 349512 Fax 01234 211520
◆ ORIENTOURS PILGRIMAGES
Tel. 0181 346 9144 Fax 0181 343 0579
◆ WORLDWIDE CHRISTIAN TRAVEL
Tel. 01179 732120
Fax 01179 732434

IN THE US
◆ PETER'S WAY INTERNATIONAL
Tel. (516) 997 6506
Fax (516) 997 4388
◆ PEL TOURS
Tel. (212) 987 4373
Fax (212) 987 4374

In the early 19th century artists, writers, and later, photographers traveled extensively and began to make the Holy Land more widely known. For some, it was a quest for the sources of Western Christian civilization. The French writer Chateaubriand was among the first to "return" to Jerusalem. He was followed by the Scottish artist, David Roberts, who became famous several decades later for his collection of engravings and watercolors of the Near East. Félix Bonfils was the first in a distinguished line of photographers to visit the Holy Land and pioneer a new technique in the field of communication: photojournalism.

19TH-CENTURY TRAVELERS

It goes without saying that 19th-century travel, whether on foot, on horseback, or by camel, was much slower than travel today, and routes were often dangerous. Brigands and bandits held travelers for ransom on the basis that they must have been rich to afford such a long journey. Chateaubriand was the pioneer of modern tourism, completing his journey through Palestine in record time – less than two weeks. Roberts, on the other hand, adopted a more leisurely pace and stayed for over three months in the Holy Land. Félix and Adrien Bonfils actually lived there, often visiting Palestine from Beirut. The journeys outlined in this section can be made using public transport. *Itinéraire de Paris à Jérusalem* chronicles Chateaubriand's eleven-month journey around the Mediterranean. Although the Holy Land appears to have been the ultimate destination on this long journey, the writer only spent a fortnight there, disembarking in Jaffa on October 1, 1806 and leaving on October 13, having gone as far as the Dead Sea and visited Bethlehem, Jerusalem and Jericho en route.

David Roberts' journey from Cairo to Beirut.

Félix Bonfils' ambition was to record the traces of the civilizations (Phoenician, Roman, Muslim, Jewish and Christian) that formed the cultural tapestry of the Holy Land.

7-day tour: Tel Aviv, Ramla, Latrun, Jerusalem, Bethlehem, Mar Saba, Qumran, Jericho, Qasr Hisham (Hisham's Palace), Bethany, Jerusalem, Tel Aviv.

◆ To meet an increasing demand for pictures of the Orient, the French photographer Félix Bonfils set up studios in Beirut (in 1867) and later in Cairo and Alexandria, selling his photographs (on albuminized paper) of the archeological sites of the Near East to tourists. His successful lighting techniques enabled him to take the first satisfactory shots of church interiors, especially the Church of the Nativity in Bethlehem and the Holy Sepulcher in Jerusalem. His son, Adrien, carried on the family business until 1890 and together they produced the most complete (over 1,600 photographs) and the most technically sophisticated photographic record of the Holy Land.

14-day tour: Jaffa, Lod, Ramle, Jerusalem, Bethlehem, Solomon's Pools, Hebron, Mar Saba, Dead Sea, Jericho, Mount of Temptation, Bethany,

Nablus, Nazareth, Mount Tabor, Tiberias, Mount Carmel, Akko, Tel Aviv.

◆ David Roberts visited the Holy Land between February and May 1839, on his way from Egypt to Syria. On his return to England his drawings and watercolors, published in the form of engravings and prints, were extremely successful. His reputation as a landscape artist gained him entry to the most sacred mosques, a privilege hitherto denied to Europeans. The Pasha Muhammad Ali was one of the first subscribers to the original edition of 1842.

21-day tour: St Catherine, Mount Sinai, Petra, Ein Gedi, Mar Saba, Jerusalem, Bethlehem, Hebron, Bet Guvrin, Bethany,

Jericho, Nablus, Shomeron, Mount Tabor, Nazareth, Cana, Tiberias, Akko, Tel Aviv, Ashkelon, Ashdod, Ramle, Lod.

STEPHENS, J.L: *Incidents of Travel in Egypt, Arabia Petraea and the Holy Land*, 1837 (Harper and Bros., New York).

CURZON, R: *A Visit to the Monasteries of the Levant*, 1848 (John Murray, London).

POCOCKE, R: *A Description of the East and some other Countries*, 1738, (J.R. Knapton, London).

◆ ARCHEOLOGY IN THE HOLY LAND

The Holy Land, with its rich historical past and many excavation sites, is an archeologist's paradise. Organized "digs" are directed by researchers from Israel, Palestine and other countries and are often the subject of international cooperation. Students of archeology are taken on by scientific missions to help with the excavations on two conditions: they must be willing to give their services free of charge (or even, as is frequently the case, pay to take part) and agree to perform often unrewarding tasks. Archeology is strictly controlled, however, and visitors cannot undertake "digs" by themselves.

DUTIES OF AN EXCAVATOR

At one time excavations were carried out in a disorganized and haphazard manner with the result that some of the most valuable legacies of the past are now gracing private collections. Today excavations are carefully monitored and it is difficult to gain access to a site without prior permission. The primary concern is to facilitate the work of expert archeologists and the first duty of an excavator is to assist them in their work, which sometimes involves performing such menial tasks as pushing barrow-loads of rubble. Taking part in a "dig" is a valuable and enriching experience in many respects: as well as enabling you to discover a particular aspect of the archeological heritage of the Holy Land and contribute to its development as a member of a professional team, it also gives you the opportunity to meet the people who live there. Some missions organize special visits to sites throughout the Holy Land.

FINDING A "DIG"

In spring and summer a number of sites take on volunteers who are keen to wield a pick and trowel. Each mission has its own conditions of recruitment and accommodation, as well as deciding on the number of participants. Some missions require their volunteers to have some form of qualification and even a specialty.

In any event you usually have to be at least eighteen, have a personal insurance policy and up-to-date vaccinations. Many missions accept beginners but places are very much in demand and often reserved for residents.

So don't wait until the last minute to book. Methods of recruitment may vary or sometimes overlap.

EARTHWATCH

Earthwatch, based in both the UK and the US, organizes trips to help on archeological digs in the Holy Land. Volunteers are asked to pay a proportion of the costs of a project.

INFORMATION
IN THE UK:
Belsyre Court
57 Woodstock Road
Oxford
OX2 6HU
Tel. 01865 311600

IN THE US:
680 Mount Auburn Street
PO Box 9104
Watertown
Massachussetts
02272–9104
Tel. (617) 926 8200

YOUTH GROUPS

Every year special youth groups throughout the world recruit volunteers to assist with excavations. Living conditions are often very basic and you may even be under canvas.

ARCHEOLOGY AND ARAB-ISRAELI PEACE ACCORDS

Be prepared to wait some time if you want to take part in a "dig" on one of the archeological sites that has passed under Palestinian control. The Palestinian authorities are currently working on the development of a judicial framework with a view to regulating excavations and overseas scientific cooperation.

For information contact the archeological school at 6 Nablus Road Jerusalem East

Mosaic found at Zippori.

SOCIETY FOR THE PROTECTION OF NATURE IN ISRAEL

As well as suggesting routes and itineraries to enable you to discover the most beautiful sites in Israel, the SPNI also organizes participation in archeological "digs". Although it doesn't publish a brochure on the subject it will obtain information, on your behalf, on the places available for the current year and register you direct ◆ 430.

ARCHEOLOGICAL DIGS

To find out about archeological digs taking place in Israel, you could ask for information from universities which offer courses in archeology and the history of art, but if there are a limited number of places available, they will probably give precedence to their own students. You may also read about digs in archeological magazines, and some expeditions may advertise for help in the small-ads sections of these magazines.

ISRAELI TOURIST OFFICE
Every year the Israeli tourist office publishes a list of excavation sites which take on volunteers.

IN ISRAEL
You can obtain information from various organizations and institutions, including the Ministries of Tourism and Education and Culture. Every year the Israel Antiquities Authority publishes a list of excavation sites.

INFORMATION
Israel Antiquities Authority
PO Box 586
Jerusalem 91004
Tel: 02-29 26 07
Fax: 02-29 26 28
Ministry for Tourism
24, Hamelech
George St.
Jerusalem
Tel: 02-23 73 11

TEL YARMUT ARCHEOLOGICAL MISSION

The aim of the Franco-Israeli Tel Yarmut mission is to find evidence of, and study, the urbanization process in Palestine during the 4th and 3rd millennia BC. Each summer the mission takes on and trains volunteers who are involved with various aspects of the work, examining and processing the material excavated under expert supervision.

INFORMATION
Mission de Tel Yarmouth
65, rue d'Amsterdam
75008 Paris
Tel. (33)
1 42 80 48 57
Fax (33)
1 45 26 19 88

ITEMS TO REMEMBER
◆ a pair of sneakers or rubber-soled canvas shoes
◆ a compass and eclimeter (to measure the gradient of a slope)
◆ a drawing board, with or without a tripod, for drawing plans or making legible notes and sketches whatever the gradient

Trainee working on the restoration of mosaic floors at Zippori ▲ 389.

◆ NATURE, SPORTS AND NATURAL REMEDIES

The Holy Land is a land of many contrasts, combining the mystery of the desert with the gentler landscape of the plains and the luxuriance of its many nature reserves. It is a land where visitors can marvel at the "miracle" of the Dead Sea, be amazed by the corals of the Red Sea and enjoy the long beaches of the Mediterranean coast. Here hikers and adventure trail enthusiasts can follow the many tracks and dry wadi beds of the Negev, Sinai and Galilee, cross the desert wastes and experience the natural wealth of the Promised Land.

TOURISM AND ECOLOGY

The Society for the Protection of Nature in Israel (SPNI) suggests walking routes lasting between 1 day and 2 weeks which include sports and sightseeing visits as well as enabling you to discover the "natural" face of Israel from an ecological point of view. SPNI members qualify for special reductions on guided tours, some of which are in English.

SPNI
3, Hashefela St.
Tel Aviv
Tel. 03-537 44 25
Fax: 03-383 39 40

SPNI New York
28 Arrandale Avenue
Great Neck
NY 11024
Tel. (800) 323 0035
Field schools and hikes from Jerusalem and Tel Aviv. No age limits.

SPNI London
25 Lyndale Avenue
London NW2 2QB
Tel. 0171 435 6803
Fax 0171 794 0291

PLANT A TREE
The *Keren Kayemet Leyisrael* (Jewish National Fund) suggests you add to the forest already planted by thousands of visitors by planting your own tree. This symbolic "plant a tree" project is being carried out under the aegis of six planting centers, one of which is in Jerusalem.

TOURIST INFORMATION OFFICE
96, Hayarkon St.
Tel Aviv
Tel. 03-23 449

BIRDWATCHING

The Ussishkin Museum in the Tel Dan Nature Reserve provides a unique introduction to the natural history of the Upper Galilee ▲ *402*. It is also a major observation point during the spring and autumn migrations.
TEL DAN NATURE RESERVE
Tiberias-Kiryat Shmona Road
Tel. 06-51 579

INTERNATIONAL BIRD-WATCHING CENTER
▲ *183*
The center welcomes ornithologists from all over the world who come to watch the spectacular spring and autumn migrations. It also suggests bird-watching routes in the environs of Eilat, while its shop stocks a wide range of ornithological information.
INFORMATION
Shopping center
City Center
Hat Marin Bd.
Tel. 07-374 276

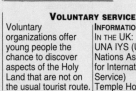

KIBBUTZIM

IN THE UK
Kibbutz Representatives
1a Accommodation Road
London NW11 8ED
Tel. 0181 458 9235
or 0181 458 5566
Fax 0181 455 7930

IN ISRAEL
"Kibbutz" program center
124, Hayarkon St.
Tel Aviv

Tel. 03-524 61 56
Fax: 03-523 99 66

VOLUNTARY SERVICE

Voluntary organizations offer young people the chance to discover aspects of the Holy Land that are not on the usual tourist route.

INFORMATION
IN THE UK:
UNA IYS (United Nations Association for International Youth Service)
Temple Hospice
Cathays, Bark,
Cardiff CF1 3AB
Tel. 01222 223088
IN THE US:
Volunteers for Peace (VFP)
43 Tiffany Road
Belmont
Tel. (802) 259 2759
VT 05730
CIEE International Workcamps
205 East 42nd Street
New York 10017
Tel. (212) 666 4177

CEREMONY OF THE THREE TEAS
The first tea tastes strong and bitter. With the second, the bitterness begins to fade. With the third, it is little more than a memory.
LAW OF THE DESERT
Drinking the first tea is an undertaking to drink the second and third teas. The first is a tea drunk by men, while the third is drunk by old men, children and those who cannot drink the first two . . . so it is whispered in the tents.

A FLIGHT OF FANCY: SKIING ON MOUNT HERMON

The resort, open from mid-December to February–March, provides accommodation, equipment and food. A bus leaves Kiryat Shmona every day at 10.15am, returning from Mount Hermon at 6pm.
In summer you can reach the summit by chair lift. Mount Hermon has unique flora as well as many different species of birds. You can also visit the area on horseback.

INFORMATION: Mount Hermon, Neve Ativ
Tel: 6-98 13 37, Fax: 6-98 12 22

The sources of the River Jordan.

Dry wadi beds near Eilat.

WATERSPORTS AND SUNBATHING

The Mediterranean coasts are especially famous for their beaches and watersports facilities, although the main diving center is Nahariya ▲ 374. There is a wide range of watersports to choose from: sailing, windsurfing, waterskiing. Lake Tiberias (the Sea of Galilee) ▲ 382 is popular for its beaches but you can also go windsurfing and waterskiing.

WALKING, CANYONING AND CANOEING

WALKING
From pleasant walks through the countryside to more energetic excursions over occasionally steep terrain in the Upper Galilee ▲ 400 or on the Golan Heights.

CANYONING
In the Judean Desert, near Wadi Qelt ▲ 322, you can rope down into caves surrounded by waterfalls. A water supply (about 6½ pints), a pair of good walking boots and a hat are essential.

CANOEING
During the dry season, water courses are dry. However you can canoe in spring and summer on the River Jordan. Information from Abu Kayak.

DIVING

The main diving centers are on the Red Sea ▲ 182 whose coral reefs have long been a source of attraction for divers, beginners and experts alike, equipped with air cylinders or a simple snorkel. There are several diving clubs at Eilat, and the Ultramarina travel agency organizes diving excursions between Eilat and Sharm el-Sheikh. Divers are, in theory, required to have an underwater fishing license. It is also worth trying the diving around Aqaba where the underwater landscape is equally remarkable. Make sure you don't climb on the coral reefs and that you are in good physical condition if you are diving with air cylinders. Finally a knife is a very useful accessory, especially if you get caught up in a fishing net.

NATURAL REMEDIES

If you are not satisfied with floating on the surface of the Dead Sea, you can always try the therapeutic qualities of its mud, used for treating psoriasis, rheumatism and asthma. The hot springs of Tiberias ▲ 380 and its environs attract those suffering from rheumatism and arthritis. Travel agents offer hotel holidays which include the cost of a health cure.

EXCURSIONS IN THE DESERT

Excursions in the desert (stone, not sand) can be made on foot, by jeep or by camel, individually or accompanied by a guide. However unless you are a first-class orienteer and mechanic, or a desert excursion expert, you are strongly advised not to set out unless you are well equipped and accompanied by a qualified guide. Never go without a map and compass, or without informing friends or a local body (the police, for example) of your intended route. Beware of wadis ● 22 which can swell drastically after rain, and always stay on the track.

BY CAR
Never drive at night and always have reserve supplies of petrol, oil and water (for you and your vehicle). Note the mileage at the start of each stage of your journey as this can be a useful indicator of distance and time.

Eilat, in particular, has a number of travel agents who organize desert excursions.

POISONOUS BITES
If you are bitten, apply an antidote immediately, make the wound bleed to flush out the poison and go straight to the nearest hospital.

There is little that has not been written about Jerusalem, the holy city of the Bible and a "must" on any visit to the Holy Land. This itinerary devotes three days to tour Jerusalem, allowing enough time to discover the rest of the country. Ideally, though, the city deserves a much longer visit – as much time as you can spare – since you cannot hope to discover all it has to offer in such a short time.

During festivals and on Fridays, the Haram al-Sharif is reserved for Muslims.

This itinerary is included in the "Holy Land in a week" (see ◆ 434, for map of the old city and suggested routes). Travel direct to Jerusalem after landing at Ben-Gurion Airport.

Your first view of the city is from Mount Scopus, the Mount of Olives and the Haas Promenade. Spend the evening at the King David Hotel.

DAY 1

Day 1 is devoted to visiting the walled the part of the city.

Start from the Jaffa Gate and walk to the Haram al-Sharif ▲ 290 via the souk and the Wailing Wall ▲ 266. After lunch – a typical and substantial falafel – in the Tariq al-Wad (Valley Road), walk along the Via Dolorosa ▲ 276 from St Stephen's Gate to the Church of the Holy Sepulcher. On the way back visit the Armenian quarter before leaving via the Jaffa Gate ▲ 254. Dine in the Nahalat Shiva area ▲ 290 before visiting the "Underground", one of Jerusalem's liveliest night spots.

Today the Citadel houses the Museum of the History of Jerusalem.

DAY 2

Most of the day is taken up with a tour of the ramparts. Start from the Jaffa Gate and visit the Citadel ▲ 252 before following the ramparts to the Garden Tomb ▲ 306. Lunch near the Notre Dame center.

Byzantine fresco found at Abu Ghosh.

In the afternoon, visit the Mount of Olives, continuing along the ramparts to the Kidron Valley and Warren's Shaft ▲ 279 and then the Siloam Pool. Return via Mount Zion and the Tomb of David ▲ 257 to the Jaffa Gate where the visit ends.

Armenian mosaic, Dome of the Rock.

The emerald domes of the Russian Cathedral of the Holy Trinity, built between 1860 and 1864, are reminiscent of the Cathedral of the Assumption of the Kremlin in Moscow.

DAY 3

The day begins with visits to the Israel Museum ▲ 298 and the Hassadah synagogue ▲ 304, followed by lunch in or near the central market. In the afternoon walk through the Ethiopian quarter and Mea Shearim ▲ 292, ending in the Russian quarter. Leave Jerusalem in the late afternoon or early the following morning.

GETTING AROUND

There is a very good and inexpensive inter-city bus network. Taxis are quicker, and inexpensive if shared by at least three people. But be careful as taxi drivers have an unrivalled reputation for conning tourists by claiming that their meter isn't working or simply refusing to start it. So make sure you either insist they put their meter on, or agree a price before you get in, and don't be afraid to haggle if the price seems too high.

A detailed map of the bus routes is available from the Tourist Office at the Jaffa Gate. Be prepared for irregular services between dusk on Friday and Saturday evening.

After the Temple was destroyed in AD 70, the menorah was taken to Rome as a symbol of Titus' victory.

TRAVELING FROM TEL AVIV TO JERUSALEM

Buses leave the central bus station for Jerusalem every ten minutes. The journey takes about one hour. Trains leave the south station every hour or so. *Sherut* (shared) taxis do the 39-mile journey in about 50 minutes and leave from Solomon Street opposite the central station. From Ben-Gurion Airport, the town of Lod is on the Tel Aviv–Jerusalem railroad line. Nesher and Megdal taxis and the no. 111 bus operate frequent services to Jerusalem. The journey takes about 40 minutes. Trains and most buses do not run on Shabbat and taxis raise their prices by around 20 percent.

THE AMERICAN COLONY ▲ 308

The elegant American Colony Hotel was the former residence of the Pasha Effendi al-Husseini, with its sophisticated oriental architecture, has welcomed such guests as T.E. Lawrence and Graham Greene. Its gardens and swimming pool are an oasis of peace and tranquility within the busy city. In the evening guests dine by candlelight on some of the best Arab specialties in the country. The American Colony is just a few minutes' walk from the Damascus Gate.

AMERICAN COLONY
1 Louis-Vincent St., Nablus Road
East Jerusalem
Tel. 02-28 51 71 Fax 02-28 35 57

◆ MAP OF THE OLD CITY

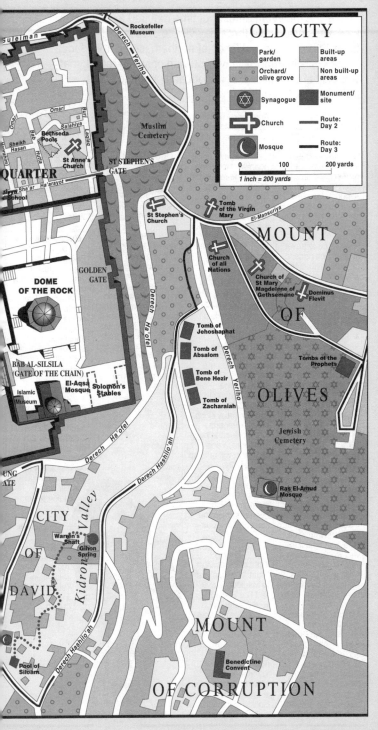

OLD CITY

- Park/garden
- Orchard/olive grove
- Synagogue
- Church
- Mosque
- Built-up areas
- Non built-up areas
- Monument/site
- Route: Day 2
- Route: Day 3

0   100   200 yards

1 inch = 200 yards

Suleiman

Rockefeller Museum

Derech Yeriho

Omari

Omari

Salahiya

Bethseda Pools

Sheikh Hasan

Laqlaq

Burj

Bab Huta

St Anne's Church

Ibrahim

QUARTER

Hayye Sha'ar

Ha'arayot

School

ST STEPHEN'S GATE

Muslim Cemetery

Tomb of the Virgin Mary

El-Mansuriya

St Stephen's Church

Church of all Nations

MOUNT

DOME OF THE ROCK

GOLDEN GATE

Derech Ha'ofel

Church of St Mary Magdelene of Gethsemane

Dominus Flevit

OF

Tomb of Jehoshaphat

Tomb of Absalom

Derech Yeriho

Tombs of the Prophets

BAB AL-SILSILA (GATE OF THE CHAIN)

El-Aqsa Mosque

Solomon's Stables

Tomb of Bene Hezir

OLIVES

Islamic Museum

Tomb of Zacharaiah

Derech Ha'ofel

Jewish Cemetery

UNG ATE

CITY

Derech Hashilo ah

Ras El-Amud Mosque

OF

Warren's Shaft

Kidron Valley

Gihon Spring

DAVID

Derech Hashilo ah

MOUNT

Pool of Siloam

Benedictine Convent

OF CORRUPTION

435

This is the minimum amount of time required to visit Israel's key sites, including a three-day visit to Jerusalem. The route focuses on the Biblical lands of northern Israel, from Judea to the Galilee, and will leave you with only one regret: that you didn't have more time. An ideal moment to start planning your next visit.

This route comprises a 7-day visit plus 2 additional days (to arrive at Tel Aviv and travel to Jerusalem, and to return to Tel Aviv in good time to catch your plane). Although there are good bus and train services, hiring a car (if your holiday budget allows) will enable you to travel at your own pace, a definite advantage when time is of the essence.

DAYS 1–3
Visit Jerusalem ▲ 432.

DAY 4
EXCURSION TO JUDEA
This excursion from Jerusalem can be made in one day, but for those who want to take their time it is well worth devoting two full days to visiting these sites. Start your day with an early morning visit to the fortress of Masada ▲ 202 and then follow the shores of the Dead Sea northward to the site of Ein Gedi ▲ 210. Carry on to Qumran, where the Dead Sea scrolls ▲ 214 were discovered, arriving in the late morning.

After lunch visit St George's Monastery ▲ 323, ensconced in the impressive Wadi Qelt, before heading northward to Jericho. Spend the rest of the afternoon visiting Qasr Hisham (Hisham's Palace) ▲ 318 to the north of the city. Once back in Jerusalem, why not have dinner at the American Colony Hotel?

DAY 5
ALONG THE VIA MARIS
Leave Jerusalem early for Tel Aviv ▲ 338 and then carry on to Caesarea ▲ 360. Visit the site before continuing northward along the shores of the Mediterranean to Acre ▲ 367 where you can have lunch on the ramparts overlooking the bay. The fortress and hammam will take up most of the afternoon, and you can round off your visit by strolling through the Muslim quarter around the souk and mosque.

DAY 6
THE LOWER GALILEE
From Acre continue to Megiddo ▲ 396 and Bet She'an ▲ 396. After lunch in Bet She'an, start the afternoon with a visit to the fortress of Belvoir ▲ 396 and then head northward to Tiberias ▲ 378 where you can swim in the Sea of Galilee. Spend the night in Tiberias.

"Horoscope" Street plaque on the heights of the old city of Jaffa.

DAY 7
SEA OF GALILEE
Spend a more restful day discovering the villages on the shores of the lake, returning in the late afternoon to Tel Aviv where the Yotvata Restaurant on the marina serves quality produce from the Yotvata kibbutz. Leave from Ben Gurion Airport the following morning.

BIRD'S-EYE VIEW OF JUDEA
Flying over the Judean Desert from Jerusalem is a truly unforgettable experience. The Kanfei Jerusalem airline company offers you this unique opportunity at affordable prices: a 30-minute flight over Jerusalem and its immediate environs ($40), or a 1-hour flight across the Judean Desert to Masada ▲ 202, returning via the Dead Sea ▲ 200, the Ein Gedi Nature Reserve ▲ 210 and Jericho ▲ 314 ($75). The company's small, single-engine planes can carry up to eight passengers.

KANFEI JERUSALEM
Atarot Airport
Jerusalem
Tel. 02-83 14 44
Fax 02-83 18 80

Make sure you are suitably dressed when visiting a mosque – short sleeves and shorts are out of the question. If necessary an attendant will lend you a veil to tie around your waist and cover your legs. Women must cover their heads, so make sure you take a scarf with you.

SHOPPING

Compared with other tourist centers, Israel is not a shopper's paradise abounding with traditional crafts. However there is plenty to satisfy visitors on the lookout for souvenirs. Among the best and most symbolic items is Dead Sea clay (at Mitzpeh Shalem) renowned for its dermatological and anti-rheumatic properties, while Caesarea is famous for its glass (found near the port and in the old city). Finally the bazaars of Jerusalem (the three souks and the Cardo), Jaffa (Kedumim Square) and St John of Acre (near the Khan el-Umdan) sell traditional crafts and jewelry at more or less reasonable prices, depending on your negotiating skills.

Map

LEBANON

Haifa
Sea of Galilee

MEDITERRANEAN SEA

Tel Aviv

Jerusalem

Gaza

Dead Sea

ISRAEL

EGYPT

JORDAN

Eilat
Aqaba

80 miles

GALILEE
Acre
Haifa
Capernaum 87
Tabgha
Tiberias
Nazareth 65
66 *Sea of Galilee*
60
Afula
Belvoir
Zichron Yaacov
Tel Megiddo
70
71
Bet She'an
Caesarea
Hadera
55
60
90
SAMARIA
4
2
55
Nablus
Jordan
Tel Aviv
1
Qasr Hisham
St George's Monastery
Jericho
1
Jerusalem
Qumran
Bethlehem
JUDEA
90 **DEAD SEA**
Gaza
Hebron
Ein Gedi
Masada
Beersheba

0 15 30 45 miles

PRACTICAL ADVICE

From October to May temperatures vary significantly from region to region. It is advisable to take warm clothing and a raincoat when visiting the Galilee and the Mediterranean coast, and summer clothes for the shores of the Dead Sea. In the desert, sunglasses, a drinking bottle and a hat are essential in all seasons. NB The pure desert air increases the burn factor, so make sure you use a high-protection cream all year round.

437

◆ THE HOLY LAND IN THREE WEEKS

For those who can spend three weeks or more in Israel, this route offers an opportunity to discover the natural, cultural and religious wealth of the Holy Land in much greater depth, and includes an excursion into Egypt to visit the main sites of the Sinai Peninsula. The length of time can be varied. For example, you can complete the route in a fortnight by omitting some of the sites and spending less time at the ones you visit. Alternatively you can extend your visit by completing the route at a more leisurely pace, savoring every moment spent in this unique and holy land.

DAY 1:
As this route starts from Eilat, Day 1 is taken up with traveling from Tel Aviv to Eilat. Alternatively you can fly to Cairo, cross the Sinai Peninsula via St Catherine's Monastery and then cross the border at Taba.

DAY 2:
Excursions into Sinai ▲ 167 from Eilat. Visit St Catherine's Monastery ▲ 174 and spend the night at the Monastir Hotel.

DAY 3:
Return to the border post at Taba, swim in the clear waters of the Gulf of Aqaba and return to Eilat in the late afternoon.

DAY 4:
Visit the town of Eilat ▲ 182 and its underwater observatory. Relax and swim on its superb beaches. Walk along the Wadi Ein Netafim.

DAY 5:
Leave Eilat early in the morning to visit the geological formations in the far south of the Negev, Amram's Pillars, Timna and the Yotvata Nature Reserve ▲ 186.

DAY 6:
An absolute must: visit the beautiful Nabatean cities of Avdat, Shivta and Mamshit ▲ 190–1.

DAY 7:
Begin with a visit to the Sdeh Boker *midrasha*, a center for research into agriculture in the arid regions, followed by a visit to the site of Ein Avdat. After lunch carry on to Dimona ▲ 192, visiting the town of Yeroham ▲ 192 on the way back to Sdeh Boker.

DAY 8:
Leave for Beersheba ▲ 199 whose market and mosque are well worth seeing. After lunch visit Tel Arad and Sodom, the site of the Biblical Sodom, with its open salt mines.

DAY 9:
Leave early in the morning for Masada ▲ 202 (the visit is more enjoyable before it gets too hot). In the afternoon follow the road northward along the shores of the Dead Sea, stopping to swim or shop en route. Visit Qumran ▲ 212, Nabi Musa ▲ 323 (said to be the site of the tomb of Moses) and then St George's Monastery ▲ 323.

DAYS 10–14:
Jerusalem ▲ 432. You can spend more time on each site than allowed for in the 3-day visit. If you do, visit the Rockefeller Museum ▲ 316, the Yemin Moshe district and the Yad Vashem Holocaust Memorial.

PETRA

During your stay in the Holy Land, take the opportunity to visit the former Nabatean capital of Petra. Due to improved diplomatic relations between Israel and Jordan it is now possible to make this trip from Eilat or Jericho, either by public transport or through an Israeli travel agent (many are beginning to offer this excursion), although as yet it cannot be done in a hired vehicle. Allow two days to fully appreciate the site as it is one of the archeological wonders of the Middle East and even the world.

438

Port Said

Gaza
Hebron
Beersheba

Ismailia

Negev
Desert

Suez

EGYPT

SINAI

Eilat
Aqaba

GULF OF SUEZ
GULF OF AQABA

Gulf of Suez

SAUDI
ARABIA

St Catherine's
Monastery

RED SEA

Sharm-
el-Sheikh

Tyre

LEBANON

Banyas

Rosh Hanikra

Hatzor
Golan

Acre

Safed
Capernaum

Haifa

Tabgha
Tiberias

*Sea of
Galilee*

Zichron
Yaacov

Nazareth

Belvoir

Tel
Megiddo

Caesarea

Bet Alfa
Bet She'an

*MEDITERRANEAN
SEA*

Nablus

Jordan

Tel Aviv

Ben Gurion
Airport

Jaffa

St George's
Monastery

Qasr
Hisham

Abu Gosh

Jericho

Latrun

Nabi Musa

Bet Shemesh

Jerusalem

Bet Guvrin

Bethlehem

Gaza

Mareshah

Lakshish

Hebron

Ein Gedi

*Dead
Sea*

Rafah

Masada

Beersheba

Arad

ISRAEL

Dimona

Sodom

Mamshit

Yeroham

To
St Catherine's
Monastery

Shivta

Nizana

Sdeh Boker
Ein Avdat

Avdat

JORDAN

Mitzpeh Ramon

*Negev
Desert*

EGYPT

SINAI

Yotvata

Timna

Pillars of Amran

Eilat

Aqaba

Taba

0   30 miles

◆ THE HOLY LAND IN THREE WEEKS

In 1947 manuscripts (written between 100 BC and AD 68) were found in the cliffs of Qumran.

A basilica and Roman theater were found at the foot of the tell at Bet She'an ▲ 396.

DAY 15:
A long excursion into Cisjordan. Leave in the morning for Jericho, whose tell has disclosed the remains of one of the oldest cities in the world ▲ 316. Visit the Mount of Temptation to the north of the city and, after lunch, Qasr Hisham (Hisham's Palace) ▲ 318 before returning to Jericho to visit the mosque.

DAY 16:
Excursion into the Sorek Valley ▲ 334. Visit Abu Ghosh ▲ 328, ancient Emmaus, the Latrun Monastery and caves on the road to Maresha and Lachish. Spend the night in Jerusalem.

DAY 17:
Head south to Bethlehem and visit the Church of the Nativity ▲ 226. After lunch continue south to Hebron. On the way back visit Beit Sahur (said to be the native village of the shepherds of the Nativity) and the Monastery of Mar Saba ▲ 230, the seat of the first anchorite orthodox monasteries. Spend the night in Jerusalem.

DAY 18:
Leave for Tel Aviv. In the afternoon visit the port of Jaffa ▲ 341 and then stroll through the old city. Spend the evening in Jaffa and dine on the ramparts.

DAY 19:
Tel Aviv: walk along the shores of the Mediterranean and through the busy Dizengoff district ▲ 344, Tel Aviv's commercial and entertainment center. It is worth spending the afternoon in the Ha'aretz ▲ 348 and Bet Hatesfutsot ▲ 350 museums.

DAY 20:
Follow the ancient *Via Maris* – which linked Egypt and Syria during the Roman occupation – from Tel Aviv to Caesarea ▲ 358, the Herodian city, later a Crusader fortress, whose underwater city is one of Israel's most impressive archeological sites. The village of Zichron Yaacov ▲ 356, on the road to Akko, is the commercial center for the delicious Carmel wines. An ideal opportunity to stop and visit the wine cellars: Spend the night in Akko.

DAY 21:
Leave for Haifa ▲ 364 in the morning and visit the Bahai Temple and the Maritime Museum. After lunch return to Akko and spend the afternoon visiting the fortress ▲ 369, the mosque and the hammam ▲ 370. Spend the night in Akko.

DAY 22:
Follow the eastern slopes of Mount Carmel to the historic site of Megiddo ▲ 394 where a succession of twenty cities has been built. Continue to the site of Bet Alpha and, further west, the Crusader fortress of Belvoir ▲ 397 overlooking the Jordan Valley. Then head north to Tiberias.

DAY 23:
Spend the day around the Sea of Galilee, visiting the sites of Jesus' ministry: Tabgha, ancient Heptapegon ▲ 390, Capernaum and the Mount of Beatitudes. In the late afternoon travel to Safed ▲ 398, capital of Upper Galilee and a holy Jewish city.

DAY 24:
Leave for the Golan Heights via Hatzor ▲ 401, Israel's largest ancient site, arriving at Banyas ▲ 403, ancient Caesarea Philippi, in the late morning. Return to Tiberias.

DAY 25:
Leave for Tel Aviv in the early hours of the morning via Afula ▲ 392 and Nazareth ▲ 388 where a visit to the monumental Basilica of the Annunciation is a must. Arrive at Ben-Gurion Airport in the early afternoon.

SHOPPING

Eilat is justly famed for its coral, sold in branches or finely crafted into jewelry, while Mitzpeh Ramon ▲ 187 is famous for its marble quarries and semi-precious stones. Beersheba market is an ideal place to pick up some wonderful Bedouin jewelry and traditional Bedouin embroidery. The typical, small coffee pans (a legacy of the Turkish occupation) make an original gift and are found notably in the Carmel market in Tel Aviv.

PRACTICAL INFORMATION

All the sites suggested above can be reached by bus or train. For short distances *sherut* taxis are much more practical and not much more expensive. Most of the tour operators listed on page 444 will organize tours covering the sites mentioned in this route.

440

USEFUL ADDRESSES

- ☆ VIEW
- **C** CENTRAL LOCATION
- ☐→ ISOLATED
- ◍ LUXURY RESTAURANT
- ◑ TYPICAL RESTAURANT
- ○ BUDGET RESTAURANT
- ⌂ LUXURY HOTEL
- ⌂ TYPICAL HOTEL
- ⌂ BUDGET HOTEL
- **P** CAR PARK
- 🚗 SUPERVISED CAR PARK
- ☐ TELEVISION
- ⌂ QUIET
- ⌄ SWIMMING POOL
- ▭ CREDIT CARDS ACCEPTED
- ☈ REDUCTIONS FOR CHILDREN
- ✗ PETS NOT ALLOWED
- ♫ MUSIC
- ⊨ LIVE MUSIC
- ☎ ROOM WITH TELEPHONE
- ★ EDITOR'S CHOICE

◆ Choosing a Hotel

442

- ♦ Under 40 sh. ($12 / £8)
- ♦♦ 80–130 sh. ($24–39 / £15–25)
- ♦♦♦ Over 130 sh. ($39 / £25)

	PAGE	PRICE	VIEW	PARKING LOT	RESTAURANT	TELEPHONE	TELEVISION	CREDIT CARDS ACCEPTED	AIR CONDITIONING	SWIMMING POOL
SINAI										
Daniela Village (St Catherine)	444	♦♦						●		
St Catherine Tourist Village	444	♦♦♦	●	●				●		●
Taba Hilton	444	♦♦♦	●	●	●	●	●	●	●	●
EILAT TO BEERSHEBA										
Adi	445	♦		●	●	●		●	●	
Carlton Coral Sea	445	♦♦♦		●	●	●	●	●	●	●
Lagoona Hotel	445	♦♦♦		●	●	●		●	●	●
Neptune (Eilat)	445	♦♦♦		●	●	●	●	●	●	●
Princess Eilat (Eilat)	445	♦♦♦		●	●	●	●	●	●	●
Youth hostel and Guesthouse	445	♦								
BEERSHEBA TO JERUSALEM VIA THE DEAD SEA										
Arad Hotel (Arad)	446	♦♦♦			●	●		●	●	
Arava Hotel (Beersheba)	446	♦			●	●		●		
Aviv (Beersheba)	446	♦				●	●		●	
Desert Inn (Beersheba)	446	♦♦		●	●	●	●	●	●	●
Ein Gedi camp site	446			●						
Ein Gedi Kibbutz-Hotel	446	♦♦♦		●	●	●	●	●	●	●
Ein Gedi Youth Hostel	446	♦		●	●				●	
Hod Hotel (Ein Bokek)	446	♦♦♦		●	●		●			
Margoa (Arad)	446	♦♦		●	●	●	●	●	●	
Metzoke Dragot holiday village (Mitzpeh Shalem)	446	♦♦		●				●		
Nirvana (Ein Bokek)	446	♦♦♦		●	●	●	●	●	●	●
BEERSHEBA TO JERUSALEM VIA HEBRON										
Mor Charbel (Bethlehem)	447	♦♦								
JERUSALEM										
American Colony Hotel	450	♦♦♦		●	●	●	●	●	●	
Caesar Hotel	450	♦♦		●	●	●	●	●	●	
Capital Hostel	450	♦								
Casa Nova Hotel	450	♦♦								
Christ Church Guest house	451	♦		●						
Christmas Hotel	451	♦		●	●					
El-Arab	451	♦	●							
El-Ahram Youth Hostel	451	♦	●							
Ein Karem Youth Hostel	451	♦								
Eretz Israel Hotel	451	♦			●					
Gloria Hotel	451	♦♦		●	●	●		●	●	
Holyland West Hotel	451	♦♦♦				●	●	●		●
Hyatt Regency Hotel	451	♦♦				●	●	●	●	
Jerusalem Hilton	451	♦♦♦				●	●	●	●	
King David Hotel	451	♦♦♦	●	●	●	●	●	●	●	●
King Solomon Hotel	451	♦♦♦		●	●	●	●	●	●	
Laromme Hotel	451	♦♦♦	●	●	●	●	●	●	●	
Lutheran Youth Hostel	451	♦♦	●							
Mitzpeh Ramat Rachel Kibbutz-Hotel	451	♦♦		●		●	●	●	●	●
Moriah Jerusalem Hotel	451	♦♦♦			●	●	●	●	●	
Mount of Olives	451	♦			●					
National Palace Hotel	451	♦♦			●	●	●	●		
New Imperial Hotel	451	♦	●							
Our Lady of Jerusalem Hotel	451	♦♦	●			●	●		●	
Our Lady of Zion	451	♦	●			●				
Palatin Hotel	451	♦♦						●		
Petra Hostel	451	♦	●							
Ritz Hotel	451	♦♦			●	●			●	
Saint Andrew's Hospice	452	♦♦	●	●		●		●		

Price legend:
- ♦ Under 40 sh. ($12 / £8)
- ♦♦ 80–130 sh. ($24–39 / £15–25)
- ♦♦♦ Over 130 sh. ($39 / £25)

	PAGE	PRICE	VIEW	PARKING LOT	RESTAURANT	TELEPHONE	TELEVISION	CREDIT CARDS ACCEPTED	AIR CONDITIONING	SWIMMING POOL
SAINT-MARON HOTEL	452	♦♦				●				
SEVEN ARCHES HOTEL	452	♦♦			●	●	●		●	
SHERATON JERUSALEM PLAZA	452	♦♦♦	●	●	●	●	●	●	●	●
YMCA THREE ARCHES HOTEL	452	♦♦	●	●		●	●		●	
JERUSALEM TO GAZA										
KIBBUTZ-HOTEL (HAFETZ HAIM)	452	♦♦		●		●		●	●	
NEVÉ SHALOM (LATRUN)	452	♦♦	●	●					●	
TEL AVIV										
CITY	454	♦♦		●	●	●	●	●	●	●
DAN HOTEL	454	♦♦♦		●	●	●	●	●	●	●
FLORIDA	454	♦♦		●	●	●	●	●	●	
GRAND BEACH	454	♦♦			●	●	●	●	●	●
HILTON TEL AVIV	454	♦♦♦	●	●	●	●	●	●	●	●
IMPERIAL	454	♦♦			●	●	●	●	●	
MORIAH PLAZA HOTEL	454	♦♦♦	●	●	●	●	●	●	●	●
MOSS HOTEL	454	♦♦		●		●		●	●	
OLD JAFFA HOSTEL	454	♦								
SHERATON HOTEL	454	♦♦♦	●	●	●	●	●	●	●	●
TEL AVIV YOUTH HOSTEL	454	♦							●	
TEL AVIV TO ROSH HANIKRA										
AKKO YOUTH HOSTEL (AKKO)	455	♦	●							
ARGAMAN HOTEL (AKKO)	455	♦♦		●				●	●	●
BETHEL HOSPICE (HAIFA)	456	♦								
CALIL (NETANYA)	457	♦♦		●	●	●	●	●		
DAN CAESARA (CAESAREA)	455	♦♦		●	●	●	●	●	●	●
DAN CARMEL (HAIFA)	456	♦♦♦		●	●	●	●	●	●	●
DAN PANORAMA (HAIFA)	456	♦♦♦		●	●	●	●	●	●	
DVIR (HAIFA)	456	♦♦			●	●	●	●	●	
MARGOA HOTEL (NETANYA)	457	♦			●	●	●	●		
NACHSHOLIM KIBBUTZ HOTEL (CAESAREA)	455	♦♦		●	●			●		●
PALM BEACH (AKKO)	455	♦♦		●	●	●	●	●	●	●
PARK (NETANYA)	457	♦♦		●	●	●	●	●		●
THE SEASONS (NETANYA)	457	♦♦♦		●	●	●	●	●	●	●
AROUND THE SEA OF GALILEE										
ARISTON (TIBERIAS)	457	♦♦		●	●	●	●	●	●	
CAESAR (TIBERIAS)	457	♦♦♦		●	●	●	●	●	●	●
CAMP SITE (HAON)	457									●
EIN GEV HOLIDAY VILLAGE (EIN GEV)	457	♦♦		●					●	
KARE DESHE Y. H. (KORAZIM)	458	♦♦	●	●						
MORIAH PLAZA (TIBERIAS)	457	♦♦♦		●	●	●	●	●	●	●
RAMOT RESORT HOTEL (RAMOT)	458	♦♦	●	●		●	●	●	●	
RON BEACH (TIBERIAS)	457	♦♦			●	●	●	●	●	
TERRA SANCTA (TIBERIAS)	457	♦								
LOWER GALILEE										
CASA NOVA (NAZARETH)	458	♦								
GRAND NEW HOTEL (NAZARETH)	458	♦♦			●	●				
UPPER GALILEE AND GOLAN										
AFIK GUEST HOUSE (HAMMAT GADAR)	459	♦♦								●
BET BENYAMIN Y. H. (SAFED)	459	♦			●					
HAGOSHRIM KIBBUTZ-HOTEL (KIRYAT SHMONA)	459	♦♦		●			●	●	●	●
KFAR BLUM KIBBUTZ (KIRYAT SHMONA)	459	♦♦				●	●	●	●	●
KFAR GILADI (KIRYAT SHMONA)	459	♦♦		●	●		●	●		
RIMON INN (SAFED)	459	♦♦		●			●		●	
RON (SAFED)	459	♦♦		●	●	●	●		●	
YOUTH HOSTEL (ROSH PINNA)	459	♦		●						

GENERAL

USEFUL INFORMATION

ISRAELI EMBASSIES
UK:
2 Palace Green
London W8 4QB
Tel. 0171 957 9500
Fax 0171 957 9555

US:
3514 International
Drive NW
Washington DC 20008
Tel. (202) 364 5500
Fax (202) 364 5423

ISRAELI CONSULATES
US:
◆ NEW YORK
800 Second Ave.
15th Floor,
NY 10017
Tel. (212) 351 5200
Fax (212) 490 9186
◆ LOS ANGELES
6380 Wilshire Blvd.
Suite 1700, CA 90048
Tel. (213) 651 5700
Fax (213) 651 3123
◆ CHICAGO
111 East Wacker Drive,
Suite 1308 IL 60601
Tel. (312) 565 3300
Also has offices in
Atlanta, Boston,
Houston, Miami, New
Orleans, Philadelphia
and San Francisco.

EGYPTIAN CONSULATE
UK:
2 Lowndes Street
London SW1X 9ET
Tel. 0171 235 9777

US:
1110 Second Avenue
New York
NY 10022
Tel. (212) 759 7120

ISRAELI GOVERNMENT TOURIST BOARD
UK:
18 Gt Marlborough St
London W1V 1AF
Tel. 0171 434 3651
Fax 0171 437 0527

US:
◆ NEW YORK
800 Second Ave,
16th floor
New York, NY 10017
Tel. (212) 499 5000
Fax (212) 499 5645
◆ LOS ANGELES
6380 Wilshire Blvd.
Suite 1700,CA 90048
Tel. (213) 658 7462
or (800) 596 1199 from
anywhere in the US

US EMBASSY IN TEL AVIV
71 Hayarkon Street
PSC 98 Box 100
APO AE 09830
Tel. (9723) 517 4338

US CONSULATE IN JERUSALEM
AMERICAN CONSULATE
GENERAL
◆ PSC 98 Box 100
APO AE 09830
Tel. 02-625 3288

TRANSPORT

AIRLINES
IN THE US:
◆ EL AL
Tel. (800) 223 6700
◆ TOWER AIR
Tel. (718) 553 8500
◆ TRANS WORLD
AIRLINES
Tel. (800) 892 4141
IN THE UK:
◆ BRITISH AIRWAYS
Tel. 0181 897 4000
or 0181 897 4567
◆ EL AL
Tel. 0171 437 9255
or 0171 439 0126

TOUR OPERATORS

IN THE US:
◆ ISRAM WORLD OF
TRAVEL
Tel. 800 223 7460
◆ AMERICAN EXPRESS
VACATIONS
Tel. 800 241 1700
◆ AYELET TOURS
Tel. (518) 437 0695
◆ BEST OF ISRAEL
Tel. (212) 984 0612
◆ CAMEO TRAVEL
SERVICE INC.
Tel. (212) 490 2880
◆ PETER'S WAY
INTERNATIONAL
Tel. (516) 997 6505
◆ PEL TOURS
Tel. (212) 987 4373

IN THE UK:
◆ EXPLORE
WORLDWIDE
Tel. 01252 344161
– CLASSIC TOURS
Tel. 0171 613 4441
◆ ORIENTOURS
PILGRIMAGES
Tel. 0181 346 9144
◆ SUPERSTAR HOLIDAYS
Tel. 0171 427 9277
◆ ISRAEL TRAVEL
SERVICE
0161 839 1111
◆ TRAVEL ISRAEL/
PROJECT 67
Tel. 0171 831 7626
◆ THE IMAGINATIVE
TRAVELLER
Tel. 0181 742 8612

◆ COX & KINGS
0171 873 5000

ST CATHERINE

CULTURE

ST CATHERINE'S MONASTERY
*Note: Visitors are
admitted to the main
church and the site of
the Burning Bush only.
Open daily 9am–noon,
except Fri., Sun., and
on Greek Orthodox
holy days. It is possible
to stay overnight at
the hermitage: requests
for accommodation
must be made before
5pm.*

HOTELS

DANIELA VILLAGE ★★
Tel. 062 749 77 32
*Very basic
accommodation, but
clean and tidy.
Half-board only.*
▭

ST CATHERINE TOURIST VILLAGE ★★★
Wadi el-Raha
Tel. 062 77 04 56
Fax 062 72 02 21
*Accommodation
consists of comfortable
bungalows.
No alcohol.*
⌕ P ⚲ ▭

TABA

HOTEL

TABA HILTON ★★★
Taba beach
Tel. 062 76 31 36
*Extremely
comfortable, deluxe
hotel. Well equipped
for a variety of
watersports.*
⌕ P ⚲ ▭ ☎
□ ▭ C

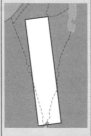

EILAT

USEFUL INFORMATION

BANK LEUMI
Commercial Center
Tel. 07-366 41 11

BRITISH CONSULATE
Tel. 07-637 23 44

EGYPTIAN CONSULATE
Mor Center
Tel. 07-637 68 82

MINISTRY OF TOURISM
Bridge House
Tel. 07-637 05 55
*On the corner of Yotam
and Arava.*

POST OFFICE
Commercial Center
(Red mall)
Hatmarim Bd
Tel. 07-637 22 19

TOURIST OFFICE
Arava Rd
Tel. 07-637 21 11
Open Sun.–Thur.
8am–8pm, Fri.
8am–3pm
and Sat. 10am–2pm.

TRANSPORT

AIRPORTS
◆ EILAT
Tel. 07-636 38 38
◆ OVDA
Tel. 07-637 58 80

BUS
EGGED TOURS
Central bus station
Tel. 07-37 31 48

CAR RENTAL
EURODOLLAR
Hatmarim Bd
Opposite the
Red Sea Hotel
Tel. 07-37 18 13
Fax 07-92 56 21
HERTZ
The Red Canyon
Tel. 07-37 66 55
Open Sun.–Thur.

8am–6pm, Fri.
8am–2pm and Sat.
8–10am

RESTAURANTS

PAGO PAGO **
Lagoona Northern
Bank
Tel. 07-37 66 60
Open lunchtime and
evenings
Thai specialties.
P ▭ C

TANDOORI **
King Wharf Lagoona
Tel. 07-33 38 79
Open lunchtime and
evenings
*Traditional music.
Indian cuisine.*
P ▭ C

THE LAST REFUGE **
Coral Beach
Tel. 07-37 24 37
*Nautical décor. Fish
and shellfish specialties.*
▭ C

THE TENT **
Lagoona Hotel
Tel. 07-636 66 66
Open evenings
Closed Fri.
*Traditional nomad
cuisine in a Bedouin
tent in the Lagoona
Hotel.*
P ▭

HOTELS

ADI *
Tsoffit
Town center
Tel. 07-37 61 51
Fax 07-37 61 54
Hotel with restaurant.
P ☎ ▭ C ⌁

CARLTON
CORAL SEA ***
Coral Beach
Tel. 07-633 35 55
Fax 07-633 40 88
Hotel with restaurant.
P ☎ ▯ ▭ ⌁

LAGOONA HOTEL ***
North Beach
Tel. 07-636 66 66
Fax 07-636 66 99
Hotel with restaurant.
P ▭ C

NEPTUNE ***
North Beach
Tel. 07-636
93 69
Fax 07-633
43 89
Hotel with restaurant.
P ☎ ▯ ▭ C
⌁

PRINCESS-EILAT ****
Taba Beach
Tel. 07-36 55 55
*Luxury hotel with
restaurant.*
P ☎ ▯ ▭ C ⌁

YOUTH HOSTEL
AND GUESTHOUSE *
Arava Rd
Near Sonesta Hotel
Tel. 07-637 00 88
Fax 07-637 58 35
Open 24 hours

SPORT

AQUA SPORT
INTERNATIONAL
Coral Beach
Po Box 300
Tel. 07-637 07 38
*Diving equipment and
underwater safaris in
the Sinai. Underwater
photography.*

CORAL BEACH
RESERVE
8 miles south of Eilat,
toward the Egyptian
border
Tel. 07-637 66 66
Open Sun.–Thur.
8.30am–4.30pm.
Fri. 8.30am–3pm.
Closed Sat.

DESERT FOX
Shell Center
Tel. 07-637 14 77
*Jeep treks in the
desert.*

DESERT SAFARI
CENTER
Marina
Tel. 07-633 01 34

*Jeep and camel treks,
climbing. Bedouin
encounters.*

DESERT SHADE
4 Max Elimelech
Center
Tel. 07-633 53 77
Open 8am–7pm
*Desert exploration by
jeep or camel; walking
and climbing.*

DOLPHIN REEF
South Beach
2 miles south of Eilat
Tel. 07-637 18 46
*A popular place to go
swimming with the
dolphins.*

THE JULES VERNE
EXPLORER GLASS-
BOTTOMED BOAT
North Beach Marina
Tel. 07-637 77 02
open 8.30am–10pm
*Glass-bottomed boat.
Exploration of the coral
reef and Japanese
gardens. Outings at
10am, 12.30pm, 3pm
and 5pm.*

LUCKY'S DIVERS CLUB
Galei Eilat
Tel. 07-637 66 55
Diving.

RED SEA SPORT CLUB
The King's Wharf
North Beach
Tel. 07-637 96 85
*Diving, parascending,
windsurfing and
horseriding are all
available.*

SNUBA SHALLOW
WATER DIVING
TOURS LTD
Coral Beach Reserve
Tel. 07-637 27 22

THE YELLOW
SUBMARINE
Coral Beach
Tel. 07-637 66 66
Open Sat.–Fri.
8.30am–4.30pm
Closed Sun.
*Inside the underwater
observatory at Coral
Beach. Exploration of
the ocean depths down
to 160 feet. Trips
Mon.–Sat. at 10am,
11.15am, 1pm, 2pm,
3pm and 3.30pm.*

UNDERWATER
OBSERVATORY
Coral Beach
Tel. 07-637 66 66
Open Sat.–Fri.
8.30am–4.30pm
and Fri. 8.30am–3pm

YOTVATA

CULTURE

TOURIST CENTER
Tel. 07-637 60 18

YOTVATA KIBBUTZ
25 miles north of Eilat
Tel. 07-635 74 44
Fax 07-635 74 00
*Zoological, botanical,
archeological and
geological exhibitions.
Combine a trip with one
to the Hai Bar Reserve.*

MITZPEH RAMON

CULTURE

TOURIST CENTER
Tel. 07-58 86 20
Open 9am–5pm.

NATURE RESERVE
Makhtesh Ramon
Tel. 07-58 86 91
Access via highway 40.

HOTEL

YOUTH HOSTEL
POB Mizpé Ramon
80 600
Tel. 07-658 84 43
Fax 07-658 80 74
*The only hostel in Israel
offering a range of
activities, including
excursions and sports.*

SDEH BOKER

CULTURE

SDEH BOKER KIBBUTZ
Tel. 07-55 56 84
Open Sun.–Thur.
8.30am–3.30pm,
Fri. and eves of festivals
8.30am–2.30pm and
Sat. 9am–2pm
*Visits to David Ben
Gurion's house and
family tomb.*

TIMNA

CULTURE

PARK
20 miles from Eilat; turn
left onto a side road
which leads to the park
Tel. 07-635 62 15
Fax 07-635 62 15
Open 7.30am–dusk

BEERSHEBA

USEFUL INFORMATION

BANK LEUMI
54 Haaztmaut St
Tel. 07-46 28 11

BUS
BUS EGGED
Bus station
Tel. 07-637 51 61
Open Sun.–Thur.
9am–4pm,
Fri. and evenings
of festivals
9am–2pm
Closed Sat.

CAR RENTAL
HERTZ
5 Ben Zvi St
Tel. 07-27 38 78
Open 8am–6pm

TOURIST OFFICE
6A Ben Zvi St
Tel. 07-23 60 01

CULTURE

ABRAHAM'S WELL
1 Hebron St
Tel. 07-23 37 75
Open Sun.–Thur.
8am–7pm, Fri.
8am–2pm
Closed Sat.

BEDOUIN MARKET
Hebron St
Tel. 07-46 36 66
Open Thur.
6am–2pm

MUSEUM OF BEDOUIN CULTURE
Lahav Kibbutz
Tel. 07-91 85 97
Fax 07-91 98 89
Open Sun.–Thur.
9am–4pm,
Fri. 9am–2pm
and Sat. 9am–4pm

NEGEV MUSEUM
Haatzmaut St
Tel. 07-28 20 56
Open Sun.–Thur.
11am–5pm, Fri. and
evenings of festivals
10am–1pm and Sat.
7–9pm.

TEL BEERSHEBA
Omer Rd
Tel. 07-46 72 86
Open 10am–1pm
and 4–6pm
Exhibition of Bedouin culture.

RESTAURANT

CAPRICE *
1 Herzl St
Tel. 07-23 23 92
Central European cuisine.

NARGILA
Central bus station
Tel. 07-623 50 30
A veritable oasis in the desert. Famous for its hospitality. Yemen-influenced Israeli cuisine.

HOTELS

ARAVA HOTEL *
37 Hahistadrut St
Tel. 07-27 87 92
▢

AVIV *
40 Mordei
Hagetaot St
Tel. 07-27 80 59
☎ ▢ C

DESERT INN **
North of the old town
Tel. 07-42 49 22
Fax 07-41 27 72
Hotel with restaurant.
P ☎ ▢ ▭ C ⌫

YOUTH HOSTEL
79 Independence Rd
Tel. 07-627 14 90

ARAD

USEFUL INFORMATION

JEEP TOUR
PO Box 669
unit no. 28
municipal market
Tel. 07-95 23 88
Jeep excursions in the Negev.

CULTURE

TOURIST CENTER
28 Ben Yair St
Tel. 07-995 44 09
Open Sat.–Thur.
9am–5pm, Fri. and eves
of festivals 9am–2pm
Exhibitions about the desert.

HOTELS

ARAD HOTEL **
6 Hapalmach St
Tel. 07-95 70 40
▢ C

MARGOA **
6 Hapalmach St
Tel. 07-995 70 14
Fax 07-995 77 78
Thermal cures, asthma treatment. Hotel with restaurant.
P ☎ ▢ ▭ C ⌫

YOUTH HOSTEL
4 Arad Rd
Tel. 07-995 71 50

EIN BOKEK

HOTELS

HOD HOTEL **
Mobile Post
Dead Sea
Tel. 07-658 46 44
Fax 07-658 46 06
Thermal cures.
P ☎ ▢ ▭ C ⌫

NIRVANA **
Highway 90, between
the Masada and
Mitzpeh Zohar roads
Tel. 07-658 46 28
Hotel and nursing home. Center for thermal cures. Hotel with restaurant.
P ☎ ▢ ▭ C ⌫

EIN GEDI

CULTURE

EIN GEDI NATURE RESERVE
Highway 90
Tel. 07-659 47 60
Open Sun.–Thur.
8am–1 hour before
sundown, Fri. 8am–2pm
Closed Sat.

RESTAURANT

EIN GEDI
Tel. 07-658 45 44
Vegetarian cuisine.

HOTELS

EIN GEDI CAMP SITE
Tel. 07-658 44 44
Private beach.
P

EIN GEDI KIBBUTZ-HOTEL
***
Tel. 07-659 42 22
Private tennis courts and beach. Shuttle to the hot sulfur springs. Hotel with restaurant.
P ☎ ▢ ▭ C ⌫

EIN GEDI YOUTH HOSTEL *
Bet Sarah
At the entrance to the
Nahal David Nature
Reserve
Tel. 07-658 41 65
Fax 07-658 44 45
On the shore of the Dead Sea.
⌲ C

MASADA

CULTURE

FORTRESS
Tel. 07-658 44 62
Accessible by cable car Sat.–Fri. 8am–4pm and by foot daily 5am–5pm. Son et lumière at 7pm Sep. and Oct. and 9pm Apr. and Aug.

MITZPEH SHALEM

HOTEL

METZOKE DRAGOT HOLIDAY VILLAGE**
North of Ein Gedi on
the shore of the
Dead Sea
Tel. 02-996 45 01
Fax 02-996 45 05
Kibbutz-hotel. Organizes desert trips.
P C

NEVEH ZOHAR

CULTURE

BET HAGOTZER MUSEUM
Highway 90
Tel. 07-658 41 58
Open by request only; contact Mr Shlomo Drori.

QUMRAN

CULTURE

ATRAKTZIA
Kalia Beach
North of the Dead Sea
Tel. 07-994 23 91
Open 9am–5pm
*Aquatic park 5 mins
by car from Qumran.
Private pool and
beach.*

BETHLEHEM

USEFUL
INFORMATION

TOURIST OFFICE
Manger Sq.
Tel. 02-74 15 81

CULTURE

**BASILICA OF
THE NATIVITY**
Tel. 02-74 10 20
Open 6am–
6pm

HERODION
Open 8am–5pm,
Apr.–Sep., 8am–4pm,
Oct.– March. Closes
one hour early Fri. and
eves of festivals.

MAR SABA
Highway 398. On the
right past Ubediya
Open 8am–4pm
*Monastery; no
women permitted.*

MILK GROTTO CHURCH
Tel. 02-74 38 67

Open 8–11am and
1–4pm

HOTELS

MOR CHARBEL ★★
Wadi Maali Rd
Tel. 02-74 21 55
Fax 02 27 28 21
*Hostel which is run by
Maronite nuns.*

HEBRON

CULTURE

**TOMB OF THE
PROPHETS**
Open 7.30–11am,
1–2.30pm
and 3.30–5pm
Closed Fri.
and Sat. am

JERUSALEM

USEFUL
INFORMATION

BANKS
BANK HAPOALIM
1 Kikar Zion
Tel. 02-620 71 71

BANK HAPOALIM
97 Yafo St
Tel. 02-625 63 76

BANK LEUMI
– 21 Rambar St

Tel. 02-75 45 11
– 21 Yafo Rd
Tel. 02-629 16 11
– 19 King David St
Tel. 02-625 74 71

**CHRISTIAN
INFORMATION CENTER**
Jaffa Gate
PO Box 14308
Tel. 02-27 26 92
Fax 02 28 64 17
Open 8.30am–12.30pm
Closed Sun.
*Religious and tourist
information covering
the whole of the
Holy Land.*

**GOOD MORNING
JERUSALEM**
Binyani Ha'ooma
1 Shazar Bd
PO Box 6001
Tel. 0251 12 70
Fax 0251 12 72
Open Sun.–Thur.
9am–7pm,
Fri. 9am–1.30pm
Closed Sat.
and Jewish festivals
*Situated opposite the
central bus station.
Hotel reservations
and home-stay
apartment reservations
for in and around
Jerusalem.*

**MAIN POST
OFFICE**
23 Yafo St
  Open Sun.–Thur.
  8am–6pm,
 Fri. 8am–2pm
Closed Sat. and
Jewish festivals

**MUNICIPAL
TOURIST
OFFICE**
22 Yafo St
Tel. 02-24 22 32
Open Sun.–Thur.
8.30am–5pm,
Fri. 8.30am–2pm
  Closed Sat., Jewish
  festivals and evenings
  of festivals.

TOURIST OFFICE
Jaffa Gate
Tel. 02-28 22 95
Open Sun.–Thur.
8am–4pm, Fri.
8.30am–2pm
Closed Sat.

**SOLAN
TELECOMMUNICATION
AND COMPUTERS
LIMITED**
Ramallah Rd
Tel. 02-95 05 05
*Mobile phone
rentals.*

TRANSPORT

ATAROT AIRPORT
North of Jerusalem
Tel. 02-583 39 80

AIRLINES
ARKIA
Klal Center
97 Yafo Rd
Tel. 02-623 48 55

DELTA AIRLINES
15 Shamay St
Tel. 02-622 24 19

EL AL
11 Hillel St
Tel. 02-625 69 34

GALILEE TOURS
3 Hillel St
Tel. 02-625 88 66

BUSES
BUS ARABES
Central Station
Sultan Suleyman Rd
EGGED TOURS
224 Yafo Rd
Tel. 02-530 45 55

UNITED TOURS
Annex, King David Hotel
Tel. 02-25 21 87

CAR RENTAL
AVIS
22 King David St
Tel. 02-624 90 01

EURODOLLAR
8 King David St
Tel. 02-623 54 67

HERTZ
Hyatt Hotel
Tel. 02-581 50 69

RENT A CAR
14 King David St
Tel. 02-624 82 04

**SHERUT NESHER
TOURS LTD**
21 King George Ave
Tel. 02-623 12 31
*Shared taxis. Useful for
the airport. Reservation
one day in advance.*

TOUR OPERATORS

**ARCHEOLOGICAL
SEMINARS**
34 Habad St
Tel. 02-627 35 15
Fax 02-627 26 60

Closed Fri., Sat.
and Jewish festivals
*Tours of the old town.
Reserve in advance.*

WALKING TOURS LTD
26 Alkavez St
Tel. 02-52 25 68
Fax 02 29 07 74
Open 8am–8pm
Closed Sat.
Guided tours of the city

CULTURE

AMMUNITION HILL
Eshkol Bd
Tel. 02-82 84 42
Open Sun.–Thur.
8.30am–5pm, Fri. and
eves of festivals
9am–1pm Closed Sat.

ASCENSION MOSQUE
Mount of Olives
Ring for admission.

BASILICA OF
ALL NATIONS
Garden of Gethsemane
Mount of Olives
Tel. 02-628 32 64
Open 8.30am–noon
and 2.30–6pm in
summer
Open 8.30am–noon
and 2.30–5pm in winter

BIBLE LANDS MUSEUM
25 Granot St
Tel. 02-561 10 66
Open Mon.,
Tue. and Fri.
9.30am–3.30pm,
Wed. 9.30am–9.30pm,
Fri. 9.30am–2pm
and Sat. 11am–3pm

BIBLICAL ZOO
Malcha quarter
Tel. 02-643 01 11
Open Mon., Wed. and
Sat. 9am–5pm, Fri.
9am–4.30pm
*Near T. Kolek
stadium.*

BOTANICAL GARDEN
Campus of Givat Ram
Hebrew University
Tel. 02-58 43 51
Open Mon.–Fri.

Dead Sea manuscripts

BURNT HOUSE
2 Tiferet Israel
Old City – Jewish
quarter
Tel. 02-628 72 11
Open Sun.–Thur.
9am–5pm, Fri.
9am–1pm
Closed Sat.

CAVE OF
GETHSEMANE
Garden of Gethsemane
Mount of Olives
Tel. 02-628 32 64
Open 8.30–11.45am
and 2.30–5pm

CENACLE (HALL OF
THE LAST SUPPER)
Zion Gate
Tel. 02-671 35 97
Open Sat.–Fri.
8am–noon and 3–6pm
Open Fri. 8am–4pm

CHURCH OF ST JOHN
THE BAPTIST
Ein Karem
Tel. 02-641 36 39
Open Mon.–Sat. 8am–
noon and 2.30–6pm,
Sun. 8am–noon and
2.30–5pm

CHURCH OF THE
HOLY SEPULCHER
Via Dolorosa
Tel. 02-627 33 14
Open 4–7.30pm

CHURCH OF THE
VISITATION
Ein Karem
Tel. 02-641 72 91
Open 8–11.45am
and 2.30–6pm in
summer
Open 8–11.45am
and 2.30–5pm in
winter

CITY OF DAVID
Tel. 02-28 81 41
Open Sun.–Thur.
9am–4pm, Fri.
9am–1pm
Closed Sat.

DOME OF THE ROCK
Tel. 02-27 23 58
Open 8–11am
and noon–3pm
Open 8–11am, during

Ramadan.Closed Fri.
and Muslim festivals

DOMINUS FLEVIT
Mount of Olives
Tel. 02-27 49 31
Open 8am–noon and
2.30–6pm in summer
(5pm in winter)

DORMITION CHURCH
Mount Zion
Tel. 02-671 99 27
Open 8am–noon
and 2–6pm

EL-AQSA MOSQUE
Temple Mount
Open 8–11am and
noon–3pm
Open 7.30–11am during
Ramadan
Closed Fri. and Muslim
festivals

FOUR SEPHARDI
SYNAGOGUES
Old City – Jewish
quarter
Tel. 02-28 05 92
Open Sun.-Mon. and
Wed.–Fri. 9.30am–4pm,
Tue., Fri. and eves of
festivals 9.30am–
12.30pm. Closed Sat.
and Jewish festivals

GARDEN OF
GETHSEMANE
Mount of Olives
Open 8.30am–noon and
2pm–sundown

GARDEN TOMB
Nablus Rd
Tel. 02-627 27 45
Open 8am–noon and
2.30–5pm
Closed Sun.

GREAT SYNAGOGUE
58 King George St
Tel. 02-624 71 12
Open 7am–1pm Prayers
Fri. and Sat. only.

HADASSAH
SYNAGOGUE
Hadassah Hospital
Tel. 02-41 63 33
Open Sun.–Thur.
8am–1pm and
2–3.45pm, Fri.
8am–12.45pm

Closed Sat.
*Windows by Marc
Chagall.*

HERODIAN
QUARTER
Old City – Jewish
quarter
Tel. 02-28 34 48
Open Sun.–Thur. 9am–
5pm, Fri. 9am–1pm
Closed Sat.

ISLAMIC MUSEUM
OF THE TEMPLE
MOUNT
Dome of the Rock
Tel. 02-628 33 13
Open Sat.–Fri. 8–11am
and noon–3pm
Open Sat.–Fri. 8–11am
During Ramadan
Closed Fri. and Muslim
festivals

ISRAEL MUSEUM
AND SHRINE OF
THE BOOK
Ruppin St
Tel. 02-670 88 11
Open Mon., Wed., Fri.
and Sun. 10am–5pm,
Fri. and eves of
festivals 10am–2pm,
Sat. 10am–4pm.
Open Tue. 10am–10pm
(Shrine of the Book)
and 4–10pm
(Israel Museum)

KHAN THEATER
2 David Remez Sq.
Tel. 02-71 82 81
*Cultural center in
an old caravanserai.
It incorporates a
theater, cabaret
(traditional
shows), a café
and a disco.*

KNESSET
Givat Ram
Tel. 02-675 33 33
Open Fri. and Sun.
8.30am–2.30pm
*Take your passport
with you.*

MARY'S TOMB
Garden of Gethsemane
Mount of Olives
Open 6 –11.45am and
2.30–5pm

MODEL OF THE SECOND TEMPLE
Holy Land Hotel
Bayit Vegan, at end of Uziel St
Tel. 02-678 81 18
Open Sun.–Thur. 8am–8pm, Fri. and Sat. 8am–5pm

MONASTERY OF THE CROSS
Ben Zvi Av.
Tel. 02-79 09 61
Open 10am–1.30pm
Closed Fri. and Sun.

MONASTERY OF THE FLAGELLATION
Via Dolorosa St
Tel. 02-28 29 36
Open 8am–noon and 1–6pm in summer
Open 8am–noon and 1–5pm in winter

MUSEUM OF THE HOLOCAUST
Mount Zion
Tel. 02-671 51 05
Open Sun.–Thur. 8.30am–6pm, Fri. 8.30am–3pm; closed Sat. and Jewish festivals

MUSEUM OF ISLAMIC ART
2 Hapalmach St
Tel. 02-66 12 91
Open Sun.–Thur. 10am–5pm, Sat. 10am–1pm. Closed Fri.

MUSEUM OF NATURAL HISTORY
6 Mohilever St
Tel. 02-563 11 16
Open Mon. and Wed. 8.30am–6pm, Tue., Fri. and Sat. 8.30am–1pm, Sat. 10am–2pm
Closed Fri.

MUSEUM OF OLD YISHUV
Old City – Jewish quarter
Tel. 02-628 46 36

Open Sun.–Thur. 9am–2pm
Closed Fri. and Sat.

OPHEL ARCHEOLOGICAL EXCAVATIONS
Tel. 02-628 81 41
Open Sun.–Thur. 9am–4pm
Closed Fri.

ROCKEFELLER MUSEUM
Arun Rashid St
Tel. 02-629 26 27
Open Sun.–Thur. 10am–5pm, Fri., Sat. and Jewish festivals 10am–2pm
Guided tours Fri. and Sun. 11am.

ST ANNE'S CHURCH
1 Mujahidin St
Tel. 02-628 32 85
Open 8am–noon and 2–6pm in summer.
Open 8am–noon and 2–5pm in winter.
Closed Sun.

SUPREME LAW COURTS
Shaareï Mishpat Road
Tel. 02-675 96 66
Visits by appointment.

THEATER OF JERUSALEM
20 Marcus St
Tel. 02-61 71 67
Theater and dance.

TICHO HOUSE
7 Harav Kook St
Tel. 02-624 50 68
Open Sun.–Mon. and Wed.–Fri. 10am–5pm, (Tue. 10pm, Fri. 2pm, Sat. 1pm)

TOMB OF DAVID
Mount Zion
Tel. 02-71 97 67
Open 8am–sundown

TOURJEMAN MUSEUM
4 Heil Hahandasa St
Tel. 02-628 12 78
Open Sun.–Thur. 9am–4pm, Fri. 9am–1pm
Closed Sat.

TOWER OF DAVID AND MUSEUM OF THE HISTORY OF JERUSALEM
Jaffa Gate
Tel. 02-627 41 11
Open Sun.–Thur. 10am–4pm, Fri. 10am–2pm
Guided tours in English Sun.–Fri. 11am. In summer, "son et lumière" in English Mon., Wed. and Sat. 9.30am

TUNNEL IN THE WESTERN WALL
2 Haomer St
Tel. 02-27 13 33
Visit by prior arrangement only.
Take boots and torch.

WARREN'S SHAFT
Tel. 02-28 23 56

YAD VASHEM
Mont Herzl
Tel. 02-675 16 11
Open Mon.–Thur. 9am–5pm, Fri. 9am–2pm
Closed Sat.

Allow at least 2 hours for the visit.

BARS

CHAMPS PUB
Yoel Salomon St
Zion Sq.
Nahalat Shiva quarter
Open 7pm–2am
English pub.
Happy hours 7–9pm.

UNDERGROUND DISCO PUB
Zion Sq.
Nahalat Shiva quarter
Disco where you can just go for a drink. Popular with young Israelis.

RESTAURANTS

CAFÉ ATARA
7 Ben Yehuda St
Tel. 02-25 01 41
Meeting place (supposedly) for the city's intellectuals.

CAFÉ CHAGALL
5 Ben Yehuda St
Tel. 02-23 33 31
Pizza, pâtes, salads, pastries.

CHEESECAKE *
23 Yoel Salomon St
Tel. 02-24 50 82
Open Sun.–Thur. 9am–midnight, Fri. 9am–4pm, Sat. after Sabbath
Snacks.
Specialties include cheesecakes, salads, soups and desserts.
▭

COFFEE SHOP
Maronite St
Jaffa Gate
Tel. 02-589 40 90
Closed Sun. and Christmas Day
Snack bar decorated with ceramics. Part of the Christ Church religious hostel.
★

EL GAUCHO **
22 Rivlin St
Tel. 02-625 66 65
Closed Fri. and Sat.
lunchtime
*Specialties: Argentinian
meat dishes.*

ETNACHTA *
12 Yoel Salomon St
Nahalat Shiva quarter
Tel. 02-625 65 84
Vegetarian cuisine.

FINK'S **
2 Histadrut St
Tel. 02-623 45 23
Open lunchtime
and evenings
Closed Fri. and Sat.
lunchtime
*Western and eastern
European cuisine.*
⊡ C

GILLY'S **
Corner of Hillel St and
Yoel Salomon St
Nahalat Shiva quarter
Tel. 02-625 59 55
Open Sun.–Thur.
noon–4pm and 6–11pm,
Fri. noon–4pm,
Sat. 19 –11pm
Closed Rosh Hashanah,
Passover, Yom Kippur,
10 days in Sep.
and Apr.
*Meat specialties.
Western cuisine.*
★

JACK'S
8 Ben Yehuda St
Nahalat Shiva quarter
Open 5–10pm
*American ice-cream
specialties.*

KAMIN **
4 Rabbi Akiva St
Corner of Hillel St
Tel. 02-25 64 28
Open 10am–midnight
Closed Yom Kippur
and the night of
Passover
*In a pretty ivy-covered
house. Terrace. French
and Italian cuisine.*
★ P ⊡

LA BELLE
18 Rivlin St
Tel. 02-24 08 07
Open lunchtime and
evenings
Closed Sat.
Western cuisine.
P ⊡ C

LITTLE ITALY *
38 Keren Hayesod
St
Tel. 02-61 76 38
Open 10 –minuit
Closed Fri., Sat. and
Yom Kippur
*Italian cuisine. A wide
range of fish dishes and
pasta.*
★ ⊡ 🏠

MAGRITTE *
9 Yoel Salomon St
Nahalat Shiva quarter
Tel. 02-23 44 99
*Simple, light cuisine;
generous portions.*

**MISHKENOT
SHA'ANANIM** **
Yemin Moshe
Tel. 02-24 46 96
Open lunchtime and
evenings
Western cuisine.
P C

MOONLIGHT
Mounbaz St
Tel. 02-23 29 29
*One of the most
pleasant cafés in the
Russian quarter.
Beautiful view from the
terrace of the Cathedral
of the Holy Trinity.*
★

**MOSES RESTAURANT –
CITADEL BAR** *
Jaffa Gate
Tel. 02-28 09 75
Open 9 am–10pm
*Local and western
cuisine.*
🌅 C

PIPO *
16 Yoel Salomon St
Nahalat Shiva quarter
Tel. 0224 04 68
Open Mon.–Fri.,
lunchtime and evenings,
and Sat. evenings
*International cuisine.
In an old building with
music and a good
variety of dishes. Good
for a quick meal.*

**PUNDAK EIN
KAREM** **
13 Hamayas St
Tel. 02-643 74 72
Open 10.30am–1am
Closed Yom Kippur
*You can get there by
bus no. 17.
Magnificent view over
Ein Karem. From May to
Oct. meals are served
in Bedouin tents.
Western and local
cuisine.*
★ 🌅 ⊡ C

SERGIO'S FRIENDS *
Botanic garden
Givat Ram
Tel. 02-79 37 95
*Ideal location by a
stretch of water
opposite the botanic
gardens. Excellent
Italian cuisine.*
★

TICHO HOUSE CAFÉ
7 Harav Kook St
Tel. 02-624 41 86
*Small terraced
café where you
can stop for a quick
snack after a visit to
the museum.*

**TSRIFF
RESTAURANT** **
5 Horkanos St
Tel. 02-624 24 78
Open 10 am–2am
Closed Yom Kippur
*A restaurant popular
with Israelis. Seafood
specialties.
Franco-Moroccan
cuisine.*

**TSRIFF
RESTAURANT** **
26 King David St
Tel. 02-624 65 21
Open 8 am–midnight
Closed Yom Kippur
*In a 1930's colonial
building, one of the best
restaurants in
Jerusalem, serving
Franco-Moroccan
cuisine. Not to be
missed: the seasonal
entrées.*
★ ⊡

**TWIN TOWERS
COFFEE SHOP** *
Our Lady of Jerusalem
PO Box 20531
Tel. 02-27 91 11
Open 9 am–11.30pm
*Opposite the New Gate,
within the precincts of
Our Lady Church.
Ideal for a light lunch.*
P 🌅 C

Saint Maron Hotel

HOTELS

**AMERICAN COLONY
HOTEL** ***
Nablus Rd
Tel. 02-627 97 77
Fax 02-627 97 79
*Turkish palace built in
the 1860's by a rich
merchant, the American
Colony is without a
doubt one of the most
beautiful hotels in the
country and a peaceful
haven in the heart of
East Jerusalem.
Beautiful gardens and
Middle Eastern
architecture. Famous
non-kosher restaurant.
The "economy" rooms
are very affordable.
Hotel with restaurant.*
P ☎ ⧠ ⊡ C

**CAESAR
HOTEL** **
208 Jaffa Rd
Tel. 02-538 21 56
Fax 02-538 28 02
Hotel with restaurant
P ☎ ⧠ ⊡ C

**CAPITAL
HOSTEL** *
1 Solomon St
Zion Square
Tel. 02-625 19 18
*Youth hostel ideal for
exploring the city's
nightlife. Free entry to
the Underground
Disco Pub for
patrons.*

CASA NOVA HOTEL*
New Gate
Po Box 1321

Tel. 02-628 27 91
Fax 02-589 43 70
*Good value for money.
Pilgrims made
particularly welcome.*

Casa Nova Hotel

**CHRIST CHURCH
GUEST HOUSE ***
Jaffa Gate
Po Box 14037
Tel. 02-627 77 27
Fax 02-627 77 30
*Run by the Anglican
Church, this is a calm
establishment full of
charm, frequented by
Arabs, Jews and
Christians. Pretty
interior courtyard
where you can drink
coffee. One of the best
addresses in the city.
Warning: lights out at
11pm.*
★ P

**CHRISTMAS
HOTEL ***
1 Ali Ibn Abi Taleb St
East Jerusalem
Tel. 02-628 25 88
Fax 02-628 78 96
Hotel with restaurant
P

EL-ARAB *
Khan Al-Zeit St
Tel. 02-628 35 37
*Arranges tours in the
Occupied Territories.*
⊁

**EL-AHRAM
YOUTH HOSTEL ***
Al-Wed St, Via Dolorosa
Po Box 51841
Tel. 02-628 09 26
Communal cooking.
⊁ ✝

**EIN KAREM
YOUTH HOSTEL ***
Ein Karem
Tel. 02-641 62 82

**ERETZ ISRAEL
HOTEL ***
51 King George St
Tel. 02-624 50 71

*Neat, quiet hotel
run by an Orthodox
Jewish couple.
A good way of
witnessing traditional
Jewish home life.
Very good value for
money.
Hotel with restaurant.*
★

GLORIA HOTEL **
33 Latin Patriarcate St
Tel. 02-628 24 31
Fax 02-628 24 01
Hotel with restaurant.
P ☎ ⌐ C

**HOLYLAND
HOTEL *****
Bayit Vegan
Tel. 02-643 77 77
Fax 02-643 77 44
*Situated in a rather
out-of-the-way location,
at the end of Uziel St,
this hotel houses a
model of Jerusalem
during the time of the
Second Temple,
which non-residents
may come in to
admire.*
⌂ ⬜ ⌐

**HYATT REGENCY
HOTEL ****
32 Lehi St
Tel. 33 12 34
Fax 81 59 47
*Free shuttle bus to the
city center from 9am to
1pm and from 4pm to
8pm.*
⌐ ☎ ⬜ C ⌂

**JERUSALEM HILTON
HOTEL *****
Givat Ram
Tel. 0258 14 14
Fax 0251 45 55
Hotel with restaurant.
⌂ ☎ ⬜ C

KING DAVID HOTEL ***
23 King David St
Tel. 02-625 11 11
Fax 02-623 23 03
*The first luxury hotel
constructed in
Jerusalem, since its
opening in 1931, the
King David has been
the setting since for a
number of important
national and
international political
and diplomatic
events. The 1930's
decor combines luxury
and good taste.
Beautiful gardens with a
view of the city walls.
Hotel with restaurant.*
★ P ⊁ ☎ ⬜
⌐ C ⌂

**KING SOLOMON
HOTEL *****
32 King David St
Tel. 02-869 55 55
Fax 02-24 17 74
Hotel with restaurant.
P ☎ ⬜ ⌐ C

New Imperial Hotel

LAROMME HOTEL ***
3 Jabotinsky St
Liberty Bell Garden
Tel. 02-675 66 66
Fax 02-675 67 77
Hotel with restaurant.
P ⊁ ☎ ⬜ ⌐ C ⌂

**LUTHERAN
YOUTH HOTEL ****
Saint Mark Rd
Po Box 14051
Tel. 02-28 21 20
Fax 02-89 47 34
Open 6 am–10.45pm
Closed for two to four
weeks in Jan.
*Youth hostel and
guest house.
Guests must be under
32 years old. No visitors
admitted to the rooms.
Lights out at 10.30pm.*
⊁ ✝

**MITZPEH RAMAT
RACHEL KIBBUTZ-
HOTEL ****
M.P. North Judea
Ramat Rachel
Tel. 02-670 25 55
Fax 02-673 31 55
*The only kibbutz-hotel
in Jerusalem.
Regular bus service
to Jerusalem all day
until 11.45pm.*
⌂ P ⌐ ☎ ⬜ ⌐ C

MOUNT OF OLIVES *
Mount of Olives Rd
Tel. 0228 48 77
Fax 0289 44 27
Hotel with restaurant.

**MORIAH JERUSALEM
HOTEL *****
39 Keren Hayesod St
Tel. 02-623 22 32
Fax 02-623 24 11
Hotel with restaurant.
⌂ ☎ ⬜ ⌐ C

**NATIONAL
PALACE HOTEL ****
4 Az-Zahra St
East Jerusalem
Tel. 02-27 32 73
Fax 02-28 21 39
Hotel with restaurant
⬜ ⌐ C

**NEW IMPERIAL
HOTEL ***
Jaffa Gate
Old City
Po Box 14085
Tel. 02-28 22 61
Fax 02-27 15 30
*Large hotel in a
good location.
Slightly crumbling,
but full of charm.*
⊁ ⌐

**OUR LADY OF
JERUSALEM
HOTEL ****
New Gate
Po Box 20 531
Tel. 02-627 91 11
Fax 02-627 19 95
*Hostel for religious
pilgrims. Terrace.
Twin Towers Café.*
⊁ ⬜ ☎ C

**OUR LADY OF
ZION***
Convent of Ecce
Homo
PO Box 19056
Tel. 02-27 72 93
Fax 02-28 22 49
*Welcoming hostel
run by the Sisters of
Our Lady of Zion.
Very beautiful
terraces.
Warning: lights
out at 10pm.*
★ ⊁

**PALATIN
HOTEL ****
4 Agripas St
Tel. 02-23 11 41
Fax 02-25 93 23
C

PETRA HOSTEL *
David St
Jaffa Gate
Tel. 02-628 23 56
*Constructed on the
orders of Tsar
Nicholas I to shelter
early Russian Orthodox
pilgrims in the Holy
Land. Minimal comfort.
Terraces.*
⊁ ✝

RITZ HOTEL **
8 Ibn Khaldoun St
Tel. 02-627 32 33
Fax 02-628 24 15
Hotel with restaurant.
⌐ ☎ ⬜ ⌐ C

SAINT ANDREW'S HOSPICE ∗∗
1 David Bemiz St
PO Box 8619
Tel. 02-73 24 01
Fax 02-73 17 11
This Scottish inn is located right in the heart of modern Jerusalem.
View of the walls of the Old City.
★ 🅿 🌂 ☎ ▭

SAINT-MARON HOTEL ∗∗
25 Maronite
Convent St
Jaffa Gate
Po Box 14 219
Tel. 02-28 21 58
Fax 02-27 28 21
This hotel is run by Maronite nuns. The rooms are sunny and have been constructed around a patio. Lebanese cuisine. (Reservation essential)
★ ☎

SEVEN ARCHES HOTEL ∗∗
Mount of Olives
Tel. 02-27 75 55
Fax 02-27 13 19
Hotel which also has a restaurant.
☎ ▭ ©

SHERATON JERUSALEM PLAZA ∗∗∗
47 King George St
Tel. 02-25 91 11
Fax 02-23 16 67
Hotel which also has a restaurant.
🅿 🌂 ☎ ▭
© 〰

YMCA THREE ARCHES HOTEL ∗∗
26 King David St
Po Box 294
Tel. 02-25 71 11
Fax 02-23 51 92
This hotel is extremely well located and has a great deal of charm with its handsome 1930's décor and its simple but comfortable rooms. The YMCA is also contains a sports club (free entry is offered to anyone staying at the hotel). The sports club's main attraction is a magnificent swimming pool decorated with mosaics.
🅿 🌂 ☎
▭ © 〰

SPORTS

MUNICIPAL SWIMMING POOL
Emek Refaim St
Tel. 02-61 13 36
Open-air swimming pool.

JERICHO

CULTURE

NABI MUSA
Route 90
Between Jerusalem and Jericho, in the direction of Almog
Ring for entry.

QASR HISHAM
Route 90
Tel. 02-92 25 22
Open 8am–4pm during the winter and 8am–5pm during the summer.

ST GEORGE'S MONASTERY
Open 9am–4pm the winter and 9am–5pm during the summer
One hour's walk west of Jericho, going up the far side of wadi Qelt toward Jerusalem.

TEL JERICHO
Route 90
Tel. 02-92 29 09
Open 8am–sundown

RESTAURANTS

AL-KHAYYAM PARK ∗
El-Sultan St
Tel. 02-92 24 77
Middle Eastern cuisine.

NABLUS

CULTURE

JACOB'S WELLS
Tel. 09-37 51 23
Open 9am–noon and 3–5pm
Ring for entry.

ABU GOSH

CULTURE

CRUSADER CHURCH
Tel. 02-34 27 98
Open 8.30–11am and 2.30–5pm
Closed Thur. and Sun.

RESTAURANTS

ABU GOSH RESTAURANT ∗∗
On the main street of the village
Tel. 02-33 20 19
Middle Eastern cuisine. Specialty: hummus.

CARAVAN INN ∗
Tel. 02-34 27 44
On the main street of the village
Open 11am–11pm
Closed Yom Kippur
Delicious Middle Eastern cuisine in a lively atmosphere. Specialties: mezze and roast lamb.
🅿 ✝

ASHKELON

USEFUL INFORMATION

HAPOALIM BANK
4 Hanassi St
Tel. 07-71 15 51

TOURIST OFFICE
Afridar center
Tel. 07-677 01 73

CULTURE

NATIONAL PARK
West of the town by the sea
Tel. 07-673 64 44

ZOOLOGICAL GARDENS
Magen Kibbutz
Tel. 07-998 30 39

BET SHEMESH

CULTURE

CAVES OF SOREK
Tel. 02-91 11 17
Open Sat.-Thur.
8.30am–4pm,
Fri. 8.30am–1pm
The caves are situated one mile to the east of Bet Shemesh

HAFETZ HAIM

HOTEL

KIBBUTZ-HOTEL HAFETZ HAIM ∗∗
Tel. 08 59 38 88
Fax 08 59 34 58
🅿 🗗 ☎ ▭ ©

LATRUN

CULTURE

MONASTERY
Highway 1
west of Jerusalem
Tel. 08 22 00 65
Fax 08 35 50 84
Open 8–11.30am and 2.30–5pm
Closed Sun.
Wine making.

HOTEL

NEVE SHALOM ∗∗
West of Latrun
Highway 3
Tel. 08 91 71 60
Fax 08 91 71 42
Bungalows and a youth hostel situated in a moshav, which brings together Jews and

Arabs. The village is in open country dominated by the Judean Hills. Wonderful view.
★ 🅿 ⛷ 🅒

KIRYAT YEARIM

CULTURE

MONASTERY OF THE ARK OF THE COVENANT
Tel. 02-34 28 18
Open 8.30–11.30am and 2.30–6pm
Ring for entry.

TEL AVIV

USEFUL INFORMATION

BANKS
BANK HAPOALIM
171 Dizengoff St
Tel. 03-522 92 95

BANK HAPOALIM
104 Hayarkon St
Tel. 03-520 06 06

BANK LEUMI
– 50 Dizengoff St
Tel. 03-526 04 44
– 130 Ben Yehuda St
Tel. 03-520 37 37

TOURIST OFFICE
5 Shalom Aleichem St
Tel. 03-521 82 14
Fax 03 521 83 96

Open Sun.–Thur.
8.30am–5pm, Wed.
and eves of festivals
8am–2pm
Closed Sat. and Jewish festivals.

MIKVE ISRAEL POST OFFICE
7 Mikve Israel
Tel. 03-564 36 50
Poste restante.

MAIN POST OFFICE
132 Allenby St
Tel. 03-564 37 64

AMERICAN EMBASSY
71 Hayarkon St
PSC 98
Box 100
APO AE 09830
Tel. 03-517 4338

SOLAN TELECOMMUNICATION AND COMPUTERS LIMITED
13 Frishman St
Tel. 03-522 94 24
Mobile phones for sale and rent.

TRANSPORT

BUS
DAN
39 King Saul Road
Tel. 03-693 33 33

AIRLINES
AMERICAN AIRLINES
1 Ben Yehuda St
Tel. 03-510 43 22

ARKIA
Tel Aviv Terminal
11 Frishman St
Tel. 03-524 02 20

DELTA AIRLINES
29 Allenby St
Tel. 03-620 11 01

EL AL
32 Ben Yehuda St
Tel. 03-526 12 22

CAR RENTAL
AVIS
113 Hayarkon St
Tel. 03-527 17 52

HAGAR RENT A CAR LTD.
106 Hayarkon St
Tel. 03-522 22 90

HERTZ
144 Hayarkon St
Tel. 03-522 33 32

TOUR OPERATORS
EGGED TOURS
59 Ben Yehuda St
Tel. 03-527 12 12

GALILEE TOURS
42 Ben Yehuda St
Tel. 03-546 63 33

UNITED TOURS
57 Ben Yehuda St
Tel. 03-522 55 52

CULTURE

AYARKON PARK
Rokah road, to the northwest of Tel Aviv, along the Ayarkon river.
Open daily
Park attractions, lake, bird sanctuary, snake display.

BEN GURION'S HOUSE
17 Ben Gurion Ave
Tel. 03-522 10 10
Open Sun.–Thur.
8.30am–3pm,
Fri. 8.30am–1pm
and Sat. 10am–1pm

BIALIK HOUSE
22 Bialik St
Tel. 03-525 45 30
Open Sun.–Thur.
9am–5pm,
Sat. 10am–2pm
Closed Fri.

BOTANICAL GARDEN
Tel Aviv University
Klausner St
Tel. 03-640 93 99

DIAMOND MUSEUM
1 Jabotinsky St
Ramat-Gan
Tel. 03-576 02 19
Open Sun.–Thur.
10am–4pm, Tue.
10am–7pm
Closed Fri. and Sat.

HA'ARETZ MUSEUM
Ramat-Aviv
Tel. 03-641 52 44
Open Mon., Wed., Thur.
and Sun. 9am–2pm,
Tue. 9am–5pm
and Sat. 10am–2pm
Closed Fri.

HABIMA NATIONAL THEATER
Tarsat Ave
Tel. 03-526 66 66
Israeli theatrical productions with simultaneous translation into English over headphones.

HELENA RUBINSTEIN PAVILION
6 Tersat Blvd
Tel. 03-528 71 96
Open Sun.–Thur.
10am–8pm, Fri.
10am–2pm and Sat.
10am–3pm

INDEPENDENCE HALL
16 Rothschild Bd
Tel. 03-517 39 42
Open Sun.–Thur.
9am–2pm
Closed Fri. and Sat.

MUSEUM OF THE DIASPORA (BET HATEFUTSOT)
Klausner St, Ramat-Aviv
University campus
Tel. 03-646 20 20
Open Sun.–Tue.
and Thur. 10am–5pm,
Wed. 10am–7pm
and Fri. 9am–2pm
Closed Sat.

MUSEUM OF HAGANAH (BET HAHAGANA)
23 Rothschild Av.
Tel. 03-560 86 24
Open Sun.–Thur.
8.30am–3pm, Fri. and eves of festivals
8.30am–noon
Closed Sat. and Jewish festivals

RABAT GAN SAFARI
Ramat Gan South
The largest zoological garden in Israel.

RUBIN MUSEUM
14 Bialik St
Tel. 03-525 42 30
Open Mon., Wed., Thur.
and Sun. 10am–2pm,
Tue. 10am–1pm
and 4–8pm
Closed Fri. and Sat.
Paintings by Israeli artists.

RESTAURANTS

BISTROT PICASSO ★★
114 Hayarkon St
Tel. 03-524 675
Popular with young residents of Tel Aviv. Pleasant, friendly atmosphere. Specialties: French and Italian cuisine.

CACTUS RESTAURANT ★★
66 Hayarkon St
Tel. 03-510 59 69
Open until midnight
Mexican cuisine.
🅿 🍽 🅒

CHIMNEY ★★
2 Mendele St
Tel. 03-523 52 15
*Pub-restaurant.
Simple but good
cuisine. Extensive wine
and cocktail lists.*
★

ELLA ★★
16 Kiker Kedumin St
Old Jaffa
Tel. 03-682 53 53
Closed Sun.
*Fish specialties.
French cuisine.*
☼ ⴲ

IZAKAYA ★★
105 Hahashmonaim St
Po Box 20760
Tel. 03-561 09 71
Open 12.30–3pm
*Japanese snack bar
where lunch is served
from 12.30pm to
5.30pm. Good-quality
cuisine.*
★

KEREN ★★★
12 Eilat St
Jaffa
Tel. 03-681 65 65
Closed Fri. and Sat.
lunchtime
*In a wooden house
which was transported
from the US to the port
of Jaffa in 1866.
French cuisine.*
🅿 ⬚ 🄲

LOFT ★★★
Hangar no. 1
Port of Jaffa
Tel. 03-518 28 35
Open 10am–midnight
*A huge industrial
warehouse decorated
with strange sculptures.
A large bay window
overlooks the port.
Extensive wine list.*
★ ☼ ⬚

PALOMA PICASSO ★★
114 Hayarkon St
Tel. 03-524 18 75
*Restaurant of the Tel
Aviv Hotel. A variety
of simple dishes.
Western and Middle
Eastern cuisine.*

PASTALINA ★★
16 Elifellet St
Tel. 03-683 64 01
Closed Fri. evening
and Sat. lunchtime
*A wide variety of
pastries. Italian
cuisine.*
🅿 ⬚ 🄲

PATATI ★
8 Haasbah St
Tel. 03-562 45 02
*A good place for a light
lunch with a glass of
wine. Western
cuisine.*

PUNCH LINE ★★
6 Ha-Arbaa St
Tel. 03-561 07 85
Open 11.30am–2pm
*The waiters are also
singers.*
★

**WHITE HALL
STEAK HOUSE** ★★
6 Mendele St
Tel. 03-524 92 82
Open noon–midnight
Closed Sat. lunchtime.
Western cuisine.

**THE CHICAGO
PIZZA PIE
FACTORY** ★
63 Hayarkon St
Tel. 03-517 75 05
*Happy hours.
American/Italian cuisine.*

**THE PROMENADE
IN TEL AVIV** ★
Gordon Frishman
Promenade
Tel. 03-510 33 33
Sandwiches and salads.

**UPKOD CAFÉ-
RESTAURANT** ★★
15 Kdumin Sq.
Old Jaffa
Tel. 03-518 11 47
Open 9am–midnight
*Housed in an old stone
building which is always
cool inside.*
ⴲ

**YOTVATA
RESTAURANT
IN THE CITY** ★★
80 Herbert Samuel
Promenade
Tel. 03-510 79 84
Open 7am–4am
*The food (salads,
fish, fruit and dairy
produce) all come
from Yotvata
Kibbutz.
A fashionable
and busy spot
where you may
have to wait.*
★

HOTELS

CITY ★★
9 Mapu St
Tel. 03-524 62 53
Fax 03-524 25 20
Hotel with restaurant.
🅿 ☎ ▢ ⬚ 🄲 ⋈

DAN HOTEL ★★★
99 Hayarkon St
Tel. 03-530 25 25
Fax 03-524 97 55
Hotel with restaurant.
🅿 ☼ ☎ ▢
⬚ 🄲

FLORIDA ★★
164 Hayarkon St
Tel. 03-524 21 84
Fax 03-524 72 78
Hotel with restaurant.
🅿 ☎ ▢ ⬚ 🄲

GRAND BEACH ★★
250 Hayarkon St
Tel. 03-546 65 55
Fax 03-527 83 04
Hotel with restaurant.
☎ ▢ ⬚ 🄲 ⋈

**HILTON
TEL AVIV HOTEL** ★★★
Independence Garden
Tel. 03-520 22 22
Fax 03-527 27 11
Hotel with restaurant.
🅿 ☼ ☎ ▢
⬚ 🄲 ⋈

IMPERIAL ★★
66 Hayarkon St
Tel. 03-517 70 02
Fax 03-517 83 14
Hotel with restaurant.
🅿 ☎ ▢ ⬚ 🄲

**MORIAH PLAZA
HOTEL** ★★★
155 Hayarkon St
Tel. 03-527 15 15
Fax 03-527 10 65
Hotel with restaurant.
🅿 ☼ ☎ ▢
⬚ 🄲 ⋈

MOSS HOTEL ★★
6 Nes Ziyona St
Tel. 03-517 16 55
Fax 03-517 16 55
🅿 ☎ ⬚ 🄲

**OLD JAFFA
HOSTEL** ★
8 Dlay Zion St
Tel. 03-682 23 16
Fax 03-682 23 16

**SHERATON
HOTEL** ★★★
115 Hayarkon St
Tel. 03-521 11 11
Fax 03-523 33 22
Hotel with restaurant.
🅿 ☼ ☎ ▢
⬚ 🄲 ⋈

**TEL AVIV
YOUTH HOSTEL** ★
36 Rehov Bnei Dan St
Tel. 03-544 17 48
*Youth hostel situated
on the banks of the
Yarkon, near the
tourist area.*
🄲

the Crusader citadel and the ticket is valid for the Turkish baths, the crypt and the citadel.

BAHAI GARDENS AND TEMPLE
Genua Sq.
Tel. 04-991 17 64
Temple open Mon., Fri.–Sun. 9am–noon.
Gardens open daily 9am–5pm.

PRISONERS MUSEUM
10 Haganah Rd
Tel. 04-991 82 64
Open 8am–4pm
Closed Fri. and Sat.

HOTELS

AKKO YOUTH HOSTEL *
Po Box 1090
Tel. 04-991 19 82
An attractive youth hostel housed in the old palace of a Turkish governor. Rooms 7, 8 and 9 have sea views.

ARGAMAN HOTEL **
Sea front
Po Box 153
Tel. 04-991 66 91
Fax 04-991 66 90

PALM BEACH **
Sea Shore
Tel. 04-981 58 15
Fax 04-991 04 34
Hotel with restaurant.

CAESAREA

RESTAURANTS

CHARLEY'S **
Sea front, Old Town
Tel. 06-36 30 50
Open lunchtime and evenings
Western cuisine.

HOTELS

DAN CAESAREA GOLF HOTEL **
Tel. 06-36 22 66
Fax 06-36 23 92
Golf.
Hotel with restaurant.

NACHSHOLIM KIBBUTZ HOTEL **
Nachsholim sea front
Tel. 06-39 95 33
Fax 06-39 76 14

SPORT

AVIV YACHT SERVICE
36 Gordon St
Tel. 03-544 32 47
Boat and yacht rental, with or without equipment.

SHOPPING

DIZENGOFF CENTER
50 Dizengoff St

FLEA MARKET
In the old Jaffa area

GAN HA'IR
7 Ibn Guirol Blvd
Shopping arcades.

NARLAT BENJAMIN RD
Pedestrianized area with various attractions and a choice of restaurants.

RAMLA

CULTURE

CHURCH AND HOSPICE OF ST NICODEMOS
Bialik St

Open 8–11.30am.
Closed Sun.

GRAND MOSQUE
Shlomo Hamelech St
Tel. 08-22 50 81
Open 8–11am
Closed Fri. and Sat.

REHOVOT
CULTURE

WEIZMANN INSTITUTE
Tel. 08-534 32 30
Closed Fri., Sat. and Jewish festivals

RESTAURANT

HAMIR PESAND *
169 Herzl St
Tel. 08-46 98 73
Open 8am–2pm
Closed Fri., Sat. and Yom Kippur
Vegetarian cuisine.

RISHON LEZION
CULTURE

CARMEL WINE CELLARS
25 Carmel St
Tel. 03-964 20 21
Open 8am–4pm
Closed Sat. and Jewish festivals.

RISHON LEZION MUSEUM
Hameyesdim Sq.
Tel. 03-964 16 21
Open Sun., Tue.–Thur. 9am–2pm, Mon. 4–8pm and Fri. 9am–1pm
Closed Sat.

RESTAURANT

THE WELL *
19 Rothschild St
Tel. 03-966 81 04
Closed Jewish festivals
International cuisine.

AKKO
CULTURE

AL-JAZZAR MOSQUE
Open 8am–6pm

CRUSADER CITY AND TURKISH BATHS
Al Jazzar St
Tel. 04-991 17 64
Open Sat.–Thur. 8am–7pm, Fri. 8.30am–1.45pm
The ticket offices are in

EIN HOD

CULTURE

DADA JANCO MUSEUM
Artists' Village
Tel. 04-84 23 50
Open Sun.–Thur.
9.30am–5pm, Fri.
9.30am–4pm
Closed Sat.

HAIFA

USEFUL INFORMATION

BANKS
BANK HAPOALIM
28 Haneviim St
Tel. 04-861 20 20

BANK LEUMI
27 Yafo St
Tel. 04-854 71 11

MAIN POST OFFICE
Sederot Hapalyam St
Tel. 04-830 43 54

MUNICIPAL TOURIST OFFICE
City Hall
14 Hertzel St
Tel. 04-866 65 21

TOURIST OFFICE
Port of Haïfa
Tel. 04-866 39 88

TRANSPORT

BUS
BUS EGGED
Bus station
Haaliyya
Hasheniyya St
Tel. 04-854 94 86

EGGED TOURS
4 Nordau St
Tel. 04-862 31 31

AIRLINE
ARKIA
80 Haatzmaut St
Tel. 04-872 22 20

CAR RENTAL
AVIS
7 Ben Gurion Bd
Tel. 04-851 30 50
Open Sun.–Thur.
8am–6pm,
Fri. 8am–2pm
and Sat. 9am–12pm

HERTZ
90 Haatzmaut St
Tel. 04-852 32 39
Open 8am–6pm

TAXIS MERKAZ MIZPEH
7 Balfour St
Tel. 04-866 25 25

TOUR OPERATORS
CARMEL TOURING
126 Hanassi St
Tel. 04-838 22 77

UNITED TOURS
5 Nordau St
Tel. 04-866 56 56

CULTURE

BAHAI TEMPLE AND GARDENS
Hatzionut Av.
Tel. 04-851 03 44
Temple open 9am–noon
Gardens open 8am–5pm

CARMELITE MONASTERY
Stella Maris Rd
Tel. 04-833 17 58
Open 6am–1.30pm
and 3–6pm.

DAGON ARCHEOLOGICAL MUSEUM
1 Pulmer Sq.
Tel. 04-866 42 21
*Free guided tours only,
at 10.30am or by
arrangement.
Closed Sat.*

ELIJAH'S CAVE
230 Allenby St
Tel. 04-852 74 30
Open Sun.–Thur.
8am–5pm,
Fri. 8am–1pm.
Closed Sat.

MANI-KATZ MUSEUM
89 Yefeh Nof St
Tel. 04-38 34 82
Open Mon., Wed., Thur.
and Sun. 10am–4pm,
Tue. 2–6pm
Fri. 10am–1pm
and Sat. 10am–2pm.

MUSEUM OF ANCIENT AND MODERN ART, MUSIC AND ETHNOLOGY
26 Shabbettai Levi St
Tel. 04-852 32 58
Open Fri. and Sun.
10am–1pm,
Tue. and Thur.
5–8pm
Sat. 10am–3pm
and 5–8pm

NATIONAL MARITIME MUSEUM
198 Allenby St
Tel. 04-53 66 22
Open Sun.–Thur.
10am–4pm,
Sat. 10am–1pm
Closed Fri.

OLIVE MUSEUM
2 Tovim St
Industrial zone
Tel. 04-65 43 33
Open Sun.–Thur.
8.30am–2.30pm
Closed Fri. and Sat.

RAIL MUSEUM
Hativat Golani St
Tel. 04-56 42 93
Open Sun., Tue.
and Thur. 9am–12pm
Closed Fri. and Sat.

REUBEN AND EDITH HECHT MUSEUM
Aba Rushi Rd
Haifa University
Tel. 04-25 77 73
Open Tue. 10am–7pm,
Sun.–Thur. 10am–4pm,
Fri. 10am–3pm and Sat.
10am–noon

TECHNION
Technion Campus
Institute of Technology
Tel. 04-832 06 64
Open Sun.–Thur.
8am–2pm. Closed Fri.,
Sat. and festivals
*National museum of
science and technology.*

RESTAURANTS

DOLPHIN ★★
13 Sderot Bat-Galim
Tel. 04-852 38 37
Open lunchtime and
evening
Seafood specialties.
🅿 ⊡ 🅲

LA TRATTORIA ★★★
119 av. Hanassi
Tel. 04-37 90 20
Open lunchtime and
evening.
Western cuisine.
🅿 ⊡ 🅲

THE PINE CLUB ★★
Bet Oren Bd
Mount Carmel
Tel. 04-32 35 68
Open Tue.–Sun. evening
and Sat. lunchtime
French cuisine.
🅿 ⊡ 🅲

VOILÀ ★★★
21 Nordeau Rd
Tel. 04-866 45 29
*Comfortable setting,
friendly atmosphere.
Elegant French
cuisine.*

HOTELS

BETHEL HOSPICE ★
40 Hagefen St
Tel. 04-52 11 10

DAN CARMEL ★★★
87 Hanassi St
Tel. 04-38 62 11
Fax 04-38 75 04
Hotel with restaurant.
🅿 ☎ ▯ ⊡ 🅲 ⌇

DAN PANORAMA ★★★
107 Hanassi St
Tel. 04-35 22 22
Fax 04-35 22 35
Hotel with restaurant.
⌇ 🅿 ☎ ▯ ⊡ ⌇
🅲

DVIR ★★
124 Yafe Nof St
Tel. 04-38 91 31
Fax 04-38 10 68
*Hotel with restaurant.
Guests can use the
swimming pool at the
Dan Panorama Hotel.*
☎ ▯ ⊡ 🅲

NETANYA

USEFUL INFORMATION

TOURIST OFFICE
Haatzmaut Sq.
Tel. 09 82 72 86

CULTURE

MUSEUM OF THE JEWISH LEGION
Moshav Ayihayil
Bet Hagdudim
Tel. 09 82 22 12
Open 8am–2pm
Closed Fri. and Sat.

RESTAURANTS

PUNDAK HAYAM ★
1 Harav Kook St
Tel. 09 34 12 22
*Near the main
beach. Middle
Eastern and Western
cuisine.*

SAMOVAR **
4 Tel Hai St
Tel. 09 33 47 74
Russian cuisine.

HOTELS

CALIL **
18 Nice Bd
Tel. 09 62 44 55
Fax 09 62 44 55
Hotel with restaurant.
P ☎ □ ⌂ C

MARGOA HOTEL *
9 Gad Machnes St
Tel. 09 62 44 34
Hotel with restaurant.
☎ □ ⌂ C

PARK **
7 David Hamelech St
Tel. 09 62 33 44
Fax 09 62 40 29
Hotel with restaurant.
⌇ ☎ □ ⌂

THE SEASONS ***
Nice Bd
Tel. 09 60 15 55
Fax 09 62 30 22
Hotel with restaurant.
P ☎ □ ⌂ C ⌇

ROSH HANIKRA

CULTURE

CAVES OF ROSH HANIKRA
Tel. 04-985 71 05
Access via cable car
Sat.–Thur.
8.30am–4pm,
Fri. 8.30am–3pm.

ZICHRON YAACOV

CULTURE

WINE CELLAR
Tel. 06-39 01 19
Open Sun.–Thur.
9am–3pm, Fri.
9am–1pm
Closed Sat.

BARON ROTHSCHILD'S GARDENS AND TOMB
Tel. 06-39 01 19
Open Sun.–Thur.
8am–3pm, Fri.
8am–12pm
Open Sat. 8am–4pm
(gardens only).

TIBERIAS

USEFUL INFORMATION

BANK HAPOALIM
3 Habanim St
Tel. 06-79 84 11

TOURIST OFFICE
23 Habanim St
Tel. 06-72 56 66
Open Sun.–Thur.
8.30am–5pm,
Fri. and evenings of
festivals 8.30am–1pm
Closed Sat.

MAIN POST OFFICE
Hayarden St
Open Sun–Tue. and
Thur. 8am–12.30pm and
3.30–6pm,
Fri. and Wed.
8am–12.30pm
Closed Sat.

TRANSPORT

BUS EGGED
Central bus station
Tel. 06-79 10 80

BIKE RENTAL
Hotel Aviv
Galil St
Tel. 06-72 00 07

CAR RENTAL
AVIS
Central bus station
Tel. 06-72 27 66

HERTZ
Jordan River Hotel
Habanim St
Tel. 06-72 39 39

AVIV SHARED TAXIS
Tel. 06-72 22 34

CULTURE

ARCHEOLOGICAL MUSEUM
Habanim St
Tel. 06-39 09 50
Open daily.

RESTAURANTS

PAGODA **
Lido beach
Tel. 06-79 25 64
Open lunchtime and
evening
Closed Shabbat
Chinese cuisine.
P ⌂ ⌂ C

THE HOUSE **
Gdud Barak St
Tel. 06-79 23 53
*This restaurant is
famous for its Thai
cuisine.*
P ⌂ C

HOTELS

ARISTON **
19 Herzl Bd
Tel. 06-79 02 44
Fax 06-72 20 02
P ☎ □ ⌂ C

CAESAR ***
103 Hatayeland St
Tel. 06-72 33 33
Fax 06-79 10 13
Hotel with restaurant.
P ☎ □ ⌂ C ⌇

MORIAH PLAZA ***
Habanim St
Tel. 06-79 22 33
Fax 06-79 23 20
*Watersports facilities.
Hotel with restaurant.*
☎ □ ⌂ C

RON BEACH **
Gdud Barak St
Tel. 06-79 13 50
Fax 06-79 13 51
Hotel with restaurant.
P ☎ □ C

TERRA SANCTA *
Old Town
Po Box 179
Tel. 06-72 29 55
Fax 06-72 00 07
By the lake.

SPORTS

TIBERIAS ROWING CLUB
At the end of the
promenade on the
sea front
Open 3.30—5.30pm
*Watersports on
the Sea of Galilee.*

BET GABRIEL

RESTAURANT

BET GABRIEL **
Tel. 06-75 02 22
*Stylish interior.
View of the lake. High
standard cuisine; fish
specialties.*
P ⌇ ⌂

CAPERNAUM

CULTURE

CHURCH AND MUSEUM
Tel. 06-72 10 59
Open daily
8.30am–4.30pm

EIN GEV

HOTEL

EIN GEV HOLIDAY VILLAGE **
East of Sea of Galilee
Tel. 06-75 80 27
Fax 06-75 05 90
*Private beach.
Bungalows.*
P C

GINNOSAR

CULTURE

FISHING BOAT OF CHRIST'S TIME
Bet Yigal Allon
Kibbutz Ginnosar
Access via Highway 90
Tel. 06-72 29 05
Open Sun.–Thur.
8am–4pm, Fri. 8am–1pm
and Sat. 9am–4pm

HAON

HOTEL

CAMP SITE
Southeast shore of the
lake.
Tel. 06-75 75 55
Private beach.
⌇

KORAZIM

CULTURE

NATIONAL PARK
Northwest of the lake
Tel. 06-93 49 82

*Traces of a town and
synagogue from
Talmudic times.*

RESTAURANT

**VERED
HAGALIL** **
North of Korazim
Tel. 06-93 57 85
Open morning,
lunchtime and evening
*Charming restaurant.
Grilled meat specialties.
Visa accepted.*
P ▭ C

HOTEL

**KARE DESHE
YOUTH HOSTEL** **
Mobile post-Korazim
Tel. 06-72 06 01
*Charming hotel.
Beautiful modern
architecture inspired by
old caravanserais.
Private beach.
Excellent value for
money.*
★ P ☼

MOUNT OF THE BEATITUDES

CULTURE

**CHURCH OF THE
BEATITUDES**
Northwest of the lake
Tel. 06-79 09 78
Open 8am–12pm
and 2.30pm–5pm

RAMOT

HOTEL

**RAMOT
RESORT
HOTEL** **
Northeast of the lake
Tel. 06-73 26 36
Fax 06-79 35 90
*Kibbutz-hotel
and holiday village.
Little bungalows
with a private garden.*
P ☼ ☎
▭ ▭ C

TABA

CULTURE

**CHURCH OF THE
MULTIPLICATION OF
THE LOAVES**
Tel. 06-72 10 61

ST PETER'S CHURCH
Tel. 06-72 47 67
Open 8am–5pm

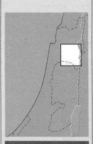

BET SHE'AN

CULTURE

**FORTRESS
OF BELVOIR**
Near Gesher Kibbutz
About 7 miles north of
Bet She'an
Tel. 06-58 70 00
Open 8am–5pm in
summer, 8am–4pm in
winter. Closes one hour
earlier on Fri.

**MUSEUM OF GAN
HASHLOSHA**
National Park
Highway 669
Between Nir-David and
Bet Alpha Kibbutzes
Tel. 06-58 30 45
Open Sun.–Fri.
8am–2pm,
Sat. 10.30am–1pm.

**SYNAGOGUE
OF BET ALPHA**
Hefzibah Kibbutz
About 4 miles east of
Bet She'an
Tel. 06-53 14 00
Open Sun.–Thur.
8am–4pm, Fri. 8am–2pm
and Sat. 10am–2pm

TEL OF BET SHE'AN
Tel. 06-58 52 00
Open Sat.–Thur.
8am–5pm,
Fri. 8am–4pm

BET YERAH

CULTURE

TEL OF BET YERAH
6 miles south of Tiberias
on the shore of the lake

CANA

CULTURE

**CHURCH OF THE
WEDDING AT CANA**
Tel. 06-51 70 11
Open 8am–12pm
and 2.30–5pm in
summer, 8am–noon
and 2.30–4pm in winter.

EIN HAROD

CULTURE

**SHTURMAN
ARCHEOLOGICAL
MUSEUM**
Ein Harod Kibbutz
Tel. 06-53 16 05
Open Sun.–Thur.
8am–1pm and
3–4.30pm, Fri.
8am–12pm and Sat.
9.30am–12.30pm

MEGIDDO

CULTURE

TEL MEGIDDO
6 miles west of Afula
Tel. 04-89 11 00
Open 8am–5pm in
summer, 8am–4pm in
winter. Closes one hour
earlier Fri.

MOUNT TABOR

CULTURE

**CENTER OF
BEDOUIN CULTURE**
Corner of Kfar Shibli
Near Kfar Tavor
Tel. 06-76 78 75
Open 8am–5pm

NAZARETH

USEFUL INFORMATION

BANK HAPOALIM
701 Harashi St
Tel. 06-57 09 23

TOURIST OFFICE
6 Casanova St
Tel. 06-57 30 03

CULTURE

**BASILICA OF THE
ANNUNCIATION AND
ST JOSEPH'S
WORKSHOP**
Paul VI St
Tel. 06-57 25 01
Open 8.30am–12pm
and 2–4.30pm in winter,
2–5.30pm in summer.
Closed Sun. am.

**NAZARETH
SYNAGOGUE**
Tel. 06-56 84 88
Open 8.30am–6pm
Ring for entry.

HOTELS

CASA NOVA *
Po Box 198
Opposite the
Basilica of the
Annunciation
Tel. 06-57 13 67

**GRAND NEW
HOTEL** **
Po Box 177
Hamotran St
Tel. 06-57 33 25
Fax 06-57 62 81
Hotel with restaurant.
☎

ZIPPORI

CULTURE

**ARCHEOLOGICAL
SITE**
North of Nazareth
Route 79
Tel. 06-56 82 72
Open 8am–5pm,
Apr.–Sept., 8am–4pm,
Oct.–Mar.

NIMROD

CULTURE

NIMROD'S FORTRESS NATIONAL PARK
16 miles east of Kiryat Shmona
Tel. 06-94 04 00
Information available from Dan Kibbutz.

KATZRIN

CULTURE

GAMLA NATURE RESERVE
Tel. 06-97 19 18
Open Sat.–Thur. 8am–4pm (Fri. 3pm) in winter.
Open Sat.–Thur. 8am–5pm (Fri. 4pm) in summer.

GOLAN ARCHEOLOGICAL MUSEUM AND WINE CELLAR
Tel. 06-96 13 50
Open Sun.–Thur. 8am–4pm, Fri. 8am–1pm and Sat. 10am–4pm
Wine cellar closed Sat.

SPORT

ABU KAYAK
Hayarden park
Near Arik Bridge
Tel. 06-92 10 78
The Jordan by kayak.

MOUNT HERMON SKI RESORT
Tel. 06-98 13 37
Israel's only ski resort.

KIRYAT SHMONA

USEFUL INFORMATION

AIRLINE
ARKIA
Pal Building
Tel. 06-95 99 39

CULTURE

TEL DAN RESERVE
6 miles east of Kiryat Shmona
Tel. 06-95 15 79
TEL HATZOR
Near Ayeland Heshacher Kibbutz
Tel. 06-93 48 55

HOTELS

**HAGOSHRIM KIBBUTZ HOTEL **
3 miles east of Kiryat Shmona near Hurshat
Tel. 06-95 62 31
P ☐↔ ☎ ☐ ☐ C

**KFAR GILADI **
2 miles north of Kiryat Shmona
Metula Road
Tel. 06-94 14 14
Access via no. 9 bus
P ☐↔ ☎ ☐ ☐ C

**KFAR BLUM KIBBUTZ **
4 miles from Kiryat Shmona north of the Hula Valley
Tel. 06-94 36 66
Fax 06-94 85 55
☐↔ ☎ ☐ ☐ C

ROSH PINNA

USEFUL INFORMATION

AIRLINE
ARKIA Airport
Tel. 06-93 53 02

HOTEL

**ROSH PINNA YOUTH HOSTEL **
Tel. 06-93 70 86
At Rosh Pinna, take the Safed road (Highway 89), to the top of the village.

SAFED

USEFUL INFORMATION

TOURIST OFFICE
50 Jerusalem St
Tel. 06-92 06 33

TRANSPORT

BUS
BUS EGGED
Bus station
Tel. 06-92 11 22

CULTURE

BET HAMEIRI MUSEUM
Old town
Tel. 06-97 13 07
Open 9am–2pm
Closed Sat.

BIBLICAL MUSEUM OF ISRAEL
Citadel
Tel. 06-97 34 72
Open Sun.–Thur. 10am–6pm, Sat. 10am–2pm.
Closed Fri.

PRINTING MUSEUM
Artists quarter
Tel. 06-97 13 07
Open Sun.–Thur. 10am–noon and 4–6pm
Fri. 9am–2pm,
Sat. 10am–2pm

HOTELS

BET BENYAMIN YOUTH HOSTEL *
Lokamei Hagetast St
Tel. 06-92 10 86
Fax 06-97 35 14
In the town center Hotel with restaurant.

**RIMON INN **
Artists quarter
Tel. 06-92 06 65
Fax 06-92 04 56
P ☐ ☐ C

**RON **
Hativat Yiftah St
Tel. 06-97 25 90
Fax 06-97 23 63
Hotel with restaurant.
P ☎ ☐ C

HAMMAT GADAR

HOTEL

**AFIK GUEST HOUSE **
Afik Golan Heights Kibbutz
Tel. 06-76 42 40
Fax 06-76 30 31
☐

APPENDICES

BIBLIOGRAPHY, *462*
LIST OF ILLUSTRATIONS, *466*

ESSENTIAL
◆ READING ◆

◆ BEN-GURION (D.): *Israel: Years of Challenge*, Blond, London, 1979
◆ BEN-SASSON (H.H.) ET AL, EDS.: *A History of the Jewish People*, Weidenfeld and Nicolson, London, 1976
◆ KAYYALI (A.W.): *Palestine: A Modern History*, Croom Helm, London, 1978
◆ UNTERMAN (A.): *The Dictionary of Jewish Lore and Legend*, Thames & Hudson, London, 1991

◆ GENERAL ◆

◆ AHARONI (Y.): *The Land of the Bible, a historical geography*, trans. Rainey (A.F.), Burns and Oates, London, 1967
◆ AHRENDT (H.): *Eichmann in Jerusalem, a report on the banality of evil*, Penguin Books, Harmondsworth, 1976
◆ ASHRAWI (H.): *Hanan Ashrawi, a passion for peace*, trans. Victor (B.), Fourth Estate, London, 1995
◆ BREMRIDGE (M.): *Oasis in the Desert. A story of exile from the Holy Land*, Arab League Office, London 1969
◆ BRENNER (F.): *Israel*, Collins Harvill, London, 1988
◆ BROWNING (I.): *Petra*, Chatto & Windus, London, 1973
◆ CASSON (L.): *Ships and Seamanship in the Ancient World*, London, 1971
◆ CONDER (C.R.): *Palestine*, George Philip & Son, London, 1889
◆ DOUGLAS-HOME (C.): *The Arabs and Israel*, Weidenfeld & Nicolson, London, 1967
◆ FINKELSTEIN (L.) ED.: *The Jews: Their History, Culture and Religion*, Philadelphia, 1960
◆ FROST (H.): *Under the Mediterranean*, Routledge & Kegan Paul, London, 1963
◆ GOITEIN (S.D.F.): *Jews and Arabs, Their Contacts Through the Ages*, Schocken Books, New York, 1955
◆ GROSSMAN (D.): *Sleeping on a wire: conversations with Palestinians in Israel*, trans, Watzman (H.), Jonathan Cape, London, 1993
◆ HOLLIS (C.) AND BROWNRIGG (R.): *Holy Places*, Weidenfeld & Nicolson, London, 1969
◆ JARVIS (C.S.): *Desert & Delta*, John Murray, London, 1938
◆ KEDOURIE (E.) ED.: *The Jewish World: Revelation, Prophecy and History*, Thames & Hudson, London, 1979
◆ LAWRENCE (T.E.): *Seven Pillars of Wisdom*, Cape, London, 1976
◆ LEIBOWITZ (Y.): *Judaism, human values and the Jewish state*, Harvard University Press, Cambridge, 1992
◆ LEWIS (B.): *The Political Language of Islam*, University of Chicago Press, Chicago, 1988
◆ LOWI (M.R.): *Water and Power, the politics of a scarce resource in the Jordan River Basin*, Cambridge University Press, Cambridge, 1993
◆ MEIR (G.): *My Life*, Weidenfeld & Nicolson, London, 1975
◆ MITTELBERG (D.): *Strangers in paradise, the Israeli kibbutz experience*, Oxford, New Brunswick, c.1988
◆ MURRAY (M.A.): *Petra, the Rock City of Edom*, Blackie & Son, London and Glasgow, 1939
◆ OZ (A.): *The Slopes of Lebanon*, Chatto & Windus, London, 1990
◆ RANDALL (R.): *Jordan and the Holy Land*, Frederick Muller, London, 1968
◆ ROBERTS (D.): *The Holy Land*, Day & Son, London 1855
◆ RODINSON (M.): *The Arabs*, trans. Goldhammer (A.), Croom Helm, London, 1981
◆ RODINSON (M.): *Europe and the mystique of Islam*, trans. Veomis (R.), I.B. Taurus, London, 1988
◆ ROTHENBERG (B.): *God's Wilderness*, Thames & Hudson, London, 1961
◆ SAID (E.): *Orientalism*, Routledge & Kegan Paul, London, 1979
◆ SCHWEID (E.): *The land of Israel: national home or land of destiny*, Herzl Press, New York, c. 1985
◆ SHIPLER (D.K.): *Arab and Jew: wounded spirits in a promised land*, Bloomsbury, London, 1987
◆ SPENDER (S.): *Learning Laughter*, Weidenfeld and Nicolson, London, 1952
◆ TAYLOR (J.): *Petra*, Aurium, London, 1993
◆ THOMSON (W.D.): *The Land and the Book*, London, 1859
◆ WHITFIELD (D.): *A Land with People, a report from occupied Palestine*, Morning Star, London, 1982
◆ WOOLLEY (C.L.) AND LAWRENCE (T.E.): *The Wilderness of Zion*, Jonathan Cape, London, 1936
◆ YADIN (Y.): *The Art of Warfare in Biblical Lands*, Weidenfeld & Nicholson, London, 1963

◆ HISTORY ◆

◆ BARON (S.W.): *A Social and Religious History of the Jews*, Columbia University Press, New York, 1960
◆ BEN-SASSON (H.H.) ET AL, EDS.: *A History of the Jewish People*, Weidenfeld and Nicolson, London, 1976
◆ BRIGHT (J.): *A History of Israel*, SCM Press, London, 1972
◆ HOURANI (A.): *A History of the Arab Peoples*, Belknap Press of Harvard University Press, Cambridge, 1991
◆ JOHNSTON (L.): *A History of Israel*, Sheed and Ward, London and New York, 1964
◆ NETANYAJU (B.) ETC, EDS.: *The World History of the Jewish People*, First Series, Ramat-Gan, London, 1964–77; Second Series, Ramat-Gan, London, 1966–76
◆ NOTH (M.): *The History of Israel*, trans. Godman (S.), Adam & Charles Black, London, 1960
◆ OESTERLEY (W.O.E.) and ROBINSON (T.H.): *History of Israel*, London, 1932

ANCIENT
◆ HISTORY ◆

◆ COOK (E.M.): *Solving the mysteries of the Dead Sea Scrolls*, Paternoster, Carlisle, 1994
◆ FURNEAUX (R.): *The Roman Siege of Jerusalem*, Hart-David MacGibbon, London, 1973
◆ HARDEN (D.): *The Phoenicians*, Thames & Hudson, London, 1962
◆ HERMANN (S.): *A history of Israel in Old Testament times*, trans. Bowden (J.), SCM Press, London, 1975
◆ MANN (J.): *The Jews in Egypt and in Palestine under the Fatimid Caliphs*, 2 vols., Humphrey Milford, London, 1973
◆ MELLART (J.): *Earliest Civilisations of the Near East*, Thames & Hudson, London, 1965

◆ MOSCATI (S.): *The World of the Phoenicians*, Weidenfeld & Nicolson, London, 1965

◆ ROBINSON (E.): *Biblical Researches in Palestine*, John Murray, London, 1887

◆ SHANKS (H.) ED.: *Ancient Israel, a short history from Abraham to the Roman Destruction of the Temple*, Prentice Hall, London, 1988

◆ SILBERMANN (N.A.): *The hidden scrolls, Christianity, Judaism and the war for the Dead Sea scrolls*, Heinemann, London, 1995

◆ SMALLWOOD (E.M.): *The Jews Under Roman Rule*, Brill, Leiden, 1976

◆ SMITH (G.A.): *The Historical Geography of the Holy Land*, Hodder & Stoughton, London, 1894

◆ DE VAUX (R.): *The Early History of Israel*, trans. Smith (D.), Darton, Longman & Todd, London, 1978

◆ WILKINSON (J.): *Jerusalem Pilgrims before the Crusades*, Aris & Phillips, Warminster, 1977

◆ WILSON (E.): *The scrolls from the Dead Sea, Israel and the Dead Sea scrolls*, Farrar, Strauss, Giroux, New York, 1978

◆ WISEMAN (D.J.) ED.: *Peoples of Old Testament Times*, Clarendon Press, Oxford, 1973

◆ CRUSADES ◆

◆ BROWN (R.): *The Children's Crusade*, Picador, London, 1990

◆ MAALOUF (A.): *The Crusades through Arab eyes*, trans. Rothschild (J.), Al Saqi, London, 1984

◆ PRAWER (J.): *The Latin Kingdom of Jerusalem: European Colonialism in the Middle Ages*,

Weidenfeld & Nicolson, London, 1972

◆ PRAWER (J.): *The World of the Crusades*, Cambridge University Press, Cambridge, 1951

◆ RUNCIMAN (S.): *The History of the Crusades*, Cambridge University Press, Cambridge, 1951

◆ SMAIL (R.C.): *The Crusades in Syria and the Holy Land etc.*, Thames and Hudson, London, 1973

◆ DE VINSAUF (G.) AND DEVESEZ (R.): *Chronicles of the Crusades*, Bohn's Antiquarian Library, London, 1847

◆ MODERN HISTORY ◆

◆ BEGIN (M.): *The Revolt*, W.H. Allen, London, 1964

◆ BEN GURION (D.): *Israel: Years of Challenge*, Blond, London, 1979

◆ BRELIN (I.): *Chaim Weizmann*, Weidenfeld & Nicolson, London, 1955

◆ BETHELL (N.): *he Palestine Triangle, the struggle between the British, the Jews and the Arabs*, André Deutsch, London, 1979

◆ BUBER (M.): *On Zion*, East & West Library, London, 1973

◆ CHOMSKY (N.): *Peace in the Middle East? Reflections on Justice and Nationhood*, Pantheon Books, New York, 1974

◆ CAMERON (J.): *The Making of Israel*, Secker & Warburg, London, 1976

◆ COHEN (A.): *Israel and the Arab World*, trans. Hodes (A.), Handelman (N.) and Shimeoni (M.), W.H. Allen, London, 1970

◆ DAYAN (M.): *The Story of my Life*, Weidenfeld & Nicolson, London, 1976

◆ GILBERT (M.): *Exile and Return: The Emergence of Jewish Statehood*, Weidenfeld & Nicolson, London, 1978

◆ GILMOUR (D.R.): *Dispossessed – The Ordeal of the Palestinians 1917–1980*, Sidgwick & Jackson, London, 1980

◆ GLUB (SIR J.B.): *Peace in the Holy Land*, Hodder & Stoughton, London, 1971

◆ GLUB (SIR J.B.): *A Soldier with the Arabs*, Hodder & Stoughton, London, 1957

◆ GREEN (S.): *Living by the Sword: America and Israel in the Middle East 1968–1987*, Faber and Faber, London, 1988

◆ HALPERN (B.): *The Idea of the Jewish State*, Harvard Middle Eastern Studies, Cambridge Mass., 1969

◆ HERZOG (C.): *Who Stands Accused? Israel Answers its Critics*, Weidenfeld & Nicolson, London, 1978

◆ KAYYALI (A.W.): *Palestine: A Modern History*, Croom Helm, London, 1978

◆ MASALHA (N.): *Expulsion of the Palestinians*, Institute for Palestine Studies, Washington D.C., 1992

◆ PALUMBO (M.): *The Palestinian Catastrophe*, Faber and Faber, London, 1987

◆ PRITTIE (T.): *Whose Jerusalem?*, Frederick Muller Ltd, London, 1981

◆ SAID (E.): *The Question of Palestine*, Routledge, London, 1979 / Vintage, New York, 1980

◆ SAYIGH (R.): *The Palestinians: From Peasants to Revolutionaries*, Zed Press, London, 1979

◆ SCHWARTZ (W.): *The Arabs in Israel*, Faber

and Faber, London, 1959

◆ WEIZMANN (C.): *Trial and Error*, Hamish Hamilton, London, 1949

◆ TRAVELERS' TALES ◆

◆ BURTON (R.): *The Land of the Midian, Revisited*, C. Kegan Paul & Co., London, 1879

◆ CONDER (C.R.): *Lieut. Claude R. Conder's Reports*, Palestine Exploration Fund, 1873

◆ CONDER (C.R.): *Tent Work in Palestine*, R. Bentley, London, 1879

◆ CURZON (R.): *A Visit to the Monasteries of the Levant*, John Murray, London, 1849

◆ HORNBY (E.): *Sinai and Petra. The Journals of Emily Hornby in 1899 and 1901*, James Nisbet & Co., London, 1907

◆ LEAR (E.): *Edward Lear's Journals: A Selection*, ed. Van Thal (H.), Arthur Barker Ltd., London, 1952

◆ MACGREGOR (W.): *The Rob Roy on the Jordan*, John Murray, London, 1869

◆ POCOCKE (R.): *A Description of the East and Some Other Countries, 1738*, J.R. Knapton, London, 1743–1745

◆ STEPHENS (J.L.): *Incidents of Travel in Egypt, Arabia Petraea and the Holy Land*, Harper and Bros., New York, 1837

◆ WILDE (W.R.): *Wilde's Narrative*, Curry, Dublin, 1840

◆ WRIGHT (T.) ED. *Early Travels in Palestine*, Henry G. Bohn, London, 1848

◆ RELIGION AND SOCIETY ◆

◆ BEN-SASSON (H.H.): *Jewish Society through the Ages*, Valentine, Mitchell, London, 1971

◆ Bibliography

◆ Fohrer (G.): *History of Israelite Religion*, trans. Green (D.E.), S.P.C.K., London, 1973

◆ Freud (S.): *Moses and monotheism*, trans Jones (K.), Hogarth Press, London, 1939

◆ Hanauer (J.E.): *Folklore of the Holy Land, Moslem, Christian and Jewish*, Press, London, 1935

◆ McCall (H.): *Mesopotamian Myths*, British Museum, London, c.1990

◆ Rosenthal (E.I.J.): *Judaism and Islam*, Thomas Yoseloff, New York and London, 1961

◆ Unterman (A.): *The Dictionary of Jewish Lore and Legend*, Thames & Hudson, London, 1991

◆ Vriezen (T.C.): *The religion of ancient Israel*, trans. Hoskins (H.), Lutterworth Press, Guildford, 1967

◆ Archeology ◆

◆ Downey (G.): *Gaza in the early sixth century*, University of Oklahoma Press, Norman, c. 1963

◆ Glucher (C.A.M.): *The City of Gaza in the Roman and Byzantine Period*, B.A.R., Oxford, c. 1963

◆ Glueck (N.): *The Other Side of the Jordan*, American School of Oriental Research, USA, 1940

◆ Glueck (N.): *Rivers in the Desert*, Weidenfeld & Nicolson, London, 1959

◆ Glueck (N.): *Dateline: Jerusalem*, Hebrew Union College Press, Jerusalem, 1968

◆ Glueck (N.): *Exploration in Eastern Palestine*, American School of Oriental Research, USA, 1934

◆ Kenyon (K.M.): *Digging up Jericho*, Ernest Benn, London, 1957

◆ Kenyon (K.M.): *Jerusalem: excavating 3000 Years of History*, Thames & Hudson, London, 1967

◆ Kenyon (K.M.): *Royal Cities of the Old Testament*, Barrie & Jenkins, London, 1971

◆ Linder (E.): *Underwater Archeology. A New Dimension in the Study of Israel in Antiquity*, Israel, 1971

◆ Macalister (R.A.S.): *A Century of Excavation in Palestine*, R.T.S., London, 1925

◆ Negev (A.) Ed: *Archeological encyclopedia of the Holy Land*, Weidenfeld and Nicolson, London, 1972

◆ Petrie (F.): *Researches in Sinai*, ed. Currelly (C.T.), John Murray, London, 1906

◆ Rothenberg (B.): *Timna: Valley of the Biblical Copper Mines*, Thames & Hudson, London, 1972

◆ Shanks (H.): *Judaism in stone, the archeology of ancient synagogues*, Harper & Row, New York and London, 1979

◆ Wilkinson (J.): *Jerusalem as Jesus Knew It: Archeology as Evidence*, Thames & Hudson, London, 1978

Art and Architecture ◆

◆ Israel Exploration Society: *The Architecture of Ancient Israel (From the Prehistoric to the Persian Periods)*, Israel Exploration Society, Jerusalem, 1992

◆ Kennedy (A.): *Petra, its History and Monuments*, London, 1925

◆ Kennedy (D.) and Riley (D.): *Rome's Desert Frontier*, University of Texas Press, Austin, 1990

◆ Kroyanker (D.) and Wahrman (D.): *Jerusalem Architecture, Periods and Styles: The Jewish Quarter and Public Buildings outside the Old City walls, 1860–1914*, Jerusalem, 1983

◆ Mackenzie (J.): *The architecture of Petra*, Oxford University Press, Oxford, 1990

◆ The Metropolitan Museum of Art: *Treasures of the Holy Land*, The Metropolitan Museum of Art, New York, 1986

◆ Schiller (E.): *The Old City (The First Photographs of Jerusalem)*, Ariel Publishing House, Jerusalem.

◆ Sukenik (E.L.): *Ancient Synagogues in Palestine and Greece*, British Academy, Schweich Lectures, London, 1934

◆ Tordai (J.C.), Morris (H.): *Into the Promised Land*, Tordai (J.C.), Morris (H.) and Cornerhouse Publications, Manchester, 1991

◆ Weyl (M.): *Treasures of the Israel Museum*, Thames & Hudson, London (on behalf of Israel Museum, Jerusalem), 1985

◆ Wigoder (G.): *Jewish Art and Civilisation*, Seuil, New Jersey, 1972

◆ Literature ◆

◆ Agnon (S.Y.): *A dwelling place of my people, sixteen stories of the Chassidim*, trans. Weinberg (J.) and Russell (H.), Scottish Academic Press, Edinburgh, 1983

◆ Amichai (Y.): *Selected Poems*, trans. Bloch (C.) and Mitchell (S.), Penguin, Harmondsworth, 1983

◆ Appelfeld (A.): *The age of wonders*, trans. Bilu (D.), Quartet, London, 1993

◆ Appelfeld (A.): *The Immortal Bartfuss*, trans. Green (J.M.), Weidenfeld and Nicolson, London, 1990

◆ Badr (L.): *A Compass for the Sunflower*, trans. Cobham (C.), Women's Press, London, 1989

◆ Bellow (S.): *To Jerusalem and Back*, Secker & Warburg, London, 1970/

◆ Carmi (T.): *The brass serpent*, trans. Moraes (D.), André Deutsch, London, 1964

◆ Darwish (M.): *Memory for Forgetfulness – August, Beirut, 1982*, trans. Muhawi (I.), University of California Press, Berkeley, 1995

◆ Darwish: *The Music of Human Flesh*, ed. and trans. Johnson-Davies (D.), Heinemann, London, 1980

◆ Darwish (M.) and al-Qasim (S.): *Victims of a Map*, trans. al-Udhari (A.), Al Saqi Books, London, 1984

◆ Dor (M.) and Zach (N.) Eds.: *The Burning Bush, poems from modern Israel*, W.H. Allen, London, 1984

◆ Faqir (F.): *Nisanit*, Aidan Ellis Publishing Ltd., Nuffield, 1987

◆ Graves (R.): *King Jesus*, Cassell & Co., London, 1946

◆ Grossman (D.): *See under: Love*, trans. Rosenberg (B.), Pan in assoc. with Cape, London, 1991

◆ Habiby (E.): *The Secret life of Saeed – the pessoptimist*, trans. Jayyusi (S.K.) and Le Garsick (T.), Zed Books, London, 1985

◆ Jayyusi (S.K.) ed.: *An Anthology of Modern Palestinian Literature*, Columbia University Press, New York, 1992

◆ Kaniuk (Y.): *The*

Acrophile, trans. Shapiro (Z.), Chatto and Windus, London, 1961

◆ KANIUK (Y.): *Confessions of a good Arab*, trans. Bilu (D.), Halban, London, 1987

◆ KANIUK (Y.): *Himmo, king of Jerusalem*, trans. Shachter (Y.), Chatto and Windus, London, 1969

◆ KHALIFEH (S.): *Wild Thorns*, trans. Le Garsick (T.) and Fernea (E.), Al Saqi, London, 1985

◆ MEGGED (A.): *The Living on the Dead*, trans. Louvish (M.), Cape, London, 1970

◆ MEGGED (A.): *Fortunes of a fool*, trans. Hodes (A.), Victor Gollancz, London, 1962

◆ MELVILLE (H.): *Journal of a Visit of Egypt and the Levant*, Princeton University Press, Princeton, 1955

◆ MICHAEL (S.): *Refuge*, trans. Grossman (E.), Jewish Publication Society, Philadelphia, 1988

◆ MUHAWI (I.) AND KANAANA (S.) EDS.: *Speak bird, speak again: Palestinian Arab Folktales*, University of Calfornia Press, Berkeley, 1980

◆ OZ (A.): *Elsewhere, perhaps*, trans. de Lange (N.), Harcourt Brace Jovanovitch, New York, 1973

◆ OZ (A.): *My Michael*, trans. de Lange (N.), Chatto and Windus, London, 1972

◆ OZ (A.): *A Perfect Peace*, trans. Halkin (H.) Chatto and Windus, London, 1985

◆ OZ (A.): *Touch the water, touch the wind*, trans de Lange (N.), Chatto and Windus, London, 1975

◆ SHABTAI (Y.): *Past Continuous*, trans. Bilu (D.), Schocken Books, New York, 1985

◆ SHAHAR (D.): *News from Jerusalem*, trans. Bilu (D.), Houghton Mifflin, Boston, 1974 /

Elek, London, 1976

◆ SHAMMAS (A.): *Arabesques*, trans. Eden (V.), Viking, London, 1988

◆ SOBOL (J.): *Ghetto*, version by Lan (D.), Hern, London, 1989

◆ SPARK (M.): *The Mandelbaum Gate*, The Reprint Society, London, 1966

◆ TAMMUZ (B.): *Castle in Spain*, trans. Schachter (J.), Victor Gollancz, London, 1974

◆ TAMMUZ (B.): *Minotaur*, trans. Parfitt (K.) and Budny (M.), New American Library, New York 1981 / Enigma, London, 1983

◆ TWAIN (M.): *The Innocents Abroad or the New Pilgrims' Progress*, American Publishing Company, Hartford, 1895

◆ YEHOSHUA (A.B.): *A Late Divorce*, trans. Halkin (H.), Harvill, London, 1984

◆ YEHOSHUA (A.B.): *The Lover*, trans. Simpson (P.), Heinemann, London, 1979

◆ YEHOSHUA (A.B.): *Mr. Mani*, trans. Halkin (H.), Peter Halban, London, 1993

GRATEFUL ACKNOWLEDGEMENT IS MADE TO THE FOLLOWING FOR PERMISSION TO REPRINT PREVIOUSLY PUBLISHED MATERIAL:

◆ A & C BLACK (PUBLISHERS) LIMITED and LIVERIGHT: Excerpt from *Letters of Gertrude Bell* published by Ernest Benn Publishers Ltd, an imprint of A & C Black (Publishers) Ltd in 1929 Reprinted by permission of A & C Black (Publishers) Limited and Liveright in the US.

◆ GEORGES BORCHARDT, INC and LIVERIGHT: Excerpt from *The Mandelbaum Gate* by

Muriel Spark, copyright © 1965 by Copyright Administration Limited. Reprinted by permission of Georges Borchardt, Inc.

◆ THE CARCANET PRESS LIMITED: Excerpt from "Identity Card" from *Leaves of the Olive Tree* by Mahmoud Darwish, translated by I. Wedde and F. Tirqan, published 1973 by Carcanet Press Limited. Reprinted by permission.

◆ DEVIN-ADAIR, PUBLISHERS, INC.: Excerpt from *The Letters of Eric Gill*, edited by Walter Shewring (1947), copyright by Devin-Adair, Publishers Inc. Reprinted by permission of Devin-Adair, Publishers, Inc. Old Greenwich, CT 06870. All rights reserved.

◆ HARCOURT BRACE & COMPANY: Excerpt from *A Perfect Peace* by Amos Oz, copyright © 1982 by Amos Oz and Am Oved Publishers Ltd., Tel Aviv; English translation by Hillel Halkin copyright © 1985 by Amos Oz. Reprinted by permission of Harcourt Brace & Company.

◆ HARPERCOLLINS PUBLISHERS LTD.: Excerpt from *On the Shores of the Mediterranean* by Eric Newby (London: HarperCollins Publishers Ltd, 1984). Reprinted by permission of HarperCollins Publishers Ltd.

◆ HARPERCOLLINS PUBLISHERS INC.: "What Entanglement in This Small Country" from *Yehuda Amichai: A Life of Poetry 1948–1994* by Yehuda Amichai, copyright © 1994 by HarperCollins Publishers, Inc. Hebrew-language

version copyright © 1994 by Yehuda Amichai; excerpt from *Twelve Cities* by John Gunther, copyright © 1967, 1968, 1969 by John Gunther. Reprinted by permission of HarperCollins Publishers, Inc.

◆ HARVARD UNIVERSITY PRESS: Excerpt from *The Letters of Gustave Flaubert*, selected, edited and translated by Francis Steegmuller © 1979, 1980 by Francis Steegmuller. Reprinted by permission of the Belknap Press of Harvard University Press, Cambridge, MA.

◆ THE JEWISH PUBLICATION SOCIETY: Excerpt from *Past Continuous* by Yaakov Shabtai, translated by Dalya Bilu (1985). Reprinted by permission of the Jewish Publication Society.

◆ PETERS FRASER & DUNLOP GROUP LTD: Excerpt from *Labels – A Mediterranean Journey* by Evelyn Waugh (London: Duckworth, 1930). Reprinted by permission of Peters Fraser & Dunlop Group Ltd.

◆ PRINCETON UNIVERSITY PRESS: Excerpt from *Journal of a Visit to Europe and the Levant* by Herman Melville, copyright © 1955, copyright renewed 1983 by Princeton University Press. Reprinted by permission.

◆ REED CONSUMER BOOKS: Excerpt from *To Jerusalem and Back*, by Saul Bellow, published by Martin Secker & Warburg, London. Reprinted by permission of Reed Consumer Books.

◆ KING JAMES BIBLE: All Bible quotes in the book were taken from this version.

◆ LIST OF ILLUSTRATIONS

1 Jerusalem, Damascus Gate, anon. photo, early 20th century, priv. coll.

2–3 Jerusalem, the ramparts, anon. photo, early 20th century, priv. coll.

4–5 The village of Askar, east of Nablus, anon. photo, early 20th century, priv. coll.

6–7 Jaffa, the inner harbor, anon. photo, early 20th century, © École Biblique et Archéologique Française de Jerusalem.

9 Jerusalem, Dome of the Rock, photo, late 19th century, priv. coll.

16 D. Tal/Albatross (top), Z. Radovan (bottom and middle)

17 F. Bony/Gallimard (top)

18 P.J. Dubois/Gallimard

20 F. Bony/Gallimard

23 F. Bony/Gallimard

26 C. Rives/Ardoukoba-Visa

27 K. Amsler/Visa (top left), A. Folley/Visa (top right)

28 A. Fossi/ISR – Akko

29 A. Fossi/ISR – Yasour

30 Z. Radovan

32 D. Tal/Albatross (top and middle), R. Nowitz/Explorer (right), Z. Radovan (bottom left)

32–3 P. von Stroheim/Cosmos (background)

33 Z. Radovan (top right), A. Keler/Cosmos (top right), D. Halleux/Bios (middle), D. Tal/Albatross (right)

34 Z. Radovan

35 Map of the world with Jerusalem at the center in *Itinerarium Sacrae Scripturae* by H. Bünting, 1585, © Zev Radovan.

38 Terracotta figurines, 4000 BC, Museum of Israel, Jerusalem, © E. Lessing/Magnum. Terracotta house 2900–2290 BC, National Museum of Aleppo, Syria, © E. Lessing/Magnum.

39 The Temple of Jerusalem, illustration of a *haggadah*, German, 18th century, all rights reserved. Captive Jews on the road into exile, bas-relief from the palace of Sennacherib at Niniveh, Mesopotamia (Iraq), commemorating the capture of Lakshish, British Museum, London, © E. Lessing/Magnum.

40 *Jesus before the Sanhedrin*, painting, Flemish school, 15th century, Thomas Dobrée Museum, Nantes, France.

41 Constantine and Helen, ivory dyptich, Bibl. Nat., Paris.

42 Muslim warrior on a camel, Arab ms., Bibl. Nat., Paris. Arrival of the first British High Commissioner in Palestine, anon. photo © Institute of Palestinian Studies.

43 Illustration from cover of

Time, © L. de Selva/Tapabor. Sealing the Gaza/Jericho agreement, © J.L Atlan/Vu.

44 Canaanite weapons, British Museum, London. Canaanite jewelry, 1400–1300 BC, Israel Museum, Jerusalem.

44–5 Anthropomorphic vase, Jericho, 1300–1200 BC, Israel Museum, Jerusalem, © Zev Radovan.

45 Pottery, 600 BC, © Zev Radovan. Canaanite statues © E. Lessing/Magnum. Sarcophagus in human form from Deir el Balah, 1400–1300 BC, © Zev Radovan.

46 Map of twelve tribes of Israel by M. Servetius, 1530. all rights reserved. Model of Solomon's Temple, terracotta, Louvre, Paris, © R.M.N. David and Solomon, engraving by L. Spirito in *Libro de la Sorte e de la Ventura*, 16th century, Bibl. Nat. Marciana, Venice, © Giraudon.

47 Seal of a servant of Jeroboam, c. 1000 BC, © Zev Radovan. Black Obelisk from Salmanazar, British Museum, London. Attack and capture of Jerusalem by Nebuchadnezzar in *Beatus de Liebana*, c. 970, Seo de Urgel, © Lauros-Giraudon.

48 Galate warrior being trampled by an elephant, terracotta, middle of 2nd century BC., Myrina, Turkey, Louvre, Paris, © R.M.N. Episode from the history of the Maccabean brothers, 11th century Bible, Laurenziana lib., Florence, © Édimédia.

49 Priests, detail of a fresco from Doura Europos, 75 BC, National Museum, Damascus, © Dagli Orti. Coin from time of John Hyrcanus, all rights reserved.

50 Terracotta tile showing *Judea Capta*, 1st century AD, Ostie, © Tournus. Entrance of Herod and his army into Jerusalem by J. Fouquet, Bibl. Nat., Paris. Imperial quadriga, panel from the Arch of Titus, Rome, © Scala.

51 Coins from the era of Bar Kokhba, Israel Museum, Jerusalem. The Triumph of Titus, panel from the Arch of Titus, Rome, © Artephot. Bronze statue of the emperor Hadrian, Israel Museum, Jerusalem. *Haggadah* illuminated by J. de Leipnik, 18th century, Rosenthaliana Lib., Amsterdam.

52 Standard of Mohammed, miniature in a Turkish religious book, 19th century, Bibl. Nat., Paris. Caravan on the move, Arab ms., Bibl. Nat., Paris.

52–3 Jerusalem, Dome of the Rock, photo, end 19th century, priv. coll.

53 Pilgrims in front of the church of the Holy Sepulcher guarded by Saracens, miniature in *Le Livre des Merveilles*, Bibl. Nat., Paris. Baghdad, miniature by Matraqi in *Description of the military campaigns of Sultan Suleyman the Magnificent in the two Iraqs*, 1534, Library of Istanbul University, © R. & S. Michaud. Arab sailors, miniature in *Makamat* by al Hariri, 1222, Bibl. Nat., Paris.

54 Arms from the First Crusade in *Recueil de Blasons* by Ch. Gavard, 12th century, Musée du Château, C.ailles. Massacre of the Saracens, miniature in *Roman de Godefroy de Bouillon et de Saladin*, 14th century, Bibl. Nat., Paris. Godfrey of Bouillon leaving for the First Crusade, miniature in *Histoire d'outremer*, 13th century, Bibl. Munic., Boulogne-sur-Mer.

54–5 Death of Roger le Preux, miniature in *Roman de Godefroy de Bouillon et de Saladin*, 14th century, Bibl. Nat., Paris.

55 Saladin brandishing a sword and intimidating Christians, letter in *Secreta fidelium crucis*, 13th century, Bodleian Library, Oxford. The Horns of Hittim, miniature, Bibl. Nat., Paris. Saint Louis leaving for the Crusades, in *Vie et miracles de Saint-Louis*, Bibl. Nat., Paris.

56 Portrait of Théodor Herzl, anon. photo, priv. coll. Israeli postage stamp, 1994. Arab demonstration on the road to Amman against the Balfour Declaration © Roger-Viollet.

57 The ship "Jewish State" arriving at the port of Haifa, © Keystone. Declaration of the Independence of the State of Israel in 1948 by David Ben Gurion, © Keystone. Palestinian camp at Nahr el-Bared, © UNRWA. Palestinians expelled into the sea near Gaza, 1949, © UNRWA.

58 Letter in *Miscellanae de Hambourg*, parchment, 1477, Library of Hamburg University. Poster "Learn Hebrew for you and your Children", Lavon Institute, Tel Aviv, all rights reserved.

59 Hebrew/Arabic alphabet. Turkish school for children of Bedouin tribes around Beersheba, © Roger-Viollet.

60 Pupil at a Jewish agricultural school in Russia, 1920/1930, American Jewish Joint Distribution Committee, New York. With the permission of Bet Hatefutsot, Tel Aviv. "Hebrew", poster of the

cultural service of Tsahal, in the 1950s, all rights reserved.

62 Philistine beer jug, Musée Bible et Terre Sainte, © Tournus. Clay, © P. Léger. Pilgrim's gourd, Musée Bible et Terre Sainte, © Tournus. Poids, Musée Bible et Terre Sainte, © Tournus.

63 Women of Ramallah making pots, anon. photo, 1905, © Library of Congress D.C. Decorated jar, Museum of Mankind, London. Household pots from the Biblical period, © Zev Radovan.

65 Oil lamp, Roman period, Maritime Museum, Haifa, © E. Lessing/Magnum.

66 Palestinian woman, painting by A.-M. Esprit, 1914 priv. coll. Clothing, coll. Widad Kamel Kawar, Rautenstrauch-Joest-Museum, Cologne. Festival dress from Beit-Dajan, idem.

66–7 Festival dress found in Ramallah c. 1870, idem.

67 Palestinian women near the Dome of the Rock in Jerusalem, © W. Braun/Zefa. Bedouin headdress, c. 1930, coll. Widad Kamel Kawar, Rautenstrauch-Joest-Museum, Cologne. Embroidered cushions from Hebron, c. 1930, idem. Dress from Gaza, found c. 1910, idem.

68 Jewish wedding ring, gold and enamel, Venice, end 16th century, Musée de Cluny, Paris, © R.M.N. Gold filigree necklace, Israel Museum, Jerusalem, © D. Harris/Asap. Yemenite Jewish bride, © M. Hayaux du Tilly. Stone necklaces, Bronze Age, Israel Museum, Jerusalem, © E. Lessing/Magnum.

68–9 Gold necklace from Tunisia, Hechal Shlomo Museum, Jerusalem, © D. Harris/Asap.

69 Gold Bedouin nose rings, coll. Widad Kamel Kawar, Rautenstrauch-Joest-Museum, Cologne. Gold earrings from Boukhara, Hechal Shlomo Museum, Jerusalem, © D. Harris/Asap. Palestinian collar, coll. Widad Kamel Kawar, Rautenstrauch-Joest-Museum, Cologne. Gold filigree earrings from Kurdistan, Hechal Shlomo Museum, Jerusalem, © D. Harris/Asap. Bedouin woman from Sinai, © M. Bar'Am/Magnum.

70 Shofar player, all rights reserved. Musician, © M. Hayaux du Tilly.

70–1 *The Jewish Orchestra*, painting by Mani Katz, 20th century, coll. privée, © Édimédia.

71 Traditional instruments in *L'Encyclopédie* by D. Diderot

and J. d'Alembert, 18th century, © Édimédia.
David playing the psalterion, miniature, 9th century, Bibl. Nat., Paris, © Édimédia.
Musicians on a kibbutz, © R. Capa/Magnum.
72 *Dance around the Golden cow*, painting by N. Bertin (1668–1736), Musée des Beaux-Arts, Quimper, © Giraudon.
Jewish Yemenite dancer © M. Hayaux du Tilly.
73 Soufis in extacy, miniature moghole, 17th century © R. & S. Michaud.
Bedouin dance at Sina, anon. photo, end 19th century, École Biblique et Archéologique Française de Jerusalem. Israeli dance, © D. Seymour/Magnum.
74 Rite of Seder in *Haggadah Ashkenazi*, Hebrew ms, 15th century British Library, London. Stages in the preparation of pita, © É. Guillemot.
75 Arab market in the Old City of Jerusalem, © F.Mayer/Magnum. Stages in the preparation of challah, © É. Guillemot.
76 Olive trees in Samaria, © Zev Radovan. Ancient olive press, © S. Nick. Stone olive press, © Zev Radovan. Wooden press, © Zev Radovan. Olive market. © S. Grandadam.
Women of Ramallah pressing olives, anon. photo early 20th century, all rights reserved.
78 *The Story of Abraham*, painting by Shalom de Safed, 20th century, Israel Museum, Jerusalem, © R. Terry.
The transmission of the Torah, *Haggadah*, German, 15th century, Israel Museum, Jerusalem.
Scroll of Ester, Italian, 1620, © Zev Radovan.
79 Ancient scroll of the Torah, © G. Nalbandian/Asap. Talmudist, postcard, early 20th century, priv. coll.
The Prophet Elijah, painting by Sassetta (1423-1426), National Gallery of Sienna, © A. Held/Artephot.
80 Seder rite in *Haggadah Ashkenazi*, Hebrew ms., 15th century, British Library, London.
Poster for the festival of Purim, 1930, Israel Museum, Jerusalem. Jerusalem, Festival of Succot, © L. Goldman/R.N.Y./Rapho.
81 Woman with a Zionist banner, chromolithograph, New-York, 1905, © N. Feuillie/M.A.H.J.
Jerusalem, the Wailing Wall, photo, early 20th century, © Roger-Violet.
A Menorah, Hebrew Bible, 1299. National Library, Lisbon, © Dagli Orti.
Calendar of Umer, Pologne,

1866, Israel Museum, Jerusalem, © L.-Y. Loirat/Explorer.
Two rabbis, *Haggadah*, 15th century, Bibl. Palatine, Parma, © Dagli Orti.
83 School in the Mea Shearim quarter in Jerusalem, © Magnum. Immigrants, 1948, © R. Capa/Magnum. Orthodox Jews in Jerusalem, © G. Sioen/Rapho.
84 *Christ teaching Nicodemus*, painting by J. Jordaens, 17th century, Musée des Beaux-Arts, Tournai, © Giraudon.
The altar of Saint Peter, painting on wood, Spain, 13th cenruty, Museum of Catalan Art, Barcelona, © Giraudon.
84–5 Canon of the evangelists, Evangelist of Saint Médard de Soissons, Bibl. Nat., Paris.
The four evangelists, detail of frontispiece of codex no. 3, 12th century, Greek Patriarcate, Istanbul, © M. Babey/Artephot.
85 Aramean inscription "Jésus", sarcophagus, 1st century AD, Israel Museum, Jerusalem, © E. Lessing/ Magnum.
Paul the Apostle, Rembrandt, 17th century, Louvre, Paris, © R.M.N.
Jerusalem, detail of the mosaic of Madaba, 6th century, Jordan, © E. Lessing/Magnum.
Crusader, fresco from Minutolo Chapel, detail, 14th century, Dome of Naples, © Roger-Violet.
86 Pilgrims in Bethlehem on Christmas Day, photo, end 19th century, © Bonfils.
Jerusalem, procession of the Cross, © L. Goldman/Rapho. The flames of the true faith, © M. Milner.
87 *The Assumption of the Virgin*, painting by Ph. de Champaigne, 17th century, Musée des Beaux-Arts, Marseilles, © Giraudon.
The Ascension, painting on wood by A. Mantegna, 15th century, Uffizi Gallery, Florence, © Alinari-Giraudon.
The Transfiguration, painting on wood by A. Roublev, 1405, coll. of the Cercle de l'art, Moscow, © Édimedia
Pentecost, miniature in *Heures à l'usage de Rome*, 16th century, château d'Écouen, © Giraudon.
88 Orthodox priest in a church, © S. Grandadam/ Fotogram-Stone.
89 Russian Orthodox priests in Jerusalem, © M. Bertinetti/Rapho.
Martin Luther, painting anon., 1561, National Museum, Copenhagen, © Dagli Orti. Portrait of a Maronite priest, anon. photo, end 19th century, © Édimédia.

Ethiopian Christian in Jerusalem, © F. Mayer/ Magnum.
90 The Angel Gabriel, Turkish miniature, 15th century Topkapi Museum, Istanbul © R. & S. Michaud. Mohammed, Turkish miniature, 18th century, Topkapi Museum, Istanbul, © Mandel/Artephot.
90–1 Koran, Egyptian ms. 16th century, © J.-L. Charmet.
91 Hadith of Mohammed, Persian ms., 16th century, Bibl. Nat., Paris.
Sanctuary at Medina, Iranian ms., 16th century, Israel Museum, Jerusalem. *Prayer in the Mosque*, painting by Bartolini, © ACR Éditions.
The *shahada*, Turkish ceramic plaque, 16th–17th century, Museum of Islamic Art, Cairo, © Giraudon.
Mecca, © Arikan/Sipa Press
92 Birth of the Prophet, Persian miniature, 16th century, © S. Halliday. Perpetual calendar from the Ottoman period. © Savel/ IMA, Paris.
92–3 Calligraphy of the word Mohammed, all rights reserved.
Jerusalem, Muslim festival in front of the Dome of the Rock © D.Harris/Asap.
93 Arab horsemen, miniature in *Les Séances d'al-Hariri*, 1237, Bibl. Nat., Paris. Meal, Idem.
Mohammed's ride from Mecca to Jerusalem, Persian ms., 1494, British Library, London. Sacrifice of a sheep. © M. Bar'Am/Magnum.
94 Lineage of the Prophet, Persian miniature, Bibl. Nat., Paris.
The enemies of the faith, fresco, Ispahan, Iran, © Dagli-Orti.
94–5 Druzes of Mount Carmel, photo, end 19th century, © Roger-Violet.
95 Palestinian, © L. Freed/ Magnum. Center of Shi'ite studies in Qum, Iran, © Abbas/ Magnum.
132 Pioneers constructing a kibbutz, anon. photo, early 20th century, priv. coll.
133 Idem.
135 David Roberts drawing, lithograph, Victoria & Albert Museum Library, London.
136 *The Jewish Wedding*, painting by Mani Katz, 20th century, priv. coll, © Édimédia.
136–7 *Orange Market in Jaffa*, painting by F. Brangwyn, Jaffa, 1893, © ACR Éditions.
137 *The Crowd*, painting by S. Mansour, 1985, © Ph. Maillard/IMA, Paris. *Street Scene in Jaffa*, detail, painting by G. Bauernfeind, © Mathaf Gallery, London.

138–9 *Temple Mount*, painting by N. Gutman, priv. coll.
140 Celestial Jerusalem, Bible, 12th century, National Library, Madrid.
At the Gates of Jerusalem, painting by M. Ardon, 1967, Israel Museum, Jerusalem, © Dagli Orti.
141 *Gethsemane*, detail, tempera on wood by A. Mantegna, 15th century, National Gallery, London, © Faillet/Artephot.
142 *The Western Wall*, painting by J.-L. Gérôme, priv. coll, © ACR Éditions. *Bethlehem*, painting by H.D. S. Corrodi, 19th century, priv. coll, © Édimédia.
143 Portrait of J.-L. Gérôme, anon. photo, end 19th century, © ACR Éditions.
144 M. Chagall, 1934, © Lipnitzki/Viollet. Tapestry from the Gobelins after a drawing by M. Chagall, 1964, © Lauros-Giraudon.
145 Young European immigrants, © R. Capa/Magnum.
147 Mount Sinai, engraving, 19th century. all rights reserved.
148 *The Angel pointing out Jerusalem to Saint John*, engraving by G. Doré, 19th century.
Crusader paying hommage, British Library, London.
150 *Jesus preaching on the Lake of Gennesaret*, engraving by G. Doré, 19th century.
151 Absalom's tomb in Jerusalem, photo, early 20th century, priv. coll.
152–3 Miniature by Loyset Liédet in *Chronicle of the Emperors* by D. Aubert, 15th century, Bibl. de l'Arsenal, Paris, © J. Vigne.
154 Promenade at a "Victoria", engraving, early 20th century, © L'Illustration/ Sygma
154–5 The Wailing Wall, anon. photo, early 20th century, priv. coll.
156–7 Immigrants arriving at the port of Haifa, 1948, © Keystone
160, © C. Tordai.
161 *The Mosque of Omar*, lithograph by D. Roberts, Victoria & Albert Museum Library, London.
162, © S. Grandadam.
162–3, © S. Grandadam.
163, © Zev Radovan.
164–5, © Duby Tal/Albatross, Tel Aviv.
166, © Duby Tal/Albatross, Tel Aviv.
167 *Mount Sinai*, painting by L. Bonnat, Musée Francisque Mandet, Riom.
168 *Moses and the Ten Commandments*, lithograph by M. Chagall, 1956, priv. coll, © Édimédia/Archives

Loudmer. The Hebrews enslaved, pentateuch said to be from Tours, 7th century, Bibl. Nat., Paris, © Édimédia. Moses and the burning bush, miniature in *Le Psautier de Saint-Louis*, 13th century, Bibl. Nat., Paris.

168–9 The Exodus of the Jewish people in *Haggadah Ashkenazi*, British Library, London.

169 Moses and Pharoah, the plagues of Egypt, Mozarabe Bible, 10th century, Bibl. San Isidoro, Leon, © Dagli Orti. Enamel cross, detail, attributed to G. Clare de Huy, 12th century, British Museum, London, © Édimédia. Parting of the Red Sea, miniature in *Rylands Haggadah*.

170 Moses receiving the Ten Commandments, Charles le Chauve Bible, early 9th century, Bibl. Nat., Paris, © Édimédia. *Moses on Mount Sinai*, painting by Rosselli, 15th century, Cistine Chapel, Vatican, © Giraudon. *Adoration of the golden cow*, painting by L. van Leyden, Rijksmuseum, Amsterdam.

171 *Moses making water spring from a rock*, painting by F. Lippi, 15th century, National Gallery, London, © Édimédia. *Gathering manna from Heaven*, painting by Maître de la manne, 15th century, Musée de la Chartreuse, Douai, France, © Giraudon.

172 Bedouins of the Sinai, © Zefa.

172–3 *Approach to Mount Sinai*, lithograph by D. Roberts, Victoria & Albert Museum Library, London.

174 Saint Catherine's monastery, © G. Degeorge. Saint Catherine's monastery, detail, © G. Degeorge. Saint Catherine's library, detail, © N. Levallois.

174–5 *The Monastery of Saint Catherine on Mount Sinai*, painting by A. Dauzats, 19th century, Louvre, Paris, © R.M.N.

175 Greek Orthodox monks. © M. Hayaux du Tilly. The monks' quarters. © M. Hayaux du Tilly. Saint Catherine, Saint-Simeon

176 Saint Catherine, © M. Hayaux du Tilly.

176–7 View of the Oasis, © Roger-Viollet.

177 Sinai, Wadi Feiran. © W. Braun/Zefa.

178 Bedouin woman from Sinai, © M. Hayaux du Tilly. Sinai, near Dahab, © J.-P. Ferrero/Explorer.

179 *The Red Sea*, painting by J.-L. Gérôme, Musée Georges Garret, Vesoul. Bedouin fisherman. © J.-P. Ferrero/Explorer.

180 The Red Sea, coral island, © Zefa. *The Members of the Expedition*, watercolor by W. de Famars Testas, Rijksmuseum van Oudheden, Leyde.

181, © Zefa.

182 Fish from the Red Sea, © Sunset.

183 Idem. The Gulf of Aqaba, © U. Kluyver/Zefa.

184 The pillars of Amram, © C. Fouré. Timna, © M. Hayaux du Tilly. Timna Park, "The mushroom" © C. Sappa/Rapho.

186–7 Crater at Mitzpeh Ramon, © F. Bony.

187 Agriculture, © J. Thomas/Explorer.

188 Nabatean coins, Museum of Aman, Musée Bible et Terre Sainte, Paris, © Tournus. British Museum, London. Detail of a lithograph by D. Roberts, Victoria & Albert Museum Library, London.

189 Petra, Temple of Deir. © Fotogram-Stone. Bedouin horseman at the entrance of a tomb, © D. Hanson/Fotogram-Stone. Temple of El-Khazneh, lithograph by D. Roberts, Victoria & Albert Museum Library, London. Nabatean cup, Museum of Aman.

190 Citadel of Avdat, all rights reserved. Nabatean leopard, all rights reserved.

191 Nabatean jewelry, all rights reserved. Basilica at Shivta, all rights reserved. Baptistry, all rights reserved.

192 Ein Avdat, © F. Bony. D. Ben Gurion at Sdeh Boker kibbutz, 1961. all rights reserved.

193 Bedouin woman, © Lipnitzki/Rapho.

194 Generations in the lap of Abraham, letter, Bible de Souvigny, 12th century, Bibl. Munic., Moulins, © Lauros-Giraudon. Vocation d'Abraham, miniature in *Le Miroir de l'Humaine Salvation*, 15th century, Musée Condé, Chantilly, © Lauros-Giraudon. Sara and Hagar, miniature in *Chronique Unic.elle* de R. von Ems, 13th century, Faksimile Verlag, Lucerne

195 *Éliezer et Rébecca*, painting de A. Coypel (1661–1722), Louvre, Paris, © R.M.N. *Lot and his daughters*, painting by L. de Leyde, 16th century, Louvre, Paris, © Édimédia.

196 Modern Beersheba, © M. Bar'Am/Magnum.

197 Bedouin market, © L.-Y. Loirat/Explorer. The Beersheba Memorial, sculpture by D. Karavan,

© D. Rubinger.

198 Bedouin nomad grinding coffee, © Roger-Viollet. Negev shepherd, © C. Tordai.

199 Tel Arad, © G. Degeorge. *The brass serpent*, painting by P.-H. Subleyras, 18th century, Musée des Beaux-Arts, Nîmes, © Giraudon.

200 The Dead Sea, © C. Sappa/Rapho. The Dead Sea, near Sodom, "Lot's wife", © Zefa

201 Mud baths, © G. Sioen/Rapho, © Martin H./Vloo. Beach at Ein Gedi. © P. Wysocki/Explorer. The Dead Sea, anon. photo, end 19th century, © J. Vigne.

202 Coin from the first revolt, showing the ritual chalice, Musée Bible et Terre Sainte, Paris.

210 Ein Gedi Kibbutz, © L.-Y. Loirat/Explorer.

211 Nubian ibex, © G. Lacz/Sunset. Ein Gedi Kibbutz © G. Sioen/Rapho. Cactus plantation, © P. Wysocki/Explorer. Oasis of Nahal David, © S. Grandadam.

212 Pitcher with silver tetradrachmas, © É. Puech. "The office" near the dining room, © Idem.

212–3 Aerial view of the site of Qumran, © Zev Radovan.

213 The rules of the community, also known as the "Manual of Discipline", scroll from cave no. 1, Israel Museum, Jerusalem. Pick, bowl, © É. Puech. The *mikveh*, © Idem. Piece of alphabet, © Idem. Ink well, Roman period, © Zev Radovan.

214 Interior of cave no. 1, © Zev Radovan. Qumran, © É. Puech. The first columns of the scroll of Isiah, cave no. 1, c. 100 BC., House of Books, Israel Museum, Jerusalem.

215 Earthen jar for holding manuscripts, from cave no. 1, © D. Harris/Asap. Copper scrolls, © É. Puech. Fragment of the Book of Psalms, c. 30-50 BC, parchment found in cave no. 2. all rights reserved.

216–7 The oak of Mambre, miniature, Bibl. Nat., Paris. *Consecration of King David*, painting of the Amiens school, 15th century, Musée de Cluny, Paris, © Giraudon.

216–7 *The Adoration of the Magi*, painting by A. Dürer, Uffizi Gallery, Florence, © Artephot.

217 *Summer, or Ruth and Boaz*, painting by N. Poussin, 17th century, Louvre, Paris, © Lauros-Giraudon. *Nativity*, painting on wood, 15th century, Musée de la Chartreuse, Douai, © Giraudon.

218 "The General

Organization of Hebrew Workers", propaganda poster, 1948, all rights reserved.

219 Bedouins in the Negev, photo, early 20th century, priv. coll.

220 Noah in *The Bible*, film by J. Huston, 1966. © Christophe L. The village of Der Samet, © Zev Radovan.

220–1 *Hebron*, lithograph by D. Roberts, Victoria & Albert Museum Library, London.

221 The oak of Mambre, photo, early 20th century, © Roger-Viollet. Abraham in *La Bible*, film by J. Huston, 1966, © Ciné +.

222 Muslim dignitaries talking in the courtyard of the Ibrahimi Mosque in Hebron, 1947, priv. coll.

223 Threshing corn, anon. photo, early 20th century, Library of Congress, Washington D.C. Women weaving near Hebron, © Zev Radovan.

226 *Massacre des Innocents*, painting by P. Brueghel le Jeune (1564–1636), Musée Munic., Lons-le-Saulnier, © Lauros-Giraudon.

226–7 Bethlehem, photo, end 19th century, priv. coll.

227 Saint Brasius, fresco in the Church of the Nativity in Bethlehem. All rights reserved.

228 Bethlehem, photo, end 19th century, priv. coll. *Shatwas*, headdresses of the women of Bethlehem, coll. Widad Kamel Kawar, Rautenstrauch-Joest-Museum, Cologne. Women of Bethlehem, © M. Hayaux du Tilly.

229 Herod, illumination by J. Fouquet in *Antiquités judaïques*, 15th century, Bibl. Nat., Paris.

230 Monastery of Mar Saba, © Zev Radovan. Monks, photo, early 20th century, © Harlingue-Viollet.

231 Jerusalem in the 7th century, Byzantine mosaic, © H. Champollion/Top.

234 The story of David, painted tablet by H.S. Beham, 16th century, Louvre, Paris, © R.M.N. King David and the Ark of the Covenant, Venetian psalter, 12th century, Bibl. Communale, Mantoue, © Dagli Orti.

235 Offering God the first fruits of the harvest, manuscript, Bibl. de l'Arsenal, Paris, © Artephot. Celestial Jerusalem, miniature in *L'Apocalypse* by Saint Jean de Lorvao, arch. nat. de Torre do Tombo, Lisbon, © Giraudon. Sultan Umar ordering the Temple of Jerusalem to be rebuilt, miniature in *History of the Conquest of Jerusalem* by G. of Tyre, 15th century, Bibl. Nat., Paris, © Giraudon.

236 *The Sacrifice of Abraham*, enamel plaque, 12th century, Louvre, Paris, © Giraudon.

236–7 Miniature in *Commentaire de l'Apocalypse de Beatus*, 11th century, Bibl. Nat., Paris.

237 *Jacob's Dream*, painting by J. W. Baur, 17th century, Kunstmuseum, Bâle, © Giraudon.

238 *Jesus and the officials of the Temple*, painting by Duccio, 13th century, mus. de l'Opera Metropolitana, Sienne, © Scala.

Jesus healing the blind man, fresco, Capoue, © Fabbri/Artephot.

The entrance to Jerusalem, Armenian ms., 13th century, © Édimédia.

238–9 *The Last Supper*, painting by Ph. de Champaigne, 17th century, Louvre, Paris, © Giraudon. Jerusalem, miniature, Bibl. Nat., Paris.

239 *The Last Judgement*, painting of the Sienna School, 14th century, Musée des Beaux-Arts, Angers, © Lauros-Giraudon.

240 Tapestry, 1510, Saint Vincent Church, Châlon-sur-Saône, © Lauros-Giraudon. King David, Amiens School, c. 1500, Musée de Cluny, © Édimédia.

241 Saint Constantine, Saint Helena Saint Agatha, Russian icon, Icon Museum, Recklinghausen, © Lauros-Giraudon.

Crusader seal of Jerusalem showing the Holy Sepulcher, the Dome of the Rock and the Citadel. © Zev Radovan.

C. Heston in *Ben Hur*, film by W. Wyler, 1959, © Cat's.

242 Crusader map of Jerusalem, 12th century, © Zev Radovan. Portrait of Suleyman the Magnificent, painting by Titian, 16th century, Innsbruck Museum, © E. Lessing/Magnum. Journey of Wilhelm II to Jerusalem, diary of 11/2/1898, priv. coll, © J.-L. Charmet.

243 Jerusalem divided. © L. Freed/Magnum. Entrance of General Allenby to Jerusalem, 11 Dec. 1917, photo anon, priv. coll.

244 *Tughra* of Suleyman, 1552, Library of Topkapi Museum, Istanbul, © J. Hyde. Portrait of Suleyman, c. 1579, Library of Topkapi Museum, Istanbul, © J. Hyde.

247 Wilhelm's carriage, © Zev Radovan.

254 Studio of the photographer C. Raad at Jaffa Gate, photo, early 20th

century, priv. coll. Jerusalem, the Tower of David, photo, early 20th century, © Roger-Violet.

255 The Cardo, © S. Grandadam. Muslim trader in the Old City. © J.-P. Ferrero/Explorer. Tailor's shop, © H. Champollion/Top. Street trading, photo, early 20th century, © Roger-Violet.

256 Typical Jewish home at the start of the century. © Zev Radovan.

256–7 Ruins of the Hurva Synagogue, © H. Champollion/Top.

257 Interior of the synagogue, painting by K. J. Polak, Israel Museum, Jerusalem, © Dagli Orti. *The Talmudist*, painting by B. Borvine Frenkel, 1970, priv. coll, © Édimédia.

258–9 Detail of the Wailing Wall, © S. Grandadam. The Wailing Wall, photo, early 20th century, © Roger-Violet.

259 Women praying, anon. photo, early 20th century, priv. coll.

260 Greek inscription forbidding non-Jews to enter the Temple, 4th century BC, Rockefeller Museum, Jerusalem, © E. Lessing/Magnum.

264 Christ's entrance to Jerusalem, miniature, 12th–13th century, Armenian Museum, Ispahan, © Giraudon. The Armenian quarter, priest in a library. © L. Freed/Magnum.

265 Mosaic from the Cathedral of St James © H. Champollion/Top. Interior of the Cathedral of St James, © G. Nalbandian/Asap. Courtyard in the Armenian quarter, © D. Harris/Asap.

266 St Stephen's Gate, photo, early 20th century, © Roger-Violet. View of Jerusalem in 1900, © Zev Radovan.

267 Model of the fortress of Antonia, © Zev Radovan. Arch of *Ecce Homo*, lithograph, 1864, all rights reserved. Bone dice from the Roman period, © Zev Radovan. The Via Dolorosa, photo anon., 1905, priv. coll.

268–1 Icon, all rights reserved. The Crucifixion, all rights reserved. Jesus is placed on the cross, all rights reserved. Veronica, all rights reserved. Jesus is condemned to crucifixion, all rights reserved. Jesus carries the cross, all rights reserved. Jesus falls for the first time, all rights reserved. Jesus meets his mother, all rights reserved. Jesus is helped by Simon

of Cyrene, all rights reserved. Jesus falls for the second time, all rights reserved. Jesus consoles the women of Jerusalem, all rights reserved. Jesus falls for the third time, all rights reserved. Jesus is stripped of his clothes, all rights reserved. Jesus is placed on the cross, all rights reserved. Jesus dies, all rights reserved. Jesus taken down from the cross is placed in his mother's arms, all rights reserved. Jesus is placed in the tomb, all rights reserved.

274 Panorama of Jerusalem on the day of the Crucifixion, drawing, 19th century, coll. R. Bornecque.

276 Ethiopian monk, © I. Talby/Rapho. The Muristan and the Church of the Redemption, anon. photo, 1905, priv. coll.

277 Harvesting olives, © S. Grandadam. The Jewish cemetery on the Mount of Olives, © S. Grandadam. The Garden of Gethsemane, painting by E. Lear, 19th century, priv. coll.

278 The Church of St Mary Magdalene on the Mount of Olives, © D. Harris/Asap.

278–9 Procession on Palm Sunday on the Mount of Olives

279 Absalom's tomb, watercolor by J. Clark, 19th century, Palestine Exploration Fund, London. Postcard produced during the visit of Wilhelm II to the holy places, 1898, priv. coll.

280 Damascus Gate, photo, early 20th century, © Roger-Violet. Water carrier, anon. photo, early 20th century, © Zev Radovan.

281 The souks of Jerusalem, © S. Grandadam, © S. Grandadam/Fotogram-Stone, © J.-M. Truchet/Fotogram-Stone, © T. Boulley/Fotogram-Stone, © B. Lewis/Network/Rapho, © R. Burri/Magnum.

282 Fountain opposite the Dome of the Rock. © Zev Radovan. Minbar, photo, early 20th century, © Roger-Violet.

282–3 Mosque of Umar, lithograph by D. Roberts, Victoria & Albert Museum Library, London.

283 El-Aqsa Mosque, photo, end 19th century, priv. coll. Wooden panel carved in the Omayyad period from El Aqsa Mosque, Rockefeller Museum, Jerusalem, © Zev Radovan.

284 The Dome of the Rock. © N. Beer/Fotogram-Stone. The Rock seen from the Dome, © G. Nalbandian/Asap.

288 *Wilson's Arch*, watercolor

by W. Simpson, 1869, Palestine Exploration Fund, London. Cisterns carved out of rock beneath Robinson's Arch, 1871, idem.

288–9 The village of Silwan, photo, early 20th century, © Roger-Violet.

289 Interior of a house in Silwan, watercolor by J. Clark, 1886, Palestine Exploration Fund, London. Idem. Rachel's tomb, anon. photo, early 20th century, priv. coll.

290 Jerusalem Street, watercolor by J. Clark, 1886, Palestine Exploration Fund, London. The Montefiore windmill, © G. Sioen/Top. Portrait of E. Ben Yehuda, Ben Dov archives, Israel Museum, Jerusalem.

291 Mezzuza, © J. L'Hoir/M.A.H.J., Paris. Front page of the *Jerusalem Post*, © P. Léger.

292 The Queen of Sheba in Jerusalem, Abyssinian painting, coll. R. Pankhurst, © E. Tweedy. Shopfront in Mea Shearim, © T. spiegel/Rapho.

292–3 *Jerusalem, moments in time*, © F. Brenner/Rapho.

293 Mea Shearim quarter, © Zev Radovan. Wrought iron *khamsa*, © D. Kroyanker/Asap. *Jerusalem, moments in time*, © F. Brenner/Rapho.

294 General Allenby, © L'Illustration/Sygma. The YMCA tower, © Asap.

295 Jerusalem station, photo early 20th century, © Roger-Violet. A Jerusalem market, © S. Stone/Fotogram-Stone. Clock on the front of a house, © Zev Radovan.

296 Laying of the first stone of the Hebrew University of Jerusalem, 1924, photo anon., priv. coll.

296–7 Hebrew University of Jerusalem, © R. Milon/Asap.

297 Debate in the Knesset, © M. Milner/Sygma. Ceramic tiles on Nashabishi House, © D. Kroyanker/Asap.

298 The Shrine of the Book, © P. Wysocki/Explorer. Sennacherib's prism, 691 BC, © E. Lessing/Magnum. Rothschild Manuscript, 15th century, Israel Museum, Jerusalem. Sceptre in the shape of an ibex, 4000 BC., Israel Museum, Jerusalem, © E. Lessing/Magnum.

299 Detail of a painted strip of the Torah, German, 1792, Israel Museum, Jerusalem, © Dagli Orti. Bronze mirror, Late Bronze Age, Israel Museum,

Jerusalem, © E. Lessing/Magnum.

Gold pendant, Late Bronze Age, Israel Museum, Jerusalem, © E. Lessing/Magnum.

A Village, painting by Egon Schiele, 20th century, Israel Museum, Jerusalem, © E. Lessing/Magnum.

300 Sculpture by Calder, © A. Parinet/Explorer. © S. Grandadam.

Warrior, sculpture by A. Bourdelle, © A. Picou/Fotogram-Stone. © S. Grandadam.

300–1 View of the Sculpture Garden, Israel Museum, Jerusalem.

301 Ascension, sculpture by O. Freundlich, Israel Museum, Jerusalem.

302 Cover of book by T. Herzl, priv. coll. Portrait of T. Herzl, anon. photo, priv. coll. Monument to the victims of the holocaust, © S. Grandadam.

303 Russian Orthodox Monastery, © F. Mayer/Magnum. Aerial view of Mount Herzl, © D. Tal/Albatross.

304 Signature of M. Chagall, © Roger-Violet. Window by M. Chagall, Hadassah Synagogue, Jerusalem, © D. Harris/Asap.

305 Idem.

306 Sheep market. © H. Champollion/Top.

307 The Garden Tomb, © Zev Radovan. Father Lagrange in Jerusalem, anon. photo, 1890, École Biblique et Archéologique Française de Jerusalem. Stonemasons in Jerusalem, photo, end 19th century, priv. coll.

308 The American Colony in Jerusalem, photo, 1919, Musée Albert Kahn, Boulogne-Billancourt. Mosaic from the American Colony, © G. Degeorge.

308–9 Head of a bull, terracotta, 1500-1200 BC., Rockefeller Museum, Jerusalem, © E. Lessing/Magnum.

309 Paintings celebrating return from pilgrimage to Mecca, © D. Kroyanker/Asap. Head of a Crusader, 14th century, Rockefeller Museum, Jerusalem, © E. Lessing/Magnum.

311 Traditional agriculture, © Zev Radovan. Harvesting olives, anon. photo, early 20th century, priv. coll.

312 Entrance of Nablus, lithograph by D. Roberts, Victoria & Albert Museum Library, London. Soap-making in Nablus, anon. photo, early 20th century,

priv. coll. "The Samaritans, Palestinian guardians of Jewish Law" © C. Le Tourneur/GLMR.

313 Idem. Roman colonnade in Samaria, photo, early 20th century, © Roger-Violet.

314 Jericho, photo, end 19th century, priv. coll. Jericho, © D. Rubinger/Rapho. © Zev Radovan.

315 Palestinian refugee camp at Ein el Sultan, © UNRWA. Palestinian exodus, © UNRWA. The Tree of Hell © S. Zeghidour.

316 The tell, © J.–O. Héron. Wall of Jericho, all rights reserved. Tower of Jericho, all rights reserved.

316–317 Skull covered in clay, all rights reserved.

317 View of the Tell of Jericho, all rights reserved. Skull covered in clay, all rights reserved. Rectangular dwelling, all rights reserved.

318 Detail of the palace of Hisham, © Domitille Héron. Colonnades of the palace of Hisham, all rights reserved.

319 View of Qasr Hisham, © J.–B. Héron. Mosaics in the baths, © J.–B. Héron. Diwan, © Domitille Héron. Omayyad décor, all rights reserved.

320 Human figure, © Zev Radovan.

321 Human figures, © Zev Radovan. The tree of life, all rights reserved.

322 St George's Monastery, © S. Grandadam.

323 Monk of St George's Monastery, © C. Harbutt/Rapho. St George's Monastery, © F. Bony. Mosque of Nabi Musa, © C. Fouré. Idem. Day of pilgrimage at Nabi Musa, École Biblique et Archéologique Française de Jerusalem.

324 The Revenge of Samson, painting by J.-G. Platzer, 18th century, Oesterreichische Galerie, Vienne, © E. Lessing/Magnum. The Ark of the Covenant falls into the hands of the Philistines, miniature, Bibl. Nat., Paris.

324–5 King David bringing the Ark of the Covenant to Jerusalem, fresco by L. Ademollo, 18th century-19th century, Galerie Pitti, Florence, © Dagli Orti.

325 The Pilgrims of Emmaus, painting by Rembrandt, 17th century, Louvre, Paris, © Giraudon. Baptism of the Ethiopian eunuch by Philip, painting by L. Sustris, 16th century, Louvre, Paris, © Giraudon. God granting victory,

miniature, Bibl. Nat., Paris.

326 Roman, © J.–O. Héron.

327 The village of Abu Gosh, anon. photo, early 20th century, priv. coll.

328 Fresco at Abu Gosh, all rights reserved.

329 Idem.

330 Railway in the Soreq Valley. All rights reserved. Vines, © T. Spiegel/Rapho.

331 The cycles of sowing and harvesting carved on a stele, © Zev Radovan. King David, film by B. Beresford, 1985, © Ciné +. Jewish tomb, © M. Hayaux du Tilly.

332 Battle of Lachish, 701 BC., bas-relief from the palace of Sennacherib at Nineveh, Mesopotamia (Iraq), British Museum, London, © E. Lessing/Magnum. Ashkelon, ruins of the Roman Agora, © Dagli Orti.

333 Crouching cat, ivory figurine from the temple of Lachish, 15th–13th century BC., Rockefeller Museum, Jerusalem, © E. Lessing/Magnum. Ashkelon, the excavations. © G. Degeorge. Hellenistic statue, © G. Degeorge.

334 Uncovering sarcophagi from the 14th–13th centuries BC, © Zev Radovan. Detail of a floor mosaic from the synagogue at Gaza, 4th century AD, © Zev Radovan.

334–5 Ahmed Mosque, c. 1914, École Biblique et Archéologique Française de Jerusalem.

335 Poster, © A. Gesgon/Cirip. Gaza, © C. Tordai. © G. Degeorge. Painting by T. Barakat, IMA, Paris.

336 Fisherman near Gaza, © UNRWA. Fish market, © S. Nick. Fisherman from Gaza, © S. Nick.

337 Bauhaus style building, all rights reserved.

339 Jonah swallowed by the whale, Hebrew Bible, 1299, Lisbon nat. lib, © Giraudon. Jaffa, engraving by D. H. Bartlett, 19th century, © Édimédia. Jaffa, photo, early 20th century, © Roger-Violet.

340 Jaffa, © S. Nick.

340–1 The orange: From harvest to sale, photos, early 20th century, priv. coll.

341 Jaffa street signs, © C. Fouré. The port of Jaffa, © S. Nick. Old Jaffa, © C. Sappa/Rapho.

342 Proclamation of the foundation of Tel Aviv, © Zev Radovan. Travel ticket, Tel Aviv, c. 1950, © A. Gesgon/Cirip. Israeli poster, 1977, © A. Gesgon/Cirip.

343 Tel Aviv buildings in the International style. All rights reserved.

344 Portrait of the architect, all rights reserved. Dizengoff Square. All rights reserved. Tel Aviv, 1948. R. Capa//Magnum.

345 Carmel Market, © S. Nick. © S. Nick. © Explorer. Habima Theater, © I. Talby/Rapho.

346 Diamonds, © Ch. Bossu Picat/Fotogram-Stone.

346–7 Tel Aviv seen from Jaffa, © O. Benn/Fotogram-Stone.

347 Tel Aviv, the Promenade, photo c. 1940. All rights reserved. Sculpture by Dani Karavan, © A. Hay.

348 Glass pitcher, 1st century AD. © E. Lessing/Magnum. Kernos from Aredebil, Iran, 1000 BC, © E. Lessing/Magnum. Pitcher, Cyprus, 7th–6th century BC, © E. Lessing/Magnum.

349 Reconstruction of a primitive home, © C. Fouré. Cylindrical piller with human images, 11th century BC, © E. Lessing/Magnum. Judean coin struck with a lyre. All rights reserved. Athlete throwing the javelin, 5th century BC, © E. Lessing/Magnum.

350 Diagram of communities, © Museum of the Diaspora. Synagogue, © Museum of the Diaspora. Scribe, © Museum of the Diaspora.

350–1 The meal, © Museum of the Diaspora.

351 Menorah, © Museum of the Diaspora. Icons, © Museum of the Diaspora.

352 Ramle, the White Mosque, © Zev Radovan.

352–3 Grapes of Rishon Lezion, Ben Dov Archives, Israel Museum, Jerusalem.

353 Chaim Weizmann, © Keystone.

354 Portrait of Baron E. de Rothschild, Ben Dov Archives, Israel Museum, Jerusalem.

354–5 Vines in the desert, © R. Nowitz/Explorer.

355 Detail of a mark verifying the kosher character of a wine, early 20th century. all rights reserved. Bottles of Israeli wine, © P. Léger. Rothschild Manuscript, 15th century, Sanctuary of the Book, Israel Museum, Jerusalem.

356 Vineyards in Zichron Yaacov, anon. photo, all rights reserved. Bust of Herod, © Eretz magazine, Israel.

358 The Arrest of Saint Paul, painting by L. di Tommé, 14th century, National Gallery of

Sienna, © Dagli Orti.
358–9 Caesarea, the aqueduct, © M. Hayaux du Tilly.
359 Portico of the Crusader fortress, © *Eretz magazine*, Israel.
360 Roman amphitheater constructed in the time of Herod the Great, 1st century BC, © Dagli Orti. Crusader architecture in Caesarea. © Zev Radovan. Mosaic showing comedy mask, Museum of Ancient Art, Haifa. All rights reserved.
361 Underwater excavations at Caesarea, © I. Grinberg. Glassware from the Roman period, Israel Museum, Jerusalem.
Aerial view of the port of Caesarea, © Zev Radovan.
364 Haifa, Carmelite Monastery, © G. Sioen/Rapho.
364–5 Haifa at the foot of Mount Carmel, engraving in *La Terre Sainte* by V. Guérin, 1884, © Édimédia.
365 Druzes at Mount Carmel, © Le Diascorn/Rapho. Idem. Wines of Israel. © A. Parinet/Explorer.
366 Poster for the festival of Haifa, c. 1930, © L. de Selva/Tapabor.
Window open on Haifa, painting by Mani-Katz, 20th century, priv. coll, © Édimédia.
367 Votive boat, terracotta, c. 700 BC., Maritime Museum, Haifa, © E. Lessing/Magnum. The Bahai Temple, © B. Wolman/Fotogram-Stone. Sculpture Garden, © S. Nick.
368 Port of Saint John of Acre, © Vloo.
368–39 Crusader fortress of Saint John of Acre, photo, early 20th century, © Roger-Viollet.
369 Reliquary of the Holy Thorn, 14th century, British Museum, London. Crusader knights, miniatures in *The Military Order of the Passion of the Saviour*, 14th century, Bodleian Library, Oxford.
371 *Steam baths*, painting by J.-L. Gérôme, priv. coll., © ACR Éditions.
372 The El-Jazzar Mosque, © G. Sioen/Rapho. Festival of Acre, © D. Tal/Albatross.
373 Jewelers of the Old Town, Acre, photo, early 20th century, priv. coll. Market in Acre, © F. Lagrange. The caravanserai, © F. Lagrange.
374 Palestinian Christians. © E. Baitel/Gamma. Rosh Hanikra, © D. Tal/Albatross.
375 Fishermen of Galilee, photo, early 20th century, priv. coll.

376 Calling of Saint Peter and Saint Andrew, miniature by Fra Angelico, c. 1430, San Marco Museum, Florence, © Orsi Battaglini-Giraudon. Jesus and the sick man, Byzantine illumination from Mount Athos, 12th century, Athens National Library, © E. Lessing/Magnum.
The Miraculous Catch, painting by Raphael, 16th century, Victoria & Albert Museum, London, © Bridgeman-Giraudon.
377 *The sermon on the Mount*, fresco by Roselli, 15th century, Cistine Chapel, Vatican, © Giraudon.
The Miraculous Catch, retable of Saint Peter, 15th century, Museum of Art and History, Geneva, © A. Held/Artephot.
The Feeding of the 5000, wood engraving by M. Wohlgemuth, Nuremberg, 1491, © J.-L. Charmet.
379 The Sea of Galilee, © L. Goldman/Rapho. Tiberias, photo early 20th century, priv. coll.
380 Details of the Zodiac, the Virgin and the Scales, mosaic from Hammath near Tiberias, 4th century, all rights reserved. Menorah, 2nd–3rd century AD, from a synagogue near Tiberias, Israel Museum, Jerusalem, © Dagli Orti. Tiberias, watercolor in *Under Syrian Sun* by A. C. Buchbold, 1906, © Édimédia.
381 Talmudist school, © M. Hayaux du Tilly. Statue of Maimonides, © Aisa.
382 Fishermen on the Sea of Galilee, photo, end 19th century, priv. coll. Mosaic from Tabgha, 6th century, © E. Lessing/Magnum.
382–3 Christ walking on the water, miniature, 12th–13th century, Armenian Museum, Ispahan, © Giraudon.
383 The Ark of the Covenant in the synagogue of Capernaum, 3rd century AD, © E. Lessing/Magnum. Graeco-Roman portico of the synagogue of Capernaum, © Dagli Orti.
384 Detail of a poster by Keren Hayesod on the Jewish colonization of Palestine, 1925. all rights reserved. Mizpa, near Tiberias, photo, early 20th century, © Roger-Viollet.
385 Detail of a poster by Keren Hayesod on the Jewish colonization of Palestine, 1925. all rights reserved.
386 *Christ at the Wedding at Cana*, detail, painting by Q. Varin, 16th–17th century, Musée des Beaux-Arts, Rennes, © Giraudon.
Joseph the Carpenter, painting by G. de La Tour, 17th century, Louvre, Paris, ©

Lauros-Giraudon.
Christ's Mission, painting of the Dutch School, 15th century, Musée des Beaux-Arts, Tournai, © Dagli Orti.
The Wedding at Cana, painting by G. David, 15th–16th century, Louvre, Paris, © Giraudon.
387 *The Annunciation*, painting by D. Bouts, 15th century, Prado Museum, Madrid, © Giraudon.
388 Woman embroidering in Nazareth, photo, early 20th century, © Roger-Viollet. Cigarette manufacture in Nazareth, photo, c. 1940, priv. coll.
389 Choir in Nazareth, © IMA, Paris. Bedouins in Nazareth, © Lawson/Rapho. Aerial view of Mount Tabor, © W. Braun/Zefa.
390 Shell frieze showing Chariots of the Canaanite War, British Museum, London. The beast of the Apocalypse, 10th century, Museum of the Cathedral of Gerona, © Artephot. Coffin of Tutankhamun, National Museum of Cairo, © A. Held/Artephot.
391 *The Transfiguration*, painting by G. Bellini, 15th century, Correr Museum, Venice, © Alinari-Giraudon.
392 Open-air school, photo, early 20th century. all rights reserved.
392–3 Details of a poster by Keren Kayemet advertizing colonization of the Valley of Jezreel in Palestine, 1930. all rights reserved.
393 Kibbutz near Ein Havod, © W. Braun/Zefa.
394 View of the Tell, © J.-O. Héron. Ivory head of the Goddess Hathor, 2000–1000 BC., Rockefeller Museum, Jerusalem, © E. Lessing/Magnum. Fragment of a painted jar showing a Canaanite, 1300 BC., Israel Museum, Jerusalem, © E. Lessing/Magnum.
394–5 Pot in the form of a fish, 2000 BC., Rockefeller Museum, Jerusalem, © E. Lessing/Magnum.
395 Incense vase from Bet She'an, 11th century BC, Israel Museum, Jerusalem, © E. Lessing/Magnum. Ivory box from Megiddo, 12th century, Rockefeller Museum, Jerusalem, © E. Lessing/Magnum.
396 Ivory woman's head from Megiddo, Rockefeller Museum, Jerusalem, © E. Lessing/Magnum. Canaanite alter from Megiddo, © Tournus. Mount Gilboa, © Zev Radovan.
397 Bet She'an, © G.

Degeorge.
Mosaic from the synagogue of Bet She'an, 4th century, Israel Museum, Jerusalem, © Dagli Orti.
398 Festival coat from around Safed, 1880, coll. Widad Kamel Kawar, Rautenstrauch-Joest-Museum, Cologne. Safed, © Delval/Rapho. Rabbi reading the Zohar, © M. Hayaux du Tilly.
399 Safed, Cabalist tomb © G. Sioen/Rapho.
400 *Safed*, watercolor by J. Zaritsky, 1924, Israel Museum, Jerusalem. Synagogue in Safed, © F. Brenner/Rapho. Safed, the Artists' quarter © G. Sioen/Rapho.
401 Woman cooking bread © C. Harbutt/Rapho. Terracotta ossuary, 4000 BC., © Zev Radovan. © R. Burri/Magnum.
402 Baniyas, © L. Goldman/Rapho.
403 Greek inscription on a stone from Tell Dan, 2nd century BC, © Zev Radovan.
404 Mount Hermon, engraving in *La Terre Sainte* by V. Guérin, 1884, © Édimédia. Ruins of Nimrod's fortress. , © Zefa.
405 Druzes, © F. Brenner/Rapho. Druze village near Mount Hermon, © Zefa. Majdal Shams, © S. Zeghidour.
406 *The Baptism of Christ*, painting by L. Sustris, 16th century, Musée des Beaux-Arts, Caen, © Giraudon.
406–7 The Jordan, anon. photo, end 19th century, © J. Vigne.
407 The Jordan, detail of a mosaic from Madaba, 6th century, Jordan, © E. Lessing/Magnum. Fertility goddess from the Jordan Valley, terracotta., 6000 BC., Israel Museum, Jerusalem, © E. Lessing/Magnum.
408 Bottling the water of the Jordan, an American enterprise, 1906, © Roger-Viollet.
414 Air France publicity poster, © L. de Selva/Tapabor.

INDEX

Page numbers in bold refer to the Practical information section.

◆ A ◆

Abbasids 42, 52, 53, 241
Abdul Hamid II, Sultan 340, 373
Abimelech, King 198
Abraham 36, 78, 93, 194–5, 198, 216, 220, 221, 236, 240, 282, 284, 406
Absalom, Tomb of 279
Abu Bakr 91, 94
Abu Diuk 315
Abu Ghosh 129, 327, **424, 440, 452**
– Crusader Church 128, 326, 328–9
– Monastery 328–9
– Mosque of 115
accommodation **412, 421, 442–3, 444, 445, 446, 447, 450–2, 454, 455, 456, 457, 458, 459**
Acre see Akko
Adam 221
Adonis-Tammuz 226
Afula 392–3, **440**
Agam, Yaacov 344
Agrippa II 380
Ahab 314, 362, 393
Ain Karim 219
Ain Quniya 404
air travel **414, 417, 436**
Akiba, Rabbi 380
Akko (Acre) 128, 368–73, **427, 436, 443, 455**
– Al-Jazzar Mosque 115, 117, 372–3
– Church of St John 373
– Citadel 369
– Crusaders' town 369
– Hammam al-Pasha 370–1
– khans 373
– Museum of Heroism 369
– port 369
– souks 373
Al-Ashraf 368
Al-Atrach, Sultan 405
Al-Ghadiriyeh 116
Al-Ghawanima 117
Al-Hakim, Caliph 266, 276
Al-Husseini, Rabah 308
Al-Jazzar 365, 368–9, 369, 370, 372, 373
Al-Khader 223
Al-Khalil see Hebron
Al-Maghtas 407
Al-Omariyeh 117
Al-Qala 116
Al-Rashid, Caliph 276
Al-Salam Canal 172
Al-Tih Desert 172
Al-Walid I 115, 286
Al-Zahir, Caliph 286
Alexander the Great 36, 39, 40, 240, 334, 339, 368
Alexander III, Tsar 113, 278

Alexander Jannaeus 49, 202
Allenby, General 42, 43, 243, 294, 339
Allenby Bridge 315, 407
Amichai, Yehuda 158
Amorites 45
Amran's Pillars 184, **438**
Amud Valley 401
Antigonus (Mattathias) 202
Antiochus III 48
Antiochus IV Epiphanes 40, 48, 240
Antoninus Pius 41
Aqaba, Gulf of 26, 172, 178, **431, 438**
Aqabat al-Jar camp 315
aqueducts 224–5
ar-Riha 314
Arab-Israeli Wars 37, 43, 56, 57
Arabic (language) 59
Arabs 41–2, 57
– dance 72–3
– music 70–1
Arad 199, **442, 446**
Arafat, Yasir 43, 57
Aramean (language) 58
Arava Valley 18–19, 186
Arbel 384
archaeology **428–9**
Archelaus 40
architecture 106–34
– Bauhaus 343
– Byzantine 124–5
– churches 112–13
– Crusader 128–9
– early 118–19
– Herodian 120–1
– for irrigation 224–5
– Islamic 126–7
– mosques 116–17
– Roman 122–3
– synagogues 108–9
Ardon, Mordecai 139, 140
areisheh 131
Aristobulus 378
Aristobulus II 40
Ark of the Covenant 106, 234, 324–5, 327, 331
Armenians 88
army, Israeli 374
Artas 223
arts 62–72
Ashdod **427**
Ashkelon 333, **427, 452**
– Roman Agora 332
Ashkenazi 256
Assassins (Hashishin) 404
Assyrians 39, 46, 47, 299, 378, 401
Atlit 357
Augustus, Emperor 313
Avdat 113, 190–1, **438**
Averbuch, Genia 344
Ayalon, battle of 325
Ayalon, valley of 324
Ayyubids 55, 286

◆ B ◆

Ba'al ha-Nes, Rabbi Meir 380
Bab al-Oued Pass 326
Babylon 39, 46, 47
Baghdad 53
Bahaism 367
Baldwin I 54
Baldwin II 54
Balfour Declaration 42, 56
Bani Naim 222
banks 413
Banyas 403, **440**
Bar Kochba 50, 51, 210, 241, 380
Bar-Yochai, Rabbi Simon 401
Barakat, Tayseer 335
Bauhaus style 343
Baurenfeind, Gustav 137
Bedouins 134, 172, 177, 178, 180, 218, 220, 306
– market 197
– Museum of Bedouin Culture 198
Beersheba 194–7, **422, 438, 442, 446**
– Bedouin market 197, **440**
– Negev Museum 196, 197, 198
Beit Sahur **440**
Bell, Gertrude 150–1
Bellow, Saul 154–5
Belvoir, Fortress of 128, 129, 397, **436, 440**
Ben Ali, Arieh L. 366
Ben-Gurion, David 43, 57, 192, 218, 342, 345
Ben Nachman(ides), Rabbi Moshe 256
Ben Yehudah, Eliezer 58, 290, 292
Ben Zakkai, Yohanan 257, 380
Bernice 380
Bertrandon de la Brocquiàre 149
Bet Alpha 396–7, **440**
– synagogue 108, 109
Bet Gabriel 383, **457**
Bet Guvrin 331, **427**
Bet-Sahour 228
Bet She'an 122, 397, **436, 440, 458**
Bet Shemesh 331, **452**
Bet Yerah **458**
Bethany **424, 427**
Bethel 310–11
Bethlehem 216, 217, 226–8, **424, 427, 440, 442, 447**
– Basilica of the Nativity 143, 226–7, **424**
– Casbah 228
– Cave of Milk 227
– Central Market 228
– minaret 116
– Mosque of Omar 228
– Museum of Old Bethlehem 228
Bialik, Haim Nahman 345

Bible 78, 140, 214–15, 339, 354
– Beersheba to Jerusalem:
– via Dead Sea 194–5
– via Hebron and Bethlehem 216–17
– Exodus from Egypt 168–9
– Gospels 84
– Jerusalem 234–9
– Jerusalem to Gaza 324–5
– language 58, 215
– Lower Galilee 390–1
– Mount Carmel 362–3
– Nazareth 386–7, 388
– Sea of Galilee 376–7
Bir Aeit 311
bird migrations 24–5
birdwatching holidays 430
boat services 414
Boaz 216, 217, 228
Bonfil, Adrien **426, 427**
Bonfils, Félix **426, 427**
border posts 415
Borot Lodz 187
Bourdelle, Emile 300
Brangwyn, Sir Frank 136
bread 74–5
British Mandate 42, 56, 58, 243, 335, 339, 367
bus services 416
Butler, Reg 300
Byzantine period 41

◆ C ◆

Caesarea 356, 358–61, **436, 437, 440, 443, 455**
– aqueducts 224, 359
– Crusader fortress 359, 360
– minaret 116
– port 361
– Roman hippodrome 359
– Roman Theater 360
Caesarea Philippi 403, **440**
Calder, 300
calendars 96
Caligula 40
calligraphy 115, 127
Calvary 146
Cana 146, 148, 385, 386, **424, 427, 458**
Canaanite civilization 38, 44–5
Canaanites 45, 299, 317, 332
Capernaum 382–3, **440, 457**
– House of St Peter 113, 382
– synagogue 382–3
car travel 418
Castel, Moshe 139
Catherine, St 174, 176
Ceremony of the three teas **430**
Chagall, Marc 144,

297, 304–5, 346
Charlemagne 276
Chateaubriand, François René de 364, 373, 426
Chosroes II 41
Christianity 41, 42, 53, 216, 226, 277
– calendar 96
– days of rest 420
– festivals 86–7, 411
– groups in Holy Land 88–9
– origins and history 84–5
– pilgrimages 85, 424–5
churches:
– architecture 112–13, 124
– layout 110–11, 124
Clarke, Edward Daniel 146
Claudius 40
Cleopatra 339
climate 411, 437
clothing 412, 437
Conon 388
Constantine, Emperor 41, 191, 226, 241, 272
copper mine 185
Copts 88
Coral Island 180
coral reef 26–7
Cordovero, Moses 399
Corrodi, Hermann 143
costume:
– army berets 374
– Bedouin 306
– Hasidic 262–3, 292
– Nazareth 388
– orthodox 423
– Palestinian 336
– Safed 398
credit cards 413
crosses, Christian 110, 111
Crusaders 42, 54–5, 85, 221, 242, 244, 264, 266, 272, 277, 286, 326, 327, 333, 334, 339, 358, 365, 373, 381, 385, 397, 403
– architecture 128–9
Curzon, Robert 152
Customs formalities 410
Cyrus 36, 39, 240

◆ D ◆

Dahariyeh 218–19
Daher al-Omar 365, 368, 369, 373
dances, Arab and Jewish 72–3
Darwish, Mahmoud 159–60
David 36, 39, 46, 144, 210, 216, 232, 234, 240, 257, 325, 327, 331, 334
Dead Sea 165, 166, 200–1, 427, 431, 436, 438
– banks of 200–1
Dead Sea Scrolls 214–15, 298, 299
Deir al-Balah 334, 336

desert excursions 431
Diadochi 40
Dimona 192, 438
Diocletian 41
Doura 220
Druzes 94, 365, 401, 405

◆ E ◆

ecology 430
Egeria 278
Eilat 26, 182–3, 411, 430, 438, 440, 442, 444–5
– International Birdwatching Center 183
– Underwater Observatory 183
Eilat, Mountains of 184
Ein al-Fourtaga 180
Ein Avdat 192, 438
Ein Bokek 201, 442, 446
Ein Feshka 213
Ein Gedi 210–11, 427, 436, 442, 446
– Cave of the Shulemite 210
– Chalcolithic Temple 118, 210
– National Park 210–11, 436
Ein Gev 443, 457
Ein Harod 458
Ein Hemed National Park 326
Ein Hod 456
Ein Karem 296, 303
Ein Nashut, synagogue 109
Ein Netafim 184
Eleazar ben Yair 206, 209
electricity 421
Elijah 362–3, 364, 393, 403
Elisha 315, 363
Elkan, Beno 297
embroidery, Palestinian 66–7, 222
Emmaus 325, 327, 330, 424, 440
English language 60
Ethiopians 89
Eudoxia, Empress 307, 334
Eusebius, Archbishop of Caesarea 358
Exile 39, 46
Exodus 168–71, 173, 182
Ezekiel, Prophet 201
Ezra 48

◆ F ◆

Falashas 292
fauna 18–25, 30–1, 149–50, 186–7, 210, 211, 402
Feiran Oasis 177
festivals:
– Christian 86–7, 411
– Jewish 80–1, 134, 411, 420
– Muslim 92–3, 306, 411
fish and fishing 28–9
Flaubert, Gustave 148

flora 18–22, 30–1, 210, 315, 403, 405, 408
food 74–5, 420
Foucauld, Father 389
fountains 115, 127
Franks 54, 55, 241, 266
French language 60
Frendlich, Otto 301
fruits 34
Fulk, King 331, 397, 400

◆ G ◆

Galilee 51, 378, 411
– Lower 384–5, 388–91, 396–7, 436, 443, 458
– Upper 398–405, 430, 443, 459
Galilee, Sea of 376–7, 378, 411, 431, 436, 443, 457–8
Gamla 405
Gaza 334–6
– Church of St John the Baptist 336
– Great Mosque 335, 336
– Museum of Popular Arts and Traditions 336
– Napoleon's Castle 336
– Philistine sarcophagi 334
– visiting 418
Gaza Strip 335
Geddes, Sir Patrick 344
Geoffrey Plantagenet 397
geography 16–17
geology 16–17
George, St 223, 403
Gérime, Jean-Léon 143, 180, 371
Gibeonites 39
Gill, Eric 153
Ginnosar 381, 457
glass 360, 361
glossary 98–104
Godfrey of Bouillon 54, 242
Golan Heights 404–5, 431, 440, 443
Goliath 331
Gomorrah 195
Gordon, General 306
Goren National Park 401
"Green Line" 218
Gunther, John 155
Gutman, Nahum 139, 346

◆ H ◆

Haag, Carl 143
Hadjar al-Nassara 384
Hadrian, Emperor 50, 51, 226, 241, 356
Hafetz Haim 443, 452
Hagar 194
Hahassid, Rabbi Yehuda 256
Hai Bar (Yotvata) Nature Reserve

186–7, 438
Haifa 364–5, 440, 443, 456
– Bahai Temple 367
– Bet Pinchas Museum 365
– Carmel quarter 365–6
– Carmelite Monastery (Stella Maris) 364
– Gan Haem Park 365
– Hadar Hacarmel 366–7
– Haifa Museum 367
– Mané-Katz Museum 366
– modern 366
– Museum of Clandestine Immigration 367
– National Maritime Museum 366
– port 367
– Reuben and Edith Hecht Archeological Museum 365–6
– Sculpture Garden 367
– University 365
Halhoul 223
Halutza 191
Hammat Gadar 443, 459
Haon 443, 457
Harmon, Q.L. 294
Harrison, Austin St Barbe 309
Hashishin 404
Hasidism 83, 292–3
– costumes 262–3
Hasmoneans 40, 48–9, 229, 241, 331
Hatzor 401
health 410, 420
– poisonous bites 431
Hebrew (language):
– Biblical 58
– Israeli 58
– learning 423
Hebron 216, 220–2, 379, 422, 427, 440, 447
– Byzantine Church 221
– Casbah 222
– Cave of the Patriarchs 221
– Jewish Quarter (Haret al-Yahoud) 222
– minaret 117
– Municipal Museum 222
– Synagogue 221
– tanners' quarter (Haret al-Qittun) 222
– Tomb of the Patriarchs (Haram al-Khalil) 117, 220–1
– Women's Mosque 221
Hebron, Valley of 218–19
Helena, Empress (Saint) 226, 241, 272, 278
Hellenistic period 36, 40
Heraclius, Emperor 41
Herod Agrippa I 40, 241
Herod Antipas 40,

378, 379
Herod the Great 40,
50, 120, 121, 202,
220–1, 226, 229, 241,
258, 260, 266, 313,
322, 339, 358, 359,
378, 403
Herodian dynasty 40
Herodion 120, 229
Herzl, Theodor 42, 56,
302, 351
Herzliya 356
Hezekiah, King 225,
233, 288
Hinnom Valley 294
Hiram, King 234
Hisham, qasr (palace)
of 318–21, **436, 440**
Histadrut (union) 218
history 36–57
Horns of Hittim 55,
381, 384–5
hotels **412**, **421**,
**442–3, 444, 445, 446,
447, 450–2, 454, 455,
456, 457, 458, 459**
houses:
– Arab 289
– Israelite 118
– of Jericho 317
– Jewish 349
– Mamluke 127
– painted 309
– Palestinian 130–1,
220
– rectangular 118
– round 118
Hula, Lake 402
Hyrcanus II 40

◆ I ◆

insurance **410**
Intifada 315, 335
irrigation 32–3, 224–5,
233
Isaac 198, 221, 236,
284
Isfahan Shah 283
Islam 277, 280
– calendar 96
– conquests 36, 52–3,
54–5
– days of rest **420**
– festivals 92–3, 306,
411
– groups in Holy Land
94–5
– Jihad 52
– origins and history
90–1
– pilgrimages 91, 309,
323
– yad Fatima 293
Israel, Kingdom of 36,
46–7, 240
Israel, State of 37, 43,
56–7, 200, 218
– local transport
416–17
Israelites 39, 45, 47
itineraries **422–40**

◆ J ◆

Jabal Foureidis 229
Jacob 198, 221, 237,
311
– Well 313
Jaffa 116, 338–41,
427, 436, 437, 440
– Al-Mamoudiyeh

Mosque 340
– Andromeda's Rock
341
– Arab quarter 341
– Gan Hapisga 341
– Museum of
Antiquities 341
– old town 340–1
– paintings of 136–7
– port 341, **440**
– Souk Hapishpeshim
340
James the Greater, St
265
James the Minor, St
265
Janco, Marcel 139
Jazzar Pasha 115
Jebaliye 176
Jebusites 232, 234,
240
Jehu, King 39, 47
Jenin 314
Jereboam II 39
Jeremiah 309
Jericho 117, 121,
314–15, **427, 436,
440, 452**
– ancient 316–17
– Elisha's Spring
(Ein al-Sultan) 315
– Herod's Palace 322
Jeroboam I 47
Jerusalem 39, 163,
232–309, 379, **417,
422, 423, 424, 427,
430, 432–5, 436, 437,
438, 442–3, 447–52**
– Absalom's tomb 279
– Achrabiya 283
– Al-Abuqhdi turba126
– Al-Aqsa Mosque 52,
241, 242, 283, 286–7
– American Colony
(hotel) 308, **433**
– Ammunition Hill 293
– Antonia 266, 268
– Archeological
Gardens 288
– Armenian Cemetery
265
– Armenian quarter
264–5
– Art Museum 302
– Bait al-Mal 283
– Basilica of the
Annunciation 112
– Batei Mahasseh 257
– Bible Lands
Museum 297
– Biblical College 307
– Biblical Zoo 302
– Billy Rose Sculpture
Garden 300–1
– Bishopric of St
George 307
– Bloomfield Garden
290
– Bokharan quarter
293
– British quarter
294–5
– Burnt House 257
– Cardo 123, 124, 255
– Cathedral of the
Latin Patriarchate 112
– Cathedral of St
James 264, 265
– Children's Memorial
302–3
– Christ Church 254
– Christian quarter

266–79
– Church of the
Archangels 265
– Church of the
Redemption 276
– Church of St Anne
113, 128, 242, 253,
266
– Church of St John
the Baptist 129, 276,
303
– Church of St Mary
the Little 276
– Church of St Mary
Magdalene 113, 278
– Church of St Peter
in Gallicante 279
– Church of the
Visitation 303
– Citadel 252, 254,
432
– City of David 288
– Convent of
Flagellation 267
– Convent of the
Moscovite Church 303
– Convent of the
Sisters of Zion 303
– Damascus Gate
244, 255, 280, 291,
306
– Davidka Square 291
– Davidoff House 293
– Dome of the
Ascension 283
– Dome of the Chain
283
– Dome of the
Prophet 283
– Dome of the Rock
52, 143, 156–7, 162,
233, 241, 242, 253,
258, 265, 282, 284–5,
432
– Dominus Flevit 278
– Dormition Abbey
279
– Double Gate 244
– East 306–9
– Ecce Homo, arch of
122, 267
– Ein Karem 296, 303
– Ethiopian Orthodox
Monastery 276
– Ethiopian quarter
292
– festivals **411**
– Garden Tomb 306
– gates 244–7
– Gethsemane 277
– Golden Gate 244,
277
– Golgotha 267, 268,
272
– Governor's Palace
294
– Hadassah Hospital
296, 304
– Hadassah
Synagogue 304–5
– Haram al-Sharif
260, 280, 282–7,
432
– Harav Kook Street
291, 292
– Hebrew University
296
– Herodian quarter
257
– Herodian Temple
253, 286
– Herod's Fortress

267
– Herod's Gate 244,
309
– Herzl Museum 302
– history 42, 232–3,
240–3
– Holy Sepulcher 41,
113, 128, 129, 147–8,
153, 241, 242, 252,
266, 272–5
– Holy Trinity Church
291, **433**
– hotels **442–3, 450–2**
– House of Caiaphas
265
– Hulda Stairs 288
– Hurva Synagogue
256
– Independence Park
295
– Institute of Islamic
Art 296
– Israel Museum 214,
297, 298–301
– Istambuli
Synagogue 257
– Italian Hospital
112
– itinerary **432–5**
– Jaffa Gate 244, 254,
255
– Jaffa Road 295
– Jeremiah's cave 309
– Jerusalem Theater
296
– Jewish Cemetery
277
– Jewish quarter 242,
254–9
– Karaite Synagogue
256
– King David Hotel
294, 308
– King David Street
295
– Knesset 297
– Liberty Bell Park
290
– Madrasa Othmaniya
283
– Maghreb (Dung)
Gate 244, 282
– Mahaneh Yehuda
market 295
– Mandelbaum Gate
243, 292, 306
– Mea Shearim
quarter 242, 292–3
– Minbar Burhan al-
Din 282
– Mishkenot
Sha'ananim quarter
242, 290
– modern 242, 290–7
– Monastery of the
Cross 297
– Monastery of
St John of the Desert
303
– Morasha quarter
292
– Mosque-Church of
the Ascension 278
– Muristan 276
– Museum of Heroism
291
– Museum of
Holocaust History 302
– Museum of Islamic
Art 283
– Museum of the Old
Yishuv 256

– Muslim quarter 52, 280–9
– Nahalat Shiva quarter 242, 290–1
– Nea (New) Church (of St Mary) 255
– Neapolis Gate 123
– New Gate 244
– New Imperial Hotel 254
– Omariyeh College 266
– Ophel 288
– Orient House 308
– painted houses 309
– paintings of 138–43, 248
– Pater Noster 278
– Petra Hotel 254
– plan 248, **434–5**
– Pools of Bethesda 266
– Rachel's Tomb 289
– Rambam Synagogue 242, 256
– Rehavia quarter 296
– Residence of the President of the Republic 296
– residential quarters 296
– Robinson Arch 288
– Rock of the Agony 277
– Rockefeller Museum 214, 309
– Room of the Last Supper 279
– Rose Garden 297
– Russian Church 291, **433**
– Russian compound 291
– St Andrew's Church 294
– St George's Anglican Cathedral 112
– St Stephen's (Lions') Gate 244, 266
– St Thonos' Chapel 264
– Saladin Street 309
– Sanhedria quarter 293
– Science Museum 297
– Seminary 265
– Sephardic Synagogues 256, 257
– Sergei House 291
– Sheikh Jarrah quarter 308
– shopping **423**, **437**
– Solomon's quarries 306, 307
– souk 280
– Stations of the Cross 267–71
– stone 307
– Street of the Chain 126
– Street of the Prophets 291, 292
– Sultan's Pool 294
– Supreme Court 297
– Synagogue of Elijah 257
– synagogues 256
– Tabor House 291
– Talbieh quarter 296, 297

– Temple Mount (Mount Moriah) 232, 233, 260–1, 282, 288
– Temples of Solomon 46, 47, 119, 234, 260, 261, 339
– Ticho House 292
– Tomb of David 257
– Tomb of the Kings 308
– Tomb of Mujir al-Din 277
– Tomb of the Virgin 277
– topography 232
– Tower of David Museum 252–3
– Valley of the Cross 297
– Via Dolorosa 122, 266, 267–71
– walls 143, 240, 241, 244–7, 258–9
– Warren's Shaft 288
– West 296
– Western (Wailing) Wall 50, 155, 255, 258–9, 282, **422**
– Wilson's Arch 288
– in writings 152–7
– Yad Vashem 302–3
– Yemin Moshe quarter 290
– YMCA 294, 295
– Zachariah's Tomb 279
– Zion Gate 244, 255
– Zion Square 291
Jerusalem, Latin kingdom of 42, 54–5
Jerusalem, Statute of 43
Jesus 84, 86, 217, 238–9, 266, 267, 268–71, 277, 306, 313, 314, 322, 325, 355, 376–7, 382–3, 385, 386–7, 389, 403, 406, 407–8
– pilgrimage to sites **424–5**
Jethro 384
jewelry 68–9
Jewish Revolts 41, 50–1
Jews 53, 56–7
– see also Judaism
– dance 72–3
– houses 349
– jewelry 68–9
– music 70–1
– pilgrimage 422–3
– wedding 137
– wines 354–5
Jezebel, Queen 362, 393
Jezreel 393
Jezreel, Valley of 390, 392–3
Jihad 52
John the Baptist, St 219, 303
John the Damascene, St 230
John Hyrcanus 49, 213, 313, 332
John Paul II, Pope 85
Jonah 223, 339
Jordan, River 406–8, **431**
– valley 166, 408
Joseph of Arimethea

268, 352
Joseph (son of Jacob) 198
Josephus, Flavius 206, 212, 229, 252, 267, 322, 358, 380, 384, 392
Joshua 240, 314, 402
Josiah, King 199, 396
Judah, Kingdom of 36, 39, 46, 47, 199, 240
Judaism 277
– see also Jews
– calendar 96
– days of rest **420**
– festivals 80–1, 134, **411**, **420**
– groups in Holy Land 82–3
– origins and history 78–9
Judas Maccabeus 48
Judea 41, 358, **436**
Judean Desert **436**
Judean Hills 222–3
Judeo-Christians 388
Judges 39
Julian, Emperor 41, 334
Justinian, Emperor 41, 174, 176, 226, 255
Juttah 219

◆ K ◆

Kabbalism 398, 399–400
Karaites 256
Karavan, Dani 197, 347
Katzrin 405, **459**
Kaufman, Richard 132
Kefar Bir'am, synagogue 109
Kemelman, Harry 295
Khan Yunis 336
Khirbet al-Mafjar 318
kibbutzim 37, 132–3, 392, **430**
Kidron Valley 230, 279
Kings 30
Kiryat Gat 333
Kiryat Shmona **443**, **459**
Kiryat Yearim **453**
Kleber, Jean Baptiste 392
Knights of the Hospital of St John 129, 276, 368, 369
Knights of the Hospitallers Order, German 129, 369
Kollek, Teddy 243
Koran see Qur'an
Korazim 383, **443**, **457–8**
Kosher food **420**
Kursi 383

◆ L ◆

Lachish 332–3, **440**
Lagrange, Father 307
Lahav, Kibbutz 198
Lake Hula Reserve 402
Lamartine, Alphonse de 254, 314, 379
lamps (oil) 64–5
languages 58–60, 215
– learning **423**

Latrun 330, **440**, **443**, **452**
Lauras 230, 323
Leah 221
Lear, Edward 149–50
Licinius 41
Lod **427**
Lot 194, 195, 222
Loti, Pierre 258
Lot's wife 200
Louis IX (Saint) 55, 358, 404
Luria, Isaac 399

◆ M ◆

Macarius, St 265
Maccabees 314, 330
– rebellion 40, 48, 241, 331
Madaba (Jordan) 125
Magidovitz, Yehuda 344
mail **419**
Maillol, Aristide 300
Maimonides (Moses ben Maimon) 380, 381
Majdal Shams 404–5
Makhtesh Ramon 187
Malbin, Ursula 367
Mamlukes 37, 42, 54, 242, 334, 339, 352, 358, 373
Mamre, oak of 221
Mamshit 191, **438**
Manasseh, King 294
Mané-Katz, Emmanuel 137, 366
Mansur, Sliman 137
Mantegna, Andrea 140
Ma'on 108
Mar Saba 230, **427**, **440**
Maresha 332, **440**
Mark Anthony 266, 339
Maronites 89
Marsa Murah 180
Mary, Virgin 217, 219, 266, 268, 277, 303, 386–7, 388
Mary Magdalene 239
Masaada 404
Masada 50, 51, 201, **436**, **438**, **446**
– fortress 121, 202–9, **436**
– Herod's Palace 121, 202
– siege 209
– synagogue 108
Mattathias 48
media **420**
medical services **420**
Mediterranean belt 30–1
Megiddo 243, 396, **436**, **440**, **458**
– altars 396
– city gate 119
– Hill of Battles 396
Megiddo Pass 389, 390
Meir, Golda 218
Meir Ba'al ha-Nes, Rabbi 380
Melchizedek 240
Melville, Herman 147–8
Mendelsohn, Eric 353

menorah 109
Metzokeh Dragot 211
Mezad Boqeq 201
Minguzzi, Luciano 300
Mishna 51, 58, 78
Mitzpeh Ramon 187,
440, 445
Mitzpeh Shalem 211,
437, 442, 446
Monastery of St Elias
(Elijah) 228
Monastery of St John
the Baptist **424**
Monastery of St John
in the Desert 303
money **413**
Montefiore, Moses
256, 289, 290
Montfort Castle 401
Moore, Henry 300
Moses 78, 106,
168–71, 176, 177,
182, 199, 323, 407
moshavim 132–3
mosques:
– layout 114–15
– minaret styles
116–17
Mount Ararat 264
Mount of Beatitudes
382, **424, 440, 458**
Mount Carmel 362–3,
364, 365, 366–7, 368,
389, 390, **427, 440**
– Bet Pinchas
Museum 365
– Gan Haem Park 365
Mount Gerizum 312
Mount Gilboa 393
Mount Hamor 392–3
Mount Hermon 389,
402, 404, **411, 431**
Mount Herzl 302–3
Mount Meron Nature
Reserve 401
Mount Nebo 323
Mount of Olives
162–3, 238, 277,
278
Mount Scopus 296
Mount Sinai 170, 176,
427
Mount Tabor 389,
390, 391, 392, **424,
427, 458**
Mount of Temptation
322, **424, 427, 440**
Mount Zion 279
Mu'awiya, Caliph 42,
52
Muhammad (Prophet)
52, 90–1, 92–3, 114,
241, 280, 283, 287,
372
music 70–1
Muslims *see* Islam

◆ N ◆

Nabateans 185,
188–9
Nabi Musa 323, **438**
Nablus 312, **422, 427,
452**
Nahal Arugot 210,
211
Nahal David 210, 211
Nahal Hever 210
Nahal Mishmar
210–11
Nahalal 132–3
Nahariya 374, **431**

Naim 392, **424**
Nameans 222
Napoleon Bonaparte
42, 334, 336, 339,
340, 352, 392
Nasb Wadi 178
Nasser, President 43
natural remedies
431
nature 16–34, 149–51
– holidays **430**
Nazareth 148, 386–9,
**424, 427, 440, 443,
458**
– Basilica of the
Annunciation 388–9
– Convent of the
Sisters of Nazareth
389
– Franciscan Museum
388
– St Joseph's Church
389
Nebi Salah 352
Nebuchadnezzar 39,
46, 47, 240, 258, 306,
309, 333
Negev 16, 165, 166,
184, 187, **438**
– Nabateo-Byzantine
cities 190–2
– Negev Steppe 20–1
Nehemiah 39, 48, 240
Netanya 164, 356,
443, 456–7
– Hasharon Museum
356
– Museum of the
Jewish Legion 356
Neveh Zohar 201, **446**
Nevi Shamuel 326
Newby, Eric 156–7
newspapers **420**
Nicomedes 352
Niemeyer, Oscar 365
Nimrods fortress 404,
459
Nineveh 332
Nizana 191
Noah 220, 264
Nogushi, Isamu 300
nomads' dwellings
134–5
Nur ad-Din 36, 54,
404
Nuseirat 336
Nuweiba 180

◆ O ◆

Oboda I 190
oil lamps 64–5
olives 76
Ottomans 37, 42, 219,
242, 243, 244, 256,
264
Oz, Amos 158–9

◆ P ◆

paintings 136–44, 248
Palestine 41, 43, 50
– chieftaincies 130
– Muslim 52–3
– traditional villages
130–1
Palestinians:
– dress 336
– embroidery 66–7,
222
– exiles 56–7
– jewelry 68–9

Pann, Abel 139
Parthians 332
passports and visas
410
Paul, St 85, 358
Persian rule 36, 39,
339
Peter, St 383, 389,
403
Petra 188, 189, **427,
438**
Pharisees 40, 49, 238
Philip (Apostle) 325
Philip (son of Herod)
40
Philistines 39, 45, 62,
198, 311, 324, 325,
330, 331, 333, 339
Phoenicians 339
photography **412**
Picasso, Pablo 346
Pilate, Pontius 267,
268
pilgrimages 146–8
– Christian 85, **424–5**
– Jewish **422–3**
– Muslim 91, 309, 323
Pillars of Amram 184,
438
Pompey 40, 241, 332
post offices **419**
pottery 45, 62–3, 189,
202, 331
prehistory 38
Premonstratensians
326
press **420**
Prophets 79, 90
Protestantism 88, 89
Ptolemies 240

◆ Q ◆

Qais tribes 218, 219,
223
Qalaat al-Bourak 223
qasr 131
Qasr Hisham 318–21,
436, 440
Qumran 212–13, **436,
438, 440, 446–7**
– caves 214
– manuscripts 214–15
Qur'an 90, 140, 280,
370

◆ R ◆

Rachel 216
– Tomb 289
radio **420**
Rafah 336
Ramah 326
Ramallah 310
Ramla 352, **427, 455**
– Great Mosque 352
– Square Tower 352
– White Mosque 352
Ramot **443, 458**
Ras Muhammed 179
Rebekah 195, 221
Rechter, Yaacov 347
Red Sea 26, 172, **431**
Rehoboam, King 47,
229
Rehovot 352, 353,
455
religions 78–96
restaurants **420**,
445–59
Richard the Lionheart
55, 330, 333, 339

Rishon Lezion 352,
353, 354, **455**
Rivlin, Rabbi Joseph
290
road signs 418
road travel 415
Roberts, David 248,
251, 426, 427
Rockefeller, John D.
309
Roman legion 326
Romans 185
– rule by 40–1, 50–1,
122, 241, 334
Rosh Hanikra 374,
457
Rosh Pinna **443, 459**
Rothschild, Baron
Edmond de 353, 354,
356
Rothschild, Wolf 257
Rubin, Reuvin 139,
345
Russian language 60
Ruth 216, 217, 228

◆ S ◆

Sabas, St 230
Sadducees 40, 49
Safed 379, 398–400,
422, 440, 443, 459
– artists' quarter 400
– Crusader fortress
400
– Hebrew Museum of
Printing Art 400
– Jewish cemetery
398
– Medinim Square
400
– silks of 398
– Synagogue of Isaac
Abuhav 400
– Synagogue of Isaac
Luria 400
– Synagogue of
Joseph Caro 400
– Synagogue of Rabbi
Habannai 400
St Catherine's
Monastery 174–6,
427, 438, 444
St Catherine's Mount
176
St George's
Monastery 323, **436,
438**
St Mary of the
Germans 129
Salah al-Din (Saladin)
36, 54, 55, 117, 221,
242, 266, 276, 283,
287, 323, 333, 339,
358, 381, 385
Samaria 39, 46, 47,
313
Samaritans 312, 313
Samoa 219
Samson 324, 333
Samuel 326
Sanhedrin 40, 41, 51,
379
Sarah 194, 216, 221
Sargon II 39, 313
Sasa 401
Saul, King 39, 46,
210, 325, 397
Schick, Conrad 291,
292
Schiele, Egon 299
Sdeh Boker 192, **438,**

445
Sdot Yam kibbutz 358, 360
Sectarians 48, 49, 212, 214
Sedom see Sodom
Seleucids 40, 49, 240
Seljuq Turks 42, 241
Sennacherib 39, 299, 332
Sephardic Jews 256, 257
Shabtai, Yaakov 151
Shaira Col 179
Shapiro, Z.H. 296
Sharm al-Sheikh 179, **431**
Sharon, Arieh 343, 344
shatwa 228
Shatz, Boris 139
Sheba, Queen of 182, 292
Shechem 313
Shephelah, plain of 331
Sherover, Gitta 383
Shi'ites 94, 95
Shiloh 311
Shivta 191, **438**
Shomeron **427**
shopping **420**, **423**, **437**, **440**
Shura al-Manquata 179
Sicarii 50, 206
Sidron Valley 230
Siloam aqueduct 225
Silva, Flavius 206, 209
Silwan 289
Sima, Miron 139
Simon the Just 308
Sinai Peninsula 168–80, **438**, **442**, **444**
Sinai War 37, 43
Six-Day War 37, 43, 335, 407
Slaughter of the Holy Innocents 226
Sodom 194, 195, 200, 222, **438**
Solomon 39, 46, 182, 185, 199, 232, 240, 283, 292, 306, 401, 407
Solomon, Pools of 223, 224, **427**
Solomon, Temples of 46, 47, 119, 234, 260, 261, 339
Solomon's Gorges 184
Sorek Valley 303, **440**
Spafford, Horatio and Anna 308
Spanish language 60
Spark, Muriel 156
sports holidays **430–1**
Stephen, St 307
Strouthion, pool of 225
Suez, Gulf of 177
Suleyman Abd al-Malek 352
Suleyman the Magnificent 42, 127, 242, 244, 276, 282, 284, 294, 306

Suleyman Pasha 372, 373
Sumerians 317
Sunnis 94, 95
Sychar **424**
synagogues 106–7
– layout 107
– Roman and Byzantine, architecture 108–9
Syria 48

◆ T ◆

Taba 180, **438**, **444**, **458**
Tabgha 381–2, **424**, **440**
– Church of the Multiplication of the Loaves 381–2
– Church of the Primacy of Peter 382
Taffoah 222
Talmud 42, 51, 78, 379, 381
Tanach 78
Tantura-Dor 356–7
taxes **413**
taxis **417**
Tegoah 229
Tel Arad 199, **438**
Tel Aviv 338, 342–51, **417**, **422**, **427**, **433**, **436**, **440**, **443**, 453–5
– see also Jaffa
– Airport **414**
– Art Museum 345
– Bialik Street 345
– Bible Museum 345
– Cameri Theater 345
– Charles Clore Garden 346
– Cultural Centre 345
– Diaspora Museum 347, 350–1
– Dizengoff Square 344
– Ha'aretz Museum 347, 348–9
– Habima Theater 345
– Hayarkon Park 347
– Historical Museum 345
– hotels **443**, **454**
– House of Meir Dizengoff 345
– Independence Park 347
– Kikar Atarim 346
– Magen David Square 344
– Museum of the Haganah 345
– Promenade 346–7
– Ramat Aviv 347
– Ramat Gan quarter 346
– Rothschild Boulevard 345
– seaside 346–7
– Shalom Tower 345
– Souk Hacarmel 345
– Tel Qasile 347, 348
– Wolfson Park 347
– Yemenite quarter 345
Tel Beersheba 198
Tel Dan 402
Tel Dan Nature

Reserve **430**
Tel Gezer 330–1
Tel Goded 331
Tel Gorem 211
Tel Hatzor 401
Tel Jericho 316–17
Tel Megiddo 396
Tel Qasile 347, 348
Tel Roumeïda 222
telephone **419**
television **420**
tell, archaeology 394–5
Templars, Order of 279, 287, 341, 369
tents, nomads' 134–5
theaters, Roman 122
Theodosius I (the Great) 41
Thutmose III 330, 334, 339
Tiberias 148, 379–81, **422**, **427**, **431**, **436**, **440**, **443**, **457**
– Bernice quarter 380
– Byzantine church 381
– Hammat Tiberias 379
– Roman theater 380–1
– St Peter's Church 381
– Synagogue of Severus 379, 380
– tomb of Akiba 380
– tomb of Ben Zakkai 380
– tomb of Maimonides 380
– tomb of Meir Ba'al ha-Nes 380
Tiberias, Lake see Galilee, Sea of
Tiberius, Emperor 379
Ticho, Anna 139, 292
time differences **412**
Timna Nature Reserve 185, **438**, **445**
tipping **413**
Titus 50, 51, 241, 258, 266, 380
Torah 78, 107, 215, 398
tourist information **412**
trains **417**
travel:
– local **416–17**
– to Holy Land **414–15**
Tree of Hell 315
Tribes of Israel, Twelve 36, 39, 46, 304–5
Twain, Mark 152–3

◆ U ◆

Umar I 42, 52, 94, 241, 286
Umayyads 42, 52, 53, 219, 241, 320, 321
useful addresses **441–59**
useful information **410–13**
Uyun Musa 177

◆ V ◆

vaccinations **410**
vegetables 34

Vespasian 50, 201, 326
villages:
– Arab 289
– Palestinian traditional 130–1
Vogüé, Marquis Melchior de 312
voluntary service **430**

◆ W ◆

Wadi al-Khalil 218–19
Wadi al-Sheikh 177
Wadi Ein Netafim **438**
Wadi Qelt 322, 323, **431**, **436**
– Herod's Palace 322
– St George's Monastery 323
wadis 22–3, 165
War of Independence 37, 197, 256, 335
watchtowers 133
Waugh, Evelyn 148
Weizmann, Chaim 296, 353
Wilhelm II 242, 244, 254, 279, 295
Willibald, St 146
wines 330, 353, 354–5, 356, 365, 404
writers, on Holy Land 146–60

◆ Y ◆

Ya'ar Yehudiya Nature Reserve 405
Yad Vashem 302–3
Yadin, Yigal 202
Yamans 218, 219
Yavneh (Yibna) 51, 257
Yeroham 192, **438**
Yiddish 58, 60
Yom Kippur War 43
Yotvata 186, **438**, **445**
young people, travel **412**

◆ Z ◆

Zaccheus 314
Zachariah, Tomb of 279
Zacharias 219
Zaritsky, Yossef 139, 400
Zealots 50, 206
Zedekiah, King 306
Zengi, Lord of Mosul 54
Zerubabel 240
Zichron Yaacov 354, 356, **440**, **457**
Zionists 42, 56, 60, 82–3, 294, 302, 326, 339, 353
Zippori 389, **429**, **458**
zodiac 109

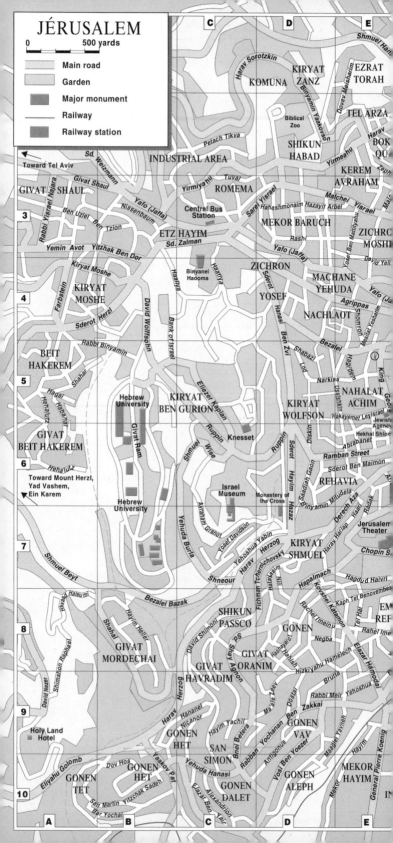